Deuteronomy

Themes and Issues in Biblical Studies
Series Editors:
Diana V. Edelman, University of Oslo
Philippe Guillaume, University of Berne

The edited volumes in this series are intended to complement traditional verse-by-verse commentaries and study bibles and introduce readers to the main themes and issues associated with the books forming the Hebrew Bible and the New Testament. The field of biblical studies has been in flux over the past half-century. The questions asked of the text are changing and with that, new theoretical frameworks are being applied to the texts that render some of the traditional methods and their underlying presuppositions unhelpful.

Consensus positions are being challenged as long-standing controversies are also being revisited in light of newer developments and evidence. Readers will gain insight into the current state of affairs relating to a specific book and the latest ideas being proposed, making the series the go-to source for cutting edge research.

Deuteronomy
Outside the Box

Edited by Diana V. Edelman
and Philippe Guillaume

SHEFFIELD UK   BRISTOL CT

Published by Equinox Publishing Ltd.

UK: Office 415, The Workstation, 15 Paternoster Row, Sheffield, South Yorkshire S1 2BX

USA: ISD, 70 Enterprise Drive, Bristol, CT 06010

www.equinoxpub.com

First published in book form 2024
The chapters of this volume were first published online by Equinox Publishing Ltd
Chapters 1, 2 and 4–12 published 2022. Chapters 15 and 17 published 2023. Chapters 3, 13, 14, 16, 18 and 19 published 2024

© Diana V. Edelman, Philippe Guillaume and contributors 2024

All rights reserved. No part of this publication may be reproduced or transmitted in any form or by any means, electronic or mechanical, including photocopying, recording or any information storage or retrieval system, without prior permission in writing from the publishers.

British Library Cataloguing-in-Publication Data

A catalogue record for this book is available from the British Library.

ISBN-13	978 1 80050 371 7	(hardback)
	978 1 80050 612 1	(paperback)
	978 1 80050 372 4	(ePDF)
	978 1 80050 623 7	(ePub)

Library of Congress Cataloging-in-Publication Data

Names: Edelman, Diana Vikander, 1954- editor. | Guillaume, Philippe, editor.
Title: Deuteronomy : outside the box / edited by Diana V. Edelman and Philippe Guillaume.
Description: Sheffield, UK ; Bristol, CT : Equinox, 2024. | Series: Themes and issues in biblical studies | Includes bibliographical references and index. | Summary: "This inaugural volume in the series, Themes and Issues in Biblical Studies, includes articles that, collectively, provide readers with informed presentations of a range of current debates concerning Deuteronomy as well as key themes and their implications"-- Provided by publisher.
Identifiers: LCCN 2024035794 (print) | LCCN 2024035795 (ebook) | ISBN 9781800503717 (hardback) | ISBN 9781800506121 (paperback) | ISBN 9781800503724 (epdf) | ISBN 9781800506237 (epub)
Subjects: LCSH: Bible. Deuteronomy--Commentaries.
Classification: LCC BS1275.53 .D47 2025 (print) | LCC BS1275.53 (ebook) | DDC 222/.1506--dc23/eng/20240924
LC record available at https://lccn.loc.gov/2024035794
LC ebook record available at https://lccn.loc.gov/2024035795

Typeset by Sparks – www.sparkspublishing.com

Contents

Preface		vii
1.	Saying Goodbye to the Theory of the Influence of Esarhaddon's Succession *Adê* on Deuteronomy 13 and 28 Diana V. Edelman	1
2.	The Role of the Oath-Bound Agreement (*Bᵉrît*) in the Book of Deuteronomy Diana V. Edelman	35
3.	Deuteronomy in Dialogue with Ancient Near Eastern Law Collections Megan B. Turton	73
4.	Geographical Dimensions of the Book of Deuteronomy Diana V. Edelman	95
5.	Ethnic Israel and Power in Deuteronomy Kåre Berge	134
6.	Basic Tools to Figure Out the Economy of Deuteronomy 12–26 Philippe Guillaume	168
7.	Yhwh (Ha)'Elohim and a Reconceived Yahwism Diana V. Edelman	209
8.	Master-Scribe and Forefather of a Scribal Guild: Moses in Deuteronomy Benedetta Rossi	247
9.	Between Self-Legitimation and Propaganda: Torah in Deuteronomy Benedetta Rossi	278
10.	Deuteronomy's Fearsome "Pedagogy" Kåre Berge	305
11.	Pragmatic, Utopian and Dystopian Deuteronomy Philippe Guillaume	320

12.	Deuteronomic Parenting *Philippe Guillaume*	335
13.	Deuteronomy as Utopia: New Possibilities for Reading an Old Friend/Foe *Madhavi Nevader*	354
14.	The Role of Deuteronomy in the Pentateuch *Richard D. Nelson*	372
15.	Deuteronomy: The Samaritan Version *Sidnie White Crawford*	389
16.	Where and When Might Deuteronomy Have Been Written? *Diana V. Edelman*	403
17.	Deuteronomy's Ethics *Georg Braulik*	434
18.	Deuteronomy's Influence on the Formation of the Psalter *Bernard Gosse*	476
19.	Landscape in Deuteronomy: What Were the Literati Imagining and Why? *Ehud Ben Zvi*	496

Author Index	515
Biblical Index	522
Subject Index	533

Preface

Deuteronomy: Outside the Box is the inaugural print volume in the series, Themes and Issues in Biblical Studies. All articles have been available through Equinox Publishing Ltd as e-publications within a month of entering the copy-editing queue. Chapters 1, 2, and 4–12 were published in 2022, chs. 15 and 17 in 2023, and chs. 3, 13, 14, 16, 18, and 19 in 2024. The only changes between the e-versions and the hardback and paperback versions are some added cross-references to other articles in the collection, which were able to be added in hindsight. The print versions also have indexes.

The underlying philosophy of this new series is to produce high-quality scholarship that is accessible to advanced-level undergraduate students as well as graduate students and colleagues. It remains difficult to find suitable reading options for upper level undergraduate classes on a specific biblical book, a focused collection of books, or a broader theme or issue. All authors are asked to try to avoid jargon as much as possible, to define technical terms at their first use when they are important to the larger discussion, and to presume no reading knowledge of Hebrew or Greek.

The focus of each volume in the series is on themes and issues relating to a given book of the Hebrew Bible. We feel it is as important to reassess the status quo of entrenched hypotheses that have become factoids and to identify ideas that have passed their "sell-by" date as to produce a line-by line commentary. Each serves a different but equally important function. We also are encouraging volume editors to include articles that situate their book in the contemporary world and show how it can be of relevance today. Editors are given great freedom in crafting the contents of their particular volume and adressing the twin goals just described. Certain volumes will have more of the former and others more of the latter. Some might strike an approximate balance.

The current volume on Deuteronomy engages heavily with a number of factoids that have developed over time. Because there has been a long-standing trend to compare the book to ancient Near Eastern law collections and a shorter trend making comparisons with Esarhaddon's oath documents and Hittite Royal Instructions, and because there are issues involved in Deuteronomy being part of the sacred scriptures of the Samaritans as well as the Jews, there is a stronger focus on its ancient context than on its relevance to the modern world, though the latter has been addressed.

This volume will probably be unlike the others in that it contains mutiple contributions by more than one author. This situation is due to ten of the chapters having originated as the result of the ongoing collaboration of Kåre Berge, Diana Edelman, Philippe Guillaume, and Benedetta Rossi after the official end of a three year grant (April 2017–June 2020) entitled "The Production, Purpose, and Ideology of Deuteronomy" funded by the Faculty of Theology at the University of Oslo. They were going to be published as an edited volume, but when the Themes and Issues in Biblical Studies was approved by Equinox Publishing Ltd, an additional nine chapters were added to make the final volume conform more closely to the philosophy of the new series.

The 19 articles in this book cover a wide range of topics that should stimulate thought and debate among students and colleagues alike. By the end of the volume, a reader can expect to be informed about key issues and themes in the book and know something of the history of debate, learn some novel solutions, and walk away feeling much better informed about past and present understandings of the significance of the book in its originating culture and its ongoing potential to influence contemporary culture.

Diana V. Edelman and Philippe Guillaume, co-editors of
Deuteronomy: Outside the Box and managing co-editors of the series,
Themes and Issues in Biblical Studies, June, 2024

Chapter 1
Saying Goodbye to the Theory of the Influence of Esarhaddon's Succession *Adê* on Deuteronomy 13 and 28

Diana V. Edelman

Abstract

The discovery in 2012 of an eleventh copy of Esarhaddon's succession *adê* at Tel Tayinat, a Neo-Assyrian provincial seat, has allowed a reassessment of the hypothesis, based on the nine copies naming city-lords from the Zagros mountains previously found at Kalḫu in 1955, that all Assyrian vassals, including Judah, had been required to swear to uphold the specified terms in addition to Assyrian citizens. It is now understood that the nine Zagros rulers were formally part of the Assyrian Empire, under the control of local governors, not vassals. Thus, there is no evidence that vassals had been included in the empire-wide oath-swearing, eliminating the likelihood of Judahite scribal access to a copy of the *adê* locally. In addition, a review of the proposed parallels in Deut 6:5; 13:1–12; 28:15–45; that point to dependency on the *adê* document demonstrates that, instead, the proposed wordings were part of a wider ancient Near Eastern koine associated with curse formulae, themes of political loyalty, and contexts of asserted authority in the present and future.

Keywords: Esarhaddon's succession *adê*, treaty, oath, curses, vassal loyalty, Tel Tayinat, Kalḫu, Tablets of Destinies

A theory has been growing in acceptance among biblical scholars that those responsible for the earliest form of Deuteronomy (*Urdeuteronomium*), usually considered to consist of all or most of chs. 12–26, had direct oral or written access to a copy of the document known variously as the Vassal Treaty of Esarhaddon (VTE), Esarhaddon's Succession Treaty (EST), or Esarhaddon's Succession Oath Documents (ESOD). They posit that one or more Judahite scribes drew on it to formulate the wording in 13:2–18 [1–17], 28:15–45, and possibly 6:5. When the theory was formulated, ten examples of this document were known from two locations: one from the city of Assur, excavated between 1903 and 1914, consisting of three fragments published in 1939–40, and the rest from the Nabû temple complex in the city of Kalḫu, excavated in 1955, with the 350 fragments restored as at least nine documents and published in 1958. The reconstructed copies of the *adê* agreement from Kalḫu served as the basis for postulating that all nine rulers from the Zagros region named on the tablets had been Assyrian vassal kings who had been required to take the oath. By extension, it was assumed that all thirty-nine Assyrian vassals would have done so, including King Manasseh of Judah, and all would have received a copy of the document to display or take back home for reference.

Both further study of the status of these rulers in the Zagros region and the discovery in 2012 of an eleventh example of the *adê* tablet in Kulania/Kinalua (Tel Tayinat), the seat of the Assyrian province of the same name (Radner 2006b, 61), make the time ripe to re-examine the validity of this theory of dependence (for data on the text versions, see conveniently Watanabe 2014; Lauinger 2019, 88). As will be argued, the theory needs to be abandoned, as do also proposals that the *adê* had been used to produce a short loyalty oath administered to the citizens of Judah, which then was used in turn by a writer or redactor of Deuteronomy.[1]

The plural term *adê* has been translated in various ways that have impacted on scholarly conceptions of how to classify Esarhaddon's succession document. Common renderings have been "treaty," "oath," or

---

1 The following presentation is based on my own assessment of the evidence and secondary literature. It agrees in large measure with the assessments made in the MA thesis of Tina Rinde, entitled "One Lynchpin Down: Challenging the Deuteronomists' Reliance on Esarhaddon's Succession Oath Document," successfully defended at the Faculty of Theology, University of Oslo, in Spring 2019. I was her supervisor. She selected this topic out of three possible options relating to Deuteronomy, the one book of the Old Testament that is studied in depth in the Faculty's theological curriculum. Since I had a vested interest in the subject as part of my funded research project, I read much of the same literature that spring and we had long conversations about it. It is hard not to reach the same conclusion when the evidence is reviewed.

"loyalty oath." The *Chicago Assyrian Dictionary* (*CAD* 1.1, 131–33 [*adû* A]) provides perhaps the most neutral definition: "a type of formal agreement" associated with religious ceremonies, curses, and oaths. This genre was used for a wide range of formal agreements between contracting human parties, between deities, and between deities and men (Parpola 1987, 181–82). Jacob Lauinger proposes a definition for the genre as "sworn pacts of loyalty imposed by a sovereign party upon one or more subordinate parties" (2013, 105, n. 25). The term is first attested in the eighth century BCE to refer to this type of agreement; it either is an Aramaic loanword (e.g. Tadmor 1982b, 455–58; Fitzmyer 1995, 57–59; Watanabe 2014, 162) or is a development from Old Babylonian *adû*, derived in turn from the Sumerian term $a_2.du_3$ meaning "work assignment" (so e.g. Durand 1991, 70; Lauinger 2013, 100, 115; Radner 2019, 312). Whatever its origin, it replaced the Old Babylonian term *isiktum*, meaning "assignment" or "duty," and the Middle Assyrian term *riksu* or *rikiltu*, meaning "bond" (Lauinger 2013, 100), as the preferred designation for "any solemn, binding agreement" (Parpola 1987, 182).

1. The Historical Context for the Creation of Esarhaddon's Oath Document

In 672 BCE, during a period of unrest and threatened coups that had begun after his failed first military campaign against Egypt in 673 BCE, King Esarhaddon proclaimed his plans for succession (for differing timelines of these events, see Leichty 1995, 951–57; Eph'al-Jaruzelska 2016, 134–39). He was chronically ill and widowed within the same year. His first son, Sin-iddina-apla, had apparently died prematurely. He announced that upon his own death, his next eldest son, Šamaš-šum-ukin, would ascend the throne of Babylonia and that Assurbanipal, possibly his third son born to the former Queen Ešarra-ḫammat, would assume the throne of Assyria (for issues of birth mothers and birth order, see Novotny and Singletary 2009). This decision was controversial, as indicated in a letter written to the king by the royal exorcist, Adad-šum-uṣur, who claimed it was not a plan done in heaven but done by the king on earth to place the eldest on the lesser throne (SAA 10 185; Parpola 1983, 117–19). In the hopes of securing the smooth enactment of his stated preferences, Esarhaddon ordered the production of numerous exemplars of an *adê* document stating them and the consequences for failing to enforce them; curses make up 34% of the total document (Watanabe 2017, 488). Officials and representatives throughout the Assyrian Empire participated in oath-swearing ceremonies at designated locales where prepared *adê* tablets bearing three seals of the deity Aššur appear to have been displayed inside a temple or temple complex after the ceremonies. The seals made each artifact a divine Tablet of Destinies (e.g. Steymans 2003, 93; Lauinger 2013, 108–10; Watanabe 2014, 161–62; Lauinger 2019, 92–93; Radner 2019, 315–16; Watanabe 2020, 73–74, 84–85) that §7, lines 71–72 in the Tel Tayinat exemplar specify, "is set up before you like [or as] your god – you shall guard it" (Lauinger 2012, 107). Also in §35b, lines 405–9 state that the tablet "which is sealed ... by the seal of Aššur, the king of the gods, [has been] placed ... in front of you as your god" (Watanabe 2020, 72). The extant tablets bear the dates, 12–18 Iyyar (in May), 672 BCE.

The eleven recovered examples of the *adê* seem to represent two recensions of an original master text in which the preamble was lengthened in one version. Three fragments of a single tablet were found in excavations conducted at the city of ancient Aššur (Qal'at Sherqat), but the find spots were not recorded so their originating context is lost (Watanabe 2014, 245–46). A smashed tablet was recovered within surface debris inside the inner sanctum of Temple Building 16 in the upper city at Tel Tayinat, ancient Kulania/Kinalua. It was lying on a podium beside an altar-like installation among at least eleven texts that probably had been displayed there, based on the presence of various means to hang or mount all of them in a frame. Both sites containing tablets were situated within the boundaries of the Assyrian Empire under formal Assyrian administration (Lauinger 2011, 10–12).

Finally, 350 fragments of at least nine smashed tablets were recovered from inside what initially had been assumed to be a throne room (e.g. Pongratz-Leisten 1994, 103–4) but now has been identified instead as the Dais of Destinies of the *akītu* house (Lauinger 2019, 94–95), adjacent to the temple of Nabû, known as the Ezida, in ancient Kalḫu, the military headquarters of the cavalry and chariotry (Wiseman 1958, 1–2; Barcina 2016, 34). Assurbanipal had been enthroned as Esarhaddon's successor at Kalḫu, fulfilling the terms of the oath document. Only the names of six of the nine rulers have been preserved, but they were all from the Zagros mountain region, which had become subjected to direct Assyrian political control before the reign of Esarhaddon to create a loyal buffer zone against a long-standing enemy, Urartu. The Zagros region was a source of horses and brave warriors but little else; it was hard to secure and police (Lanfranchi 2003, 81–83, 97–104, 114; Radner 2003, 42–43, 61).

While these nine individuals remained hereditary rulers whose successors had to be confirmed by the king of Assyria, they were also formally subject to the closest Assyrian provincial governor. Thus, they were not strictly vassal kings, as had been assumed in earlier discussions. They bore the lesser title of "city lord" (*bēl āli*), not the title of king (*šarru*) that had been used formerly in correspondence with some of the rulers from the region before their becoming part of greater Assyria

(Lanfranchi, 2003, 87–88, 92–96, 108–16; Radner 2003, 49–50, 53–56, 60). Instead, they were officials of the larger Assyrian Empire, and as such had sworn the oath to make Assurbanipal king at Esarhaddon's death along with other Assyrian provincial administrators. §1 states the *adê* is binding on the sons and grandsons, present and future, of the named city lord, as well as the men in his hands, young and old, as many as there are from sunrise to sunset, all those over whom Esarhaddon, king of Assyria, exercises kingship and lordship (Parpola and Watanabe 2014, 28).

The Tel Tayinat tablet includes a long list of generic categories of people as the oath-takers rather than the name of the single city-lord found on each tablet recovered at Kalḫu:

> ... the governor of Kulania/Kinalua, the deputy, the majordomo, the scribes, the chariot-drivers, the third men, the village managers, the information officers, the prefects, the cohort commanders, the charioteers, the cavalrymen, the exempt, the outriders, the specialists, the shi[eld-bearers (?)], the craftsmen, [and] with [all] the men [of his hands], great and small, as many as there are – [wi]th them and with the men who are born after the adê in the [f]uture, from the east [...] to the west, all those over whom Esarhaddon, King of Assyria, exercises kingship and lordship ... (§1) (Lauinger 2019, 112)

In all instances, those who functioned in an official capacity swore an oath on behalf of the commoners under their control, even if commoners might have been present at the ceremony. The wording suggests an intention to include as wide a swath of Assyrian citizens as possible and to make the oath binding on the current generations and multiple ones to come.

According to Hayim Tadmor (1982a, 148), the distant provinces of Media over which these "chieftains" ruled as Assyrian functionaries constituted "a natural refuge for any possible contender to the throne. Thus, securing their loyalty would have been a top priority, even when they technically were Assyrian officials. Yet it seems their presence at Assurbanipal's enthronement in Kalḫu may not have been due primarily to a concern about their loyalty in particular (Lanfranchi 2003, 89) but rather, due to their status as official representatives of population groups living within the provincial framework of the Assyrian Empire.

There is insufficient data to allow more than mere speculation about their presence at that particular site for the oath-taking and why their Tablets of Destinies were displayed on the Dais of Destinies of the *akītu* house in Kalḫu afterwards rather than taken back home to be placed in their own sanctuaries (for proposals, see e.g. Steymans, 2013, 9–10, who perpetuates modern stereotypes about mountain-dwelling "nomads" vs. Radner 2003, 41, 52; 2019, 314; Lauinger 2013; 2019, 94–96). The unique standing of the Zagros city lords within the Empire as both Assyrian citizens and local rulers must underlie the situation in some way. The possibility they had supplied men who formed part of Assurbanipal's bodyguard or corps within the royal standing army (so e.g. Liverani 1995, 59–62; Lanfranchi 1998, 105, 107; 2003, 114; Radner 2003, 59–60; Zehnder 2009a, 360–65) remains an option even after the discovery of the Tel Tayinat tablet, involving categories of citizens, including military forces swearing an oath in that regional capital. However, the supplying of bodyguards or troops no longer should be seen to be the underlying reason why the Zagros city-lords were required to participate in the empire-wide adê ceremony in 672 BCE. The likelihood that all eleven tablets recovered to date had been displayed inside temple complexes must be factored into a satisfactory explanation, regardless of any possible involvement of men from the Zagros region as royal bodyguards or an elite corps.

Morton Cogan (1974, 47) has pointed out that no native Median gods are invoked in the curse sections of the adê tablets. This would seem to corroborate the status of the nine Zagros city lords as provincial "Assyrians," not vassal kings. In addition, both the shorter and longer recensions of the text appear among these nine examples, so it cannot be argued that one version of wording had been developed for vassals and another for Assyrians (Lauinger 2015, 287, 296, contra e.g. Watanabe 2014, 147).

The nine tablets belonging to city lords of the Zagros mountains have been cited as evidence that vassals, including King Manasseh of Judah, were required to swear the loyalty oath in 672 BCE. As argued, however, they do not support that understanding. Tadmor (1982a, 150) had already noted that "Neither is there evidence that every vassal throughout the empire was obliged to take these oaths of loyalty upon his master's accession to the throne" as a standard practice, let alone in this extraordinary case.

Nor does the statement made in the name of Assurbanipal on Prism A support the inclusion of all Assyrian vassals in swearing the oath of loyalty. There it is said that Esarhaddon had "convened the people of Assyria, great and small, from the Upper Sea to the Lower Sea [and] made them swear a treaty oath by the gods and made a binding agreement to protect my crown-princeship and future kingship over Assyria" (Streck 1916, 4, lines 18–19). The king includes only Assyrian citizens as the oath-takers, which undoubtedly meant in practical terms representatives of the people and government officials, as demonstrated in particular by the Tel Tayinat tablet. These representatives resided within the seventy-one provinces of the Empire. It did not include the additional thirty-nine client vassal kings who ruled over land outside the imperial territory proper (Zehnder 2009a, 366; Lauinger 2015, 289–90; *pace* Wiseman 1958, 4). Given the expansive language in the wording, bragging about the inclusion of all foreign vassal kings under his control as well would have enhanced the message, implying it had not been part of the official policy.

2. §§54–55 of ESOD and Implications for the Inclusion of Vassals in the Oath Ceremonies

In light of the number of extant queries made to the deity Šamaš about the loyalty of a number of subject peoples alongside royal family members, palace staff, the military, and royal administrators and appointees, it is possible that some vassals whose loyalties were suspect in the case of a succession might have been included in the proceedings alongside suspect population groups already living in Assyrian provinces. Judah does not appear among the fifteen named groups.[2] The Philistines, Sidonians, and Arameans do, however.

The Tel Tayinat copy of the oath document contains a section of five curses, written in Babylonian, invoking western deities that had not been legible on any of the restored Nimrud exemplars but likely had been an integral part of the text of all copies (so e.g. Lauinger 2012, 119; Steymans 2013, 4). §§54–55 invoke the gods Aramiš of the city and land of Qarnê and the city and land of Aza'i, Adad and Šala of Kurba'il, Šarrat-Ekron, "Queen of Ekron," Bethel and Anat/Bethel without an accompanying location, and Kubaba and Karḫuḫa of Carchemish. It seems that all but one of the cities named were Assyrian provincial seats in 672 BCE, when the oath document was written.

Qarnê was a city located in the Hauran, east of the Sea of Galilee, probably at Šēḫ Saʻd. It is thought to have become the seat of the province of the same name in 732 BCE under Tiglath-Pileser III (Lipiński 2000, 353, 365–66; Radner 2006b, 61–62; Lauinger 2012, 119; Steymans 2013, 4). Aza'i is likely either to have been a territory in the al-Ghab Plain whose seat was located at Rasm et-Tanjara (Athanassiou 1977, 327, n. 7, cited by Lauinger 2012, 119) or a province and provincial seat adjoining Qarnê created in former Aramean territory at the same time in 732 BCE. In the

---

2 Those named in the letters that have survived include the Itua'eans, the Elamites, the Hittites, the Gurreans, the Manneans, the Medes, the Cimmerians, the Akkadians, the Arameans, the Philistines, the Sidonians, the Nubians, the Egyptians, the Qedarites, and the Šabuqeans. The tabulation is made in Eph'al-Jaruzelska 2016, 12. The wider collection of queries among which those concerning these vassals appear have been collected and published in Starr 1990.

first instance, the cult might have been transplanted with deportees from Qarnê; in the second, it would have been a deity whose territory included or sphere of influence extended over at least two political units, like Yhwh, with Israel and Judah.

The location of Kurba'il is not known but two possibilities have been proposed. It might have lain in the province of Ninūa/Nineveh, northwest of Nineveh proper, in an area subject to flooding (Kinnier Wilson 1962, 98-99), although since it seems to have been a provincial seat itself, it would make more sense to argue that it lay northwest of the province of Ninūa/Nineveh, east of Tarbiṣu, and possibly north of Dūr-Šarru-ukīn (Schwemer 2001, 596). Alternatively, because it is mentioned together with Kalḫu in some texts, it might have lain in territory adjoining Kalḫu, between Ḥazir and the Great Zab, south of Ğabal Zirga Bardareš (Radner 2006b, 47), west of the province of Arba'il (Steymans 2013, 4). The deities of Kurba'il are Semitic in origin, certainly, and the city name seems to be Aramaic. It would already have been located within an Assyrian province under Shalmaneser III, who dedicated a statue to Adad of Kurba'il, thanking him for his recent victories over his enemies i.e. Hazael of Damascus and Kati, king of Quē, ca. 838 BCE (Kinnier Wilson 1962, 95-96; Schwemer 2001, 598; Radner 2006b, 47). However, the presence of temples to Adad and Šala at Kalḫu, the cavalry center where Asshurbanipal's coronation occurred, and to Bel Kurba'il (lord of Kurba'il) in the capital city of Ashur (Kinnier-Wilson 1962, 98) might suggest that the cult of this divine couple had spread in the first instance southeastward, perhaps with transplanted Arameans serving in the military and central administration and with Aramean traders, or in the second instance, westward and northwestward.

Bethel and Anat-Bethel were Aramean deities probably worshipped over a wide geographical area and so not limited to a specific locale. It is noteworthy that in the treaty between Esarhaddon and Baal, king of Tyre, dated 677 BCE, the pair are invoked in §4, lines 6-7 to deliver the king to the paws of a man-eating lion if he breaks a treaty stipulation (Parpola and Watanabe 2014, 27). They appear last within the section of Assyrian and Akkadian gods, §4, lines 1-7, ahead of a summary invoking the great gods of heaven and earth, the gods of Assyria, the gods of Akkad, and the gods of Eber Nari (line 8). Following that summary are specific curses overseen by the gods of Eber Nari: Baal Shamaim, Baal Malagê, and Baal Saphon (lines 10-13), concluding with curses overseen by Melqart, the patron deity of Tyre, Eshmun, an important deity of Sidon, and Astarte, the wife of Melqart (lines 14-9).

In 717 BCE, Sargon II conquered Carchemish and made it an Assyrian provincial seat. Thus, its deities Kubaba (and) Karḫuḫa became part of the imperial Assyrian pantheon thereafter.

Finally, Ekron was one of the three Philistine cities existing at the time as an independent kingdom; Gath had ceased to be inhabited and Ashdod had become an Assyrian province under Sargon II in 711 BCE (Radner 2006b, 58). In 667 BCE, Ekron's king, Ikausu/Achish, supplied auxiliary troops for Assurbanipal's first campaign to conquer Egypt (Na'aman 2003, 84). It was the only one of the sites mentioned in §§54–55 that was still a vassal, not an Assyrian provincial seat or city.

Both the Arameans and the Philistines appear among the fifteen groups about whom enquiries concerning loyalty were made by Esarhaddon to Shamash. Since it appears that Aramaic-speaking groups already had become Assyrian citizens living in Assyrian provinces carved out from their former independent polities, while Ekron was a vassal, the choice of these western deities was not predicated on the status of the deities within the imperial system. The inclusion of a small sampling of deities worshipped by Aramaic speakers would have made the document meaningful for the large number of such citizens living in the western provinces and deportees and their descendants who had ended up in eastern provinces. The singling out of one Philistine deity vs. one Phoenician deity might have been random. The Sidonians, like the Philistines, had been the subject of an enquiry to Shamash. The point seems to have been to include a local deity from the southern Levant from an ethnic group whose loyalty had been suspected or who represented a segment of the regional population considered noteworthy by the Assyrians.[3]

3. The Role of Vassals in ESOD

Vassals are mentioned only once in the *adê* document, in §14, line 162. They are the potential source of an evil, improper or ugly word about Esarhaddon, which, if heard, is to be reported to the crown prince. Allies also appear only once, in §10, line 112, in a list that includes Assyrians, courtiers or any living being, as potential instigators of rebellion and insurrection; if this happens "you", i.e. the one swearing an oath of loyalty, are to take your stand with and protect Assurbanipal. In neither case are vassals or allies included in the "you" being directly addressed. Thus, it would seem they were not envisioned as part of the intended

---

[3] Perhaps the main goddess of Ekron was included because the scribes compiling the *adë* had access in their archives to a copy of a vassal treaty made between the king of this city and Sennacherib, after he quashed a rebellion by the city nobles and restored King Padi to his throne, ca. 701 BCE, or a subsequent vassal treaty renewed by Esarhaddon.

audience of the tablet used at the oath-taking ceremonies that took place from 12–18 Iyyar, 672 BCE.

As just seen in the preceding section, it is possible but not confirmed that the king of Ekron might have been required to participate in the oath ceremony administered at one of the western provincial seats like Ashdod or Samerina, or even in the Assyrian heartland. Such a possibility does not prove by extension, however, that all vassals would have sworn the oath and would have received a copy of the document to display or deposit back home in their temples (*pace* e.g. Frankena 1965, 151; Levinson and Stackert 2012, 132; Steymans 2013, 2, 4, 11). Logically, if all vassals had been ordered to participate, one would have expected a curse to be included for each and none for the Arameans, who already were citizens. That is not what is present in the text, however.

The fact that so many curses are written in Babylonian in the curse sections of Esarhaddon's *adê* (e.g. §35, lines 397–402a and §§37–56, lines 414–93) points to a concern for non-compliance from that part of the imperial citizenry. The *adê* is composed 81% in Assyrian vs 19% in Babylonian, but the use of Babylonian is concentrated in the consequential clauses of conditional curses attached to specific deities and then in §56 to "the great gods of heaven and earth residing in the world, as many as their names are called in this tablet" (Watanabe 2017, 474, 476–82). Many fewer curses are written in Assyrian: §57, lines 511–12, §63, lines 526–29, §64, lines 530–33, §65, lines 534–36, §69, lines 547–50, §70, lines 551–54 (Watanabe 2017, 482–85).

Let us turn now to Judah specifically. Even if access to Esarhaddon's succession *adê* in Judah cannot be proven and is not likely, a copy of the treaty established when Judah became a vassal of Assyria or a subsequent, updated vassal treaty with Assyria would have been kept in Judah. Tadmor (1982a, 150–52) considers it possible that Assyria established an *ardūtu* ("servitude") type of relationship with Israel and Judah and other western kingdoms that did not include a formal vassal treaty and that the latter was instituted quite late in Judah. "The only king of Judah who definitely took the *adê* oath was Zedekiah" (2 Kgs 24:20) (p. 152), which is signaled indirectly by saying he rebelled against the king of Babylon, not of Assyria.

This is an argument from silence, however, which, given the selective nature of the accounts of the reigns of Judah's kings in 2 Kings, cannot carry much weight in indicating when Assyria would have executed a formal *adê* agreement with Judah. The term [w]ardu[m]/ [w]ardūtu[m] designates a servant/servantship or a vassal/vassalship (CAD 1, part 2, 243–53). Tadmor (1982a, 150–52) points out that in Assyrian texts, only some vassals are said to have rebelled against or transgressed an *adê*; this seems to lead him to his assumption. But he has not cited textual evidence that shows that new vassals were bound by an oral oath only or that the tribute and any other conditions would not have been put in writing. Perhaps we should not expect the nature of the preserved texts to contain such a policy, however. The written stipulations would serve as the basis for eventually confiscating and annexing the lands of a rebellious vassal, usually after a third transgression. With each of the first and second transgressions, the overlord would have raised the tribute assessment.

Angelika Berlejung thinks a formal Assyrian vassal treaty existed with the king of Judah by the time of Manasseh but that the document stating the stipulations would have been housed at the residence of the local Assyrian *qēpu*-official, whose job it would have been to see that it was enforced, not at the royal court in Jerusalem (2012, 23, 32). The *qēpu*'s residence likely was the palatial complex at Ramat Raḥel south of Jerusalem (stratum Va; for a description, see Lipschits et al. 2011, 10–12, 20, 22). It is a point of debate whether the treaty would have been written in Assyrian only or also in Aramaic for accessibility for this western vassal. Be that as it may, the problem is that nothing is known of its contents, so it has not been considered a potential source for Deuteronomy by biblical scholars. The Assyriologist, Karen Radner (2006a), advanced such a possibility, however, when rejecting any dependence between Deuteronomy and Esarhaddon's succession *adê*. It certainly is more likely that a vassal treaty with Judah existed than that a copy of Esarhaddon's *adê* ended up in Judah.

A copy of Esarhaddon's *adê* document should have ended up in the Assyrian province of Samerina, however. Thus, those who want to argue for dependency should either be advocating a northern origin for the book, which none does, or need to follow the lead of William B. Morrow. He has argued that Judahite scribes potentially could have learned the contents of Esarhaddon's *adê* document through oral interaction with Assyrian scribes and officials in Samerina and other regional contexts (2009, 232; 2010, 377–78; 2019, 139).

To summarize the discussion in Sections 1–3 so far, no proof exists that all thirty-nine Assyrian vassals were required to attend an oath-taking ceremony at one or more designated Assyrian locations in 672 BCE, where they would have received a copy of Esarhaddon's succession document. No evidence exists that a copy of this document ended up in Judah. No evidence exists that Judahite scribes accessed its contents in written or oral form in a neighboring Assyrian province like Samerina or possibly at the chancellery of the court of Ekron, if its king had been asked to swear the oath of loyalty as a vassal, which is by no means certain.

4. A Close Look at the Proposed Dependencies Between Deuteronomy and ESOD

Without the opportunity of direct contact with or accessibility to ESOD being able to be established, further proposed parallels demonstrating dependency lose their force. Even so, when one looks at the proposed parallels, the first thing that becomes evident is that they represent a very small proportion of both Esarhaddon's *adê* document and the book of Deuteronomy. While this does not disqualify the proposed parallels *per se*, it leads one to wonder why more of this source would not have been used. Beyond this preliminary observation, when the details are examined, many questionable assertions and conclusions have been made.

4.1 Deuteronomy 28:15–45

The first attention focused on the curses in Deut 28:15–45. Donald J. Wiseman (1958, 87–88) had noted that lines 444–45 in §47 of Esarhaddon's *adê* had similarities to Deut 28:17 and that lines 528–29 in §63 recalled the wording in Deut 28:23–24. Riekele Borger (1961, 191–92) then expanded on the second observation by asking if the Deuteronomist might have drawn this curse from a treaty between the Assyrians and the Judahites. This was a logical deduction. Borger's insight was dismissed, however, when focus subsequently narrowed to the curses in 28:25–33. In 1965, Moshe Weinfeld picked up on the comment by Wiseman (1958, 25) that in §§37–63, "apart from the five [deities] first named, [i.e. Aššur, Ninlil, Anu, Sin, and Šamaš], the order has no significance," as well as his observation concerning the closeness in wording between the curse in §63 and Deut 28:23–24. He proceeded to follow the immediate lead of Delbert Hillers (1964, 13), however, who had adapted Wiseman's comment to claim instead, "where curses by individual gods occur in series they are usually listed in strict order of the gods' rank within the pantheon."

Instead of focusing only on the order of the first five gods, Hillers opened the way for himself and others to consider curses overseen by additional deities in the list and to eliminate the chief couple, Aššur and Ninlil, as well as Anu, the third deity in Wiseman's list of five, from necessary inclusion. Weinfeld (1965, 418–20; 1972, 119) then pointed out that the order of curses in Deut 28:26–35 appears random on its own but mirrors almost exactly the order in §§39–42 of Esarhaddon's succession *adê*, which follows the standard hierarchical order of the Assyrian pantheon. These are leprosy, blindness, exposure of those killed, rape of the wife, plundering, and the enslavement of children. He and others have argued the biblical text follows the logic dictated by the order of the Assyrian pantheon and so must have derived from Esarhaddon's succession *adê* specifically (so e.g. Steymans 1995b, 132–34, 138–39; Tigay 1996, 497; Levinson and Stackert 2012, 134; contrast Koch 2008, 216–30, who has reviewed the evidence and rejected any dependency).

The "almost" involves the fact that in the Assyrian text, pestilence and unburied bodies is the third curse, while in Deuteronomy it is the first. So basically, the order is not the same and does not follow the supposed hierarchy of the Assyrian pantheon since it would place Ninurta at the head of the list of gods being considered, not sixth after Sin and Šamaš but before Venus, or third, once Aššur, Ninlil, and Anu are removed and one begins the list with Sin and Šamaš. Also, the fact has often been overlooked that the Assyrian text specifies leprosy alone, while the biblical text refers to four different skin disorders, but not leprosy explicitly. The suggestion by Hans Ulrich Steymans (2013, 7–9) that the order of curses in §§38A–42 was altered by a biblical writer in 28:25-33 to elaborate on a topic he found in the vassal oath section in §56 does not solve the inconsistency convincingly.

In a second publication that appeared in 1965, Rintje Frankena pointed to more extensive parallels between Deut 28:20-57 and §§37-56 (lines 414-493) (pp. 144-50), not only the small cluster Weinfeld has focused on. "The correspondences between the texts, in my opinion, are more than mere accidental parallels caused by the use of the same sources, (sic!) in some instances, the resemblance is so close that the phrasing of some curses in Deut. xxviii may be supposed to be an elaboration of an Assyrian 'Vorlage', whereas the curse sequence of Deut. xxviii roughly follows the Assyrian text" (1965, 145). In the summary of this discussion, he states, "the order of the curses in Deut. xxviii is not the same as in the vassal treaties [of Esarhaddon] …" (1965, 146).

Frankena cited parallels for two of the three curses that head the curse section of the *adê*, §§37, 38, which Weinfeld did not include in his parallels because the corresponding verses in Deut 28 did not appear sequentially before vv. 25-33. Frankena (1965, 145) linked the curse in §37 that Aššur decree an evil and unpleasant fate for the one who breaks the stipulations, not granting him long-lasting old age and the attainment of extreme old age with 28:20 (Parpola and Watanabe 2014, 45). He then paired the second curse involving Mullissu/Ninlil (§38A) ("May Mullissu/ Ninlil, his beloved wife, make the utterance of his mouth evil and may she not intercede for you"; Parpola and Watanabe 2014, 45) with 28:29b. Weinfeld could have included this proposed parallel in his discussion of 28:26-33 but at the expense of another disruption to the "hierarchical order."

Neither scholar cited a parallel for Anu's curse, §38A, which is present in all but one of the extant tablets. "May Anu, king of the gods, let disease, exhaustion, malaria, sleeplessness, worries and ill health rain upon all your houses" (Parpola and Watanabe 2014, 45). Hans Ulrich Steymans (1995a, 299-300), however, aligned it with Deut 28:34-35, even though there is no overlap in wording between the two. This proposed parallel can be dismissed (so François 2017, 171-72).

It is noteworthy that Frankena proposed pairing Deut 28:25 with the curse Ištar was to oversee in §48. Weinfeld, however, chose to begin the parallel sections only with v. 26, even though it continues a curse that begins in v. 25. Technically, then, v. 25 needs to be included in Weinfeld's clusters being compared, as others have recognized and done in subsequent analyses. Thus, in addition to the above disorder that would place Ninurta ahead of Sin and Šamaš, the proposed parallels skip the head divine couple, Aššur and his wife Mullissu/Ninlil and Anu, the third deity, but include Venus, because the curse she oversees resembles the last in the cluster of curses in Deut 28:25-33 to some degree.

Spencer L. Allen (2013, 5-10, 13) has now problematized the existence of a normative hierarchical order of the Neo-Assyrian pantheon. He has demonstrated that by the eighth century BCE, the tradition popularized in scribal tradition by the "Code of Hammurapi" had become "somewhat malleable" and that the order of deities varied in different Neo-Assyrian genres. In addition, he has noted that while Weinfeld assumed a long-standing link between deities and specific curses in Assyro-Babylonian tradition, the evidence reveals that multiple deities had been associated with specific curses over time (2013, 15-16). While his observations do not disprove the contention that there is a certain amount of overlap between §§39-42 of Esarhaddon's *adê* and Deut 28:25-33, they require the elimination of the argument that the order of curses in the latter follows the order of the Assyrian pantheon.

A comparative reading reveals that parts of the Assyrian curses in §§39-42 are not present in Deut 28:25-33. "May Sin forbid you from entering into the presence of the gods or king; roam the desert like the wild ass and the gazelle!" in §39 is absent from 28:27. In §40, the only punishment to be dispensed by Šamaš is blindness, so that one will walk about in darkness. In 28:28-29, however, the punishments are to be madness, blindness, and confusion of mind, and while groping in darkness is mentioned, so also is continual abuse and robbery, which appears nowhere in §40.

In §41, Ninurta is invoked to kill the one who breaks the terms of the *adê* with an arrow, fill the plain with his blood and feed his flesh to the eagle and vulture. In Deut 28:25-26, however, the one who breaks the covenant will be defeated by his enemies, flee before them in seven ways, and become an object of horror to all the kingdoms of the earth. Their corpses will be food for every bird of the air and animal of the earth, with no one to frighten them away. Both deal with the realities of death and non-burial in war but not in identical terms.

§42 mentions wives lying in the lap of the enemy and sons who will not inherit the house because the enemy will divide your goods. Deuteronomy 28:30–33 deals in general with the same theme of what happens to individuals when enemies conquer, but the examples are not identical. Here, a man will be engaged to a woman but another man will lie with her. One will build a house but not live in it and plant a vineyard but not enjoy its fruit. Animals will be confiscated; children will become prisoners of war, and strangers will eat the fruit of the ground and of one's labors while one personally will be repeatedly abused and crushed."

Additional parallels between sections in Esarhaddon's succession *adê* and those in Deut 28:14–50 have been proposed beyond the popularly drawn parallels just discussed between Deut 28:26–33 and §§39–42. In addition to revisiting those just presented, Mark S. François (2017, 80–174) has examined in depth the following: Deut 28:15 and lines 194–96 in §17; Deut 28:17 and lines 433–435 in §47, Deut 28:20 and §37; Deut 28:20–44 and §56; Deut 28:21 and §49; Deut 28:22 and §52; Deut 28:23–24 and lines 528–533 in §§63–64; Deut 28:25 and §48; Deut 28:34–35 and §38A; Deut 28:38 and lines 442–445 in §47; Deut 28:53–57 and lines 448–451 in §47. He concludes that of these passages, only three likely had some sort of potential direct or mediated relationship: 28:23–24 with lines 442–445 in §47 and 28:53–57 with lines 448–451 in §47, and 28:25a, 2633 and §§39–42 as a third instance, with reservations. In his view, the parallels are best explained by a close common tradition, shared cultural values/ experiences, internal textual developments and influences from other sources rather than a mediated, non-vertical genetic relationship (2017, 253–56). Thus, he rejects any proposed direct dependency of curses in Deut 28 on curses in Esarhaddon's succession *adê*.

Finally, a recent study by C. L Crouch and Jeremy M. Hutton of translation techniques of Akkadian treaty documents into Aramaic at Tell Fekheriyeh has included a consideration of whether Deut 28:22, 23–24, 30, and 31–32 might have utilized similar "optimal translation" practices in translating sections of ESOD into Aramaic or Hebrew. They reject the possibility that the writer of Deuteronomy was attempting translation *per se*. They conclude instead that he likely was familiar with a broad range of ancient Near Eastern curse formulae and themes and used some of them to compose his text (2019, 231–55, 300).

It is becoming increasingly recognized that the curses in Deut 28:15–45 reflect standard tropes used in the wider ancient Near Eastern treaty tradition (so e.g. Zehnder 2009b, 518, 520–27, 530, 532; Crouch 2014,

146, 180–81), the Assyrian treaty tradition from which the curses in Esarhaddon's succession *adê* also drew (so e.g. Radner 2006a, 374–75; Koch 2008, 231), or possibly a West Semitic Aramaic or northwest Semitic curse tradition (so e.g. Ramos 2016, 206–7, 213, 218; Quick 2018, 156–57, 162–77). They draw on cross-culturally shared experiences of the realities of war, famine, drought, and pestilence and their aftermaths. Thus, on literary grounds alone, the likelihood that the author of Deuteronomy composed four of the eighteen or so curses in ch. 28 from his knowledge of the contents of §§39–42 of Esarhaddon's succession *adê* is minuscule.

4.2 Deuteronomy 13

The direct influence of ESOD on Deut 13 has been discussed both in terms of §4 and what has been called the "canon formula" in 13:1, found also in Deut 4:2, as well as the proposed dependency of vv. 2–6 [1–5] and vv. 7–12 [6–11] on §§10 and 12. Each proposal will be examined in this sub-section, beginning with the more widely discussed second pair.

The similarity in language and ideology concerning the handling of political sedition in §§10 and 12 of Esarhaddon's succession *adê* and two of the three subsections concerning sedition in the form of religious apostasy in Deut 13 has led some scholars to posit a direct link between the two (so e.g. Dion 1991, 203–5; Levinson 2001, 236–41; Otto 1999, 64; Rüterswörden 2002, 190; Steymans 2003, 97–105, Levinson 2010, 337–40, 344–47; Otto 2016, 1, 239–61). In developing a case, however, scholars have included §§6, 8, 9, 11, 18, 22, 24, 26, 35–37 and 57 in the larger discussion. I will only deal with §§10 and 12.

§10 requires the following:

> If you hear any evil, improper, ugly word which is not seemly or good to Assurbanipal, the great crown prince designate, son of Esarhaddon, king of Assyria, your lord, from the mouth of his enemy or from the mouth of his ally, or from the mouth of his brothers or from the mouth of his uncles, his cousins, his family, members of his father's line, or from the mouth of your brothers, your sons, your daughters, or from the mouth of a prophet, an ecstatic, and inquirer of oracles, or from the mouth of any human being at all, you shall not conceal it but come and report it to Assurbanipal, the great crown prince designate, son of Esarhaddon, king of Assyria. (Parpola and Watanabe 2014, 33)

§12 requires the following:

> If anyone should speak to you of rebellion and insurrection (with the purpose) of ki[lling], assassinating, and eliminating Assurbanipal, the [great crown] prince designate, son of Esarhaddon, king of Assyria,

your lord, concerning whom he has concluded (this) treaty with you, or if you should hear about it from the mouth of anyone, you shall seize the perpetrators of insurrection and bring them before Assurbanipal, the great crown prince designate. If you are able to seize them and put them to death, then you shall destroy their name and their seed from the land. If, however, you are unable to seize them and put them to death, you shall inform Assurbanipal, the great crown prince designate, and assist him in putting to death the perpetrators of rebellion. (Parpola and Watanabe 2014, 34)

One notes that §10 deals with any word or matter that is potentially negative toward the future king, which is to be reported to the crown prince without presenting the source in person. It applies to a long list of potential speakers, some of whom also appear in the lists of those committing apostasy in Deut 13, while the second deals with plans for assassination. In the latter case, one should try to seize the conspirator(s) directly and present him/them to the crown prince. If possible, he/they should be put to death by the one who was trying to be recruited to the cause of rebellion; no hearing is mentioned, but perhaps none was needed since the official would be acting on his certain knowledge of attempted personal recruitment. If such an individual cannot physically seize the traitor(s), however, the one who was being approached to join the cause is to report his knowledge of the plot to the crown prince and help him kill the traitors. In the second option it is unclear if aiding in the physical apprehension of the traitors is envisioned as a prior step to helping physically to execute them, or whether the implication is that once the traitors have been apprehended by other royal agents, the one who reported it is to testify against them, thereby justifying their being put to death by order of the king, using his own executioner. The "you" being addressed in both paragraphs are officials within the Assyrian imperial administration and representatives of the citizenry, seen in the list of generic office-holders in the version of the *adê* found at Tel Tayinat.

Deuteronomy 13 falls into three sections: vv. 2–6 [1–5], where the enticer to apostasy is a prophet or dream-diviner and is to be put to death for urging disloyalty in others through a sign or portent; vv. 7–12 [6–11], where the enticer is a relative or close friend who speaks secretly about apostasy, who is to be stoned by the one approached first, followed by the rest of the people thereafter; and vv. 13–18 [12–17], where the enticers are scoundrels who have subverted the other inhabitants of their town to commit apostasy by worshipping other gods. In this case, where knowledge of the situation apparently has spread by rumor, an investigation is explicitly to take place. If it is confirmed to be accurate, the entire town population and its animals are to be placed under ban and killed, with its spoils burnt along with the town itself as a holocaust to Yhwh Elohim. It is to remain a perpetual ruin.

Immediately, it is apparent that the third section has no parallel in the wording of the *adê*. Also, in order to make the alleged borrowing work, scholars have to enlist the aid of §12, because there is no mention of killing anyone in §10 as there is in all three sections of ch. 13. Once that is done, they argue that §12 presents a case of summary execution without a trial that parallels the situation in v. 4 [5] for an apostate prophet or dream-diviner and in v. 10 when dealing with family members and close friends, but which otherwise contravenes the due process of a trial and conviction on the basis of a formal investigation that is specified in the case of an entire city turned apostate (v. 15 [14]) or in 19:15, which requires testimony from two or three witnesses (so e.g. Levinson 1995, 37, 59–63).

The statement in v. 10 [9] that the accuser is to be the first to throw a stone before the others join in, however, implies that a trial has preceded the execution (Weinfeld 1972, 95). The stoning is carried out by a group of residents who then collectively are responsible for executing a prescribed punishment. By the same token, as already noted, it is not necessarily the case in §12 that there would not have been some sort of hearing to extract a confession of guilt after the arrest of the traitor and before his execution, to substantiate the claims of treason.

The gradations of rebellious behavior and their accompanying responses do not align between the political sedition in §§10 and 12 and the religious sedition in ch. 13. In the *adê*, the negative words that could be spoken by a long list of people in §10 are less of an immediate threat and can be left to the king to investigate as he sees fit after he receives reports; death is not a necessary outcome. Only those plotting assassination must be killed. In all three cases in Deuteronomy, there are those who have committed apostasy and so are to be killed, whether or not they have managed to persuade others to join them. Also, in the *adê*, the family members precede the religious personnel, whereas in Deut 13, the apostate prophets and dream-diviners precede the family members, who also include the mother's relatives, not just the father's side of the family, and close friends, who are absent in the *adê*. On the other hand, the enemies and allies of the *adê* are missing in Deuteronomy. What seem to be close connections at first glance are less so upon more careful examination (those who reject such a connection include e.g. Veijola 1995, 310; Pakkala 2006, 129–34; Koch 2008, 166–68; Berman 2011, 33–35; Crouch 2014, 138–45).

In addition, however, during the debates that have taken place over these proposed parallels, new evidence from extant ancient Near Eastern treaties has been added into the mix, which provides even closer parallels than the combination of §10 and 12. In particular, the Hittite Ismerika treaty (CTH 133) provides close parallels in §§9, lines 21-24, to 13:7-12 [6-11] (so e.g. Dion 1991, 201; Veijola 1995, 301-2; Koch 2008, 154; Zehnder 2009b, 514-15; Berman 2011, 29-31) and also, according to Christoph Koch (2008, 164-65), vv. 25-26 with 13:13-19 [12-18] and, according to Berman, §10, lines 25-28, with 13:13-18 [12-17] (31-33), although Veijola (1995, 304-7) preferred to draw a parallel between §2, lines 16-18 of the treaty the Hittite King Šuppiluliuma made with King Sunaššura of Kizzuwatna and Deut 13:15, 16b, 17aα, ββ, 18. A parallel to the treaty between Šuppiluliuma's father, Tudhaliya II, and the same King Sunaššura of Kizzuwatna concerning informing the overlord if someone enters a city, incites a revolt, and begins a war and Deut 13:12-14 has also been put forward (Zehnder 2009b, 514). Others have proposed that lines 12-13 of the Aramaic Sefire Treaty Stele #3 also provides a parallel to 13:13-18 [12-17] (so e.g. Weinfeld 1972, 99, n. 4; Dion 1991, 202-3; Zehnder 2009b, 514; Berman 2011, 35), while Koch (2008, 164-65) has cited lines 1-4 and 9-14 of the treaty as potential parallels to ch. 13. None of the proposed alternate texts has a parallel for the case of seditious prophets and diviners, however. Together, these four treaties demonstrate that sedition was common among royal family members and court officials and that the defection of an entire city that housed the leader of insurrection was perceived as a real threat in many kingdoms and empires. Both became standard issues to be included in treaty stipulations, as deemed necessary.

Koch (2008, 152-65), for example, notes that references to friends as sources of sedition appear in other Hittite treaties and Zakutu's succession *adê*. He also points out the language in 13:9, "to hear and (then) conceal," is a typical obligation in Hittite and Assyrian vassal treaties and loyalty oaths and so should not be seen to derive from one particular exemplar. He concludes that the writer responsible for ch. 13 selected concerns that were typical in treaty stipulations and expressed them in a West Semitic treaty idiom. Others who have recognized that analogies to elements in ch. 13 and the main theme of sedition can be found in ancient Near Eastern treaties include e.g. Moshe Weinfeld (1972, 91-100), Timo Veijola (1995, 320), and Markus Zehnder (2009b, 511-28).

Joshua Berman (2011; 2013) has helped dismantle any ability to claim a sole reliance on §§10 and 12 of Esarhaddon's succession *adê* by the person who created Deut 13 in his detailed examination of the parallels found in the late Bronze Age Hittite Ismerika treaty. He has not, however, drawn the logical conclusion that dealing with seditious elements was a standard treaty trope, and speedy execution was the typical punishment for traitors. Whether the execution was always or ever to be done without a trial remains a point needing further clarification. He notes, however, that in CTH 133, lines 27–28, when a seditious household or individual is found, the verb used to refer to their execution, "*ak(k)*- implies 'being put to death by judicial sentence; be legally executed'" (2011, 31). He leaves open the issue of "how Hittite forms became reflected in biblical accounts of the covenant" yet proposes the possibility that "the laws of Deuteronomy 13 may represent a highly refracted reworking of a tradition that we witness today only in Hittite tradition" (2011, 44). This idea resonates with the proposal made here that the native Judahite treaty tradition had its roots in the Late Bronze Age international treaty tradition, inherited from the scribes of Jerusalem, but that the tradition would also have been influenced over time by evolved Aramaic and Assyrian treaty forms, both of which also would have had roots in the same Late Bronze Age international tradition.

As in the case of the alleged dependency of ch. 28 on Esarhaddon's succession *adê*, what emerges in examining proposed close parallels between §§10 and 12 and Deut 13 is that sedition from various sources was a common reality. As such, it would have been a standard issue to be addressed in the stipulations of vassal treaties and succession documents. There is little point in looking for a specific "foreign" source for the three potential sources of religious sedition in ch. 13, and the three forms of execution of the guilty: killing in general; stoning in particular; and putting under a total ban. It makes much better sense to assume that the biblical writer drew on his native Judahite treaty tradition, which probably shared many traits with a wider West Semitic treaty tradition (so Morrow 2004, 114–15; Zehnder 2009b, 534, but mis-using Israelite to represent Judahite; and ch. 3 in this volume).

Let us turn now to the statement in 13:1 [12:32], "The entire word I am commanding you, it you shall observe to do; you shall not add to it or take away from it." It has a close variant in 4:2: "You shall not add to the word I command or take away from it" and another in Jer 26:2, where Yhwh commands Jeremiah to stand in the court of the temple and speak to all the cities of Judah that come to worship in the house of Yhwh, "all the words that I command you to speak to them; do not hold back (*'al-tigra'*) a word." Finally, one can add, "All the speech of God proves true …; do not add to its words lest it rebuke you and you be found a liar (Prov 30:5–6) and "I perceived that whatever God does endures forever; nothing can be added to it, nor anything taken from it. God has done it, so that people fear before him" (Eccl 3:14).

It appears this idiom was known and used within the ancient Mediterranean world in similar but not identical wordings (Oeming 2003, 122–30). I will give four examples. It appears, for example, in the epilogue of the stela of Hammurabi (reigned ca. 1792–1750 BCE) (Roth 1995, 135–36), where it is emphasized that no future king should "… alter the judgments

I rendered and the verdicts I made, nor remove my engraved image" (xlviii 59–94) or "… reject my judgments, change my pronouncements, or alter my graven image" (xlviii 95–xlix 17). If one should "… overturn the judgments I rendered, change my pronouncements, alter my engraved image, [or] erase my inscribed name and inscribe his own name" or have another do so (xlix 18–44), the gods are to deprive him of kingship and curse his destiny. A second example is found in the Erra Epic (ca.1000–666 BCE): "It was revealed to him in the night, and when he spoke in the morning, he did not leave out a single line, nor did he add one to it" (Weinfeld 1972, 262).

The expression also occurs in at least one treaty. In the written terms of the treaty between Muwatallis (II) of Hatti and Talmi-sarruma of Aleppo, dating to the late fourteenth or early thirteenth century BCE, §2 reports the fact that the earlier tablet that his father, Muwatallis (II), had made for the king of Aleppo had been stolen, so Muršili (II) has written another tablet for him. "I have sealed (it) with my seal, and have given (it) to him. In the future nobody shall change a word of the text of this [tablet]. The word of the Tabarna, the Great King, shall neither be abrogated, nor broken" (no. 67; Kitchen and Lawrence 2012, 541; I thank Ada Taggar-Cohen for the reference). Additionally, scholars have noted similar language in the closing sections of Greek treaties (for various examples from the ancient Near East and Greece, see Weinfeld 1972, 261–74; Reuter 1989, 109–10; Hagedorn 2004, 76–78, 163; Levinson 2009, 26).

Finally, a close parallel to the wording in 13:1 and 4:2 occurs in §8 of the "fifth" plague prayer of Muršili (II) addressed to the assembly of the gods (CTH 379). The immediately preceding section (§7) dealt with Egypt, although only the country's name remains intact. Apparently, it referred to a tablet concerning a formal agreement made between Hatti and Egypt by a preceding king. The second plague prayer of Muršili (II) to the storm-god of Hatti (CTH 378.II) contains a report in §§4–5 of how Muršili's father broke his treaty with Egypt after Egyptians murdered his son; he attacked and defeated the infantry and chariotry of Egypt. After Egyptian prisoner-of-wars arrived in Hatti, a plague broke out. This might be the incident that had been detailed again in §7 (no. 11; Singer 2002, 58–59; 67), or possibly a new incident. §8 goes on: "To this tablet I did not add a word nor did I take one out. O my lords, look, I do not know whether any of those who were kings before (me) added [a word] or took one out" (no. 14; Singer 2002, 67; Weinfeld, 1972, 262, n. 4. I thank Ada again for suggesting Singer's presentation). While the phrase occurs in a written prayer, it is used in connection with a treaty tablet, which seems to be what prompted its presence.

Yet, the occurrence in §4 of Esarhaddon's adê has been singled out among the other known examples as the specific source from which the writer of Deuteronomy or a subsequent editor or redactor borrowed the phrase when writing 13:1 and 4:2. Some scholars have argued that the first verse of ch. 13 is a late addition, which would link it to a secondary scribal hand (e.g. Mayes 1979, 231–32, Veijola 2004, 284; Otto 2016, 1,218–21,1,226). Another issue involves whether it functions as the closing to ch. 12 or as the opening to ch. 13. A decision in favor of one or the other possibility affects whether the phrase, kol haddābār, "the entire word/matter," refers back to the call for a single altar and the concomitant changes that follow from it as outlined in ch. 12 or introduces collectively the regulations that begin in ch. 13 (for this issue and other grammatical irregularities, see e.g. Driver 1902, 151; Reuter 1989, 110; Rütersworden 2010, 19–23; Levinson 2009, 31, 33, 36; Hagedorn 2013, 90–92; Otto 2016, 1,213–14, 1,218–22, 1,226, 1,234–38). Whether original or secondary and functioning to close ch. 12 vs. open ch. 13, the issue is whether these two examples of what was a known expression can be determined to be interdependent. The answer is no, unless it can be established that the writer of Deuteronomy had access to the text of ESOD, which has been argued in the preceding section to be unlikely.

Paragraph 4, lines 57–61 read: "You shall neither change nor alter the word of Esarhaddon, king of Assyria, but serve this very Assurbanipal, the great crown prince designate, whom Esarhaddon, king of Assyria, your lord, has presented to you, and he shall exercise the kingship and dominion over you" (Parpola and Watanabe 2014, 31). Once again, for convenience, Deut 13:1 reads: "The entire word that I am commanding you, it you shall take care (literally, "guard" or "keep") to do; you shall not add to it nor take from it." Instead of the two synonyms, "change" and "alter," that appear in §4, in Deuteronomy one finds two antonyms, "add to" and "take away from."

Bernard M. Levinson (2009, 31) argues that the writer of 13:1 has deliberately employed the common ancient Near Eastern scribal technique known as inverted citation or Seidel's law, reversing the order of the prohibition followed by a positive command found in §4 while signaling his reuse of an older text. He goes on to attribute the change of the two synonyms in the prohibition to two antonyms to derive from a desire "to create a merism expressing totality," calling it "a creative reworking" of §4. Yet the latter approach is not more effective than the former, so why one would bother is not clear. Finally, he argues this creative reworking has "subverted the treaty's demand not to alter the 'word' of Esarhaddon" (2009, 32).[4]

---

4   Levinson (2019, 36) goes on to apply the same principle of inverted citation to argue that the wording in 13:1 has been inverted by the later writer responsible for 4:2. The reason he has not suggested that 4:2 was based on §4 rather than

In a subsequent article co-authored with Jeffrey Stackert, the two argue that the phrase is used in ESOD in a context of legal succession, which has inspired its use in Deuteronomy to convey the ideology that the law given on the plains of Moab is the legitimate successor to the law proclaimed at Sinai/Horeb (2012, 137–39). Yet this understanding overlooks the probable nature of each ESOD tablet as a Tablet of Destinies, displayed inside a sanctuary (Lauinger 2019, 92–93; Watanabe 2020, 73–74). That likelihood places the phrase about not changing or altering the declared written words of Esarhaddon in a different context; the words Esarhaddon declares are the will of the deity Aššur, three of whose seals are imprinted into each tablet. Both ESOD and Deuteronomy, then, use the phrase not as "a rhetorical expression of succession" (2012, 137) but instead as a rhetorical expression of authority. Whether that authority is invoked to legitimate the new, exegetical oral interpretation of older biblical traditions, as suggested, for example, by Udo Rüterswörden (2010, 23, 27), or the written text of Deuteronomy itself (e.g. Levinson 1998, 28–34, 48; 2003, 7, 12), which provides such exegesis in relation to Exodus and perhaps also materials currently found in Leviticus and Numbers, remains a point of dispute. In his study, Manfred Oeming also fails to note the authoritative nature of the source of the text that undergirds the use of the formula in the ancient Near Eastern and biblical texts (2003, 130–31). In ESOD it is the royal authority of Esarhaddon who allegedly is initiating divine destiny; in 13:1 it is the teaching, prophetic, or scribal authority of Moses, who elsewhere in the book enjoys divine endorsement, and in 4:2 it is divine authority relayed by Moses and his teaching. In the epilogue of Hammurabi's stela, the treaty between Muwatallis II of Hatti and Talmi-sarruma of Aleppo, and the "fifth" plague prayer of Muršili (II), it is royal authority. The uses of the idiom in treaties, law collections, prayers, and proverbs share with Deuteronomy and ESOD a concern that future generations continue to hold the contents of the text in question as authoritative.

Levinson's analysis presupposes the additional dependencies on or "creative reworkings" of ESOD found in Deut 13:2–12 [1–11] and 28:25–33. Without these other suggested connections, it is highly unlikely

> 13:1 likely is his assumption that 13:1 lies within the so-called "core" that he would identify as *Urdeuteronomium* while 4:2 falls within the "frame" that he assumes is a later expansion. The application of this technique to establishing an intentional dependency between 4:2 and 13:1 seems appropriate, even with the difference between the second person singular and plural forms in the merism. Which text is citing the other remains an open point of debate, however. In the storyworld, 13:1 is quoting 4:2, but in terms of the growth of the book, either scenario is possible.

he would have made the arguments he has; he readily acknowledges the wider occurrence of the ancient Near Eastern idea concerning not changing words in any way. In light of the counter-arguments that have been made here concerning the lack of evidence of access to the ESOD by Judahite scribes as well as the superficial similarities between paragraphs in ESOD and Deut 13:2–12 [1–11] and 28:25–33, this proposed origin for the statement about not adding to or taking away from the words in 13:1 and 4:2 should be rejected. Instead, it should be understood to be an expression that was part and parcel of Judahite and Judean scribal language for contexts of asserted authority in the present and future that has been used in four separate books in the collection comprising the Hebrew Bible.

4.3 Deuteronomy 6:5

In contrast to the three foregoing arguments for direct dependency, the situation of the possible dependency of Deut 6:5 on Esarhaddon's succession *adê* has been widely dismissed in favor of the recognition that "to love" and "with all your heart" derive from the wider ancient Near Eastern vassal treaty tradition (so e.g. McCarthy 1965, 144–47; Hillers 1969, 152; McKay 1972, 426–35; Weinfeld 1972, 334; Tigay 1996, 77; Zehnder 2009a, 347–48, 355–56; Arnold, 2011, 552–62; in favor of dependency, see e.g. Otto 1999, 61–62; 362–63; Hardmeier 2005, 229, 245). A vassal had an oath-bound duty to be loyal to his overlord that was expressed using these phrases. In addition, Susan Ackerman (2002, 440–47, 457) has noted that in interpersonal relationships in the texts of the Hebrew Bible, the subject of the verb "to love" and the noun "love" is usually the hierarchically superior party in the relationship, whether that is human-divine, male-female, or parent-child. Esarhaddon's succession *adê*, which was modeled in many ways on a vassal treaty document, is but one example of the use of this language to express oath-bound duty.

William L. Moran (1963) appears to have been the first to propose this wider context, even though he based his conclusion on royal correspondence between overlords and vassals rather than actual treaties; the former confirmed the existence of the latter, which have not survived. The eleven sections (§§4, 5, 8, 11, 17, 18, 19, 20, 24, 25, 34) that have been cited from Esarhaddon's *adê* in connection with Deut 6:5 have provided illustrations of the concept of oath-bound loyalty; they have not been argued to have been the exclusive source.[5] Perhaps the very limited nature of the

---

5   All have been cited by Kazuko Watanabe (2014, 164). Eckart Otto has cited §§18 and 24 (1999, 361–63), Christof Hardmeier §§18, 24, and 34 (2005, 245),

two expressions has led scholars not to seek exact parallels in a certain document, or perhaps the fact that Moran's discussion already pointed to multiple sources for comparisons headed off such a search. Even so, once one argues or accepts that the composer of Deut 13 and 28 used a copy of Esarhaddon's succession *adê* or an intermediate Judahite document that had extracted §§10, 12 and §§39–42 or modeled contents on them as a source, it is possible to suggest that one or more of the occurrences of "to love" one's overlord and "with all one's heart" in this specific document sparked its formulation in Deuteronomy or the hypothetical intermediate document (so e.g. Frankena 1965, 153). It is a slippery slide.

5. ESOD as the Source of a Proposed Early Judahite Loyalty Oath

Proposals that a derivative, short intermediary Judahite document was drawn up in Hebrew using selected sections of the Assyrian text and eventually used by a writer or redactor of Deuteronomy as a source must also be rejected. As demonstrated earlier, there is no proof that King Manasseh participated in an oath-swearing ceremony to uphold Esarhaddon's succession *adê*, which does not appear to have been mandated for the thirty-nine vassal kings of Assyria unless perhaps their past behavior had given reason for suspicion, as the king of Ekron's might have done. It is highly unlikely, then, that a copy of the *adê* tablet, written in Assyrian and Babylonian cuneiform like the other known examples or even in an Aramaic translation, for which no proof currently exists, found its way to the Assyrian *qēpu*'s residence at Ramat Raḥel or the royal palace or temple complex in Jerusalem. Thus, the suggestion that the scribes of King Manasseh used a copy of this document as a model to create a loyalty document against potentially rebellious elements within the kingdom of Judah and subjected sections §§10 and 56 in particular to "creative revision" to produce Deut 13:2-12 [1-11] and 28:20-44 (so Levinson and Stackert 2012, 131) lacks supporting evidence (Morrow 2019, 139).

For the same reasons, the idea that with Assyrian power waning, King Josiah had his scribes subvert Esarhaddon's succession *adê* by drawing up a document in Hebrew based on it that asserted that Judah owed its loyalty to Yhwh alone (so Otto 1999, 67–69; 2000, 62–65; Morrow 2009, 228–29, 231–33) is to be rejected. The seeds for this position were already laid by Frankena and Weinfeld. Frankena (1965, 152–53) had suggested that Josiah's covenant renewal with Yhwh had substituted

---

Bernhard Lang §§25 and 34 (2002, 39), and Udo Rüterswörden §24 (2006, 235).

for the former treaty with Assyria and his cult reform had removed all vestiges of the influence of Assyrian deities; both moves were to have signaled his regained political and religious independence. Weinfeld (1972, 100) had argued that Deut 13 was part of the covenant between king and people, on the one hand, and Yhwh on the other, mentioned in 2 Kgs 23:1–3. Both equated the new document with *Urdeuteronomium* rather than an independent document that later was used as a source for *Urdeuteronomium* and argued it replaced the treaty with the king of Assyria as an act of rebellion. Both also argued that ch. 13 has wording similar to that about sedition in Esarhaddon's succession *adê*. Weinfeld (1972, 91–100) noted, however, this was a standard element in Hittite, Aramean, and Neo-Assyrian treaties; he did not assume a single external source necessarily. In his discussion of Deut 13 in his commentary, however, Otto seems to have abandoned his earlier idea of the Hebrew document in favor of a direct use of the succession *adê* by the creator of *Urdeuteronomium* (2016, 1,238–41).

Conclusion

The idea that Esarhaddon's succession *adê* was used as a direct or secondary source for composing any part of Deuteronomy should be abandoned. The lack of proof that all vassals were required to participate alongside Assyrian officials and representatives in the oath-swearing ceremonies that appear to have taken place in various locales around the Assyrian Empire in May, 672 BCE removes the needed evidence that the writer of Deut 13 and 28 would have been able to access the document in written or oral form. No copy was known to have ended up in Judah, be that at Manasseh's court or at the residence of the Assyrian *qēpu*, likely at Ramat Raḥel. In addition, many of the proposed parallels are not unique to the Esarhaddon succession *adê* but, rather, reflect standard tropes in curses and real threats of sedition from within the royal family and court and from the wider population that are present in extant ancient Near Eastern vassal treaties. Rather than look for an outside source from which the ideas would have been derived, it is logical to propose instead that the ideas expressed in chs. 13 and 28 were familiar from the native monarchic Judahite treaty template, which would have included a standard list of curses to be drawn upon to suit the particular circumstances. It likely would have shared much in common with other regional templates, because treaties were an international genre. At the same time, however, it would have had its own particular preferences and format.

The removal of Esarhaddon's succession *adê* as a source for Deuteronomy opens up the issue of the dating of the composition of the book anew, be that any early hypothetical short form as well as the extended book form. The unsubstantiated link to ESOD has been relied upon to corroborate the reliability of the biblical story of the finding of "the scroll of the teaching" in the temple during repairs undertaken in the reign of Josiah (2 Kgs 22:3–23:3). What has been considered to be almost a consensus in support of a Josianic date of the composition for *Urdeuteronomium* needs urgent reassessment, with alternate proposed datings and their accompanying rationales given serious consideration.

Works Cited

Ackerman, Susan. 2002. "The Personal is Political: Covenantal and Affectionate Love ('āhēb, 'ahābâ) in the Hebrew Bible." *Vetus Testamentum* 52: 437–55.

Allen, Spencer L. 2013. "Rearranging the Gods in Esarhaddon's Succession Treaty (State Archives of Assyria 2 6:414–465)." *Die Welt des Orients* 43: 1–24.

Arnold, Bill T. 2011. "The Love–Fear Antimony in Deuteronomy 5–11." *Vetus Testamentum* 61: 551–69.

Athanassiou, Homer. 1977. "Ras et-Tanjara: A recently Discovered Syrian Tell in the Ghab. Part I, Inventory of the Chance Finds." PhD thesis, University of Missouri-Columbia.

Barcina, Cristina. 2016. "The Display of Esarhaddon's Succession Treaty at Kalḫu as a Means of Internal Political Control." *Antiguo Oriente* 14: 11–51.

Berlejung, Angelika. 2012. "The Assyrians in the West: Assyrianization, Colonialism, Indifference, or Development Policy?" Pages 21–60 in *Congress Volume Helsinki 2010*. Edited by Martti Nissinen. Supplements to Vetus Testamentum 148. Leiden: Brill.

Berman, Joshua A. 2011. "CTH 133 and the Hittite Provenance of Deuteronomy 13." *Journal of Biblical Literature* 130: 25–44.

------. 2013. "Historicism and Its Limits: A Response to Bernard M. Levinson and Jeffrey Stackert." *Journal of Ancient Judaism* 4: 297–309.

Borger, Riekele. 1961. "Zu den Asarhaddon-Verträgen aus Nimrud." *Zeitschrift für Assyriologie* 54: 173–96.

Cogan, Morton. 1974. *Imperialism and Religion: Assyria, Judah and Israel in the Eighth and Seventh Centuries B.C.E.* Society of Biblical Literature Monograph Series 19. Missoula, MT: Scholars Press.

Crouch, Carly L. 2014. *Israel and the Assyrians: Deuteronomy, the Succession Treaty of Esarhaddon, and the Nature of Subversion*. Ancient Near Eastern Monographs 8. Atlanta, GA: Society of Biblical Literature.

------ and Jeremy M. Hutton. 2019. *Translating Empire: Tell Fekeriyeh, Deuteronomy, and the Akkadian Treaty Tradition.* Ancient Near Eastern Monographs 135. Tübingen: Mohr Siebeck.

Dion, Paul E. 1991. "Deuteronomy 13: The Suppression of Alien Religious Propaganda in Israel during the Late Monarchical Era." Pages 147–216 in *Law and Ideology in Monarchic Israel.* Edited by Baruch Halpern and Deborah W. Hobson. Journal for the Study of the Old Testament Supplement Series 124. Sheffield: JSOT.

Driver, S. R. 1902. *A Critical and Exegetical Commentary on Deuteronomy.* 3rd edition. Edinburgh: T. & T. Clark.

Durand, Jean-Marie. 1991. "Précurseurs syriens aux protocoles néo-assyriens." Pages 13–72 in *Marchands, diplomates et empereurs: Études sur la civilisation mésopotamienne offertes à Paul Garelli.* Edited by Dominique Charpin and Francis Joannès. Paris: Recherche sur les civilisations.

Eph'al-Jaruzelska, Izabela. 2016. "Esarhaddon's Claim of Legitimacy in an Hour of Crisis: Sociological Observations." *Orient* 51: 123–42.

Fitzmyer, Joseph A. 1995. *The Aramaic Inscriptions of Sefîre.* Revised ed. Biblia et Orientalia 19/A. Rome: Pontifical Biblical Institute.

François, Mark S. 2017. "Something Old, Something Borrowed, or Something New? The Relationship Between the Succession Treaty of Esarhaddon and the Curses of Deuteronomy 28." PhD thesis, University of St. Michael's College.

Frankena, Rintja. 1965. "The Vassal Treaties of Esarhaddon and the Dating of Deuteronomy." Pages 122–54 in *Kaf he 1940–1965.* Edited by P. A. H. de Boer. Oudtestamentische Studiën 14. Leiden: Brill.

Hagedorn, Anselm C. 2004. *Between Moses and Plato: Individual and Society in Deuteronomy and Ancient Greek Laws.* Forschungen zur Religion und Literatur des Alten und Neuen Testaments 204. Göttingen: Vandenhoeck & Ruprecht.

------. 2013. "Canonical Formation: Canons and Curses: Some observations on the 'canon-formula' in Deuteronomy and its afterlife." Pages 89–105 in *Biblical Interpretation and Method: Essays in Honour of John Barton.* Edited by Catherine J. Dell and Paul M. Joyce. Oxford: Oxford University Press.

Hardmeier, Christof. 2005. "Die Weisheit der Tora (Dtn 4,5–8). Respekt und Loyalität gegenüber JHWH allein und die Befolgung der Gebote – ein performatives Lehren und Lernen." Pages 155–84 in *Erzähldiskurs und Redepragmatik im Alten Testament. Unterwegs zu einer performativen Theologie der Bibel.* Ancient Near Eastern Monographs 46. Tübingen: Mohr Siebeck.

Hillers, Delbert R. 1964. *Treaty-Curses and the Old Testament Prophets.* Biblia et Orientalia 16. Rome: Pontifical Biblical Institute.

------. 1969. *Covenant: The History of a Biblical Idea*. Baltimore: The Johns Hopkins Press.
Kinnier Wilson, J. V. 1962. "The Kurba'il Statue of Shalmaneser III." *Iraq* 24: 90–115.
Kitchen, Kenneth A. and Paul J. N. Lawrence. 2012. *Treaty, Law, and Covenant in the Ancient Near East. Part 1: The Texts*. Wiesbaden: Harrassowitz.
Koch, Christoph. 2008. *Vertrag, Treueid und Bund: Studien zur Rezeption des altorientalischen Vertragsrecht im Deuteronomium und zur Ausbildung der Bundestheologie im Alten Testament*. Beihefte zur Zeitschrift für die altestamentische Wissenschaft 383. Berlin: De Gruyter.
Lanfranchi, Giovanni B. 1998. "Esarhaddon, Assyria, and Media." *State Archives of Assyria Bulletin* 12: 99–109.
------. 2003. "The Assyrian Expansion in the Zagros and the Local Ruling Elites." Pages 79–118 in *Continuity of Empire(?): Assyria, Media, Persia*. Edited by Giovanni B. Lanfranchi, Michael Roaf, and Robert Rollinger. Padova: Sargon.
Lang, Bernhard. 2002. *The Hebrew God: Portrait of an Ancient Deity*. New Haven, CT: Yale University Press.
Lauinger, Jacob. 2011. "Some Preliminary Thoughts on the Tablet Collection in Building xiv from Tell Tayinat." *Journal of the Canadian Society for Mesopotamian Studies* 64: 5–14.
------. 2012. "Esarhaddon's Succession Treaty at Tell Tayinat: Text and Commentary." *Journal of Cuneiform Studies* 64: 87–123.
------. 2013. "The Neo-Assyrian *adê*: Treaty, Oath, or Something Else?" *Zeitschrift für altorientalische und biblische Rechtsgeschichte* 19: 99–115.
------. 2015. "Neo-Assyrian Scribes, 'Esarhaddon's Succession Treaty', and the Dynamics of Textual Mass Production." Pages 285–314 in *Texts and Contexts: The Circulation and Transmission of Cuneiform Texts in Social Space*. Edited by Paul Delnero and Jacob Lauinger. Studies in Ancient Near Eastern Records 9. Boston, MA: De Gruyter.
------. 2019. "Literary Connections and Social Contexts: Approaches to Deuteronomy in Light of the Assyrian *adê*-Tradition." *Hebrew Bible and Ancient Israel* 8: 87–100.
Leichty, Erle. 1995. "Esarhaddon, King of Assyria." Pages 949–58 in vol. 2 of *Civilizations of the Ancient Near East*. Edited by Jack M. Sasson. New York: Charles Scribner's Sons.
Levinson, Bernard M. 1995. "'But You Shall Surely Kill Him': The Text-Critical and Neo-Assyrian Evidence for MT Deuteronomy 13:10." Pages 37–63 in *Bundesdokument und Gesetz: Studien zum Deuteronomium*. Edited by Georg Braulik. Freiburg: Herder. Reprinted as pages 166–92 in *"The Right Chorale": Studies in Biblical Law and Interpretation*. Ancient Near Eastern Monographs 54. Tübingen: Mohr Siebeck, 2008.
------. 1998. *Deuteronomy and the Hermeneutics of Legal Innovation*. New York: Oxford University Press.

------. 2001. "Textual Criticism, Assyriology, and the History of Interpretation: Deuteronomy 13:7a as a Test Case." *Journal of Biblical Literature* 120: 236–69.

------. 2003. "'You Must not Add Anything to What I Command You': Paradoxes of Canon and Authorship in Ancient Israel." *Numen* 50: 1–51.

------. 2009. "The Neo-Assyrian Origins of the Canon Formula in Deuteronomy 13:1." Pages 26–43 in *Scriptural Exegesis: The Shapes of Culture and the Religious Imagination. Essays in Honor of Michael Fishbane*. Edited by Deborah A. Green and Laura S. Lieber. Oxford: University Press.

------. 2010. "Esarhaddon's Succession Treaty as the Source for the Canon Formula in Deuteronomy 13:1." *Journal of the American Oriental Society* 130: 337–47.

------ and Jeffrey Stackert. 2012. "Between the Covenant Code and Esarhaddon's Vassal Treaty: Deuteronomy 13 and the Composition of Deuteronomy." *Journal of Ancient Judaism* 3: 123–40.

Lipiński, Eduard. 2000. *The Arameans: their Ancient Culture, History, and Religion*. Orientalia Lovaniensia Analecta 100. Leuven: Peeters.

Lipschits, Oded, Yuval Gadot, Benjamin Arubas, and Manfred Oeming. 2011. "Palace and Village, Paradise and Oblivion: Unravelling the Riddles of Ramat Raḥel." *Near Eastern Archaeology* 74:1–49.

Liverani, Mario. 1995. "The Medes at Esarhaddon's Court." *Journal of Cuneiform Studies* 47: 57–62.

Mayes, Andrew D. H. 1979. *Deuteronomy*. London: Marshall, Morgan & Scott.

McCarthy, Dennis J. 1965. "Notes on the Love of God in Deuteronomy and the Father-Son Relationship between YHWH and Israel." *Catholic Biblical Quarterly* 27: 144–47.

McKay, J. W. 1972. "Man's Love for God in Deuteronomy and the Father/Teacher - Son/Pupil Relationship." *Vetus Testamentum* 22: 426–43.

Moran, William L. 1963. "The Ancient Near Eastern Background of the Love of God in Deuteronomy." *Catholic Biblical Quarterly* 25: 77–87.

Morrow, William B. 2004. "*Fortschreibung* in Mesopotamian Treaties and the Book of Deuteronomy." Pages 111–23 in *Recht und Ethik im Alten Testament. Beiträge des Symposiums "Das Alte Testament und die Kultur der Moderne" anlässlich des 100. Geburtstags Gerhard von Rads (1901-1971) Heidelberg, 18.-21. Oktober, 2001*. Edited by Bernard M. Levinson and Eckart Otto. Altes Testament und Moderne 13. Münster: LIT.

------. 2009. "The Paradox of Deuteronomy 13: A Post-Colonial Reading." Pages 227–39 in *"Gerechtigkeit und Recht zu üben" (Gen 18, 19). Studien zur altorientalischen unde biblischen Rechtsgeschichte, zur Religionsgeschichte Israels, und zur Religionssoziologie: Festschrift für Eckart Otto zum 65. Geburtstag*. Edited by Reinhard Achenbach and Martin Arneth. Wiesbaden: Harrassowitz.

------. 2010. "'To Set the Name' in the Deuteronomic Centralization Formula: A Case of Cultural Hybridity." *Journal of Semitic Studies* 55: 365–83.

------. 2019. "Have Attempts to Establish the Dependency of Deuteronomy on the Esarhaddon Succession Treaty (EST) Failed?" *Hebrew Bible and Ancient Israel* 8: 133–59.

Na'aman, Nadav. 2003. "Ekron under the Assyrian and Egyptian Empires." *Bulletin of the American Schools of Oriental Research* 332: 81–91.

Novotny, Jamie and Jennifer Singletary. 2009. "Family Ties: Assurbanipal's Family Revisited." *Studia Orientalia* 106: 167–77.

Oeming, Manfred. 2003. "'Du sollst nichts hinzufügen und nichts wegnehmen' (Dtn 13,1). Altorientalisch Ursprünge und biblische Funktionen der sogenannten Kanonformel." Pages 121–37 in *Verstehen und Glauben. Exegetische Bausteine zur einer Theologie des Alten Testaments*. Bonner biblische Beiträge 142. Berlin: Philo. Reprint of Christoph Dolmen and Manfred Oeming, *Biblischer Kanon, warum und wozu? Eine Kanontheologie*, 68–90. Quaestiones Disputatae 128. Freiburg: Herder, 1992.

Otto, Eckart. 1999. *Das Deuteronomium. Politische Theologie und Rechtsreform in Juda und Assyrien*. Beihefte zur Zeitschrift für die altestamentische Wissenschaft 284. Berlin: De Gruyter.

------. 2000. "Political Theology in Judah and Assyria: The Beginning of the Hebrew Bible as Literature." *Svensk exegetisk årsbok* 65: 59–76.

------. 2016. *Deuteronomium 12:1–23,15*. Herders Theologischer Kommentar zum Alten Testament. Freiburg: Herder.

Pakkala, Juha. 2006. "Der Literatur- und religionsgeschichtliche Ort von Deuteronomium 13." Pages 125–37 in *Die deuteronomischen Geschichtswerke. Redaktions- und religionsgeschichtliche Perspektiven zur "Deuteronomismus" - Diskussion in Tora und Vorderen Propheten*. Edited by Marcus Witte, Konrad Schmid, Doris Prechel, and Jan Christian Gertz. Beihefte zur Zeitschrift für die altestamentische Wissenschaft 365. Berlin: De Gruyter.

Parpola, Simo. 1983. *Letters from Assyrian Scholars to the Kings Esarhaddon and Assurbanipal, Part II: Commentary and Appendices*. Alter Orient und Altes Testament 5,2. Kevelaer: Butzon & Bercker and Neukirchen-Vluyn: Neukirchener Verlag.

------. 1987. "Neo-Assyrian Treaties from the Royal Archives of Nineveh." *Journal of Cuneiform Studies* 39: 161–89.

------ and Kazuko Watanabe. 2014 *Neo-Assyrian Treaties and Loyalty Oaths*. State Archives of Assyria 2. Helsinki: Helsinki University Press. Original version 1988.

Pongratz-Leisten, Beate. 1994. *Ina šulmi īrub. Die kulttopographische und ideolkogische Programmatik der akītu-Prozession in Babylonien unde Assyrien im 1. Jahrtausend v. Chr.* Baghdader Forschungen 16. Mainz am Rhein: P. von Zabern.

Quick, Laura. 2018. *Deuteronomy 28 and the Aramaic Curse Tradition*. Oxford Theology and Religion Monographs. New York: Oxford University Press.

Radner, Karen. 2003. "An Assyrian View on the Medes." Pages 37–64 in *Continuity of Empire(?): Assyria, Media, Persia*. Edited by Giovanni B. Lanfranchi, Michael Roaf, and Robert Rollinger. Padova: Sargon.

———. 2006a. "Assyrische ṭuppi adê als Vorbild für Deuteronomium 28." Pages 351–78 in *Die deuteronomistichen Geschichtswerke. Redaktions- und religionsgeschichtliche Perspektiven zur "Deuteronismus"-Diskussion in Tora und Vorderen Propheten*. Edited by Markus Witte and J. F. Diehl. Beihefte zur Zeitschrift für die altestamentische Wissenschaft 365. Berlin: De Gruyter.

———. 2006b. "Provinz, C. Assyrien." Pages 42–68 in *Reallexikon der Assyriologie*, vol. 11/1-2. Edited by Michael P. Streck. Berlin: De Gruyter.

Ramos, Melissa. 2016. "A Northwest Semitic Curse Formula: The Sefire Treaty and Deuteronomy 28." *Zeitschrift für die alttestamentliche Wissenschaft* 128: 205–22.

———. 2019. "Neo-Assyrian Treaties as a Source for the Historian: Bonds of Friendship, the Vigilant Subject and the Vengeful King's Treaty." Pages 309–28 in *Writing Neo-Assyrian History: Sources, Problems, and Approaches. Proceedings of an International Conference Held at the University of Helsinki on September 22-25, 2014*. Edited by Giovanni B. Lanfranchi, Raija Mattila, and Robert Rollinger. State Archives of Assyria 29. Helsinki: The Neo-Assyrian Text Corpus Project.

Reuter, Eleonore. 1989. "'Nimms nicht davons weg und füge nichts hinzu': Dtn 13:1, seine alttestamentlichen Parallelen und seine altorientalischen Vorbilder." *Biblische Notizen* 47: 107–14.

Roth, Martha T. 1995. *Law Collections from Mesopotamia and Asia Minor*. Atlanta, GA: Scholars Press.

Rüterswörden, Udo. 2002. "Dtn 13 in der neuern Deuteronomiumforschung." Pages 185–204 in *Congress Volume Basel 2001*. Edited by André Lemaire. Supplement to Vetus Testamentum 92. Leiden: Brill.

———. 2006. "Die Liebe zu Gott im Deuteronomium." Pages 229–38 in *Die deuteronomisischen Geschichtswerke: Redaktions- und religionsgeschichtliche Perspextiven zur "Deuteronismus"-Diskussion in Tora und Vorderen Propheten*. Edited by Markus Witte and J. F. Diehl. Beihefte zur Zeitschrift für die altestamentische Wissenschaft 365. Berlin: De Gruyter.

———. 2010. "Die sogennante Kanonsformel in Dtn 13,1." Pages 19–29 in *Juda und Jerusalem in der Seleukidenzeit. Herrschaft-Widerstand-Identität. Festschrift für Heinz-Josef Fabry*. Edited by Ulrich Dahmen. Bonner biblische Beiträge 159. Göttingen: Vandenhoeck & Ruprecht.

Schwemer, Daniel. 2001. *Die Wettergottgestalten Mesopotamiens und Nordsyriens im Zeitalter der Keilschriftkulturen. Materialen und Studien nach den schriftlichen Quellen.* Wiesbaden: Harrassowitz.

Singer, Itamar. 2002. *Hittite Prayers.* Writings from the Ancient World 11. Atlanta, GA: Society of Biblical Literature.

Starr, Ivan. 1990. *Queries to the Sungod: Divination and Politics in Sargonid Assyria.* State Archives of Assyria 4. Helsinki: Helsinki University Press.

Steymans, Hans Ulrich. 1995a. *Deuteronomium 28 und die* adê *zur Thronfolgeregelung Asarhaddons. Segen und Fluch im Alten Orient und in Israel.* Orbis Biblicus et Orientalis 145. Freiburg: Universitätsverlag.

———. 1995b. "Eine assyrische Vorlage für Deuteronomium 28,20–44." Pages 119–41 in *Bundesdokument und Gesetz. Studien zum Deuteronomium.* Edited by Georg Braulik. Freiburg: Herder.

———. 2003. "Die neuassyrische Vertragsrhetorik der 'Vassal Treaties of Esarhaddon' und das Deuteronomiums." Pages 89–152 in *Das Deuteronomium.* Edited by Georg Braulik. Österreichische biblische Studien 23. Frankfurt am Main: Peter Lang.

———. 2013. "Deuteronomy 28 and Tell Tayinat." *Verbum et Ecclesia* 34: 1–13.

Streck, Maximillian. 1916. *Texte: Die Inschriften Assurbnipals und der letzen assyrischen Könige.* Vol. 2 of *Assurbanipal und die letzen assyrischen Könige bis zum Untergange Nineve's.* Leipzig: J. C. Hinrich.

Tadmor, Hayim. 1982a. "Treaty and Oath in the Ancient Near East: A Historian's Approach." Pages 127–52 in *Humanizing America's Iconic Book: Society of Biblical Literature Centennial Addresses 1980.* Edited by Gene M. Tucker and Douglas A. Knight. Chico, CA: Scholars.

———. 1982b. "The Aramaization of Assyria: Aspects of Western Impact." Pages 449–70 in *Mesopotamien und seine Nachbarn. Politische und kulturelle Wechselbeziehungen im alten Vorderasien vom 4. bis 1. Jahrtausend v. Chr.* Edited by Hans-Jörg Nissen and Johannes Renger. Second improved ed. Berliner Beiträge zum Vorderen Orient 1. Berlin: Dietrich Reimer.

Tigay, Jeffrey. 1996. *Deuteronomy.* JPS Torah Commentary. Philadelphia, PA: Jewish Publication Society.

Veijola, Timo. 1995. "Warheit und Intoleranz nach Deuteronomium 13: Lothar Pelitt zum 65. Geburtstag." *Zeitschrift für Theologie und Kirche* 92: 287–314.

———. 2004. *Das 5. Buch Mose Deuteronomium, Kapitel 1,1–16, 17.* Das Alte Testament Deutsch 8.1. Göttingen: Vandenheock & Ruprecht.

Watanabe, Kazuko. 2014. "Esarhaddon's Succession Oath Documents Reconsidered in Light of the Tayinat Version." *Orient* 49: 145–70.

———. 2017. "A Study of Assyrian Cultural Policy as Expressed in Esarhaddon's Succession Oath Documents." Pages 473–92 in vol. 2 of *"Now It Happened in Those Days": Studies in Biblical, Assyrian, and Other Ancient Near Eastern Historiography Presented to Mordechai Cogan on His 75th Birthday.* Edited by Amitai Baruchi-Unna, Tova Forti, Shmuel Ahituv, Israel Eph'al, and Jeffrey H. Tigay. Winona Lake, IN: Eisenbrauns.

------. 2020. "Adoration of Oath Documents in Assyrian Religion and its Development." *Orient* 55: 71–86.

Weinfeld, Moshe. 1965. "Traces of Assyrian Formulary in Deuteronomy." *Biblica* 46: 417–27.

------. 1972. *Deuteronomy and the Deuteronomic School*. Oxford: Clarendon.

Wiseman, Donald J. 1958. "The Vassal-Treaties of Esarhaddon." *Iraq* 20: 1–99 + plates.

Zehnder, Markus. 2009a. "Building on Stone? Deuteronomy and Esarhaddon's Loyalty Oaths (Part 1): Some Preliminary Observations." *Bulletin for Biblical Research* 19: 341–74.

------. 2009b. "Building on Stone? Deuteronomy and Esarhaddon's Loyalty Oaths (Part 2): Some Additional Observations." *Bulletin for Biblical Research* 19: 511–35.

About the Author

Diana V. Edelman is professor emerita at the Faculty of Theology, University of Oslo. Her research interests focus on the history, archaeology, and literature of the ancient Southern Levant more generally, and on Judah and Samaria in the Iron Age, Neo-Babylonian, and Persian periods more specifically.

Chapter 2
The Role of the Oath-Bound Agreement (B^erît) in the Book of Deuteronomy

Diana V. Edelman

Abstract

Comparative ancient Near Eastern terminology suggests that the Hebrew term *b^erît* (ברית) designated a formal, oath-bound agreement with two constituent elements: the *'edut*, "written specifications," and the *'ālâ*, "oath" or "curse." Its use in Deuteronomy can be construed either as an example of a formal vassal treaty entered into between Yhwh and Israel or as the written terms of formal contracts, whose Hittite examples have been dubbed "instructions," being entered into by various groups of "royal" (divine) employees, who participated in an oath-swearing ceremony to uphold the stipulated terms. In Deut 12:1–26:15, *haḥuqqîm w^ehammišpāṭîm* represent the directives for the behavioral norms of the *b^erît* being entered into in the storyworld. They do not adhere to the formulation of known units in ancient Near Eastern legal collections; they are best construed either as treaty stipulations or as instructions to royal employees. Finally, explanations for why Yhwh's people are designated Israel, not Judah, are examined.

Keywords: treaty, instructions, *b^erît*, *'edut*, *'ālâ*, Israel, legal collections

With the help of ancient Near Eastern analogies, it has become clear that the Hebrew term *bᵉrît* (ברית) designates a formal, oath-bound agreement. In early Akkadian, two terms had been used to refer to such a pact: *rikiltu/rikistu/riksu u māmitu*, "bond and oath," where the first element designated the written terms and the second the oath. In Neo-Assyrian, the preferred phrasing was (*ṭuppu*=tablet) *adê māmitu* or *adê tāmīti* (see e.g. Weinfeld 1972, 67; Otto 1999, 20–32; Morrow 2004, 114–16). Similarly, in the Hittite sphere, such agreements were known as *išḫiul* and *lengai* "bond and oath." In both spheres, it was possible to use the first element only, "bond," as a shorthand to refer to the official document and oath. In later Assyrian and Aramaic, use of the single shorthand term, *adê*, came into vogue, which appears to have implicitly included the oath. The Hebrew term *bᵉrît* likewise seems to be the primary term used to designate this type of agreement, designating the bond between the two parties but implicitly including the oath that sealed the bond. Two additional terms appear in Deuteronomy that seem to designate the two constituent elements: *ʿedut*, "written specifications," which likely is cognate to *adê*, and *ālâ* (אלה), "oath" or "curse."

The element translated "bond" in both Hittite and Akkadian has a range of meanings, depending on the context. According to Ada Taggar-Cohen (2011, 462, 469), the noun *išḫiul* means "obligation, duty, regulation, law, or treaty" and should not be limited in translation to the concept of a political treaty. Assyriologists are divided over how best to conceive of the genre the *adê* represented; options have included "work assignment, duty, treaty, covenant, a solemn binding oath agreement, and oath documents" (see Parpola 1987; Durand 1991, 70; Lauinger 2013; Watanabe 2017, 476).

In the case of both the extant Akkadian and Hittite examples, the range of possible meanings has made it clear that the genre had sub-types. Two that are particularly relevant to the current discussion are the vassal treaty made between two kings and a category referred to as "royal instructions" in Hittite literature. The latter corresponds to extant exemplars of Assyrian succession oath documents as well, however, with potential reflexes in the Hebrew Bible. The sub-type of the vassal treaty has been applied for over 90 years to the texts of Deuteronomy and Exodus; the implications of the latter sub-type, royal instructions, are only recently receiving much overdue attention. Both will be examined in this contribution.

The storyworld of Deuteronomy is set on the plains of Moab, east of the Jordan River, on the eve of crossing the watercourse to conquer and take possession of the promised land (1:1–5). Moses looks back to two previous formal, oath-bound agreements in Israel's shared memory: the one with Abraham and his descendants concerning the inheritance of the promised land (1:8, 11, 35; 4:37; 6:10, 23; 7:12; 9:5, 27; 26:7; 29:12; 30:20; 34:4), and the one made at Mt. Sinai. He chooses consistently to avoid the latter designation, however, and instead calls it Mt. Horeb (see ch. 4). He refers to the *bᵉrît* made there (Deut 4:13, 23, 31; 5:2; 8:18; 9:9, 11, 15; 10:8; 29:24 [25]; 31:9, 25–26) and the people's failure to keep its stipulations or directives during their wilderness sojourn (1:6–4:43). In a subsequent, long speech (4:41–26:19), he provides instructions relating to the existing oath-bound agreements, with new requirements that are to apply in the promised land. The consequences of following and not following them are presented. The writer has the people affirm these new terms and has Yhwh Elohim also conditionally affirm Israel's status as the deity's holy, treasured people, thereby concluding a new agreement in the storyworld (26:16–19), which subsequently is said to have been solemnized or sealed by oath (29:13 [14], 18–20 [19–21]). This formal agreement made on the plains of Moab is referred to within the book itself by the term *bᵉrît* on a number of occasions (5:3; 8:18; 17:2; 28:69 [29:1], 29:8 [9], 11 [12], 13 [14], 20 [21]; 31:16, 20).

References to the agreement concerning the land promised to Abraham in Gen 15 and reaffirmed subsequently by Yhwh to Isaac (Gen 26:2–5) and Jacob (Gen 28:13–15) situate the events taking place in Deuteronomy within the larger storyworld extending from Genesis through 2 Kings. The conquest of the promised land is narrated immediately after the formal, oath-bound agreement made in the plains of Moab, and the exile from it after multiple failures of the king and the people of both Israel and Judah to uphold the mandates of the Sinai/Horeb *bᵉrît* in 2 Kings completes the meta-narrative covered in the Enneateuch. The inclusion of this theme in the book has been seen as both original (e.g. Arnold 2017) and secondary (e.g. Van Seters 1972, 451–52; Römer 1990, 266–71, 568–75).

Another dimension of the patriarchal *bᵉrît* promising land is highlighted by Ehud Ben Zvi (2015, 128–29). The intended and actual audiences of Deuteronomy identified with a transtemporal Israel remembered as having existed both in the land and outside it. The land promise could be broken without too high a cost to the identity of the community identifying over time as Israel. In contrast, the idea of Israel as Yhwh's oath-bound, chosen community was essential to the identity of the audience. The social and ideological costs of doubting this promise would continue in the future were "too high for the processes of shaping self-identity and social reproduction."

While Deuteronomy is not a formal treaty document nor a formal set of royal instructions, in talking about the *bᵉrît* between Yhwh Elohim and his people, Israel, the writer has included many elements that would have been integral to each. After reviewing how Deuteronomy does and does not include such elements of both sub-categories of the formal, oath-bound agreement, the reason for conceiving the relationship between Israel and its god in terms of this genre will be addressed and the reason why the name Israel was chosen to designate the group will be considered.

1. The Sub-Category of the Treaty and Deuteronomy

Texts of formal, oath-bound agreements made between the kings of two countries have been excavated and reveal that while a generic template existed with a list of options, different regions favored the inclusion of different elements over time. The elements selected for use also depended on the specific historical circumstances of the contracting parties. One cluster of such documents are Hittite treaties, which likely reflect the conventions in place in the Late Bronze period in the Levant (ca. 1550–1200 BCE) and favored by the Hittites, who were a world power at the time. Another cluster originates in Assyria in the Neo-Assyrian period, although they are few in comparison to formal agreements contracted between kings and groups of people concerning the succession to the throne that represent the second sub-type to be examined below (§2). A third cluster are Aramean treaties, which share features found in both the Late Bronze Age Hittite treaties and the subsequent Neo-Assyrian treaties. Located geographically between these two powers, Aramean kingdoms entered into formal agreements with both powers in their heydays and apparently adapted their scribal practice over time to accommodate both, producing in the process a new regional template.

When these regional templates are compared to elements recounted in Deuteronomy concerning the process that resulted in a formal, oath-bound agreement between Yhwh and Israel, there is overlap with the three delineated traditions, but it seems that Judahite scribes could have developed their own tradition for such formal political pacts, which was maintained by their Judean successors. The monarchic-era scribes likely inherited the Hittite model that was in use in the region in the Late Bronze period, but they modified it over time to include elements favored by both the Arameans and the Neo-Assyrians (similarly, Brekelmans 1978, 34; Morrow 2004, 114–15). The kingdom of Judah had dealings with political units from both regions.

Since we have little written evidence from the kingdom of Israel, it is hard to know if its scribes would have shared the same template used in Judah. As independent kingdoms, the two could have developed independent practices. The bulk of the Hebrew Bible is a product of Judahite and Judean tradition, so what it contains most likely reflects southern practices. However, since the Pentateuch was accepted as authoritative in both Samarian and Judean circles, and a minority voice in scholarship has proposed a northern origin for Deuteronomy in particular for almost one hundred years, we cannot say definitively that the covenant template being presumed was only Judahite. It is possible that Deuteronomy was a joint venture with input from northern scribal circles or even penned in its initial form as a book by a Samarian scribe.

1.1 The Hittite *Išḫiul*-Template and Deuteronomy

Having already presented the relevant information in a previous publication (Edelman 2021b) and not finding it easy to vary the wording in what needs to be covered, what follows concerning the three templates for the sub-category of treaty and how they relate to Deuteronomy overlaps directly with that earlier discussion. Beginning with the Hittite *išḫiul* template, there were six standard elements:

1. The preamble, which begins, "These are the words of" + the name of the more powerful contracting "king": 1:1–5, where Moses is the speaker on behalf of Yhwh and Israel is the other "receiving" partner.
2. The historical prologue that gives the background for the current imposition of the treaty: 1:6–11: 32. As noted by Moshe Weinfeld (1977, 267), these prologues often refer to the history of the relationship between the two parties and may dwell on the rebelliousness of the vassal's ancestors and its consequences. The same ideas are found in references to the promises to the fathers (Deut 4:37–38; 7:8; 9:5) and to the rebellion during the wilderness wanderings (Deut 1:26–28, 43; 4:3–5). There frequently is a reference in the prologue to the land given to the vassal by the suzerain and an urging of the vassal to take possession of it, found also in Deut 1:8, 21, as well as to the boundaries of the assigned land. In contrast, Dennis J. McCarthy (1981, 186) limits the historical-paranetic prologue of the central treaty discourse to chs. 5–11. He considers 4:44–28:68 to be the basic draft of the book or the "core" that was expanded with the addition of later chapters.
3. The stipulations: Deut 12:1–26:15, phrased primarily in first and second person.
4. Reference to one or more tablets and provision for deposit in the temple before the gods and periodic reading: Deut 10:1–5; 17:18–20; 31:9, 10–13, 25–27. Provision for the deposit of the tablets with the words of Yhwh Elohim in the divine ark that was to be kept in the temple occurs in 10:1–5. Provision for the deposit of "the scroll of this teaching" beside the ark occurs in 31:25–27 as well as its

conveyance to the priests and the elders in 31:9 and for the periodic recitation of the scroll before the public every seven years in 31:10-13. Meanwhile, the king is to study it daily (17:18-20).

5   A list of the gods that witness the agreement: 4:26; 30:19; 31:19-21, 25-28; 32:46. In Deuteronomy, the sole deity that exists is the contracting superior party rather than a human king, which eliminates the possibility of divine witnesses. Nevertheless, Heaven and Earth are invoked as witnesses (4:26; 30:19; 31:28), as they are in the Hittite treaty tradition (*COS* 2.17a, b; 2.18=Hallo 2002, 93-98, 100-6). In addition, the Song of Moses (32:1-43) serves as a witness against the Israelites (31:19-21; 32:46), as does the written scroll containing all the words (31:25-27; 32:46 possibly).

6   Finally, curses and blessings: Deut 11:13-17, 26-28; 27:14-28:45. The Hittite "blessings" consist of the protection of the gods that oversee the treaty and the curses, while the curses consist of destruction sent by those same deities on the king personally, his family, his city, and his land. They are generic, with no specific examples given. In contrast, here there are detailed examples of both blessings and curses, which go well beyond the Hittite custom in a vassal treaty.

It can be seen that all five elements occur in the narrative of Deuteronomy but not in the order one would expect. The list of witnesses comes after the curses and blessings, although both of these elements are anticipated already in the historical prologue section, where they appear in the expected order: witnesses (4:26) and blessings and curses (11:13-17, 26-28). The Hittite king, the more powerful contracting partner, was to maintain the vassal in his position and to secure the possession of throne by his heir, which he swore to do by oath. The vassal, on the other hand, swore an oath to uphold all the other stipulations of the treaty (Altman 2003, 178-84). Even so, in Neo-Assyrian vassal treaties, there are no conditions or obligations placed on the more powerful overlord in the written document. In Deuteronomy, Yhwh similarly seems to commit to the obligation of maintaining Israel as its 'am sᵉgullâ in 26:18 if the people obey its commands. According to Moses's teaching, this divine commitment includes the blessings listed in 11:13-15, 26-27 and 28:2-14 (Edelman 2021b, 43-44).

1.2. The Neo-Assyrian *Adê*-Template and Deuteronomy

If the Neo-Assyrian *adê* template for a treaty is followed instead, much less of the text is accounted for. Working with the seven elements proposed by Jacob Lauinger (2015, 286–87), two are missing, and Deuteronomy does not follow the Neo-Assyrian sequence:

1. preamble: Deut 1:1–5;
2. list of the gods: Heaven and Earth, the Song of Moses, and the larger scroll of *tôrâ* (4:26; 30:19; 31:28);
3. stipulations: Deut 12:1–26:15;
4. curses only: Deut 11:16–17, 28;
5. the words of the oath: missing, but a reference to the spoken words of both the people and the suzerain, Yhwh, is found in 26:17–19, as though a parity treaty were being established;
6. another series of curses: 27:14–26; 28:15–45;
7. a final colophon: missing.

The first list of witnesses is not in the expected sequence; it precedes rather than follows the stipulations. Under the missing oath, it can be noted that all but two references to a sworn oath in Deuteronomy have Yhwh as subject, not the people. The majority refer to Yhwh having sworn to the fathers previously to give them land (1:8, 4:21; 6:10, 18, 23; 7:13; 8:1; 10:11; 11:9, 21; 19:8; 26:3, 15; 28:11; 30:20; 31:7, 20, 21, 23, 34:4) or to a covenant with the fathers (4:31; 7:8, 12 implicitly; 8:18; 9:5 implicitly; 13:17 implicitly; 29:13 implicitly). Only in 28:9 and in the reference to Yhwh having spoken in 29:13 does it seem Yhwh has sworn a current oath to the people. A separate oath Yhwh swore at Horeb to destroy the people is mentioned three times in 1:34–35; 2:14. There are only two instances where the people swear, and in both cases they are commanded always to swear an oath in whatever circumstance it might be required in the name of Yhwh only (6:13; 10:20). In all extant examples of Neo-Assyrian *adês*, the suzerain never swears an oath to the lesser party. It is noteworthy, however, that in the Hittite treaty tradition, a mutual exchange of oaths took place in a ceremony in which the written contents of the treaty document were ratified (e.g. *COS* 2.17b=Hallo 2002, 96–98; Altman 2003, 178–84).

Simo Parpola and Kazuko Watanabe (2014, xxxv) add four elements to Lauinger's list. They are seal impressions after the preamble (#2 of 11); a historical introduction before the stipulations and after the oath that in their list comes after the list of divine witnesses and oath (#5 of 11), not after the stipulations; a violation clause (#7 of 11) before the first set of curses; and a vow (#9 of 11) between the two sets of curses. The differences between the Neo-Assyrian *adê* and the biblical *bᵉrît* are clear enough when using the shorter list of expected elements. Nevertheless, for the sake of completeness, one can note the following concerning the proposed additional four elements. The seals would be absent. The historical introduction to the treaty stipulations found in two Assyrian texts only would be ch. 11 perhaps. The violation clause would be Deut 27:10 for the ceremony to take place at Mt. Ebal and 28:15 for the ceremony on the plains of Moab. Finally, the vow would be 26:18 (Edelman 2021b, 44–45).

1.3 The Aramaic *Adê*-Template and Deuteronomy

For the Aramaic *adê* template, the first Sefire Stele, the longest and most complete of the three extant stelae, will be used as a template, with the subheadings proposed by Joseph Fitzmyer (1995, 40–55). There is an ongoing debate about whether the term *adê* is Old Babylonian but ultimately of Sumerian derivation (so Durand 1991, 70; Lauinger 2013, 100, 115; Radner 2019, 312) or is of Aramaic origin, becoming a loanword in Akkadian (so Tadmor 1982, 455–58; Fitzmyer 1995, 58; Watanabe 2014, 162):

1. a title, introducing the contracting parties: Deut 1:1–5;
2. a list of gods serving as witnesses to the agreement: Heaven and Earth, the Song of Moses, and the larger scroll of *tôrâ* (Deut 4:26; 30:19; 31:28);
3. curses against the vassal if he violates the pact: Deut 11:16–17, 28;
4. curses with accompanying rites: missing;
5. a restatement of the contracting parties that includes the sons and grandsons of both kings as well as the gods of both cities as contracting parties to the pact, plus an obligation to read out the treaty publicly: Deut 31:9–13 contains the provision for public reading and 6:1–3 might be loosely construed as a restatement of the contracting parties, but this element basically is missing;
6. the stipulations: Deut 12:1–26:15;
7. a statement that the pact is to serve as a reminder or memorial for the future generations: Deut 29:13–27 [Engl. 14–28];
8. one "blessing" or non-curse, which resembles the Hittite tradition rather than the Neo-Assyrian one: Deut 11:13–15, 26–27; 28:2–14;
9. a few curses, which resembles the Hittite tradition more than the Neo-Assyrian one: Deut 11:16–17, 26, 28; 27:15–26; 28:15–45.

As in the case of the Neo-Assyrian *adê*, only a few of the elements are lacking, but the sequence of their occurrence in Deuteronomy does not follow the Aramaic *adê* treaty tradition closely, and there are many more blessings and curses in Deuteronomy than expected. Nor is all of the material in Deuteronomy accounted for. If one adopts this subcategory as most relevant for understanding Deuteronomy, the absence of a historical prologue in this tradition might be due either to an adoption of Neo-Assyrian practice on this point or to the nature of the

Sefire pact as a parity treaty rather than a vassal treaty (Altman 2008, 26–40). Importantly, however, the inclusion of the gods of both cities as contracting parties alongside the human rulers in the second statement of the contracting parties provides a precedent for a deity as a contracting party in a formal treaty (Edelman 2021b, 46).

It could be argued that some of the differences in order or missing elements are due to the circumstance that in the storyworld, Moses is potentially talking about a treaty rather than potentially reading the words of a written treaty aloud to the contracting parties. The text includes teaching by him as commentary on the stipulations in 12:1–26:15, which are framed by statements defining them as *haḥuqqîm wᵉhammišpāṭîm* in 11:32 and 26:16. Nevertheless, after the lengthy stipulations, he also announces that a *bᵉrît* has been entered into "today" after both Israel and Yhwh exchange unspecified words in 26:17–19. This exchange of declarations would seem to relate to the subsequent references to the oath, אלה, in 29:13 [14], 17 [18] and 19 [19]. The *hiphil* of *'mr* was used commonly in the west Semitic world in juridical contexts to signal consent (Vriezen 1963, 207–10).

1.4 Assessment

It seems, then, that the author of Deuteronomy might be envisioning a two-step process of treaty-making involving a written set of formal commands or stipulations (*bᵉrît; 'ēdut*) that are proclaimed before a declarative oral affirmation under oath is made (*'ālâ*) in order to enact a formal and binding pact. This same two-part process was used by the Hittites and the Assyrians, as evidenced by the compound name of such agreements, which included an oath alongside specified terms. It is implicit in the Aramean tradition. The logical deduction to be drawn is that when concluding treaties in the ancient Near East, the document containing the stipulations was usually separate from the formal oaths sworn by the parties before the gods (e.g. Korošec 1931, 26–28, 34–36; Beckman 2006, 283). The oath that sealed the agreement was not recorded but was an integral element in the completion of a formal agreement.

Rather than posit that the scribe(s) responsible for Deuteronomy was/were directly familiar with international scribal conventions for treaties in vogue at the time he/they composed the book, the simpler solution would be to posit their use of a native Judahite/Judean template for writing treaties. The creator of Deuteronomy might have chosen to depict the socio-ethnic bond of members of Israel in terms of a formal contract with Yhwh as their direct sovereign. The genre of political treaty (b^eriît) could have become theologized, with Yhwh replacing the earthly suzerain and the people replacing the vassal king (so Edenburg 2015, 134).

2. The Sub-Category of "Royal Instructions" and Deuteronomy

The second relevant sub-category involves a king issuing a set of "instructions" or duties to serve as behavioral norms to various types of royal employees or the entire nation, which are made binding through the latter group swearing an oath to uphold them that often involved curses. The royal archives from Ḫattuša contained numerous examples that led Hittite scholars to recognize this sub-category within the genre of the išḫiul; it can be identified in Assyrian and biblical usage as well.

2.1 Hittite Royal Instructions

While often described under the heading, Hittite "Instructions," Ada Taggar-Cohen (2011, 469–72; 2020, 26) has demonstrated that a group of išḫiul texts presents the partially preserved, written terms of formal contracts being entered into by various groups of royal employees, who participated in an oath-swearing ceremony to uphold the stipulated terms. Jared Miller (2013, 1) prefers to characterize the employees as "a professional class or classes within the internal state administration." Extant examples involve royal servants (#2); military officers and frontier post governors (#7), "all the men," used in a military context (#10); princes, lords, and military officers (#12); the mayor of Ḫattuša (#13); perhaps the royal majordomo (#15); frontier post governors alone (#17); military commanders (#18); priests and temple personnel (#20); supervisors (#21); priests and diviners (#24); the UKU.UŠ troops (#25); lords, princes, and courtiers (#26); courtiers alone (#27); and the men of Ḫattuša (#28) (Miller 2013, 7 for list and the ToC for specific texts).

The išḫiul was "a legal means by which the Hittite king anchored the loyalty of his 'servants'; he created an obligatory connection of master and servant through a ceremonius (sic!) oath" taken in a public place in the presence of the (icons of) witnessing deities (Taggar-Cohen 2020, 24, quote on p. 26). Unlike the treaties, the "instructions" documents had no set structure, even though they tended to share with treaties a number of components, including the name of the king issuing the directives, occasionally a description of the circumstances for the creation of the document, the detailed instructions, and a mention of the oath and the punishments (Taggar-Cohen 2020, 26). Both Taggar-Cohen (2020, 25, n. 46) and Miller (2013, 2) note that the oath would have been unilateral, with only the subordinates swearing before the gods, not the king. This point distinguishes the Hittite treaty from Hittite royal instructions; in some examples of the former, the king swore an oath or was bound in some way to one.

The instructions, directives, or prescriptions are written in both second person singular and plural and third person singular or plural, almost equally, and can alternate among the four options in the same document. They are "a mixture of prescriptive and prohibitive clauses. Occasionally positive, but more often negative, consequences are added, including blessings and imprecations, often with reference to the oath deities, sometimes of an entirely secular, penal nature" (Miller 2013, 6–7). Historical examples in narrative form can appear, as in a treaty, as well as rationalization, and the oath usually is referred to but occasionally cited explicitly in first person (Miller 2013, 7). From time to time the king also speaks in first person. Sentences providing motives or warnings occur in some documents, particularly the instructions to priests and temple personnel (#20), but true conditional motive clauses are few, if any.

2.2. Assyrian Royal Succession Oath Documents

More recently it has been noted that Esarhaddon's *adê* document is not a vassal treaty *per se*, as it had been labelled in early discussions, but instead an oath document that exemplifies the sub-category of the *adê* involving royal instructions issued under oath to subordinates (Watanabe 2014, 145–46; Miller 2013, 70). Since it deals with royal directives concerning protocols for royal succession, it most closely parallels Hittite texts #11, "For the Successions of Tudḫaliyas I and III," #24, "Tudḫaliya IV's Instructions and Loyalty Oath Imposition for Lords, Princes, and Courtiers," and #27, Tudḫaliya IV's Instructions and Loyalty Oath Imposition for Courtiers" (Miller 2013, 154–67; 282–93; 294–306). The specific historical circumstances differ among the cases, however, and the Hittite examples tend to deal with oaths imposed after "irregular" successions.

Three extant Neo-Assyrian documents exemplify this sub-category, and all three deal with oaths imposed on royal employees to ensure the enthronement of a successor who was not the one expected by birth order. They include Sennacherib's succession oath document (VAT 11449; Parpola and Watanabe 2014, 18), Queen Zakutu's succession oath document (ABL 1239 + JCS 39 189; Parpola and Watanabe 2014, 62–64), and Esarhaddon's succession oath document (ND 4336 and duplicates; Parpola and Watanabe 2014, 28–58). The copy of Esarhaddon's *adê* excavated at Tel Tayinat, ancient Kulania/Kinalua, illustrates how the majority of the sealed copies would have read within the Empire, indicating that the tablets from Kalḫu, ancient Nimrud, involving at least nine rulers from the Zagros mountain region who also were Assyrian citizens, were exceptions to the rule because of the unusual arrangements put in place to manage this mountainous border zone after it had been incorporated into Assyria (see ch. 1 in this volume). Those to take the binding oath include:

> ... the governor of Kulania/Kinalua, the deputy, the majordomo, the scribes, the chariot-drivers, the third men, the village managers, the information officers, the prefects, the cohort commanders, the charioteers, the cavalrymen, the exempt, the outriders, the specialists, the shi[eld-bearers (?)], the craftsmen, [and] with [all] the men [of his hands], great and small, as many as there are – [wi]th them and with the men who are born after the adê in the [f]uture, from the east […] to the west, all those over whom Esarhaddon, King of Assyria, exercises kingship and lordship ... (§1) (Lauinger 2012, 112)

The document of Queen Zakutu (Naqia), mother of Esarhaddon and grandmother of crown prince Ashurbanipal, imposes the oath upon the following:

> Šamaš-šumu-ukin, [Ashurbanipal's] equal brother, Šamaš-metu-uballiṭ, and the rest of his brothers, the royal seed, magnates, governors, the bearded and the eunuchs, the royal entourage, the exempts and all who enter the Palace, and Assyrians high and low (lines 3–7). (Parpola and Watanabe 2014, 62)

Exemplars of Esarhaddon's *adê* tablets uniquely are impressed with three seals of the deity Aššur, turning them into divine Tablets of Destiny (Lauinger 2019, 92–93; Radner 2019, 315–16; see ch. 1 in this volume). Lines 405–9 in §35b state that the tablet "which is sealed ... by the seal of Aššur, the king of the gods, [has been] placed ... in front of you as your god" (Watanabe 2020, 72). This move reflects a strategy to impress upon Assyrian oath-takers empire-wide that Ashurbanipal's succession to the throne was divinely endorsed. Even so, the tablets are designated *adê* documents and are formatted otherwise as royal directives to subordinates who are sworn by oath to enact them and who will bring upon themselves a series of curses should they not carry them through.

2.3. Possible Examples of Royal, Oath-Bound Agreements in the Hebrew Bible

The Hebrew *bᵉrît* also seems to have had a sub-category that involved a formal, oath-bound pact the king imposed on representatives of the people or the people at large during the monarchy, in addition to a political treaty (Weinfeld 1972, 85–91). It is mentioned in connection with Joash's coronation under unusual circumstances and is mediated by the priest Jehoiada in the narrative (2 Kgs 11:4–20). According to the story line, the throne had been usurped by Athaliah and was being returned to its rightful heir, Joash, who was a minor. Two more incidents, however, involving the active participation of the people of the land in installing Azariah as the rightful heir to his assassinated father Amaziah (2 Kgs 14:21) and Josiah as Amon's rightful heir after the latter's assassination (2 Kgs 21:19, 23–24, 26; 22:1) might imply that an oath-bound pact had been imposed on the people by both kings concerning their plans for succession before their assassinations, like the three neo-Assyrian examples. Finally, Josiah's b^{e}rît made with the people to observe the contents of the scroll found in the temple during repairs (2 Kgs 23:1–3), together with the first of two agreements mediated by Jehoiada in 2 Kgs 11:17 that the king and people would be Yhwh's people, reflect this sub-category of royal, oath-bound instructions. Both lead to cultic reforms, which are envisioned to be the main topic of the underlying b^{e}rît.

3. The Nature of Deut 12:1–26:15: Law Code, Treaty Stipulations, Royal Directives, or Something Else?

In Deut 12:1–26:15, *haḥuqqîm w^{e}hammišpāṭîm* represent directives for the behavioral norms of the b^{e}rît being entered into in the storyworld. They are delineated by an *inclusio*-framework that describes what follows 11:32 and precedes 26:6 as constituting these two elements. In addition, this material is summarily described in three ways: as *miṣwâ*, "command" (Deut 5:31; 6:20; 7:11) or *miṣwôt*, "commands" (11:1); *'ēdōt/'ēdut*, "a document containing stipulations" (4:45; 6:20),[1] and *tôrâ*, "teaching" (4:8).

Translations of the two terms have been heavily influenced by the assumption that the material constitutes a once-independent legal code. *Haḥuqqîm* has been commonly translated as "statutes" and has been associated with cultic law (Alt 1953, 278–332; Levin 1996, 118) or situations where secular jurisdiction is powerless to intervene, so that prohibition, positive duty, and curse are invoked to gain compliance (Carmichael 1974, 41). *Mišpāṭîm*, meanwhile, has been translated "ordinances" and associated with secular case law (Alt 1953, 278–332; Levin 1996, 118) or with situations where secular jurisdiction can enforce a penalty for

---

1   The Masoretes vocalized this text as a defective plural; it seems more likely that the intended term was a Hebraicized form of the technical term *'adê*. For this meaning, see de Vaux 1961, 103, 147, 301; Kutsch 1973, 56 n. 29; Yeivin 1974.

infraction (Carmichael 1974, 41). An alternate approach to understanding the two terms would see their distinguishing trait to be whether they are conditional or unconditional written regulatory formulations. *Ḥuqqîm* would be second or third person statements expressed unconditionally, both positively and prohibitively, while *mišpāṭîm* would be second or third person statements expressed conditionally in the format, "if...then..." (Edelman 2021b, 32).[2]

There are two strong indications that the collection of conditionally and unconditionally phrased materials in 12:1–26:15 was not conceived to be a legal collection equivalent to the so-called Hittite and Assyrian law-codes. Both involve conventions present in the materials that are atypical of such legal collections (for other arguments, see Milstein 2021). The first is the extensive use of second person formulations, both conditionally and unconditionally, with first person language interspersed. All extant "legal" collections from the ancient Near East are formulated in third person and almost exclusively as conditional statements; unconditional injunctions, prohibitions, or regulations occur rarely (for all examples, see Paul 1970, 115 nn. 1 & 2; Sonsino 1980, 31, 34). In Deuteronomy, of the sixty-five conditional statements made with *kî* or *'im*, only fifteen, or 23% (19:11; 21:5; 21:18; 22:13, 20, 22, 25, 28; 24:1, 5, 7; 25:1, 2; 25:5, 7), are part of a third person hypothetical example, sometimes with second person motive or paranetic clauses immediately following. The remaining fifty instances, or 77%, are part of second person hypotheticals, also with motive or paranetic material in second person when included (Edelman 2021b, 38).[3] In ancient Near Eastern literature, conditional formulations in second person are common in the phrasing found in instructional material associated with wisdom, formal political agreements that include stipulations, private legal documents, and letters, while unconditional direct address formulated both positively and negatively in second person is used in Hittite and Syrian treaty stipulations, wisdom instructions, collections of proverbs, disciplinary warnings, royal instructions, tomb inscriptions, prescriptive ritual texts, recipes, and training texts (Sonsino 1980, 36–38; Morrow 1994, 138, 140–47).

---

2 This understanding would be consistent with the underlying meanings of the root of both words. *Ḥ-q-q* means "to carve or inscribe," so that a more general categorization of *ḥōq/ḥuqqâ* would be a formal or official regulation, command, or proclamation that has been written down and has binding force. *Š-p-ṭ* means "to judge," so the *mem*-performative noun *mišpāṭ* would be a judgement or verdict which, by implication, has been written down (though not as a formal law) and also has binding force.

3 In the MT, Deut 12:20, 21, 29; 13:2, 7, 13, 19; 14:24; 15:7, 11, 12, 13, 16, 21; 17:2, 8, 14; 18: 6, 9, 21; 19:1, 8, 9, 16; 20:1, 10, 11, 12, 19; 21:1, 10, 14, 22; 22:2, 6, 8, 11, 23; 23:22, 23, 25, 26; 24:10, 12, 19, 20, 21; 25:11; 26:11, 12.

The second indication that Deut 12:1–26:15 was not representing a collection of laws is the extensive presence of motive clauses, in contrast to their rare appearance in the extant ancient Near Eastern legal collections. Roland de Vaux, for example, noted that "unlike all other Eastern laws, its [biblical] prescriptions are often supported by a justifying motive" (1961, 149). Building on the work of Berend Gemser (1953) and Pinchas Doron (1978), Rifat Soncino (1980, 65–69, 93, 153–67) tallied 111 examples among the 225 prescriptions presented, slightly less than 50%. Yet only a handful appear in the "Laws of Hammurapi" and the Middle Assyrian legal collection together, out of all extant examples of ancient Near Eastern legal collections (Paul 1970, 115 nn. 1 & 2). Such dependent clauses provide a justification or incentive for complying with the preceding command or regulation, formulated either conditionally or unconditionally. They can be grouped broadly into four categories: humanistic motives; motives that emphasize Israel's election; clauses whose motives consist of a promise of divine reward; and motive clauses of a didactic nature (Doron 1978, 73–77; contrast Gemser 1953, 56–60). The additional presence of paranetic statements in 12:1–26:15 that summon the people to obedience, formulated as independent clauses, is another convention that sets the biblical collection of *haḥuqqîm wᵉhammišpāṭîm* apart from ancient Near Eastern legal collections, which lack such clauses.

Assnat Bartor (2010) sees the inclusion of the motive clauses and extensive use of second person address to stem from their belonging to a biblical genre she calls narrative law, in contrast to the typical presentation of legal material in a third person, "if...then..." format deriving from case law in other ancient Near Eastern collections. With the telling of such short legal stories in second person address alongside casuistically presented non-narrative, third person formulations, the audience is involved directly and better able to grasp the import of the instruction being presented. In her view, "The laws ... motivate the story plot, since the continued survival of the nation is dependent on receiving and observing them" in Deuteronomy (2010, 20). She notes further, "Moses' role does not end with the establishment of norms"; he also "must guarantee their transmission and see that they are instilled, taught, and explicated so that the addressees understand the nature of the laws, recognize their righteousness, and are persuaded to uphold them" (2010, 68). To this end, Moses is portrayed as systematically interrupting his delivery of the bare substance of the regulations to clarify, emphasize, and persuade (2010, 69).

A possible explanation of the anomalous nature of Deut 12:1–26:15 might be that in the storyworld, this material combines the divine words constituting the actual directives or stipulations for normative behavior, mediated through Moses, with Moses's personal commentary or "teaching" relating to them interspersed. This understanding would be consistent with much of Bartor's narrative reading of the "laws." Moses's teaching would be clearly distinguished from the divine directives he is mediating if the motive clauses and paranetic material were assigned to him and the remaining second and third person conditional and unconditional formulations to Yhwh. The first person statements in the book, meanwhile, clearly identify Moses or Yhwh as the speaker beforehand, leaving no ambiguity about who is saying what.

However, while Bartor's explanation would account for the extensive use of motive clauses to separate Moses's teaching from Yhwh's directives, it would not seem to resolve the issue of the extensive use of second person conditional and unconditional formulations in what she dubs narrative law. Narratives are usually presented in the third person unless direct speech is involved, like the so-called ancient Near Eastern law collections.

The underlying problem seems to be the assumption that 12:1–16:15 constitutes some form of law or legal philosophy. The stylistic inconsistencies are easily resolved by reconceiving the contents of these chapters as either treaty stipulations or royal oath-bound instructions interspersed with Moses's teaching, found in the motive clauses and paranetic material. The presence of second and third personal conditional and unconditional statements, in singular and in plural, is typical of the oath-bound agreement genre as well as didactic material, but motive clauses are typical of instructional material associated with wisdom.[4] The proposed mixing of these two genres in 12:1–26:15 is fully consistent with the designation of the *ḥuqqîm* and *mišpāṭîm* as both a statement of duties and obligations (*miṣwâ*/ *miṣwôt*; 5:31; 6:20; 7:11; 11:1) in written form (*ēdōt*/*ʿēdut*; 4:45; 6:20),[5] and instruction (*tôrâ*; 4:8).

---

[4] Many have identified an influence from what commonly is dubbed a wisdom tradition or sapiential literature. For the debate over whether or not a professional wisdom school or professionally grounded wisdom tradition had existed in Judah or Yehud, see Crenshaw 1981, 28–29 (pro) and Whybray 1974, 31, 33–43, 46, 54, 69–70 (con); Sneed 2011, 61–64 (con); Cohen 2018, 42–56 (con). For the identification of wisdom elements or wisdom-like conventions in Deuteronomy, see Malfroy 1965; Carmichael 1967; 1974; Murphy 1967; Weinfeld 1967; Boston 1968; Lindars 1968, 129; Crenshaw 1969; Geller 1994; O'Dowd 2009, 47; Cohen 2018.

[5] The Masoretes pointed this text as a defective plural; it seems more likely that the intended term was a Hebraicized form of the technical term *ʿadê*. For this meaning, see de Vaux 1961, 103, 147, 301; Kutsch 1973, 56 n. 29; Yeivin 1974.

4. The Potential Source of the Idea Underlying Israel's Formal, Oath-Bound Agreement with Yhwh Elohim

Underlying the collection of *ḥuqqîm* and *mišpāṭîm* in 12:1–26:15 is a worldview predicated on a divine preference for order vs. chaos. Normally, human kings are tasked by their national gods with ensuring the maintenance of that order by, among other things, overseeing the dispensation of justice in their societies. So, for example, the Code of Lipit-Ishtar (ca. 1900 BCE) states that Anu and Enlil called Lipit-Ishtar, king of Isin, to establish justice in the land, to banish complaints, to turn back enmity and rebellion by force of arms, and to bring well-being to the Sumerians and Akkadians (e.g. Roth 1995, 24–25). The prologue of the so-called Code of Hammurabi states that Anu and Bel called Hammurabi (ruled ca. 1728–1686 BCE) to cause justice to prevail in the land, to destroy the wicked and the evil, to prevent the strong from oppressing the weak ... to enlighten the land and to further the welfare of the people (Roth 1995, 76–77). The king of Judah similarly was considered chosen by Yhwh Ṣebaôt to ensure maintenance of divinely sanctioned order and justice and to be the conduit for blessings and abundant harvests. The terms of the oath-bound agreement being envisioned as being made on the plains of Moab allows for a future, native king who will spend his time studying and presumably enacting "this teaching" (17:14–20), but is predicated in the first instance on Yhwh Elohim serving directly as Israel's king. In line with that understanding, the covenantal stipulations or divine "instructions" depict the deity's primary concerns to be the maintenance of order over chaos, which involves behavioral norms that enact principles of justice in towns and cities. When the people assent to these imposed behavioral norms, they take on the direct responsibility, both collectively and individually, to ensure their enactment, with or without the mediation of a human king.

The optionality of a native king in this formal agreement suggests a situation of composition at some point after the kingdoms of Israel and Judah had been conquered and turned into an Assyrian province in the case of Israel, or a Neo-Babylonian province in the case of Judah, or subsequently, an Achaemenid province. As rightly noted by Wolfgang Oswald (2015, 63), the concept of a polity with no human king in charge, which also is envisioned in Exod 18–24, would have been considered treasonous; an assault on the king, if written during the monarchic period. The need to reground group identity and prevent fragmentation in light of diasporic communities seems to have led to the adaptation of former royal "covenantal" ideology to suit the new situation.

As already argued, it is likely the writer of Deuteronomy was drawing on one of the sub-categories associated with the literary genre known as the oath-bound agreement, the b*e*rît, when describing what was taking place in the storyworld. But was that a political treaty, now modified to have Yhwh Elohim the overlord and Israel the vassal? Or was it royal instructions, in which Yhwh Elohim, the divine king, is setting out behavioral directives for his subordinate people, Israel? Or, might a third likely sub-category, an oath-bound agreement a king entered into with the national god upon succession to the throne, possibly be what the writer drew upon?

The single example of such a contract between god and king in the HB is mentioned at Joash's enthronement. He received the crown and the written contract of the covenant (2 Kgs 11:12; 2 Chr 23:11). The tradition of the covenant between Yhwh and the house of David can be seen to point indirectly to such a written pact as well, however (2 Sam 7:8–16; 2 Sam 23:1–7; Pss 89:20–38; 132:11–12).

The same practice of a contract between god and king is attested in at least three extant documents from around the ancient Near East that span two millenia. The earliest refers to a covenant between the deity Ningirsu and the *ensi* of Lagash, Urukagina (died ca. 2371 BCE). The second is a text in which Marduk proclaims, "That prince shall rule all the lands. I alone, all you gods, have a covenant with him" (twelfth century BCE). The third (K2410) relates to the investiture of Esarhaddon, king of Assyria (reigned 681–669 BCE) (Lewis 1996, 405–8).

In the third instance, a peace agreement (*šulmu*) recorded on an oath-bound agreement tablet (*ṭuppi adê*) had been placed before the statue of Aššur. After an oracle from Aššur was given, sacrifices and an oil libation were made and incense burned. Then the tablet was taken up and read to the new king, Esarhaddon, suggesting it contained the terms of a formal agreement between the deity and the king (for the full text, see Parpola 1997, 22–27; for its relevance to the biblical concept of a royal covenant, see e.g. Otto 1999, 79–86 and Nissinen 2000, 251–54). Roland de Vaux (1961, 103) found a similar practice in Egypt in an unspecified text of Thutmoses III.

All three named kings, Joash, Urukagina, and Esarhaddon, had been involved in abnormal successions, so it remains unclear whether these formal written agreements were exceptions or the rule.[6] Were this

---

6 According to the books of Kings, eight coup d'états took place in the kingdom of Israel, each of which resulted in a successful change in dynasty (1 Kgs 15:25–29; 16:8–14, 15–16; 2 Kgs 9:14, 24; 15:8–10, 13–14, 23–25, 30). The Judean author of Kings has mentioned nothing of a covenant or pact in any of these instances. Our knowledge about kingship ideology and coronation procedures in the Israelite kingdom is virtually non-existent, which precludes our knowing whether a formal pact between the king and Yhwh of Samaria had ever been

sub-category to have served as a model for the writer of Deuteronomy, Yhwh Elohim would have filled the role of the deity, and the people, Israel, would have replaced the king.

Finally, a fourth potential sub-category of *adê/bᵉrît* might have involved a formal, oath-bound agreement between a deity and a group of people (Lewis 1996, 408–10), which would require no adaptation to have served as the underlying model. One example is known, and it is not the text of such an agreement but instead a reference to the existence of such an agreement between a group of people and the deity Aššur on an Aramaic incantation plaque found near Arslan Tash in Upper Syria and dated paleographically to the early seventh century BCE (*KAI* 27=Donner and Röllig 2002, 7). The owner of the plaque is not named, but in the first four lines an incantation is directed against the goddess Anat, the god Smm, son of Pidrašiša, and the "Strangler of lambs" not to enter his house or tread his court. The remaining eight lines state that "Aššur has established a covenant with us. All the sons of the gods have established with us, and the leader of the council of holy ones, a covenant of heaven and earth forever, a covenant of Ba'al, Lord of the earth, a covenant of Ḥoron, whose mouth is bound, and his seven mates and the eight wives of the Lord of the sanctuary" (Zevit 1977, 111–12, 116; contrast the translation of Cross and Saley 1970). Ziony Zevit (1977, 116) signaled the importance of this plaque as evidence that the gods named in lines 5–12 "had granted the religious community to which the plaque's owner belonged a covenant," making it "the first clearly attested non-Israelite covenant theology from the ancient Near East."

He and others have failed to note, however, that the wording on the plaque is consistent with the inclusion of deities as contracting parties in Aramaic political treaties alongside the two kings, as seen above in the Sefire treaty. In fact, this practice might reflect an underlying understanding that the national god already stood in a formal, oath-bound pact with the ruling king established at his enthronement, making the deity more than a guarantor of the terms of the covenant but one bound by them as well. Thus, the reference to the covenant with Aššur may be to a political treaty between the plaque-owner's city or country and Assyria, in which the various deities named were made parties to the covenant along with the head Assyrian god, Aššur. In this case, Zevit's suggestion that the covenant would be with a religious community would not be correct. It appears that in the Aramaic scribal tradition of ancient Syria, gods

> normal protocol or had been used in cases of usurpation to seek legitimacy and support.

could enter into formal treaties with kings and by extension, indirectly, with the citizens of their lands.

Any of the proposed four sub-categories of *bᵉrît* could have been envisioned by the writer of Deuteronomy to have been applicable in the storyworld. The last one would require no adaptations but also is the most tenuous, with no extant example of the text of such an agreement between a deity and a group of people. If the treaty is preferred, it could include both parties swearing an oath, as in the Hittite tradition but not in the Neo-Assyrian. The situation is unclear in the extant Aramean tradition. Judahite tradition could have routinely included both parties swearing an oath, as they do in Deut 26:17-19 and 29:13, 18-20 [14, 19-21]. Or, in light of the unusual, adapted circumstances, the writer could have included Yhwh voluntarily making a conditional declarative statement in 26:18-19 in response to the people's unconditional declarative statement in 26:17 as part of their sworn oath. In the case of royal directives, only the subordinates swore an oath, not the king. One would need to argue, then, that the writer included Yhwh making a conditional response to the people's declarative portion of the oath spontaneously, without being obligated or expected to do so. In the case of the oath-bound agreement between a deity and a king, it is likely the god was not bound by oath, only his subordinate, the king. Thus, the same explanation of 26:17-19 as in the preceding case of royal instructions would apply.

In the larger storyworld of Deuteronomy, Moses looks back to the oath-bound agreement entered into at Mt. Horeb. Since Israel has already become Yhwh's people by then, it might make more sense to interpret what is happening on the plains of Moab as the mediated delivery of new directives to Israel by its divine king, on the eve of the settlement of the land, rather than a second or renewed "treaty" meant to reconfirm Israel's status as Yhwh's "vassal," which is the standard scholarly view.

Interestingly, Taggar-Cohen (2020, 33) argues that the *bᵉrît* in Exodus is closer to the "royal instructions" sub-category than to the treaty sub-category, "for it includes laws which are the instructions for the people on how to fulfil their role as servants of the god." At the same time, "They are the basis of the social structure, and thus also are for the administrative structure of Israelite society." She does not comment on the *bᵉrît* in Deuteronomy, even though the same observations apply. If she is correct, then the status of Israel as the people of Yhwh is not presented as first being established at Sinai via a treaty but would seem to trace back to the formal pact Yhwh entered into with Abraham and his descendants (e.g. Deut 7:8, 12). In Exodus, a greatly multiplied Israel already are Yhwh's subjects, who are sworn to uphold a set of divine instructions that will become relevant in the extended storyworld of Genesis-2 Kings, because

Israel has left Egyptian slavery and now will need to have in place its own social and administrative structures.[7]

William B. Morrow (2023) suggests that the behavioral norms presented in Exod 20:24–23:12 and Deut 12–26 minus ch. 13, 17:2–7, and 28:21–44 both were once part of formal Judahite, monarchic-era documents belonging to the sub-category of royal instructional documents written in times of change. He considers the original audience of both to have been officials associated with the palace and temple. He admits, however, that they would have been extracted from the older documents, so that the original texts of both are no longer preserved or accessible. Thus, whether the writer of Deuteronomy has extracted most of the contents of 12–26 from a pre-existing written document or whether he might have assembled these chapters himself for the first time, drawing on existing materials in many instances but adapting them to suit his purposes (Edelman 2021b), remains open to debate.

The impetus to reconceive the people as part of an oath-bound community with Yhwh as king may have come from Achaemenid imperial administrative policy and royal ideology. On inscriptions and friezes at Persepolis, the Achaemenid kings proclaimed themselves rulers over many lands and peoples and appear to have left local administrative practices and social customs in place unless it was not to their advantage, providing their own, ethnically Persian appointees to oversee local operations and secure Persian interests (for various aspects of royal ideology, see Herrenschmidt 1976; Briant 2002, 165–254; Lincoln 2012; Silverman 2016). One notable change was the removal of the tax-exempt status of many temples in Assyria, Babylonia, and Egypt (Briant 2002, 60–61, 73–74, 480–81, 492–93). Creating a sense of peoplehood not predicated on the lost monarchy but adapting former royal ideology would have been in line with the policy of recognizing such groups and endorsing their means of social self-regulation.

At the same time, however, the concept of a binding contract allowed a means of formal endorsement of what probably had involved strategies of informal authority claimed or asserted by the priests and literati after the collapse of monarchic authority. Under the monarchy, they would have enjoyed official authority within the royal bureaucracy by virtue of their professions, but they also likely would have included symbolic strategies employed by informal groups, like mythologies of descent, intergroup marriage, ritual beliefs of practices, moral exclusiveness, and lifestyle, to reinforce the boundaries and cohesiveness of their particular

---

7   She argues further that the *bᵉrît* in Josh 24 reflects the sub-category of treaty, where new documents are written when there is a change in political circumstances (2020, 34).

sub-group (Cohen 1974, 65–89). In Babylonia they might have continued many of their symbolic strategies, even if some might have been assigned new meanings in the changed circumstances, as a way to assert entitlement to informal authority among the Judean deportees.

In the wake of the rebuilding of the temple in Jerusalem and the repatriation of some of these former elites to serve as the local agents of Achaemenid imperial administration in Yehud, those in power once again enjoyed formal imperial authority. However, it appears they wanted to augment their informal symbolic strategies to assert their right to authority within the community conceived as Israel as well, which was not coterminous with the province (Berge 2021, 294–301). They jointly represent the tribe of Levi, whom Yhwh endorses to be his representatives in society for the dispensing of higher justice beyond the level of the local elders and for overseeing the proper enactment of the stipulated ethical norms, values, and festival calendar honoring the divine king (Deut 10:8–9; 17:9, 12, 18; 18:1–8; 19:17; 20:2; 21:5; 24:8; 26:3; 27:9, 14; 31:9; 33:8–11). Some no doubt were among the provincial literati, so that the creator of the book wrote himself and his scribal colleagues into positions of local influence and power among those in Yehud who self-identified as members of Israel.

Effectively, the priests and Levitical literati claim divine endorsement to become the contacts between the imperial representatives and the group at large. Practically speaking, they position themselves as agents of the imperial administration. For purposes of inner group prestige and hierarchy, however, they do not appeal to their confirmation in office by the local foreign imperial overseers but instead, to their endorsement by Yhwh Elohim, Israel's acknowledged highest authority (for a power struggle in Yehud between the scribal and cultic elite reflected in the book, see Rossi 2021).

John Kessler (2006, 99–107) applied an alternate sociological concept of a re-founding "charter group" to the leaders of the immigrant Mesopotamian Judean group responsible for introducing the new concept of Yhwh and *torah*-grounded program into Yehud, based on events portrayed in the books of Ezra and Nehemiah. In his understanding, the transplanted elite was given authority by the Persian crown and also enfranchised by the ex-pat *golah* community in Babylonia. Thus, in his view, they would not have needed to employ mechanisms of informal authority to establish or justify themselves. However, unless they were perceived by the non-*golah*, local population of Yehud as "insiders" who were entitled to leadership by virtue of insider criteria, as "outsiders" they would have had to impose their authority by force and expect non-cooperation on a regular basis.

5. Why Israel, Not Judah?

A final conundrum warranting comment is the curious situation that the group identity being advocated in Deuteronomy for those of Judahite descent and ties to the former kingdom of Judah in the central Judean highlands is as Israelites, not as Judeans. The book has a pan-Israelite perspective, including the traditional twelve tribes, and thus the territory from Dan in the north to the Brook of Egypt in the south, with the two and a half tribes that chose to settle in Transjordan before the main invasion of Canaan also involved. The Hebrew Bible contains multiple tribal configurations that are called Israel; this is but one (Davies 2007, 39–126). Israel had not existed as the name of a kingdom since 721 BCE, and with its demise, the Assyrian province that replaced it was named Samerina, not Israel. The Israel envisioned in this book is generally considered not to correspond to any known political unit in historical reality; the "United Monarchy" under David and Solomon is considered to be a literary construct providing "a Golden Age" and imperial identity in "Israel's" past, although a more recent trend is arguing for the historicity of David ruling over a kingdom that included settlements in Benjamin and the Samarian hills as well as settlements in the hill-country of Judah concurrently, possibly called Israel at the time (see ch. 4 on ethnicity for more about the concepts of tribal Israel and "all Israel").

The explanation for this anomaly in name adoption remains elusive. Philip Davies (2007, 129–77) suggested that Benjaminite scribes based at the Yehudite regional seat of Mizpah during Neo-Babylonian imperial control appropriated Israelite traditions preserved at Bethel, which had become part of Judahite territory (Josh 18:21–24) before that time. They created the concept of the new, theocratic community of tribal Israel as part of an early historiographical work that featured the leadership of Benjamin among the northern tribes (excluding Judah) until the death of Saul at Gilboa. This work was later modified and expanded so that Judah would play the primary role instead of Benjamin, resulting in the Deuteronomistic History collection (Deut-2 Kgs). In the process, Judah became an integral part of "all Israel," one of its tribes, and voluntarily associated itself with the concept of Israel as Yahweh's chosen, oath-bound community.

Nadav Na'aman (2014b, 117–19) built on but modified this idea by proposing that a writer, probably based at Bethel during the Neo-Babylonian period when the site was under Yehudite control, composed the Abraham, Isaac, and Jacob stories, drawing on both northern and southern oral and written traditions in combination with his own creative imagination. He created a story of common origins for all

Yhwh-worshippers living in the territories of the former kingdoms of Israel and Judah. They constituted a "new Israel."

In an earlier article (2010), Na'aman had argued that, on analogy with the political, cultural and ethnic rivalry between the adjoining kingdoms of Babylonia and Assyria, with Assyria appropriating the textual and religious heritage of Babylonia, Judah sought to appropriate Israelite cultural heritage after the disappearance of the independent kingdom of that name. He situated the initial move to do so in the reign of Josiah. Taking advantage of waning Assyrian power, he accepts as historically reliable the report of Josiah undertaking cultic reforms in Judah and in Bethel (2 Kgs 23) and annexing southern Benjamin (Josh 18:21–24). "Religious reform of the kind attributed to Josiah is a natural place to seek a new identity embracing all Yhwh devotees under a single umbrella" (2010, 19). Thus, he proposes that the southern adoption of Israelite identity took place in stages that began toward the end of the Judahite monarchy but proceeded during the Neo-Babylonian period. While he notes the elites of the provinces of Samerina and Yehud would have competed over the heritage of Israel, one can observe that the books of Genesis-Deuteronomy that provide the founding myths for the "new Israel" came to be accepted by both communities and their sub-groups, shaping the identities of both.

Finally, in an even earlier article (2009), Na'aman argued that the pre-Deuteronomistic stories about Saul and David had been passed down orally in court circles in Jerusalem and had dealt with the emergence of the kingdom of Judah; stories of the emergence of the Northern Kingdom have only been preserved fragmentarily in biblical historiography. The territory dominated by these two kings was larger than Judah, including especially Gilead, which later on had belonged to the northern Israelite kingdom. Since the name Israel no longer was attached to the Northern Kingdom when the stories were written down, no earlier than the late eighth century BCE, the historian adopted Israel as a flexible term that he could apply to all or part of the territory formerly ruled by the kingdom of Israel. It thus became "a 'literary' designation for the nation of devotees of Yhwh, who had inhabited the territories of Israel and Judah since early times" (2009, 344–48; quote from 348). Yet, why would the name that Saul or David had used to designate their political kingdoms, which grew and waned over time just like the subsequent kingdom of Judah had, have been forgotten in oral tradition, necessitating this move?

Israel Finkelstein and Neil A. Silberman (2006) associated the transfer of Israelite traditions to Judah and the formation of a pan-Israelite identity with a major influx of Israelite refugees in the wake of the conversion of the kingdom of Israel to the Assyrian province of Samerina in 721 BCE. They suggest that the situation "must have presented a challenge to the southern leadership and created an urgent need to unite the two segments of the new Judahite society – Judahites and Israelites – into a single national entity" (2006, 269). In their view, King Hezekiah responded by centralizing the cult in Jerusalem to prevent the immigrants, whom they claim numbered half if not more of the population of Judah, from maintaining their northern cult traditions and making pilgrimages to Bethel in Samerina (274). He also commissioned the writing of the story of the early Davidides, the "History of David's Rise" and the "Succession History," to reconcile two traditions about the early days of the Jerusalem dynasty: the positive Judahite one of David and Solomon and the negative one preserved among the northern immigrants that held memories of a pro-Saulide perspective (278–79). The resulting texts were "an instrument of reconciliation *within* Judah, and a vehicle for the rise of pan-Israelite ideology," creating "a United Monarchy *within* the borders of Judah, certainly not in all ex-Israelite territories, which were under direct Assyrian rule" (279).

Proposals concerning Hezekiah's response to a purported influx of immigrants from the southern Samarian hills country and Benjaminite plateau are problematic. First, Nadav Na'aman (2007, 2014a) tied the expansion of Jerusalem in the late eighth century to policies that offered Judahites from the countryside protection in light of a planned revolt against Assyria and possible Assyrian reprisals. Thus, it is not certain that large numbers of refugees from Samaria fled south, and as an Assyrian vassal, Hezekiah would have been obligated to return them to authorities in Samerina.

Establishing Jerusalem as Judah's cultic center would not have precluded Israelite immigrants from crossing into Samerina to go on pilgrimage to Bethel unless Hezekiah stationed guards at crossing points to turn them back. As long as the immigrants paid taxes in Judah and honored Jerusalem's royal deity, Yhwh Ṣebaôt (and his wife, Asherah) at the appropriate festivals dedicated to this deity, who, where, and how they worshipped were of no concern to the king.

Similarly, whatever traditions and cultural practices potential immigrants might have brought with them from the kingdom of Israel were not sources of subversion that Hezekiah needed to be worried about. The people were now living under a new political regime and would have been expected to have conformed to its royal mandates and practices and adapt to its culture outside the household. They were now Judahites. No king would have catered to immigrants by altering local Davidic history to respond to their concerns.

Finally, Finkelstein and Silberman have not really explained why Hezekiah or Judahite scribes would have chosen to equate Judah with Israel or subsume Judah within a twelve-tribe or pan-Israelite identity.

The historical scenario they have sketched more logically should have led to Israel being subsumed into Judah and the development of a pan-Judahite identity.

Daniel Fleming proposes yet another scenario. The memory that David's fame was based on his rule over Israel "forges an ancient bond between the founder of the southern kingdom and the northern realm" (2012, 49). Accepting the suggestion of Hugh G.M. Williamson (2011) that Isa 8:14 accurately records a sentiment alive during the monarchic period in its mention of "the two houses of Israel," they both deduce from this phrase that "the house of David never gave up its heritage as onetime rulers over Israel" (2012, 49). Fleming also accepts Williamson's suggestion that a link between Yhwh and Israel could have survived in the Jerusalemite temple, even though it almost certainly had been lost in ordinary Judahite life and culture (2012, 49).

Other textual examples that Fleming thinks illustrate the process of either the preservation of Davidic rulership over Israel or the process of the appropriation of Israelite identity after the fall of the Northern Kingdom in 721 BC include Ps 78:41, Jer 2, Mic 1:5; 3:1, 8–10 (2012, 48–50). Kristin Weingart (2014, 360–61) shares many of his views. She identifies the Succession Narrative (2 Sam 9–20; 1 Kgs 1–2) Hos 5,9, Isa *1–11, and Mic*1–3 as clear examples that demonstrate that the name Israel had been applied to Judah before the demise of the kingdom of Israel in 721 BCE.

In addition, Fleming notes that by the time Chronicles is composed (c. 350–250 BCE), Israel is identified "with what the Jews had become, the whole people of God. Judah needs no separation" (2012, 53). In summing up, he notes that in a no-doubt lengthy and obscure process, "the name 'Israel' was applied to the descendants of Judah. Judah could claim to be part of a larger Israel from high antiquity, but non-Judahites from that larger Israel could participate in the life of Israel only after the monarchies if they came to Jerusalem – at least figuratively – and worshiped on Judah's terms" (2012, 55). While he has provided a partial answer to why this appropriation took place after the demise of the Northern Kingdom by pointing out someone in Judah must have perceived a basis for the connection, he has not fully explained what was gained by the appropriation, or in what life settings, other than possibly the cult, it would have functioned before or after the appropriation. My final critique of Finkelstein and Silberman remains unanswered here as well.

Building on the work of all the preceding scholars, Wolfgang Schütte (2018) has proposed that not only were there a number of Israelite refugees who settled in Judah after Israel was converted to the Assyrian province of Samerina in 721 BCE (2018, 154–56), but also that much of the territory of Judah may have been controlled by the kingdom of Israel in the ninth century, which established fortresses at strategic locations (e.g. Arad) and outside of Judah, the trading post at Quntillet 'Ajrud. The "house of David" mentioned in the Tel Dan Stele would essentially have been an independent city-state that had been established by David, an "Israelite" in origin from Bethlehem, who managed to conquer the older site and make it the seat of a continuing dynasty. Over time, it had aligned itself with Israel, perhaps as a vassal, and any local chiefdoms in the territory also would have been aligned with either or both of these polities (2018, 163).

It seems that Schütte combines two separate models for how Judah became "Israelitized." One traces the Davidic dynasty and its early followers to roots within a social group called Israel, whose members were conceived of as kin-related (so Weingart 2014, 362–66; 2019, 26). It should be noted, however, that the name Israel might already have been applied to a political entity as well in David's time, i.e. Saulide Israel, with which David might have been affiliated before or after he conquered Jerusalem.

In this scenario, some clans living in Judah would have been part of Saulide Israel and so could have perpetuated an Israelite social identity, even after the Jerusalemite city-state eventually grew into a territorial state named Judah and took control of the Judean hills from the territorial state of Israel; these clans would have had a political identity as Judahites but possibly could have perpetuated a social identity as Israelites (so also Sergi 2022).

Then, according to the second model, an influx of Israelites into Judah in the wake of the conversion of Israel to the province of Samerina would have introduced a fresh wave of Israelite collective identity, in which a combined social and political identity would have changed to a social Israelite identity only over time, alongside a Judahite political identity for these immigrants. Neither scenario, however, explains ultimately the decision of the literati in Jerusalem to adopt the identity of pan-Israel as a social or quasi-political unit in which Judah was one of a number of constituent tribes instead of creating the idea of a pan-Judah that included a number of tribes formerly affiliated with Israel or sticking with the biblical imagery of "Israel and Judah" as related but separate entities.

Hermann Michael Niemann (2019) provides an alternative scenario for why Hezekiah or his scribes might have "Israelitzed" Judah. He argues that David had been a member of the Ephrathite clan of Ephraim or Benjamin and thus was ultimately of Israelite background. The clan had members located both north and south of Jerusalem (2019, 8–10). David established a dynastic political unit known as the House of David, mentioned on the

Tel Dan Stele in the mid-ninth century BCE. His northern roots became obscured over time, however, when Jerusalem came to be the capital of what was called the kingdom of Judah instead of Beth-David, by ca. 750 BCE. Court historiographers located Bethlehem in Judah over time and made David a Judahite in origin (209, 17).

Niemann argues that the view of a unified Israel with Jerusalem as its center first emerged under Hezekiah. Asking why the name "Israel" was chosen instead of "Judah" for this unified entity, he suggests, in the form of another question, "Did Hezekiah's pan-Israelite ideology use 'Israel' to conceal problematic features in the stories of David and Solomon such as the alleged origin of the dynasty from Judah?" (2019, 20). Thus, his proposal would seem to be that Hezekiah's scribes decided to set the record straight about the dynasty's Israelite origin.

A final scenario can be proposed. It now appears that Judah was ruled directly by Israelite kings for the second half of the ninth c. BCE (Frevel 2016, 203–28; Edelman 2021a, 114–17). Thus, the writer of the books of Kings would not have been implementing Niemann's proposed impulse toward historical accuracy by Hezekiah's scribes in adopting the pan-Israelite ideology. Instead, they were obscuring the fact that three Israelite kings had occupied the throne of Beth-David, effectively incorporating it into the kingdom of Israel. Instead, it seems that a memory of being part of Israel in the distant past could have led Judean scribes to resurrect and repurpose this old name, which had not been used to designate the Northern Kingdom since 721 BCE and possibly a century or more earlier. The Assyrians had called the kingdom the land of Samaria and the province that replaced it Samerina.

Those responsible for reconceiving the beliefs and ritual practices prevalent during the monarchy and presenting them within the corpus of texts that came to be the Hebrew Bible sought to create a new identity for those who worshipped Yhwh in various forms and lands. They presented the cult of Yhwh Elohim as a form of henotheism/monolatry, likely in the hopes of attracting adherents more easily than they would have had they advocated strict monotheism. The concept of a tribal "Israel" allowed them to direct their message to Yahweh-worshippers in the Galilee, the central hill country, the Judean hill country, and Transjordan, the geographical regions that had comprised the kingdom of Israel at various times during its existence, as well as the diasporic communities of the former kingdoms of Israel and Judah in Syria, Babylonia, and Egypt. It allowed them to build simultaneously a sense of social community and cohesion not predicated on a dynastic monarchy that could have been perceived as a threat to the imperial power of the time.

One factor influencing the Judean adoption of a modified Israelite identity might have been a decision to include all territory where Yhwh had been traditionally worshipped in localized forms under the potential future jurisdiction of Levitical control. A related, second factor might have been the decision to influence the administration of justice in as wide a swath of the Achaemenid satrapy of Eber Nari ("Across the River") as possible. Galilee, Samaria, and Yehud were included, and possibly Transjordan. The possibility that the gentilic "Hebrew," *'ibrî*, used in Deut 15:12, refers to a person originating in this province has been raised (Davies 2007, 176).

A third factor might be that in light of the new conception of deity being espoused as well as the changes envisioned in household cult in Deuteronomy, a deliberate decision was made to resurrect an old name associated with occupants of the southern Levantine hill country to designate the group as a corporate people. In this way, the group's core agenda potentially could be developed and spread over a wider territory than Yehud alone, allowing the Levitical leadership to extend its tentacles and sphere of influence with imperial backing while trying to replace traditional Yahwistic beliefs and practices still being followed in Samaria and Yehud with the new ones they advocated. The Achaemenid Empire tended to distinguish among its subject population groups, applying gentilic labels that associated various people either with geographical regions or kinship-based descent groups, real or fictive, with language likely a third association (for more on this, see ch. 5 on ethnicity).

A fourth influencing factor might have been the recognition that unfulfilled hope plays a central role in a group's identity (Lebel 2022). Having inherited the twelve-tribe scheme, the writers of Deuteronomy might have deliberately seen its potential to allow them to embed hope in the new vision of its "theocratic Israel." They wanted to persuade others to espouse their vision for the future and its underlying beliefs and ways of acting. By projecting its success "one day" to become an "Israel" occupying a wide territory in both Cisjordan and Transjordan, as it allegedly had done before in the past though not successfully, they might have hoped to demonstrate to potential new group members that they planned to become the main vision for "theocratic Israel" over other visions being espoused; they would be the one that accomplished the widest territorial spread.

While in theory the label Israelite should have been inherited at birth into one of the traditional twelve tribes, regardless of physical location, in the storyworld of Deuteronomy, Israelites must choose individually if they will accept the oath-bound directives imposed by the divine upon subordinate Israel, thereby choosing life and blessing, or if they will choose death and the enactment of the curses (30:15–19) (for a study of the theme of life, see Markl 2014). The same choice is being impressed on the reader. As a result, not everyone born an "Israelite" (e.g. Ephraimite,

Danite, Benjaminite; Samarian, Galilean, Judean) will necessarily self-identify with that label and its implications. Those who want to continue monarchic-era beliefs about a pantheon and the mediating role of deified ancestors and family gods and the use of physical representations of the head divine couple, Yhwh Ṣebaôt and Asherah, will not choose life and insider status (see ch. 7 for more information about monarchic-era religion).

Conclusion

Because Deuteronomy describes the making of a formal, oath-bound agreement between Yhwh Elohim and Israel in the plains of Moab before crossing the Jordan River to take possession of the Cisjordanian portions of the promised land, many elements that were included in the written forms of such formal agreements are presented in the narrative. A review of preserved examples of the Hittite *išḫiul*, the Aramaic *adê* and the Neo-Assyrian *adê* has shown that two prominent sub-categories, the vassal treaty and royal instructions, need to be considered when determining what the writer meant when using the Hebrew term *bᵉrît* and how he was conceiving of Israel's relationship to Yhwh and what was taking place on the plains of Moab. Two additional sub-categories, the formal agreement between a deity and the reigning king and possibly between a deity and a group of people, have also been considered as possibly having belonged to the genre of *bᵉrît*.

Chapters 12–26 do not follow the conventions used for ancient Near Eastern legal collections; instead they follow the conventions found in the genre of the formal, oath-bound agreement. Thus, in the storyworld, they do not function as a legal code; instead, they serve as either the stipulations of a vassal treaty or the behavioral directives of royal instructions. If one favors the first option, then a new treaty is being made on the plains of Moab in anticipation of Israel's conquest of and settlement in Cisjordan. If one follows the second instead, then the divine king Yhwh is establishing a new set of binding behavioral norms on his subordinates, Israel, to be in force during the conquest of the promised land and once the land is settled.

The decision to present this "theocratic Israel" as formally bound to its divine leader is likely a deliberate adaptation of monarchic-era royal ideology in a situation where there was no longer an independent native king or kingdom; the audience likely lived in an imperial reality. The scholarly understanding that Achaemenid imperial administrative policy favored supervised self-regulation by recognized socio-ethnic groups within the Empire probably contributed to this self-description as Israel by those who sought to gain authority within it via the internal consent of the group, which would then also endorse them as imperial middlemen.

Finally, six proposals have been reviewed for why, in this and other books that came to form the Hebrew Bible, Israel was the name chosen to present the vision of a theocratic, ethnic entity rather than Judah. The envisioned group did not need a political identity realized in historical time to exist. Yet the name of a former kingdom that had once existed hundreds of years earlier was resurrected and repurposed, and a decision was made not to use Judah or its successor Yehud, where most of the biblical books were composed, but Israel instead.

Works Cited

Alt, Albrecht. 1953. "Die Ursprünge des israelitischen Rechts." Pages 278–332 in volume 1 of *Kleine Schriften zur Geschichte des Volkes Israel.* Munich: C. H. Beck.

Altman, Amnon. 2003. "Who Took an Oath on a Vassal Treaty – Only the Vassal King or Also the Suzerain?" *Zeitschrift für altorientalische und biblische Rechtsgeschichte* 9: 178–84.

———. 2008. "What Kind of Treaty Tradition Do the Sefire Inscriptions Represent?" Pages 26–40 in *Treasures on Camels' Humps: Historical and Literary Studies from the Ancient Near East Presented to Israel Eph'al.* Edited by Mordechai Cogan and Dan'el Kahn. Jerusalem: The Hebrew University Magnes Press.

Arnold, Bill T. 2017. "Reexamining the 'Fathers' in Deuteronomy's Framework." Pages 10–41 in *Torah and Tradition: Papers Read at the Sixteenth Joint Meeting of the Society for Old Testament Study and the Oudtestamentisch Werkgezelschap, Edinburgh, 2015.* Edited by Klaas Spronk and Hans M. Barstad. Oudtestamentische Studiën 70. Leiden: Brill.

Bartor, Assnat. 2010. *Reading Law as Narrative: A Study in the Casuistic Laws of the Pentateuch.* Ancient Israel and Its Literature 5. Atlanta: Society of Biblical Literature.

Beckman, Gary. 2006. "Hittite Treaties and the Development of the Cuneiform Treaty Tradition." Pages 279–301 in *Die deuteronomistischen Geschichtswerke. Redaktions- und religionsgeschichtliche Perspektiven zur "Deuteronomismus"-Diskussion in Tora und Vorderen Propheten.* Edited by Markus Witte et. al. Beihefte zur Zeitschrift für die altestamentische Wissenschaft 365. Berlin: Walter de Gruyter.

Ben Zvi, Ehud. 2015. "A Balancing Act: Settling and Unsettling Issues Concerning Past Divine Promises in Historiographical Texts Shaping Social Memory in the Late Persian Period." Pages 109–29 in *Covenant in* the Persian Period: From Genesis to Chronicles. Edited by Richard J. Bautch and Gary Knoppers. Winona Lake, IN: Eisenbrauns.

Berge, Kåre. 2021. "Dynamics of Power and the Re-Inventing of 'Israel' in Persian Empire Judah." Pages 293–321 in *Levantine Entanglements: Local Dynamics of Globalization in a Contested Region*. Edited by Terje Stordalen and Øystein S. LaBianca. Sheffield: Equinox Publishing Ltd.

Boston, James R. 1968. "The Wisdom Influence upon the Song of Moses." *Journal of Biblical Literature* 87: 198–202.

Brekelmans, Christianus. 1978. "Wisdom Influence in Deuteronomy." Pages 28–38 in *La Sagesse de l'Ancien Testament*. Edited by Maurice Gilbert. Bibliotheca Ephemeridum Theologicarum Lovaniensium 51. Louvain: Louvain University Press.

Briant, Pierre. 2002. *From Cyrus to Alexander: A History of the Persian Empire*. Translated by Peter T. Daniels. Winona Lake, IN: Eisenbrauns.

Carmichael, Calum M. 1967. "Deuteronomic Laws, Wisdom, and Historical Traditions." *Journal of Semitic Studies* 12: 198–206.

------. 1974. *The Laws of Deuteronomy*. Ithaca: Cornell University Press.

Cohen, Abner. 1974. *Two-Dimensional Man: An Essay on the Anthropology of Power and Symbolism in Complex Societies*. Los Angeles: University of California Press.

Cohen, Yoram. 2018. "Why 'Wisdom'? Copying, Studying, and Collecting Wisdom Literature in the Cuneiform World." Pages 41–59 in *Teaching Morality in Antiquity: Wisdom Texts, Oral Traditions, and Images*. Edited by T. M. Oshida with Susanne Kohlhaas. Orientalische Religionen in der Antike 29. Tübingen: Mohr Siebeck.

Crenshaw, James L. 1969. "Method in Determining Wisdom Influence upon 'Historical' Literature." *Journal of Biblical Literature* 88: 129–42.

------. 1981. *Old Testament Wisdom: An Introduction*. Louisville: John Knox.

Cross, Frank Moore, Jr., and Richard J. Saley. 1970. "Phoenician Incantations on a Plaque of the Seventh Century B. C. from Arslan Tash in Upper Syria." *Bulletin of the American Schools of Oriental Research* 197: 42–49.

Davies, Philip R. 2007. *The Origins of Biblical Israel*. Library of Hebrew Bible/Old Testament Studies 485. New York: T & T Clark.

Donner, Herbert and Wolfgang Röllig. 2002. *Kanaanäische und aramäische Inschriften*, Volume 1. 5th ed. Weisbaden: Harrassowitz.

Doron, Pinchas. 1978. "Motive Clauses in the Laws of Deuteronomy: Their Forms, Functions, and Contents." *Harvard Annual Review* 2: 61–77.

Durand, Jean-Marie. 1991. "Précurseurs syriens aux protocols néo-assyriens." Pages 13–72 in *Marchands, diplomates et empereurs. Études sur la civilization mésopotamienne offertes à Paul Garelli*. Edited by Dominique Charpin and Francis Joannès. Paris: Éditions recherche sur les civilizations.

Edelman, Diana. 2021a. "Creating the Memory of an Unbroken Davidic Dynasty in the Book of Kings in Response to Political Discontinuity."

Pages 109–24 in *Negotiating Memory from the Romans to 21st Century: Damnatio Memoriae*. Edited by Øivind Fuglerud, Kjersti Larsen, and Marina Prusac-Lindhagen. Routledge Studies in Cultural History. London: Routledge.

———. 2021b. "Deuteronomy as the Instructions of Moses and Yhwh vs. a Framed Legal Code." Pages 25–75 in *Deuteronomy in the Making: Studies in the Production of Debarim*. Edited by Diana Edelman, Benedetta Rossi, Kåre Berge, and Philippe Guillaume. Beihefte zur Zeitschrift für die altestamentische Wissenschaft 533. Berlin: de Gruyter.

Edenburg, Cynthia. 2015. "From Covenant to Connubium: Persian Period Developments in the Perception of Covenant in the Deuteronomistic History." Pages 131–49 in *Covenant in the Persian Period: From Genesis to Chronicles*. Edited by Richard J. Bautch and Gary Knoppers. Winona Lake, IN: Eisenbrauns.

Finkelstein, Israel and Neil A. Silberman. 2006. "Temple and Dynasty: Hezekiah, the Remaking of Judah and the Rise of Pan-Israelite Ideology." *Journal for the Study of the Old Testament* 30: 259–85.

Fitzmyer, Joseph A. 1995. *The Aramaic Inscriptions of Sefîre*. Revised ed. Biblica et Orientalia 19/A. Rome: Pontifical Biblical Institute.

Fleming, Daniel. 2012. *The Legacy of Israel in Judah's Bibkle: History, Politics, and the Reinscribing of Tradition*. New York: Cambridge University Press.

Frevel, Christian. 2016. *Geschichte Israels*. Kohlhammer Studienbücher Theologie 2. Stuttgart: Kohlhammer.

Geller, Stephen A. 1994. "Fiery Wisdom: Logos and Lexis in Deuteronomy 4." *Prooftexts* 14: 103–39.

Gemser, Berend. 1953. "The Importance of the Motive Clause in Old Testament Law." Pages 50–66 in *Congress Volume Copenhagen 1953*. Edited by G. W. Anderson et al. Supplements to Vetus Testmentum 1. Leiden: Brill. Reprinted in 1968 as pages 95–115 in *Adhuc Loquitur: Collected Essays of Dr. B. Gemser*. Edited by Adrianus van Selms and Adam S. van der Woude. Leiden: Brill.

Hallo, William W. 2002. *Monumental Inscriptions from the Biblical World*. Vol. 2 of *The Context of Scripture*. Leiden: Brill.

Herrenschmidt, Clarisse. 1976. "Désignation de l'empire et concepts politiques de Darius 1er d'après ses inscriptions en vieux perse." *Studia Iranica* 5: 33–65.

Kessler, John. 2006. "Persia's Loyal Yahwists: Power Identity and Ethnicity in Achaemenid Yehud." Pages 91–122 in *Judah and the Judeans in the Persian Period*. Edited by Oded Lipschits and Manfred Oeming. Winona Lake, IN: Eisenbrauns.

Korošec, Viktor. 1931. *Hethitische Staatsverträge. Ein Beitrag zu ihrer juristischen Wertung*. Leipziger rechtswissenschaftliche Studien 60. Leipzig: T. Weicher.

Kutsch, Ernst. 1973. *Verheissung und Gesetz. Untersuchungen zum sogennanten "Bund" im Alten Testament*. Beihefte zur Zeitschrift für die altestamentische Wissenschaft 131. Berlin: de Gruyter.

Lauinger, Jacob. 2012. "Esarhaddon's Succession Treaty at Tell Tayinat: Text and Commentary." *Journal of Cuneiform Studies* 64: 87–123.

——. 2013. "The Neo-Assyrian *adê*: Treaty, Oath or Something Else?" *Zeitschrift für altorientalische und biblische Rechtsgeschichte* 19: 99–115.

——. 2015. "Neo-Assyrian Scribes, 'Esarhaddon's Succession Treaty,' and the Dynamics of Textual Mass Production." Pages 285–314 in *Texts and Contexts: The Circulation and Transmission of Cuneiform Texts in Social Space*. Edited by Paul Delnero and Jacob Lauinger. Studies in Ancient Near Eastern Records 9. Boston: de Gruyter.

——. 2019. "Neo-Assyrian Treaties as a Source for the Historian: Bonds of Friendship, the Vigilant Subject and the Vengeful King's Treaty." Pages 309–28 in *Writing Neo-Assyrian History: Sources, Problems, and Approaches. Proceedings of an International Conference Held at the University of Helsinki on September 22-25, 2014*. Edited by Giovanni B. Lanfranchi, Raija Mattila, and Robert Rollinger. State Archives of Assyria 29. Helsinki: The Neo-Assyrian Text Corpus Project.

Lebel, Efi. 2022. "The Survival of the Identity Group: A Case Study of the Survival of the Jewish People during the Second Temple Period." PhD dissertation, University of Haifa.

Levin, Christoph. 1996. "Über den 'Color Hieremianus' des Deuteronomiums." Pages 107–26 in *Das Deuteronomium und seine Querbeziehungen*. Edited by Timoo Veijola. Suomen Eksegeettisen Seuran julkaisuja 62. Helsinki: Finnish Exegetical Society.

Lewis, Theodore J. 1996. "The Identity and Function of El/Baal Berith." *Journal of Biblical Literature* 115: 401–23.

Lincoln, Bruce. 2012. *"'Happiness for Mankind': Achaemenian Religion and the Imperial Project*. Acta Iranica 53. Leuven: Peeters.

Lindars, Barnabas. 1968. "Torah in Deuteronomy." Pages 117–36 in *Words and Meanings: Essays Presented to D. Winton Thomas*. Edited by Peter R. Ackroyd and Barnabas Lindars. Cambridge: Cambridge University Press.

Malfroy, Jean. 1965. "Sagesse et loi dans le Deuteronome: études." *Vetus Testamentum* 15: 49–65.

Markl, Dominik. 2014. "This Word is Your Life: The Theology of 'Life' in Deuteronomy." Pages 71–96 in *Gottes Wort im Menschenwort. Festschrfit für Georg Fischer SJ zum 60. Geburtstag*. Edited by Dominik Markl, Claudia Paganini and Simone Paganini. Österreichische biblische Studien 43. Frankfurt am Main: Peter Lang.

McCarthy, Dennis J. 1981. *Treaty and Covenant: A Study in Form in the Ancient Oriental Documents and in the Old Testament*. Analecta Biblica 21A. Rome: Pontifical Biblical Institute.

Miller, Jared. 2013. *Royal Hittite Instructions and Related Administrative Texts.* Writings from the Ancient World 31. Atlanta: Society of Biblical Literature.

Milstein, Sara J. 2021. *Making a Case: The Practical Roots of Biblical Law.* New York: Oxford University Press.

Morrow, William S. 1994. "A Generic Discrepancy in the Covenant Code." Pages 136–51 in *Theory and Method in Biblical and Cuneiform Law: Revision, Interpolation, and Development.* Edited by Bernard M. Levinson. Journal for the Study of the Old Testament Supplement Series 181. Sheffield: JSOT Press.

———. 2004. "*Fortschreibung* in Mesopotamian Treaties and the Book of Deuteronomy." Pages 111–23 in *Recht und Ethik im Alten Testament. Beiträge des Symposiums "Das Alte Testament und die Kultur der Moderne" anlässlich des 100. Geburtstags Gerhard von Rads (1901–1971) Heidelberg, 18.–21. Oktober, 2001.* Edited by Bernard M. Levinson and Eckart Otto. Altes Testament und Moderne 13. Münster: LIT.

———. 2023. "The Laws in the Covenant Code and Deuteronomy as *Dienstanweisungen.*" *Scandinavian Journal of the Old Testament* 37: 28–147.

Murphy, Roland E. 1967. "Assumptions and Problems in Old Testament Wisdom Research." *Catholic Biblical Quarterly* 29: 407–18.

Na'aman, Nadav. 2007. "When and How Did Jerusalem Become a Great City? The Rise of Jerusalem as Judah's Premier City in the Eighth-Seventh Centuries." *Bulletin of the American Schools of Oriental Research* 347: 21–56.

———. 2009. "Saul, Benjamin and the Emergence of Biblical Israel." *Zeitschrift für die altestamentische Wissenschaft* 121: 211–24, 335–49.

———. 2010. "The Israelite-Judahite Struggle for the Patrimony of Ancient Israel." *Biblica* 91:1–23.

———. 2014a. "Dismissing the Myth of a Flood of Israelite Refugees in the Late Eighth Century BCE." *Zeitschrift für die altestamentische Wissenschaft* 126:1–14.

———. 2014b. "The Jacob Story and the Formation of Biblical Israel." *Tel Aviv* 41: 95–125.

Niemann, Hermann Michael. 2019. "Judah and Jerusalem: Reflections on the Relationship between Tribe and City and the Role of Jerusalem in Judah." *Zeitschrift des Deutschen Palästina Vereins* 135: 1–31.

Nissinen, Martti. 2000. "Spoken, Written, Quoted, and Invented: Orality and Writtenness in Ancient Near Eastern Prophecy." Pages 235–71 in *Writings and Speech in Israelite and Ancient Near Eastern Prophecy.* Edited by Ehud Ben Zvi and Michael H. Floyd. Atlanta: Society of Biblical Literature.

O'Dowd, Ryan. 2009. *The Wisdom of Torah: Epistemology in Deuteronomy and the Wisdom Literature.* Forschungen zur Religion und Literatur des Alten und Neuen Testaments 225. Göttingen: Vandenhoeck & Ruprecht.

Oswald, Wolfgang. 2015. "Correlating the Covenants in Exodus." Pages 59-73 in *Covenant in the Persian Period: From Genesis to Chronicles.* Edited by Richard J. Bautch and Gary Knoppers. Winona Lake, IN: Eisenbrauns.

Otto, Eckart. 1999. *Das Deuteronomium. Politische Theologie und Rechtsreform in Juda und Assyrien.* Beihefte zur Zeitschrift für die altestamentische Wissenschaft 284. Berlin: de Gruyter.

Parpola. Simo. 1987. "Neo-Assyrian Treaties from the Royal Archives of Nineveh." *Journal of Cuneiform Studies* 39: 161-89.

------. 1997. *Assyrian Prophecies.* State Archives of Assyria 9. Helsinki: Helsinki University Press.

------ and Kazuko Watanabe. 2014. *Neo-Assyrian Treaties and Loyalty Oaths.* State Archives of Assyria 2. Helsinki: Helsinki University Press. Reprint of 1988 original version.

Paul, Shalom M. 1970. *Studies in the Book of the Covenant in the Light of Cuneiform and Biblical Law.* Supplements to Vetus Testamentum 18. Leiden: Brill.

Radner, Karen. 2019. "Neo-Assyrian Treaties as a Source for the Historian: Bonds of Friendship, the Vigilant Subject and the Vengeful King's Treaty." Pages 309-28 in *Writing Neo-Assyrian History: Sources, Problems, and Approaches. Proceedings of an International Conference Held at the University of Helsinki on September 22-25, 2014.* Edited by Giovanni B. Lanfranchi, Raija Mattila, and Robert Rollinger. State Archives of Assyria 29. Helsinki: The Neo-Assyrian Text Corpus Project.

Römer, Thomas. 1990. *Israels Väter. Untersuchungen zur Väterthematik im Deuteronomium und in der deuteronomistichen Tradition.* Orbis Biblicus et Orientalis 99. Freiburg: Universitätsverlag and Göttingen: Vandenhoeck & Ruprecht.

Rossi, Benedetta. 2021. "'Not by Bead Alone' (Deut 8:3): Elite Struggles over Cultic Prebends and Moses's Torah in Deuteronomy." Pages 329-63 in *Deuteronomy in the Making: Studies in the Production of Debarim.* Edited by Diana Edelman, Benedetta Rossi, Kåre Berge, and Philippe Guillaume. Beihefte zur Zeitschrift für die altestamentische Wissenschaft 533. Berlin: De Gruyter.

Roth, Martha T. 1995. *Law Collections from Mesopotamia and Asia Minor.* Writings from the Ancient World 6. Atlanta: Scholars Press.

Schütte, Wolfgang. 2018. "Were There Israelites in "Judean Exile?" *Antiguo Oriente* 16: 147-80.

Sergi, Omer. 2022. *The Two Houses of Israel.* Atlanta: Society of Biblical Literature.

Silverman, Jason M. 2016. "Was There an Achaemenid 'Theology' of Kingship? The Intersections of Mythology, Religion, and Imperial Religious Policy." Pages 172-96 in *Religion in the Achaemenid Persian*

Empire: Emerging Judaisms and Trends. Edited by Diana Edelman, Anne Fitzpatrick-McKinley, and Philippe Guillaume. Orientalische Religionen in der Antike 17. Tübingen: Mohr Siebeck.

Sneed, Mark. 2011. "Is the 'Wisdom Tradition' a Tradition?" *Catholic Biblical Quarterly* 73: 50–71.

Sonsino, Rifat. 1980. *Motive Clauses in Hebrew Law*. Chico, CA: Scholars.

Tadmor, Hayim. 1982. "The Aramaization of Assyria: Aspects of Western Impact." Pages 449–70 in *Mesopotamien und seine Nachbarn. Politische und kulturelle Wechselbeziehungen im alten Vorderasien vom 4. bis 1. Jahrtausend v. Chr.* Edited by Hans-Jörg Nissen and Johannes Renger. Second improved ed. Berliner Beiträge zum Vorderer Orient Texte 1. Berlin: Dietrich Reimer.

Taggar-Cohen, Ada. 2011. "Biblical covenant and Hittite *išḫiul* reexamined." *Vetus Testamentum* 61: 461–88.

――――. 2020. "The Hebrew Biblical *Bérit* in Light of Ancient Near Eastern Covenants and Texts." *Canon and Culture* 14: 5–50.

Van Seters, John. 1972. "Confessional Reformulation in the Exilic Period." *Vetus Testamentum* 22: 448–59.

Vaux, Roland de. 1961. *Ancient Israel: Its Life and Institutions*. Translated by John McHugh. London: Dartman, Longman & Todd.

Vriezen, Theodor C. 1963. "Das Hiphil von *'amar* in Deut 26.17, 18." *Jaarbericht van het Vooraziatisch-Egyptisch Gezelschap (Genootschap) Ex oriente Lux* 17: 207–10.

Watanabe, Kazuko. 2014. "Esarhaddon's Succession Oath Documents Reconsidered in Light of the Tayinat Version." *Orient* 49: 145–70.

――――. 2017. "A Study of Assyrian Cultural Policy Expressed in Esarhaddon's Succession Oath Documents." Pages 473–92 in vol. 2 of *"Now It Happened in Those Days": Studies in Biblical, Assyrian and Other Ancient Near Eastern Historiography Presented to Mordechai Cogan on his 75th Birthday*. Edited by Amitai Baruchi-Unna et al. Winona Lake, IN: Eisenbrauns.

――――. 2020. "Adoration of Oath Documents in Assyrian Religion and Its Development." *Orient* 22: 71–86.

Weinfeld, Moshe. 1967. "Deuteronomy: The Present State of Inquiry." *Journal of Biblical Literature* 86: 249–62.

――――. 1972. *Deuteronomy and the Deuteronomic School*. Oxford: Clarendon.

――――. 1977. "B^{e}rîth." Pages 253–79 in volume 2 of *Theological Dictionary of the Old Testament*. Edited by G. Johannes Botterweck and Helmer Ringgren. Translated by John T. Willis. Grand Rapids, MI: Eerdmans, 1977.

Weingart, Kristin. 2014. *Stämmevolk-Stattsvolk-Gottesvolk*. Forschungen zum Alten Testament 2.68. Tübingen: Mohr Siebeck.

――――. 2019. "'All of These Are the Twelve Tribes of Israel': The Origins of Israel's Kinship Identity." *Near Eastern Archaeology* 82: 24–31.

Whybray, Roger N. 1974. *The Intellectual Tradition in the Old Testament.* Beihefte zur Zeitschrift für die altestamentische Wissenschaft 135. Berlin: Walter de Gruyter.

Williamson, Hugh G.M. 2011. "Judah as Israel in Eighth Century Prophecy." Pages 81–95 in *A God of Faithfulness: Essays in Honour of J. Gordon McConville on His 60th Birthday.* Edited by Jamie A. Grant Alison Lo, and Gordon Wenham. London: T. & T. Clark.

Yeivin, Shmuel. 1974. "Ēdūth." *Israel Exploration Journal* 24: 17–20.

Zevit, Ziony. 1977. "A Phoenician Inscription and Biblical Covenant Theology." *Israel Exploration Journal* 27: 110–18.

About the Author

Diana V. Edelman is professor emerita at the Faculty of Theology, University of Oslo. Her research interests focus on the history, archaeology, and literature of the ancient Southern Levant more generally, and on Judah and Samaria in the Iron Age, Neo-Babylonian, and Persian periods more specifically.

Chapter 3
Deuteronomy in Dialogue with Ancient Near Eastern Law Collections

Megan B. Turton

Abstract

The very heart of Deuteronomy, chs.12–26, is comprised of legal discourse. Early critical scholarship identified the "Deuteronic Code" in chs. 12–26 as a "core," distinct in some sense from the surrounding narrative frames in chs. 1–11 and 27–34. Subsequent scholarship has detected a complex literary history in the book's legal and narrative chapters, positing pre-exilic, exilic, and post-exilic layers. There is considerable debate regarding what might be identified as the first layer of Deuteronomy and the dating of this stratum. Some scholars theorize that select Deuteronomic laws, especially from chs. 21–25, may have circulated separately prior to their integration into the "Deuteronomic Code," as one among a number of ancient law collections that, despite being produced by various peoples and cultures of ancient West Asia or the ancient Near East (ANE), share certain characteristics in form and content. Yet, when we put Deuteronomy's legal writings in dialogue with the cuneiform laws, it reveals intriguing contrasts and continuities, prompting all sorts of questions regarding the dating, compositional history, character, purpose, and function of Deuteronomic law. Comparing Deuteronomy's laws on different forms of adultery and sexual violation (Deut 22:22–29) with their ANE counterparts reveals that at least portions of Deut 21–25 are part of a broader ANE legal tradition. Nonetheless, Deuteronomy also presents a unique legal ideology and theology, promoting exclusive loyalty to Yhwh's law, rather than to a foreign empire or native king.

Keywords: Deuteronomic law, ancient Near Eastern law collection, treaty, narrative, casuistic law, adultery, sexual violation

1. Introduction

Of the five books that make up the Pentateuch, it is the final book, Deuteronomy, that provides the most sustained treatment of what we might call "law." Exodus contains a small legal collection, sometimes called "the Covenant Code" (Exod 20:22–23:19), while Exodus, Leviticus, and Numbers present a series of priestly regulations of cultic and ethical significance interspersed throughout the narrative, along with a distinct set of laws in the "Holiness Code" of Lev 17–26. The very heart of Deuteronomy, chs. 12–26, is comprised of legal discourse. Already in the nineteenth century, critical scholarship identified the "Deuteronic Code" in chs. 12–26 as a "core," distinct in some sense from the surrounding narrative frames in chs. 1–11 and 27–34, which, despite depicting the journeying of the Israelites to the plains of Moab before entering the promised land, appear to reflect the experience of exile (e.g. Harvey and Halpern 2008, 47–85).

Subsequent scholarship, especially in Europe, has detected a complex literary history in the book's legal and narrative chapters, positing pre-exilic, exilic, and post-exilic layers. Much ink has been spilled in the effort to identify the first layers of Deuteronomy, an *Urdeuteronomium*, with perhaps a majority of scholars contending that cornerstones of a "legal core" can be found in the centralization laws of Deut 12, plus the loyalty provisions in Deut 6:4–5 and ch. 13 along with the accompanying curses in ch. 28. From this perspective, the laws of centralization adapt provisions in the Covenant Code, including the altar law (Exod 20:24), while Deut 6:5; 13:1, 2–12; 28:20–44 bear resemblance to Esarhaddon's Succession Treaty (EST), §§ 4, 10, 12, 39–42, 56. These core texts are often linked to the seventh century, the period of Josiah's cult-centralization reform (2 Kgs 22–23) and Assyrian imperialism (e.g., Levinson 1997, 145–57; 2010; Otto 1999, 14–90; 2013, 222–28; Levinson and Stackert 2012). Others, however, emphasize the virtual absence of the monarchy in Deuteronomic law and the narrative that undergirds it and contend that even the earliest stratum of Deuteronomy cannot be dated before the collapse of the Judahite monarchy and its institutions in 587 BCE (e.g. Pakkala 2009, 2019).

But Deuteronomy is a multifaceted book, and a number of scholars also identify the Deuteronomic laws as one among a number of ancient law collections that, despite being produced by various peoples and cultures of ancient West Asia or the ancient Near East (ANE), share certain characteristics in form and content (Westbrook 1985, 247–48; Wells 2005, 200). Nine such documents within this proposed genre have survived, but only one other collection comes to us through the Hebrew Bible in the form of the *mišpāṭîm*, "legal cases," of Exod 21:1–22:17. The remaining seven collections are written on clay tablets in cuneiform, a script developed by the Sumerians and adopted by the administrative systems and educated elite of later civilizations. The cuneiform law collections come from a range of historical periods and cultures: the Sumerian laws of Ur-Nammu (LU), ca. 2100 BCE and Lipit-Ishtar (LL), ca. 1930 BCE; the Old Babylonian Laws of Eshnunna (LE), ca. 1770 BCE and Hammurabi (LH), ca. 1750; the Hittite Laws (HL), ca. 1650–1500 and ca. 1400–1180 BCE; the Middle Assyrian Laws (MAL), ca. 1076 BCE; and the Neo-Babylonian Laws (NBL), ca. 700 BCE (see Roth 1997 for dating and English translations).

As we shall see, comparisons between the law collections *within* the Pentateuch and with the cuneiform collections and other law-texts *outside* the Bible have prompted all sorts of questions regarding the dating, compositional history, character, purpose, and function of biblical law. Many of these discussions center around Deuteronomy, the book which also connects the first four books of the Torah (Gen–Num) with the rest of the Israelite/Judahite historiography (Josh–2 Kgs).

2. The Deuteronomic Laws and ANE Laws: Connections and Contrasts

Before we engage more closely with the ANE law collections, it is instructive to make some broad observations about the characteristics of Deuteronomy and its legal materials. Deuteronomy 12:1–26:15 is framed by the legal descriptors *ḥuqqîm* and *mišpāṭîm* "statutes" and "legal cases" (11:32; 26:16), terms that are elsewhere equated with *miṣwâ*, "commandment" (6:1; 7:11), but also *'ēdōt*, "testimony" (4:45; 6:20) and *tôrâ* (4:8) (Edelman 2021, 30). *Tôrâ*, which may be translated as "law" but also more broadly as "teaching" or "instruction," is the term used most frequently to collectively describe the speeches of Moses that make up Deuteronomy (see Deut 4:8, 17:8, 17:19, 27:3, 27:8, 27:26, 28:58, 28:61, 29:20, 29:28, 30:10, 31:11, 31:12, 31:26, 32:46). As Assnat Bartor recognizes, Deuteronomy is part of a complex narrative delivered by an unidentified narrator that begins in the book of Genesis and ends in the book of Kings (Bartor 2010, 17–22). The laws of Deuteronomy are embedded within this story-world but are delivered through the first-person narration of Moses. Having received divine revelation, he is depicted as delivering a series of speeches (see Deut 1:6–4:43, 4:44–28:69, 29:1–30:20) on behalf of Yhwh to the Israelites on the plains of Moab, before the Israelite people enter the land (Tigay 1996, xii). There is, therefore, an intimate interconnection and dialectic between law and narrative in Deuteronomy.

For example, Deuteronomy frequently uses the singular or plural second-person "you" in its formulation of law. The second-person address is absent in only five laws: Deut 21:15–17; 22:13–19; 22:28–29; 24:5;

25:5-10 (Bartor 2010, 36). From the standpoint of the reader/listener, the use of the second person draws attention to how the laws are addressed to the characters within the story, Moses and the Israelite people, at particular points in the narrative but also to the reader/listener, insofar as they identify with the characters (Nasuti 1986, 10-11; Bartor 2010, 36-37). Moreover, Deuteronomy recurrently employs "motive clauses" that provide the motivation, reason, justification, or incentive for a legal provision. According to Rifat Sonsino, there are 111 motive clauses among the 225 prescriptions found in Deut 12-26 (Sonsino 1980, 93). Motive clauses can be explanatory, ethical, religious, and historical and often create links between the laws and the narrative framework (Gemser 1953, 50-66). For example, the laws on the treatment of Hebrew indentured slaves in Deut 15:12-14 encourage compliance by reminding the people that "...you were a slave in the land of Egypt, and Yhwh your God redeemed you" (Deut 15:15). As an "embedded story" in the law, the mentioning of historical redemption from slavery in Egypt "opens a window" onto the frame-story for the law's addressees/readers, so that the purpose of the law and the reason for adhering to it is situated within the wider story (Nasuti 1986, 12-13; Bartor 2011, 17-22). The rhetorical, persuasive, and pedagogical nature of these features also hint that the laws were not necessarily backed by officially mandated violent acts but were perhaps more in keeping with didactic instruction or teaching that was passed down through the family, as found within the wisdom literature like Proverbs (e.g. Prov 6:20; see Deut 6:7-9) (Sonsino 1980, 174-75; Watts 1999, 62-67; Frymer-Kensky 2003, 979; Edelman 2021, 55-66).

When we put these stylistic features of Deuteronomy's legal writings in dialogue with the cuneiform laws, it reveals intriguing contrasts and continuities. To begin with contrast, the use of the first-person narrative by the lawgivers, Moses and Yhwh, is unique to the delivery of biblical law and unknown in other ANE law collections, which limits first-person narration to "prologue" and "epilogue" frames (Bartor 2010, 23-24). The use of the second-person, "you," in either conditional "if-you" statements ("casuistic" law, see Alt 1966, 79-132) or unconditional "you shall/shall not" statements ("apodictic" law, see Alt 1966, 79-13), is also absent in ANE law (see Paul 1970, 115, n. 1 for a list of unconditional statements in the cuneiforms laws – but they are not formulated in the second person). However, within Akkadian scribal practice, second-person formulation is used in treaties, loyalty oaths, prescriptive ritual texts, recipes, training texts, and royal decrees (Morrow 1994, 140-47). Furthermore, while motive clauses are sporadically present in LH and MAL, they are mostly absent in the ANE law collections (Sonsino 1980, 153-67, 172-74). According to Sonsino's count, the percentage of the corpus containing motivated legal prescriptions is 6% for LH and 5% for MAL (167).

Chapters 12–18 of Deuteronomy present material that does not substantially overlap with cuneiform law. Deuteronomy 12:1–16:17 (and 16:21–17:1) focus on cultic matters – worship and sacrifice requirements, tithes, dietary regulations, and the festival calendar, which are partly a reworking of laws from the "Covenant Code" (Exod 20:22–23:19), adapted according to Deuteronomy's vision of cult-centralization (Levinson 1997; for a different perspective, see Van Seters 2003; Edenburg 2022). Deuteronomy 16:18–18:22 present Israel's ideal political configuration or "constitution," prescribing and delimiting the role of various office bearers, judge, king, priest, and prophet (Levinson 2006, 2008a). It is significant that in the Deuteronomic laws and narrative framework, there is only one mention of the king (Deut 17:14–20). As we shall see when we look closer at the cuneiform law collections, there was a strong tradition in ancient Western Asia of the king being perceived – or promoting himself – as the guardian of justice and the one responsible for producing and promulgating "just laws." Yet in the story-world of Deuteronomy, Yhwh replaces the king as the source of law and Moses, who is human but not a king, is responsible for communicating divine law (Levinson 2008a, 58–62; Schmid 2013, 121–26).

Nonetheless, biblical law is at least partially the product of its cultural context, a context that is shared with other peoples and cultures of the area. This is particularly obvious for the book of Exodus, where the *mišpāṭîm* found in Exod 21:2–22:17 utilize the same casuistic style of the cuneiform laws in the third person, "if ... then ..." and present very similar legal matters, including the famous cases of the goring ox (Exod 21:28–32, 35–37) and a fetus lost in miscarriage (Exod 21:22–25), which will be discussed below.

Parts of the Deuteronomic law collection also demonstrate considerable overlap in form and content with the cuneiform legal tradition. Deuteronomy 19–25 utilize the impersonal third-person formulation known from the ANE law collections. If one were to isolate the casuistic laws in Deuteronomy that are, apart from the occasional rationale or motive clause, formulated entirely in the third person, the results would be as follows (Wells 2010, 94–95; Seitz 1971, 111–13):

Deut 21:15–17 law concerning the inheritance of the birthright when a man has two wives, one loved and one hated
Deut 21:18–21 law concerning a rebellious son
Deut 22:13–21 law concerning a slandered bride
Deut 22:22 law governing ordinary adultery (LH §129, MAL A §§12–16)
Deut 22:28–29 law governing sex with an unmarried and unbetrothed woman (MAL A §§ 55–56)

Deut 24:1–4	law prohibiting the restoration of a particular marriage
Deut 24:5	law exempting a newly married man from military service for one year
Deut 24:7	law on kidnapping (LH §14, HL §§ 19–21)
Deut 25:5–10	law on levirate marriage (cf. HL §193, MAL A §30)

Furthermore, a number of additional laws within this section contain casuistic expression with only a few second-person forms (again, apart from motive clauses and other admonitory material) or deal with "classic" legal themes that resonate with ANE legal tradition. These laws and their counterparts in the cuneiform laws may be represented as follows (adapted from Wells 2010, 95–96):

Deut 19:4–5+11–12	law on slayer who flees to another city
Deut 19:16–19	law on false accusation (LL §17, LH §§1–4)
Deut 21:1–7	law on unknown murderer (LH §§22–24, HL §IV)
Deut 22:8	law on negligent homicide (LE §58; LH §229)
Deut 22:23–27	law governing adultery-while-betrothed/sexual violation (LE §26, LH §130, HL §§197–198)
Deut 25:1–3	law on flogging a convicted person
Deut 25:11–12	law concerning a woman grabbing a man's genitals (MAL A §8)

The similarities between Exod 21:2–22:17; Deut 19–25 and the ANE law collections raise the question of connection. Did Israelite/Judahite scribes have access to cuneiform laws and directly base their own cases on these traditions (so Wright 2009)? Or, might ANE traditions have been received by Israelite/Judahite scribes via oral transmission (Greengus 1994, 77–87) or by living within the general cultural milieu of ancient Western Asia (e.g., Wells 2006, 115–18)? What specific conditions might have facilitated the transmission and reception of legal traditions, and in which period would this be most likely? The answers to these questions are not just pertinent for reconstructing the compositional history of Deuteronomy but also for discerning the possible character, purpose, and function of the Deuteronomic laws. There has been much discussion on the nature of the ANE collections and if the "Deuteronomic Code" – or part of it – is of the same genre, then findings on the ANE law collections arguably apply to Deuteronomic law as well.

3. The Character, Purpose, and Function of the Cuneiform Law Collections

Most of the discussion on the nature and function of the cuneiform laws has focused on LH, which was discovered in 1901. It is one of the most complete texts, still extant on dozens of tablets and as a monument, where the legal provisions were inscribed on a black stone stele, framed by a prologue and epilogue that emphasize the gods' appointment of Hammurabi as king and testify to his role in bringing justice and peace to the land (Roth 1997, 71–76). Initially, interpreters deemed the text an early example of "legislation" or "law code" in the modern sense of the term. The Enlightenment ideal of "law code" that developed into the civil law jurisdictions of Europe required law codes to be coherent, comprehensive, and systematic; law codes aspired to govern all branches of law. The text, comprised of general, abstract terms, was considered the sole repository of a fixed and stable law that overrode all other sources and was to be strictly applied through deductive reasoning (Mousourakis 2015, 287–309). Subsequent studies on LH, however, have identified many issues with applying this idea of law to the Babylonian collection (Eilers 1932, 8–9; Landsberger 1939, 221–22; Kraus 1960, 283–96; Westbrook 1989, 201–22).

In a now seminal article, French Assyriologist Jean Bottéro integrated and expanded prior arguments, contending that the listed provisions found on Hammurabi's monument cannot be regarded as a "law code," because the law code of a land is "... a complete collection of the laws and prescriptions that govern that land: 'the totality of its legislation'" (Bottéro 1992, 161). Bottéro even questions whether LH can be categorized as "legislation" or "law," defining law as "an imperative rule of social conduct, laid down and enforced by legitimate authorities. Hence, it is something general, something universal" (Bottéro 1992, 161). According to this analysis, LH is neither a law code nor law, because of its content, its illogicality, and because there is no evidence that it was ever enforced.

Bottéro's analysis and conclusions have been complemented, nuanced, and critiqued by later studies. Nevertheless, a number of his observations remain relatively uncontroversial. First of all, in terms of content, the stipulations of LH are far from exhaustive, neglecting important legal issues, including a law that deals directly with murder (Bottéro 1992, 161; Wells 2005, 201). Even if all the legal topics and material from every cuneiform law collection were combined, they would not cover all the legal areas that were known to be regulated (Greengus 1994, 80). Moreover, the legal provisions are sometimes highly specific, because they employ what is known as the "conditional" or "casuistic" style, which describes a particular situation, usually in the third person and introduced by "if" (the protasis), followed by the resolution or sanction that restores balance "then…" (the apodosis): "*If* a man commits robbery and is then seized, [*then*] that man shall be killed" (LH §22). This formulation predominates throughout most of the cuneiform law collections. Because the provisions are articulated in a way that begins with the specific and particular, by which general principles may be extrapolated, they do not present as universal or general in the same way as modern statutes (Roth 2001, 243–54; Bottéro 1992, 161–62, 170–72; Westbrook 2003, 20). The articles are grouped according to topics and associations. Clusters of law were generated by scribes who would start with one case, but then generate others by modifying one or more factors: the status of the perpetrator or victim, the nature of the injury or damage, the *mens rea* of the defendant. This same method of composition was also used in other scribal treatises, including medical and omen collections (Bottéro 1992, 159, 173–77; Westbrook 2003, 10–11; Milstein 2021, 60–61).

Scholars have also detected, at least on the surface of the text, illogicality in and inconsistency between some of the individual provisions of LH. For example, in LH §7, an agent who has received the personal property of someone without a written title or without witnesses is considered the thief of that property, and he is condemned to death. However, in LH §123, the agent who receives property for safekeeping without witnesses or contracts can deny his involvement, and the case is not subject to claim (Bottéro 1992, 162–63; Fitzpatrick-McKinley 1999, 89–90).

The most critical evidence that has been brought to bear on the status of LH is that there is no direct evidence that its provisions were cited and applied by judges or other officials to resolve legal disputes or that the populace referred to the provisions in their legal practices. This has been demonstrated by comparing LH with the hundreds of contemporary Babylonian trial records and thousands of transactional documents (Roth 1997, 5; Bottéro 1992, 162–63). It would appear that legal decisions and practices were largely determined by forms of custom and unwritten law, underlying principles of truth and justice (*kittu and mêšaru* in Akkadian), and the viewpoints of kings, judges, and officials (Bottéro 1992, 179–85; Wells 2005, 205–6; see examples in Démare-Lafont and Fleming 2023, 21–22; see also 1, 4, 12–13). The conclusion that we must draw is that LH, and perhaps the other cuneiform law collections, did not function as comprehensive law codes, or even as legislation or statute. What, then, were the purposes or functions of these documents? Three predominant positions have been put forward, which are not necessarily mutually exclusive: academic treatise, royal apologia or propaganda, and precedent.

Following a critical article by F. R. Kraus in 1960, scholarship has emphasized the scribal characteristics of the ANE law collections, classifying them as academic or scientific treatises. As indicated above, the collections of laws were likely created by the same scribal schools (é.dub. ba.a in the Old Babylonian period) that produced other "scientific lists": lexical lists, god lists, astronomical lists, omen lists, mathematical lists, and medical lists. These anthologies are formulated using conditional phrases, which represent a type of scientific framework. A premise or hypothesis is posited and then a conclusion or judgment is drawn, based upon the elements of that hypothesis (Kraus 1960, 288–90; Bottéro 1992, 170–71; Westbrook 1985, 151–53). The extent to which the cases accurately reflected legal practice is a matter of debate. Raymond Westbrook and Bruce Wells envision that some of the cases, if not the majority, were drawn from real-life situations (Westbrook 1989; Wells 2005, 202), while others emphasize the speculative, hypothetical, and exceptional nature of individual provisions and the compositions as a whole (Eichler 2009; Fried 2001, 76–78; Fitzpatrick-McKinley 1999, 95, 99–100; Kraus 1960, 290). For example, there is a reappearance of the same, unusual legal situations within multiple collections, including the goring ox who inflicts injury or causes death (LE §§53–55; LH §§250–52; Exod 21:28–32, 35–37), and the loss of a fetus after blows are inflicted upon the mother (LH §§ 209–14; MAL §§ 21, 50–52; HL §§17–18; Exod 21:22–25) (Finkelstein, 1981, 19, 21; Malul 1990, 129). For some, these reoccurring cases suggest the literary transmission of theoretical cases within the curriculum of scribal schools (Westbrook 1985, 257; Finkelstein, 1981, 18). Alternatively, some experts have suggested that because select cases contain unique variations on the same legal theme, they reflect cultural particularisms and the practice of local courts (Otto 1993, 16–18; Lafont 1994, 93, 108–9).

For J. J. Finkelstein, the lower Mesopotamian collections should be conceptualized as "royal apologia" or "royal propaganda." LU, LL, and LH had prologues and epilogues that bracket the laws and draw attention to their religious and political function. Within Mesopotamia, the king was considered the divinely authorized guardian and administrator of justice, and for many scholars, the laws along with their literary frames should be read in light of the king's need to legitimize his rule and present himself as a "just king" to his subjects and to the gods (Finkelstein 1981, 100–4; see also Bottéro 1992, 166–69, 179–84; Charpin, 210, 78–79; Roth 1996, 15–19, 21–24; 1997, 80–81).

LH and the other law collections have also been conceived as a compendium of legal precedent, in origins, form, and use. The casuistic form and the specific details provided in the conditions and outcomes of each case are suggestive of legal decisions that have been stripped of their contingent elements and reformulated in the logical and impersonal language of scribal thought (Westbrook 1985, 251; 1989, 204, 218–19; Otto 1994, 160–63; Bottéro 1992, 164–66). Raymond Westbrook and Eckart Otto contend that the law collections, as compilations of exemplary cases, could have had an intended or actual use as a guide or reference work for judges and officials in their decision-making (Westbrook 1985, 253–64; Otto 1994, 163). HL and MAL were found in what appear to be royal archives, where they could have been available for consultation (Wells 2005, 201). Other scholars, however, argue that there is little indication within the laws themselves that they were intended to be binding upon judges; nor do the documents of practice suggest that judges consulted or cited lawbooks (Fitzpatrick-McKinley 1999, 95–100; Fried 2001, 78–79).

It is likely that each of these perspectives holds some truth (Bottéro 1992; Charpin 2010, 71–82). Law is a complex phenomenon that defies simplistic definition, exhibiting diverse features and used for a variety of purposes (Pirie 2013, 1–25). The aforementioned functions for legal writings are confirmed by comparison to other historical examples. The formal law collections of the ANE were written by and were partly the creation of educated elites who were trained in scientific and analogous thinking, imagining new legal situations and hypothesizing just outcomes. Similarly, the *responsa* (written opinions) of Rome, the early Anglo-Saxon common law, and the Islamic *shari'a* were the intellectual products of elite jurists and lawyers (Pirie 2013, 73–105, 118–21). The similarities in content and form between the collections certainly suggest a degree of legal borrowing between cultures through scribal schools. Nevertheless, it is also likely that some provisions were drawn from local judicial records, and it is possible that some of the collections were intended to function as reference works or collections of precedent. There is little evidence of any law collection being cited and explicitly applied to decide a legal case, but their *influence* on legal thinking and practice is harder to gauge. At the very least, the collections were intended for education, presenting exemplary cases to demonstrate a particular way of thinking, to inculcate underlying principles. Differently from the civil law in Europe, the case-based English common law developed in much the same way (Roth 2001, 252–54; Berman 2014, 20–22). The presence of epilogues and prologues in the lower Mesopotamian law collections that extol the virtue of the king confirm that the legal writings were not purely "functional" in their character but were sometimes literary vehicles of idealism, ideology, and even propaganda. This is a somewhat common characteristic of law: for example, the adoption of entirely impractical Latin lawbooks by Germanic kings in medieval Europe was most certainly ideologically motivated, a matter of "image-building" to emulate the famous Roman achievement (Wormald 1999, 25).

Bottéro very effectively demonstrated that LH did not operate like modern law codes or legislation and paved the way for scholarship to reconsider the character, purpose, and functions of legal writings in ancient Western Asia; however, each of the characteristics identified reflect legitimate expressions of law and potentially throw light on the character of the Deuteronomic legal provisions.

4. A (pre-)Deuteronomic Law Collection?

Questions surrounding the character and function of the ANE collections have been applied to biblical law (see Westbrook 1985, 1989; Fitzpatrick-McKinley 1999; LeFebvre 2006; Wells 2008). As both Dale Patrick and Bernard Jackson have pointed out, while there are virtually no Judahite or Israelite documents of practice to which we can compare Pentateuchal law, studies on the biblical narratives, histories, and prophetic books reveal that relevant laws were not necessarily applied by kings, judges, or officials to decide legal cases or by the people to determine their own legal practices (Jackson 2000, 114–21; Patrick 1985, 193–98). Instructions to judges do not adjure the application of written law but of principles of justice: honesty, fairness, and impartiality (Exod 18:21; 23:1–3, 7–8; Deut 1:16–17; 16:19–20) (Patrick 1985, 191–93). Like cuneiform law, biblical law had diverse functions, but these were not strictly "legislative": monumental (Josh 8:38), archival (Deut 31:26; 1 Sam 10), didactic (Deut 17:18–20), and ritual (Deut 31:9–13; 2 Kgs 23:1–3) (Jackson 2000, 121–41).

Some scholars have identified the production of Deuteronomy as a decisive moment for catalyzing the transformation of biblical law into something like "legislation" that had a more direct bearing on legal practice (e.g. Westbrook 1985, 219–22; Patrick 1985, 189–90, 200–4). Konrad Schmid has emphasized the moment when the Covenant Code and the book of Deuteronomy were ascribed to the deity and imbued with the authority and normativity of divine origins (Schmid 2013, 121–25). This may relate in some way to the binding nature of the Neo-Assyrian vassal treaties, which call for unconditional loyalty (see Deut 6:4–5) and strict submission to the Neo-Assyrian king (see Deut 13) under the threat of curses (see Deut 28). As indicated above, it has been suggested that in the late seventh century, scribes in ancient Judah adopted this concept and transformed it, perhaps subversively, so that loyalty and strict submission was directed not towards the Neo-Assyrian king but the Israelite God (Otto 1999). Thus, law is both "authored" by God and becomes the decisive factor in the relationship between God and humankind in the form of covenant (treaty) stipulations.

This theory is not without controversy: some recent critics dispute the direct influence of the Neo-Assyrian treaty-format on Deuteronomy (Crouch 2014, 179–84; Morrow 2019; Edelman 2021, 41–52), while others posit a post-587 dating (see references in Pakkala 2019). Another group question whether there is evidence of Deuteronomic law being applied before the exilic period and even beyond (Davies 1999, 54–71; LeFebvre 2006 55–95; Vroom 2018, 72–74).

Returning to the idea of a Deuteronomic law collection in the ANE tradition, several scholars posit that one or more law collections existed in ancient Judah or Israel prior to the existence of any text that could be recognizable as Deuteronomy. These laws may have circulated separately prior to their integration into the "Deuteronomic Code" and so sit within a wider tradition of ANE law (Wells 2010, 94–98). For Raymond Westbrook, this collection consists of chapters 21–25, albeit reworked and interspersed with hortatory and other non-legal material (Westbrook 1985, 248). More specifically, Alexander Rofé identifies a series of laws in Deut 21–25 on sexual and family matters that originated in a single, older written tractate dating to around the eighth century BCE, which was expanded and altered in the seventh century, when it was incorporated into Deuteronomy (Rofé 2002, 169, 191–192). This older document included Deut 21:15–17, 18–21; 22:13–21, 22:22–29; 24:1–4, Deut 25:5–12. Similarly, Eckart Otto theorizes the existence of a "pre-Deuteronomic" and independent collection of family laws that in the seventh century was integrated into Deuteronomic law alongside the revised laws of the Covenant Code, but the motive clauses in 22:22b, 24b and 22:26 were added by a "Deuteronomic redactor" (Otto 1998, 131–32, 140–41; 2013, 220–21). Both Rofé and Otto draw parallels between this set of laws and MAL Tablet A – a collection of over sixty laws pertaining almost entirely to women (Otto 1998, 133–34; Rofé 2002, 170; Pressler 1993, 21–22, n. 2).

By contrast, Cynthia Edenburg isolates a smaller collection of "women's sex laws" in Deut 22:13–29. She conjectures that in light of the literary parallels, the scribe responsible for the compilation may have based some cases directly on LH §§129–30 and MAL A, both of which may have been copied as part of the West Semitic or Judahite scribal school curriculum (Edenburg 2009, 48, 53, nn. 30 and 31). Moreover, for Edenburg, Deut 22:13–29 were revised by and integrated into the Deuteronomic laws by a "Deuteronomistic scribe" after the fall of Judah in 587 BCE (Edenburg 2009, 59).

More recently, Sara Milstein has discerned a different kind of association between the Deuteronomic laws and the cuneiform legal tradition. She isolates a selection of Deuteronomic laws (19:4–6; 21:15–17; 22:13–19, 28–29; 24:1–4; 25:5–10) that she believes were originally private cases with pecuniary penalties. She identifies affinities between these laws and a genre of Mesopotamian texts that Milstein calls "legal fictions." These were legal-pedagogical texts that scribes copied in the course of their education, including contracts, trial narratives, sequences of cases with varying details, and legal phrasebooks (Milstein 2021, 20–52). "Hebrew Legal Fictions," possibly based upon Mesopotamian antecedents, were likely accessible to Israelite/Judahite scribes as lists of common legal clauses, a theory supported by the presence of one fragment of such a cuneiform list at the Late Bronze Age Canaanite sites of Hazor (also Emar and Ugarit) (Milstein 2021, 82–85; Horowitz, Oshima, and Sanders 2006, 73–74; Schniedewind 2019, 72, 89).

Each of these theories on the literary and redactional history of Deut 21–25, its relation to the rest of the Deuteronomic laws, and its relation to parallel laws in the ANE collections lead to varying conclusions concerning the collection's purpose, ideology, and application in the legal practice of ancient Israel (Edenburg 2009, 43–44). This can be illustrated by focusing on laws concerning different forms of adultery and sexual violation.

5. Laws on Adultery and Sexual Violation in Deut 22:22–29 and the ANE Law Collections

Deuteronomy 22:22–29 may be broken down into four related cases pertaining to adultery and sexual violation – whether or not these acts constitute "rape" in the modern sense (see Kawashima 2011, 1–22):

Deut 22:22	Adultery
Deut 23:23–26	Adultery-while-betrothed
Deut 23:25–26	Violation of a betrothed woman
Deut 28–29	Violation of an unbetrothed woman

Deuteronomy 22:22a covers adultery *in flagrante delicto*, "caught in the act." Both the man and the married woman are to be killed, an outcome that is also required in LH §129, MAL A §13, §15, and HL §197b. However, unlike the cuneiform laws, the Deuteronomic provision does not explicitly contemplate a choice for the wronged husband to pardon his wife and her adultery partner or provide the option of a reduced sentence (MAL A §14, §15; HL §198; LH §129). In the ANE laws, adultery appears to be similar to a tort in private law: the husband, being the "injured party," is entitled to decide upon the execution of the punishment (see also Jer 3:8; Hos 2:4–7; Prov 6:32–35). Deuteronomy 22:22b, however, seemingly conceptualizes adultery as a sin against God that threatens the purity of the land and places adultery into the realm of criminal law, where the entire community is implicated: "So you shall purge the evil from Israel" (Deut 22:22b) (Rofé 2002, 181–84).

Neither does Deuteronomy here allow for varying levels of culpability between the wife and the fornicator. MAL A §12 and HL §197a, by contrast, attempt to differentiate between consensual adultery and rape by reference to where the intercourse took place. It is considered rape if the act occurs in the open, a public thoroughfare (MAL A §12) or the mountainside (HL §197a), and in such cases the man alone is subject to punishment (Edenburg 2009, 51–52). The alternate scenario is considered in LU §7, MAL A §14, §16, and HL §197a, where the woman is considered be at fault, because the man did not know she was married (MAL A §14, §16), or the woman invited the man into her house (HL §197a). In these cases, the man is cleared, but the wife is punished.

Intriguingly, it is in the laws dealing with adultery-while-betrothed and sexual violation (Deut 22:23–27) that Deuteronomy attempts to differentiate between consensual and nonconsensual intercourse, similar to MAL A §12, HL §197, but also MAL §55. If the betrothed woman meets with the man in town and does not cry for help, then it is assumed she willingly participated (vv. 22–24). Both the man and the woman are to be stoned at the town gate, "So you shall purge the evil from your midst" (v. 24b.). But, if the event happens in the open country, then it is assumed that the woman may have cried for help without being heard and only the man is punishable by death (vv. 25–27). While HL §197 presents a similar case and counter-case – but where the woman is *married* (see above) – MAL A §55, deals with the rape of an *unbetrothed* virgin. In this case, different places and circumstances are also considered (the act occurred in the father's house, the city, countryside, the main thoroughfare, the granary, at night, during the city festival) in order to establish the principle that, *regardless* of the place or time of assault, the man is at fault and must provide for the girl and compensate her father for the loss of her bride-price (Edenburg 2009, 53–54). Only LE and LH contain laws that actually cover the violation of a *betrothed* woman, but they do not provide the same detail on how to establish the woman's consent, mandating the death of the perpetrator who forces himself on a betrothed woman by kidnapping (LE §26) or while a woman is in her father's house (LH §30).

Finally, Deut 22:28–29 deal with the rape of an *unbetrothed* virgin. If a man rapes her and they are caught in the act, he is required to pay fifty shekels to her father (the virgin's bride-rice), marry her, and never divorce her. The law is closely related to the similarly drafted law on seduction in Exod 22:15–16 (Rofé 2002, 134; Otto 1998, 131–32; Edenburg 2009, 55). As indicated above, MAL A also presents laws on this topic and requires the perpetrator to marry his unbetrothed victim and pay silver triple "her value" (MAL A §55).

6. Implications and Conclusions

What do we make of this complex array of differences and similarities between Deut 22:22–29 and the various ANE law collections? First, there is enough correspondence between 22:22–29 and their cuneiform counterparts to confirm that at least portions of Deuteronomy 21–25 are part of a broader ancient Near Eastern legal tradition. This is despite the narrative framing, along with the first-person voicing and the second-person address, which present the Deuteronomic laws as the product of a spontaneous divine revelation, providing the content for a unique covenant between the Israelite people and Yhwh.

Furthermore, although the exact nature of the connection between Deut 22:21–25 and the ANE legal tradition is uncertain, it is likely that some Deuteronomic provisions are examples of legal borrowings or scribal creations. Otto, for example, comparing Deut 22:22–29 to the redactional structure of MAL A §§12–16, describes Deut 22:23–27 as an internal extension of Deut 22:22, 28–29 that was "scholarly" in character. He adds, "there was a lot of juridical sophistication and legal theory in these laws" and we do not know how many were "really executed in pre-canonical times" (Otto 1998, 134 and 140). Although coming from a different perspective, Milstein also advocates for the scribal character of Deut 22:22–29. For Milstein, Deut 22:28–29 was one of a number of "Hebrew Legal Fictions" that were incorporated into Deuteronomy, while Deut 22:22–24; 25–27 were all provided by a later scribe to supplement the older, private case law and create the illusion of a cluster of laws on "illicit intercourse" (Milstein 2021, 69–72).

Second, there are significant differences between this cluster of Deuteronomic laws and their cuneiform counterparts, at least in the form in which we receive them. On the one hand, we cannot rule out the possible influence of local custom or case law, as Otto speculates for Deut 22:22a, 28–29//Exod 22:15–16 (Otto 1998, 132–33; Edenburg 2009, 56). On the other hand, some variances likely arose at the redactional level: adultery in Deuteronomic law is (re)cast as a "criminal" matter that requires the death sentence (Deut 22:22b, 23–24); the husband is not free to elect for a reduced punishment or pecuniary penalty, unlike the father in the case of the unbetrothed virgin who is raped (Deut 22:28–29). The act of adultery is portrayed as a sin against God that also endangers the whole community. This is underscored by the use of the second-person "you" four times throughout vv. 22–26 and the motive clauses, "so you shall purge the evil from Israel/your midst" (vv. 22b, 24b. See also the motive clause in 26b, which exonerates a betrothed woman who is raped, "because this case is like that of someone who attacks and murder a neighbor"). Furthermore, these features and the mode of enacting the death in penalty in Deut 22:24, "you shall bring both of them to the gate of that town and stone them to death," correlate with the provisions mandating the death penalty for apostasy (Deut 13:5; 17:5, 7) or enticement to apostasy (13:9–10). This association suggests that maintaining exclusive fidelity toward Yhwh (Deut 13:2-18; 17:2-7) also required strict loyalty in the social order, represented here by marriage (Deut 22:22-27) (Edenburg 2009, 56-60; Milstein 2021, 70-72, 85-89). This has ramifications for how women are viewed and treated within the laws (Pressler 1993; Edenburg 2009; Otto 1998).

For Rofé, the systematic approach taken by the redactor of the laws of illegal sexual relationships (Deut 22:22-29) and the transformation of private law to criminal law (Deut 22:22-24) brings these provisions closer to "legislation" or "modern statute law," as the writer managed "to transform procedure and thereby influenced subsequent practice" (Rofé 2002, 185-86). But Edenburg rightfully points out that their uncompromising nature marks the laws "as part of a utopian program in which absolutely fidelity replaces consideration of exigent circumstances and contingences" (Edenburg 2009, 58-59). Yet, in the laws on adultery and sexual violation, the influence of the ANE legal scribal tradition lingers and exerts its reasoning. Despite the seemingly uncompromising stance on adultery-while-married expressed in Deut 22:22, the provisions that differentiate between consensual and nonconsensual sex on behalf of the betrothed woman (Deut 22:23-26) may be retrojected in Deut 22:22 (Otto 1998, 134). Private law and pecuniary penalty is retained in Deut 22:28-29, in the case of the violated unbetrothed woman (in contradiction to Deut 21:20-21), and privately negotiated penalties for adultery short of death almost certainly continued in continuity with ANE legal practice (Wells 2015, 297-300; McKeating 1979, 57-72).

Milstein considers the links between Deut 13:2-19; 17:2-7 and 21-25 as indicative of "an interest beyond the scope of legislative concerns" and contends that the product is no longer "law" in the ANE sense, but the "illusion" or "guise" of law that blurs the lines between law and cult (Milstein 2021, 60, 88-89, 152-58). This may be slightly overstating the point: Deuteronomic law, like ANE law, likely consisted of scholarly cases, local customs and rulings, and didactic instructions; it also possessed ideological motivations behind its drafting that go beyond the regulation of the social order – but the *type* of ideology behind Deuteronomy is contrapuntal to that of the lower Mesopotamian collections and the ANE treaty format. Whether this developed in the pre-monarchic or post-monarchic period, the ideology and theology of Deuteronomy does not promote exclusive loyalty to the king of a foreign empire or even to a native king – who is instead subject to Torah and its divine laws (Deut 17:14-20) – but to Yhwh and the deity's legal judgments and statutes, while judges facilitate the bringing of justice and righteousness to the land (Deut 16:18-20).

Works Cited

Alt, Albrecht. 1966. "The Origins of Israelite Law." Pages 79–132 in *Essays on Old Testament History and Religion*. Translated by R. A. Wilson. Garden City: Doubleday.

Bartor, Assnat. 2010. *Reading Law as Narrative: A Study in the Casuistic Laws of the Pentateuch*. Society of Biblical Literature Ancient Israel and Its Literature 5. Atlanta: Society of Biblical Literature.

Berman, Joshua. 2014. "The History of Legal Theory and the Study of Biblical Law." *Catholic Biblical Quarterly* 76: 19–39.

Bottéro, Jean. 1992. "The 'Code' of Hammurabi." Pages 156–84 in *Mesopotamia: Writing, Reasoning, and the Gods*. Translated by Zainab Bahrani and Marc Van de Mieroop. Chicago: University of Chicago Press.

Charpin, Dominique. 2010. "The Status of the Code of Hammurabi." Pages 71–82 in *Writing, Law, and Kingship in Old Babylonian Mesopotamia*. Translated by Jane Marie Todd. Chicago: University of Chicago Press.

Crouch, Carly L. 2014. *Israel and the Assyrians: Deuteronomy, the Succession Treaty of Esarhaddon, and the Nature of Subversion*. Ancient Near East Monographs 8. Atlanta: Society of Biblical Literature.

Davies, Philip R. 1999. "'Law' in Early Judaism." Pages 3–33 *in Judaism in Late Antiquity III. Where we Stand: Issues and Debates in Ancient Judaism*. Edited by J. Neusner and A. J. Avery-Peck. Leiden: Brill.

Démare-Lafont, Sophie, and Daniel E. Fleming, eds. 2023. *Judicial Decisions in the Ancient near East*. Atlanta: Society of Biblical Literature.

Edelman, Diana. 2021. "Deuteronomy as the Instructions of Moses and Yhwh vs. a Framed Legal Code." Pages 25–75 in *Deuteronomy in the Making: Studies in the Production of Debarim*. Edited by Diana Edelman et al. Beihefte zur Zeitschrift für die alttestamentliche Wissenschaft 533. Berlin: De Gruyter.

Edenburg, Cynthia. 2009. "Ideology and Social Context of the Deuteronomic Women's Sex Laws (Deut 22:13–29)." *Journal of Biblical Literature* 128:43–60.

------. 2022. "Messaging Brothers in Distant Lands." *Hebrew Bible and Ancient Israel* 11: 204–23.

Eichler, Barry L. 2009. "Examples of Restatement in the Laws of Hammurabi." Pages 365–400 in *Mishneh Todah: Studies in Deuteronomy and Its Cultural Environment in Honor of Jeffrey H. Tigay*. Edited by Nili Sacher Fox, David A. Glatt-Gilad, and Michael J. Williams. Winona Lake: Eisenbrauns.

Eilers, Wilhelm. 1932. *Die Gesetzesstele Chammurabis*. Leipzig: Hinrichs.

Finkelstein, J. J. 1961. "Ammiṣaduqa's Edict and the Babylonian 'Law Codes.'" *Journal for Cuneiform Studies* 15:91–104.

------. 1981. *The Ox That Gored*. Transactions of the American Philosophical Society. Philadelphia: American Philosophical Society.

Fitzpatrick-McKinley, Anne. 1999. *The Transformation of Torah from Scribal Advice to Law*. Journal for the Study of the Old Testament Supplement Series 287. Sheffield: Sheffield Academic.

Fried, Lisbeth. 2001. "'You Shall Appoint Judges': Ezra's Mission and the Rescript of Artaxerxes." Pages 63–89 in *Persia and Torah: The Theory of Imperial Authorization*. Edited by James W. Watts. Symposium Series 17. Atlanta: Society of Biblical Literature.

Frymer-Kensky, Tikva. 2003. "Israel." Pages 975–1046 in Vol. 2 of *A History of Ancient Near Eastern Law*. Edited by Raymond Westbrook and Gary M. Beckman. Handbook of Oriental Studies 72. Leiden: Brill.

Gemser, Berend. 1953. "The Importance of the Motive Clause in Old Testament Law." Pages 50–66 in *Congress Volume Copenhagen 1953*. Edited by G. W. Anderson et al. Supplements to Vetus Testamentum 1. Leiden: Brill.

Greengus, Samuel. 1994. "Some Issues Relating to the Comparability of Laws and the Coherence of the Legal Tradition." Pages 60–87 in *Theory and Method in Biblical and Cuneiform Law: Revision, Interpolation and Development*. Edited by Bernard M. Levinson. Journal for the Study of the Old Testament Supplement Series 181. Sheffield: Sheffield Academic.

Harvey, Paul B., Jr and Baruch Halpern. 2008. "W. M. L. de Wette's 'Dissertatio Critica …': Context and Translation." *Zeitschrift für altorientalische und biblische Rechtsgeschichte* 14:47–85.

Horowitz, Wayne, Takayoshi Oshima, and Seth Sanders. 2006. *Cuneiform in Canaan: Cuneiform Sources from the Land of Israel in Ancient Times. Alphabetic Cuneiform Texts*. Jerusalem: Israel Exploration Society and the Hebrew University of Jerusalem.

Jackson, Bernard S. 2000. *Studies in the Semiotics of Biblical Law*. Journal for the Study of the Old Testament Supplement 314. Sheffield: Sheffield Academic.

Kawashima, Robert S. 2011. "Could a Woman Say 'No' in Biblical Israel? On the Genealogy of Legal Status in Biblical Law and Literature." *Association for Jewish Studies Review* 35:1–22.

Kraus, F. R. 1960. "Ein zentrales Problem des altmesopotamischen Rechtes: Was ist der Codex Hammurabi?" *Genava* 8:283–96.

Lafont, Sophie. 1994. "Ancient Near Eastern Laws: Continuity and Pluralism." Pages 91–118 in *Theory and Method in Biblical and Cuneiform Law*. Edited by Bernard M. Levinson. Journal for the Study of the Old Testament Supplement Series 181. Sheffield: JSOT Press.

Landsberger, Benno. 1939. "Die Babylonischen Termini far Gesetz und Recht." Pages 219–34 in *Symbolae ad iura orientis antiqui pertinentes Paulo Koschaker dedicatae*. Edited by Johannes Friedrich et al. Studia et documenta ad iura Orientis antiqui pertinentia 2. Leiden: Brill.

LeFebvre, Michael. 2006. *Collections, Codes, and Torah: The Re-characterization of Israel's Written Law.* The Library of Hebrew Bible/Old Testament Studies 451. New York: T. & T. Clark.

Levinson, Bernard M. 1997. *Deuteronomy and the Hermeneutics of Legal Innovation.* New York: Oxford University Press.

———. 2006. "The First Constitution: Rethinking the Origins of Rule of Law and Separation of Powers in Light of Deuteronomy." *Cardozo Law Review* 27.4:1, 853–88.

———. 2008a. "Deuteronomy's Conception of Law as an 'Ideal Type': A Missing Chapter in the History of Constitutional Law." Pages 52–86 in *"The Right Chorale": Studies in Biblical Law and Interpretation.* Forschungen zum Alten Testament 54. Tübingen: Mohr Siebeck.

———. 2010. "Esarhaddon's Succession Treaty as the Source for the Canon Formula in Deuteronomy 13:1." *Journal of the American Oriental Society* 130:337–47.

Levinson, Bernard M., and Jeffrey Stackert. 2012. "Between the Covenant Code and Esarhaddon's Succession Treaty: Deuteronomy 13 and the Composition of Deuteronomy. *Journal of Ancient Judaism* 3:123–40.

Malul, Meir. 1990. *The Comparative Method in Ancient Near Eastern and Biblical Legal Studies.* Alter Orient und Altes Testament 227. Kevelaer: Butzon & Bercker.

McKeating, Henry. 1979. "Sanctions against Adultery in Ancient Israelite Society, with Some Reflections on Methodology in the Study of Old Testament Ethics." *Journal for the Study of the Old Testament* 4:57–72.

Milstein, Sarah J. 2021. *Making a Case.* Oxford: Oxford University Press.

Morrow, William. 1994. "A Generic Discrepancy in the Covenant Code." Pages 136–51 in *Theory and Method in Biblical and Cuneiform Law: Revision, Interpolation and Development.* Edited by Bernard M. Levinson. Journal for the Study of the Old Testament Supplement Series 181. Sheffield: Sheffield Academic.

———. 2019. "Have Attempts to Establish the Dependency of Deuteronomy on the Esarhaddon Succession Treaty (EST) Failed?" *Hebrew Bible and Ancient Israel* 8:133–58.

Mousourakis, George. 2015. *Roman Law and the Origins of the Civil Law Tradition.* Cham: Springer.

Nasuti, Harry P. 1986. "Identity, Identification, and Imitation: The Narrative Hermeneutics of Biblical Law." *Journal of Law and Religion* 4:9–23.

Otto, Eckart. 1993. "Town and Rural Countryside in Ancient Israelite Law: Reception and Redaction in Cuneiform and Israelite Law." *Journal for the Study of the Old Testament* 57:3–22.

———. 1994. "Aspects of Legal Reforms and Reformulations in Ancient Cuneiform and Israelite Law." Pages 160–96 in *Theory and Method in Biblical and Cuneiform Law: Revision, Interpolation and Development.* Edited by Bernard M. Levinson. Journal for the Study of the Old Testament Supplement Series. Sheffield: Sheffield Academic.

------. 1998. "False Weights in the Scales of Biblical Justice? Different Views of Women from Patriarchal Hierarchy of Religious Equality in the Book of Deuteronomy." Pages 128–46 in *Gender and Law in the Hebrew Bible and the Ancient Near East*. Edited by Victor H. Matthews, Bernard M. Levinson, and Tikva S. Frymer-Kensky. Journal for the Study of the Old Testament Supplement Series 262. Sheffield: Sheffield Academic Press.

------. 1999. *Das Deuteronomium: Politische Theologie und Rechtsreform in Juda und Assyrien*. Beihefte zur Zeitschrift für die alttestamentliche Wissenschaft 284. Berlin: De Gruyter.

------. 2013. "The History of the Legal-Religious Hermeneutics of the Book of Deuteronomy from the Assyrian to the Hellenistic Period." Pages 211–50 in *Law and Religion in the Eastern Mediterranean: From Antiquity to Early Islam*. Edited by Anselm C. Hagedorn and Reinhard G. Kratz. Oxford: Oxford University Press.

Pakkala, Juha. 2009. "The Date of the Oldest Edition of Deuteronomy." *Zeitschrift für die alttestamentliche Wissenschaft* 121:388–401.

------. 2019. "The Influence of Treaties on Deuteronomy, Exclusive Monolatry, and Covenant Theology. *Hebrew Bible and Ancient Israel* 8:159–83.

Patrick, Dale. 1985. *Old Testament Law*. Atlanta: John Knox.

Paul, Shalom M. 1970. *Studies in the Book of the Covenant in the Light of Cuneiform and Biblical Law*. Supplements to Vetus Testamentum 18. Leiden: Brill.

Pirie, Fernanda. 2013. *The Anthropology of Law*. Oxford: Oxford University Press.

Pressler, Carolyn. 1993. *The View of Women Found in the Deuteronomic Family Laws*. Beihefte zur Zeitschrift für die alttestamentliche Wissenschaft 216. Berlin: De Gruyter.

Rofé, Alexander. 2002. *Deuteronomy: Issues and Interpretation*. Old Testament Studies. London: T. & T. Clark.

Roth, Martha. 1996. "Mesopotamian Legal Traditions and the Laws of Hammurabi." *Chicago-Kent Law Review* 71:13–39.

------. 1997. *Law Collections from Mesopotamia and Asia Minor*. 2nd ed. SBL Writings of the Ancient World. Atlanta: Scholars.

------. 2001. "Reading Mesopotamian Law Cases PBS 5 100: A Question of Filiation." *Journal of the Economic and Social History of the Orient* 44: 243–92.

Seitz, G. 1971. *Redaktionsgeschichtliche Studien zum Deuteronomium*. Beiträge zur Wissenschaft vom Alten und Neuen Testament 93. Stuttgart: Kohlhammer.

Schmid, Konrad. 2013. "The Genesis of Normativity in Biblical Law. Pages 119–36 in *Concepts of Law in the Sciences, Legal Studies, and Theology*.

Edited by Michael Welker and Gregor Etzelmüller. Tübingen: Mohr Siebeck.

Schniedewind, William M. 2019. *The Finger of the Scribe: How Scribes Learned to Write the Bible.* New York: Oxford University Press.

Sonsino, Rifat. 1980. *Motive Clauses in Hebrew Law.* Society of Biblical Literature Dissertation Series 45. Chico CA: Scholars.

Tigay, Jeffrey H. 1996. *Deuteronomy: The Traditional Hebrew Text with the New JPS Translation.* The JPS Torah Commentary. Philadelphia: Jewish Publication Society.

Van Seters, John. 2003. *A Law Book for the Diaspora: Revision in the Study of the Covenant Code.* Oxford: Oxford University Press.

Vroom, Jonathan. 2018. *The Authority of Law in the Hebrew Bible and Early Judaism: Tracing the Origins of Legal Obligation from Ezra to Qumran.* Supplements to Journal for the Study of Judaism 187. Leiden: Brill.

Watts, James W. 1999. *Reading Law: The Rhetorical Shaping of the Pentateuch.* The Biblical Seminar 59. Sheffield: Sheffield Academic.

Wells, Bruce. 2005. "Law and Practice." Pages 198–211 in *A Companion to the Ancient Near East.* Edited by Daniel C. Snell. Malden MA: Blackwell Publishing.

------. 2006. "The Covenant Code and Near Eastern Legal Traditions: A Response to David P. Wright." *Maarav* 13:85–118.

------. 2008. "What Is Biblical Law? A Look at Pentateuchal Rules and Near Eastern Practice." *Catholic Biblical Quarterly* 70: 223–43.

------. 2010. "Competing or Complementary? Judges and Elders in Biblical and Neo-Babylonian Law." *Zeitschrift für Altorientalische und Biblische Rechtsgeschichte* 16:77–104.

------. 2015. "Sex Crimes in the Laws of the Hebrew Bible." *Near Eastern Archaeology* 78.4:294–300.

Westbrook, Raymond. 1985. "Biblical and Cuneiform Law Codes." *Revue Biblique* 92:247–64.

------. 1989. "Cuneiform Law Codes and the Origins of Legislation." *Zeitschrift für Assyriologie* 79:201–20.

------. 2003. "The Character of Ancient Near Eastern Law." Pages 1–90 in Vol. 1 of *A History of Ancient Near Eastern Law.* Edited by Raymond Westbrook and Gary M. Beckman. Handbook of Oriental Studies 72. Boston: Brill.

Wormald, Patrick. 1999. *Legal Culture in the Early Medieval West: Law as Text, Image and Experience.* London: Hambledon.

Wright, David P. 2009. *Inventing God's Law: How the Covenant Code of the Bible Used and Revised the Laws of Hammurabi.* New York: Oxford University Press.

About the Author

Megan B. Turton is a Lecturer in Hebrew Bible and Language at Whitley College, the University of Divinity, Melbourne. With a previous degree in law, her research focuses on the books of Exodus and Deuteronomy, biblical and ancient Near Eastern law, and the legal texts of the late Second Temple period. Her doctoral dissertation, "Continuity or Contrast? The Character and Extent of Legal versus Narrative Textual Variation in the Hebrew Manuscripts of Exodus 19–24," completed through the University of Sydney, will be published in the Mohr Siebeck series, Forschungen zum Alten Testament. It investigates the character and extent of textual fluidity in the laws and narratives of Exodus 19–24, and evaluates the implications of textual diversity for understanding the character, purpose, and function of biblical law.

Chapter 4
Geographical Dimensions of the Book of Deuteronomy

Diana V. Edelman

Abstract

A number of geographical issues relating to Deuteronomy are explored. The physical characteristics of Cisjordan are described before moving on to the implications of Israelitizing the promised land and the phenomenon of cities of refuge. The chapter ends with an examination of three geographical anomalies. First is the use of the designation Seir/Mt. Seir vs. Edom in the book. Second is the favoring of (Mt.) Horeb instead of (Mt.) Sinai as the name of the site of the giving of the law and covenant-making after leaving Egypt. Finally, why the mountains of Gerizim and Ebal next to Shechem are the place where the words of the Moab covenant are to be inscribed and a commemorative ceremony is to take place, rather than the town of Shechem, Mt. Zion, or Jerusalem, is considered.

Keywords: cities of refuge, Horeb, Seir, Gerizim, Ebal, promised land, Cisjordan

Geography is a central concern in the storyworld of Deuteronomy. A recurring theme is how Yhwh Elohim is confirming his promise to the fathers to possess "the land," which is a direct allusion to the stories now found in the book of Genesis. At the same time, however, this geographical emphasis is the result of a larger storyline that begins in Genesis and is not completed until either the book of Joshua or, perhaps, the books of Kings. In that wider context, the book anticipates the conquest and occupation of the land, and even the eventual exile from that land for repeated failures to worship Yhwh alone (4:25-30; 28:58-68; 30:1-8; 31:16-18). Thus, it would be unwise to emphasize Israel's ties to the promised land as the primary message of the book. Rather, the centrality of the Torah/teaching to the very existence and identity of Israel is the central message. This Torah is from Yhwh Elohim, mediated through Moses, but also enhanced and made understandable by Moses's own instruction.

1. The Boundaries of the Promised Land

The boundaries of the promised land are given in 1:6-8 as the hill country of the Amorites (that includes the Wadi Eschol [1:2], Hormah [1:44], and Heshbon [2:24], with Kadesh Barnea located just beyond its limit or just within it [1:20],) and the neighboring areas of the Arabah, the hill country, the Shephelah, the Negeb, the seacoast, the land of the Canaanites, and the Lebanon as far as the Great River, i.e. the River Euphrates. The northern boundary is consistent with the delineation of the land in Gen 15:18. The hill country of the Amorites seems to end somewhere close to Kadesh Barnea, which would be consistent with a termination point along with Brook of Egypt also found in Gen 15:18. Thus, there seems to be deliberate allusion to the Genesis passage. The boundaries are also more or less consistent with those given in Exod 23:31 (e.g. Milgrom 1976, 6), even if the terminology is somewhat different and there is no marking of the eastern border as the *yam sûp*. There, the southern border is the wilderness (*midbār*). The boundaries appear again in 11:24 in a more schematic form: from the wilderness (*midbār*) to the Lebanon and from the River – the Euphrates River – to the Western Sea (Mediterranean). This time, the Euphrates marks the eastern limit, not the northern, as in Gen 15:18, but the designation of the southern extent as the wilderness is consistent with Exod 23:31, even if the Lebanon is a new boundary not found in either earlier passage. They appear a final time in 34:1-4, where the northernmost limit is only Dan and the southernmost Zoar, in the Arabah valley south of the Dead Sea. This final description is not dependent on Gen 15:18 or Exod 23:31, in spite of an explicit statement put in the mouth of Yhwh in v. 4 that "This is the land of which I swore to Abraham, Isaac and Jacob, 'I will assign it to your offspring.'" The southern boundary near Zoar might be loosely based on the land Abra(ha)m is to possess after Lot chooses to separate and move east into the plain of the Jordan in Gen 13:7-12, but this is only a possibility. It has been suggested that the borders in the first two instances reflect the province of Eber Nari, put in place by the Neo-Babylonian imperial administration and continued under the Achaemenids (Davies 2007, 176).

In the storyworld, Moses's speeches to the people of Israel take place on the plains of Moab, east of the Jordan River. The tribes of Reuben, Gad, and half-Manasseh have already occupied territory in Transjordan from the northern side of the Wadi Arnon in the south to Gilead (2:31-36), including the Arabah on the east side of the Jordan from the Dead Sea to Lake Chinnereth (3:17; 4:47-49) to as far north as Mt. Hermon (3:8-10). All this territory is included within the boundaries of the promised land (3:12-17), even if that is not immediately clear from the initial description in ch. 1. The men of these two and a half tribes must cross over and help the other tribes occupy Cisjordan and receive allotments there. Their wives, children and livestock can, however, remain on their already allotted land in Transjordan (3:18-20).

2. Physical Characteristics of the Promised Land

Various traits of the promised land are given. It is a good land (6:19, 8:7) that consists of both hills and valleys, from which streams, perennial and seasonal (8:7; 21:4), springs, and fountains issue (8:7). It is a land of mountains and valleys, a land that soaks up the early and late rains of heaven (11:11, 14; 28:12, 24; 32:2). Its rocks are iron and its hills contain copper that can be mined (8:9).

Its arable soil (e.g. 26:15) yields many crops and produce: wheat and barley, vines (=grapes and wine), figs, pomegranates, olive oil, (8:8; 11:14; 23:25-26 [24-25 Engl]; 24:19-21; 28:39-40, 51; 32:13-14), and orchards (20:19) (for a detailed discussion of agricultural practices in the Iron Age and beyond that would apply across the southern Levant, see conveniently Borowski 2002). The references to "honey" (*dᵉbāš*) in 6:3; 8:8; 11:9; 26:9, 15; 27:3; 31:20; 32:13 have been thought more likely to refer to date syrup (*silan*) made by boiling dates than to honey produced by bees (e.g. Crane 1975, 457; in the Mishna, m. Ter. 11:2-3; m. Bik. 1:3, 3:9; m. Ned. 6:8-9). However, since date trees were limited to oasis areas in the Jordan Valley, the Arabah Valley, the southern coastal plain near el-Arish and Gaza, and the desert (Zohary 1982, 60-61), they would not have yielded a widely used product but, instead, one more likely limited to elite consumption.

Assuming the "you" in the storyworld is primarily "the people in general" and not the socially elite members more narrowly, a more plausible option would be carob molasses (*dibs el kharrub*). Carob trees grew in the coastal plain and throughout the forested and maquis regions up to 300 m. in altitude in the western foothills and on the eastern slopes of Galilee and Samaria of Cisjordan, providing wide access to their pods by all levels of society for boiling to produce the sweet syrup (Zohary 1982, 29, 33–34, 63).

The land also contains grazing habitats (11:15) that support herds and flocks (8:13; 28:31, 51; 32:13–14). They supply milk and rennet for food products like soft and hard cheeses, yoghurt, and kefir, as well as meat, wool for weaving clothing, blankets, and curtains, sinews, horns for tool handles, and hides for various uses. Cattle also were used to plow fields for planting. The presence of soil types that support a mixed subsistence economy based on a combination of agriculture, horticulture, viticulture, and animal husbandry led to a summary characterization of the promised land as "a land flowing or dripping with kefir (fermented milk) and carob (or date?) syrup" (6:3; 11:9; 26:9, 15; 27:3; 31:20).

The physical environment supports much wildlife: deer, gazelle, roebuck, wild goat, ibex, antelope, mountain sheep, hares, hyraxes, ostriches, boars, eagles, vultures, buzzards, kites, falcons, ravens, nighthawks, varieties of hawks and owls, bustards, hoopoes, bats, and winged insects (14:3–19), including locusts (28:38) and cicadas (28:42), as well as worms or grubs (28:39). Along the Mediterranean coast, one can find pelicans and sea gulls and along the coast and in freshwater marshlands cormorants, storks, and varieties of heron. Fish are found in the Sea of Galilee and the Mediterranean Sea (14:3–19). The landscape is controlled and exploited by many great polities whose citizens inhabit great man-made cities with sky-high walls (9:1; 19:14, 27:17).

Deuteronomy envisions Israel as living in the pre-existing walled towns and cities in the land after the occupation. This is signalled, on the one hand, by their conquest of the territories of King Sihon and King Og in Transjordan (2:32–36; 3:3–7), in which the women and children settle according to their assignments (3:19), and their anticipated conquest of such cities in Cisjordan that Yhwh has given to them to occupy, relieving them of the burden of building from scratch (e.g. 19:1; 20:10–20; 28:52). These cities in Cisjordan are currently occupied by the Hittites, Girgashites, Amorites, Canaanites, Perizzites, Hivites, and Jebusites, seven groups bigger and more numerous than Israel (7:1). Yet, Yhwh, Israel's king, will ensure that the conquest of the cities in Cisjordan is gradual, not a blitzkrieg, so that the wild beasts do not grow too numerous for Israel (7:22). This statement recognizes the tenuous balance between order and chaos; cultivated land is orderly while wilderness is chaotic, and it is the responsibility of the king, divine or human, to prevent reversion to chaos.

On the other hand, Israel's intended occupation of the pre-existing walled cities and towns is made clear from the many references to the activities that are to take place after successful occupation and settlement "in your gates." In certain passages, "your gates" is used to designate the settlements Yhwh is giving Israel (e.g. 16:18) (Berge 2021). The city gates were the traditional venue used to settle legal disputes, but chs. 12:1–26:15 regulate many aspects of urban life.

This being the case, the book names very few cities in the promised land: Heshbon, Jahaz, Aroer, Salcah, Edrei, Bezer, Ramoth, and Golan in Transjordan, and only Gilgal and Jericho in Cisjordan. The vicinity of Shechem is referred to, but not the city itself by name in the MT text. Instead, the storyworld assumes a landscape dominated by walled cities built by previous generations and cultures that is to remain more or less intact. The Israelites will take over what is there. They will give new names to some of those places as a way to claim them as theirs, but if a pre-existing name is adopted, the new occupants will embody the place as part of Israelite culture (Casey 1996, 34). In either instance, as noted by Edward S. Casey, "The world comes bedecked in places; it is a place-world to begin with" (1996, 43), whose places become deeply inscribed with time and history, the diachronic media of culture (44).

The Israelites will continue to work the land surrounding each city, as the previous inhabitants had. Rain-dependent agriculture and livestock-raising are to continue as the mainstay of the economy (e.g. 8:10–14; 11:13–15). Even so, they will do so according to Israelite customs and practices, even if many of these will overlap with those of the preceding cultures (see ch. 6; for types of land tenure, see Guillaume 2011, 9–55).

3. Israelitizing the Promised Land

The promised land is to be the setting for the future daily lives of the Israelite people. There, through the application of Moses's teaching, they will follow rules of behavior and adopt a shared worldview, values, and rituals that will help them understand who they are. Using a social memory perspective, Ehud Ben Zvi notes how the lack of specificity about physical characteristics of the walled towns or the contrasting space designated "the place" helps highlight for readers the need to apply Moses's teaching in both types of spaces. The physicality of the promised land serves only as a backdrop in the storyworld for the enactment of the divine directives (2023).

The physical terrain and occupied towns will contribute to the creation of new elements of collective memory, with various places becoming powerful emotional and cultural symbols. At the same time, the Israelites will gradually modify their local environments as they respond to constraints and opportunities as well as adapt their culture to live successfully in their local terrain and ecological niches. The formerly independent cities belonging to the seven groups in the land (7:1) will become occupied places in the geographical territory included in Israel's promised land that now is to be settled by a majority ethnos (Knox, Marston, and Nash 2010, 5–7). Yet the writers anticipate the presence of non-native residents (*gērîm*) living within the Israelite towns as a minority; they are entitled to justice alongside Israelites (24:17; 27:19) and may participate in the annual rejoicing before Yhwh at the chosen place at the festivals of Weeks and Sukkot, though not Passover (Deut 16:11, 14; 26:11).

Thus, the anticipated conquest and occupation is to yield places and regions that will become Israelite. The physical shape of places will be altered in some cases. For example, all the places on high mountains, hills, and under every leafy tree where the former groups worshipped their gods are to be destroyed, along with the paraphernalia used there (Deut 7:5; 12:2–3; cf. 12:29–31; 14:1–21; 18:9–14). Instead, a new site will be designated by Israel's divinity for animal sacrifices (12:5–6, 10–12). The inevitable destruction of houses and buildings and the creation of breaches in city walls during the conquest will require some rebuilding and reshaping of existing space over time. Although some physical structures and landmarks will remain in place, they will gain new significance within embodied Israelite cultural experience.

Once the Israelites settle in the conquered and cleansed cities, they will be "set apart" or made holy by their status as Yhwh's people who are loyal to this deity alone, who is their covenant partner, and they will dedicate their gifted territory to its divine donor exclusively. As a result, they and their inhabitants will come under the direct protection of Yhwh Elohim. This protection is to be signalled through the writing of "these words" on the doorposts of city gates and at entries into houses or housing complexes and worn as an amulet on the body (6:6–9; 11:18–20). The words, whichever are selected, will mark those places and persons as belonging to the deity exclusively, replacing former practices that would have looked to family gods and ancestors to protect houses and local city gods to protect individual cities. The use of amulets to protect individuals may well have been an existing practice that now was to represent the exclusive protector, Yhwh Elohim, through selected words vs. former imagery or symbolism. These envisioned practices are two explicit ways the reoccupied cities and their new inhabitants will be "Israelitized."

For the writer of this book, the local is the main focus, expanding out at times to the regional level but rarely if ever the "global" i.e. imperial level. In addition to the seven local groups that are to be dispossessed in 7:1, mention is made of Moabites, Ammonites, Edomites, and Egyptians, providing a narrow southern Levantine regional focus on both sides of the Jordan River, where members of the twelve tribes will settle, as well as the past place where Israel remembers having lived in slavery before moving to its new homeland as freed people. There is no mention, however, of Arameans, Arabs, Philistines, or Phoenicians, who lived in the wider southern Levant, nor of imperial groups further afield like Assyria, Babylonia, or Persia.

The place Yhwh will choose to set the divine name or reputation (šēm) to remain out of all the tribes or in one of the tribes (12: 5, 14) is to serve mentally as a central place after the occupation and settlement of the promised land. The location is not necessarily the physical, geographical center of the territory, but it will function as a supra-tribal ritual center and tribunal. In subsequent books the site is claimed to be Jerusalem by Judeans/Yehudites, while the Samarians claimed it was Mt. Gerizim, based on the ceremony to take place there described in Deut 11: 29-30 and 27:1-8. Both are too far south to represent a mid, north-south point from the River Euphrates to the Brook of Egypt, although Mt. Gerizim is more centrally positioned if the boundaries from Dan to Beersheba are in view.

The narrative to be remembered about this "place" by Israelites as well as outsiders who hear about it is its selection by Yhwh Elohim (e.g. 12:5, 11, 14, 26). Thus, it is to constitute the earthly place where the šēm (divine name/reputation) will remain while the deity will remain in heaven (26:15) (for place, see e.g. Casey 1996; Cresswell 2004, 8, 85-86; Knox, Marston and Nash 2010, 41-45).

In the latest form of the received text, in various manuscripts and translations, the place (māqôm) will contain a temple (23:19 [18]) with an open-air altar, where Levitical priests will "stand to serve" Yhwh Elohim or his name (10:8; also 17:12; 18:5, 7 and 21:5); the root šrt ("to serve") is normally understood to refer to formal duties performed by cultic specialists when applied to priests and Levites in divine service. They will offer the blood of voluntary sacrifices brought by the people over the course of the year (12:6, 11, 26-27) and of the offerings of firstborns from the flock (15:19-23). It is to be the location of a court where cases that are too difficult for local town courts to decide can be heard as necessary, with a binding verdict rendered (17:8-13).

The inclusion of a temple with a year-round functioning priesthood and a lawcourt may not have been part of the original vision of the book, however. The māqôm may only have been meant to serve as a place of pilgrimage once or three times in the year, where family and community feasting would occur, assemblies of Israelite males would take place, and difficult, unresolved law cases could be resolved before those gathered (12:7, 11–12, 17–18; 14: 22–26; 16:1–16; for one reconstruction of the pre-Deuteronomic role of the *māqôm*, see Guillaume 2021). In the final form of the book, the divinely designated *māqôm* will be where events take place that co-locate space and time (Casey 1996, 38).

Implicitly, the eventual temple will house the ark that contains the tablets written by the finger of Elohim atop Mt. Horeb, associated with the covenant made there between Yhwh and Israel (10:3–8). Beside it is to be kept "this scroll of teaching" relating to the covenant on the plains of Moab, written down by Moses and entrusted to the Levitical priests for safe-keeping: Deuteronomy (31:9, 25–26). Thus, the unnamed place will be famous because it is the religious center of a holy people (7:6; 14:2, 21; 26:19; 28:9) and a treasured people (*'am sᵉgullâ*; 7:6; 14:2) who constitute Yhwh's inalienable possession (*'am naḥᵃlâ*; 4:20; 9:29). Within the storyworld of this book, any prior narrative that might have attached to the chosen place is to be forgotten, and any subsequent narrative will be of secondary importance to the primary, founding narrative presented here.

4. Cities of Refuge

An arguably new concept in Deuteronomy is cities of refuge (4:41–43; 19:1–13), although whether they are specifically designed to replace an older system involving altars of asylum remains disputed (e.g. Rofé 1986, 213–14, 226–27, 235–36; Clements 1989, 25; Stackert 2006, 41–44; contrast Barmash 2005, 80–81). Leaving aside the question of possible historical evolution, the creation of the three cities of Bezer, Ramoth, and Golan as cities of refuge in the territory already conquered in Transjordan is narrated in 4:41–43. Then, in 19:1–13, the rationale for three future sites in Cisjordan after the conquest is provided in 19:3, 6. First, the way/route is to be established (תכין לך הדרך), and afterwards, the territory is to be divided into three parts (v. 3). This is so that anyone who has killed another unintentionally may reach the closest of the three locations before he is overtaken by an angry avenger of blood in hot pursuit "because the way/route is long." The point is for the person who has committed manslaughter to be able to be safe from summary execution by a blood relative of the person who has died. Instead, a trial is to take place that will decide his ultimate fate. The phrase "because the way/route is long" appears to refer back to the opening phrase in v. 3, but it remains unclear what is being assumed by either. Verse 3 might indicate that the eventual choices of location were to be tied to accessibility by established routes. Verse 6, however, seems to imply that the provision of three sites is to be instead of a single site of refuge because in the latter case, if it lay quite distant from the killer's home, he might be overtaken by a blood-avenger before reaching safety.

Within the storyworld of Deuteronomy, the humanly designated cities of asylum would seem to be a practical solution to a problem connected to the envisioned, single divinely "chosen place," where one might otherwise expect those who unintentionally commit manslaughter to seek asylum under the auspices of its priests. If this is the case, then two related points follow logically. Elsewhere in the book, "the place" chosen by Yhwh Elohim will house the only legitimate temple with a sacrificial altar in the land (23:19 [18]; 10:8; 12:6, 11, 27; 15:19-23; 18:5, 7; 21:50); as a corollary, the three future cities of asylum will not contain functioning altars. The relationship to the provision for asylum for a person who kills another accidentally in Exod 21:12-14 can now be considered.

In the legal case described in Exod 21:12-14, if the killer does not lie in wait for his victim but happens onto the other person and ends up killing him, presumably after a dispute that escalates to violence, ending in death, he may flee to "the place that Elohim (MT) (or 'they' in the Syriac version)[1] will appoint" (vv. 12-13). While the selection of a single place (*māqôm*) for asylum is only implied as a rejected option in Deuteronomy, here it is stated explicitly in the MT. In both cases, it is to take place only after entering and occupying the promised land. In Deuteronomy, Yhwh Elohim implicitly will choose the site that will house his temple but which will not serve as a place of asylum; in MT Exodus, Elohim will explicitly appoint a place that will serve as the sole place of asylum.

Verse 21:14 then adds that if a man attacks another wilfully, to kill him through cunning, "[then] from [being] with my altar you shall take him, to die." This verse ostensibly indicates that Yhwh will appoint a place that will contain an altar and that the practice of asylum for unpremeditated manslaughter is envisioned to involve seeking refuge at this sanctuary. The claim that v. 14 intends to emphasize the seriousness of the act of premeditated murder by stating that anyone who commits such a crime could even be arrested at an altar is possible syntactically but not likely (e.g. Barmash 2005, 78). Most portions of temple precincts were inaccessible to ordinary people, although it might have been possible to admit asylum seekers as an exception, upon request made at the temple gates. More tellingly, had this been the case, one would have expected

---

1   It is likely that the Syriac version has been changed by scribes to harmonize with the procedure described in Deut 19:2-3 for the Israelites to use to establish cities of refuge for themselves in the promised land.

the presence of a particle like *gam* expressing the sense of "even" before or after the phrase "from with my altar." Thus, Exod 21:12–14 envisions what is implicitly rejected in Deut 19:6: a single, divinely appointed site containing a sacrificial altar that will serve as the single, designated place of asylum for those who murder unintentionally. At the same time, a clear contrast is drawn between the divinely appointed single site of asylum with an altar in Exod 21:12–14 and the three sites the people will choose for asylum in Cisjordan in Deut 19:1–13, which will lack altars.

In Deut 19:1–13, three equally spaced towns without functioning temples containing sacrificial altars, located in the future Cisjordanian territory occupied by ten and a half tribes of twelve-tribe Israel, will be set up by the Israelites as places of asylum for those who commit involuntary manslaughter. In them, blood revenge (*lex talionis*) cannot operate after a person has stood trial in absentia, apparently in his home town, and his innocence of premeditated homicide has been determined by his elders (19:4–7). If, on the other hand, he has been found guilty by his elders, he is to be extradited to his home town from the city of refuge where he has been residing and handed over to the blood-avenger there to be put to death (Deut 19:11–13).[2] According to Josh 20:7, the three towns eventually are established at Kedesh in Galilee, in the territory of Naphtali; at Shechem in the hill country of the tribe of Ephraim, and at Hebron in the hill country of the tribe of Judah.[3]

The internal logic of the book of Deuteronomy indicates this provision of three towns of asylum is a response to what otherwise would have been a single site of asylum at "the chosen place" that eventually

---

[2] It is noteworthy that Josh 20 seems to envision a different understanding of the trial. When one arrives at a city of asylum, he must explain his situation and what has occurred to the elders at the city gate, who then are to give him a place to remain and not turn him over to a blood-avenger. The fugitive is to stay put until his standing before the council/congregation for a verdict (or?) until the high priest in office at the time dies. Then he may return to his home town. Numbers 35:12 also notes that the city of asylum makes the fugitive safe from an avenger so that the one who has slain may not die before his standing before the council/congregation. What is not clear here is the location where the council/assembly holds the trial. Is it back in the fugitive's home town or in the city of refuge or in the city where Yhwh will place his name? Here, it takes place after the fugitive has fled. That is not specified in Deuteronomy, where the asylum is not said to be temporary.

[3] One can note that in Num 35:1–8, these six cities of refuge are subsumed under a new concept of 48 Levitical cities within the land belonging to the other tribes. Each is to be surrounded by pasture land extending 1,000 cubits in all directions, to be used by the resident Levites for their domestic animals, personal property, and all their animals.

would house the sole temple and the only legitimate place to offer animal sacrifice. Since that undetermined site might lie a great distance from eventual Cisjordanian settlements, this solution was to be implemented to allow someone who committed unintentional manslaughter to escape from a blood avenger to safety until his town elders could review the facts of what had taken place and provide a binding ruling as to whether the homicide was intended or unintended murder. This is a means to place the practice of *lex talionis* ("eye for an eye"; life for a life) under formal local judicial control. It is unclear if Exod 21:12-14, which anticipates a single, divinely appointed place of asylum with a functioning altar, is original in its context or a later addition, so it is best to reserve judgment about both literary and historical precedence between it and Deut 19:1-13.

5. Three Geographical Anomalies in the Book

Three anomalies occur in geographical names used in the book. There is a strong preference for describing the region south of the Beersheba Valley as Seir, not Edom (e.g. 1:2, 46; 2:1, 4, 5, 8, 29). There also is a consistent designation of the place where the first covenant was made as (Mt.) Horeb (1:2, 6, 19; 4:10, 15; 5:2; 9:8; 18:16; 28:68 [29:1 Engl.]). (Mt). Sinai occurs only once in the book, in 33:2 in a poem that was incorporated as a whole into the text. Finally, the location of a commemorative ceremony once the land has been possessed is given as near the terebrinth(s) of Moreh, involving Mt. Gerizim and Mt. Ebal, not Shechem more specifically, and not Mt. Zion associated with Jerusalem either. The underlying reasons for all three are not often addressed.

5.1 Seir

The preference for Seir/Mt. Seir rather than Edom as the name of the territory inhabited by Edomites or the descendants of Esau might be yet another appeal to Genesis, where Mt. Seir is used as the name of a territory belonging to the autochthonous Horites and is particularly associated with Esau (Gen 14:6; 33:14, 16; 36:8, 9; 36:20-21; 36:30); once it is directly equated with Edom (Gen 32:4 [3]). Another possible influencing factor in its use in both Genesis and here might have been a desire to designate the Negev highland territory more specifically and to distinguish it from the former Transjordanian kingdom of Edom and perhaps the subsequent province of Idumea as well.

Related to this observation, however, is the explicit mention of Edom/Edomites three times, in 2:4 [3], 8 [7] and 23:8. In 2:4, your brothers, the people of Esau, live in Seir, and Yhwh has given Mt. Seir to them as a possession (v. 5). As a result, the deity will not give any of their land to Israel (v. 5). Clues to Seir's location are provided by the six occurrences of the term in the description of the route that led from Horeb to the current location in the storyworld in Transjordan in the wilderness, in the Arabah opposite Suph, between Paran and Tophel, Laban, Hazerot, and Dizahab (1:1). First, the narrator reports "[it is] eleven days from Horeb by the way/route of Mt. Seir to Kadesh Barnea" (1:2), where the Israelites encamped for a period of time. If Mt. Seir is the eastern terminal point of the route, which seems likely, with Kadesh Barnea located on it, all that can be deduced it that Mt. Seir lay east of Kadesh Barnea. Then, in 1:44, after the Israelites disobey Yhwh and Moses and decide to fight the Amorites in the hill country north of Kadesh Barnea on their own, the Amorites pursue them as bees do and crush them in Seir, as far as Hormah (1:44). This implies a location for Mt. Seir in the Negev Highlands and/or southern Judean hill country, which lay east and north of Kadesh Barnea.

The remaining three mentions of Mt. Seir in 2:1, 4, 5 and 8 together provide the third clue. In 2:1, the Israelites leave Kadesh Barnea[4] and circle around (root *sbb*) Mt. Seir for many days again before finally being told by Yhwh to turn north (*ṣāpōnāh*) and cross into the territory (*bigḇûl*) of "your brothers, the sons of Esau, who live in Seir." This statement and the ensuing one in 2:5 that Yhwh has given Mt. Seir to the Edomites

---

4   The text states they head in the direction of *yam sûp*. The Greek translators rendered the Hebrew phrase *eryrthra thalassa,* leading to an association with the Red Sea in the Hellenistic period, either via the Gulf of Suez or the Gulf of Aqaba. This tradition was perpetuated by the Vulgate translation (*mare rubrum*). It likely was influenced by uses in other biblical books, especially Num 21:4; 33:10–11; 1 Kgs 9:26, and Jer 49:21, where it must indicate the Gulf of Aqaba. Another argument going back to Jerome and Rashi is that it means "sea of reeds," which would indicate a shallow lake or marsh area in the Nile Delta region of Egypt. Options include one of the Ballah lakes, Timsah Lake, or Bitter Lake (Huddlestun 1992, 638). Another option for meaning would be "sea of ending/termination/destruction (*yam sôp or śûp*)," symbolizing the mythological watery chaos from which creation took place and, as a corollary, a new beginning after order is restored (Snaith 1965, 397; Ahlström 1977, 287). In the latter case, there likely would be no intended equation with a known sea, lake, or marsh. For helpful discussions of the various options, see e.g. Snaith 1965; Batto 1983; Huddlestun 1992; Dozeman 1996. It would seem the writer of Deut 1–2 probably was envisioning Israel setting out southeastwards toward the Gulf of Aqaba, since in the ensuing vv. 4, 5, and 8, they eventually head northward along the route from Elath and Ezion-geber toward the Arabah.

as a possession ($y^eruššâ$) seem to indicate that their prior wanderings in 2:1 circumvented Mt. Seir and only now the Israelites will enter Seir from the south *en route* to their final stop in the Arabah of Moab in the storyworld (1:1). This in turn suggests Seir extended further south from the Beersheba Valley and Negev Highlands into northern Sinai. Verse 6 goes on to state that the Israelites "pulled away from" their brothers, the sons of Esau living in Seir, from the way/route of the Arabah from Elath and from Ezion-geber and turned and went along the path/route of the wilderness of Moab. The wording suggests they followed the route going north from Elath and Ezion-geber to Edom but branched off where it might have turned west to go to the Negev Highlands and southern Judean hill country, or possibly east to go to the Edomite plateau and hill country above the eastern side of the Arabah. They then took a new route that continued north toward the Dead Sea and then along its eastern shore to the Rift Valley at the northern tip of the Dead Sea below the Moabite plateau.

Thus, Esau appears to be located in unspecified wilderness territory west of the Arabah in the mind of the writer. This would be consistent with a Persian-era reality and possibly also a Neo-Babylonian reality (Edelman 2022). That territory might also extend to the eastern side of the Arabah, to the traditional area of the kingdom of Edom with its capital at Bosrah in the late eighth-sixth centuries BCE, depending on the date of composition, but only implicitly, since all six references in chs. 1–2 arguably locate Mt. Seir west of the Arabah. Only two, 1:2 and 2:8, both dealing with the names of routes, might allow for a location east of the Arabah as well, but need not do so.

The reference to the sons of Lot is noteworthy; it likewise alludes to Genesis. The Moabites and Ammonites are descendants of Abra(ha)m's nephew Lot (Gen 19:30–38) who, as a member of Abra(ha)m's extended family, is not supposed to go with him to the promised land but does (Gen 12:1, 4–5). Eventually, he separates from his uncle, taking the *'arabah* (Gen 13:5–13) and the land to its east (19:30–38) as a possession. According to Deut 2:8–23, Yhwh has granted them their lands to possess.

In the storyworld of Genesis, both Esau and Lot are Abra(ha)m's kin, but only Abra(ha)m's direct descendants are included as recipients of the promised land, and among them, only the favored line, which passes through Esau's twin brother, Jacob. Nevertheless, like the Moabites and Ammonites, Yhwh has given the sons of Esau a territory to possess outside the promised land, and Gen 36 provides a genealogy for "Esau- that is Edom" as well as a list of kings. It includes territory on the east side of the Jordan, well beyond Seir.

Finally, Deut 23:1–8 states who may "enter" (verb *bw'*) the assembly (*qāhāl*) of Yhwh and who may not. Three categories are forbidden forever:

no eunuch, i.e. male with crushed testicles or a removed penis (v. 2 [1]); no *mamzēr*, i.e. an illegitimate child or any descendant thereof (v. 3 [2]), and no Moabite or Ammonite or any descendant thereof, because they did not supply food and water when Israel passed by after leaving Egypt and also because they hired Balaam to curse Israel (vv. 4-7 [3-6]). Two categories are allowed: the Edomite, because he is your brother, and the Egyptian, because you were a *gēr* in his land. Children born to either may enter the assembly of Yhwh in the third generation (vv. 8-9 [7-8]).

The first two prohibited groups have no explanation supplied; apparently the reasons were obvious. A eunuch was considered deformed or no longer a complete man and therefore either was unworthy of entering sacred space or not entitled to participate in adult male rituals or assemblies.[5] The term *mamzēr* occurs only twice in the Hebrew Bible: here and in Zech 9:6, where the context seems to indicate either that a no longer ethnically pure Philistine group will dwell at Ashdod or that due to impending foreign conquest, women who survive and remain will give birth to illegitimate children after being raped. Either way, the *mamzēr* prohibition would seem to reflect the priestly principle of avoiding the mixing of two distinctive substances or categories (*kil'āyim*), like the prohibition of letting two breeds of cattle mate, of sowing a field with two kinds of seeds, or of wearing cloth made of two types of material (Deut 22:10-11; Lev 19:19).

The explanations for excluding the Moabites and Ammonites appeal to a shared narrative of the group's past, but only the Balaam story is recounted in a biblical text, in Num 22-24, and there it is Moab and the Midianites, not the Ammonites, who hire Balaam. There is no account of Moab and Ammon failing to provide Israel with food and water, and according to Deut 2:29 [28], the Moabites who dwell at Ar as well as the descendants of Esau who dwell in Seir supply requested food and water in exchange for payment. King Sihon of Heshbon is the first to refuse the request for food and water, and by divine design and decree, his territory marks the beginning of the conquest of the promised land (2:30-31 [29-30]). In Num 16-18, as Israel is *en route* to the land of Moab, Yhwh supplies water for them at Beer, but there is no story before or after concerning Moab's refusal to supply water. Moab and Ammon are the first of four politico-ethnic groups to be mentioned, in contrast to the previous two categories, so perhaps explanations were deemed necessary in each case.

---

5   The exclusion of eunuchs was or became a point of contention. In Isa 56:4-5, eunuchs who keep sabbath and the covenant will be included in Israel; Yhwh will give them an everlasting name in his house and inside his walls a monument and name/reputation better than sons or daughters.

The reasons given for the Edomites and Egyptians eventually being allowed to be included in the assembly appeal to stories in the book of Genesis. This is where we learn that Esau is Jacob's elder twin brother but he sells his birthright to Jacob, which is confirmed by Isaac through a deceptive ruse hatched by his wife, Rebekah (Gen 25:19–27:45). We learn of Esau's connection with Mt. Seir (Gen 14:6; 33:14, 16; 36:8, 9; 36:20–21; 36:30) as well as his Edomite affiliation (Gen 32:4 [3]; 36:1). It is also in this book that Abra(ha)m is a temporary *gēr* at the court of pharaoh (12:10–20), and the prediction in Gen 15:13 of 400 years of Egyptian oppression includes an initial status as *gērîm*, followed by that as slaves (*waʿăbādûm*). Joseph, who arrives in Egypt as a slave, implicitly wins his freedom (41:37–46) and works as a resident *gēr* under another pharaoh, securing the land of Goshen for his brothers and their families as a place of temporary residence (Gen 46:31–47:1–12).

Returning to the anomalous explanation for the exclusion of Ammonites and Moabites forever, the key to understanding the current justification seems to be provided in Deut 2:2–23: these are the children of Lot. They are cousins of the Israelites and Edomites. While the Israelites are told explicitly by Yhwh that they must purchase food from their brothers, the Edomites, no such stipulation is made concerning their cousins, the Moabites or Ammonites, only that Yhwh has provided territories for both of them.

The charge brought in 23:5 [4] is that neither cousin anticipated/met (*lōʾ qiddemû*) you with food and water along the way when you went out of Egypt, i.e. they did not provide hospitality to extended family in the neighborhood. With no other tradition to draw on that provided a good excuse involving both groups, this one appears to have been fashioned by building on traditions in Genesis concerning the sons of Lot and was then supplemented with the Balaam story in Numbers, in spite of its involving only one of the two groups. It was the only quasi-relevant material available. Whether this explanation was part of the original text or was added subsequently is not clear. In any event, the two references to the sons of Edom in 2:4 [3], 8 [7] and the one to the Edomite in 23:7 constitute, along with the reference to the Moabites and Ammonites as the sons of Lot, additional instances of deliberate inter-Pentateuchal allusion.

5.2 (Mt). Horeb Instead of (Mt). Sinai

A few explanations of the second geographical anomaly, (Mt.) Horeb instead of (Mt.) Sinai, have been offered. One is that, in a desire to eliminate a potential reference to the moon god Sin in the name Sinai, Horeb was substituted to imply the heat of the sun, yielding a more acceptable image. Yhwh had been associated with solar traits (e.g. Gall 1898, 2; Hyatt 1971, 203). But the underlying trait of the root *ḥ-r-b* seems to be dryness or drought, not heat, and thus, an absence of water, not an excess of sunshine. A second explanation is that Horeb was a neutral term or a cipher to designate a "wasteland" that was used to avoid negative connotations associated with Sîn and Seir/Edom. A generic term was chosen because the specific location of the mountain was no longer known (Perlitt 1977, 315–19). If the tradition of *tōrâ*-giving and entering into a covenant at Mt. Sinai were already established in cultic circles, however, then the name of the place where the event occurred would not have easily been forgotten, even if the specific physical location became fuzzy over time. The very fact we still have the name indicates it was not forgotten.

A third explanation is that the two terms are not entirely coterminous. Sinai would have been the name of the mountain proper, while Horeb would have been a wider regional designation. M. H. Segal (1961, 90) has noted that Rephidim, like Sinai, was also located in Horeb in Exod 17:6. There Moses struck a rock to produce water in front of the elders; the spot was subsequently called Massah and Meribah (17:7). In addition, in Exod 3:1 and 1 Kgs 19:8, the mountain of Elohim lay within the wider region of Horeb (*ḥōrēbâ*, with locative *heh*). In Exod 18:5, this region is described as wilderness (*midbār*). For this reason, the writer could not say in Exod 19:2 that the Israelites journeyed from Rephidim and arrived at Horeb; they arrived at Mt. Sinai, which also lay in the region of Horeb. Segal reasons that Horeb is used extensively in Deuteronomy because once Israel was encamped on the plains of Moab that lay quite far away from Mt. Sinai, it made more sense to use the wider geographical term than the specific name of the mountain alone.

A review of biblical texts indicates that Hebrew *hār* can mean both "mount" when referring to specific mountain peak as well as a region that contained multiple peaks that collectively could be designated by the singular term in the sense of "mountainous or hilly terrain or country." Yet in Exod 33:6, the reading seems to be Mt. Horeb, not the hill-country of Horeb, especially in light of the characterization of the nature of the landscape of Horeb in 18:5 as wilderness, not hill-country. In addition, the writer of Exodus refers to the wider region as the wilderness of Sinai (*midbar sînay*) (19:1, 2) and the area between Elim and Sinai as the wilderness of Sin (*midbar sîn*) (16:1). There is a single reference to Horeb in the context of the covenant at the mountain of God in Exod 3:1. One has to wonder if this is not an editorial addition meant to harmonize the accounts of covenant-making in the wilderness after the escape from Egypt in Exodus and Deuteronomy.

The writer of Deuteronomy has consistently avoided referring to Mt. Sinai or any possible hill-country of Sinai in his narrative. Instead, he talks about what transpired in Horeb (1:2, 6, 19; 4:10, 15; 5:2; 9:8; 18:16; 28:69 [29:1]). He never uses the construct chain *har ḥōrēb*, yet in 1:6 he talks about "the mountain" located there, which has no specific name. References to an assembly of the people to hear the divine words (4:10; 18:16), Yhwh speaking out of fire (4:15; 18:16), and the making of a covenant with Yhwh our Elohim at Horeb (5:2) or just with Yhwh (28:69 [29:1]) occur, which in Exodus take place at Mt. Sinai, and implicitly here, at "the mountain" first introduced in 1:6. It is highly unlikely that he did not know the Mt. Sinai tradition, so the logical inference is that he was deliberately avoiding use of the name Mt. Sinai for some reason.

There is a single reference to Sinai in a poem incorporated wholesale into Deuteronomy in ch. 33. There is three-way parallelism between Sinai, Seir, and Mount Paran in v. 2. According to Segal's logic, Mount Paran would be the specific name of God's mountain and Sinai and Seir regional entities with some geographical overlap in which Paran was located. Many scholars consider ch. 33 to be a later addition to the book, in which case one could posit that an editor deliberately used a tradition referring to Sinai, perhaps for purposes of harmonization with Exodus, just as the reference to Horeb in Exod 3:1 might be an editorial harmonization. On the other hand, however, as already noted, as it stands in v. 2 of the poem, Sinai is a wider regional designation; there is no mention of Mt. Sinai but, instead, one of Mt. Paran. Thus, the creator of the book of Deuteronomy could conceivably have taken up this poem and allowed the reference to Sinai to stand because it could be construed regionally.

A fourth explanation proposes a deliberate change in the name to make a theological point. In priestly writings, Mt. Sinai is the home of Yhwh, associated with a tradition of divine theophany in natural phenomena like earthquake, thunder, lightning, thick cloud, and fire. The tent of meeting is required to contain Yhwh's physical presence among the people until the temple is built on Mt Zion in Jerusalem as the deity's new permanent home in the midst of its people. By designating the location of the first giving of divine instruction (Torah) as Mt. Horeb, an arid place without water to sustain life,[6] the priestly concept of Yhwh having an earthly home and place where divine *kabod* would manifest could be de-emphasized or even undermined in favor of the view that Yhwh has manifested instead in the written instruction. The physical place this

---

6   While not describing Horeb specifically, the wilderness the Israelites crossed after leaving the mountain is similarly characterized as "a waterless land (*ṣimmāʾōn*) with no water in it" except for that which Yhwh Elohim brought forth from the flinty rock (8:15).

instruction was given is of no importance and has no ability to sustain life. Yhwh Elohim is located in heaven, not on earth (Deut 26:15). It is the revealed instruction itself that sustains life and serves as a wellspring (Edelman 2015, 329–30).[7]

The writers of both Deuteronomy and Exodus use Horeb/Sinai as a symbolic place. Unlike biblical stories that locate past events in the local terrain, which often are etiological but which also have instructional value in terms of social values, custom, and shared past, the event of the giving of divine instruction is attached to a location outside the promised land. Examples of stories associated with places inside the local land include the origin of the sanctuary at Bethel in Gen 28:10–22, the origin of the heap of ruin at Ai in Josh 8, and the origin of the prohibition of eating the sinew of the thigh-vein that is over the hollow of the thigh of any animal in Gen 32:25. Also, both situate myths and stories in physical places they inhabit, as a means of teaching wisdom or survival skills.

Because of its location "far away," Horeb/Sinai is not a place Israelites will visit regularly to recall the giving of divine instruction there through the agency of Moses and the importance of Torah for living their lives as the people of Yhwh Elohim. In this specific case, then, the writer has employed the practice of tying a crucial event in the formation of the Israelites to what is presumably a physical place, allowing the mneumonic function of such a practice to be triggered when either the term Torah or Horeb/Sinai is heard. But the other bodily senses cannot be engaged in the way they are when a person experiences a place directly.

Perhaps the desire to situate the giving of Torah outside the promised land in order to make it binding on Israelites living anywhere – in Cisjordan and Transjordan as well as in diasporic locations – was a motivating factor for this slight anomaly (e.g. Römer 2015, 238–39). More importantly, perhaps the tradition of Mosaic Torah was a rather late innovation, a part of incipient Judaism, which had no traditional ties to a physical location in Cisjordan that could be used as the site of the revelation of the divine teaching and its annual commemoration. Instead, however, the place Yhwh will choose to place his name to dwell within one of your tribes (12:5, 14) is to become the center of annual commemorative celebrations of that past event at Horeb/Sinai (see ch. 8), obviating the need for pilgrimage into the wilderness to the "original place," whose specific location was not known or remembered even in antiquity. The scroll containing the teaching delivered on the plains of Moab, i.e. the book of Deuteronomy (31:9, 26), will eventually be housed inside the sanctuary at that place, beside the ark that contains the two tablets inscribed with

---

7   P ideas return in 31:15–18.

the Ten Commandments. Thus, Horeb/Sinai, a symbolic location in its essence, can be "mapped onto" the chosen place that is to house its principle audio-visual artifacts.

5.3 Mt. Gerizim and Mt. Ebal vs. Shechem, Mt. Zion, or Jerusalem

The final anomaly is why the mountains next to Shechem are the place where the words of the Moab covenant are to be inscribed and a commemorative ceremony to take place in 11:29–30 and 27:1–8 rather than Shechem proper, Mt. Zion, or Jerusalem. The answer might lie in a further appeal to Genesis and the story of Abra(ha)m's arrival in the promised land. After reaching the land of Canaan, he travels south until he reaches "the terebrinth/oak of Moreh" in the vicinity of Shechem. There Yhwh appears to him and announces, "I will assign this land to your offspring." In response, he erects an altar (Gen 12:6–7). In the MT version of Deut 11:29–30, Moses instructs the people to set a blessing on Mt. Gerizim and a curse on Mt. Ebal, which are located "beside the terebrinths/oaks of teaching." The Samaritan version, on the other hand, reads "beside the terebrinth/oak of Moreh in front of Shechem." While the MT version has trees in the plural vs. the singular tree in Gen 12:6, there is little doubt that the passage intends to recall the Abrahamic story.[8] The Samaritan version makes that even more explicit, reduplicating the singular terebrinth/oak of Moreh and locating it explicitly near Shechem. These are the only references in the Hebrew Bible to such a tree or grove of teaching; both are in the immediate vicinity of Shechem.[9]

The wording of 11:30 in the MT text is awkward, which may have contributed to the proposal that it is a later addition that allegedly interrupts a logical connection between the commandments with which Moses opens his speech in 6:4–11:25 and the "statutes and ordinances" he

---

[8] In this case, the MT version may well have been altered to the plural to weaken the original allusion, while the SP version may have added the reference to Shechem to make the link even more explicit.

[9] By implication, this is likely to be the same terebrinth/oak tree near Shechem under which Jacob buried "the gods of the foreigner" and earrings in possession of members of his household in Gen 35:4 after returning from Aram Naharaim. While this tree is represented in Hebrew by the form *'ēlâ*, not *'ēlôn*, the diminutive or adjectival ending *-ôn* does not alter the shared underlying root. The *'ēlâ* in or near the sanctuary of Yhwh (*miqdaš yhwh*) at Shechem in Josh 24:25–26 is almost certainly another reference to the same tree, even though it also lacks the qualifier *mōreh*, as is also the terebrinth/oak of the erected stone (*'ēlôn muṣṣāb*) in Shechem where Abimelech is said to have been crowned king in Judg 9:6.

had laid down in that speech (Na'aman 2000, 144, 153–55). The location of Mt. Gerizim and Mt. Ebal is given as "across the Jordan, beyond/following the way/route of the setting of the sun in the land of the Canaanite living in the Arabah opposite the stone circle/Gilgal, near the terebrinths/oaks of Moreh." In English at least, we would have avoided making the phrase "near the terebrinths/oaks of Moreh" a dangling modifier by positioning it as the first element in the description or the second, after "across the Jordan."

The reference to "the land of the Canaanite living in the Arabah opposite the stone circle/Gilgal" seems to function as the eastern terminus or starting point of a route going westward from the Cisjordanian Arabah into the central hill country. Frequently, a specific city served as a terminal or destination point for a route, like the Timnah route (Gen 38:14), the Beth-Shemesh route (1 Sam 16:12), or the Beth-Horon Ascent route (Jos 10:10). There also are routes in the Hebrew Bible, however, that are named by regional destination, like the Bashan route (Num 21:33; Deut 3:1), the Mt. Seir route (Deut 1:2), the Arabah route (Deut 2:8), and the Wilderness of Moab route (Deut 2:8) (Dorsey 1991, 47–51). The decision to describe the eastern terminus for a Cisjordanian route that went from the western side of the Jordan rift valley westward in this somewhat circumlocutionary way is consistent with the larger trend in the book that avoids mentioning most cities in the land to be occupied by name. The same trend is illustrated in the preference for naming routes by region in the book.

In the MT version of Deut 27, Moses commands that when the people have occupied the land, they are to set up plastered stones inscribed with "this instruction" on Mt. Ebal. They are to build an altar and offer burnt offerings and offerings of well-being there, eating and rejoicing before Yhwh their Elohim. Finally, they are to announce a series of twelve curses, one for each tribe. In the Samaritan Pentateuch, the site in v. 4 is Mt. Gerizim instead. Opinion is divided over which is the older reading, although the trend now is to favor Mt. Gerizim. In either case, there is no direct statement that this is the place Yhwh will choose or has chosen to set his name to dwell inside a temple that will house the ark, with the book of Deuteronomy beside it, where animal sacrifices will be made year round and where three annual festivals will be held. Instead, it is the site of a one-time ceremony commemorated by stones inscribed with the contents of the Mosaic teaching.

Eduard Nielsen (1955, 54) pointed out that the prominence given to Shechem in Deut 11:29–31 and 27:1–8 might have derived from its having been the site of the first sanctuary built in Canaan (Gen 12:6–7; 33:18–20). It appears, in fact, that the ceremony to take place near Shechem in Deuteronomy is intended to mark the fulfilment of the first divine promise to give the land to Abra(ha)m's offspring by having it take place at the same locale (e.g. Wenham 1971, 106–7). As such, in the storyworld it will be partially commemorative in nature, recalling the initial promise of "this land" to Abra(ha)m's descendants. At the same time, however, it closes the circle relating to the promised land, making it a reality in a one-time ceremony with an altar purpose-built for the occasion. The order of the tribes to partake in the blessings and curses in 29:11–13 follows the enumeration in Gen 49 and is likely based on the latter text (Nielsen 1955, 72), as another echo of Genesis in the book.

Unlike in the book of Exodus, where the initial covenant with Israel is made outside the promised land, here the renewal of the covenant made on the plains of Moab or yet a new covenant is made within the boundaries of the promised land.[10] Whether correct or not, those responsible for Deuteronomy in its present form are deliberately wanting to associate Israel with a territory, as a potential *goy*, a political unit, beyond just an *'am*, people, or in addition to that status (4:6–8; 34). It can be noted that the promises to Abra(ha)m and Sarai/Sarah in Gen 12:12; 17:5–6, 16, 20; 18:18; 21:13, 18 and to Jacob in Gen 35:11, 46:3 are for one or more polities to spring from these forefathers. Thus, perhaps the concentrated references to Israel as a *goy* in Deut 4 also are meant to allude to the promises to Abra(ha)m and his direct descendants, alongside the boundaries of the promised land in 1:6–8; the references to Israel being as numerous as the stars of heaven in 1:10, 10:22, and 28:62 that recall Gen 15:5, 22:17, and 26:4; the reference to blessings in 1:11 and 7:12 recalling Gen 12:2; and the use of Seir to designate the land of Edom.

The accumulated references and allusions discussed above to a number of passages in Genesis in the "frames" of Deuteronomy, chs. 1–11 and 26:16–34:12, demonstrate that those responsible for creating the book intended to link it to Genesis as well as the books of Exodus and Numbers. Thus, while Deuteronomy currently forms the conclusion to an extended

10 One can note a potential discrepancy in the larger text. In 6:1, Moses announces that the regulations and judgments constituting collectively what is commanded (*miṣwâ*) are to be observed "in the land you are crossing over to inherit," i.e. Cisjordan. That does not rule out their application also in Transjordan among the two and a half tribes whose inherited land lies there once the men return from the conquest, but such a situation is implicit only. At the same time, in the immediate context in the storyworld, Moses is focused on the occupation of Cisjordan as the impending future event involving all the tribes, not past conquest, which has been reviewed already in a previous speech. The forward focus could account for the limited scope of applicability. Nevertheless, he could have said that the *miṣwâ* was to be observed in "all your inherited lands" if Transjordan were considered part of the promised land when ch. 6 was written, as it is explicitly in chs. 2–4.

biography of Moses that begins in the book of Exodus, it was designed to include the patriarchal narratives as well as an integral part of Israel's common past. In the storyworld, the forefathers include the patriarchs as well as the Exodus generation, the parents of those standing on the plains of Moab and being addressed by Moses (Arnold 2017, 19–30, 33–36, 42–44 *pace* Römer 1990).

At the same time, the activities to take place at Mt. Gerizim and Mt. Ebal beside the terebrinths/oaks of Moreh in 11:29–31 and 27:1–8 seem to point forward to events in Josh 8:30–35 and 24:1–28. The first text, Josh 8:30–35, explicitly recounts the fulfilment of all the specified actions in both texts, although it fails to mention the plastering of two stones before writing upon them a copy of "the teaching/torah of Moses" in v. 32 or the terebrinths/oaks in Deut 11:30. Nevertheless, it refers to Moses five times in the space of five verses, including references to Moses as "the servant of Yhwh" (vv. 31, 33), the scroll of the teaching of Moses (v. 31), a copy of the teaching of Moses being written on the stones (v. 32), and the words that Moses commanded (v. 33). Moses is accentuated as the pre-eminent source of authority in this unit of text.

In addition, the writer of Josh 8:30–35 has used the literary technique of inverted citation, also known as Seidel's law, in which the order of elements in a source are reversed, thereby signaling that the new text is a reuse of an older one. In Deut 27:2–8, the stones are first to be plastered and "the words of this teaching" written on them (vv. 2–4)[11] before the altar is built and holocausts and peace offerings are made upon it. In Josh 8:30–35, the altar-building takes place first, with sacrifices of holocaust and peace offerings made upon it (vv. 30–31), before moving to the writing of a copy of the teaching of Moses (v. 32). The writer then deftly uses the constituents of the assembly described in Deut 29:9 to describe this new ceremony, which includes the sojourner in both cases (v. 33). He finishes by reporting the fulfilment of the attachment of the blessing and the curse to Mt. Ebal and Mt. Gerizim in Deut 11:29 during the ceremony by having the people divided on either side of the ark, half in front of Mt. Gerizim and half in front of Mt. Ebal, "as commanded at the first." The priests then read out "all the words of the teaching, the blessing, and the curse according to all written in the scroll of teaching" (v. 34), which may allude to or be based on the law-reading commanded every seven years

---

11 Although v. 8 reports the actual writing after the sacrifices, it has been recognized that it resumes the command made initially in v. 3a and is intended close to a frame around material that was added secondarily in vv. 3b–8 concerning the specific location of the stones as Mt. Ebal in the MT and Mt. Gerizim in the Samaritan Pentateuch and the building of an altar and offering of sacrifices thereon (e.g. Fishbane 1985, 162).

at Sukkot in Deut 31:9-13 (e.g. Nihan 2007, 219). There is no doubt that Josh 8:30-35 is intended to recount the fulfilment of the two sets of commands in Deut 11:29-32 and 27:4-8.

It needs to be noted, however, that many scholars consider both Deut 11:29-32 and 27:1-8 or parts thereof to be secondary additions to the book (Na'aman 2000 for a good overview, esp. 143-47; Van Seters 2003, 64; Nihan 2007, 200-13). Both interrupt the narrative flow where they are situated. Together, they form an inclusio or frame around the *ḥuqqîm ûmišpāṭîm* that begin in Deut 12:1 and end in 26:16, followed immediately by the concluding of a formal covenant in 26:17-19.

Unravelling the complex history of both Deut 11:29-32 and 27:1-8 is probably no longer possible, although it is noteworthy that 27:5-7 cite the altar law in Exod 20:24-26, not the one in Deut 12, and seem also to allude more widely to Exod 20-24 (e.g. Nihan 2007, 210-12, 215). The allusion to the altar law in Exod 20:24-26 can be seen to function as a means of justifying the altar that will be used for the one-time commemorative ceremony; it is not meant to become a permanently functioning altar (pace Nihan 2007, 215-16, 223). It can be noted that both 11:30 and 27:4 contain two conflicting locations for the actions to take place after crossing the Jordan: the vicinity of Gilgal and the vicinity of Shechem. This is in spite of the possible but awkward reading of the reference to the land of the Canaanites in the Arabah opposite Gilgal in 11:30 as the eastern terminus of a route heading westward. Joshua 4:19-34 recounts the erection of twelve stones near Gilgal, recalling the ceremony that took place at Sinai in Exod 24:3-8, with further parallels drawn between the crossing of the Jordan River (Josh 3:1-4:24) and the crossing of the Sea of Destruction (*yam sûp*) in Exod 14:21-31.

As already noted, Josh 8:30-35 recounts the fulfillment of the combined commandments in Deut 11:29-32 and 27:1-8 in a ceremony in the vicinity of Shechem. Yet, it, too is considered to be a secondary addition in that book, dependent upon the additions made to Deuteronomy (e.g. Na'aman 2000, 141, 155; Nihan 2007, 217-18). Is it logical to suggest, as has Nadav Na'aman (2000, 152-58), that the two additions to Deuteronomy were made by a Judean redactor trying to legitimate the cult at Shechem that had been established after the destruction of both Jerusalem and Bethel and their temples by the Neo-Babylonians?

Alternative scenarios are possible. So, for example, Christophe Nihan has proposed that a Judean editor added Deut 11:29-32 and 27:1-8 at the time of the formation of the Pentateuch to accommodate Samarian Yahwists. Since they would only have the first five books in their collection, they needed an endorsement of their already existing sanctuary on Mt. Gerizim (2007, 223).

Two more options can be considered. The first would be that a later Judean redactor added the details in Deut 11:29–32 and 27:1–8 for a one-time commemorative ceremony to take place on Mt. Gerizim originally, which later was changed to Mt. Ebal when anti-Samarian tensions heated up. He would have had an ulterior motive of critiquing any Samarian claims at the time that Gerizim was the divinely chosen place to establish a permanent temple and cult (e.g. Amit 2014, 240). He also would have assumed the split references to the one-time ceremony would be acceptable to Samarians.

The second would be that a Samarian redactor could have added the passages with an ulterior motive to set a precedence for their claim that Mt. Gerizim was the intended "place" Yhwh chose to place his name but deliberately worded it as a one-time ceremony to gain support from Judeans. It should be noted that in the Samaritan book of Exodus, the first two of the ten commandments are combined to make room for a new, tenth commandment (Exod 20:14). It specifically anticipates the language in Deut 11:29–30 and 27:2–7 to make the sanctity of Mt. Gerizim part of the original revelation at Sinai, going beyond the subsequent command by Moses to build an altar there, sacrifice, rejoice, and have in place a copy of the text of the *tôrâ* written on plastered stones. The purpose of the added commandment is to have Yhwh directly single out Mt. Gerizim as his chosen place.

Four options to explain the addition of Deut 11:29–31 and 27:1–8 to the book of Deuteronomy have been reviewed; more no doubt are possible. It is noteworthy that the additions seem intended to draw on the traditions about Shechem in Gen 12:6, 8, and 35:2, 4, yet they do not mention Shechem directly, as does Josh 24. Instead, 11:29 refers to Mt. Gerizim and Mt. Ebal, and in 27:4 the location for the commemorative ceremony is specified as Mt. Gerizim in the Samaritan Pentateuch and Mt. Ebal in the MT. The latter, in particular, is the location of the Persian-era Yahwistic temple in Samaria. Thus, these added references can be seen to fulfill multiple purposes. They look both backward to the beginning of the Pentateuch and forward to the ceremony reported in Josh 8:30–35 and, as such, help construct the idea of a Hexateuchal collection. They also situate a one-time commemorative ceremony at the site where a permanent temple eventually is situated in the Persian period, perhaps with the intention of critiquing the latter facility. Whether part of an original intention or not, this dimension would have emerged once the Samaritans opted for the Pentateuch as their collection of authoritative texts rather than the Hexateuch. For a Judean audience, the message conveyed was that the permanent temple built on Mt. Gerizim was illegitimate; Yhwh had chosen Jerusalem as the single, permanent place where the name would dwell. Any solution proposed for the underlying reason for the addition of these two passages must be able to offer a plausible explanation for why both Judeans and Samarians could accept and include them in their versions of both Deuteronomy and their authoritative collections of writings.

In contrast, what takes place in Josh 24:1-28 does not fulfil any of the explicit commands in Deuteronomy, although the MT does mention a terebrinth/oak, which it locates in the sanctuary of Yhwh in Shechem. The OG text, however, locates the events at Shiloh instead and makes no mention in v. 26 of a sanctuary; instead, v. 25 has a plus stating that the events took place "before the tent of the God of Israel," and in v. 26, the sacred tree is located "before Yhwh" (vv. 1, 25-26), referring back to the setting that began in 18:1. Recently, Ville Mäkipelto (2022) has made a strong case that the Hebrew text used as the basis for the OG translation had been changed by a Jerusalemite scribe to read Shiloh instead of Shechem and to omit any mention of a sanctuary at Shechem, due to growing anti-Samaritan sentiments in the late Hellenistic period after ca. 200 BCE. The likelihood that Shiloh is a secondary reading has been argued for a long time, however (e.g. Nielsen 1955, 86-87; Sperling 1987, 120; Anbar 1992, 30). Yet, oddly enough, both versions contain many of the elements recounted previously in 8:30-35 that took place at Mt. Ebal and Mt. Gerizim, but in a different order, and they leave out any mention of Moses as prophetic mediator and the ark. What is going on?

In the MT, after the partial conquest of Cisjordan and the allocation of tribal lands there, Joshua gathers the tribes of Israel to Shechem a second time (cf. 8:30-35). The choice of Shechem might depend on 8:30 -35 and with it Deut 11:29-31 and 27:1-8, if it was written after those texts. However, as noted by a number of scholars (e.g. Anbar 1992, 117 -20; Blum 1997, 200; Römer and Brettler 2000, 413; Nihan 2007; Schmid 2018, 24), it might instead (or also) be an appeal to Gen 12:6, 8 and the first altar Abra(ha)m constructs in the promised land. "Israel's history in Genesis through Joshua ends where it began" (Schmid 2018, 24). Then, in their presence, with their representatives, the elders, heads, judges, and scribes (šōṭᵉrîm), which echoes Deut 29: 9 and secondarily, Josh 8:33, he provides a historical summary quoting Yhwh the God of Israel (compare 1 Sam 10:17-19) of their shared past that serves as the historical prologue to a new covenant to be established that day. It begins with Abra(ha) m's call in Gen 12 outside the land in Harran (v. 2) and ends with the current situation in which they collectively have been given land they have not grown weary/struggled for, dwell in cities they did not build, and enjoy the fruits of vineyards and olive groves they did not plant (v. 13). Joshua then provides those gathered with the terms of a covenant (vv. 14-20), which center on loyalty to Yhwh Elohim alone. The people agree initially; Joshua pronounces a single blessing for obedience and curse for disobedience (v. 20), and then the people assent a second time (v. 21). Joshua proceeds to state the people are witnesses for/against each other concerning their individual commitment to serve Yhwh (alone) (v. 22), which the people confirm. Joshua then repeats Jacob's command to his family while they were at Shechem in Gen 35: 2 to "put away all the foreign gods that are among you," and the people confirm their decision to serve Yhwh and listen to his voice a third and final time.

The story continues in v. 25 with the narrator stating that Joshua made a covenant that day and set/established for them ḥoq ûmišpāṭ, usually translated "a statute and an ordinance," in Shechem. He then wrote "these words/matters" in the scroll of the teaching of God/scroll of divine teaching before setting up a large stone under the terebrinth/oak in the sanctuary (miqdāš) of Yhwh. He announces it is to serve as a witness against all those assembled because it has heard all the oral presentations of Yhwh that he has spoken with us and thus will serve as a witness lest you (pl.) deny your (pl.) God (for its structure and potential links to other biblical texts, see e.g. Giblin 1964, Koopmans 1990; Anbar 1992).

It is noteworthy that there is no mention of Mt. Gerizim or Mt. Ebal, only of Shechem. There is no plastering of two large stones that will have written on them all the words of "this teaching" or the building of an altar of unhewn stones (27:4–8), perhaps because a sanctuary (miqdāš) already existed (24:26). Nor is there any setting of the blessing and curse on Gerizim or Ebal or any presence of the ark. At the same time, the historical retrospect picks up phraseology from a number of different books, not just the Pentateuch but also Samuel, Kings and prophetic books (e.g. Van Seters 2003, 146–49; Anbar 1992, 98–100; Sperling 1987, 122–33; Edenburg 2017, 171–73; Mäkipelto 2018, 172–97). Thus, it seems to be a late pastiche assembled from forms of these written scrolls. Unlike 8:30–35, this second ceremony does not seem intended to narrate the fulfillment of the commands in Deut 11:29–31 and 27:1–8 and need not presume the account of the commemorative ceremony in 8:30–35 either, which might post-date it.

What stands out in Josh 24 is how Joshua becomes a covenant-mediator and law-giver in his own right between the people and Yhwh Elohim. In the MT, Moses only appears in the summary of the past relating to Egypt, alongside Aaron, as having been sent by Yhwh before the plagues (v. 5); the reference is missing altogether in the LXX and probably has been added secondarily in the MT.[12] Thus, at most, Moses is presented in the MT as a past leader. The initial "law-giving" and covenant at Sinai/Horeb

---

12 Interestingly, the only other text that refers to the "sending" of Moses and Aaron is 1 Sam 12:8, the very text that claims that Moses (and Aaron) "brought forth you fathers from Egypt and settled them in this place."

is nowhere mentioned; nor is Moses's second revelation of regulations and the making of a second covenant on the plains of Moab. What is the logical explanation for these anomalies?

Certainly, whether one considers 24:1–28, in whole or in part, original or secondary to its current location will affect one's attempt to unravel its function. In particular, deciding if the references to Joshua setting a *ḥoq ûmišpāṭ* in 25b and writing "these words" in the scroll of the divine teaching/teaching of God in v. 26a were original or added is crucial.

When vv. 25b and 26a are left to the side, 24:1–28 narrates a covenant reaffirmation ceremony that took place at Shechem under Joshua's leadership, soon before his death. There is nothing particularly odd about that; the covenant on the plains of Moab in Deuteronomy is arguably a first example of such a ceremony, and Josh 24 would be a second. There seems to be such a renewal at key points in the periodized story of Israel's past.

There is a similar occasion on the threshold of "the period of the United Monarchy" in 1 Sam 12, which ends the "period of the Judges," although it is not strictly a covenant renewal. Nevertheless, Samuel is reported to have written the custom/case for kingship (*mišpaṭ hammᵉlūkâ*) on a scroll in 1 Sam 10:25 and laid it to rest before Yhwh. At Gilgal, in the wake of Saul's coronation as first king, he admonishes the people, possibly in light of contents of the scroll, although it is not mentioned specifically in ch. 12. They confess they have sinned by asking for a king (v. 19) and Samuel warns them to fear Yhwh and serve him faithfully, and if they fail to do so they and their king will be swept away.[13]

There is a *bone fide* third ceremony of covenant reaffirmation led by King Josiah after the finding of the "scroll of the covenant" during temple repairs toward the end of the monarchy in 2 Kgs 23:3, to which the people also were party. All involved agree to perform the words in the book. It takes place on the verge of "the period of the exile."

A further example then takes place in "the period of restoration." In Neh 9–10, the nobles as well as the common people make a covenant in the wake of the reading of the Torah scroll and the first celebration of Sukkot in Jerusalem to observe the commandments contained in the scroll. Prior to that, in Ezra 9:1–10:5 the people swear an oath to follow the prohibition of mixing with "the people of the land" found in the "teaching of Moses that Yhwh the God of Israel had given" after Ezra had

---

[13] It is not clear if Samuel is intending the people to think back to the content of the scroll he had reportedly written in the storyworld containing *mišpaṭ hammᵉlūkâ*, "the practices of kingship," which he laid to rest before Yhwh in 10:25 or not or if the confession of sin is intended to refer back to this written document or not.

introduced that teaching as the official set of regulations and statutes in Israel (7:10). The oath there is related to one regulation explicitly, however, but perhaps all in the teaching of Moses implicitly. All the direct and indirect reaffirmations of the covenant just sketched are presided over by the main leader of the era.

Proponents of a current trend argue Josh 24 is a late addition (e.g. Van Seters 1984, 154; Blum 1997; Na'aman 2000, 155, 158; Nihan 2007, 196–99; Popović 2009, 92–96; Wildenboer 2015; Schmid 2017, 151–55; Edenburg 2017; Krause 2017; Mäkipelto 2018, 224), countering a former view that favored it as pre-monarchic or monarchic and either original or added secondarily to the book (e.g. Noth 1930, 66–75; Nielsen 1955, 86–141; Perlitt 1969, 239–84; Sperling 1987, 136). Even so, that does not preclude subsequent alterations to the text, which are apparent in the various versions.

Turning to vv. 25b–26a, there may not be any substantive difference in meaning between the singular forms of *ḥoq ûmišpāṭ* used as collective nouns in Josh 24:25, with parallels in Exod 15:25b, 1 Sam 30:25; Ps 81:5; and Ezra 7:10, and the plural forms *ḥuqqîm ûmišpāṭîm* used together a number of times in Deuteronomy (4:1, 5, 8, 14, 40, 45; 5:1, 31; 6:1, 20; 7:11; 11:32; 12:1; 26:16–17). Nevertheless, the singular, collective forms never appear together in the latter book, and in spite of the many references to Moses in prior chapters of Joshua and the need for Joshua and the people to heed "all the teaching Moses commanded you" (1:7) and obey all (things) Moses commanded (1:17; 8:35; 22:2), the use of the singular forms may be deliberate. There may be an intentional move to include "all the teaching of Moses" found in the books of Exodus–Deuteronomy and not just the *ḥuqqîm ûmišpāṭîm* of Deuteronomy within a single collection. While Josh 8:32 and 22:5 seem to relate the teaching of Moses specifically to the book of Deuteronomy, other references to Moses's commands are vaguer and, in one instance, relate to events that took place already at Kadesh Barnea in Num 13 (14:6). Another exception is the late text, 8:31, which cites Exod 20:25 as belonging to the scroll of the teaching of Moses; whoever wrote that passage considered regulations in Exodus already to be integral to that written text.

This singular *ḥoq ûmišpāṭ*, then, could go hand in hand with the reference to the scroll of the Torah of God/divine teaching in v. 26a, which might be intended to distinguish it from a scroll or combination of scrolls that constitute "the teaching of Moses." Thomas Römer (2017, 214–15) argued that the report that Joshua wrote "these words" in the scroll of the teaching of God was intended, along with a number of other passages in Genesis–Joshua, to endorse the creation of a Hexateuch rather than a Pentateuch as an authoritative foundation story for Israel. Joshua's account of the taking of the promised land and its division among the remaining tribes who had not received land in Transjordan is now included in Israel's defining metanarrative of origins (see also Nelson 1997, 268; Römer and Brettler 2000). Agreeing with Joachim J. Krause (2017, 185) who cites Erhard Blum (1997, 232–35; 2012, 70–71), Römer suggests that the scroll of the teaching of God in v. 26a is a designation for the Hexateuch, in contrast to the scroll of the teaching of Moses, which designated the nascent Pentateuch.

"The scroll of the Torah/teaching of God" (sēper tôrat 'ĕlōhîm) is found only in Josh 24:26a. An almost identical phrase, "the scroll of divine Torah/teaching" (sēper tôrat hā'ĕlōhîm), occurs in Neh 8:18, with the definite article before 'ĕlōhîm, making the latter more likely to be intended to serve as an adjective. The phrase in Neh 18:18 is clearly equated with "the scroll of the teaching of Moses" (sēper tôrat mōšeh) in 8:1, the scroll of teaching (sēper hattôrâ) in 8:3, the scroll (hassēper) i.e. the divine teaching (tôrat hā'ĕlōhîm) in 8:8, the scroll of the teaching of Yhwh your Elohim (sēper tôrat yhwh 'ĕlōhêhem) in 9:3, and the scroll of Moses (sēper mōšeh) in 13:1. Thus, it is synonymous with six other expressions that designate the same body of teaching that has Yhwh Elohim as its ultimate source but which was conveyed and perhaps amplified by Moses. The same body of text(s) is being referenced in the storyworld in Neh 8:1–9:3.

The situation in Nehemiah is consistent with the tendency to designate Yahweh or Elohim as the source of the teaching (tôrâ) in the so-called legal codes in Exodus and Deuteronomy. Yhwh is the originator in Exod 13:9; 16:4, 28; 24:12; Deut 30:10; see also 2 Kgs 17:34, 37; Ps 78:10; 1 Chr 16:40; 2 Chr 17:9 and Elohim in Exod 18:16, 20; see also Isa 1:10; Hos 4:6. Moses sets the divine regulations before the people as an intermediary only (Deut 4:8, 44; see also e.g. Josh 1:7; 8:31, 32; 23:6). In line with this trend, in 2 Kgs 10:31 one finds a reference to the teaching of Yhwh the God of Israel and in Neh 8:18 and 10:28, 29 to the teaching of Elohim/divine teaching, while in Ezra 7:10 one finds the teaching of Yhwh and in Neh 9:13 the teaching of Yhwh Elohim. References to the teaching of Moses occur in 1 Kgs 2:3; 2 Kgs 23:5; 2 Chr 23:18; 25:4; 31:3; 35:26. However, in most other instances that refer to Moses's teaching, care is taken to make it clear that Yhwh is the source of such teaching (e.g. 2 Kgs 21:8; 2 Chr 30:16; 33:8; Ezra 3:2; Neh 2:3; 8:14; 9:14; Mal 3:22 [4:4 Engl]; Dan 9:11, 13). There is no clear indication, then, that "the scroll of the Torah/teaching of God" (sēper tôrat 'ĕlōhîm) in Josh 24:26 is intended to be something separate from any of the expressions used in Neh 8:1–9:3 and elsewhere to designate written divine instruction. If a distinction were intended, as suggested, it was done in such a subtle fashion that it made little, if any, impact.

It is the case, however, that the collective ḥoq ûmišpāṭ whose words Joshua wrote in the scroll of the teaching of God could be argued to endorse the inclusion of all the collections of regulations now found in Exodus–Deuteronomy as a single authoritative corpus, beyond Deuteronomy alone. This, then, raises the larger issue of whether within the corpus of books comprising the Hebrew Bible, a terminological distinction is made among the seven phrases used to describe what Ezra read out and used as the basis of study in Neh 8:1–9:3 between these two options or not. A related issue to be explored is whether the content of the referent phrases might have changed over time.

Either way, the failure to refer to Moses in the early form of ch. 24 (v. 5 is missing from the OG) could have stemmed from a desire to avoid any confusion between the scroll of the more limited torah (Deut or acc. to Römer, Gen–Deut) and the scroll of the more expansive torah (Exod–Deut or acc. to Römer, Gen–Josh). The same desire could have led to the decision to emphasize Elohim as the source of the expansive teaching. Both alternatives are consistent with a possible desire either to create a separate Hexateuch (Wildenboer 2015; Römer 2017) or at least to mark off a sub-phase within a larger Enneateuchal meta-narrative that begins in Gen 12 and extends through the end of 2 Kings (so Schmid 1999, 209–30; Otto 2000; Kratz 2002; Aurelius 2003; Achenbach 2005; Becker 2006; Krause 2017, 182–83). The book-ends of the phase are the promise of land to Abra(ha)m when he arrives at Shechem (Gen 12:6–7) and the covenant affirmation ceremony at Shechem in Josh 24:1–28, after a large chunk of the conquest and the division of the land has been accomplished.

In regards to this debate, it can be noted that Josh 24:1–28 anticipates subsequent acts in the Enneateuch in which the people abandon their promise made in MT Josh 24 at Shechem and appoint Abimelech king in place of Yhwh (Judg 9) and Jeroboam in place of Yhwh's endorsed line of Davidic kings (1 Kgs 12), both at Shechem (Mäkipelto 2018, 191–9). Nihan (2007, 223) prefers to look backward from 2 Kings and suggests that in Josh 24, Torah is presented "as the true foundation for the new unity between Judeans and Samarians after the fall of the two kingdoms and the end of the monarchical state." Yet, the depicted twelve-tribe unity is a feature of the foundational narrative that continues in the Enneateuchal narrative from the sons of Jacob in Genesis until the "Divided Monarchy" in 1 Kgs 12:20. The storyworld requires this unity; it is not limited to Joshua 24 by any means. The centrality of the divine teaching for the tribes that will eventually become the residents of the northern and southern kingdoms is emphasized from Exodus–2 Kings.

The account of a covenant-making ceremony at Shechem that took place in a sanctuary that already existed there in the storyworld would not have posed any particular threat to an intended Judean audience (Schmid 2017, 59; 2018, 26, but he includes an intended Samarian audience as well). They would have presumed that Jerusalem was the sanctuary Yhwh Elohim would choose eventually, but it did not yet exist in narrative time. Thus, the use of other sanctuaries for ceremonies would have been expected in the storyworld, before the time of David and Solomon and the temple-building in Jerusalem.

Two other reasons for the composition of Josh 24 have been proposed. The first is that the chapter intends to depict Joshua as the next "prophet like Moses" by having him emulate Moses and also establish a law and a covenant between Israel and its deity (Nicholson 1967, 77; Knauf 2014, 77). In favor of this view, it can be noted that Joshua employs the prophetic formula, "Thus, says Yhwh," in v. 2 and goes on to quote Yhwh's direct speech in vv. 3-13. This prophetic role coheres with Yhwh's speaking directly to Joshua throughout the book.

Yet, even as Yhwh vows to be with Joshua as he was with his servant, Moses, the deity declares, "you will put this people in possession of the land that I swore to their ancestors to give them" (1:2-6). The noun "prophet" is absent entirely from the book. Because Yhwh is masterminding the conquest, the deity's directions have to get conveyed to Joshua, the military leader, in some manner. The author has chosen direct divine communication between Yhwh and Joshua that implies a prophetic-like ability of Joshua to receive the divine words. Nevertheless, his role is not defined overtly as that of a prophet but rather as a Torah-obedient, pious leader.

Had the intention of vv. 1-28 always been to portray Joshua as "a prophet like Moses," one might have expected a direct confirmation of that point by having the narrator state directly that Joshua was emulating Moses's previous actions of concluding (two) covenants between Yhwh Elohim and Israel, setting *ḥuqqîm ûmišpāṭîm*, and writing words in a scroll of divine teaching. In addition, a direct confirmation that Yhwh had selected Joshua as the next "prophet like Moses" would have eliminated any question. This direct approach to referencing passages in Deuteronomy was used in the insertion in 8:30-35, for example.

In addition, there is no reference to Joshua in Deuteronomy that explicitly anticipates or confirms his role as Moses's *prophetic* successor (Deut 1:38; 3:21, 28; 31:3, 7, 23; 32:44, and 34:9). The statement in 32:44 by Yhwh that "I will be with you" often follows the command, "Fear not," as a form of divine assurance before war, and thus is not likely to allude in some way to the prophetic office. The statement in 34:9 that Joshua bin Nun was "full of the spirit of wisdom" (see e.g. Exod 28:3; Isa 11:2) after Moses laid his hands on him likewise has no routine connection to prophecy.

Thus, nowhere in Deuteronomy is Joshua portrayed as the next "prophet like Moses." At most, one could suggest that the author of Josh 24:28 or even a subsequent editor decided to cast him in such a role retrospectively, using Deut 18:15 as a prompt or even adding it to Deuteronomy to justify his depiction.[14] It should be noted that the eventual creation of an unbroken chain of prophetic successors in the former and latter prophetic books (Joshua–Malachi) would have needed to be anchored in the kind of promise found in Deut 18:15-19 (Knauf 2009, 133-35; 2014, 77). This is the case regardless of whether the original intention of 18:15-19 would have been the sporadic sending of a prophet (e.g. Von Rad 1966, 123-24; Mayes 1979, 282; Miller 1990, 155) or a permanent institution (e.g. Driver, 1902, 227; Smith 1918, 233; Philips 1973, 126). Another scribe could have subsequently added 34:10 to deny any prophetic role to Joshua or at least make sure he was not seen as Moses's equal.

As a second additional proposal for why ch. 24 was added to the end of Joshua, Cynthia Edenburg has proposed that the covenant-making in Josh 24 might be intended to serve as a written acknowledgement that the Diaspora would persist. In her view, its purpose could have been to encourage them to maintain loyalty to Yhwh alone in their multicultural settings in the eastern Diaspora. She concludes that loyalty to Yhwh is the only covenant obligation Joshua puts on the people in ch. 24 (2017, 174-76, 179).

Her proposal has not explained, however, the function of vv. 25b-27, which refer to Joshua setting a *ḥoq ûmišpāṭ*, his writing of the "these words" in the scroll of God/divine scroll, or the standing stone that serves as a witness. Perhaps she envisions the singular form of the nouns together to refer to the single requirement to serve Yhwh alone (vv. 14, 20, 23); what, though, are "these words" in v. 26a? As John Van Seters

---

14   Two curious passages could point to earlier traditions in which Joshua and Moses were rivals for the position of leader of the Exodus from Egypt, covenant-making, teaching, and the conquest of Canaan. The plus in LXX Josh 24:31a states that Joshua led the people out of Egypt, not Moses, and that the people buried the flint knives Joshua used to circumcise the sons of Israel at Gilgal in his tomb with him, as Yhwh commanded them to do; they are there until this very day. It is likely the MT text was changed to remove the claim for Joshua's role in the Exodus in v. 3; at the same time, the reference to Moses (and Aaron) in v. 5 that is absent from the LXX was probably added (Mäkipelto 2017, 223, 231-32). Then, 1 Sam 12:8 states that Moses and Aaron led the people into the promised land, not Joshua (Ahlström 1980). This version of the past is very similar to the story an unnamed Jew in Alexandria told Hecateus of Abdera (lived in the fourth century BCE). Assuming it was accurately recorded, the metanarrative had Moses lead the people across the Jordan, into an empty land in which no kings had previously ruled. He proceeded to establish Jerusalem and the temple (Stern 1974, 26-35). If so, their rivalry was eventually resolved through editorial work that assigned each a part of the larger set of tasks.

(1984, 151) has pointed out, there are parallels in Josh 24 to the covenant ceremony in Exod 19–24, and it is reasonable to assume that the covenant-making in v. 25a includes the acts of setting of the *ḥoq ûmišpāṭ* in v. 25b, its inscribing in the scroll of the teaching of God (v. 26a), and the erection of the stone as a witness in vv. 26b–27 as integral acts of the process. Thus, there seem to be wider stipulations involved in this covenant than mere loyalty to Yhwh; the contents of the *ḥoq ûmišpāṭ* that become part of the scroll of divine teaching are conditions of the covenant. And this conundrum returns us to the earlier discussion concerning the import of vv. 25b–26a in particular and the failure to mention Moses in this chapter (following the OG omission of v. 5) in spite of the numerous references to him elsewhere in the book. They include mentions of his teaching but primarily of his commands concerning the conquest and land distribution.

Fortunately, the current discussion does not require a solution to the larger, weighty issues concerning the role of Joshua 24 in the Hexateuch or the Enneateuch. Rather, the focus has been on whether any passages in Deuteronomy, but particularly 11:29–31 and 27:1–8, look forward to Josh 24. The answer to that more limited question is no; they both are potentially late additions to Deuteronomy, and they find their explicit fulfillment in Josh 8:30–35, which also is likely a late addition to Joshua. All three emphasize how a one-time commemorative ceremony is to take place on Mt. Gerizim once the land has been conquered. Beyond that, whether they are meant to lay the groundwork to legitimate the Samarian temple built on Mt. Gerizim by ca. 450 BCE or to discourage an equation of that temple with the place Yhwh will choose for the divine name/reputation to dwell remains an open issue.

Conclusion

Many facets of geography are operational in Deuteronomy, due in large part to the setting of the book on the verge of the occupation of the western half of the promised land. The writer delineates a set of boundaries for Cisjordan and also describes physical features in the landscape and natural resources found therein, as well as a multi-pronged economy based on rain-dependent crops and livestock. He envisions how the invading Israelites will occupy pre-existing cities with their vineyards and olive groves and make that space "Israelite" by removing the religious practices and associations of local landmarks with the customs and folkways of the previous inhabitants and replacing them with Yahwistic religious practices and Israelite stories of association that reinforce a common identity. These include a central "place" to celebrate pilgrimage festivals that commemorate the Exodus event and founding of the covenanted people, a single altar for animal sacrifice, the use of *mezuzot* and *tefillin*, and the creation of three additional cities of asylum. Otherwise, the book envisages virtually no change to the natural landscape. Finally, the anomalous uses of Seir in place of Edom, of Horeb in place of Sinai, and of Mt. Gerizim and Mt. Ebal instead of Shechem, Mt. Zion, or Jerusalem have been explored, with various proposed explanations and implications presented.

Works Cited

Achenbach, Reinhard. 2005. "Pentateuch, Hexateuch und Enneateuch: Eine Verhältnisbestimmung." *Zeitschrift für altorientalische und biblische Rechtsgeschichte* 11: 122–54.

Ahlström, G. W. 1977. "Judges 5:20f. and History." *Journal of Near Eastern Studies* 36: 287–88.

------. 1980. "Another Moses Tradition." *Journal of Near Eastern Studies* 39: 65–69.

Amit, Yairah. 2014. "How to Slander the Memory of Shechem." Pages 231–43 in *Memory and the City in Ancient Israel*. Edited by Diana V. Edelman and Ehud Ben Zvi. Winona Lake, IN: Eisenbrauns.

Anbar, Moshe. 1992. *Josué et l'alliance de Sichem: Josué 24:1-28*. Beiträge zur biblischen Exegese und Theologie 25. Paris: Peter Lang.

Arnold, Bill T. 2017. "Reexamining the 'Fathers' in Deuteronomy's Framework." Pages 10–41 in *Torah and Tradition: Papers Read at the Sixteenth Joint Meeting of the Society for Old Testament Study and the Oudtestamentisch Werkgezelschap, Edinburgh, 2015*. Edited by Klaas Spronk and Hans M. Barstad. Oudtestamentische Studiën 70. Leiden: Brill.

Aurelius, Erik. 2003. *Zukunft jenseits des Gerichts: Eine redaktionsgeschichtliche Studie zum Enneateuch*. Beihefte zur Zeitschrift für die alttestamentliche Wissenschaft 66. Berlin: de Gruyter.

Barmash, Pamela. 2005. *Homicide in the Biblical World*. Cambridge: Cambridge University Press.

Batto, Bernard F. 1983. "The Reed Sea: Requiescat in Pace." *Journal of Biblical Literature* 102: 27–35.

Becker, Uwe. 2006. "Endredaktionelle Kontextvernetzungen des Josua-Buches." Pages 139–61 in *Die deuteronomistischen Geschichtswerke: Redaktions- und religionsgeschichtliche Perspektiven zur "Deuteronomismus"- Diskussion in Tora und vorderen Propheten*. Edited by Markus Witte, Konrad Schmid, Doris Prechel, and Jan Christian Gertz. Beihefte zur Zeitschrift für die alttestamentische Wissenschaft 365. Berlin: de Gruyter.

Ben Zvi, Ehud. 2023. "'Your Gates'-Evoking a Landscape of Fortified Cities in Deuteronomy: Meanings, Implications, and Comparative

Considerations with Other Constructions of the Israelite Past." *Scandinavian Journal of the Old Testament* 37: 17-33.

Berge, Kåre. 2021. "Cities in Deuteronomy: Imperial Ideology, Resilience, and the Imagination of Yahwistic Religion." Pages 77-96 in *Deuteronomy in the Making: Studies in the Production of* Debarim. Edited by Diana V. Edelman, Kåre Berge, Philippe Guillaume, and Benetta Rossi, Beihefte zur Zeitschrift für die alttestamentische Wissenschaft 533. Berlin: de Gruyter.

Blum, Erhard. 1997. "Der kompositionelle Knoten am Übergang von Josua zu Richter: Ein Entflechtungsvorschlag." Pages 181-212 in *Deuteronomy and Deuteronomic Literature: Festchrift C. H. W. Brekelmans*. Editd by Marc Vervenne and Johan Lust. Bibliotheca Ephemeridum Theologicarum Lovaniensium 133. Leuven: Peeters. Reprinted as pages 249-80 in *Textgestalt und Komposition: Exegetische Beiträge zu Tora und Vordere Propheten*. Edited by Wolfgang Oswald. Forschungen zum Alten Testament 69. Tübingen: Mohr Siebeck, 2010.

Borowski, Oded. 2002. *Agriculture in Iron Age Israel*. Boston: American Schools of Oriental Research.

Casey, Edward S. 1996. "How to Get from Space to Place in a Fairly Short Stretch of Time: Phenomenological Prolegomena." Pages 14-52 in *Senses of Place*. Edited by Steven Feld and Keith H. Basso. Santa Fe: School of American Research.

Clements, Ronald E. 1989. *Deuteronomy*. Old Testament Guides. Sheffield: Sheffield Academic.

Crane, Eva. 1975. *Honey: A Comprehensive Survey*. London: Heinemann [for] the Bee Research Association.

Cresswell, Tim. 2004. *Place: A Short Introduction*. Malden, MA: Blackwell.

Davies, Philip R. 2007. *The Origins of Biblical Israel*. Library of Hebrew Bible/Old Testament Studies 485. New York: T & T Clark.

Dorsey, David A. 1991. *The Roads and Highways of Ancient Israel*. Baltimore: The Johns Hopkins University Press.

Dozeman, Thomas. 1996. "The *yam-sûp* in the Exodus and the Crossing of the Jordan River." *Catholic Biblical Quarterly* 58: 407-16.

Driver, S. R. 1902. *A Critical and Exegetical Commentary on Deuteronomy*. International Critical Commentary 5. Edinburgh: T. & T. Clark.

Edelman, Diana. 2015. "The Metaphor of Torah as a Life-Giving Well in Deuteronomy." Pages 317-33 In *History, Memory, Hebrew Scriptures: A Festschrift for Ehud Ben Zvi*. Edited by Ian. D. Wilson and Diana V. Edelman. Winona Lake, IN: Eisenbrauns.

------. 2022. "Late Historical Edom and Reading Edom, Seir, and Esau in the Prophetic Literature through Persian Lenses: Preliminary Observations." Pages 392-428 in *About Edom and Idumea in the Persian Period: Recent Research and Approaches from Archaeology, Hebrew Bible Studies and Ancient Near East Studies*. Edited by Benedikt Hensel, Ehud

Ben Zvi, and Diana V. Edelman. Worlds of the Ancient Near East and Mediterranean. Sheffield: Equinox Publishing Ltd.

Edenburg, Cynthia. 2017. "A Diaspora-oriented Overriding of the Joshua Scroll." *Hebrew Bible and Ancient Israel* 6: 161–80.

Fishbane, Michael. 1985. *Biblical Interpretation in Ancient Israel*. Oxford: Clarendon.

Gall, A. Freiherr von. 1898. *Altisraelitische Kultstätten*. Beihefte zur Zeitschrift für die alttestamentische Wissenschaft 3. Giessen: J. Ricker.

Giblin, Charles H. 1964. "Structural Patterns in Joshua 24,1–25." *Catholic Biblical Quarterly* 26: 50–69.

Guillaume, Philippe. 2011. *Land, Credit and Crisis: Agrarian Finance in the Hebrew Bible*. BibleWorld. Sheffield: Equinox Publishing Ltd.

———. 2021. "Deuteronomy's *Māqōm* before Deuteronomy." Pages 195–217 in *Deuteronomy in the Making: Studies in the Production of Debarim*. Edited by Diana Edelman, Benedetta Rossi, Kåre Berge, and Philippe Guillaume. Beihefte zur Zeitschrift für die alttestamentische Wissenschaft 533. Berlin: de Gruyter.

Huddlestun, John R. 1992. "Red Sea." *Anchor Bible Dictionary* 5: 633–42.

Hyatt, J. P. *Commentary on Exodus*. New Century Bible Commentary. London Oliphants, 1971.

Knauf, E. Axel. 2009. "Kings among the Prophets." Pages 131–49 in *The Production of Prophecy: Constructing Prophecy and Prophets in Yehud*. Edited by Diana V. Edelman and Ehud Ben Zvi. BibleWorld. London: Equinox Publishing Ltd.

———. 2014. "Why 'Joshua'?" Pages 73–84 in *Deuteronomy-Kings as Emerging Authoritative Books: A Conversation*. Edited by Diana V. Edelman. Ancient Near Eastern Monographs 6. Atlanta: Society of Biblical Literature.

Knox, Paul L., Sallie A. Marston, and Alan E. Nash. 2010. *Human Geography: Places and Regions in Global Context*. Third Canadian edition. Toronto: Pearson Prentice Hall.

Koopmans, William T. 1990. *Joshua 24 as Poetic Narrative*. Journal for the Study of the Old Testament Supplement Series 93. Sheffield: JSOT.

Kratz, Reinhard G. 2002. "Der vor- und nachpriesterschriftliche Hexateuch." Pages 295–323 in *Abschied vom Yahwisten: Die Komposition des Hexateuchs im der jüngsten Diskussion*. Edited by Jan Christian Gertz, Konrad Schmid, and Markus Witte. Beihefte zur Zeitschrift für die alttestamentische Wissenschaft 315. Berlin: de Gruyter.

Krause, Joachim J. 2017. "Hexateuchal Redaction in Joshua." *Hebrew Bible and Ancient Israel* 6: 181–202.

Mäkipelto, Ville. 2017. "The Four Deaths of Joshua: Why the Septuagint is Pivotal for the Study of Joshua 24." *Hebrew Bible and Ancient Israel* 6: 217–42.

———. 2018. *Uncovering Ancient Editing: Documented Evidence of Changes in Joshua 24 and Related Texts*. Beihefte zur Zeitschrift für die alttestamentische Wissenschaft 513. Berlin: de Gruyter.

———. 2022. "Rewriting Joshua Traditions in Late Second Temple Judaism: Judean-Samaritan Relations as a Catalyst for Textual Changes." Pages 239–264 in *Scriptures in the Making: Texts and Their Transmission in Late Second Temple Judaism*. Edited by Raimo Hakola, Jessi Orpana, and Paavo Huotari. Leuven: Peeters.

Mayes, Andrew D. H. 1979. *Deuteronomy: Based on the Revised Standard Version*. New Century Bible Commentary 5. Grand Rapids, MI: Eerdmans.

Milgrom, Jacob. 1976. "Profane Slaughter and a Formulaic Key to the Composition of Deuteronomy." *Hebrew Union College Annual* 47: 1–17.

Miller, Patrick D. 1990. *Deuteronomy*. Interpretation: A Bible Commentary for Teaching and Preaching. Louisville: John Knox.

Na'aman, Nadav. 2000. "The Law of the Altar in Deuteronomy and the Cultic Site Near Shechem." Pages 141–61 in *Rethinking the Foundations: Historiography in the Ancient World and in the Bible: Essays in Honour of John Van Seters*. Edited by Steven L. McKenzie and Thomas Römer. Beihefte zur Zeitschrift für die alttestamentische Wissenschaft 294. Berlin and New York: de Gruyter.

Nelson, Richard D. 1997. *Joshua*. Old Testament Library. Louisville: Westminster John Knox.

Nicholson, E. W. 1967. *Deuteronomy and Tradition: Literary and Historical Problems in the Book of Deuteronomy*. Philadelphia: Fortress.

Nielsen, Eduard. 1955. *Shechem: A Tradito-Historical Investigation*. Copenhagen: G.E.C. Gad.

Nihan, Christophe. 2007. "The Torah between Samaria and Judah: Shechem and Gerizim in Deuteronomy and Joshua." Pages 187–233 in *The Pentateuch as Torah: New Models for Understanding Its Promulgation and Acceptance*. Edited by Gary N. Knoppers and Bernard M. Levinson. Winona Lake: Eisenbrauns.

Noth, Martin. 1930. *Das System der zwölf Stämme Israels*. Beiträge zur Wissenschaft vom Alten (und Neuen) Testament 4.1. Stuttgart: Kohlhammer.

Otto, Eckart. 2000. *Das Deuteronomium im Pentateuch und Hexateuch: Studien zur Literaturgeschichte von Pentateuch und Hexateuch im Lichte des Deuteronomiumrahmens*. Forschungen zum Alten Testament 30. Tübingen: Mohr Siebeck.

Perlitt, Lothar. 1969. *Bundestheologie im Alten Testament*. Wissenschaftliche Monographien zum Alten und Neuen Testament 36. Neukirchen-Vluyn: Neukirchener Verlag.

———. 1977. "Sinai und Horeb." Pages 302–22 in *Beiträge zur alttestmentlichen Theologie: Festschrift für Walther Zimmerli zum 70. Geburtstag*. Edited by

        Herbert Donner, Rudolph Smend, and Robert Hanhart. Göttingen: Vandenhoeck & Ruprecht.

Philips, Anthony. 1973. *Deuteronomy*. Cambridge Bible Commentary 5. Cambridge: Cambridge University Press.

Popović, Mladen. 2009. "Conquest of the Land, Loss of the Land: Where Does Joshua 24 Belong?" Pages 87–98 in *the Land of Israel in Bible, History, and Theology: Studies in Honour of Ed Noort*. Edited by Jacques van Ruiten and J. Cornelius de Vos. Supplements to Vetus Testamentum 124. Leiden: Brill.

Rad, Gerhard von. 1966. *Deuteronomy: A Commentary*. Translated by Dorothea Barton. London: SCM.

Rofé, Alexander. 1986. "The History of the Cities of Refuge in Biblical Law." Pages 205–39 in *Studies in Bible*. Edited by Sara Japhet. Scripta Hierosolymitana 31. Jerusalem: Hebrew University Magnes Press.

Römer, Thomas. 1990. *Israels Väter. Untersuchungen zur Väterthematik im Deuteronomium und in der deuteronomistichen Tradition*. Orbis Biblicus et Orientalis 99. Freiburg: Universitätsverlag and Göttingen: Vandenhoeck & Ruprecht.

———. 2015. *The Invention of God*. Translated by Raymond Geuss. Cambridge: Harvard University Press.

———. 2017. "The Date, Composition, and Function of Joshua 24." *Hebrew Bible and Ancient Israel* 6: 203–16.

Römer, Thomas and Marc Brettler. 2000. "Deuteronomy 34 and the Case for a Persian Hexateuch." *Journal of Biblical Literature* 119: 401–19.

Schmid, Konrad. 1999. *Erzväter und Exodus. Untersuchungen zur doppelten Begründung der Ursprünge Israels in den Geschichtsbüchern des Alten Testaments*. Wissenschaftliche Monographien zum Alten und Neuen Testament 81. Neukirchen-Vluyn: Neukirchener Verlag.

———. 2017. "Jews and Samaritans in Joshua 24." *Hebrew Bible and Ancient Israel* 6:148–60.

———. 2018. "Overcoming the Sub-Deuteronomism and Sub-Chronicism of Historiography in Biblical Studies: The Case of the Samaritans." Pages 17–29 in *The Bible, Qumran, and the Samaritans*. Edited by Magnar Kartveit and Gary N. Knoppers. Studia Judaica 104. Berlin: de Gruyter.

Segal, Moses H. 1961. "The Composition of the Pentateuch – A Fresh Examination." Pages 68–114 in *Studies in the Bible*. Edited by Chaim Rabin. Scripta Hierosolymitana 8. Jerusalem: Magnes Press

Smith, Sir George Adam. 1918. *The Book of Deuteronomy*. Cambridge, UK: Cambridge University Press.

Snaith, N. H. "The Sea of Reeds: The Red Sea: ים סוף." *Vetus Testamentum* 15 (1965): 395–98.

Sperling, S. David. 1987. "Joshua 24 Re-examined." *Hebrew Union College Annual* 58: 119–36.

Stackert, Jeffrey. 2006. "Why Does Deuteronomy Legislate Cities of Refuge? Asylum in the Covenant Collection (Exodus 21:12–14) and Deuteronomy (19:1–13)." *Journal of Biblical Literature* 125: 23–49.
Stern, Menahem, ed. 1974. *From Herodotus to Plutarch*. Vol. 1 of *Greek and Latin Authors on Jews and Judaism*. Jerusalem: Israel Academy of Sciences and Humanities.
Van Seters, John. 1984. "Joshua 24 & the Problem of Tradition." Pages 139–58 in *In the Shelter of Elyon: Essays on Ancient Palestinian Life and Literature in Honor of G. W. Ahlström*. Edited by W. Boyd Barrick and John R. Spencer. Journal for the Study of the Old Testament Supplement Series 31. Sheffield: JSOT.
——. 2003. *A Law Book for the Diaspora: Revision in the Study of the Covenant Code*. New York: Oxford University Press.
Wenham, Gordon J. 1971. "Deuteronomy and the Central Sanctuary." *Tyndale Bulletin* 22: 103–18.
Wildenboer, Johan. 2015. "Joshua 24: some literary and theological remarks." *Journal for Semitics* 24: 484–502.
Zohary, Michael. 1982. *Plants of the Bible: A Complete Handbook*. New York: Cambridge University Press.

About the Author

Diana V. Edelman is professor emerita at the Faculty of Theology, University of Oslo. Her research interests focus on the history, archaeology, and literature of the ancient Southern Levant more generally, and on Judah and Samaria in the Iron Age, Neo-Babylonian, and Persian periods more specifically.

Chapter 5
Ethnic Israel and Power in Deuteronomy

Kåre Berge

Abstract

This chapter argues that different aspect of what may be called an "Israelite identity" in Deuteronomy first and foremost serve the social powerand the exclusive position of an elite group of literati standing behind this biblical book. The ethnic ideology of the book is part of a utopian vision that primarily is concerned with Israel as a religious, learning community. It makes sense to regard Deuteronomy as an attempt to present "Israel" as an "ethnic" entity in order to situate themselves vis-à-vis the Achaemenid imperial administration or at least to serve an "internal-Israelite" purpose. The vision serves to establish and legitimate the informal authority of the authorial group, which probably belonged to Deuteronomy's "Levitical priests."

Keywords: Israel, ethnicity, kinship, tribes, nation, power

In the "frames" of Deuteronomy (chs. 1–11 and 27–34), "Israel" is portrayed as an *ethnic* entity; the idea is implied but not made explicit in the "core" (chs. 12–26). What do we mean when we characterize Israel in this way, and why might the scribe(s) who created the book have chosen this strategy for conceiving Israel? Ethnicity is a modern concept that needs to be adapted when applied to the ancient book of Deuteronomy.[1] To be

---

1   In addition to the works being cited in the following presentation, Diana Edelman (1996) and Elizabeth Bloch-Smith (2003) have presented different views on ethnicity in "early Israel." This discussion does not directly affect the issue of ethnicity in Deuteronomy, although it does contribute to the question of methodology.

an operable concept in a study of Deuteronomy, it has to be applicable to some aspects assigned to "Israel" in the book, though not all. Although the modern term itself has fuzzy borders, most if not all the typical traits listed by some central students of ethnicity are applicable to elements in Deuteronomy.

This chapter argues that different aspects of what may be called "ethnicity" first and foremost serve the social power and the exclusive position of an elite group of literati standing behind this biblical book. To appear as a limited, distinct, and differentiated social and cultural entity, the audience, the whole people of Israel, needs to learn from the literati's teaching and to obey their instructions. The main terms used to describe "all Israel" and its tribes actualize descent and common origin, which are founding premises of ethnicity, while other important premises, like a homeland, a shared language, and shared customs and solidarity, are also present in the book. The ethnic ideology of the book is part of a utopian vision that primarily is concerned with Israel as a religious, learning community. The vision serves to establish and legitimate the informal authority of the authorial group, which probably belonged to Deuteronomy's "Levitical priests."

I also argue that invention of a pan-"Israelite" sense of ethnicity makes sense under Achaemenid rulership. Its imperial administration classified different groups according to their "ethnicity."

Theoretical Basics of Ethnicity

Ethnicity became a field of study, both in biblical and social/anthropological studies, in the 1990s and beginning 2000s. There are several, mostly converging definitions of ethnicity. The anthropologist Anya Peterson Royce, for example, defines it as follows:

> An "ethnic group" is a reference group invoked by people who share a common historical style (which may be only assumed) based on overt features and values, and who, through the process of interaction with others, identify themselves as sharing that style. "Ethnic identity" is the sum total of feelings on the part of group members about those values, symbols, and common history that identify them as a distinct group. "Ethnicity" is simply ethnic-based action (1982, 18).[2]

---

2 For ethnic identity as a sentiment more deeply rooted and potent than non-kinship groups like common class, religion or locale, see also e.g. Connor 1992, 53; for ethnicity as a social activity, see also e.g. Miller 2008, 172.

She deliberately uses the term "style" in place of the more commonly used term "tradition." She wants to avoid evoking the ideas of stability and lengthy existence that often are associated with tradition conceived of as old customs, old symbols, and old modes of behavior. In her opinion, this common association "probably never corresponded very closely to reality. Humans constantly acquire new traits, change and rework old ones, abandon some features altogether" (1982, 9).

In contrast, Elizabeth Bloch-Smith, a Syro-Palestinian archaeologist, includes a sense of primordiality as integral to an ethnic group (2003, 402). Kenton L. Sparks, a biblical scholar, likewise embraces a primordial grounding for ethnic groups (1998, 11, 16–17). He considers shared corporate ethnic sentiments to arise from human affections for family that are extended to those who are (or appear to be) like us. He rejects any idea that they are "mere 'instruments' of socioeconomic manipulation" (1998, 21).[3]

Dermot A. Nestor pursues the same track. Following the lead of Jacques Berlinerblau (1999, 193), who criticizes the idea of ideology as a possession, intentionally constructed, promulgated, and imposed by ancient intellectuals, Nestor claims that at least parts of Deuteronomy's idea of ethnicity are not intentionally created by the Deuteronomists, and that extended kinship and ethnic "brotherhood" were in existence long before (his dating of) the Deuteronomic core to Josiah's reform (2010, 200).

Royce summarizes ethnicity using three Ps: power, perception, and purpose. Ethnic perception takes concrete form as symbols and stereotypes. Powerholders may vary within a given ethnic group. The power to assign roles and lay down rules is a privilege of the dominant group, which includes defining subordinate groups as ethnie. Royce seems interested in these subordinates—"Everyone in a subordinate position is potentially an ethnic [group-member]"—while dominant groups rarely define themselves as ethnic groups (1982, 3).[4] Hence, ethnic perception

---

[3] There is a (mostly schematical) opposition between "primordialism" and "constructionist" positions in studies of ethnicity and nationality, see, e.g. Hylland Eriksen 2004, 49. Montserrat Guibernau and John Hutchinson (2004, 2) use the terms primordial (nations are perennial or even primordial to the human condition) and constructed and instrumental (i.e. constructed by some national entrepreneurs). Smith discusses "primordialism and perennialism" (1999, 3–4), explaining that nations are "primordial" when they were seen as natural, ubiquitous and universal in humanity. His contrasting term is "modernism" (p. 6).

[4] Ethnicity as a border phenomenon originates primarily from the Norwegian anthropologist Fredrik Barth (1966, 1969). Accordingly, interaction is regarded as a central factor in creating and maintaining ethnic identity. Some would even regard conflict as functional in ethnicity formation.

may also belong to a subordinate group within a larger group, whose purpose is to improve their inferior position (1982, 4–6). The three Ps apply equally to "being different from others" outside and inside the ethnic group. Following Royce, an asymmetrical relationship is often implied in ethnic notions. This is also emphasized by David Small (1997, 272) with regard to biblical ethnicity.

Sociologist Anthony D. Smith (1999, 13) has provided different versions of a list of criteria identifying ethnic communities or ethnies (a plural Greek term; the singular is ethnos). He includes 1) an identifying name or emblem, 2) a myth of common origin and descent, which seems to ground a sense of putative kinship that can be biological and/or spiritual (1999, 15), 3) shared historical memories and traditions, 4) one or more elements of common culture, 5) a link with a historic territory or "homeland" (ethnoscape), and 6) a measure of solidarity, at least among the élites (for similar lists, see Edelman 1996; Leoussi and Grosby 2007, 5; Garmann 2007, 114–15.) These criteria are widely cited, yet it is unclear how they differ from the traits of "nation."

As a concept, ethnicity is situated between kinship and the nation. Central to this and other works in the present study is Jonathan M. Hall's (1997) study of ethnic identity in Greek Antiquity. While kinship signals smaller groups comprising communities of people connected through real or imagined descent and filiation who know each other (Barth 1973, 3), "nation" is a modernist concept designating an entity larger than families, villages, or city-states that is primarily connected by mass education and industrialization. For this reason, few theorists would talk about nations in a pre-modern era, although some do (see below). Ethnic groups are non-corporate communities that, on the one hand, are larger than kin or locality groups; they transcend face-to-face interaction (Royce 1982, 24–25; Bloch-Smith 2003, 402). On the other hand, they are less than a nation on the scale of size.

To situate "ethnicity" in recent research relating to Deuteronomy specifically, I will summarize the work of two scholars, beginning with the more recent study. Philip R. Davies spoke of "an ethnicizing agenda" in the book (2014, 28). However, he also claimed that Deuteronomy seeks to define Israel in terms of its *religion* and not by its genealogical descent or its monarchic cult and political status (28).[5] In his view, Deuteronomy's corporate identity cannot be expressed in terms of feudalism or

---

5 The combination of ethnicity and religion is quite normal, but some scholars have argued that the notion of ethnicity in Deuteronomy, which is exclusionary, collides with the religious commitment (status with regard to Yhwh), which may also include foreigners/*gerim* (Sparks 1998, 228).

patronage but only through religion, lineage, and custom.[6] The book's *ethne* is organized within large empires and is no longer a monarchic state (38). Its pan-"Israelite" ethnic identity requires, however, both local and "national" dimensions, according to Davies, but this "national" element does not, in his view, appear to lie in the political sphere in terms of monarchy, nor in the cult in terms of sacrifices.

Davies caught important aspects of Deuteronomy's ethnicity. He also suggested a clear rationale for a post-monarchic dating and function of the book. Playing a religious function, ethnicity is not tied to the political sphere as a monarchic political agenda.

Kenton L. Sparks goes in another direction. Distinguishing between chs. 1-4 and 5-26, he argues that chs. 5-26 are of northern Israelite origin but are to be read in the context of seventh-century Judah and King Josiah's reform (1998, 226-29). Sparks defines Deuteronomy's ethnic sentiment more or less along the same line as Davies, but his view on the origin and dating is different. Having argued that its land theology and the ethnic separation from the peoples of the land point to the eighth century BCE when Assyria transplanted foreign deportees into the newly created province of Samerina (234), he regards the brotherhood concept as part of the ethnic sentiment (236-38). This is, according to him, "a new agenda by the Josianic redactor" (237). Sparks fails to account for the predominance of the "ethnic" brotherhood in the frame (chs.1-11 or 12), and especially in chs. 1-3, a part of the book that unanimously is regarded as post-monarchic by redaction critics.

Modern Ethnic Traits and the Abstract/ Imagined Community in Deuteronomy

All the "ethnic" features in Smith's list presented in the previous section are recognizable in Deuteronomy:

1. A specific name, Israel.
2. Myths of a shared origin include references to the forefathers and the promise of the land to Abraham and his descendants as well as the Exodus from Egypt (Deut 6:10; 7:8). Kinship underlies the concept of Israel as twelve tribes descended from twelve brothers

---

6   Davies refers to "national religion" (2014, 31) and "national identity" (38), but he did not seem to mean a nation or a state because he explained it by religion, lineage, and custom. Subsequently, he equated the "national" (sic) dimension with a "pan-'Israelite' ethnic identity" (38). This is also the way I use "national:" as a pan-Israelite vision and concept with no association with modern nationalism.

and is reinforced within the text by the use of the term "brother" to refer to fellow Israelites in some but not necessarily all uses (Deut 1:16, 28; 3:18, 20; 10:9; 15:7, 12; 17:15, 20; 18:2, 15, 18; 24:7; 33:16, 24; Guillaume 2021, 290–94, 309).

3. Shared "historical" memories in Moses' appeals to past events during the wilderness wanderings after leaving Mt. Horeb until the arrival at the plain of Moab, in both the frames and the core (e.g. chs. 1–3 and 9).

4. Shared cultural elements include food customs, exemplified in the list of clean and unclean animals and food preparation restrictions (14:3–21). The annual three pilgrimage festivals that commemorate the formative Exodus event, even if *gērîm* can be included as guests, are another shared cultural practice. In addition, habits, custom, or "a way of doing things," perhaps covered by the term משפט, *mišpāṭ* (so Davies 2021, 16; e.g. Deut 17:8, 9, 11; 18:3; 21:17; 24:17; 25:1) underlies many of the prescriptions in the "core" chs. 12–26 (e.g. 12 and 13; 14:1–2; 17:2–7; for further examples, see also Markl 2012, 230).

5. The concept of a homeland is reflected in the anticipated occupation of the promised land (Deut 6:10).

6. A measure of solidarity is expected of the people in terms of not following the religious practices of those they will dispossess (chs. 7 and 12) and, for example, in the command to root out religious apostasy at the family and the town level, acting as a group to kill any offenders, including a prophet or dreamer of dreams, who speak in the name of another deity (Deut 13:2–17). There is no question that an "ethnic" understanding of Israel is present in this book, even meeting modern criteria and definitions of ethnicity and of an *ethnie*.[7]

The modern concept of an "abstract/imagined community" (James 1996; Anderson 2006) might also aid in the conceptualization of Deuteronomy's ethnicity. The concept refers to an entity too large for its members to be personally acquainted, but one where members know about each other through the newspaper. While this form of communication was unknown in the ancient world, the modern concept nevertheless has some affinities with Deuteronomy. Physical attendance at the envisioned three annual pilgrimage festivals would have provided the opportunity

---

[7] The term was introduced by Smith (1986) and applied to the ancient Mediterranean world by Garmann (2007, 113). In modern politics, ethnicity is questioned and sometimes even banned. For a short survey of romantic, evolutionary theories of ethnicity leading to racism, see Hall 1997, 7–13, 19–20.

to meet and interact with Israelites from other towns and regions, even if temporarily. Beyond that, however, the knowledge that other Israelites would be participating in these festivals and keeping the sabbath in theory, if not always in reality, makes the people in Deuteronomy's storyworld aware that they are contemporaneous with group members they do not know, which is a feature of Anderson's definition. The common festivals compensate for the large size of the population, something that resembles Anderson's idea of the abstract community bound together by ideas of common time (dated celebrations).

The term "abstract/imagined community" also dovetails with the elusive "you" in the book, a polysemic entity that seems to be the audience addressed but, in some cases, obviously is its representative authorities at court, as in Deut 17:4–5, 8–10, which probably refers to the *sofetim* and *soterim* in 16:18. While the former term *sofetim* means judges, the latter (*soterim*) should be scribes, probably functionaries at the local courts, since the term is Aramaic for "scribe." This general "you" (sg./pl.) envisions an "Israel" that goes far beyond face-to-face relationships and a reciprocal community, thus complying with the concept as developed by James and Anderson. The idea in Deuteronomy of Israel as a community listening to the discourse of the priests when they read or teach the Law of Moses is congruent as well with Hall's conclusion that ethnicity is "ultimately constructed through written and spoken discourse" (1997, 2). This does not preclude an intersubjective reality. It does mean, however, that in Deuteronomy, ethnicity may respond in varying degrees to the reality of the authors but may even be completely utopian. As a discourse, "ethnicity" in Deuteronomy is also envisioned as something to be practiced in the land they are going to occupy, for instance through the triannual festivals (Deut 16).

Ethnicity in the Ancient World and in Deuteronomy

How does the ethnic look in the ancient Near East? For what purpose and benefit do social groups identify themselves as ethnic entities? At Persepolis, for example, the Apadana northern stairway documents Achaemenid awareness and recognition of multiple group identities existing within the Empire, which accordingly appears as multi-ethnic. Different members of the tribute-bearing procession are distinguished by styles of dress and hairdos that emphasize the diversity. The Fortification Tablets, stemming from the reign of Darius the Great (around 500 BCE) and recording the transfer of food commodities to different groups of workers, likewise document a number of ethnonyms; 26 appear in the 5,000 edited texts (Henkelman and Stolper 2009, 273; see the list on 274).⁸ Examples include Indians, Babylonians, Carians, Arabs, Greeks, and Egyptians. They are mostly identified by the -b(e)/p(e), -r(a) ending in Elamite, which is the equivalent of what is called in Hebrew a gentilic ending (-î). This adjectival ending can express kinship or geographical affiliation or a language.

Wouter F. M. Henkelman and Matthew W. Stolper regard the "ethnic" entities named at Persepolis as deriving from administrative labelling. On analogy to Herodotus's comment that the workers at Mt. Athos were divided *kata ta 'ethnea* "according to their ethnic groups" (2009, 278), they propose that the underlying administrative list might have detailed work gangs gathered from around the Empire to help construct the capitol and its complex of buildings. In so far as they represent ethnonyms, then, all the groups are named primarily after their areas of origin (toponyms), then perhaps by their language, which might overlap with the geographical regions, and perhaps finally by their craft skills or possibly other cultural signifiers. What is unclear, however, is precisely how the gentilics relate to the underlying reality that they were teams of experts sharing a specific trade. The same applies to the shared team language: does this mean that the gentilic also designates a language spoken? A possible solution is that the Persian administration put together gangs of skilled workers of common origin, i.e. coming from the same area and speaking the same language, to facilitate the efficient completion of the common work to which they had been assigned.

This is how their place would have been defined in the administrative imperial system. Thus, the gentilic markers serve to designate expatriated groups from regions that predominantly had become provinces but in some cases, like the Sidonians or Arabs, had remained vassal kingdoms or tribes.

There are no Israelites/Samarians or Judeans among those depicted and named at Persepolis, but that does not exclude their constituting an *ethnos* or separate *ethnoi* within the Empire. Likewise, there are no Ammonites, Moabites, Edomites, or Philistines. As the list mentions "Assyrians" (probably Syrians according to Henkelman and Stolper 2009), Egyptians, Cypriotes, and other groups within the province of Across the River (or its precursor, Babylonia and Across the River), this absence is conspicuous. The Israelites/Samarians and Judeans either were subsumed under the majority population of their province, were not sources of work gangs used in imperial building projects in the region of Fars, or were considered too insignificant to be included.

---

8   For the text and translation, see Hallock (1969).

Judeans appear elsewhere, however, in Babylonian archives, and the use of the gentilic seems to follow the same main trend as at Persepolis. *Ia-a-hu-da-a-a*, "Judean," found in some Babylonian-era private archives detailing business and agricultural matters, seems to refer primarily to an individual's territorial place of origin rather than being a statement of ethnicity. The place-name *alu sa Yahudaia*, "Judahville," found in some of the documents in the David Sofer-Collection (Pearce 2006, 2016; Pearce and Wunsch 2014), indicates that a group of deported Judahites was resettled near Borsippa, though this was not the only place they ended up. The evidence locates others in the regions of Nippur and Uruk (Zadok 1979, 34–35). The common imperial practice, dating back to the Assyrians, was to group deportees together by their countries of origin in towns, especially in rural areas where they would cultivate the land and serve the crown through corvée obligations tied to the land (e.g. Zadok 1979, 34–35, 49, 79; Machinist 2003, 255). It is hard to say if these gentilic labels are solely geographical (place of origin) in nature or also are meant to reflect a shared sense of putative kinship and common origin, in addition perhaps to a shared spoken language. All three meanings could have been applicable simultaneously in some cases.

The division of regions populated by *ethnoi* is well established in Hellas around 500 BCE (Hansen 2013, 264). In this case, however, an *ethnos* might be political, e.g. the population of a single *polis* (Hall 1997, 34), or the citizens of a group of *poleis* might have regarded themselves as belonging to one *ethnos*. Emily Mackil discusses the origin and development of the *koinon* (Greek, federal state), a group of *poleis*, "a form of regional state comprised of multiple poleis" (2013, 304), distinct from military alliances, religious organizations (like the Delphic-Anthelic amphictyony), and unitary *poleis* with local councils, sometimes also called an *ethnos*, in mainland Greece and the Peloponnese. Mackil says that in this area, "eleven of the twenty regions … were politicized, that is, they had a regional government in the form of a *koinon*" (305), and in mainland Greece and the Peloponnese to 323 BCE, at least 183 of 456 *poleis* were members of one *koinon* or another. The *ethnos*, she remarks, not an intrinsically political concept, still labelled politicized population groups (306–7). Common to these "politicized" groups was a sense of group identity in the form of descent from a common ancestor, the occupation of a shared territory, and the sharing of one or more sanctuaries (307).

Some of these features resemble Deuteronomy: descent from common ancestors, shared territory, and one sanctuary. But the idea noted in Mackil's list that they were driven out from their original place is lacking. If we do not assume a direct influence or a regional common arbiter (see Sparks below), we might still think that there is a connection. It is hardly incidental that two such parallel phenomena occur around the same time. Both Deuteronomy and the Greek phenomena originated in the fifth–fourth centuries BCE. Greece and the originators of Deuteronomy faced the same imperial reality: the Persians. If the picture of this group formation is somehow correct, one might tend to think that there existed some conditions in the Achaemenid imperial government that encouraged non-Persian population groups or smaller political entities to organize into larger entities. In Greece they were called a *koinon* or an *ethnos* (among other terms), and in Judah or among the Judeans, an *'am* or a *goy* called "all Israel" with clearly ethnic traits. What benefit and whose interests it may have served is more difficult to say and would need a separate investigation.

I will not revive the old amphictyony hypothesis, which was connected with the scholarly concept of the pre-monarchic "twelve tribes of Israel," neither will I present it in a new fashion as an explanation of the pan-Israelite idea in post-monarchic time. It is worth noting, however, that Deuteronomy models "all Israel" not only as a religious community but also as a judicial and military entity and even as a possible kingdom. In addition, while the entity is not described as a league of *poleis*, nevertheless its sub-units are cities, not the hamlets and villages that comprised the main settlement pattern in Judah/Yehud in exilic and post-exilic time. While the Greek *koinon* may have one or more sanctuaries, Deuteronomy concentrates all Israel around one sanctuary (of whatever character).

As noted, a direct influence from Greece on Deuteronomy is hardly demonstrable. Among biblical scholars, Sparks (1998, 51–53, 261–63) argues there are several similarities between the Greek ideology of ethnicity presented by Herodotus and Deut 1–4, and additional similarities with other parts of Deuteronomy. He cautiously argues that Deuteronomy, "especially its Deuteronomistic sections" (261), which in his reading is basically reduced to chs. 1–4, shows signs of influence from Greece "or perhaps from a common cultural arbiter between Israel and Greece" (261), which may have been Phoenicia (263). In addition to the similarities mentioned above, Sparks notes a derogatory conceptualization of the peripheral peoples, the primeval inhabitants of Palestine (262). Yet most distinguishing Israelite in Deuteronomy (deuteronomistic part: chs. 1–4) is the idea that Yhwh is the giver of the land to Edom, Ammon, and Moab in addition to Israel. Suggestive but less conclusive is Seth Schwartz's opting for "a family resemblance to Athenian democracy" in "the Torah and related documents," with all distribution of resources placed in the hands of the nation as a whole, not an aristocracy (2013, 189–90). Schwartz concludes, rightly in my opinion, that in the Torah, Israel is neither a political "constitution" nor a Platonic utopian fantasy, but still is "manifestly idealized and countercultural" (190).

To conclude, there seems to be some kind of common denominator in the (late) Persian period that triggered the formation of super-clan/super-*polis* "ethnic" entities. This arbiter may have been the practice used by the Persian administration to designate different *ethnoi* by gentilic labels that seem to have designated common kinship, a shared original territory, and language. A common profession might have been a practical corollary to this, probably because common origin and language facilitated their work.

In Deuteronomy, Israel is depicted as an ethnic entity. Its character consists of common kinship (a number of clans or tribes), a geographical territory, and implied in the text, common language. Everything said about the people presupposes the Israelites' occupation of the land or a possible lost hold over something still regarded as the land of Israel, its kinship origin, and its shared religion. A shared homeland is one of the most significant characteristics of the people, alongside its common history (Wilson 2005, 112), but as Smith has argued (see above), it does not mean that one really inhabits or occupies this land at present. In Deuteronomy, the land is a land to be, a future territory from which Yhwh will drive out all the indigenous inhabitants so Israel can possess it, but it is already given to their ancestors and, if read in the storyline from Genesis, also partly taken into possession by the ancestors as the land of promise (Gen 13:14–17). Parts of the promised land were even already in the possession of the patriarchs (Gen 23; 33:19). Its religious character is also evident. Yet it is difficult to establish a hierarchy among these three aspects of biblical Israel.

The elements of kinship and territory are also visible in the characterization of other "nations," whether a gentilic is used specifically to designate them or not. The territorial connection is present in Deut 1:4, 7, where Sihon, king of the Amorites (a gentilic), had lived in Heshbon and Og, the king of Bashan, in Ashtarot and Edrei before the Israelites conquered them. Both territory and kinship are associated with the Moabites in 2:8, 9, where they are called the descendants (literally sons) of Lot, their eponymous ancestor, and with the descendants (literally sons) of Ammon. Yhwh has given the region of Ar to the Moabites and other adjoining land to the Ammonites (2:19–23). Language, the third possible aspect associated with a gentilic, is not mentioned directly in the text, but we know that these four groups of peoples spoke northwest Semitic languages related to, but different from, Hebrew.

Key Terminology Associated with Israel as an *Ethnos*

Within Deuteronomy, the following expressions are used to characterize or describe the audience listening to Moses' speeches in the storyworld as well as the intended ancient audience reading or hearing the book and its message: Israel, "all Israel" (כל ישראל), "descendants/children (literally sons) of Israel" (בני ישראל), "tribes" (שבטים), "nation" (גוי), and "kinspeople" (עם).

"Israel"

This term, without modifiers, appears frequently in the book: Deut 1:38; 2:12; 4:1; 5:1; 6:3–4; 9:1; 10:2; 17:12, 20; 18:1; 19:13; 20:3; 21:8, 21; 22:19, 21–22; 25:6,–7, 10; 26:16; 27:9; 29:10; 31:9, 30; 33:10, 28–29; 34:10. For the audience in the storyworld as well as the intended audience, the term Israel is familiar and carries with it shared, inbuilt associations that do not require explanation.[9]

The term Israel is used in three discernible ways. First, it denotes an entity possessing the land by destroying the inhabitants (1:38; 2:12; 20:3); an entity of warfare whose actions always result in success with no casualties. It is not led by the king, although there is (or may be) a king "in Israel" (17:20). Second, it is a listening and learning community, which appears primarily in the frame (4:1, 5:1, 6:3–4, 9:1, 20:3; for a connection with 31:12–13, see Markl 2012, 62–66). Third, it is the community subject to religious and moral purification (17:4, 17:12, 19:13, 21:8 [atonement], 22:21, 22:22 ["the virgins of Israel"], 22:19, 23:17 [no קדשה "sacred or holy woman"], and 26:15 [divine blessing]). All the "men of Israel" (27:14, 29:10) seem to be specifically responsible for listening, witnessing, and organizing the right Israelite community (see also the occurrences of "wise men" in 1:13, 15–17, 22–23). The assembly is also a listening entity, (31:30) (אזני כל קהל ישראל). As a whole, the term summarizes central aspects of Deuteronomy's Israel.

"All Israel"

The term "all Israel," כל ישראל, garners fourteen Accordance hits in Deuteronomy:

---

9   Use of the term "Israel" to denote Israel and Judah occurs in biblical prophetic texts probably before the exile and may have been in use in the time following 722 BCE (Kratz 2018, 507–14).

1:1: The words Moses spoke to all Israel.

5:1: Moses summoned all Israel, speaking: Listen to the statutes etc.

11:6: All Israel saw the terrible punishment that hit Dathan etc.; this picks up Num 16:34, which also speaks of all Israel in the same position.

13:12: All Israel shall listen to the punishment and fear and shall not go on to do evil.

18:6: Levite who wants to go from all gates in all Israel to the central place.

21:21: All Israel shall see the punishment and fear.

27:9: Moses and the Levitical priests spoke to all Israel, saying: Be quiet, today you have become Yhwh's people ('am).

29:2: Moses summoned all Israel saying: you have seen what Yhwh did.

31:1, 7, 11: Moses spoke to all Israel: Do not be afraid of the peoples in the land! All Israel will come together on the place … you shall read this torah.

32:45: Moses spoke to all Israel.

34:12: Remember what Yhwh did before the eyes of all Israel…

In all these cases, except for 18:6, "all Israel" is the audience in the narrative's storyworld who saw or listened, frequently reacting with fear, and who were challenged to keep the commandments and God's Torah. They were the audience of the words of Moses (1:1, 5:1). In particular, in the narrative's "today," they became a kinspeople to Yhwh your God, לעם ליהוה אלהיך, 27:9, responsible for listening to his voice and keeping his commandments. "All Israel" is a meta-subject in the book; they never act (in opposition to the addressed "you," e.g. in ch. 26). Nor are they actors in joint projects in the book except for being this audience of the past who was challenged to follow the Torah. We get no impression that "all Israel" was a political or social entity; it is just the audience of the past and, at the same time, an audience expected to react to the message now written down in the book.

"All Israel" is much less integrated into the corpus of texts. While not secondarily edited into the text, it appears to be more artificial, less specific, and there are almost no clues about how it works and functions. It bears all the marks of a constructed, theoretical, or utopian idea.

In 18:6, "all Israel" appears to designate the entire Israelite population that will live in the conquered cities in the promised land. The Levites are a component of "all Israel" but are set apart from other members by not being entitled to land heritage (18:1). Instead, they are designated to teach Jacob/Israel the divine judgments משפטיך (rather, customs, traditions?) and laws ותורתך, Deut 33:10, but they shall also "put incense in his nose, and a whole-offering upon his altar," which are traditional priestly tasks.

"Descendants of Israel"

The expression "descendants/children (literally 'sons') of Israel" (בני ישראל) is a clear demarcation of ethnicity expressing the idea of kinship. Of the nineteen occurrences, only two (23:18 and 24:7) are found in the "core" (chs. 12–26):

1:3; 3:18 brothers and *bᵉnê yiśrā'ēl kol-bᵉnê-hayil* at war

4:44, 45, 46 Torah given to *bᵉnê yiśrā'ēl* during walk out of Egypt

10:6 *bᵉnê yiśrā'ēl* set out from Be'erot ("wells") of the descendants (literally sons) of Ya'aqan) to begin desert wandering

23:17 [18] *bᵉnê* and *bᵉnôt yiśrā'ēl* are to have no sanctified ones among them, related to the house of Yhwh

24:7 if one of his brothers, of *bᵉnê yiśrā'ēl* is kidnapped

28:69 the new covenant made with *bᵉnê yiśrā'ēl* in the land of Moab

31:19, 22 write down this song, teach *bᵉnê yiśrā'ēl* the song, as a witness to them

31:23 Joshua shall lead *bᵉnê yiśrā'ēl* into the land

32:8 *'Elyon* put up borders between *'ammîm* according to the number of *bᵉnê yiśrā'ēl*

32:49, 52 the land of the Canaanites will be given to the *bᵉnê yiśrā'ēl*

32:51 Moses and Aaron acted unfaithfully among the *bᵉnê yiśrā'ēl*

33:1 Moses blessed *bᵉnê yiśrā'ēl*

34:8 *bᵉnê yiśrā'ēl* wept over Moses

34:9 *bᵉnê yiśrā'ēl* listened to Joshua

The expression בני ישראל seems to have a temporal or chronological dimension, designed to emphasize that the audience in the storyworld is the next generation of Israel after those who experienced Sinai; they are the ones prepared to enter the promised land. The kinship term does not necessarily imply bloodlines; "descendants/children of" might mean more generally, membership in a group.

"Tribes"

Israel consists of twelve tribes led by their heads. The idea of tribes is found in the frames in 3:13; 10:8; 29:7; 29:9; 29:17; 29:20; 31:28; and 33:5. Collectively, they show that those responsible for the frame wanted to present Israel as a unity of tribes. Nevertheless, its trans-tribal value is clear;[10] it not only is a league of tribes but also is presented as an integrated entity that appears more like the modern term "nation." Every attempt is made to show that the tribes exist only as building blocks of one nation. This is marked also in Deut 6:4, which insists that Yhwh is one and not many (Aurelius 2003).

In the core, Israel's tribes appear in 12:5, 14; 16:18; 18:1; and 18:5. In ch. 12, the tribes denote all Israel as seen from the perspective of the tribes/ an ethnic unity of tribes gathered around the pilgrimage center that has been selected from among the tribes. Deuteronomy 16:18 mandates administration for Israelite cities in all the tribes. Finally, 18:5 and 12 refer to one of the twelve tribes, Levi, whose members are set apart to minister in the name of Yhwh. It constitutes a brotherhood of its own, and a rival one.

The use in 16:18 is political, but without any reference to issues of unification of Israelite/Judean groups. The idea is of a people living in cities governed by the elders of the city and some other administrators or officers. This has led Joseph Blenkinsopp (1995, 5) to assume that the core constrained the authority and jurisdiction of heads of households, tribal elders, and the descent system and kinship groups. His argument is based on the appointment of state magistrates and the rejection of sacrificial practice for the dead.

There is no doubt that Israel is depicted as a group of tribes in both the frames and the core in the current form of the MT and other extant versions. However, like "all Israel," this tribal notion is constructed; it is a theoretical idea that has been only loosely integrated into the corpus of texts. A nation of tribes is a contradiction in terms, which also indicates the loose integration of the notion of tribes in the concept. However, as a nation of tribes, Israel is predominantly a listening and learning, religious people in the book. This is what its ethnic identity is about in the first instance. It is also envisioned as an administrative unit (of cities), but this is more a consequence of its religious commitment than a presupposition of it.

---

10 The terms "trans-tribal" and "trans-local" are used in Grosby 2002, 58.

(Kins)People

The term *'am/'ammîm* (עָם, עַמִּים) occurs 107 times (Accordance search) in Deuteronomy. It designates Israel in some 58 of these cases (2:4; 3:28; 4:6, 10, 20; 5:28; 7:66; 9:6, 12–13, 26–27, 29; 10:11; 13:10; 14:2, 21; 16:18; 17:7, 13, 16; 18:3; 20:5; 21:8; 26:15, 18–19; 27:1, 9, 11, 25–26; 28:9; 29:12; 31:7, 12, 16; 32:6, 9, 36, 43; 33:3, 5, 7, 21, 29). The most common translation of this term is "people," with an emphasis on connections of kinship and religious ceremonial, but it sometimes seems to designate a clan (paternal) relationship involving blood ties (*HALOT* 1, 182). Yet none of these three traits is easy to find in Deuteronomy. Even in the cases where Israel is clan-based, the term עַם is not used in the immediate context. There is a clear historical link, but this is not expressed in terms of genealogy or a clan system.

In Deuteronomy, עַם is used in three contexts to describe Israel: military, religious, and legal. First, Israel is a wandering people at war (2:4, 3:28 "be strong and firm," normally in war context, 31:7–8, 10:11). Typically, the term also denotes a people at war, a "militia" (1; 2; 17:16 immediately following עַם as the Israelite people; and 20:2, 5, 8, 9). Second, and dominantly, it is a religious entity; see the references in chs. 4, 7, 9, 14, 21, 26, 28, 29, 31:12, and 16, as well as the people responding in a ritual context in ch. 27. The third and final use of עַם to characterize Israel emphasizes that the people are participants in a legal system: 13:10; 16:18; 17:7, 13; and 18:3. The legal system, however, is closely related to Israel's religious essence (13:10; 16:20; 17:2–7; 18:3–5).

Hence, far from denoting a clan-based community (which it is), in Deuteronomy, עַם denotes instead a people regarded as a military army on the move to the land it is going to occupy as its legal property. This also corresponds to the annihilation (חרם) or destruction of the indigenous peoples and their ritual places. This wandering people is a religious entity, also with legal institutions and practices closely related to its practice of religion. All this points suggestively in the direction of the "holy war" ideology to be found later in the Deuteronomistic history. The link to holy war and the army on the move to occupy a territory would explain the predominance of עַם for Israel, even when the end result of the movements in Deuteronomy is a גוי (*goy*, "nation"). Finally, the *'am* is also a teaching/learning community when being gathered to listen and learn (4:6, 10). Hence, the Israel and the *'am* of Deuteronomy are co-extensive in the mind of the writer, with the same three traits visible.

Other groups that are seen specifically to constitute a people in Deuteronomy include: "the people greater and taller than we," Amorites, in the land to be occupied (1:28); "a people great and mighty, and tall:"

the Emim/Rephaim (2:10), the Rephaim/Zamzummim (2:21), and the Anakim (9:2); "the children of (all) *'ammîm* under the whole heaven" (2:25); and "Sihon and all his army" (2:32; see also 3:2). The majority of references to other groups are collective and non-specific, serving as "Others" outside of Israel. However, one gets the impression that all these *'ammîm* somehow relate to warfare and occupation by the Israelites, especially when they are characterized by size and strength. When it comes to specific actions, it is about a king, his land, cities, and his army (2:25, 32, 3:2 וכל עמו, 2:32).

Additionally, it should be noted that Deuteronomy contains four uses of the word *'am* followed by one or more qualifiers to define ways in which the group differs from other or surrounding groups. Israel is an *'am qādoš*, a holy people (7:6), an *'am sᵉgullâ*, Yhwh's special or treasured possession out of all peoples on the face of the cultivatable soil (7:6), an *'am ḥākām wᵉnābôn*, a people wise and understanding (4:6); an *'am naḥalâ*, a people of (Yhwh's) possession (4.20). Yet it is also an *'am-qᵉšê-'orep*, a stubborn people (9:6), clearly an insider characterization with an essentially religious function, which does not correspond to any of the six criteria listed by Smith (above). This feature seems to correspond to a genre- or template-trait in Deuteronomy, *paranesis* (instruction, counsel, advice), which even might pick up an element from penitential prayers (Exod 34:9; see Exod 33:5).

To conclude, the designation of Israel as an *'am* does not specifically point to a society based on common decent, kinship, or clans. Rather, it points to a group characterized by military strength and a religious essence derived from being connected with its God. As a religious community, it is also wise and understanding, due to its learning. The other *'ammîm* are subject to either Israel's occupation or their warfare.

"Nation"

The term *gôy/gôyîm* occurs 46 times (Accordance search) in Deuteronomy, yet only a few cases refer to Israel: Deut 4:6, 4:7, 4:34; (9:14 is about Moses); 26:5; 32:21; and 32:28. There are no references to Israel as a *gôy* in "the core." The term is said to denote a people, the "whole population of a territory," and a nation (*HALOT* 1, 183).

Israel as a גוי גדול, a great people, in 4:6-8, 4:34, and 26:5, may well refer to the promises in Gen 12:2, 17:20, 18:18, and 46:3. This designation, used even for Israel in Egypt (4:34, 26:5), is probably due to the notion in Deuteronomy's frame that Israel is emphatically placed among other *gôyîm*.[11] Remarkably, in Deut 4:6, the other peoples are העמים, and Israel will be spread among the *'ammîm* and among the *gôyîm* in 4:27, but except for this, Israel will drive out a number of *gôyîm* whenever they enter the land, 4:38; 7:1; 7:17; 7:22; 8:20 (special); 9:1–5; 9:14; 11:23; 12:2; 12:29–30; 18:9 (*tô'ᵃbōt haggôyîm*); 18:14; 19:1; 20:15; 26:19; 28:1; 28:12, 28:36; 28:49; 28:65; 29:15; 29:17; 29:24; 30:1; 31:3. Special are 15:6: they shall pledge to rule over many *gôyîm*; 17:14: wanting a king like all the *gôyîm*; and Deut 32:8, 32:21, 32:28, and 32:43. In the majority of cases, one gets the impression that *gôy/gôyîm* relates to a struggle about land. Tentatively, I follow Diana Edelman (ch. 4 in this volume), reasoning that those responsible for Deuteronomy in its present form deliberately want to associate Israel with a future territory as part of a larger meta-narrative.

"Custom"

As noted in §2, for Royce ethnicity implies a sense of "doing the same things," and in §3 I listed custom under the fourth item, shared cultural elements, in Anderson's list of ethnic traits. The term משפט, *mišpāṭ* occurs 37 times in Deuteronomy (Accordance search). The lexical meaning (as it appears in Deuteronomy) is mostly said to be "legal decision, judgment" (*HALOT* 2: 651). However, one should consider the possibility that this decision refers to tradition and custom, "ways of doing things," which appears clearly in 18:3 (so Davies 2021:16).[12] The singular form appears in the frame once only, in 1:17, and four times in the poetic chapters, in 32:4, 41, 33:10, 21. All other occurrences are in the core (16:18, 19, 17:8, 9, 11, 18:3, 19:6, 21:17, 22, 24:17, 25:1). These should be interpreted differently from the plural. Linked to the people of Israel, and with the double wording החקים והמשפטים, the phrase always occurs in the frame (4:1, 5, 8, 14, 45; 5:1, 31; 6:1, 20; 7:11 added to המצוה; 8:11 also has a different sequence; see also 26:16, 17; 30:16). This compound phrase obviously refers to the totality of Moses' teaching, which overlaps with the Torah presented by Moses (4:8). If the word means "tradition, custom," the singular משפט not accompanied by החקים signals something different from Torah, which is not custom, but in the context its communicative function should be to explain that what the Torah Moses presents is in accordance with their local customs (see below). Chapter 7 does not have the compound phrase,

---

11   Outside Deuteronomy, in Gen 20:4 גוי can hardly denote the "whole population of a territory" and hardly any kinship group. Even the distinction sometimes made by scholars that in Egypt, Israel became a large עם, not a גוי (Exod 1:8), is contradicted by Gen 46:3, which explicitly says that Jacob will become a large גוי in Egypt.

12   See also Edelman 2021, 31–32.

but the plural form of *mišpāṭ*, "because you listen to these judgments, המשפטים, ... Yhwh your God will keep with you the covenant and the love that he swore to your ancestors," הברית ואת החסד אשר נשבע לאבתיך, but it underscores the general obligations of the covenant.

A different picture emerges in Deuteronomy's core. In 17:8, 9, 11, as in 25:1, משפט refers to a case in court, either homicide or another matter, which people are to take to the central place, to the priests, the Levites, and to the judge who is there in those days, who shall render a final, binding decision. In 18:3, the term designates the customary rights of the priests; in 21:17, the right of the firstborn; and in 24:17, the right of the orphans, widows, and the *gēr* (the stranger). The latter usage also occurs in the frame in 10:18 and 27:19. Finally, in 19:6 and 21:22, *mišpāṭ* concerns homicide and in 16:18–19 righteous judges, as in the frame in 1:17. In the core, then, some uses of *mišpāṭ* are concerned with legal judgments in addition to customary practice.

The ideology of an ethnic Israel is thus connected with the local practice of custom and administrative/legal practice in the cities, i.e. with tradition. In terms of its religious commitment to the one God, ethnic Israel is equated with local, everyday practices; the practice of habits and *doxa* as described by Pierre Bourdieu (1977, 159): something that goes without saying in a society, the attitudes, habits, and practices one takes for granted, but a *doxa* made explicit in the book.

The seven different terms discussed in this section testify to an attempt in Deuteronomy to construe a sensibility of ethnic identity beyond individual or clan-based experience. This is done by playing on ideas of an inclusive "Israel," which is presented as a listening and learning community having a conspicuous martial nature. Its ethnic aspect is corroborated through 1) the idea of the annual festivals for all Israel, 2) the addressed "you," who seem to be presented or imagined as the all-inclusive population, even when the reality must have been much more limited (e.g. Deut 16:18; 17:4–5, which presuppose executive officers), and 3) the everyday interest in practical lawgiving and custom in the cities.

Does Deuteronomy's Ethnic Israel Reflect a Vision or Reality?

When one moves from the storyworld of Deuteronomy to the real world in which the kingdoms of Israel and Judah once existed, a new wrinkle intrudes on our understanding of the ethnic character of Israel as portrayed in Deuteronomy. How does the Israel portrayed in this book relate to those who created it, whenever and wherever they wrote, and how many of its ethnic traits derive from a past or present historical reality? We do not have a clear picture of the *ontological* (social) conditions that could make the idea of the Israelite entity possible. In the first instance, it is just a textual symbol; a symbol, however, that those responsible for the book attempt to *naturalize* as an entity in prehistory and *materialize* in dietary customs, festival practice, a system of tithes, judicial organization, as well as land ownership.

The notion of ethnicity has been used in several historical and archaeological studies that attempt to identify "Israel/Israelite" identity before, during, and after the historical kingdoms of Israel and Judah.

Deuteronomic Israel as a Reflection of Pre-monarchic, Tribal Israel

A number of studies have attempted to trace ethnic traits of a physical, pre-monarchic, tribal Israel (Killebrew 2005, 13–14, 149–50).[13] They have elicited skeptical responses, however, about the ability to undertake or complete such an enterprise successfully (Edelman 1996, 25; Finkelstein 1997, 217; Small 1997; Hall 1997, 2; Bloch-Smith 2003, 402, 406 but cf. 422). While the mention of a people called Israel in the coda section of the Egyptian Merneptah Stele (ca. 1209 BCE) confirms the existence of some sort of entity at that time, its relationship to biblical "Israel" remains more elusive. It is unclear how much of the reality of this pre-monarchic Israel has been handed down intact within the traditions currently found in the biblical texts, however, and how much of the depiction of early Israel in the books of Genesis–Samuel is an imagined, distant past. In any event, few if any scholars today would argue that twelve-tribe Israel was a contemporary reality at the time of the composition of Deuteronomy. In addition, as Raz Kletter (2014, 3–4) aptly comments, material culture does not equate to an ethnic identity; nor does a linguistic community.[14]

Monarchic Israel

Those who date Deuteronomy, or its core, to the late Iron Age tend to emphasize Deuteronomy's "state-character," consciously or unconsciously reading it as a reflection of what was to be an adapted reality of the situation of its creators. A few scholars prefer to conceptualize the

---

13   Daniel Fleming (2012, 239–51) presents an overview of different positions regarding the ethnogenesis of "Israel," starting in the twelfth and eleventh centuries BCE.

14   I agree with Raz Kletter (2014, 4) that even though ethnicity is a modern construct, the matter existed in Antiquity.

Israel depicted in the Hebrew Bible as a national state, even though it is commonly argued that "nation" is a modern construct. Steven Grosby claims that pre-modern nations existed in Antiquity (Grosby, 1991, 1997, 2002), while declining to use the term (patrimonial) state (Grosby, 2002, 65).

Dean McBride Jr. (1987, 230) has been the primary proponent of Deuteronomy's "state-character." He has noted that Josephus (*Antiquities of the Jews*, 4:176–331) identified the Mosaic Torah of Deuteronomy as the ancient Israelite *politeia*, not a *nomos*, although he definitely understood *politeia* to represent Hebrew *torah*.[15] On this basis, McBride interprets Deuteronomy as the constitution of Israel as a political entity, which also served as the book's historical function. A number of scholars who date the text to the pre-exilic period, notably in the reign of Josiah, have followed his suggestion. Frank Crüsemann argues that the major part of "the core" appears to be a political constitution (*Verfassung*) for a late, pre-exilic theocratic democracy *Theokratie als Demokratie* (1992, 286–88). William M. Schniedewind states plainly that Deuteronomy forms the blueprint for the Josianic reforms but curiously concludes that royal scribes did not produce the book; rather, it is "the literature of the 'people of the land'" (2004, 109, 112). Although his own presentation tends toward Israel as an ethnic group, Robert R. Wilson concludes that "Deuteronomy is intended to be a polity, a constitution for an actual state" (2005, 123).

Ernest W. Nicholson (2014, 51, 101–16) criticizes, rightly in my opinion, those who find Deut 17:14–20 (as part of 16:18–18:22) to be a "polity" representing the Israelite/Judahite kingdom, either a real one under Josiah or a utopian one during the restoration after the exile. He points out it is an altogether critical comment on kingship. Less convincing is his suggestion that Ahaz and the Assyrian Empire served as the role model behind this text.

In this volume, we reject the idea that Deuteronomy originated in Judah in the late monarchic (Josianic) period. There is simply too little that is "monarchic" in it to support such an idea. The similarities with the narrative of Josiah's reform may be due to ideological "back-writing."

It has been suggested that Deuteronomy's Israel is more like the Greek city councils than the ancient Levantine kingdoms. In §4 the issue of the Greek concept of *ethnos* being coterminous with a single city in some instances but involving multiple cities in others (the *koinon*) was discussed. As noted there, Seth Schwartz (2013) argued that the Torah's political and

---

15 "Most noteworthy here is Josephus' choice of the Greek term *politeia*, rather than *nomos* or the like, to describe the juridical substance of Deuteronomy; there is no reason to doubt that he understood *politeia* to represent Hebrew *torà* in its characteristically Deuteronomic usage" (McBride 1987, 229).

social vision resembles Athenian democracy. But where is the council in Deuteronomy? There are city elders, judges, and magistrates in the cities and at the pilgrimage center, but the elusive "you" seems to be the representatives of the general population, and they are hidden in rhetoric. We find no council, as was constituent of Greek city-states, but there is a $q^ehal\ yhwh$ in 23:1–3. The text does not offer any description of its function however.

Post-Monarchic Israel

Others find the notion of ethnicity and kinship depicted in Deuteronomy aptly connected with a post-monarchic, socio-political reality (e.g. Crüsemann 1992, 64). The focus on ethnicity and kinship as well as the "Othering" aspect may cumulatively point in the direction of intense contact with other ethnic groups in an imperial setting and the need for demarcation.[16] Those who favor this setting for the writing of Deuteronomy see its Israel either to reflect a return to a pre-state political entity and Israel as a tribal *ethnos* (e.g. Killebrew 2005, see above) in an imperial setting that is anticipated to continue in the future, or as a vision for a hoped-for, future reality in an imperial system, where the *ethnos* can experience a modicum of self-regulation (e.g. Nicholson, 2014, 50–51).[17]

In a study of Israel as a people in Deuteronomy, Dominik Markl (2012) cannot endorse an interpretation of the book as a constitution for an actual state because he dates its composition after the termination of the Judahite monarchy. Nevertheless, he acknowledges that Deuteronomy is a "compendium of political rhetoric" (2012, 55–56), so that Israel's identity is politically oriented. Chapters 12–25 evoke Israel as "the legally

---

16   Abner Cohen (1969, 2) writes that in modern Africa, retribalization "is the result, not of ethnic groupings disengaging themselves from one another, but of increasing interaction between them." Anya Peterson Royce (1982, 40), who also cites Cohen at this point, concurs. "In other words, ethnic identity is more often the product of increasing interaction between groups than the negative result of isolation" (1982, 40).

17   Jon L. Berquist argues that as a secondary state, Yehud defined itself in terms of its temple and through a temple ideology (1995, 147–50). This also serves as the ground for his view of leadership in the Yehudite state. However, Deuteronomy does not present Israel as a temple-state. Berquist also states that the immigrants were a new class of citizens for Jerusalem, distinct ethnically and culturally. This is not expressed in Deuteronomy either, unless one interprets "the peoples in the land" as those who were left in the land. Also, the authors of Deuteronomy do not correspond to Yehud's scribal school who, as presented by Berquist (1995, 163–64), "radically relativizes the temple as a source for divine truth"; this latter point is of no consequence in Deuteronomy.

constituted nation" (87), and the book "imparts ... moral identity to the people" (301). The Mosaic Deut–Torah is "the Moab covenant's law code" (301). The "hermeneutics of justice" of Israel as a political entity also has a religious quality. Accordingly, Deuteronomy "aims at a religious formation of the people" (292). In its present shape, Deuteronomy does not address a monarchic state. As noted by Nicholson, it holds a view of an imagined, future "Israel" not yet in existence.

Social Closure and the Construction of Power in Deuteronomy

It has been standard for scholars to focus on the whole of "Israel" as an entity distinguished from "the Canaanites" and other groups in the promised land. However, in order to understand the purpose of ethnicity in the communicative function of this book, we need to look at the power dynamics among group members in the socio-political setting where the book was written for a larger audience and differentiate between those who created the book and the community at large. As noted by Royce (see above), ethnic perception may belong to a subordinate group within a larger group, whose purpose is to improve their inferior position (1982, 4–6). In the preceding section I have concluded that while definitive proof is lacking, the book presumes a post-monarchic and possible diasporic setting for its composition.

Max Weber's concept of "inner social closure" (2019, 123) enhances the observations of Royce and is useful in addressing the issue of the power dynamics underlying the book. The main point is that a given society will decide on certain strategies that they cannot be certain will succeed, but they run with them anyway. Hence, he begins by defining social closure in terms of insiders and outsiders. "Social relationships are closed to outsiders to the extent that its [the society's] substantive meaning, or its prevailing rules exclude such participation or restrict or permit it only according to specific conditions" (Weber 2019, 123). Such closedness can be defined traditionally, according to Weber, and this seems to be the case in Deuteronomy, where closedness (to some outsiders) is based on Mosaic prescriptions. He then goes on to discuss "inner closure—among the agents themselves and in their relationship to each other" (2019, 125) within a given group, which is my primary focus. The latter concept acknowledges that within a given society, some members can gain exclusive control over access to certain resources or opportunities.

In Deuteronomy, such agents may be influential office holders (royal power groups) but more probably groups holding informal power not connected to the imperial administrative system. The privileges afforded the Levitical priests and those who constituted a scribal elite in the society envisioned in the book exemplify inner closure. The most visible expressions of a more restricted group hegemony appear in the frame, especially in the stipulation about the writing of the scroll of the Torah, its preservation, and its being read in public in ch. 31.

"The priests, the sons of Levi," and the elders (v. 9), addressed as "you," are given the task of reading the Torah loudly to all the Israelites (v. 11). In every other chapter but here, the "you" in Deuteronomy are common Israelites (e.g. 4:1 *passim*, 5:1, 32; 6:1-3, 4-8, etc.), which some have understood to reflect an element of a "democratic" or "egalitarian" ethos (e.g. Schwartz 2013, 190). However, it is more relevant to read the "you" addressed in all chapters but ch. 31 as the audience of the literati, and the "you" in ch. 31 as the literati, the group behind the book, who are the privileged ones able to write, read, and instruct the people.

One needs to look at who profits from the distinction made among those addressed as "you." Only through the acceptance of the authority of the scribal elites and the group handling the Torah in the name of Moses can the envisioned "Israel" become a reality:

> So now, Israel, give heed to the statutes and ordinances that I am teaching you to observe, so that you may live to enter and occupy the land that Yhwh, the God of your ancestors, is giving you. You must neither add anything to what I command you nor take away anything from it, but keep the commandments of Yhwh your God with which I am charging you." (Deut 4:1-2; NRSV, adapted)

In the storyworld, after Moses writes the scroll of the Torah, heaven and earth are to serve as witnesses against "the elders of your tribes" and your שטרים. The latter term is frequently translated "your officers" but might refer instead to a guild of scribes (see above). Both groups function as the representatives of the people understood as a community of tribes.

While it is Moses who is teaching the audience in the narrated time as well as the audience in the time of narration, a reading or hearing audience living in a post-exilic generation needs to listen as a collective to the authoritative speakers and interpreters of "Moses," i.e. scribes who hold the authoritative position of keeping, proclaiming, and interpreting the scroll of the Torah of Moses. What is more, as I have argued elsewhere (Berge 2016), the authority of this group as interpreters is enhanced through the fact that "the original" Mosaic book is subsequently lost and present only as a version of Deuteronomy. Similarly, the public speech of Moses is transmitted only through the public speech of the Levitical priests.

At the same time, however, this group has no officially sanctioned position of authority. It relies instead on what Abner Cohen has described as "informal authority," which is not supported or enforced by a government or societal law structures.[18] Instead, the authority is granted through voluntary, mutual consent by members of the group. Weber characterizes such a situation as "communalization, in which ... social action rests ... on a subjectively *felt* (affectual or traditional), *mutual sense of belonging* among those involved" (2019, 119). It is evident that the success of the vision presented in Deuteronomy depends on the voluntary acceptance of the addressees; hence, it relies at least in part on an "affective, emotional, or traditional basis" (2019, 121).

A significant aspect of the legitimation of power not addressed in Markl's 2012 study discussed in §7.3 is foregrounded by Benedetta Rossi (2021) and myself (Berge 2021): What group would benefit from Deuteronomy's presentation of Israel? Rossi notes that access to the Torah is limited to the priestly elite/the Levites. This takes the issue a significant step forward, since "political" becomes intelligible as the struggle of an informal group for societal power.[19]

Rossi demonstrates how specific groups hold exclusive knowledge and competence in the Hebrew Bible. From general considerations of symbolic capital and symbolization of power, one may expect even the most religious parts of the biblical texts to sustain (or deconstruct) societal power. This is one of the enduring insights from Pierre Bourdieu's notion of symbolic fields and cultural capital (Guillory 1993). I have also argued that aspects of Deuteronomy's presentation of the Israelite community seem to function as acts of "resilience" (2021, 91). By resilience, I mean the ability of Deuteronomy to resist imperial domination by envisioning another possibility of rule, a political imagination of renewal and transformation without provoking imperial authorities.

In summary, a look at the implied authority behind the picture of the ethnic entity of Israel and its foundations presents us with an elite group attempting to establish its informal authority in a community envisioned

---

18   I follow Abner Cohen (1969, 1974), whose anthropological work has inspired me to suggest interpreting Deuteronomy as the legitimating work of an informal group (Berge 2021).

19   The term "political" is elusive without further clarification. In studies of the contemporary world of the Hebrew Bible, it usually refers to kingdoms and empires. This is presupposed in the edited work by Jason Silverman and Caroline Waerzeggers (2015) and by Dale Launderville (2003, 1–7), who also uses the term "political theology" (5). Jan Assmann demonstrates, however, the complexity of the term "political theology" (Assmann, 2002, 15–28). One definition is "the sacral staging of the political, or the political realization of the sacred" (19). What complicates use of the term "political theology" in Deuteronomy is the presence of something that could be called personal piety (Launderville 2003, esp. 328; Assmann 2002, 113 *passim*).

to be based on the Torah—and dependent on the teaching by this group of scribes.

The Function of Ethnicity in Deuteronomy

So, what is the purpose of ethnicity in Deuteronomy? Those who date Deuteronomy (the core and the "late pre-exilic" frame) to the late monarchy tend to regard the ethnic issue as an attempt to reconcile two (or more) different peoples. This is the basic function of Deuteronomic ethnicity according to Kenton L. Sparks. Originating in the time between Hezekiah and Josiah, Deuteronomy's ethnic concept holds political significance for the kingdom.[20] In his view, the ethnic sentiment accomplishes the common identity of Judahites and Israelites; it presents "a kinship theology of brotherhood to all Judeans and Israelites" (1998, 264). The criteria for this ethnic inclusion "hinged on one's status as a 'brother' and also on one's status as a fellow heir of the forefathers" (1998, 264). Then, "the primary purpose of these ethnic expressions [the forefather tradition] was to exploit the natural sentiment of kinship as a motivational factor in the effort to promote the Deuteronomic ideal of mono-Yahwistic fidelity" (1998, 228; see also 231).

The idea that the purpose of ethnicity in Deuteronomy is to unite the people of two kingdoms should be rejected as insufficiently grounded on the text. Apart from possible Northern traditions in Deut 32,[21] there are few clear hints pointing to any project of unifying groups from different (former) kingdoms or foreign immigrants into an existing or former kingdom. The distribution of land east of the Jordan (3:12-20) expresses a "large-Israel-idea" that in other contexts also includes Samaria and Transjordan, but it belongs to post-exilic time (Otto 2012, 480). Even if

20   Sparks does not state this explicitly, but the thrust of his analysis of Deuteronomy, as also signaled in the title of this chapter (1998, 222), leads in this direction: "Josiah may have taken the challenge of Deuteronomy seriously" (235), and "the primeval inhabitants of the land (in Deuteronomy) would correspond to the foreign deportees transplanted by Assyria in the North" (234). See also p. 237: the "ethnic brotherhood" ideology corresponds to the agenda of the Josianic redactor, who is associated with Josiah's reform effort.
21   Otto, 2012, 2176-77. Nothing indicates a concern with two different kingdoms or peoples in these verses. The possibly Northern tradition (v. 10, see also Hos 9:10 and Ps 78:71) is rather a literary creation from the Psalms (also Ps 82) as a very late composition. For a text-critical discussion of $b^e n\hat{e}\ yi\acute{s}r\bar{a}'\bar{e}l$ and the added "Israel" in v. 9, see Nilsen 2018, 28-29 in addition to Otto's discussion (2012, 2, 147-48).

the latter idea should reflect a memory of the pre-exilic kingdoms, it only foreshadows the distribution of the land in Josh 12–13, 17 (and Num 32). A Northern perspective appears in the mention of Mt. Ebal and Mt. Gerizim as places of worship (ch. 27), but the idea that Deuteronomy seeks to create a new entity out of two different populations is left to heavy suggestion. It is not convincing, unless one is tempted to regard its time of origin as after the fall of Samaria (722 BCE), during the reign of Hezekiah, Manasseh, or Josiah in Judah, or another period when there was a delicate relationship between the Northern and the Judahite population. In any case, against the suggestion of Eckart Otto (2012, 485), the narrative in 3:12–20 cannot be regarded as an attempt to legitimate any historical process of unification after 722 BCE or at the time of Josiah.

"All Israel" is just what it says: the audience addressed by "Moses" (the storyline's representative of the literati/scribal elite). "All Israel" and cognate terms (see above) are simply the intended listening and learning populace, the addressees of those groups of literati who claim rights of knowledge about the right way of being "Israel." In other words, the intention of the authorial literati was to disseminate their ideology of one God, Yhwh, to a community called "all Israel" and to corroborate (or introduce) the authority of a limited group. The addressees are the well-to-do farmers, the traders, and the people living in the cities and their hinterlands; they are the crowd coming together at the festivals. These could be the elite whose hegemony the Levitical priests seek to take over for themselves. Strangers (*gērîm*) are included, to be sure, but these seem to be individuals (hired workers or officials of the imperial government) scattered throughout the cities. It is a matter for further investigation how the presence of *gērîm* inside Israel affects the Deuteronomic understanding of ethnicity.

This view of the general population, the "all Israel," is corroborated by the result of the review of the terms for ethnic Israel: they all refer predominantly to the group of people listening to, and challenged by, the teaching of Moses. Of course, the populace is told that this religious ideology implies political and economic consequences, but these are based neither on kingdom nor on empire.

The picture of ethnicity in Deuteronomy does not correspond to the real situation in the provinces of Yehud or Samerina in the Babylonian or Persian period. Also, it probably does not correspond to the exilic situation. According to Wilfred G. Lambert (1975, 191; also cited by Nicholson 2014, 47), "ordinary people might share in the spirit of the more important annual festivals, but the city temple was not a place of their devotions. For them the niche at home or the street corner shrine was the place of religion." If this is relevant to the production of Deuteronomy, we might assume that the focus on cities (in addition to the festivals) likewise reveals an elite priestly culture behind the book.[22]

So, why ethnicity? The two concepts of 1) an elective covenant and 2) ethnicity as a "destiny" work together in Deuteronomy to motivate the general population to follow the lead of the scribal elite. While Deuteronomy's call to obey the commandments, statutes, and judgments of the covenant appeals to decision and will, the book's reference to ethnicity is presented as a destiny; something unchangeable but also something that captures a sensitivity in the general population.

Ethnicity is primarily applied to peripheral or "informal" groups that are not sustained by political regimes. Thus, it is a residual political category; it follows as the result of groups' struggle for power or influence. As a discursive practice, Deuteronomy's ethnic identity defines boundaries. In order for a discourse of ethnicity to work, one needs to find an Other, but this Other (the indigenous peoples: Canaanites, etc.) seems to be a literary construct ungrounded in the historical reality at the time the text was produced. Alternatively, one should read the ethnicity issue as a pedagogical tool. This is the path taken in this chapter.

I argued elsewhere that the authors of Deuteronomy develop an "ethnic" identity for the people in order to legitimate their informal authority over this "Israel" (Berge 2021). This is done, for example, by linking the idea of one people with the practices in the cities. This cognitive approach focuses our lens on "how people see the world, parse their experience, and interpret events" (Brubaker 2004, 77); it is something people *do*. In this perspective, we do not look for things-in-the-world, but for social imagination and a way of seeing, which is just as strong a social force, although it lies in mental states.

This perspective involves two further aspects. First, stereotyping is present because it requires minimal processing. Stereotyping is not beyond conscious control, but as Rogers Brubaker argues, is rooted in ordinary cognitive processes (2004, 73). Second, "primordialism" is present because ethnicity is seen to be the result of "a deep-seated cognitive disposition to perceive human beings as members of 'natural kinds' with

---

22   Thomas Römer notes that the story of Moses' death outside the land clearly betrays a Diasporic perspective (2013, 47). He also argues that the "crisis semantics" in the Dtr History should be attributed to "Mandarin" authors, "the class of high officials of the Judean court, who (perhaps in Babylon) attempted to edit a comprehensive history in order to understand why the disaster happened" (2013, 39). As is common among redaction historians, Römer, argues that substantial revision of the Deut History took place in the Persian period, specifically (with regard to 2 Kgs 22–23) in a Diasporic situation (2013, 40).

inherited and immutable 'essences'" (2004, 4). In this regard, the authors play on the deep sensibilities of the populace.

The originators of Deuteronomy sought to evoke and call Israel into being as an ethnic group. In Brubaker's terms, by treating "Israel" as a substantial thing-in-the-world, they "contribute[d] to producing what they apparently describe[d] or designate[d]" (2004, 10). In league with Pierre Bourdieu, Brubaker calls this a performative character: "By *invoking* groups, they seek to *evoke* them, summon them, call them into being. Their categories are *for doing*—designated to stir, summon, justify, mobilize, kindle, and energize" (2004, 10).

Conclusion

What does the idea of ethnicity *do* in Deuteronomy? On one level, it limits access to the people, the covenant, and eventually, the social and political power in the entity called Israel by categorically excluding those who are distinguished as outsiders/others. However, the intention and purpose of Deuteronomy should not be reduced to one, single issue, not even in its "final form."

On another level, ethnicity serves an internal performative function of identification among the diaspora. It makes sense to regard Deuteronomy as an attempt to present "Israel" as an "ethnic" entity in order to situate themselves vis-à-vis the imperial administration or at least to serve an "internal-Israelite" purpose. The latter might have been an attempt by an elite group of literati to extend their informal authority to all Hebrew-speaking groups worshipping Yhwh (in one or more variant forms).

An elite scribal group, probably standing behind the Levitical priests, created or more probably re-invented the concept of an Israelite ethnicity in order to establish and legitimate their informal authority as social and cultural leaders of an envisioned community called "Israel." This was done more or less outside the political structures of the Achaemenid Empire.

Works Cited

Anderson, Benedict. 2006. *Imagined Communities: Reflections on the Origin and Spread of Nationalism*. London: Verso.

Assmann, Jan. 2002. *Herrschaft und Heil. Politische Theologie in Altägypten, Israel und Europa*. Frankfurt a.M.: Fischer Taschenbuch Verlag.

Aurelius, Erik. 2003. "Der Ursprung des Ersten Gebots." *Zeitschrift für Theologie und Kirche* 100: 1–21.

Barth, Fredrik. 1966. *Models of Social Organization*. Glasgow: Royal Anthropological Institute.
------. ed. 1969. *Ethnic Groups and Boundaries*. Boston, MA: Little, Brown.
------. 1973. "Descent and Marriage Reconsidered." Pages 3–20 in *The Character of Kinship*. Edited by Jack Goody. Cambridge: Cambridge University Press.
Berge, Kåre. 2016. "Mystified Authority: Legitimating Leadership through 'Lost Books.'" Pages 41–56 in *Leadership, Social Memory and Judean Discourse in the Fifth-Second Centuries BCE*. Edited by Diana Edelman and Ehud Ben Zvi. London: Equinox Publishing Ltd.
------. 2021. "Cities in Deuteronomy: Imperial Ideology, Resilience, and the Imagination of Yahwistic Religion." Pages 77–196 in *Deuteronomy in the Making: Studies in the Production of Debarim*. Edited by Diana Edelman, Benedetta Rossi, Kåre Berge, and Philippe Guillaume. Beihefte Zeitschrift für die Alttestamentische Wissenschaft 533. Berlin: de Gruyter.
Berlinerblau, Jacques. 1999. "Ideology, Pierre Bourdieu's Doxa, and the Hebrew Bible." *Semeia* 87: 193–214.
Berquist, Jon L. 1995. *Judaism in Persia's Shadow: A Social and Historical Approach*. Minneapolis, MN: Fortress.
Blenkinsopp, Joseph. 1995. "Deuteronomy and the Politics of Post-mortem Existence." *Vetus Testament* 45: 1–16.
Bloch-Smith, Elizabeth. 2003. "Israelite Ethnicity in Iron I: Archaeology Preserves What is Remembered and What is Forgotten in Israel's History." *Journal of Biblical Literature* 122: 401–25.
Bourdieu, Pierre. 1977. *Outline of a Theory of Practice*. Cambridge: Cambridge University Press.
Brubaker, Rogers. 2004. *Ethnicity without Groups*. Cambridge, MA: Harvard University Press.
Cohen, Abner. 1969. *Custom and Politics in Urban Africa: A Study of Hausa Migrants in Yoruba Towns*. London: Routledge. Paperback edition 2014.
------. 1974. *Two-Dimensional Man: An Essay on the Anthropology of Power and Symbolism in Complex Societies*. London: Routledge.
Connor, Walker. 1992. "The Nation and its Myth." *International Journal of Comparative Sociology* 33: 48–80.
Crüsemann, Frank. 1992. *Die Tora: Theologie und Sozialgeschichte des alttestamentlichen Gesetzes*. München: Chr. Kaiser.
Davies, Philip R. 2014. "The Authority of Deuteronomy." Pages 27–47 in *Deuteronomy-Kings as Emerging Authoritative Books: A Conversation*. Edited by Diana V. Edelman. Ancient Near Eastern Monographs 6. Atlanta, GA: Society of Biblical Literature.
------. 2021. "From Where Did Deuteronomy Originate?" Pages 13–24 in *Deuteronomy in the Making: Studies in the Production of Debarim*. Edited by Diana Edelman, Benedetta Rossi, Kåre Berge, and Philippe Guillaume.

Beihefte Zeitschrift für die Alttestamentische Wissenschaft 533. Berlin: de Gruyter.

Edelman, Diana. 1996. "Ethnicity and Early Israel." Pages 25–56 in *Ethnicity and the Bible*. Edited by Mark G. Brett. Biblical Interpretation Series 19. New York: Brill.

———. 2021. "Deuteronomy as the Instructions of Moses and Yhwh vs. a Framed Legal Code." Pages 25–75 in *Deuteronomy in the Making: Studies in the Production of Debarim*. Edited by Diana Edelman, Benedetta Rossi, Kåre Berge, and Philippe Guillaume. Beihefte Zeitschrift für die Alttestamentische Wissenschaft 533. Berlin: de Gruyter.

Eriksen, Thomas Hylland. 2004. "Place, Kinship and the Case for Non-Ethnic Nations." Pages 49–62 in *History and National Destiny: Ethnosymbolism and its Critics*. Edited by Montserrat Guibernau and John Hutchinson. Oxford: Blackwell.

Finkelstein, Israel. 1997. "Pots and People Revisited: Ethnic Boundaries in the Iron Age I." Pages 216–37 in *The Archaeology of Israel: Constructing the Past, Interpreting the Present*. Edited by Neil A. Silberman and D. Small. Journal for the Study of the Old Testament Supplement Series 237. Sheffield: Sheffield Academic Press.

Fleming, Daniel. 2012. *The Legacy of Israel in Judah's Bible: History, Politics, and the Reinscribing of Tradition*. Cambridge: Cambridge University Press.

Garmann, Sebastian. 2007. "Ethnosymbolism in the Ancient Mediterranean World." Pages 113–25 in *Nationalism and Ethnosymbolism*. Edited by Athena S. Leoussi and Steven Grosby. Edinburgh: Edinburgh University Press.

Grosby, Steven E. 1991. "Religion and Nationality in Antiquity." *European Journal of Sociology* 32: 229–65.

———. 1997. "Borders, Territory and Nationality in the Ancient Near East and Armenia." *Journal of the Economic and Social History of the Orient* 40: 1–29.

———. 2002. *Biblical Ideas of Nationality Ancient and Modern*. Winona Lake, IN: Eisenbrauns.

Guibernau, Montserrat and John Hutchinson. 2004. "History and National Destiny." Pages 1–8 in *History and National Destiny: Ethnosymbolism and its Critics*. Edited by Montserrat Guibernau and John Hutchinson. Oxford: Blackwell.

Guillaume, Philippe. 2021. "Brothers in Deuteronomy: Zoom in on Lothar Perlitt's Volk von Brüdern." Pages 289–328 in *Deuteronomy in the Making: Studies in the Production of Debarim*. Edited by Diana Edelman, Benedetta Rossi, Kåre Berge, and Philippe Guillaume. Beihefte Zeitschrift für die Alttestamentische Wissenschaft 533. Berlin: De Gruyter.

Guillory, John. 1993. *Cultural Capital: The Problem of Literary Canon Formation*. Chicago, IL: University of Chicago Press.

Hall, Jonathan M. 1997. *Ethnic Identity in Greek Antiquity*. Cambridge: Cambridge University Press.

Hallock, Richard T. 1969. *Persepolis Fortification Tablets*. The University of Chicago Oriental Institute Publications Volume XCII. Chicago, IL: The University of Chicago Press.

Hansen, Mogens H. 2013. "Greek City-States." Pages 259-78 in *The Oxford Handbook of the State in the Ancient Near East and Mediterranean*. Edited by Peter Fibiger Bang and Walter Scheidel. Oxford: Oxford University Press.

Henkelman, Wouter F. M., and Stolper, Matthew W. 2009. "Ethnic Identity and Ethnic Labelling at Persepolis: The Case of the Scudrians." Pages 271-323 in *Organisation des pouvoirs et contacts culturels dans les pays de l'empire achéménide*. Edited by Pierre Briant and Michel Chauveau. Paris: de Boccard.

James, Paul W. 1996. *Nation Formation*. London: Sage.

Killebrew, Ann E. 2005. *Biblical Peoples and Ethnicity: An Archaeological Study of Egyptians, Canaanites, Philistines, and Early Israel, 1300-1100 B.C.E.* Atlanta, GA: Scholars Press.

Kletter, Raz. 2014. "In the Footsteps of Bagira: Ethnicity, Archaeology, and Iron Age I Ethnic Israel." *Approaching Religion* 4: 2-15.

Kratz, Reinhard G. 2018. "Prophetic Discourse on 'Israel'." Pages 503-16 in *Archaeology and History of Eighth-Century Judah*. Edited by Zev I. Farber and Jacob L. Wright. Atlanta, GA: SBL Press.

Lambert, Wilfred G. 1975. "The Historical Development of the Mesopotamian Pantheon: A Study in Sophisticated Polytheism." Pages 191-200 in *Unity and Diversity: Essays in the History, Literature, and Religion of the Ancient Near East*. Edited by Hans Goedicke and J.J.M. Roberts. Baltimore, MD and London: Johns Hopkins University Press.

Launderville, Dale. 2003. *Piety and Politics: The Dynamics of Royal Authority in Homeric Greece, Biblical Israel, and Old Babylonian Mesopotamia*. Grand Rapids, MI: Eerdmans.

Leoussi, Athena S. and Steven Grosby. 2007. "Introduction." Pages 1-11 in *Nationalism and Ethnosymbolism: History, Culture and Ethnicity in the Formation of Nations*. Edited by Athena S. Leoussi and Steven Grosby. Edinburgh: Edinburgh University Press.

Machinist, Peter. 2003. "Mesopotamian Imperialism and Israelite Religion: A Case Study from Second Isaiah." Pages 237-64 in *Symbiosis, Symbolism, and the Power of the Past. Canaan, Ancient Israel, and their Neighbors from the Late Bronze Age through Roman Palaestina*. Edited by William G. Dever and Seymour Gitin. Winona Lake, IN: Eisenbrauns.

Mackil, Emily. 2013. "The Greek Koinon." Pages 304-23 in *The Oxford Handbook of the State in the Ancient Near East and Mediterranean*. Edited by Peter Fibiber Bang and Walter Scheidel. Oxford: Oxford University Press.

Markl, Dominik. 2012. *Gottes Volk im Deuteronomium*. Wiesbaden: Harrassowitz.

McBride, S. Dean, Jr. 1987. "Polity of the Covenant People: The Book of Deuteronomy." *Interpretation* 41: 229–44.

Miller, James C. 2008. "Ethnicity and the Hebrew Bible: Problems and Prospects." *Currents in Biblical Research* 6: 170–213. doi:10.1177/1476993X07083627

Nestor, Dermot Anthony. 2010. *Cognitive Perspectives on Israelite Identity*. Library of Hebrew Bible/Old Testament Studies 519. London, New York: T&T Clark.

Nicholson, Ernest W. 2014. *Deuteronomy and the Judaean Diaspora*. Oxford: Oxford University Press.

Nilsen, Tina D. 2018. *The Origins of Deuteronomy 32: Intertextuality, Memory, Identity*. New York: Peter Lang.

Otto, Eckart. 2012. *Deuteronomium 1,1-4,43*. Herders Theologischer Kommentar zum Alten Testament. Freiburg: Herder.

Pearce, Laurie. 2006. "New Evidence for Judeans in Babylonia." Pages 399–411 in *Judah and the Judeans in the Achaemenid Period: Negotiating Identity in an International Context*. Edited by Oded Lipschits and Manfred Oeming. Winona Lake, IN: Eisenbrauns.

——————. 2016. "Cuneiform Sources for Judeans in Babylonia in the Neo-Babylonian and Achaemenid Periods: An Overview." *Religion Compass* 10/9: 230–243.

Pearce, Laurie and Cornelia Wunsch. 2014. *Documents of Judean Exiles and West Semites in Babylonia in the Collection of David Sofer*. Edited by Laurie E. Pierce and Cornelia Wunsch. Cornell University Studies in Assyriology and Sumerology 28. Bethesda, MD: CDL Press.

Römer, Thomas C. 2013. "Conflicting Models of Identity and the Publication of the Torah in the Persian Period." Pages 33–52 in *Between Cooperation and Hostility: Multiple Identities in Ancient Judaism and the Interaction with Foreign Powers*. Edited by Rainer Albertz and Jakob Wöhrle. Göttingen: Vandenhoeck & Ruprecht.

Rossi, Benedetta. 2021. "'Not by Bread Alone' (Deut 8:3): Elite Struggles over Cultic Prebends and Moses's Torah in Deuteronomy." Pages 329–63 in *Deuteronomy in the Making: Studies in the Production of Debarim*. Edited by Diana Edelman, Benedetta Rossi, Kåre Berge, and Philippe Guillaume. Beihefte Zeitschrift für die Alttestamentische Wissenschaft 533. Berlin: de Gruyter.

Royce, Anya P. 1982. *Ethnic Identity: Strategies of Diversity*. Bloomington, IN: Indiana University Press.

Schniedewind, William M. 2004. *How the Bible Became a Book*. Cambridge: Cambridge University Press.

Schwartz, Seth. 2013. Jewish States. Pages 180–98 in *The Oxford Handbook of the State in the Ancient Near East and Mediterranean*. Edited by Peter Fibiber Bang and Walter Scheidel. Oxford: Oxford University Press.

Silverman, Jason and Caroline Waerzeggers. 2015. *Political Memory In and After the Persian Empire*. Edited by Jason Silverman and Caroline Waerzeggers. Atlanta, GA: SBL Press.

Small, David. 1997. "Group Identification and Ethnicity in the Construction of the Early State of Israel." Pages 271–89 in *The Archaeology of Israel: Constructing the Past, Interpreting the Present*. Edited by Neil A. Silberman and David B. Small. Journal for the Study of the Old Testament Supplement Series 237. Sheffield: Sheffield Academic Press.

Smith, Anthony D. 1986. *The Ethnic Origins of Nations*. Oxford: Blackwell.

------. 1999. *Myths and Memories of the Nation*. Oxford: Oxford University Press.

Sparks, Kenton L. 1998. *Ethnicity and Identity in Ancient Israel: Prolegomena to the Study of Ethnic Sentiments and their Expression in the Hebrew Bible*. Winona Lake, IN: Eisenbrauns.

Weber, Max. 2019. *Economy and Society: A New Translation*. Edited and translated by Keith Tribe. Cambridge, MA and London: Harvard University Press.

Wilson, Robert R. 2005. "Deuteronomy, Ethnicity, and Reform: Reflections on the Social Setting of the Book of Deuteronomy." Pages 107–24 in *Constituting the Community: Studies on the Polity of Ancient Israel in Honor of S. Dean McBride Jr.* Edited by John T. Strong and Steven S. Tuell. Winona Lake, IN: Eisenbrauns.

Zadok, Ran. 1979. *The Jews in Babylonia during the Chaldean and Achaemenian Periods According to Babylonian Sources*. Haifa: University of Haifa.

About the Author

Kåre Berge is professor emeritus and guest researcher at the Faculty of Theology, University of Oslo. His studies cover the Pentateuch, especially Genesis, Exodus and Deuteronomy, focusing on cultural memory, politics of identity, didacticism, and symbolization of power relations. In particular, "Dynamics of Power and the Re-invention of 'Israel' in Persian Empire Judah," pages 293–321 in *Levantine Entanglements* (edited by T. Stordalen and Ø.S. LaBianca, Sheffield: Equinox Publishing Ltd, 2021) and "Cities in Deuteronomy: Imperial Ideology, Resilience, and the Imagination of Yahwistic Religion," pages 77–96 in *Deuteronomy in the Making* (edited by D. Edelman, B. Rossi, K. Berge, and P. Guillaume, BZAW 533; Berlin: W. de Gruyter, 2021).

Chapter 6
Basic Tools to Figure Out the Economy of Deuteronomy 12–26

Philippe Guillaume

Abstract

Deuteronomy has long been held as particularly innovative, humanitarian and kind to the poor. The legal collection in the heart of the book is read here in light of ancient economic practices. Once the basic principles of any economy are understood, the practices prescribed in Deuteronomy display much common sense and their purported humanitarian traits are not devoid of self-interest.

Keywords: poverty, interests, credit, alms, debt, self-indenture

The Bible is a collection of theological works dealing primarily with moral and ethical issues, whereas economics readily evokes today stock markets and unbridled greed. Economics deals with debt while theology deals with sin, but theology and economics are no strangers: forgiveness of sins is forgiveness of debts towards God.[1] That said, economics is a modern concept for which the ancient Egyptians, Mesopotamians and the Hebrews had no term. This does not mean that issues surrounding production, distribution, exchange, and greed were born with the industrial revolution.

The Bible mentions food and drink, hunger and thirst, feasting and fasting, peace and war, rain and drought, barrenness and fertility. More

---

1 On the influence of Aramaic using the same word for sin and debt, see Anderson (2009, 27).

than any other part of the Hebrew Bible, the legal core of Deuteronomy is replete with references to economic practices: sale of carrion, tithes, silver, debt-cancellation, labor and salaries, interest, pledges, gifts, slavery, self-indenture, marriage, landmarks, transport, war spoils, inheritance, lost property, harvest, gleanings and weights. Despite the lack of quantitative data necessary for economic analysis, students of Deuteronomy are confronted with economic issues they might be ill-equipped to tackle. This chapter supplies a basic toolbox to read the most economically minded section of the Bible, starting with an outline of what "economics" is.

1. Economy and Welfare

Simply defined, economics is the branch of knowledge that covers the production, consumption and transfer of wealth. A country, state or region's economy is the result of the choices its inhabitants make to maximize their welfare under the constraints in which they live. Welfare avoids the notion of "profit" and broadens the domain of economics to a wide range of human behavior, including non-market behavior. This approach is as relevant to the modern and post-modern world as it was to ancient Mesopotamia and Israel. According to 1992 Nobel Prize laureate for economics Gary Becker (1930–2014), human preferences are fairly similar over time and across social backgrounds and cultures. Whether twenty-first-century northern Americans or second millennium BCE Babylonians, the decisions ordinary humans take are guided by a desire to maximize welfare as they conceive it (Becker 1976). These decisions involve most aspects of life (health, prestige, pleasure...), aspects that do not bear a stable relation to market goods and services. For this reason, the principle of welfare maximization applies to most if not all cultures, ages and economic actors. Whether selfish, altruistic, loyal, spiteful or masochistic, rational or irrational, humans aim at maximizing welfare *as they conceive it*. It is how they conceive welfare that is socially conditioned and varies according to times and cultures. Hence, Deuteronomy's laws provide glimpses on how their authors conceived welfare. They drew up guidelines on how to make the best choices to maximize welfare in an agrarian society, that is a society in which everyone or almost everyone produces most of the food it consumes. To grasp the implications of welfare maximization for Deuteronomy's laws, a number of misconceptions need to be cleared before delving further into the biblical text.

2. Common Misleading Assumptions

2.1 Marxist Referents

Deuteronomy tends to be interpreted today in moral terms in support of the reaction to the liberal economic model that triumphed after the bankruptcy of the Soviet Union. Now that Marxism is no longer seen as a threat, some of its categorizations are used in biblical exegesis (Boer 2015; Ro 2018) to denounce "capitalism", a fuzzy concept to designate market economies (Welborn 2017; Simkins 2020) though what is really at stake is the Neo-liberal economic model characterized by minimal state intervention and free market. This model relies on the laws of offer and demand to regulate the economy and began to be implemented during the tenures of Margaret Thatcher in the UK and Ronald Reagan in the USA, becoming dominant following the fall of the USSR.

In the 1850s, Karl Marx had crafted a controversial Asiatic Mode of Production to draw attention to the importance of ownership of the means of production (mostly land) in Ancient Near Eastern economies. Marx's followers underlined the dichotomy between domestic and palatial means of production. The domestic economy where land is owned in common by the members of the village commune was supposedly subordinated to the palatial economy operated by large temples and palace households that relied much on slave labor (Van de Mieroop 1999, 112–113). In the domestic sector farmers lived at subsistence level, any surplus being collected by the palatial sector.

Today, our understanding of the economies of ancient Mesopotamia, Egypt and the Levant has moved in leaps and bounds thanks to the processing of primary sources unearthed by archaeologists. As a result, the Asiatic Mode of Production has lost much relevance for the study of the economy of Babylonia in first millennium BCE (Jursa 2010, 18). Marxian referents nevertheless enjoy a certain popularity among biblical scholars who have not been trained to navigate the major differences between the ancient economies and the world they are accustomed to. Moreover, the denunciation of capitalism resonates with caricatural portrayals of the rich in biblical prophetic literature, i.e. the rich oppressing the poor to wallow in luxury (Amos 4:1), which provides a high moral ground for denunciations of current economic practices when the use of Marxist referents is less risky than was the case in the days of US Senator McCarthy (1908–1957). Nevertheless, a grasp of the fundamentals of the economic realities in which the biblical texts were produced and transmitted is a prerequisite for any meaningful application of biblical principles to the current situation.

2.2 The False Weights of Merchants

Ezekiel's dirge over Tyre and its leading role in Mediterranean trade (Ezek 27) and prophetic texts such as Amos 8:4–8; Hos 12:7 and Mic 6:10–13 tend to be read as clues to the inherently dishonest nature of trade. These violent critiques certainly echo the self-perception of producers across the world and across the millennia. Farmers view themselves as the victims of the merchants who buy their surpluses. When haggling, any seller declares loud and clear to the potential buyer – and to all within earshot – that he is being fleeced by the merchant who can be nothing but a crook or he would not offer such a ridiculously low price for such prime quality products as he is being offered. Hence, the prophetic denigrations of traders are faithful sound boxes of the opinion of farmers, but they purposefully ignore the point of view of the merchant and thus cannot reflect the realities of trade.

In fact, no trade can flourish on the basis of fleecing and even less by using false scales. The archives of an Assyrian trader recovered in the city of Ashur (Radner 2016) illustrate the basic principle of trade. Profits are generated by acquiring staples where they can be bought cheaply because they are abundant and then selling them at a higher price where they are in high enough demand. Between 651–614 BCE, Duri-Aššur and three partners (designated as brothers) employed four caravan leaders who drove donkeys upstream the Tigris River three times a year. The donkeys were loaded with expensive garments (hats, shoes) and textiles that served as packing material. On arrival, everything was sold, including the donkeys, to purchase expensive wine in the Jebel Sinjar. The wine was poured into skins and loaded on rafts floated down the Tigris for the return journey to Ashur where wine, skins and logs were in high demand (Radner 2017, 225). Without credit, Duri-Aššur and his partners could not have run such operations. To finance the purchase of textiles and donkeys, Duri-Aššur and his partners approached investors that were subsequently reimbursed from the proceeds from the sale of the wine, skins and logs in Ashur. The profits must have been significant enough to motivate the partners to repeat these operations over decades and their investors to continue financing them. Some investors contributed large sums, but most investments were modest ones, occasionally by women.

Were Duri-Aššur and his partners dishonest? Aquinas, as much as Marx, would not have thought so as long as the price at which Duri-Aššur sold his goods in Ashur reflected the value of the labor, costs and time invested in transporting them there (Lambert 2019). Moreover, the trade between Ashur and the mountainous regions upstream benefited all the parties involved: the herders who produced the wool and skins, the manufacturers of the fine textiles, the donkey breeders, the caravan leaders, the wine growers and the loggers as well as those who invested the funds needed to finance the caravans. The trade raised the price of staples where they were abundant by creating a demand that would have otherwise been inexistent, and delivered staples where they were in short supply. The use as weighted silver as a standard, much earlier than the invention of coinage, greatly facilitated exchange by providing a convenient measure of the value equivalent of different staples: at any given time, how much barley was a sheep or a slave of a given age worth.

Deuteronomy is immune from the prophetic denigrations of trade because the brother's "donkey fallen on the road" (Deut 22:4) is a likely reference to caravan trade. The donkey belongs not to a neighbor, as is the case in the NRSV, but to "your brother", the standard reference to an associate, i.e. someone who had invested some capital to finance the acquisition and transport of the goods on the fallen donkey, whether or not the associates had any family ties (Radner 2017, 225).[2] The mention of Edomite brothers (Deut 23:8) is a further clue that Deuteronomy's Israelites were involved with Edomite associates in a thriving trade that may eventually have caused envy and prophetic rantings against merchants.

2.3 Ethics Versus Economics

The exegesis of biblical texts dealing with economic matters requires overcoming the ingrained assumption that ethics and economics are irreconcilable. Though Deuteronomy is immune of prophetic denunciations of wealth, its laws tend to be read as pleas in favor of the poor, though not necessarily to improve their condition. Christoph Levin (2014, 71) identifies a late revision in the interest of the devout poor, a revision he ascribes to writers who did not wish to see poverty eradicated because, as is the case in the Psalms, poverty is "the mark of a religious group characterized by its special closeness to God" (Levin 2014, 59). Or Deuteronomic laws such as the release of outstanding debts (see below §3.7) are considered beyond the ability of humans to practice their "perfect selflessness; its fulfillment needs to await eschatological times" (Vogt 2008, 41). Deuteronomy would thus delineate an unattainable utopia, a subject discussed in ch. 11 of this volume.

In fact, the long tradition of Mesopotamian debt-release is now well-established. Certain types of debt were cancelled when a new king was enthroned and, later, in times of acute economic crises (Olivier 1997;

---

2   See also George (2019, 51) for Old Babylonian letters and the standard formula "If you are truly my brother" that often seem to indicate business associations rather or besides family ties.

Charpin 1990). There are important differences between Mesopotamian *mišarum* and *andarārum* edicts and the *šmiṭṭah* of Deut 15 though all of them deal with the release of certain debts, a prerequisite to any healthy credit system ancient and modern. The beneficiaries of the *šmiṭṭah* were primarily those for whom a seven-year credit cycle is relevant, hence those who are not poor by any means.

2.4 The Poor

The *šmiṭṭah* is hardly a benevolent attitude towards the poor. Subject to the *šmiṭṭah* release are loans with terms of up to seven full years, which excludes loans contracted by ordinary farmers (see below). The figure of the poor is a common trope in Deuteronomic studies. It reflects the natural tendency of scholars to opt unconsciously for the self-gratifying moral position of defender of the poor and ignore the crafty disposition of farming population that enables them to survive without waiting for alms for the wealthy.

The figure of the poor is thus good enough for theological readings but too fuzzy a category to understand the outworking of debt-release and of the Deuteronomic economy as a whole. More precise categories are a prerequisite. First of all, it is vital to note that there are no beggars in Deuteronomy, except in some manuscripts of the LXX that add a beggar (πτωχός) beside the immigrant, widow and orphan to whom the forgotten sheaf and the gleanings belong (Deut 24:19-20). The beggar represents the most acute level of poverty, the truly destitute who has lost everything, including the ability to earn his bread at the sweat of his brow, and who survives solely on alms. Such is the situation of the poor (רש) in Prov 28:27.

Deuteronomy ignores such levels of economic deprivation because its laws are meant to reduce poverty, though with an acute awareness that want can never be entirely eradicated (Deut 15:11). Deuteronomy uses two different words for reduced economic conditions. The word אביון in Deut 15:11 designates the state of need that is expected to remain in the land despite the release of debts at the end of the seventh year. Following the Greek rendering of אביון with cognates of the verb ἐπιδέω, the NRSV aptly renders this term as "needy", which does not imply the destitution of the beggar. The "opening of the hand" of verse 11 differs from that of verse 8 where it involves lending (עבט) rather than giving because the needy one is creditworthy. Hence, there is a fair chance that the borrower will be able to honor his debt. This is not the case in verse 11 that urges the addressee to open his hand again, this time to a "poor and needy neighbor" (NRSV) or more accurately "to your hard working brother and to your needy one" (לאחיך לעניך ולאבינך). This time no lending is called for and the new situation is marked by the introduction of the term עני. This term has a very broad semantic field, from "misery", "oppression", "subjection" to "insufficient property" (*HALOT* 2, 856–57).

The Alexandrian translators rendered עני as πένης. The primary meanings of πένης – from which the English "pain" is derived – are "toil" and "hard labor". In classical Greek, the πένης works hard for his living, he is a day-laborer (Liddell, Jones and Scott 1996, 359). The Greeks viewed physical labor as incompatible with political activities because a life of constant toil did not afford the laborer the leisure to perform the duties of a citizen (Coin-Longeray 2001). Manual workers were thus excluded from the citizenry of the city of Thebes and from the citizenry of Plato's ideal city (Aristotle, *Politics* II, 1278 a25).

The NRSV's rendering of the terms עני and πένης as "poor" in Deut 15:11 is too vague to be helpful. Despite the Greek aristocratic disdain for manual labor, the Alexandrian translators understood the beneficiaries of the second "opening of the hand" in verse 11 as a hard-working brother and someone in need, but not as a beggar in need of alms to survive to the morrow.

The notion of poverty is imported from the Psalms where the pair עני ואביון is found thirteen times to convey privileged access to divine favors.[3] Righteousness is equated with poverty, to the point that Matt 19:24 can claim that "it is easier for a camel to go through the eye of a needle than for a rich man to enter the kingdom of God". Small consolation for the poor for whom the ability to pass through the eye of a needle is not particularly beneficial or relevant. Using the Psalms to interpret Deut 15 is unhelpful. There are neither beggars nor destitute paupers in Deuteronomy. Yet, anyone familiar with Deuteronomic scholarship cannot help but retort, "but what about the *personae miserae*?"

2.5 *Personae Miserae*

In addition to the fuzziness of the image rendered by the term "poor", discussions of Deuteronomy are peppered with mentions of the *personae miserae*, a convenient Latin expression to designate the beneficiaries of triennial tithes (Deut 14:29): the Levite, the immigrant, the widow and the orphan. Yet, Deuteronomy *never* uses the terms עני or אביון in relation to a Levite, immigrant, widow or orphan. Logically, the so-called *personae miserae* are not poor and even less destitute (Lohfink 1991, 43).

---

[3] "Weak and needy" in Ps 35:10; and "poor and needy" in Ps 37:14; 40:17 par. 70:6; 74:21; 86:1; 109:16, 22. See Scheffler (2005).

Whether or not they are miserable is a matter of semantics, not of economics. *Personae miserae* is a misnomer that ought to be avoided, unless one infers with Harold Bennett (2003) that tithes cannot possibly cover the basic needs of immigrants, orphans and widows. To evaluate the validity of Bennett's claim, the actual ratio of beneficiaries of tithes against the number of tithe payers would be necessary.

The Levite is indeed deprived of the land lots (חלק) ascribed to the other Israelites (Deut 18:1). It is likely that the immigrant, widow and orphan are equally deprived of lots of communal land – the immigrant because he does not belong, the widow because land shares are inherited by males, and the orphan because he is not yet of age. Nevertheless, Deut 18:8 notes that the Levites have additional resources available to them from some obscure "paternal possessions" (לבד ממכריו על האבות) besides the food they are entitled to when they travel to the *maqom*, the place chosen for the joyful consumption of yearly tithes before YHWH (14:22–26). As for widows, they have gleaning rights (Deut 24:19–21), which does not imply that they are necessarily destitute. Some widows obtain loans by handing over pledges other than a cloak (Deut 24:17), which means that they are creditworthy. They might not be rich but, according to the text, they are not destitute either. They are not portrayed as miserable.

2.6 Trade Resilience

Karl Polanyi's notion of a marketless Mesopotamian society gradually gives way to a greater awareness of the role of trade in the ancient Near East, factors that had not been recognized because the activities of individual traders left few traces in the archaeological record compared to palaces and large temple institutions (Pirngruber 2021, 81). The same bias exists for Egypt, though the existence of a world of itinerant traders, private merchants, mobile populations, women involved in various types of business, independent craftsmen, rural entrepreneurs and cottage industries, is beginning to come under scrutiny. The importance of these non-institutional economic actors is underlined by the fact that they flourished especially when central authority collapsed (Moreno García 2021, 221).

The main pitfalls now flagged, the credit market delineated in Deuteronomy can now be considered in more detail.

3. How the Credit Market Works

3.1 Basics

At the risk of stating the obvious, it is necessary to set out a few basic facts. A loan is a transaction in which a lender allows a borrower to use some property or commodity – such as seeds, food, tools, labor or silver – for a set period, after which it must be returned to its original owner. Lending must not be confused with risk or venture capital, which is neither reimbursable nor interest-bearing. Participants in venture capital projects take the risk of financing a project, such as a distant maritime trading venture, and, in the event of it being successful, reward themselves by having a share in the profits. If the project fails, they lose part or all of their investment.

Lending includes the notion of credit, which is a specific term that applies to one of the most common forms of finance and is contractual, whether formally agreed to orally or in writing. The most current form of credit is the delay granted by a seller to a buyer to pay for goods or services delivered. In most cases, credit is short-term, i.e. the buyer has to pay his creditor within a day, a week, a month or up to a year. It enables the seller to make an early sale and the buyer to acquire goods or services prior to having the means to pay for them. Credit acts as a temporary buffer: the "buy now, pay later" principle, thanks to which both parties achieve their objectives. The seller is content: a sale has been made; the buyer is happy; goods or services have been acquired without having to pay for them on the spot. Of course, longer-term credit facilities can be negotiated for transactions or projects that require finance over a number of years. They are not to be confused with revolving credit, which is simply the renewal of short-term credit terms and conditions, typically found in the deals between merchants and growers that are characterized by seasonal needs.

Credit, from the Latin *credere*: to believe, is a theological concept that designates a seller or lender's faith – hence the term "creditor" – in the capacity of a buyer to pay for goods and services or a borrower to reimburse a loan.

All economies are based on credit, the elusive belief of a creditor in the creditworthiness of a debtor (from the Latin *debere*: to owe) who lacks the means to pay for goods or services immediately but who can be trusted to pay later.

Loan and credit instruments (legal documents setting out the contractual relationship between the parties) come in a variety of forms ranging from a simple oral understanding between two persons to complex mechanisms involving several parties.

Debt is simply (a) what a buyer owes a seller who has extended credit or (b) what a borrower owes a lender who has granted a loan. Among the terms of credit or the conditions of a loan, the most important aspects are: the nature of the loan or commodity (seeds, silver, etc.); the amount or quantity (the principal or goods) lent to the buyer or borrower; the duration of the loan or credit (see next paragraph); the interest rate (see §3.2 below); the guarantees offered in case of default (see §3.4 and §3.5 below) and the penalties for late payment of interest or default on the repayment of the principal.

Loans, including credit, have a set duration, i.e. the time between the date of transfer of the money or commodities (the principal or goods) to the buyer or borrower and the date at which the principal or goods must be returned or repaid to the seller or lender (the creditor). All credit, whatever its form, falls necessarily into one of two categories: short-term, i.e. of a duration of less than one year; and medium- to long-term, i.e. of a duration of more than one year. The distinction is of critical importance. Short-term credit is used chiefly to finance locally based agricultural and trading transactions between parties that, more often than not, have close connections and deal on a recurrent basis. Medium- to long-term credit serves mainly to finance longer-distance trade ventures, typically maritime ventures, and projects that require several years to complete, such as infrastructure, construction and land development, processing plants, etc. Hence, short-term credit tends to be used for smaller financing requirements while longer-term credit can reach vast proportions.

Though Deuteronomic scholarship is replete with mentions of loans granted to "the poor" (Levin 2014, 57), it must be stressed that loans are neither charity nor alms and that it makes no economic sense whatsoever to grant loans or extend credit to anyone unlikely to be in a position to reimburse their lender or supplier. For this reason, the poor receive alms, i.e. gifts, with no expectations of direct returns, which does not exclude indirect returns (see §3.8 below). Therefore, seeking a loan is neither an indicator of poverty nor the first step towards destitution. On the contrary, obtaining a loan or credit is the proof that the recipient is not destitute. The need for a loan indicates a lack of liquidity, i.e. the lack of immediately available funds, but it is also a mark of creditworthiness, in other words the ability to present convincing evidence of being able to honor a debt in time and in full, including interest where relevant.

3.2 Interests and Usury

To modern eyes, the standard interest rates of 20 percent on silver and 50 percent on grain practiced in the ancient Near East seem like outright usury. Yet, they are fair for several reasons. First, they are rates per annum, which is misleading because most loans were contracted for a number of weeks or months, rarely more than twelve months.[4] Borrowing a sack of grain at a rate of 50 percent means that a year later the borrower must return a sack and-a-half. The ordinary farmer, however, borrowed grain over four to five months, between sowing (November–December) and harvesting (April–May). He thus paid back at most a sack and-a-quarter at harvest time when his stores were at their fullest whatever the yield of that particular year. That extra quarter of a sack was grain he did not have to store, and thus did not risk being spoiled by mice, pests or mold. In the event of a poor harvest, the farmer fed his family with whatever was at hand before borrowing seeds in November and whatever else needed to tide his household over till March when unripe grain could already be eaten rather than having to wait another month for the harvest (Josh 5:11), hence reducing the duration of loans and the amount paid back as interest.

The merchant who provides grain at the rate of 50 percent might still appear to be a loan shark to modern western eyes unaccustomed to microcredit. Despite high "usurious" interest rates, the Nobel prize for economy was awarded to the founder of the Grameen Bank in 2006 because micro-finance is recognized by development agencies as an effective way of empowering small and micro-enterprises and traders (Sider 1997, 120). High interest rates are fair because they reflect the high transaction costs involved in micro-credit operations. It is less costly, less risky and usually more profitable to lend a million to a single rich borrower over 20 years than lending small sums over a number of months to numerous borrowers of modest means.

The concept of usury and its interpretation are based on a flawed understanding of Aristotle's notion of the sterility of money (Wood 2002). As a means of exchange, money was considered unnatural because it only exists by law, not in nature. Charging interest on money or commodities is condemned as "unnatural". Since money cannot be used directly as raw material or to produce goods and is employed only to facilitate the exchange of goods and services, it was said to be "sterile" because it

---

[4] Tenors (the time between the disbursement of the loan and its maturity; see the glossary at the end of this chapter for such technical terms) in numbers of months presented specific issues when an intercalary month was added and interests ran over thirteen instead of twelve months. See Csabai 2020.

cannot of itself increase wealth, as would a herd of cattle, a wheat field or a mill. Therefore the charging of interest, which Aristotle incorrectly thought to imply a direct productivity of money, was strongly condemned as contrary to nature. Aristotle considered that since money was sterile, it should be limited to settling purchase and sales transactions and not used for granting loans; "money cannot produce offspring" (Lambert 2019). Money is fungible, meaning that it is there to be spent and exchanged for anything considered to have a corresponding value, such as food, goods, services or even another currency. Likewise, commodities are fungible to the extent they can be bartered, in other words exchanged or traded for other commodities. It could be established, say, that a kilo of tomatoes is worth two kilos of potatoes or that an hour's work in the field is worth a measure of barley. Following on that concept, a loan has no trading value: the lender, having immobilized his capital for the duration of the loan, cannot spend it until it is repaid.

All this was nonsense in reality; a lender could charge interest on his loaned-out capital, which then becomes "interest-bearing" if not exactly "child-bearing" but certainly not sterile. The higher the interest rate, the greater the return on investment – or, one might say, the fecundity of the lender's capital. But what really bothered moralizing theologians was the thought that a loan should ceaselessly produce further money throughout its duration, even on the Lord's days, without the lender having to lift a finger, let alone produce food by the "sweat of his brow".

As a rule of thumb, interest rates increase in proportion to the social distance between lender and borrower and in inverse proportion to the size of the loan. In embedded societies as was the case in the ancient Near East, interest rates varied greatly and were optional. It can be ascertained that interest-free commercial loans denote a close relationship of trust between parties who would have known each other well enough and done plenty of deals together over the years. In such cases, transactional costs would have been minimal and interest would have been waived, perhaps in favor of other services rendered by the borrower.

A commercial contract might stipulate that in lieu of interest some other service is to be rendered. The following example of such a contract, in the form of a promissory note (a promise to pay), is from a Babylonian clay tablet and serves to illustrate the case in point (Cornell University Studies in Assyriology and Sumerology #8 in Pearce and Wunsch 2014, 110).

On the 18th of month IV (June–July) 551 BCE, shortly after the barley harvest, a man named Rapā obtains an interest-free loan of 1100 liters of good-quality dates and 900 liters of barley from a lender named Tūb-Yāma. Rapā promises to reimburse, first, the 1100 liters of dates to his creditor, Tūb-Yāma, three months later (i.e. in September–October) prior to the new date harvest and, next, the 900 liters of barley in the following month, i.e. month VIII (October–November).[5] Rapā's wife guarantees the deliveries (i.e. the repayment of both commodities to Tūb-Yāma), probably because the risks are high since the borrower, Rapā, intends most likely to speculate on the dates' seasonal price fluctuation. Rapā is possibly collecting barley from a number of peasants as tax or in repayment of loans. He will deliver to his creditor 900 liters from the barley he has collected just when the price of barley is at its peak at the start of the sowing season. It is quite certain that the lender, Tūb-Yāma, has no intention of consuming the barley, which is sufficient to feed four adults for a year, but plans either to lend the barley on to his peasant farmers or to deliver it to a local temple or even use it to pay his taxes to the governor. Tūb-Yāma must have counted on Rapā, a fellow Judean, to supply him with barley collected as taxes or acquired from other sources.

The fact that the loans are interest-free can be explained in two ways: either the parties have family or business ties and want to remain on good terms, or Rapā is rendering Tūb-Yāma, his creditor and supplier, other goods or services, omitted in the contract. The specification that the dates are to be of "good quality" may indicate that dates of varying grades, origin or age are traded on the markets.

What, in this contract, compensates for the absence of interest? The guarantee offered by Rapā's wife might indicate that she has means of her own and that she accepts to secure her husband's transaction because he does not have direct access to her personal fortune. The contract does not specify the terms of the guarantee. Would silver or goods have been held in escrow by a third party? Or would one or other of the witnesses named in the promissory note act as arbitrator if, on default of repayment by the due date, the lender called the guarantee?

The backing Rapā receives from his wife implies that, in case of default, she would be obliged to use funds from her own dowry to honor her husband's debt.[6] But should Rapā have been entertaining thoughts of repudiating his wife, he would find himself having to pay her back her dowry, which has all gone on settling his debt to his creditor – a perilous

---

5   For comparison purposes, an adult needed an estimated 250 kilos of barley a year to survive. During the Ur III period, institutional workers received a monthly ration of 60 liters of barley for a man and 30 liters for a woman (Waetzoldt 1987, 121–22).

6   Despite inevitable variations, the dowry is basically the capital a daughter received from her father upon marriage, whereas sons had to wait for their father's death to inherit their share of the paternal estate. The dowry was often used by the husband though the wife retained full ownership of it. The husband had to hand it back to his wife when he repudiated her or transmit it to her legitimate heirs if she died before her husband (Stol 2016, 134–45).

state of affairs. Did Rapā's wife have a vested interest in guaranteeing her husband's transaction? We shall never know.

As can be seen from the above-mentioned transaction, commercial loans need not be interest-bearing. Even so, there are easy ways in which to conceal interest. How? Deut 23:20–21 designates interests as *neshek* ("biting" נשך) and ignores *tarbit* (תרבית), the other designation for interest, which can be understood as an additional payment (Lev 25:36). Hence, *neshek* is a "bite" of the principal, i.e. a portion that is excised from the principal by the lender at the time of the transfer of the silver or commodities to the borrower, though this deduction is omitted in the promissory note (Gamoran 1971, 132). Thus, if "A" agrees to lend "B" 100 but "A" only hands over 90 to "B" who is committed to pay "A" back 100, the interest, though invisible, amounts in reality to 11.11 percent (and not 10 percent, because the borrower "B" has only had the use of 90 percent of the loan). This practice is well-attested to as a means of circumventing the ban on interest-bearing loans in cultures that prohibit interest. Another way round the ban is for the borrower to offer the lender a gift or do him a favor at the time of the transaction, knowing the lender tacitly expects this.

Yet another form of avoidance is for a "borrower" to sell property to a "lender" and then rent or lease it back from the "lender". At the end of an agreed period, the "borrower" repurchases the property at the price at which it was first sold. In actual fact the sale price of the property corresponds to a loan, the rental corresponds to the interest on the loan and the property serves as a pledge which is forfeited if the "borrower" fails to redeem it on the agreed repurchase date because the borrower's venture has failed.

This method is attested in antiquity as much as in recent centuries. For example, in the nineteenth century CE Zanzibar ivory traders needed to finance their expeditions to the Great Lakes region through what is now Tanzania. When lacking adequate funds of his own to pay the cost of porters, guards, safe passage dues and elephant tusks, a trader would seek additional funds from a financing house in Zanzibar. Being debarred by Islamic law from making interest-bearing loans, the financing institution would purchase the trader's house, for instance, and lease it back to him for a set rental to enable his family to continue living there while he went on his expedition to gather supplies of ivory. When back with his haul of ivory, the trader would repurchase his house with the proceeds of the sale of the ivory (McDow 2018, 48–55).

A similar practice existed in ancient Greece. An illustration of this is the recorded case of a phratry in 300 BCE that let out a plot of land for a period of ten years to a tenant at an annual rent of 600 drachmas with the option for the tenant to acquire the plot at the price of 5000 drachmas at any time he chose before the term of the lease.

What was quite likely, but left unsaid, was that the tenant was the original owner of the land but, needing 5000 drachmas in funds, sold his land to the phratry who leased it back to him for 600 drachmas a year with the option to repurchase it at any time at the same price at which he sold it to them. Should the tenant not repurchase his property before the term of the lease, it would be forfeited to the phratry.

The annual rental of 600 drachmas corresponds to 1 percent a month, i.e. 12 percent a year. If the tenant does not repurchase the land, he will have paid out 6000 drachmas in rent with no longer the option to repurchase his property. His choice lies between retrieving his land prior to termination of the ten-year lease or investing the proceeds he received initially from the sale of the land in a more profitable venture or in another property of greater potential value.

There is always the possibility that the tenant was never in fact the owner of the land and that he merely raised a loan from the phratry who, rather than charge him interest, leased out one of their plots of land to him at a rent that was equivalent to the interest they might have charged had they been permitted by law to do so. The option to purchase the land was only an exit ploy. But this scheme does not take into account the requirement the phratry would surely have had for some form of surety for their loan. No such guarantee is recorded, however, so the first assumption seems the more likely of the two.

In other cases, the interest started accruing once the tenor of the loan was reached. It was a penalty for the delay and a rent paid on the capital that was not restituted in time. In this way the motivation of the creditor to press for reimbursement was reduced and the borrower might sometimes have found it more profitable to pay interest on the loan than to release capital from other more profitable operations.

While interest-free loans may be seen as benevolence, their main consequence was to transform lenders into associates, as is still the case today in Islamic finance. Unable to compensate for the immobilization of funds lent out without charging interest, financiers would draw revenues instead from their share in any profit generated by the activity financed by their loan. Contrary to a banker who draws revenues by lending at a higher interest rate than that which he pays his depositors, providers of interest-free loans scrutinize the projects and transactions they finance more closely because they share with the borrowers the risks and consequent losses or profits of their venture.

3.3 Seasonal Price Fluctuations

Another factor to take into account is that the importance of interest drawn from loans is secondary to the potential profit made from seasonal price fluctuations. Though farmers reimbursed loans of grain with grain to escape price fluctuations, merchants relied on seasonal price fluctuations and price differentials between staples. An example of this is found in a Neo-Babylonian joint venture commercial contract, known as a *ḫarrānu*, written on a clay tablet (Cornell University Studies in Assyriology and Sumerology #40 in Pearce and Wunsch 2014, 162–63) dated 10 IX 5 (10th of November–December in the fifth regnal year of Darius, i.e. 517 BCE).

The two partners in the venture are a silent partner named Aḫīqam who agrees to provide a consignment of 2160 liters of dates to an acting partner named Iššûa whose job it is to invest the dates as wisely as he can by lending them to farmers who will pay him back in barley after the barley harvest.

Iššûa has six months in which to finalize all his transactions after which he is committed to pay Aḫīqam one-half of silver for the dates he received from him plus 50 percent of the profits he has made from lending the dates to farmers and perhaps also to merchants and dealers like himself.

The important points to note here are that: (a) the dates Aḫīqam advanced Iššûa were vastly overvalued: Aḫīqam priced them at one-half mina of silver when in fact their average market value was around half that amount; (b) Iššûa does not seem to object to the arrangement because he obviously has no funds of his own but he is a very smart dealer who knows precisely to whom he can most profitably lend his funds (remembering that dates were a standard form of legal tender in those times because, like grain or oil, they had a relatively long shelf-life); and (c) the farmers who borrowed dates from Iššûa were required to repay him in barley immediately after the harvest, when date prices were highest and barley prices lowest, hence securing Iššûa large amounts of barley to be lent back at sowing time.

The venture is a win-win situation for all stakeholders, but why? Let us take a look at each in turn: Aḫīqam, the silent partner, has struck a deal with Iššûa in which he, Aḫīqam, is safe in the knowledge that, by valuing the dates he provided Iššûa at something like twice their market price, he should be making a return on his investment of around 100 percent at least over six months, even in the unlikely event Iššûa were to fail to make a profit in his dealing with the farmers and other potential clients. Aḫīqam hopes to make an even greater return on his investment, however, because if Iššûa does make a profit, he will receive a 50 percent share of it. Aḫiqam agreed to the joint venture with Iššûa because he knows Iššûa's reputation in the marketplace is solid and he is confident in Iššûa's abilities, honesty and expert market knowledge. Proof of this is the fact that Aḫiqam requires no guarantees from Iššûa. They would quite likely have worked together in the past entirely to Aḫiqam's satisfaction.

Iššûa, the acting partner, has no such assurances. He probably has little or no capital of his own, which is why he has to rely on a rich investor, even if the terms seem unequal. But he knows his market and the market would certainly know him as the highly reputable agent of Aḫiqam, the rich and probably powerful merchant. Based on his past experience, Iššûa would feel confident that he can turn a profit. And the way he does so is based essentially on the strong market price fluctuations of commodities such as barley. By lending or selling dates in return for future deliveries of barley at harvest time, when the price of barley is at its lowest (because supply outstrips demand at that time of the year), Iššûa can expect to receive, in repayment (with interest) of his loans of dates, larger quantities of barley than at any other time of the year. He can also count on commissions and fees from other market dealers. All he need do is then wait until the rising market demand for barley forces prices up again, at which time he will start selling his stocks of barley in exchange for silver. As a rough guide, if we assume the market value of Iššûa's initial stock of dates is 100 and that, by lending it at interest he obtains in return barley that is worth 400 by the time he exchanges it a few months later for silver, he will have made a profit of 300. Of that 300, he will return 200 to Aḫiqam, who had valued the dates at twice their market price, and share the remaining 100 with Aḫiqam, leaving a net profit of 50 for himself and 150 for Aḫiqam. Aḫiqam takes the lion's share but that is his reward for having taken the greater risk. Iššûa's reward is the trust Aḫiqam put in him, which enabled him to earn a living without having had to risk any of his own capital and, moreover, entertain hopes of working in partnership with Aḫiqam again in the future.

The farmers who approach Iššûa for a loan of dates do so because they need working capital or bridging finance prior to the barley harvest to pay such things as food, tools for the oncoming harvest, labor, the settlement of outstanding debts, a daughter's dowry, etc. Once the crops have been harvested, they are in a position to repay their debts to Iššûa. The high rate of interest little affects them because the period is relatively short. Had they not had access to funds, they might have found themselves in awkward if not tragic situations. Iššûa represents a lifeline to them at a cost that they can readily bear if the future harvest yields are satisfactory.

One last point is worth mentioning concerning the notion of the ḫarrānu described as a commercial venture set up between partners. By modern standards, the structure of the venture and the relationship between these so-called partners might seem more like an arm's length arrangement between a rich man and an enterprising dealer with no fortune of his own. One might almost say that the relationship between them looks rather like that of a trusting master and a faithful but unpaid retainer – or possibly even an enfranchised slave – who must earn his living by his wits. The *ḫarrānu* has no legal status protecting the sole investor in the event of bankruptcy. It is a very short-lived, private arrangement, ill-balanced and grounded entirely in socially driven mutual trust. But it was in ancient times a popular way of doing business and obviously very well suited to the social and economic needs of its day. We need, however, to be wary of attempting to compare it too closely to financial partnerships or institutions as we know them in today's business world.

3.4 Risk Reduction and Collaterals

Caravans may be attacked, donkeys can break a leg or fall sick. Products may not be bought and sold at the expected price. The peasant never knows in advance how much sown grain will yield. As much as trade and agriculture, finance involves risks. There are no such things as investments with guaranteed high returns. Potential profits are proportional to the risk involved. Profits generated by farming are smaller than those made in long distance trade and finance, but the risks involved in dry grain farming are as small as the investment in labor and seeds it requires.

Nevertheless, farmers as much as traders and investors hedge their bets in different ways. The basic rule is the diversification of assets – not putting all one's eggs in the same basket – and growing different plants in separate locations in addition to raising animals. The merchant reduces his risks by taking collateral such as the pledges (עבט) mentioned in Deut 24:6–13. This time, the NRSV correctly renders the borrower as "your neighbor" (רע). As a modern banker who secures loans by mortgaging assets he distrains in case of default, Deuteronomy's addressee secures the loans he grants to his neighbors with collaterals. The creditor should wait outside the house of the borrower to receive the pledge (Deut 24:10–11). As nothing in the text suggests that the transfer of the pledge occurs following default, in most cases handing over a pledge would be part of antichretic arrangements.

3.5 Possessory Pledges: Antichresis

Contrary to pledges seized from a defaulter when the tenor of the loan was reached, many loans in the ancient Near East were reimbursed by transferring the usufruct of the pledge to the creditor during the tenor of the loan (Zaccagnini 2001, 223–29). This is usually the situation erroneously referred to as debt slavery. Antichresis is the proper economic term. The person involved is no slave. It is the labor not the person that the borrower supplies to his creditor in order to reimburse the loan. The loan is by definition fully paid back at the maturity of the loan, when the pledge returns to its family or its master if it was a slave who was provided. The return is no manumission, however. The personal status of the pledge was not altered. The creditor enjoyed the use of the pledge, not its ownership. The same applies to other assets – animal, field or house – supplied by the borrower to reimburse a loan.

The Hebrew or Hebrewess mentioned in Deut 15:12 are part of an intricate antichretic arrangement between brothers (Rossi and Guillaume 2018). Their release in the seventh year is not the result of manumission – contrary to the NRSV's heading for these verses – but the consequence of the maturity of the antichretic loan that their labor contributed to reimburse. Pledges are not freed because they were slaves, but because they have contributed all the labor that had been agreed upon to cover the loan in question. Were the pledges supplied slaves, they remained slaves after returning to the service of their master.

3.6 Agricultural Debt as Insurance

Farmers borrow over a number of months to tide them until the next harvest. Even the commercial loans recorded in the so-called documents of Judean exiles, some of them involving over fifty shekels of silver or several tons of barley and dates, have terms that hardly ever exceed 12 months (Pearce and Wunsch 2014). Contrary to commercial loans, creditors did not press for the reimbursement of agricultural loans granted to ordinary farmers because it secured them privileged access to surpluses when there were any. Nor were farmers in a hurry to extinguish their debts because their creditor had to keep them alive when the harvest failed (Guillaume 2010). Hence, agricultural debt created a lien with a trader and whatever interest paid to service the loan was an insurance premium against famine. This point needs to be underlined because it is counterintuitive. Boer (2015, 156) sums up the view among biblical scholars on loans prevailing as the first step in a spiral of destitution.
Lenders are conceived as loan sharks who lend to the poor in the hope of impounding the borrower's assets one by one until the borrower has nothing left than his own person to be seized by the loan shark. The flaw in such reasoning becomes obvious when one considers the next step after the purported loan shark has swallowed the defaulter's person, his household, animals and land.

What would the loan shark do with the slaves he acquired by impounding the defaulter? The fastest way to recoup losses would be to sell these slaves, if a demand for slaves existed. But what about the land? In the ancient world, land was not a commodity. Land had no value in itself because it was over-plentiful. What gave value to land was whatever had been invested in it to give it value: buildings, terraces, orchards, irrigation, or simply the heavy labor involved in clearing stones and bushes to prepare it for dry cultivation. Low demography, abundance of land and absence of machinery combined to make human and beast-power far more valuable than land. Additional land would be of little use for the purported loan shark without the hands to work it. Hence, his best option is to leave his debt slaves to work the land that was theirs and is now his. Less obvious but more damning, is that ancient slaves as much as modern employees require far more supervision than self-employed entrepreneurs and peasants working their own plots. This is the lesson from the parable of the manager in Luke 16: the basic rule is that estate owners often find it more profitable to save on supervision by accepting a fixed amount in rent from a tenant farmer rather than a proportion of the yield from a sharecropper. The loss of greater returns in years of bountiful harvest was further compensated by sharing the risk involved in agricultural production with the tenants who shouldered the losses in years of poor harvest (Haque 1977; Foxhall 2001).

The conclusion is that the scenario of loan sharks who lend in the hope of seizing borrowers' assets fails to grasp the essential reciprocity that ties lenders and borrowers in mutual dependence. Such reciprocity is no humanistic stance and neither side readily acknowledges the reciprocity because it is part and parcel of the tough bargaining process involved. The loan shark is a faithful reflection of the demonization of traders and lenders in prophetic literature, but it does not stand the test of economic reality.

In the real world, agricultural debt provided security thanks to intricate networks of interdependence. Farmers sought to remain in debt with a merchant. This basic principle is counterintuitive and the failure to grasp it is the source of much misunderstanding. The example of the British banks established in Mandate Palestine provides a fitting illustration of the function of agricultural debt. To save farmers from the grip of the merchants who supplied them with grain at high interest rates, the Mandate authorities opened banks that offered farmers loans at much lower interest rates than the merchants'. Yet, the farmers shunned those loans because they knew that in case of default the banks would seize the collateral. On the contrary, after a bad harvest the merchants supplied them with grain and seeds (Nadan 2005).

While loans keep the borrower in bondage, debt in the form of outstanding loans generates a degree of solidarity between borrowers and lenders. This is the grain of truth in the difference Boer (2015, 156–58) establishes between debt and credit. Keen as he is to denounce merchants as loan sharks, Boer attributes interest-bearing loans to extractive regimes, while interest-free loans granted within the community to allocate and reallocate goods would be the mark of subsistence regimes. In fact, what distinguishes the two is neither the interest rates nor the origins of the funds.

The survival of local communities depends on their ability to find external sources of grain in times of dearth because, apart from minimal differences, all the members of a farming community experience dearth and overabundance at the same time. As Boer (2015, 156) correctly notes, merchants were the main providers of loans thanks to their ready access to silver and foodstuffs. The notion of a local market in which locals barter their goods has minimal economic validity because whenever a given household has surplus grain, fruit, wool or meat to sell, that surplus has no value on a local market that is flooded by the same surpluses offered by their neighbors. Unless the local community has the means to transport its surplus where it might yield substantial returns, the surplus of isolated communities has no market value. Unless some external agency sets up a cooperative to store surpluses safely and sell them later when prices are higher, it is the reviled merchant who can provide the expertise and the networks needed to shift grain and other staples from where they are in excess towards where they are in high demand, in order to make a profit after transport costs, tolls, duties, bribes and other related costs have been covered. This is the "buying cheap and selling dear" principle criticized by Marx as mere circulation of commodities that creates no value because the seller's gain is supposedly the buyer's loss. A society without commerce, without money or based solely on local trade would experience recurrent spells of hunger and even famine from which the European continent managed to rid itself only two centuries ago.

3.7 Release of Commercial Debts

Contrary to the arrears of ordinary farmers for whom they represented an insurance premium, commercial loans could not be left running indefinitely. As the 2008 subprime crisis revealed, the upper level of the credit market is at risk if it is not purged at regular intervals. Loans between associates (brothers) involve larger sums and greater risk than agricultural credit, though they are interest-free (Deut 23:20). Hence the reluctance to lend to a needy brother when the date of the release was drawing close (Deut 15:9).

In Deut 15, the brother who seeks a loan is not living from hand to mouth. Like the women and men who provided funds to Duri-Aššur (see above §2.2), he is looking for some capital to invest in ventures that will hopefully generate greater profit than agricultural loans, but at greater risk. Therefore, the section on the šmiṭṭah release (Deut 15:1–6) closes with the recognition that all is not rosy in the best of worlds. All needs are indeed taken care of within the brotherhood, first in the form of loans and, if necessary, as the release of outstanding debts. Debt releases preserve a healthy credit market. The šmiṭṭah is a protective measure as much for the defaulter as for those involved on the credit market. Altruism is secondary and not as significant as it seems because the defaulter's position once his slate has been cleaned has changed. He is unlikely to benefit from the same advantageous conditions that he got before the release because he represents a higher risk once his debts towards his brothers were remitted after he suffered major losses due to miscalculation or to a stroke of bad luck. Having his slate cleared helps, but it does not restore his fortunes overnight. He needs fresh capital to start again, but his creditworthiness is down and the brothers who remitted his debts are in no hurry to help, at least not during the current seven-year cycle of credit.

A Babylonian example illustrates the practical consequences of debt releases. Around 1542 BCE, King Shamsu-iluna (Sun-God-is-Our-God), the son of Hammurabi, issues in the eighth year of his reign a decree cancelling debt. It is in this context that a certain Pû-ilî, a musician by trade, brings a case against a man who had let out his field in exchange for a loan of two shekels of silver:

> ... Pû-ilî the musician has testified before me in these terms: "I pledged my field [to him] and he lent me two shekels of silver. He has gathered and taken away the grain that was in the field but he has not given me back the yield from my field". This is how he has testified before me. As you know, according to the royal order, he who caused [a loan] to be repaid and has taken the yield must return them... (adapted from Charpin 2000, 196)

In other words, what Pû-ilî is complaining about is that the person who granted him a loan and who held his field as a pledge took away the entire crop instead of giving it to him. The field was pledged as collateral for the loan but the crop it yielded was the borrower's and not the lender's.

According to article 49 of the Laws of Hammurabi, this is what should have taken place:

> If a man has taken silver from a merchant and has given to the merchant a field suitable for grain or sesame, and has told him, 'Cultivate the field, harvest the grain or sesame which is produced, and take it away,' then assuming that the cultivator has produced some grain or sesame from the field, it is the owner of the field who should collect whatever grain or sesame may have been produced in the field, and he shall give the merchant grain for the silver which he received from him, as well as the interest on it, as well as for the effort of cultivating it. (Richardson 2000, 59)

In normal circumstances, Pû-ilî would have had to reimburse his debt, including interest, together with the costs incurred by the merchant lender in cultivating the land, or at least the wages of the plowman, as the land was ready for sowing (though in this particular case it would seem the merchant lender was liable for the cost of the seed). The owner of a pledged field was normally entitled to its crops, which would have meant that it was for Pû-ilî to incur all harvesting costs and subsequently to service the loan with the proceeds from the sale of the crops. But here we have a clear case of an antichretic loan where the merchant lender farms the pledged field for himself and recovers the loan he has granted Pû-ilî through the proceeds from the sale of the crops. But what if the yield were insufficient to service the loan? The previous article (§48) of Hammurabi's laws states that, in the event of force majeure, interest for that year is waived.

In the case of Pû-ilî, the problem lies in the fact that the king proclaimed a debt-cancellation edict, alluded to as a "royal order" in the text. According to the edict, confirmed from other sources, outstanding debts were cancelled and, in the event a merchant lender had nevertheless compelled a borrower to pay back a debt, that lender was obliged to give his debtor back the goods he had extorted from him. That is why our musician was claiming the merchant owed him the crop from the field he had pledged as security for the loan. The edict had cancelled his debt, therefore he owed the merchant lender nothing, other perhaps than expenses the merchant had incurred, such as the seed he had planted. The merchant lender, however, must have considered that by seizing the crop he was compensating for his losses as a result of the edict. Indeed, contrary to the edict proclaimed eight years earlier in celebration of the king's accession to the throne, this second debt-cancellation edict was proclaimed probably as a result of a disastrous harvest. If such was the case, the merchant lender had seized what little grain the field had yielded so that he could at least recover the seed he had sown.

The difference between agricultural and commercial debt should now be clearer. Agricultural debt creates a lien between farmers and merchants – clients and patrons – that neither side is in a hurry to loosen through timely and full reimbursement of loans. When necessary, loans can usually be restructured: for instance, the tenor or repayment date of the principal can be rescheduled to a later date and the interest can be capitalized by incorporating it into the principal. And should that not resolve the matter, ad hoc or recurrent releases of commercial debts may, for reasons of political expediency, prove to be a solution of the last resort to prevent the collapse of trade and thus of the economy as a whole. In the case of the šmiṭṭah, as we shall see in the next section, its systematic recurrence introduces a significant complexity in the calculation and drafting of the terms and conditions of credit transactions and generally has the effect of limiting the rescheduling of short-term loans to the time left before the next šmiṭṭah date.

3.8 Calibrating Principals

The šmiṭṭah marks off the maximum term of all commercial loans. At the end of the seventh year, any arrears from non-antichretic loans between brothers must be forgiven. In theory, arrears on antichretic loans are impossible as the creditor enjoys the use of the pledge during the term of the loan, the principal being calculated in proportion to the expected returns generated by the pledge – labor from a slave, animal or other dependent of the borrower, grain from a field, rent from a house.

The specificity of the šmiṭṭah and of the jubilee (Lev 25) is the regularity of the release, the date of which is known to all concerned and who thus know exactly the number of growing seasons and harvests before the next release. Instead of depending on the decision of a king under pressure from the different segments of the economy, it is the calendar that decides when arrears will be lost. On a specific date at the end of the seventh year, probably during a feast when merchants gather to settle accounts, each one balances what he lent with what he owes and forgives any outstanding sums instead of carrying them over to the next seven-year cycle.

Any borrower who finds himself in debt towards the brothers who granted him credit facilities is inevitably spurred on to pay back before the axe falls. Assuming his credit record is faultless, his creditors are naturally more inclined to trust him than to write off the debt because the šmiṭṭah marks a final expiry date for any rescheduling, after which any outstanding receivables are lost to them. By halting the natural tendency of the parties active on the commercial credit market to prolong indebtedness endlessly through rescheduling, the šmiṭṭah introduces a vital sense of proportion. Instead of transferring arrears from one seven-year cycle to the next and allowing the debts of the less successful trader to snowball to the point where his indebtedness threatens the economic viability of his creditors as much as his own, the šmiṭṭah ensures that on the morrow of the release, every actor begins the new cycle with a clean slate and that those who had their debts released are either retired from the market altogether or made to borrow on terms adjusted in proportion to the new risk they represent.

The corollary is that the principals are carefully calibrated in proportion to the number of months left before the next release. Even in the year immediately after the release, most if not all tenors will be shorter than seven years and any rescheduling will be correspondingly limited in time. In the sixth year, they will not exceed twelve months. The principals are set accordingly.

The drawback is a lack of flexibility as, in the event say of a succession of poor harvests, the date of the next debt-release cannot be advanced, unless an exceptional one be decreed, but by whom since the king in Deut 17:19 only reads the Torah? Nevertheless, Deuteronomy's šmiṭṭah makes far more economic sense than the 49-year interval of the jubilee release, which is far too long to have any practical economic relevance other than in the possible case of very long-term investments or leaseholds in land, buildings or infrastructure (such as a winepress, a mill or, say, an irrigation system) where arrears of debt in the form of lease payments or rent have become untenable for the debtor and further indebtedness would spell ruin and possibly enslavement.

3.9 Alms as Cash Converters

In addition to any arrears he has to forgive on the day of the šmiṭṭah, the Deuteronomic brother is expected to open his hand and distribute gifts and alms (Deut 15:11). Forgiving arrears is compulsory. Giving alms represents capital outlays too, but neither forgiving arrears nor alms-giving is without returns. While all brothers active in commercial credit benefit from the clean slates enforced by the šmiṭṭah, the alms given with no expectations of reimbursement are part and parcel of the credit market. Whatever is given to the needy (Deut 15:11) converts material wealth into social capital, a higher and more lasting form of capital (Bourdieu 1986). Generosity is a cash converter. What the right hand gives when it is under no compulsion to disburse (contrary to taxes) the left hand gets back in the form of reputation. Alms giving is the privilege of the wealthy who have enough leeway not to live from hand to mouth but have one hand free to collect what the other gives (Prov 3:16; Matt 6:3). A good name acquired through generous giving (including generous gleanings, Deut

24:19-22; Ruth 2) is beneficial in ways similar to the security generated by agricultural debt discussed above. Voluntary giving buys a good reputation that translates into lower interest rates, lower transaction costs, a pool of ready obligees in the form of keen laborers (Deut 24:14), militia men (Deut 20:1-8), favorable witnesses (Deut 19:15; 21:7), self-indentured slaves (Deut 15:16-17), to the point where the wealthy are not entirely free not to give. As is still the case today, the wealthy dedicate some of their surplus wealth to foundations and charities bearing their name, because philanthropic activities contribute positively to their image and hence to their more immediately profit-oriented economic activities. There is little new in the search for profit (Eccl 1). Therefore, this chapter closes with an appraisal of Deuteronomic laws that are commonly listed as clues of Deuteronomy's humanitarian thrust.

4. Self-Interested Altruism

Moshe Weinfeld (1961, 242) ascribed Deuteronomy to a preacher and social critic whose primary aim was "the instruction of the people in humanism". Weinfeld (1961, 241) organized the laws that supposedly reflect Deuteronomy's humanist outlook in three categories. A first category emphasizes the value of human life and human dignity: laws concerning roof battlements (Deut 22:8), the burial of executed criminals (21:22-23), whipping (25:1-3), women war captives (21:10-14), and runaway slaves (23:16). A second category includes laws dealing with the poor (15:1-11), hated wives (21:15-16), a neighbor's vineyard and standing grain (23:24-25). The third category of humanitarian laws deals with cruelty to a mother bird (22:6-7) and to a treading ox (25:4).

The idea that Deuteronomy's laws are motivated by a concern for the humanitarian treatment of others remains popular, to the point that Deuteronomy's slave laws have been deemed ancient precedents to modern human rights (Tsai 2014).

To Weinfeld's list, Bill Arnold (2021, 181-183) adds the mandate to include one's entire household in the moment of sacrifice to Yhwh (12:7.12; 14:26; 16:11.14), the prohibition of cutting fruit trees during a siege (20:19-20), the deferral of a new husband from military service (24:5) and the seizure of essential implements in pledge (24:6.10-13). In fact, the humanistic thrust of those laws is equally motivated by self-interest.

4.1 Entire Households at the *Maqom*

The mandate to include one's entire household in the moment of sacrifice to Yhwh establishes a ranking that automatically distinguishes the ordinary Israelites from an economic elite whose households count the greatest number of wives, children and slaves. For these affluent households, sharing the festive meals with aliens, Levites, widows and orphans adds to the social capital (see above §3.8) they already obtain by delivering the largest amount of food as triennial tithes for the support of the aliens, Levites, widows and orphans. As these affluent households are also the ones bringing the greatest amounts to the *maqom* to eat and drink joyfully before YHWH (Deut 14:22–26), feeding additional guests from a theoretical 10 percent of the yield represents a lighter burden than is the case for households of more modest means. Therefore, elite men gain prestige in parading their entire household – slaves included – at the *maqom* feast.

4.2 Credit

Deuteronomy prohibits interest on loans granted to brothers (not NRSV's "another Israelite"), but sets no limits on the interest accruing from loans to foreigners (Deut 23:19) whose arrears must be claimed relentlessly and never released as is the case with loans granted to brothers (Deut 15:3). The scope of the purported altruism is thus kept within narrow bounds. Interest-bearing loans to neighbors are not prohibited explicitly. The practice is left to the discretion of each brother, an essential flexibility to deal with the entire gamut of individual situations that exceed the ability of any legal system to take into account realistically. In any case, the prohibition of charging interest on loans and the obligation of erasing arrears on the seventh year are not particularly altruistic since the actual costs these laws represent for a lender correspond to savings when the same lender borrows from his brothers. The same applies to the freedom to eat from another person's unharvested crops (23:24–25). Being allowed to pluck ears and grapes from a neighbor's crops means that the neighbor is granted the same right to help himself from one's own produce before or during the harvest (23:24–25).

As stated above (§3.2), the absence of interest reveals a close relation between lender and borrower. The same can be said about collaterals (§3.4) that are mentioned when brothers lend to neighbors because neighbors represent a higher risk than brothers. The only limitations are the seizure of essential implements and the choice of the pledge granted to the borrower (24:10–11). Taking a mill stone as pledge (24:6) makes no economic sense whatsoever since it would hinder the borrower's ability to pay back the loan. The return of the coat of a poor borrower at sunset (24:12-13) is hardly a humanitarian gesture when the said coat secures a day loan. Handing back the pledge in the evening though the loan was not paid back in full would defeat the point of the pledge. The borrower could default and disappear overnight. All in all, Deuteronomy's credit laws reflect sound economic practices. Granting loans may indeed be a mark of altruism, but this is not what is usually understood as humanism.

4.3 Warfare

Deuteronomy's warfare laws distinguish between cities that accept the terms of peace and open their gates and those that reject the terms of peace (Deut 20:10-14). The distinction has clear economic motivations. The population of the cities that surrender without a fight is not spared out of kindness but because it is used as forced labor, which compensates for the absence of spoils that are taken from the cities that resisted. That the lives of women and children in stormed cities are saved is hardly humanistic either. Husbands and fathers are slaughtered while the non-combatants are enslaved. The slave trade is implicitly condoned in the ban on the abduction of any person belonging to an Israelite brother (Deut 24:7).

Warriors are given the choice of selecting the most desirable (young) women as spouses for themselves (Deut 21:10-14). The required month of mourning is the necessary time to find out whether or not the woman was pregnant when captured. This requirement saves her from being raped on the battlefield, but her feelings are not taken into consideration.

The prohibition to sell her in case of repudiation works more as a warning to her captor against marrying foreign women than benevolence for the war captive herself. Taken as spoil, the woman brought no dowry into the marriage because her father and brothers would have been slaughtered when their city was taken. Repudiation thus means sending her off empty-handed with no compensation except for her own life (21:14 לנפשה), leaving her few economic options apart from prostitution, a prospect that would contribute to make her subdued in her new home. As the fate of the children she may have born is not stated, the implication is that they remain with their father, which links the law of the desirable war captive with that of the deferral of a new husband from military service (24:5). The aim of the lawgiver is to maximize offspring, providing opportunities even for men of modest means to obtain additional wives and pregnancies.

The ban on the destruction of fruit trees (20:19-20) reflects the concerns of an audience that has every interest in preserving the economic potential of regions about to be conquered in order to extend Israelite territory (14:24; 19:8). Like the prohibition on taking the mother bird with its fledglings, the ban on felling trees is motivated by self-interest: "that it may go well with you and you may live long" (22:7).

4.4 Physical Punishment

The requirement to bury the corpse of a criminal on the day of the execution (21:22–23) avoids the additional humiliation of the family that a prolonged exposure of the corpse would generate and thus quenches any desires of vengeance. The entire village, the victims of the crime included, have no interest in feeding a cycle of violence through excessive punishment. For the same reason, flogging is limited to no more than forty lashes, "least your brother be humiliated in your eyes" (25:3). The interest of the group prevails over humanistic considerations for the guilty individual.

4.5 Sumptuary Rules

Whereas sumptuary laws impose restraint on luxury, a number of laws commonly listed as humanitarian may foster precisely the opposite stance, i.e. a conscious display of extravagance. Muzzling the threshing ox (25:4) and yoking a donkey with an ox (22:10) are ordinary practices that denote farmers living at subsistence level more than cruel treatment of animals. Taking the mother bird with her eggs (22:6) improves their diet.

Letting the treading ox eat some of the grain, yoking *two* oxen together rather than an ox with a donkey, letting the mother bird go free, have a similar motivation as abstaining from sowing the empty space in one's vineyard and the requirements of the other "miscellaneous laws" in Deut 22:5–12. The parapet built on one's roof (22:8) is more than a common-sense measure against falls. It is also a mark of luxury when the house in question has a second storey contrary to the neighboring houses that are on ground level and need no parapet.

Whereas the everyday dress code of farming populations displays little gender differentiation, wearing tassels on the four corners of cloaks (22:12) is as extravagant as abstaining to make the most of the empty space between trees, plowing with two or more oxen, wearing pure cloth (22:11) when neighbors cannot afford such luxuries. The prohibition to collect the forgotten sheaf for the benefit of the alien, widow and orphan (24:19–22) has the same motivation.

These obligations and prohibitions take into account economic considerations beyond the hard-won shekel and call to go beyond the call of duty to convert freely accepted losses and additional costs into honor and repute – i.e. social capital (Bourdieu 1986). Setting its primary audience of brothers a notch higher than their neighbors, what first appears as wasteful is in fact an investment. Only a select group involved in financial operations with foreigners and for tenors of up to seven years can afford it.

4.6 Family Law

As is the case with the war captive (see above §4.3) family law places the interest of the group above that of the individual. A double share is for the first-born son (21:15–17). Whatever the father's feelings towards his sons and wives, birth order overrides personal preferences and cuts short internal maneuvering that can tear up close kin groups. The aim is to preserve family capital and ensure smooth transmission to the next generation. Hence the law of the rebellious son hardly mitigates the case of the "glutton and drunken" son (21:20; against Arnold 2021, 183). At the request of both parents, a rare occurrence of mothers in legal proceedings (see also 13:7; 22:15), all the men of the local community execute the culprit who squanders goods instead of working hard to produce them. Depleting stores and threatening the family's creditworthiness, his behavior is a taint on the family's repute, a capital as crucial as stores of grain, wine, oil and silver.

There are no "glutton and drunken" daughters, but women represent a potential threat as sexual misconduct (22:22–27). The family's social capital is epitomized in the reputation of its daughters because the value of their suitors is a reliable measure of the family's social standing. For this reason, the damage done by the accusing husband is described in Deuteronomy as "entering a bad name on a daughter of Israel" (22:19).

Slaves are part and parcel of the household and represent an important part of the family's capital. Such precious assets are born in the household, kidnapped from non-brothers (24:4), caught in war (20:12–14) or even welcomed at no cost (23:16–17). This latter scenario is discussed further (see ch. 11 of this volume) as one instance of utopia in Deuteronomy. For the matter at hand, the purported humanism of the law of the runaway slave applies as much to the slave as to the household that is known for good treatment of its servile members. Again, altruism is self-serving as nothing indicates that the choice of deciding where the runaway shall reside entails manumission. The altruistic aspect of the asylum is limited to the possibility to escape from harsh masters and find a better slave master.

4.7 The So-Called Levirate Marriage

The custom of Levirate marriage (25:5–10) ensures a posterity for a man who died before fostering a son, but places a higher premium on offspring than on marital harmony, as is the case with the law of the desirable war captive (see §4.3).

Though designated as levirate, from the Latin *levir*, Deuteronomy's specifications for the marriage of a sister-in-law differ significantly from Roman law and from other biblical texts referred to as illustrations of levirate marriage (Gen 38; Ruth 4; Matt 22:24). First of all, three preconditions apply: the men were brothers, they resided together and the deceased left no son (25:5). Besides co-residence, "residing" involves working an undivided estate or joint ownership of assets pooled into a partnership (Milstein 2019, 56). The death of one of the partners precipitates the liquidation of the partnership unless the surviving partner takes the "wife of the dead" (v. 5). If not, the wife of the dead is free to marry again outside (חוצה) the partnership.

Then, four of the six verses of this law (25:7–10) consider the objection of the surviving brother and how to force him to comply. Why would a man hesitate to take the wife of his deceased brother and risk public shaming for himself and for his descent (25:8–10) though he is not denied the right to refuse the expected marriage?

Lastly, the wife of the dead partner is systematically designated as "the wife of the dead" (אשת המת), never as a widow. As a widow, she would be entitled to a share of triennial tithes delivered at the gate of her place of residence (Deut 14:28–29). The wife of the dead brother is not granted the status of a widow because the point is not to ensure her subsistence (against Otto 2016, 1850–53; Verburg 2019).

The untimely death of one of the partners has deleterious consequences for the partnership, all the more so if the deceased brother had invested part or the totality of his wife's dowry in the partnership. In this case, the surviving partner has to find funds to pay back what is owed to the wife of the dead brother. Had she produced an heir, she would act as guardian of her son's estate until he comes of age and the partnership would survive until then. As the dead partner left no son, the heirs of the surviving partner have a stronger claim to their uncle's share in the partnership than the wife of the dead partner. Hence the reluctance of the surviving brother and the social pressure to force him to comply (25:7–8) because impregnating the wife of the dead is against his personal interest and that of his own children. The text ignores that it might also be against the interest of the wife of the dead who may have better options at her disposal. She is presented as the one who insists on the marriage when in fact it is more a matter of public opinion and social pressure to which she is expected to comply as much as her unwilling brother-in-law. The insistence on the necessity to perpetuate the name of the dead brother sets the economic viability above the personal interest of two individuals facing a crisis.

Another aspect to be factored in is the mention of the first-born (הבכור) that v. 6 presents as the aim of the expected union. This first child, presumably a son, born by the wife of the dead is to "raise on the name" (יקום על שם). Whatever the meaning of this expression, the focus is on this first son, though the LXX renders the son as a child (παιδίον) to harmonize Deut 25 with the prescription relative to the inheritance of daughters in Num 27:1–11 (Tigay 1996, 231). The birth of a son or of a child might terminate the obligations of the surviving partner towards the wife of the dead. This is suggested by the Septuagint that mentions co-residence (συνοικέω, Deut 25:5) and thus implies a temporary union instead of a permanent marital bond (γαμβρεύω) as is the case with Tamar and Onan (Gen 38:8).

With the birth of a first-born, the wife of the dead becomes the guardian of her son's share in the partnership that is thus saved from immediate liquidation. Or the guardianship of the first-born is assumed by the surviving partner so that the wife of the dead is free to marry a man outside the partnership (איש זר). This second option might be preferable as the surviving brother would not have to deal with a woman who is both the guardian of his stepson and the wife of a man who has no stakes in the partnership. In either case, the law simply delays the marriage of the wife of the dead after the birth of an heir for the dead partner.

There is little humanitarian concern in these obligations, though this law shows that women in the Bible as much as in ancient Near Eastern economies were *de facto* economic agents, even if only as silent partners.

5. True Humanitarian Measures

While scholarship has somewhat exaggerated the humanist thrust of Deuteronomy's laws, three of them do reflect a concern for the welfare of non-elite groups, a concern that appears contrary to the immediate interest of the elite that wrote or financed the production of Deuteronomy's legal collection.

5.1 Care of the Father's Wife

The prohibition of marrying a father's wife (Deut 23:1 [English 22:30]) is another ten-word legal saying that reads like a proverb. The stated rationale is that a man must not uncover his father's wing (לא יגלה כנף אביו). Why should a son not take (לקח) one of his father's wives for himself when a brother is expected to take his sister-in-law (25:5)? Strictly from an economic point of view, taking a woman one's father divorced or left as widow would avoid what the case of the unwilling brother-in-law seeks to avoid, namely, preventing her assets from departing the family circle. Such reasoning would miss the point shared by these laws.

In cases involving a widow who is not the mother of the addressee, the law implies that the honorable thing to do is for the son to take care of the widowed wife as he would take care of his own widowed mother, without taking the widow as his wife, even if social mores allowed it. In some cases at least, a wife who survived her spouse would be much younger than her husband and still fertile, while the age difference between her and her stepson could be minimal. Hence the temptation to take her as wife since there is no kinship between them, except for the father's "wing" (כנף). In such case, the prohibition to marry one's father's wife is motivated by a humanistic consideration for a widow who has few better options than to enter her stepson's household, but not (even?) as a secondary wife.

5.2 Self-Indenture

Though never listed as a humanitarian measure, the self-indenture of members of modest means – Hebrews according to 15:12 – in affluent households deserves to be qualified as humanitarian. Obviously, the voluntary decision to enter someone's household as slave forever (15:16–17) benefits first and foremost slave masters who acquire additional slaves for free, though each additional slave entails an extra mouth to feed (well) year-round. Deuteronomy never disconnects generosity from the interest it represents to the giving side. Nevertheless, a life of slavery in a home one has learnt to appreciate – if not love as verse 16 states – after years of serving it to reimburse antichretic loans (see above §3.5) can seem preferable to a life of freedom *and* misery.

5.3 Virgin Rape

Marriages were often arranged by the parents before their children came of age. Things did not always proceed as planned, however. A young woman could be raped before her marriage, thus ruining her prospects of making a decent marriage. The rape of a married or promised woman is liable to the death penalty, wherever the rape occurred (Deut 22:23–27). If, however, the marriage agreement had not been finalized, the rapist must pay fifty shekels to the girl's father and marry his victim. Exodus 22:17 grants the father the right to refuse his daughter to the rapist. Deuteronomy ignores this right. Instead, it compensates the woman by forbidding the husband to ever repudiate her (22:29).

Being forcefully married to her rapist who had to pay a fine to her father and having to live with that man for the rest of her life appears as a double punishment (Ochshorn 1981, 207). This would certainly be the case if the young woman had really been raped, though even in this case, having to marry the man who raped her would be one of few options left for a young girl whose rape was publicly known (Weinfeld 1972, 285). The case is entirely different if the rape was pre-arranged.

Having witnesses at hand to state that they caught the pair in the act placates the *pro forma* objections the girl's father would raise to save face in front of the village. "Proof" of non-consent preserves the girl's honor as much as her family's and provides the raped girl a life-long insurance against divorce. In these conditions, rape was an insurance premium that nubile girls of families of limited means might be willing to pay in order to enter the household of men able to pay the fifty-shekel silver fine to their father. Without denying the violence involved in the transaction, the violence done to the young woman could, in some cases, function as a convenient cover-up for the pre-arranged connivence between raper and raped. By denying the father of the raped girl the option to cash the fine but retain the daughter, Deuteronomy condones the well-attested practice of bride abduction (Stol 2016, 261). As long as she acts before the completion of the marriage agreement, a young woman may marry the man of her own choice, "the husband of her heart" as Akkadian texts designate such freely chosen husband (Stol 2016, 86), against her father's will and against social mores, usually due to different social standings. Given the little attention biblical laws give to women's feelings, such a license granted to young women to override parental preference regarding the choice of a husband deserves a place of honor on the list of humanitarian laws.

Conclusion

Deuteronomy's laws provide the most comprehensive set of economic practices found in the Torah. They are consistent with practices attested in the ancient world. They call for the essential fairness in the administration of justice (witnesses, corpses, flogging, unsolved murder), respect of private property (standing crops, field boundaries), preservation of the means of production (animals, slaves, credit, conquered cities, fruit trees) and reproduction (women, female captives, first-born sons and widows), bourgeois values fostering the stability required for a thriving economy.

The generous employer is a case in point. Small end-of-contract gifts (15:14) and salaries paid on the dot (24:14–15) secure a pool of seasonal manpower from which owners of large farms can pick the best workers, besides runaway slaves seeking better working conditions and self-indentured servants seeking life employment in a good home. Nowhere are the economic advantages obtained from the humane treatment of humans and beast more obvious. Resisting the temptation of small gains procured by false weights (25:13–16) generates greater profits in the long run. A good repute is a prerequisite for success in agricultural and commercial endeavors past and present: it reduces transaction costs and secures a faithful clientele.

Whereas humanistic gestures may be conceived as self-sacrificial because they are costly, Deuteronomy's humanism is best understood as opportunities offered to Israelites to maximize their welfare as they conceive it, while taking into full consideration the constraints inherent to an agrarian society dependent on a commercial elite for credit.

Though they have conflicting interest, self-interested economic agents face dilemma resolved when each contributes some capital. Failure to resolve conflicts resulting from the dilemma can be expected to lead to mutual loss (Wagner-Tsukamoto 2008, 116). Therefore, each contributes capital in one form or another and expects returns on investment, but not necessarily in the same form of capital.

As in any society, credit is the answer for some needs, charity for those in dire straits, with no illusion about the eradication of all forms of want. Inequality of means is a prerequisite to the survival of the entire society thanks to a limited redistribution that reduces the most blatant needs without striving to attain equality of means. On the contrary, the economy relies on a general desire and hope of betterment of one's circumstances, in particular through war and conquest.

The hope of improving one's circumstances is never entirely fulfilled and is often disappointed. Impecunious laborers may find self-indenture preferable to freedom. Even the wealthy are not immune to reversals of fortune and need to be bailed off by their creditors.

Minimal redistribution in the forms of tithes, debt release and alms prevents general collapse. Such are the harsh realities of economic relations in any society, ancient and modern. The way wealth is displayed varies, but the ways to acquire and increase it are fairly similar across continents and centuries because humans seek to maximize their welfare as they conceive it. Deuteronomy is no exception. The purported humanistic thrust of its laws is not devoid of self-interest, but it is best illustrated where it was not previously identified, in the care of the father's widow, the self-indenture of members of economically deprived families and, quite remarkably, in the law of the raped virgin that grants an enterprising young woman the option to marry a man of her own choice, in particular if, contrary to the Shumanite of the Song of Songs, her beloved is not a shepherd but the son of a wealthier family than hers, the usual cause for his parents' opposition to the marriage – a happy marriage of self-interest and humanism for the daughters of families of lower means.

Nevertheless, there are a number of features in Deuteronomy 12–26 that challenge the otherwise economic realism of its laws, elements that have been considered as unrealistic or utopian. This is the subject of ch. 11 in this volume.

Glossary of Financing Terms

Antichresis: Loan where a lender has the usufruct of the borrower's pledge until the loan is repaid.
Arrears: Late or overdue payment of principal or interest.
Capital: Personal fortune or assets; funds held or invested in an enterprise.
Capitalization: Incorporation of outstanding interest or arrears into principal.
Cash converter: In the present context, gifts or donations made to enhance the giver's reputation.
Collateral: Asset pledged to a lender until a loan is repaid. In default, the lender keeps the asset.
Credit: 1. Delay granted by a seller to a buyer to pay. 2. A loan.
Creditor: 1. A seller who has granted a buyer credit. 2. A lender.
Creditworthiness: A seller or lender's perception of a buyer or borrower's solvability.
Debt: An amount a buyer owes a seller or a borrower owes a lender.
Debtor: A person who owes a seller or a lender.
Default: Failure of a debtor to make payment of interest or principal when due.
Distrain: For a lender to withhold the return of a pledge to a borrower who defaults.
Interest: What a seller charges a buyer for delayed payment or a lender charges for a loan.
Liquidity: Available funds (or readily convertible assets) to meet short-term payment obligations.

Loan: Transaction where a lender grants a borrower the use of property or funds for a set period.
Loan shark: A fraudulent lender whose objective is to dispossess borrowers of their pledges.
Long(er)-term: A period lasting more than a year.
Manumission: Release from slavery or servitude.
Maturity: Date on which a loan or obligation is due.
Microcredit: The granting of small loans (often at high interest rates) for very short durations.
Outstanding debt: Unpaid debt (it becomes overdue if still unpaid after maturity or tenor).
Pledge: Property transferred by a borrower to a lender as collateral for the duration of a loan.
Principal: Amount lent to a borrower and to be repaid by a set date (with or without interest).
Promissory note: Written promise to pay a buyer makes to a seller or a borrower to a lender.
Rate (interest): Percentage of a loan paid by a borrower over a set time (day, week, month, year).
Receivable: Outstanding payment owed to a person or an enterprise for goods or services.
Release (debt): Cancellation of a debt owed to a lender.
Rescheduling (debt): Renegotiation of the payment date of a loan.
Šmiṭṭah: Seven-yearly obligation of brothers to release their debtors from having to repay loans.
Security: Collateral (see above).
Seize: Distrain (see above).
Short-term: Period of less than one year.
Tenor: Period from the disbursement of a loan to its maturity.
Transaction costs: Expenses incurred by a lender in arranging a loan.
Usufruct: Right to use exclusively a property belonging to another person.
Usury: Rate of interest deemed excessive by custom, law or depending on circumstances.

Works Cited

Anderson, Gary A. 2009. *Sin: A History*. New Haven: Yale University Press.
Aristotle's *Politics*. 2013. Translated with an Introduction, Notes, and Glossary by Carnes Lord. Chicago: University of Chicago Press, Second Edition.
Arnold, Bill T. 2021. "Innovations of the Deuteronomic Law and the History of its Composition." Pages 163–94 in *Deuteronomy in the Making: Studies*

in the Production of Debarim. Edited by Diana Edelman, Benedetta Rossi, Kåre Berge, and Philippe Guillaume. Beihefte zur Zeitschrift für die alttestamentische Wissenschaft 533. Berlin: de Gruyter.

Becker, Gary S. 1976. *The Economic Approach to Human Behavior.* Chicago: University of Chicago Press.

Bennett, Harold V. 2003. "Triennial Tithes and the Underdog: A Revisionist Reading of Deuteronomy 14:22-29 and 26:12-15." Pages 7-18 in *Yet with a Steady Beat Contemporary U.S. Afrocentric Biblical Interpretation.* Edited by Randall C. Bailey. Atlanta: SBL.

Boer, Roland. 2015. *The Sacred Economy of Ancient Israel.* Louisville: Westminster John Knox.

Bourdieu, Pierre. 1986. "The Forms of Capital." Pages 241-49 in *Handbook of Theory and Research for the Sociology of Education.* Edited by John G. Richardson. New York: Greenwood.

Charpin, Dominique. 1990. "Les édits de restauration des rois babyloniens et leur application." Pages 13-24 in *Du pouvoir dans l'Antiquité, mots et réalités.* Geneva: Droz.

------. 2000. "Les prêteurs et le palais: les édits de mîšarum." Pages 185-212 in *Interdependency of Institutions and Private Entrepreneurs.* Edited by A.C.V.M. Bongenaar. Publications de l'Institut historique-archéologique néerlandais de Stamboul 87. Leiden: NINO.

Coin-Longeray, Sandrine. 2001. "Πενία et πένης: Travailler pour vivre?" *Revue de philologie, de littérature et d'histoire anciennes* 75: 249-56.

Csabai, Zoltán. 2020. "Intercalary Months and Interest-bearing Loans in Babylonia. A Promissory Note from the Egibi Archive." *Hungarian Assyriological Review* 1: 61-73. https://doi.org/10.52093/hara-202001-00005-000

Foxhall, Lin. 2001. "Access to Resources in Classical Greece." Pages 209-20 in *Money, Labour and Land.* Edited by Paul Cartledge, Edward E. Cohen and Lin Foxhall. London: Routledge.

Gamoran, Hillel. 1971. "The Biblical Law against Loans on Interest." *Journal of Near Eastern Studies* 30: 131-34.

George, Andrew R. 2019. "Old Babylonian School Letters." Pages 9-72 in *Old Babylonian Texts in the Schøyen Collection, Part Two: School Letters, Model Contracts, and Related Texts.* Edited by Andrew R. George and Gabriella Spada. Cornell University Studies in Assyriology and Sumerology 43. Bethesda, MA; CDL Press; Penn State University Press.

Guillaume, Philippe. 2010. "The Hidden Benefits of Patronage: Debt." Pages 107-25 in *Anthropology and the Bible.* Edited by Emanuel Pfoh. Piscataway: Gorgias Press.

Haque, Ziaul. 1977. *Landlord and Peasant in Early Islam.* Islamabad: Islamic Research Centre.

Jursa, Michael (ed.). 2010. *Aspects of the Economic History of Babylonia in the First Millennium.* Münster: Ugarit-Verlag.

Lambert, Thomas E. 2019. "Bankers as Immoral? The Parallels between Aquinas's View on Usury and the Marxian View of Banking and Credit." *Munich Personal RePEc Archive* Online. https://mpra.ub.uni-muenchen.de/97741/

Levin, Christoph. 2014. "Rereading Deuteronomy in the Persian and Hellenistic Periods: The Ethics of Brotherhood and the Care of the Poor." Pages 49–71 in *Deuteronomy-Kings as Emerging Authoritative Books: A Conversation*. Edited by Diana V. Edelman. Ancient Near Eastern Monographs 6. Atlanta: Society of Biblical Literature.

Liddell, Henry Georges, Henry Stuart Jones and Robert Scott. 1996. *Greek-English Lexicon*. Oxford: Oxford University.

Lohfink, Norbert. 1991. "Poverty in the Laws of the Ancient Near East and of the Bible," *Theological Studies* 52: 34–50.

McDow, Thomas F. 2018. *Buying Time*. Athens, OH: Ohio University.

Milstein, Sarah J. 2019. "Will and (Old) Testament: Reconsidering the Roots of Deuteronomy 25,5–10." Pages 49–64 in *Writing, Rewriting, and Overwriting in the Books of Deuteronomy and the Former Prophets. Essays in Honour of Cynthia Edenburg*. Edited by Ido Koch, Thomas Römer and Omer Sergei. Leuven: Peeters.

Moreno García, Juan Carlos. 2021. "Markets, Transactions, and Ancient Egypt: New Venues for Research in a Comparative Perspective." Pages 190–229 in *Markets and Exchanges in Pre-Modern and Traditional Societies*. Edited by Juan Carlos Moreno García. Oxford and Philadelphia: Oxbow.

Nadan, Amos. 2005 "The Competitive Advantage of Moneylenders over Banks in Rural Palestine." *Journal of the Economic and Social History of the Orient* 48: 1–39.

Ochshorn, Judith. 1981. *The Female Experience and the Nature of the Divine*. Bloomington: Indiana University Press.

Olivier, Johannes P. J. 1997. "Restitution as Economic Redress: The Fine Print of the Old Babylonian Mēšarum-Edict of Ammiṣṣduqa," *Zeitschrift für altorientalische und biblische Rechtsgeschichte* 3: 12–25.

Otto, Eckart. 1998. "False Weights in the Scales of Biblical Justice? Different Views of Women from Patriarchal Hierarchy to Religious Equality in the Book of Deuteronomy." Pages 128–46 in *Gender and Law in the Hebrew Bible and the Ancient Near East*. Edited by Victor H. Matthews, Bernard M. Levinson and Tikva Frymer-Kensky. Sheffield: Sheffield Academic Press.

––––––. 2016. *Deuteronomium 12–34: Zweiter Teilband*. Herders Theologischer Kommentar zum Alten Testament. Freiburg-Basel-Vienna: Herder.

Pearce, Laurie. E. and Cornelia Wunsch. 2014. *Documents of Judean Exiles and West Semites in Babylonia in the Collection of David Sofer*. Cornell University Studies in Assyriology and Sumerology 28. Bethesda, ML: CDL.

Pirngruber, Reinhard. 2021. "Markets, Efflorescence, and Political Economy in the Ancient Mediterranean and the Ancient Near East." Pages 71–89 in *Markets and Exchanges in Pre-Modern and Traditional Societies*. Edited by Juan Carlos Moreno García. Oxford and Philadelphia: Oxbow.

Polanyi, Karl. 1944. *The Great Transformation. The Political and Economic Origins of Our Time*. New York: Farrar & Rinehart.

Radner, Karen. 2016. "Die beiden neuassyrischen Privatarchive." Pages 79–133 in *Ausgrabungen in Assur: Wohnquartiere in der Weststadt, Teil 1*. Edited by Peter A. Miglus, Karen Radner, and Franciszek Stępniowski. Wissenschaftliche Veröffentlichungen der Deutschen Orient-Gesellschaft 152. Wiesbaden: Harrassowitz.

———. 2017. "Economy, Society, and Daily Life in the Neo-Assyrian Period." Pages 209–28 in *A Companion to Assyria*. Edited by Eckart Frahm. New Haven: Yale University.

Richardson, Mervyn Edwin John. 2000. *The Code of Hammurabi*. Sheffield: Sheffield Academic Press.

Ro, Johannes. U. 2018. *Poverty, Law, and Divine Justice in Persian and Hellenistic Judah*. Atlanta: SBL.

Rossi, Benedetta and Philippe Guillaume. 2018. "An Alternative Reading the Law of the Hebrew 'Slave' (Deuteronomy 15:12–18)." *Res Antiquae* 15:1–28.

Scheffler, E. H. 2005. "The Poor in the Psalms: A Variety of Views." *Verbum et Ecclesia* 36: Art. #1478. http://dx.doi.org/10.4102/ve.v36i1.1478

Sider, Ronald. J. 1997. "Evaluating the Triumph of the Market." Pages 112–33 in *The Jubilee Challenge. Utopia or Possibility?* Edited by Hans Ucko. Geneva: WCC Publications.

Simkins, Ronald A. 2020. *Creation & Ecology. The Political Economy of Ancient Israel and the Environmental Crisis*. Eugene, OR: Cascade.

Stol, Marten. 2016. *Women in the Ancient Near East*. Berlin: de Gruyter, 2016.

Thompson, Steven. 2006. "Was Ancient Rome a Dead Wives Society? What did the Roman Paterfamilias Get Away With?" *Journal of Family History* 31:3–27.

Tigay, Jeffrey. 1996. *Deuteronomy: The Traditional Hebrew Text with the New JPS Translation*. Philadelphia: Jewish Publication Society.

Tsai, Daisy Y. 2014 *Human Rights in Deuteronomy: With Special Focus on Slave Laws*. Beihefte zur Zeitschrift für die alttestamentische Wissenschaft 464. Berlin: de Gruyter.

Van de Mieroop, Marc. 1999. *Cuneiform Texts and the Writing of History*. London and New York: Routledge.

Verburg, Jelle. 2019. "Women's Property Rights in Egypt and the Law of Levirate Marriage in the LXX." *Zeitschrift für die alttestamentliche Wissenschaft* 131: 595–97.

Vogt, Peter. 2008. "Social Justice and the Vision of Deuteronomy." *Journal of the Evangelical Theological Society* 51: 35–44.

Waetzoldt, Harmut. 1987. "Compensation of Craft Workers and Officials in the Ur III Period." Pages 117–42 in *Labor in the Ancient Near East.* Edited by Marvin A. Powell. American Oriental Series 68. New Haven: American Oriental Society.

Wagner-Tsukamoto, Sigmund A. 2008. "An Economic Reading of the Exodus: On the Institutional Economic Reconstruction of Biblical Cooperation Failures." *Scandinavian Journal of the Old Testament* 22: 114–34.

Weinfeld, Moshe. 1961 "The Origins of the Humanism in Deuteronomy." *Journal of Biblical Literature* 80: 241–47.

——. 1972. *Deuteronomy and the Deuteronomic School.* Oxford: Clarendon.

Welborn, Larry L. 2017. "Marxism and Capitalism in Pauline Studies." Pages 361–96 in *Paul and Economics.* Edited by Thomas R. IV Blanton and Raymond Pickett. Minneapolis: Fortress.

Wood, Diana. 2002. *Medieval Economic Thought.* Cambridge: Cambridge University Press.

Zaccagnini, Carlo. 2001. "Nuzi." Pages 223–36 in *Security for Debt in Ancient Near Eastern Law.* Edited by Raymond Westbrook and Richard Jasnow. Leiden: Brill.

About the Author

Philippe Guillaume is a trained agriculturist and a lecturer at the Biblical Institute of the University of Berne (Switzerland). His current research focuses on the ancient Near East economy and agrarian matters related to biblical texts and laws, in particular in Deuteronomy with a volume dedicated to *The Economy of Deuteronomy's Core* (Sheffield: Equinox Publishing Ltd, 2022).

Chapter 7
Yhwh (Ha)'Elohim and a Reconceived Yahwism

Diana V. Edelman

Abstract

Changes in the conception of the divine and household religion, religious festivals, and other practices discernible from textual and archaeological materials relating to the monarchic era of the kingdom of Judah (ca. 975–586 BCE) vs. what is being espoused by the writer of Deuteronomy and in subsequent additions to the book are examined. The new conception of Yhwh Elohim vs. Yhwh Ṣeba'ot and this deity's assumption of the roles of other deities precedes a consideration of the suppression of the ancestors and family gods in household cult, Israel as a holy people but not a nation of priests, the endorsement of dietary restrictions, advocacy of a central place of worship, and the endorsement of three annual pilgrimage festivals to the latter site.

Keywords: pilgrimage, household cult, Yhwh Elohim, family gods, ancestral cult

In the storyworld of Deuteronomy, Yhwh *'ĕlōhîm* is to be the only deity the people of Israel acknowledge as influencing events in life and death. The underlying worldview accepts that the divine is actively involved in the human world and that acknowledgement of this "fact" in all activities in life, from the life cycle to the food production cycle, from economics to warfare and the dispensing of justice, must permeate the fabric of society. Daily behavior, including ritual practices, should bring to mind and reinforce this world view. What we call religion was not optional in the ancient world; one ignored the divine at one's own risk and should have expected bad fortune and illness to result. In this chapter, the changes that are discernible from textual and archaeological materials in the conception of the divine and household religion, religious festivals, and other practices from what can be pieced together concerning the monarchic era of the kingdom of Judah (ca. 975–586 BCE) and what is being espoused by the writer of Deuteronomy and in subsequent additions to the book will be reviewed.

1. The Attributes Accompanying the Divine Name

In Deuteronomy the deity is consistently designated Yhwh (your, my, our, his, or their) *'ĕlōhîm*; never Yhwh of hosts/armies (Yhwh ṣᵉbā'ôt)[1] or "cherubim-sitter" (yōšēb kᵉrūbîm; 1 Sam 4:4; 2 Sam 6:2; 2 Kgs 19:15; Isa 37:16; Ps 80:2; 99:1), which were the fuller designations applied to Yhwh in Judah during the monarchy and possibly beyond in other biblical texts.[2] The preference for Yhwh (your, my, our, his, or their) *'ĕlōhîm* in

1 Use of this title is extensive and is found in the books of Samuel, Kings, Isaiah, Jeremiah, Micah, Nahum, Habbakuk, Zephaniah, Haggai, Zechariah, Malachi, Psalms, and Chronicles. The four examples in Chronicles are all derived from earlier uses in Kings or in a common source both authors accessed, but 1 Chr 17:24 goes on to equate Yhwh Ṣeba'ôt with (Yhwh) 'elohe Israel. The occurrences are as follows: 1 Sam 1:3, 11; 4:4; 15:2; 17:45; 2 Sam 6:2, 18; 7:8, 26, 27; 1 Kgs 18:5; 19:10, 14; 2 Kgs 3:14; Isa 1:9, 24; 2:12; 3:1, 15; 5:7, 9, 16, 24; 6:3, 5; 8:13, 18; 9:6 [7], 12 [13]; 10:16, 33; 13:4, 13; 14:22-24, 27; 17:3; 18:7; 19:4, 12, 16-18, 20, 25; 21:10; 22:25; 23:9; 24:23; 25:6; 28:5, 22, 29; 29:6; 31:4, 5; 37:16; 37:32; 39:5; 44:6; 47:4; 48:2; 51:15; 54:5; Jer 2:19; 6:6, 9; 7:3; 21; 8:3; 9:6 [7], 14 [15], 16 [17]; 10:16; 11:17, 20, 22; 16:9; 19:3, 11, 15; 20:12; 23:15, 16, 36; 25:8, 27-29, 32; 26:18; 27:4, 18, 19, 21; 28:2, 14; 29:4, 8, 17, 21; 29:5; 30:8; 31:23; 31:35; 32:14, 15, 18; 33:11, 12; 35:17-19; 39:16; 42:15, 18; 43:10; 44:2, 11, 25; 46:18, 25; 48:1, 15; 49:7, 26, 35; 50:18, 33, 34; 51:5; 51:14; 51:19, 33, 57, 58; Mic 4:4; Nah 2:14 [13]; 3:5; Hab 2:13; Zeph 2:9, 10; Hag 1:2, 5, 7, 9, 14; 2:4, 6-9, 11, 23; Zech 1:3, 4, 6, 12, 14, 16, 17; 2:12 [8], 13 [9], 15 [11]; 3:7, 9, 10; 4:6, 9; 5:4; 6:12, 15; 7:3, 4, 9, 12, 13; 8:1-4, 6, 7, 9, 11, 14, 18-23; 9:15; 10:3; 12:5; 13:2, 7; 14: 16, 17, 21; Mal 1:4, 6, 8-11, 13, 14; 2:2, 4, 7, 8, 12, 16; 3:1, 5, 7, 10-12, 14, 17, 19 [4:1], 21 [4:3]; Ps 24:10; 46:8 [7]; 12[11]; 48:9 [8]; 59:6 [5]; 84:2 [1]; 4 [3], 13[12]; 1 Chr 11:9; 17:7, 24.
2 In the texts of Isaiah, Jeremiah, Haggai, Zechariah, Malachi, Ps 59:5 and 1 Chr 17:24, there is a consistent and deliberate policy to equate this older title with the idea of *Yhwh elohim* or *(Yhwh) elohe Israel*, leading also to the novel title, *Yhwh 'ĕlōhê Ṣeba'ôt*. The most logical explanation of this situation would be an attempt to gain acceptance for the new ideas associated with Yhwh Elohim by claiming that *Yhwh Ṣeba'ôt*, the former territorial and national deity of the kingdom of Judah, is the same basic god as Yhwh Elohim but that different divine characteristics are important now and require changes in ritual praxis as a result. It is a rhetorical strategy that simultaneously draws on two ways of

this book distinguishes it also from the prophetic books, where *'ĕlōhîm* is never used in the identical way as a concretized plural noun in tandem with the name Yhwh. Extrabiblical inscriptions reveal the existence of additional regional forms of Yhwh: at Quntillet 'Ajrud in the Wadi Quraiyah in northeastern Sinai, travelers called on Yhwh of Samaria (Shomron) and Yhwh of Teman (the "South" or a more specific region/ city named Teman) for blessing and protection (see e.g. Hutton 2010), both alongside his divine consort, Asherah (for her role, see e.g. Thomas 2017). Then, in a tomb at Khirbet Beit Lei, 8 km east of Lachish, Yhwh is designated *'lhy yršlm*, *'ĕlōhîm* of Jerusalem, and another inscription states, "I am Yhwh your *'ĕlōhîm*," as found numerous times in Deuteronomy (for these inscriptions, see conveniently Zevit 2001, 370–438; Na'aman 2011).

The Beit Lei tomb and one located 20 m to the north are cut and decorated in a style typical of the Iron II period. Persian pottery was found inside the latter cave and fragments were outside of the first, indicating most likely that both had been reused in the Persian period. No pottery or metal objects were found anywhere in the cave with the inscriptions, which is odd for the Iron Age in terms of both types of artifacts and for the Persian period in terms of pottery at least. The broken fragments outside could suggest grave robbers had removed such items in the distant or more recent past. In any case, the inscriptions could date to either period of use.

The exact import of the divine designation *'ĕlōhîm* needs clarification. In Deuteronomy, it is a plural form applied to a singular subject, the proper name of a deity, and is used with a singular verb form. Thus, while there are instances in the Hebrew Bible where the term functions as a normal plural noun, "gods," where the verb governing it is plural in form, it is the former that is the focus of discussion here.[3]

Suggestions have been made that the plural form expresses amplitude, excellence, majesty, or a superlative state or quality. However, as

> dealing with change; by setting the changes back in time so that there never was a break in continuity and by admitting a break and distinguishing between what used to be and what is now. The complete transition from one to the other on the ground would have taken at least a century.

3   Another noteworthy peculiarity is the presence in Hebrew of two nouns that appear to designate a god or the concept of divinity: *'ēl*, plural *'ēlîm*, and *'ĕlōªh*, plural *'ĕlōhîm*. Other Semitic languages have only one noun. The possibility might be worth considering that the former was the original Hebrew term and that the latter was an Aramaic loan-word that was introduced from imperial Aramaic but came to be treated as a Hebrew word morphologically and grammatically. If one were to posit the two are dialectical differences, then the latter would logically be associated with a northern, Israelite or Samarian dialect since that territory adjoined Aramaic-speaking territories.

demonstrated by Joel Burnett (2001, 23, 53), in Hebrew and other West Semitic languages, there is a grammatical category of noun that represents a concretized abstract plural, which denotes "an individual person or thing representing a certain status expressed as an abstraction." 'Ĕlōhîm is but one example and is best translated "deity." However, the same plural form also can be used as a general noun of abstraction, in which case, it is best rendered "divinity." When it appears as the second element in a construct chain, it can convey the adjectival sense of "divine." Comparative usage in Akkadian and Phoenician tends to suggest that the abstract plural was considered a more elegant and sophisticated form of expression than the corresponding singular form (Burnett 2001, 23–25, 29).

In Deuteronomy, almost all occurrences of 'ĕlōhîm bear a pronominal suffix: most frequently it is "your deity" (second person singular and plural), but "our deity," "my deity," "their deity" and "his deity" also appear. Thus, in this book, 'ĕlōhîm is not used as a title or divine attribute of Yhwh so much as a description of this particular deity's relationship to Israel; Yhwh is your deity or our deity, not the deity of other groups, like the Ammonites or Moabites (cf. Judg 11:24) or Edomites.[4] Such a view is consistent with the statement in 4:19 that the sun, moon, stars, and planets in heaven have been allotted to all the (other) people groups under heaven to worship (see also 17:2–7) and in 32:8–9 that when Most High divided humanity according to the number of divine sons, Yhwh's portion was his people, Jacob.

The monarchic-era Yhwh ṣᵉbā'ôt, who also is the "cherubim-sitter," was closely associated with the ark (e.g. 1 Sam 4:4). It might have contained a portable statue of Yhwh that was used to seek oracles during war. This is the impression of its function in a number of texts. In the storyworld in Num 10:35–36, whenever the ark set out, Moses said, "Arise,

---

4   The phrase Yhwh 'ĕlōhîm occurs without a suffix on the latter term in other books. For that reason, I am using it here as well, although technically, it is possible, had an unsuffixed form been used in this book, it might have been Yhwh hā'ĕlōhîm, where the second definite noun stood apposite to the deity's name. Unlike in the Aramaic inscriptions from Palmyrene, however, which use 'lh', "the god" i.e. the singular form of the noun with a definite article (Hillers 1998), it is harder to accept that in the phrase, Yhwh 'ĕlōhîm, the two nouns stand in apposition in Hebrew. The Hebrew form is indefinite and is a plural abstract noun, not a singular, definite noun. Thus, unless plural abstract nouns can carry a definite sense by definition, without the morphological marker ha- or a pronominal suffix, the relationship between Yhwh and 'ĕlōhîm will require a different explanation. For a discussion, see Halpern 2009, 205–7. Perhaps as a cultic phrase, Yhwh 'ĕlōhîm can be considered a poetic formulation, where the definite article was deemed dispensable.

O Yhwh, and let your enemies be scattered and let those who hate you flee before you." Upon the return of the ark, he said, "Return, Yhwh, to the ten thousands of Israel." Psalm 132:8 seems to corroborate this general idea: "Arise, O Yhwh, go to your resting place, you and the ark of your might (*'uzzekā*)." In 1 Sam 4 the ark was captured by the Philistines at the battle of Ebenezer. The statement in v. 22 that the capture of the ark signalled the departure of the glory from Israel could refer to the light reflected off a divine image with a wooden core overlaid with metal foil. At the battle of the Michmash Pass in 1 Sam 14:18-19, Saul calls for the ark of *'ĕlōhîm* "that went with the people of Israel at that time" to seek an oracle but tells the priest to "withdraw his hand" before receiving the answer because of visible commotion in the Philistine camp. Also, in 1 Sam 6:19, the divine killing of seventy men of Beth-Shemesh because they had looked upon the ark of Yhwh seems to reflect a wider tradition that seeing *'ĕlōhîm*, i.e. in physically represented form, would result in death (e.g. Exod 19:21; 24:10-11). This concept already appears to be an attempt to counter a prior tradition that considered seeing a god in physical form an acceptable practice thought to bestow blessing.[5]

Finally, the statement in 1 Kgs 8:9 that the ark of the covenant of Yhwh that was placed inside the holy of holies under the cherubim at the dedication of Solomon's temple had inside "nothing except the two tablets of stone that Moses put there at Horeb, where Yhwh made a covenant with the people of Israel, when they came out of the land of Egypt" certainly sounds like apologetic. The stress on the tablets alone certainly implies that other items once had been kept inside, either alongside or instead of them. The same point is made again less forcefully in 1 Kgs 8:21 by Solomon: "And there I have provided a place for the ark in which is the covenant of Yhwh that he made with our fathers, when he brought them out of the land of Egypt." Both passages are redefining the function of the ark. Ultimately, the ark can disappear and be replaced by the scroll of teaching i.e. Deuteronomy that was to be kept beside it; the scroll already contains the Ten Commandments, so nothing is lost unless one considers the physical artifacts vital. Eventually, many arks will house Deuteronomy and the other four books comprising Torah for use in synagogues.

In Deuteronomy, the ark is a box that contains the two stone tablets of teaching written by the divine finger at Mt. Horeb (10:1-8). The Levites are set apart to carry the ark of the covenant (*bᵉrît*) of Yhwh (10:8), but no specifications are given for its placement once the central place is

---

[5] It is possible that during the monarchy, those sent on diplomatic missions took with them portable statues of Yhwh to seek divine guidance, similar to the one Wenamun took with him of Amun on his mission to secure cedarwood from Phoenicia and to use to swear oaths, in the Egyptian "Tale of Wenamun."

established. Nevertheless, implicitly it will be housed inside the temple built at the place Yhwh your *'ĕlōhîm* has chosen/will choose (23:19 [18]), where "the scroll of this teaching" is to be set beside the ark of the covenant of Yhwh Elohim to serve as a witness (31:26). Its future function, then, is to hold "enshrined" physical artifacts that record the basis of the covenant made between Yhwh and Israel at Mt. Horeb and, as such, to testify continually to the terms to be observed in order for the foundational covenant to remain in effect, at least in the latest form of the book.[6]

Implications concerning the new conception that Yhwh *'ĕlōhîm* was to convey are able to be deduced or inferred from various statements in the book. In the lines of this text we are hearing only one side of a conversation or debate, however, and in some cases we must infer what ideas and practices were being countered when they are not prohibited directly. Even so, not every negative command necessarily modifies a previously accepted social norm. In order to avoid misconstruals, corroboration that a different belief, norm, or practice was maintained in the monarchic era from what is being advocated in Deuteronomy will be sought from other books in the Hebrew Bible collection and from archaeological remains.

The following statements appear concerning Yhwh in Deuteronomy: Yhwh is our *'ĕlōhîm* (deity); no other exists [for us]; only him alone (4:35, 39; 32:39). Yhwh [is] our *'ĕlōhîm* (deity); Yhwh [is] *eḥād* ("one; alone/only; unique") (6:4) (for the various translations, see conveniently Pessoa da Silva Pinto 2019). The deity is invisible; at Horeb, the Israelites only heard

---

6   In the book of Exodus it is consistently called the ark (25:10, 14,15, 21; 35:12; 37:1, 5; 40:20, 21) or the ark of testimony (*'ēdut*) instead (25:16, 22; 26:33-34; 30:6, 26, 31; 39:35; 40: 3, 5, 21) with no reference to Yhwh or Elohim. There is a single mention in Leviticus, with no qualifiers (16:2). In Numbers, one finds the ark (3:31; 10:35) the ark of testimony (4:5; 7:89) and the ark of the covenant of Yhwh (10:33; 14:44) thus combining the terminology from Exodus and Deuteronomy. Beyond the Pentateuch, in Joshua, the designation from Deuteronomy is taken up; the majority of references are to the ark of the covenant of Yhwh or simply the ark, with one reference to the ark of testimony (4:16). A new designation, the ark of Yhwh, is frequent in this book, while there are two references to the ark of the covenant of Yhwh your Elohim (3:3; 4:5) and two to the ark of the covenant of Yhwh of all the earth (3:11, 13). The single reference in Judg 20:27 introduces yet another new form, the ark of the covenant of Elohim or of the divine covenant, while in 1 Samuel yet other new designations appear alongside most of the ones already attested: the ark of Elohim/divine ark (3:3; 4:11, 13, 17-19, 21-22; 5:1-2), the ark of the covenant of Yhwh Seba'ot, cherubim-sitter" (4:4), and the ark of the deity of Israel (5:8, 10, 11; 6:3). Then, continuing in 2 Samuel, the most frequently used expressions are the ark of Elohim/divine ark and the ark of Yhwh, with only one mention of the ark of the covenant of Elohim/divine covenant (15:24). Usages in additional books can be found using a word search.

a voice and saw no form as the deity communicated "the words" to them (4:12, 33) and wrote them with its own finger on two tablets (4:13; 5:22; 9:10–11; 10:1–5). As a result, it is not permitted to represent Yhwh *'ĕlōhîm* by an image or to worship the sun, moon, stars, and host of heaven, which Yhwh *'ĕlōhîm* has allotted to all (other) peoples (*'ammîm*) (4:15–19). Israel must not have any gods/deity in addition to Yhwh (5:7; 6:14; 7:16; 8:19; 10:20; 11:16; 13:1–16; 17:2–5; 18:20; 27:15), and no image or idol is to be made or bowed down to or worshipped (5:8–9; 7:25; 12:3–4; 28:36, 64; 29:17–18, 26); Yhwh is a jealous god (*'ēl qannā'*) (4:24). No Asherah shall be planted–any tree–beside Yhwh's altar, and no *maṣṣēbâ* (standing stone) shall be erected; both are things Yhwh hates (16:21–22). Israelites must swear by the name of Yhwh only (6:13; 10:20) and must not intermarry so that the children of such unions will not serve other gods/another deity (7:4).

This set of characteristics points by implication to a number of changes from what had been acceptable for monarchic Yahwism. No longer is a couple, Yhwh *ṣᵉbā'ôt* ("of hosts/armies") and Asherah, the head of the divine sphere and a realm of divine and spiritual beings; Yhwh Elohim is the only deity that is to exist for Israel. There is a discernible move to henotheism or monolatry in the book, where for Israel, no other gods/ deity but Yhwh Elohim are (is) to be acknowledged or worshipped, even if they/it are/is believed to exist (MacDonald 2003, 59–96). They have been allotted to other ethnic groups.

The explicit prohibition against any image of Yhwh Elohim because none had been revealed by the invisible god at Horeb overcomes the possibility left open in the wording of the second commandment that one could be made of Yhwh, just not of other gods, because Yhwh is a jealous god. This prohibition implies that during the monarchy an image of Yhwh *ṣᵉbā'ôt* had been acceptable. The visions of Ezekiel (1:4–28; 10:1–22) and Isaiah (6:1–7) of Yhwh as an enthroned divinity are likely to be based on a statue of Yhwh as a seated god used in the Jerusalemite temple. Exodus 24:10–11 reports that the elders saw a seated or standing *'ĕlōhîm* (deity/ divinity) at Sinai. The variant readings in the LXX that refer to an *ephod*, which can designate a physical representation of a deity, rather than the ark in 1 Sam 14:3, 18; 23:9; 30:7 might also provide evidence that statues of Yhwh had been used in the past and consulted for oracles.

Thomas Römer (2007, 49–50) has pointed out additional, relevant passages. One is the LXX version of 1 Sam 2:11, where "the boy [Samuel] served the face of Yhwh before Eli the priest," which he considers to be the original reading that was deliberately altered in the MT to "the boy served Yhwh, the face of Eli, the priest" to avoid the implications that Shiloh housed a statue of Yhwh. It allows one to understand the expression in the Lucianic version of 1 Sam 1:5, "the portion of the face," to represent the sacrificial portion deposited before the divine statue. He thinks two additional prophetic passages seem to anticipate Yhwh's return to Yehud in a physical statuary form along with repatriated Judeans. Jeremiah 31:21 reads, "Pay attention to the route, to the road on which I will travel" when one follows the consonantal text without added vowels. Isaiah 52:8 says, "with their own eyes they see Yhwh returning to Zion" (Römer 2015, 141–59). Herbert Niehr (1997, 89–91) had already pointed out that the many references in the psalms to seeing the face of Yhwh or the divine face (*pānê 'ĕlōhîm*) should be understood literally as references to viewing a statue of the deity, not metaphorically. The likelihood that Yhwh was represented physically in anthropomorphic form during the monarchy is becoming more widely accepted (Niehr 1997; Uehlinger 1997; van der Toorn 2002; Niehr 2003b; Edelman 2009a; for cautionary remarks, see Sasson 2002).

Additionally, two seals dating to the seventh century BCE of the monarchic period, an unprovenanced terracotta sculpture thought to date to the late eighth or early seventh century BCE, and a coin from the Persian period have been identified as possibly bearing images of Yhwh. A seal belonging to Elishama son of Gedalyahu depicts an enthroned male deity flanked by trees of life riding in a boat, while another bearing the name '*šyhw [bn] mšmš* features a seated male deity with a crescent moon at the tip of his arm bent in a blessing gesture (Sass 1993, 232–34; Römer 2007, 45; contrast Keel and Uehlinger 1998, 307–10, #306a and #305c, who accept the figure is a deity but not Yhwh). The terracotta sculpture measures 16 cm high, stands on four short legs, and features a seated divine couple, possibly Yhwh and Asherah, with lions or sphinxes serving as arm rests (Uehlinger 1997, 150–51; Römer 2007, 45). Finally, a coin minted in the province of Yehud ca. 400–350 BCE depicts Yhwh in human form seated on a wheeled throne, recalling the visions in Ezekiel. The Achaemenid administration permitted authorized mints to select the imagery used on local coinage, so unless this coin was deliberately minted by a non-native governor of Yehud to contravene an existing aniconic practice, it indicates that in influential native circles, representing Yhwh in physical form was still accepted at this time (Edelman 1995; contrast de Hulster, 2009). Clearly, the issue of an aniconic Yhwh Elohim was contentious for centuries and aniconism only won out over time.

It is possible that this debate was carried on within Deuteronomy itself via at least one subsequent addition to the text. Römer has taken up the arguments of others that the verb *šrt* refers to service to the statue of a deity, illustrated especially by Ezek 20:23 and 44:12. He then wonders if the statement in Deut 10:8 that the Levites are to stand (*'md*) before Yhwh to serve him (*lšrtw*) does not reflect taking care of Yhwh's statue. In a footnote he also points out that in Deut 18:5, 7 and 21:5, the function of the Levites "has been altered" to state that they are to stand to serve in the name of Yhwh or that Yhwh has chosen them to serve him and to bless in/by the name, Yhwh. Since, however, the book is characterized by the theological concept that Yhwh's name represents him on earth in his chosen place while the deity remains in heaven, it is more likely that Deut 10:8 represents a later addition meant to challenge the aniconic concept associated with name theology by having the first statement one encounters concerning the duties of the divinely selected Levites to allow for their care of a statue of Yhwh in the chosen place.

2. Yhwh's Assumption of the Roles of Other Former Gods

Since Israel was to have a single deity, that deity needed now to assume the roles of former deities and spiritual entities. If Israel follows the *mišpāṭîm*, Yhwh will increase human and animal offspring and agricultural yields (7:13; 28:4–5, 11, 18; 28:38–42, 51); this deity will send rain for human food and fodder for livestock (11:14; 28:12). It is likely that during the monarchy, Ba'al would have been seen to be responsible for rain, crop yields, and the increase in herds and flocks. In addition, the ancestors are likely to have been credited with help in securing these bounties, perhaps as intermediaries with the higher gods. Hosea 2:8–13 [2:10–15 in Hebrew] indicates that Ba'al or forms thereof were considered the source of grain, wine, oil, vines, and fig trees as well as implicitly, multipliers of flocks that yielded wool (for Yhwh's absorption of Ba'al's traits and spheres of activity, see Anderson 2016).

The realm of responsibility of Asherah is not specified in the biblical texts, even though her former existence is (for this deity, see conveniently e.g. Ackerman 1992; Frevel 1995; Binger 1997; Hadley 2000; Wiggins 2007). Comparative evidence from Ugarit, where Asherah was the wife of El and mother/procreatrix of the gods, would favor her association with human fertility. Indirect evidence this was the case likely is provided by the thousands of female pillar figurines that have been found throughout the territory of Judah during the monarchic period. They are thought to have represented prayers by women for conception, successful birth, or adequate milk to feed babies (see e.g. Kletter 1996; 2001; Darby 2014; Dever 2014). Their eventual disappearance over the course of the Persian period,[7] while such figurines continued in use in surrounding cultures,

---

7 The claim made by Ephraim Stern (1989; 1999; 2006) that none has been found within the borders of Yehud or Samerina in the Persian period, indicating that a purification of the religion took place among the Babylonian exiles, who transferred it to the land of Israel upon their return, dismisses known

tends to suggest either that they had represented a female goddess and not merely a human figure or that they represented a human figure directing her petitions to a female goddess. Had Yhwh always been conceived to have granted and withheld human fertility, then there would not have been any reason to stop production of such figurines offered as prayers to this deity. The ancestors likely were also thought to be able to secure children, probably in their intercessory capacity with a more influential deity like Asherah (e.g. Edelman 2017a, 128–34; 2017b, 147–63).

It is generally assumed that the cult of the Queen of Heaven mentioned in Jer 44 as having been practiced among Judahite refugees who had resettled in Egypt was worship offered to Asherah. Those in Pathros are singled out among other settlers in Migdol, Tahpanes, and Memphis (v. 1) as rejecting Jeremiah's message spoken in the name of Yhwh that attributed their worship of other gods back home as the reason for the destruction of Jerusalem and the cities of Judah. They believe the vows, offerings involving substances turned to smoke, offerings of cakes bearing the image of the goddess, and drink offerings they, their fathers, their kings, and their officials had made to the Queen of Heaven back in Judah had brought them food and prosperity. Once they had stopped their practices, however, they lacked everything and were consumed by the sword and famine (vv. 16–19; also 7:18). Verse 8 suggests they had continued these practices in Egypt.

The prohibition against planting a tree beside the altar of Yhwh your Elohim in 16:21 relates to a former, monarchic-era practice of planting a tree as a symbol of Yhwh's consort/wife, Asherah, beside altars dedicated to him. In 2 Kgs 18:4, King Hezekiah is said to have cut down the asherah as part of his cult reforms in the temple in Jerusalem. In 2 Kgs 23:6, King Josiah is said to have ordered the high priest Hilkiah to remove the asherah from the temple precinct in Jerusalem. Hilkiah reportedly burned it beside the brook Kidron outside the city. The asherah beside the Yahwistic altar at Bethel was similarly reported removed and burned at this time (2 Kgs 23:15). In Mic 5:14 [13 in Hebrew], Yhwh announces, "I will uproot your asherahs from your midst and destroy your cities." The Jerusalemite cult at the time is described to have included cultic personnel who wove material for the deity (2 Kgs 23:7). The goddess also apparently was represented in physical form as a statue or figure with a wood core that was covered in metal foil (1 Kgs 15:13; 2 Kgs 21:7; 2 Chr 15:16). The three uses in 1 Kgs 16:33 and 2 Kgs 17:16; 21:3 imply a statue of some sort through the use of the verb "to make" rather than "to plant." Asherah was no longer to be represented or worshipped.

> examples as insignificant exceptions so they do not challenge his theological assessment.

The now forbidden *maṣṣēbâ* (standing stone) that Yhwh hates (16:21–22) likely had been used to represent a divine entity other than Yhwh during the monarchy. Perhaps, on analogy with the Katumuwa Stele and 10 Luwian stelae, it had been used to embody the spirit or former life-force of a dead person (Sanders 2013, 87, 93–94). The possibility that is could have been used to represent a range of deities or spiritual entities, including Yhwh, might have led to the decision to prohibit its employment in all instances. This would have avoided any potential usage for a divine entity other than Yhwh Elohim. At the same time, had it formerly been used to represent or embody Yhwh on earth in some settings, the prohibition would have eliminated that practice as inconsistent with the spirit of the deity's invisibility (4:15–19). Some consider standing stones to be aniconic (e.g. Mettinger 1995); what is being rejected is their use as a vehicle of embodying the divine, be that Yhwh, another god, or deified ancestors, whether in human, animal, or non-figurative form.

A number of practices of "other nations" are now forbidden. No one is to be found among Israel who allows a son or daughter to pass through fire, who practices divination (*qōsēm qᵉsāmîm*), who divines by cloud or smoke (*mᵉʿônēn*), who gives omens (*menaḥēš*), who practices sorcery (*mekaššēp*), who casts spells (*ḥōbēr ḥeber*) (18:10–11, 14), who asks an ancestral spirit (*ʾôb*) or a familiar spirit (or personal god?) (*yiddᵉʿōnî*), and finally, who seeks an oracle from (*dōrēš*) the dead. Some of these practices might have been performed by non-priestly temple personnel, but many likely were done locally by freelance practitioners. It is no longer clear in all cases what would have been involved, and some or all might have been native practices that for polemical reasons are being characterized as wrongfully adopted from "other nations" as part of a strategy of hidden polemics (Amit 2000) to deal with a sensitive, contentious topic. Irregardless, all would by now need to be eliminated from Israelite life because they involved invoking or binding the powers of gods and spiritual entities other than Yhwh Elohim.

3. Changes in Household Cult

Household cult during the monarchy would have centered on honoring and petitioning the ancestors and family god(s) (see conveniently e.g. van der Toorn 1996; Meyers 2010; Schmitt 2012b; Albertz et al. 2014; Edelman 2021, 248–53). Deuteronomy envisions a radical change in practice here. The confession concerning the sacred portion to be delivered to the priest at the central sanctuary, probably at the pilgrimage festival of Sukkot, has the Israelite confirm he has not given any of this sacred portion to the dead (26:12–14). The passage indicates that during the monarchy, the dead were considered entitled to a sacred portion because they were part of the divine realm or the spiritual-divine end of the human-divine continuum (so e.g. Lewis 1989, 115–16; Schmitt 2012a, 433; Edelman 2017a, 136–39).

The association of the ancestors with the spiritual-divine spectrum of the continuum is confirmed in other books. Given that this idea was to be supplanted by the monolatrous program being presented in Deuteronomy, it is fortunate that the few extant examples were not written out entirely over time. Two strong examples can be cited. In 1 Sam 28:13, when the dead Samuel who has been summoned for Saul by the mistress of spirits appears, he is described as an *'ĕlōhîm* (deity; divinity). In Isa 8:19–20, the question is asked, "… should a people not consult its *'ĕlōhîm*, the dead, on behalf of the living?" A third example is provided by the combination of two passages, Num 25:2 and Ps 106:28, that recall events said to have taken place during the wilderness wanderings at Ba'al Peor. The people of Israel ate sacrifices for the dead, the *'ĕlōhîm*, and bowed down to them. These passages suggest that selected ancestors either were deified or were viewed as having transformed into invisible spiritual entities (for ancestral cult, see conveniently e.g. Lewis 1989; Bloch-Smith 1992; Schmidt, 1996; Niehr 2003a; Nutkowicz 2006; Cook 2007; Hays 2011; Osborne 2011; Schmitt 2012a; Wyatt 2012; Edelman 2017b).

The ancestors likely were represented by physical objects called *tᵉrāpîm*, always plural.[8] They are found in household contexts (Gen 31; Judg 17–18; 1 Sam 19:13, 16) and were used in divination (root *qsm*, 1 Sam 15:23; Ezek 21:26) or to seek an oracle (Judg 18:5, 14; Hos 3:4; Zech 10:2) from a source other than Yhwh (Gen 31:19, 34, 35; possibly 1 Sam 15:23; possibly 2 Kgs 23:24; Ezek 21:26 [21]; Hos 3:4; Zech 10:2). Laban refers to the *tᵉrāpîm* his daughters had stolen as "my gods or my deity" (*'ĕlōhāy*; Gen 31:30), and when they subsequently are buried under the oak near Shechem in 35:2–4, they are described as "the gods or the deity of the foreigner" (*'ĕlōhê hannēkār*) (for *tᵉrāpîm*, see conveniently van der Toorn and Lewis 1995; Flynn 2012; Edelman 2012; Lewis 2014; Edelman 2017a).

Because they are children of Yhwh Elohim, members of Israel must not lacerate themselves, presumably to draw blood to use as an offering to spirits of the dead or to the deity Ba'al (e.g. 1 Kgs 18:28) or set a baldness

---

8   The question remains open as to whether this is numerical plural, a concretized abstract plural or an abstract plural more generally (Burnett 2001, 23). Thus, it might refer to a number of physical objects that represented perhaps the two most recent generations of deified ancestors still within the memory of those alive or to a single representation of a particular ancestor.

between the eyes for the dead (14:1).⁹ The latter might be another part of a ritual mourning of Baʿal's death or a different practice associated with mourning the death of a loved one (i.e. Mic 1:16; Jer 16:6; Ezek 7:18). Both must have been acceptable former practices related to the view that families deified some of their ancestors. As George Adam Smith (1918, 185) noted, "That these customs were not practised merely from excess of grief, nor only as testifying to the continuance of the mourner's blood covenant with the dead, but also in acknowledgement of the divinity of the latter and as the mourners' consecration to them is implied in the reason given in v. 2 ... Jehovah's people are *holy* and sacred to Himself alone."

The prohibitions against consulting ghosts or spirits or seeking oracles from the dead in 18:10–11, 14 warrant further comment. As already mentioned, the prohibition against setting up a *maṣṣēbâ* might have been directed at a practice associated with representing the dead, although perhaps not in household cult so much as in a dedicated mortuary cult. Also, the *tᵉrāpîm* appear to have been the primary way one or more deified ancestors had been given physical representation at the household level.

Joseph Blenkinsopp (1995) has situated the prohibition of ancestral cult in Deut 14:1; 18:9–14 as part of a wider monarchic royal policy aimed at transferring individuals' allegiance from their kinship lineage networks, especially clans (*mišpāḥôt*), to the "state." He suggests that five of the eight forbidden practices in 18:9–14 "have to do either exclusively or principally with interaction between the living and the dead" (*qōsēm qᵉsāmîm*; *mᵉʿônēn*; *šōʾēl ʾōb wᵉyiddᵉʿōnî* [counted as two]; and *dōrēš ʾel-hammētîm*) (1995, 11–15; quote on 11). He also finds a deliberate strategy being used in the "legal" section "by limiting sacrifice, sacrificial meals, and consumption of the tithe at the 'state' sanctuary at the beginning [ch. 12] and the prohibition of mortuary meals at the end (xxvi 14)" (1995, 15). In between, he detects in the "laws" the strengthening of royal control in the administration of justice and in supervising local affairs (e.g. 16:18–20; 17:8–13; 19: 15–21; 21:1–9; 21:3–5), while undermining the exercising of authority at the household level (e.g. 13:7–12, 15–16; 19:1–13; 21:15–17, 18–21; 23:15–16) (1995, 4–5).

---

9   For the latter option, which also would be a form of mourning rite used to lament the death of the fertility god Baʿal, see Mayes 1981, 239. He seems to connect both practices to the Baʿal cult. Contrast Anthony Phillips (1973, 97), who suggests both practices probably aimed to make the mourner unrecognisable to the dead person's spirit, implicitly to avoid unwanted negative attention. The same two practices are prohibited in Lev 19:27–28 alongside two new ones: marring the edges of one's beard and tattooing oneself.

If a different setting for the book is assumed, however, a different motivational logic becomes relevant. Once Yehud became a Neo-Babylonian province, without a functioning royal temple in Jerusalem, the local population naturally would have strengthened its kinship networks to cope with the new situation, whether or not they had previously been weakened. These circumstances would have continued until the temple was rebuilt and its priesthood and the administrators attached to it assumed control of administrative affairs and served as the interface with the Achaemenid authorities. At this point, the arguments put forward by Blenkinsopp would apply equally to the circumstances in imperial Yehud. However, instead of the king having a vested interest in gaining the allegiance of the locals, it would have been the priests and native imperial administrators who would have wanted to enhance their authority and gain allegiance from the local people. As agents of the imperial administration, their ability to carry out their imperial duties depended in large part on the cooperation of the local population and their ability to control them successfully, as well as inserting themselves into key judicial and supervisory roles among the people. A strategy might have been envisioned of tying the populace more closely to the temple and asserting a common, supra-clan identity based on a covenant with Yhwh Elohim that would have loosened their kinship ties and loyalties.

Yet even in this reconceived setting, is this the only explanation for the desired change in ancestral cult? Blenkinsopp does not address what the Deuteronomic agenda anticipates will happen to household cult if its regulations are followed. Specifically, is it aiming to make it disappear altogether, as it has virtually in modern, western societies? Or is it envisioning it to continue, but now with Yhwh functioning in place of the ancestors and household god(s)? In the latter case, the underlying motivation could well have been prompted primarily by the changed conception of deity represented by Yhwh Elohim, not by political expediency (e.g. Edelman 2021, 265–69). Among the population at large, which tends to follow custom and tradition, the ability to eliminate household cult altogether rather than adapting it or providing something to replace it would have met strong resistance.

Yhwh is *'ĕlōhê hā'ābôt*, "the deity of the fathers/ancestors" (1:11, 21; 4:1; 6:3; 10:15 indirectly; 12:1; 29:25). This deity swore to the fathers to give them the land after bringing them out of Egypt (6:23–34; 7:13; 8:1, 18; 10:11; 11:9, 21; 26:15; 30:20; 31:7, 20; 34:4) and kept its oath (7:8). It will maintain with Israel the covenant and the loyalty it swore to the ancestors (7:12). The phrase under discussion, "deity of the fathers/ancestors," ostensibly is emphasizing that Yhwh was worshipped by Israel's forefathers and had established a special relationship already with the patriarchs by promising their descendants land and rescuing them from bondage in Egypt. (Yhwh) *'ĕlōhê hā'ābôt* thus serves as a kind of mnemonic catchphrase for two centrally important elements in Israel's foundational myths found in previous books in the Pentateuch. An additional implication, however, is that the forefathers themselves do not warrant the status of *'ĕlōhîm*; they are dead humans who once relied on the living god, Yhwh Elohim, just as their descendants should continue to do.

In addition, Joel Burnett (2001, 68) understands the expression *'ĕlōhê hā'ābôt* to facilitate the amalgamation of a number of former personal patriarchal deities into a single one as well as the depiction of the continuity between the worship of Yhwh as the national patron and the earlier religion of the patriarchs. Both deductions are possible. However, in the present discussion, what needs to be noted is how the catchphrase subtly reinforces the prohibition of consulting dead ancestors in 18:11, which points to a concurrent belief they have become members of the spiritual-divine continuum who can be consulted for knowledge. Simultaneously, however, it conveys the message that Yhwh already had served as the personal or family god of the ancestors for multiple generations, reinforcing the novel idea that all Israelites should have Yhwh as their personal god by asserting it was a long-standing practice (Edelman 2021, 264–67). During the monarchy, a family god or pair of gods likely had served as the personal god of all family members from generation to generation. Normally, these were lower-level deities that could intercede with higher level deities, with local shrines near the family home in addition to the altar in the home (e.g. Vorländer 1975, 12–14, 84, 155–58; van der Toorn 1996, 71–87, 255–65).

The prohibition against other gods means that former family gods were to be abandoned alongside deified ancestors. Although there is no explicit statement about what was to replace the former practice, the answer is given indirectly in the claim that Israel is unique among the great polities (*gôyim gᵉdôlîm*) in having their deity near to them when they call to him (4:7). Yhwh Elohim will now become the personal god of every Israelite.

The prohibition aimed at every individual Israelite against planting an asherah beside an altar to Yhwh might also be aimed at an envisioned adapted household cult, at least in the final form of the book. It presumes that altars will exist outside the place Yhwh will choose to place his name to dwell. If the centralization of the cult is a secondary addition to the book, as argued by some (e.g. von Rad 1953, 67), this reference would be to altars at local and regional temples and shrines dedicated to Yhwh. Ordinary people would not have used Yhwh as their personal family god since he was the national high god to whom their lower tier personal god and ancestors would act as divine intermediaries. Logically, only members of the royal family, some aristocratic families, and priestly families who served Yhwh ṣᵉbā'ôt would have been in a position to have Yhwh serve as their personal family god. Since, however, the centralization mandate is generally seen to have been integral to the original formulation of the book (see below), the assumption that individuals would have had an altar to Yhwh would have presumed that Yhwh already had or was to become embedded in the household cult of families across all levels of society, not just those representing the upper echelons. Such family altars would have been used to make small daily food offerings to Yhwh, not for the ritual slaughter of animals.

Finally, two new aspects of household religion potentially are envisioned that would reinforce Yhwh's role on the household and personal level. These are the use of divine words as protective amulets in two locations. They are to be worn on the body (6:8; 11:18) and also placed on the doorposts of houses and gates of housing complexes and possibly of entire towns (6:9; 11:20). Some have argued that both ideas were meant metaphorically in the book, not literally, even if both were taken literally and implemented subsequently (e.g. Tigay 1982, 327; Cohn 2008, 40–44). Both practices are assigned commemorative and didactic functions in the wider context of 6:9–25 and are to be the object of teaching that will secure long life over generations in 11:18–21. Both seem to be part of a strategy to make Yhwh Elohim and the written Torah the new central foci of household religion by having Yhwh provide the protective functions that formerly would have been performed by the household god(s) and ancestors. Yhwh's words will now ward off evil from one's home and person.

4. Israel as a Holy People but Not a Nation of Priests

The concept of Israel as a holy people (*'am qādôš*) found in Deut 7:6; 14:2, 21; 26:19, and 28:9 overlaps to some degree with the statement in Exod 19:6 that it is a holy nation (*gôy qādôš*), but the latter then goes on to add a kingdom of priests or priestly kingdom (*mamleket kōhᵃnîm*), and in Num 16:3 that all the congregational members are holy (kol hā'('ēdâ kullām qᵉdōšîm*). How one understands the phrase *mamleket kōhᵃnîm* affects how the ensuing altar law in Exod 20:24–26 is interpreted. Assuming it means a kingdom of priests, Simeon Chavel (2015, 186–87, 192–93), for example, sees it to envision a nation of holy families, each with direct, unrestricted access to the divine king and able to serve as priests worthy of proximity and access to the deity in any place. No longer does Yhwh host Israel at his temples through the mediation of a professional class of priests; here, Israelite households build a simple altar wherever they choose from materials readily available and host the deity; it comes in response to their call or invitation, accepts their bloody food offering, and will bless them. He sees it illustrated in the young men ($n^{e'}ārîm$) sent by Moses from the children of Israel actively performing sacrifices at the ensuing covenant ceremony (Exod 24:5).

If, however, one assumes instead that the phrase means a priestly kingdom, i.e. kingdom led by priests, an entirely different scenario follows logically. The common Israelite, while a member of the holy nation, would take his animal to be sacrificed to any altar. There, implicitly, the officiating priest would manipulate the blood on his behalf and one or the other would invoke Yhwh's name in prayer or petition (e.g. the logical implication of Arnold 2016, 173-74). The report of the youths causing the offering of holocaust sacrifices (currently pointed as a *hiphil*; cf. Deut 12:13) and initiating the sacrifice of peace offerings (verb pointed as a *qal* but could be repointed as a resultative *piel*) in 24:5 would be possible to interpret as the selected assistants/subordinates ($n^{e'}ārîm$) leading the bulls to be sacrificed to waiting priests.[10]

The idea of a priestly people or kingdom is not part of the Deuteronomic concept of the "people holy" to Yhwh Elohim; this particular phrase has not been taken up, if it was known by the writer. The people are holy but are not to sacrifice on any altar wherever they choose; they must offer sacrifices for Yhwh only at the chosen place (12:26-27). In the present forms of the text at least, priests will implicitly be involved (they "serve" or "minister", root *šrt*; e.g. 10:8; 18:5, 7), and as payment, they explicitly will receive the shoulder, cheeks, and stomach of animals not offered as holocausts in addition to the first-fruits of grains and wool from the first annual shearing (12:6, 11; 18:1, 3-4). The people may slaughter animals themselves at home to produce meat for consumption, as they do with hunted animals and as priests would of animals used as sacrifices; this is due to the eventual existence of only one altar in the promised land for animal sacrifice, which might be located some distance from some of the settlements. They are to pour out the blood of any animal they kill for food onto the ground like water (12:15-16, 21-24); there is no mention made of building a simple altar beforehand, which suggests it was not deemed necessary. This sets it apart from Chavel's reading of Exod 19-24, where he argues the kingdom of priests that consists of every Israelite would always use an altar, existing or built on the spot, to kill an animal as a sacrifice to Yhwh, consuming the meat afterward in the context of worship or, implicitly, also for private use. In the "final

---

10 Chavel (2015, 196-97) argues that the concept of the kingdom of priests in Exod 19-24 is meant to wrest control of religion and the temple from royal control and patronage.

form" of Deuteronomy, the holy people are sub-divided into "laity" and "priests."

While there is no mention of home altars in Deuteronomy, as already noted, there may be implicit acceptance of household altars dedicated to Yhwh to replace those that used to be dedicated to the ancestors and family god(s), where small, token food offerings would have been made, primarily plant-based, and prayers offered. The point, however, is that when meat is to be eaten locally, it is to be slaughtered at home, without the involvement of an altar. The people are "holy" but not a "kingdom of priests" or a nation led by priests (Exod 19:6). The current form of the book acknowledges the existence of priests but underplays their influence and power, making Levitical scribes who will teach Torah to be of equal or greater importance.

5. Dietary Laws

In Deut 14:1–21 a series of prohibited and approved foods is given. Verses 1–3 introduce these wider rules from the narrower perspective of forbidden practices associated with mourning and commemorative rites for the dead; these include gashing oneself to spill blood, cutting one's hair between the eyes to create baldness (v. 1), and eating any abomination (tô'ēḇâ) (v. 3). In between comes an appeal to Israel's status as Yhwh's holy people and treasured people (v. 2), which justifies why the activities framing it in vv. 1–3 are inappropriate. Elsewhere, in Isa 65:4, the eating of pig flesh and a broth made from "tainted/offensive things" (piggūlîm) is specifically connected with some sort of ritual that takes place inside tombs and in 66:17 in gardens, where the menu includes pork, mice, and "the detestable thing" (haššeqeš) and the activity includes sanctification and purification. Scholars have suggested that pork was consumed in rituals associated with fertility cults as well as death cults (e.g. Noth 1967, 56; Zevit 2001, 535) or the cult of Asherah specifically (e.g. Ackerman 1992, 186–90).

The rationale underlying this list of living things that can be consumed as food follows typical systems used by scribes throughout the ancient Near East to make lists that classify and categorize. Land animals can be eaten that have a cleft hoof and chew the cud, domesticated or wild (vv. 4–8), and water-dwelling life forms must have fins and scales (vv. 9–10). Birds (ṣippôr) are classified as clean (ṭāhōr) and, implicitly, unclean (v. 11); the birds not to be eaten seem to share in common a diet of living or once-living creatures (vv. 12–18). Winged insects ('ôp̄) similarly are classified as clean and unclean, but no examples are given (vv. 19–20). By analogy, perhaps those that feed on other living things again are unclean.

Two final rules forbid eating any dead carcass and boiling a kid in its mother's milk. (v. 21). There is some overlap in this list with the list found in Lev 11. The more important issue is not if one is dependent on the other or if both derive from a common source, but rather, if any dietary restrictions were part of the original design of the book or were perhaps added secondarily.

The prohibition against eating pork is rationalized on the basis of its only having one of the two required traits of an animal allowed to be eaten: the cloven hoof but not a cud (regurgitated, partially digested food requiring further chewing to process) (v. 8).[11] Yet the introductory verses point to another underlying reason and stronger motive than not fitting all criteria of a class: pork was consumed in connection with rituals and activities conducted on behalf of the dead, many of whom used to become divinized ancestors and perhaps also in the cult of Asherah. Since there is a wider agenda in the book to have Yhwh Elohim replace the former gods, family god(s) and divinized ancestors, in their current presentation, headed by other prohibited practices associated with a cult of the dead, these dietary laws appear to be part of a multi-pronged approach to change household cult. Whether they are original in the book or added secondarily as another tool to undermine ancestral cult, however, cannot be determined definitively.

6. The Central Place

The concept of a central place that Yhwh Elohim will choose in the MT but "has chosen" in the Samaritan version out of all the tribes where his name is to dwell is a hallmark of the book of Deuteronomy, appearing

---

11   The Hebrew may be phrased to call attention to the immediate context and suggest more is going on than meets the eye; it reads *hû' wᵉlō' gērâ*. A verbal form would be expected normally after the negative particle *lō'*, not a noun. The particle *'ên* would normally precede the noun to convey the idea "there is no cud; it has no cud." The root *grh* occurs as a verb, in fact. It would be possible to read these three letters as a piel perfect 3 masc. sing. verb instead, meaning "it does not stir up strife" or "it does not go to court." That meaning makes little immediate sense when applied to a pig. However, it could allude to actions associated with an ancestor, who could become angry and punish the living and also act as an intercessor between the living and entities higher in the divine hierarchy in the older belief system that is trying to be phased out, denying either power to divinized dead. Thus, the reading in Lev 11:7, which corresponds to that underlying LXX versions and also found in the Samaritan text, *whw' grh l' ygwr*, "and it, a cud does not chew" is not necessarily to be "restored" as original here.

twenty-one times.[12] There has been much discussion of the compositional history of ch. 12, where this concept is first announced, which has resulted in the hypothetical identification of three to five stages of growth to produce what is in the current text and a tendency to favor vv. 13-19 or some portion thereof as the oldest statement (for a summary, see Mayes 1981, 221-22). A minority position also has questioned the import of what might be considered the earliest formula in 12:14 on two counts. First, the definite article in front of *māqôm* could be understood to have a distributive sense, yielding the meaning "any place" instead of the more common, straightforward meaning, "the place." Second, the phrase *bᵉ'aḥad šᵉḇāṭêkā* could be translated "one or any of your tribes," parallel to the phrase *bᵉ'aḥad šᵉ'ārêkā* in 16:5; 17:2; 18:6; 19:5; 23:17, "in any of your [city] gates" (e.g. Oestreicher 1923, 106; Welch 1924, 48-49; Segal 1961, 111; Halpern 2021, 98-101). The second phrase contrasts with the wording in v. 5, "from all your tribes" (*mikkol-šiḇṭêkem*), and would allow for a rotating central place or even for multiple chosen centers functioning simultaneously.

It can be noted, however, that the phrase *bᵉkol māqôm* in v. 13 serves as a deliberate contrast with *bammāqôm* in the immediately succeeding clause in v. 14, signalling the latter must indicate a single location. *Bammāqôm* similarly contrasts with *bᵉkol šᵉ'ārêkā*, "in any of your gates i.e. towns " in v. 15, also clearly implying a single place. Had multiple chosen places been envisioned, that point could have been made much more clearly by referring to places in the plural or by using *kol māqôm*, "any place," instead, as in v. 13 (see previously e.g. Nicholson 1967, 53-54; Mayes 1981, 227). Georges Minette de Tillesse (1962, 66-67) makes the slightly different but relevant point that in v. 5 "from among all your tribes" likely was an attempt to improve upon "in one of your tribes" in v. 14, which was too vague and did not exclude radically enough the possibility of multiple sanctuaries.

It is possible but not certain that 12:13-14 was written to overturn the practice described in Exod 20:24. The writer of Deuteronomy could have taken up the reference to the holocaust offerings in v. 24 as representative of sacrifices more generally and then altered the phrase *bᵉkol hammāqôm*, "in every place," to *bᵉkol māqôm*, "in any place," to be appropriate in the new context. No one would systemically offer a holocaust sacrifice at every altar he came across; the variant form of the phrase conveys a disapproval of multiple places containing altars for sacrifice by using a similar phrase but one that yields sense, not nonsense, in its new setting. However, caution is needed here, since scholars have argued for a

---

12   12:5, 11, 14, 18, 21, 26; 14:23, 24, 25; 15:20; 16:2, 6, 7, 11, 15, 16; 17:8, 10; 18:6; 26:2; 31:11.

complex development of both Exod 19:22–26 and Deut 12 (see discussions of each in commentaries).

In addition, "the place Yhwh will choose to place his name to dwell/remain" was interpreted to mean a single center in its application. In the Persian period, only two temples are known to have been erected for Yhwh in Cisjordan, the one on Mt. Gerizim in the province of Samerina and the one in Jerusalem in the province of Yehud. Both claimed the status of the single chosen place referenced in Deut 12.[13] A third temple dedicated to Yhwh was or had been located in the Cisjordanian region around Makkedah in the province of Edom during the late Persian period. It is mentioned on an ostracon alongside a temple to 'Uzza (Lemaire 2002, #283; updated translation in Lemaire 2015, 118–19).[14] It is unclear, however, if the temple was still being used or had been abandoned. It is possible it had been an older Iron Age temple that had continued in use or gone out of use, rather than being newly (re)built in the Persian period, like the temples on Mt. Gerizim and in Jerusalem. The temple to Yao on the island of Yeb before the first cataract of the Nile in Egypt had been founded during the Iron Age and continued in use until its destruction ca. 410 BCE and rebuilding shortly after 406 BCE; it was functioning in 402 BCE (Porten 1968, 292, 295; Rosenberg 2004) shortly before the settlement was abandoned.

Regardless of one's preferences for identifying redactional layers, there is widespread but not unanimous agreement that the book endorses a single place where priests will manipulate the blood of sacrifices. This is an innovation from the monarchic period. Numerous shrines, temples, and open-air facilities with altars had existed throughout the territory of the tribes, dedicated to the worship of Yhwh and other deities.

The call for a single chosen place in Deuteronomy may not, however, originally have envisioned a full-time, functioning temple with priestly personnel carrying out a restored sacrificial cult (Guillaume 2021). It may have been intended to function as a pilgrimage site used three times a year for festivals, remaining otherwise unoccupied the rest of the year. The sacrificial cult is inconsistent with the concept of an invisible Yhwh Elohim somewhere in heaven, which manifests on earth via a name or

---

13 For the view that the text was written to be deliberately ambiguous in not naming the chosen site, to allow unity among disparate Yhwh-worshipping contingents with loyalty to diverging historical cultic sites, see Knoppers 2013, 212.

14 In the original publication Lemaire also found mention of a temple to Nabu in the text. However, he has since revised his understanding and no longer includes a third temple but, instead, a monumental tomb alongside the tomb of Yinqom, which he had read earlier.

reputation made known in Torah. Such an entity no longer manifests in a statue that would need to be cared for and fed in order to entice it to remain in the temple and present in the statue via the pleasing aroma of roasting fat and entrails (e.g. Hundley 2015, 209-10). Thus, it is possible that the sole reference to the temple (23:18), the limited references to the ark, which in the monarchic period had been a piece of temple paraphernalia (10:1-9; 31:9, 25-26), were added to the book after the temple in Jerusalem was rebuilt and its priesthood gained power and influence. The same would then apply to the priests/Levitical priests carrying the ark (31:9) and serving in a sacrificial capacity (18:1, 3-4; 20:2; 26:3, 4). Their being involved as ultimate arbiters of unresolved disputes (17:8-12; 19:16-19; 21:1-9), supervising any future king in writing a copy of the scroll of teaching (17:18), and functioning as doctors/healers (24:8) might be original vs. later insertions; these responsibilities do not require a temple to take place. The book reflects a struggle for power between Aaronide sacrificial specialists and other types of personnel based at the temple, all of whom were subsumed under the broad category of *kohen*, routinely but misleadingly translated as "priest" (Edelman 2009b, 34-40), who performed more writing and text-based functions as doctors, administrators, judicial personnel, and instructors of Torah (Rossi 2021). The competing groups are presented in the "final form" of the book as members of the tribe of Levi.

The eventual restriction of sacrifices to a single altar in the place Yhwh will choose to place his name necessitates a number of changes in its wake. One is the elimination of the cultic employment of Levitical priests in outlying sanctuaries dedicated to Yhwh. They are given the option to go up to the one functioning sanctuary and while there can work and receive priestly portions from the voluntary sacrifices brought by Israelite families (18:1-8). Those who remain in outlying cities, alongside other Levites working as scribes, are to be supported by the tithes due to Yhwh every third year, along with orphans, widows, and *gērîm* ("resident foreigners"), which are to be stored within the cities rather than being consumed at the main sanctuary (14:28-29).

A positive consequence is the ability to situate at this central location a court consisting of Levitical priests and a judge in office at the time. They can adjudicate legal disputes too difficult for local town judges and scribes (17:8-13; 16:18). Their decisions are to be final, and anyone who fails to accept or carry out the verdict is to be put to death.

As already suggested, the writer of Deuteronomy might have envisioned the establishment of a central site of pilgrimage where all Israel should gather three times a year for commemoration and celebration. Israelite families were to report three times a year before Yhwh at the place the deity would choose to place his name (16:1-15), with the males being involved implicitly in assemblies once there, where they would see the face of Yhwh and each would make a gift (*matt*ᵉ*nâ*) of his hand (= of his agricultural labor and yield) according to the blessing Yhwh Elohim had bestowed (16:16–17).[15] Once the temple was rebuilt in Jerusalem as the sole center of legitimate sacrifice in Yehud, it logically became the site equated with the otherwise unspecified site of pilgrimage.

7. Pilgrimage Festivals

A few things are noteworthy in the festival calendar in ch. 16, especially when set beside those in Exod 23 and 34, Lev 23, and Num 28–29. The first is that none of the three has a fixed date for observance in Deuteronomy or Exodus; all three fluctuate annually according to the vicissitudes of the weather, which would determine when ripening and harvest cycles would take place. Pesaḥ is to be observed in whatever month or at whatever new moon the ears of barley are ripening but still green. The observance of Shavu'ôt is after the wheat is cut and Sukkôt after the fruits of the arable soil are gathered in for the year. By contrast, in Leviticus and Numbers, both a combined festival of Pesaḥ-Maṣṣôt and Sukkôt are assigned fixed dates that divide the calendar into two halves consisting of six lunar months, with an intercalated month as needed. Another is that in Deuteronomy and Exodus, there is no reference to any holy convocation (*miqrā' qōdeš*), while in Leviticus and Numbers all three festivals are so designated. In addition, in Deuteronomy there is a single reference to a *mô'ēd*, an appointed time or assembly, which refers to sunset as the time to slaughter the paschal lamb during Pesaḥ (16:6). Exodus also has a single reference to a *mô'ēd*, but it is to the month or new moon when the barley is ripe but green (23:15). In Lev 23 and Num 28–29, however, each ordained institutionalized ritual (*ḥag*) (Sanders 2013, 90) is a *mô'ēd* as well as a *miqrā' qōdeš*. Finally, there is a single reference to a closing assembly (*'aṣeret*) on the final day of Pesaḥ (Deut 16:8). This technical term is also found only in Lev 23:36 and Num 29:35. In both instances, it describes a closing assembly on the final day of Sukkôt, the eight-day autumnal festival.

---

15   The identical phrase, "they shall not appear before me without a gift," appears in the festival regulations in Exod 23:15 for Maṣṣôt alone. The phrase, "three times a year each of your males shall appear to the face of the lord (*hā'ādōn*), Yhwh" occurs in Exod 23:17, while a variant form, "Three times a year each male shall see the face of the lord, Yhwh the deity of Israel (*'ĕlōhê yiśrā'ēl*)," is used in Exod 34:23.

The slaughtering of the paschal offering from the flock or herd at sunset of the first day and its subsequent cooking and total consumption before morning must be done at the place Yhwh will choose to place his name; not at home in the cities (Deut 16:1-2, 5). It commemorates the departure from Egypt at night when Yhwh freed Israel from slavery in Egypt (16:1, 6). In addition, no leaven (*ḥāmēṣ*) is to be eaten; unleavened bread (*maṣṣôt*) is to be eaten for seven days (16:3). The bread represents bread of distress, associated with the hurried departure from Egypt, and also is to remind the celebrants of the day of the departure from the land of Egypt (16:4). The eating of the paschal meal lasts all night; in the morning, the people are to return to their tents and eat unleavened bread for six days. (16:7-8). On the seventh day there is to be an assembly (*'aṣeret*) for Yhwh Elohim that does not specify the inclusion of family members, and no business can be transacted (16:8).

Other books have differing specifications. In Exod 23:15 and 34:18, the *ḥag* is known only as Maṣṣôt. It is a set assembly (*mô'ēd*) in the month of ripening barley ears, the month when the Exodus took place, and no one is to appear before the face of Yhwh without a gift. In Exod 34:25, on the other hand, reference is made separately to the *ḥag* of Pesaḥ, whose sacrifice must be consumed ("must not pass the night") before morning. No date is specified. In Lev 23:5-8, the combined Pesaḥ-Maṣṣôt celebration has specific dates. Pesaḥ is to take place during the night of the fourteenth of the first month at twilight, and the feast of Maṣṣôt then follows immediately on the fifteenth for seven days, during which time unleavened bread must be eaten. There is to be a holy convocation (*miqrā' qōdeš*) on the first and last days of Maṣṣôt, when no business can be conducted.

Finally, in Num 28:16, the Passover for Yhwh is to take place on the fourteenth of the first month, followed by an unnamed *ḥag* festival in which unleavened bread must be eaten for seven days. This combined celebration eventually is designated a *mô'ēd* in 29:39. There is a holy convocation (*miqrā' qōdeš*) on the first and seventh days in which no one may conduct business (28:18, 25). In addition, found only here are the daily holocaust sacrifices with their accompanying grain offerings to take place during the festival, apparently on the main altar of the temple in Jerusalem, though this is not specified (28:19-24).

Shavu'ôt is to take place seven weeks after the sickle is put to the standing grain (Deut 16:9). Barley and wheat were both grown in the territory of Judah and also within the kingdom of Israel. One of the Samaria ostraca dubbed "the Barley Letter" refers to barley specifically, probably during the reign of Jeroboam II (c. 793-752 BCE) (Albright 1958, 211=*ANET* 321). It is not known, however, if farmers tended to grow both grains or limited themselves to one or the other. Wheat was more nutritional than barley and also had a higher exchange value. The barley harvest took place earlier than the wheat harvest. Logically, if the festival were to involve all local residents throughout the territory, it should have occurred after the wheat harvest so all would have something to use for the apportioned free-will offering (*missat nᵉdābâ*) that is to be given according to the blessing Yhwh has bestowed (16:10, 16–17). But since this institutionalized ritual lasted a single day, perhaps what was envisioned here was for individual farmers to appear at the central place after they completed their grain harvest to make the free-will offering along with others from their town and other locales who happened to complete at the same time and then to enjoy a festival meal with their families and the Levites, the widow, the orphan, and the resident foreigner from their towns. If so, this festival would have taken place over the course of weeks and not on a single day. It also is a time to recall the former slavery in Egypt and the need to observe "these [covenantal] regulations (*ḥuqqîm*) (16:12)."

In Exod 23:16, the second *ḥag* of the year is referred to as "the feast of the harvest of the early fruits (*bikkûrîm*) of your produce that you sow in the field." The first of the early fruits of the arable soil are to be taken to the temple of Yhwh *'ĕlōhîm* (23:19; 34:26). In Exod 34:22, on the other hand, this feast is called the Feast of Weeks, which involves more precisely the early fruits of the wheat harvest. According to Lev 23:10–14, when one reaps a harvest, he is to bring an *omer*-measure of the first of the harvest to the priest. He will wave it before Yhwh to gain favor on the day after the sabbath, and on that day holocaust sacrifices accompanied by grain offerings and libations will be offered, with a male goat to atone. Until the offering (*qorban*) to Elohim takes place, one cannot eat bread or roasted or fresh grain. It is a perpetual regulation. Then, fifty days from the date of the offering of the first *omer*, a new food offering (*minḥâ*) consisting of two loaves of baked bread made from the early grain (23:15–22) is to be presented with accompanying holocausts, grain offerings, and libations and a male goat to atone and two lambs as *šᵉlāmîm*. On this day a holy convocation will take place and no business may be transacted. This is a perpetual regulation that applies in all places of residence throughout the generations. Finally, in Num 28:26–31, this second *môʿēd* of the year is "the day of the early fruits" when one brings a new food offering (*minḥâ*) for Yhwh "in your weeks." There is to be a holy convocation and no business may be transacted. In addition to the regular holocaust sacrifice, additional holocausts with their grain offerings and libations and a male goat to atone will be made.

Sukkôt is to take place after the ingathering from the threshing floor and the vat in the autumn (Deut 16:13). The completion of these activities would have been dependent on when the rains fell in a given year and the temperatures during the ripening of the fruit and then the final processing of grapes into wine, possibly olives into oil, and the winnowing of the grain for storage. Like Pesaḥ, it was to last seven days and was to include families, the Levite, the resident foreigner, the orphan, and the widow in feasting at the central place (16:14–15). The males were to present gifts proportionate to their harvest yields (16:16–17). The confession said when the basket of first fruits is presented to the officiating priest at the chosen place contains references to both an Aramean patriarch and the Exodus story (26:1–10). Every seventh year, "this teaching" is to be read out at this final ḥag (31:11–13).

In Exodus there is no ḥag called Sukkôt; instead, there is a Feast of Ingathering ('āsîph) at the end of the year (23:16; 34:22), when one gathers in the produce from the field (23:16). The first of the early fruits of the arable soil are to be taken to the temple of Yhwh Elohim (23:19; 34:26). In Lev 23:33–36, the seven-day Feast of Sukkôt, the last of three set assemblies (môʻᵃdîm) for Yhwh, has a fixed date beginning on the fifteenth day of the seventh month. On the first day a holy convocation is to take place and no business is to be transacted. During the seven days offerings by fire ('iššeh) are to be presented to Yhwh. Then on the eighth day, there is a final holy convocation, which constitutes an assembly ('aṣeret). An offering by fire to Yhwh is to be made and no business can take place.

In Lev 23:39–44 additional information is given concerning the ḥag for Yhwh that begins when one has gathered in the yield of the land, on the fifteenth day of the seventh month, and lasts seven days. The first and eighth days are to be little sabbaths. On the first day, one is to take the fruit of a splendid tree, palm leaves, branches of a leafy tree, and poplars/willows of the stream. Every full citizen ('ezrâ) in Israel is to dwell in booths (sukkôt) for seven days, so that the generations may know that Yhwh made the children of Israel dwell in booths when he caused them to go out from the land of Egypt.

Finally, in Num 29:12–39, a ḥag for Yhwh is to begin on the fifteenth day of the seventh month with a holy convocation; no business is to be transacted. Various holocausts with their accompanying grain offerings and libations along with the male goat to be offered for atonement are listed for each of the seven days. On the eighth day, an assembly ('aṣeret) is to occur, no business may be transacted, and holocausts with grain offerings and libations and a male goat to atone are to be offered.

Deuteronomy is much closer to the regulations for the three ḥag festivals in Exodus than those in Leviticus and Numbers but stands out in one respect. As in Exodus, each institutionalized ritual remains tied to the annual weather patterns and the harvesting of barley, wheat, and grapes and olives. Uniquely, however, each festival in Deuteronomy explicitly commemorates the Exodus.[16] None of the other three books links Weeks to the Exodus, and only in Leviticus does Sukkôt also commemorate the Exodus.

There is an agenda in Deuteronomy to extend the Exodus myth of origins from its primary commemoration at the *ḥag* of *pesaḥ* celebrated on a single night to the seven-day festival of *maṣṣôt* immediately following. The unleavened bread consumed during the barley harvest is equated with the bread of distress symbolizing the hasty departure from Egypt. This might represent a reworking of a former barley harvest celebration. The mythicization trend continues with the barley harvest and the autumnal agricultural ingathering. The confession said at Sukkôt when the basket of fruits is offered to the priest adds the patriarchal promise of land to the Exodus theme as commemorative aspects of Israelite identity. Thus, agricultural festivals now become commemorations of Israel's foundational event, the Exodus, and the gift of the land promised to the patriarchs, adding an element designed to reinforce ethnic identity as well as the authoritative status of founding stories in the Pentateuch. Shabbat similarly is to be observed every seven days as a commemoration of the freeing from slavery in Egypt (5:14–15), exemplifying this same trend.

---

16 If one considers 14:22–26 to be a stand-alone regulation that does not presume any of the other information given concerning the festival calendar subsequently in the book in ch. 16 or 26, then no explicit commemoration of the Exodus is present; instead, the purpose of tithing year in and year out and feasting at the central place is "so that you may learn to revere (literally fear) Yhwh your *'ĕlōhîm* forever. At the same time, however, these verses do not state how many times a year the feasting and tithe-paying is to occur; the feasting is not said to be a *ḥag* festival involving "all Israel." Instead, if taken literally, the impression gained is that it is an individual household obligation and celebration that will be fulfilled whenever the harvests are complete and firstlings have been born, which can take place at any time over the course of the year, even if the mating of herds was encouraged during certain seasons. Presently, ch. 14 introduces the topic of annual tithing that will be paid at the *maqôm*, which includes all agricultural yield and male firstlings of the flock. It deals with logistics for those who live a distance, allowing them to convert the tithe to silver. The next section, 14:27–29, adds an exception concerning the leaving of the tithe in settlements every third year to feed non-landowners. Verses 15:1–18 move on to the remission of debts every seventh year, followed by more information about the consecration of male firstlings, before moving on to presenting the regulations concerning the three annual *ḥag* festivals that take place after agricultural harvests at the *maqôm*. Thus, it is plausible to read ch. 14 as an introductory statement concerning tithes that are to be paid in the context of celebrations at the chosen *maqôm* year in and year out, with details about the specific calendar for payment and celebration given in ch. 16.

Studies of the phenomenon of ritual pilgrimage have identified a number of functions played by the practice. The overarching one that seems most applicable to the current situation is as an integrating force for "national" identity by enacting "national" ideology, rather than the reaffirmation of social norms to maintain the "state" by closely associating royal order with divine order by appropriating sacred places or objects into "state" identities and iconographies to shore up political authority (Wolf 1958; Coleman and Elsner 1995, 206; Frankfurter 1998, 21–22; McCorriston 2011, 22, 51–53; Altmann 2011, 49–50, 53, 62–64, 69 without adopting his historical reconstruction and noting he also allows for a textually prescribed experience in addition to or instead of a physical one). The consistent appeal to the shared common history in Deuteronomy's regulations resonates with an emphasis on a common identity, even if what was being constructed was a common ethnic unit rather than a "national" one (see ch. 5). The inclusion of all twelve tribes constituting Israel in these future pilgrimage festivals to be celebrated at a single site, not just Judeans or Samarians, allowed for the reinforcement and renewing of wider, social affinities with those with whom one did not normally have contact, creating an immediate sense of identity as Israelites beyond the more restricted, everyday, regional, town, or clan identity one assumed. During the Hasmonean dynasty (ca. 140–37 BCE), a "national" identity was reinforced by the celebration of these pilgrimage festivals, even if before and after that time, ethnicity had been the central focus and became so once more after the disappearance of the relatively short-lived polity.

Three additional relevant functions of pilgrimages should be highlighted. First is the participation of all levels of society in an event where regular divisions are temporarily suspended, although some are acknowledged when patronage is involved (McCorriston 2011, 26–27, 46). The inclusion of the widow, orphan, *gēr*, and Levite in the feasting aspects of the pilgrimages in 16:9, 13 and the Levite and *gēr* in 26:11 points to both the desire to use these events to create group solidarity regardless of income and member status, and, at the same time, to allow the recognition of benefactors who would provide the food and possibly also the accommodation for some of these non-landowning groups within the larger society. The inclusion of the resident foreigner (*gēr*) at this ethnocentric celebration provided invited non-Israelite guests who could be recipients of the generosity of benefactors, illustrating the correct treatment of "the other" or outsider in contrast to how Israel had been treated in Egypt when they had been *gērîm*. At the same time, these individuals, if they were resident traders and craftsmen, could supply desirable goods for purchase or exchange during the festival.

Second, pilgrimages become occasions for males to transact business and cement new business partnerships with those one meets, particularly during the eight days one would be present for Pesaḥ-Maṣṣôt and Sukkôt (McCorriston 2011, 28–31, 39, 41). Only the final day of the first and the opening and closing days of the second eventually become periods in non-Deuteronomic festival regulations when business was forbidden, leaving six or seven days to renew old contacts and make new ones, extending one's trading network. Third, the implicit inclusion of women[17] and explicit inclusion of other family members in the legislation in ch. 16 allows for socializing, shopping, and the arranging of marriages while also reinforcing common identity through the participation in the same prescribed rituals and the affirmation of accompanying beliefs over the course of the festival.

A final economic dimension of pilgrimage is noteworthy. In the Arab world at least, temples that served as set sites of pilgrimage were maintained by tithes, taxes, and private donations paid when pilgrims arrived (McCorriston 2011, 66). The Achaemenid administration allowed the operation of temples throughout its Empire but appears to have sponsored the (re)construction of only a few, in Egypt and Mesopotamia. They seem to have expected locals to fund temples in their vicinities, or larger facilities that owned extensive lands and personnel to pay taxes and supply labor for Persian enterprises (Briant 2002, 73–74, 484). Evidence of local funding is provided by the trilingual Xanthus inscription (e.g. Teixidor 1978; Lemaire 1995) and also possibly in the list of silver collected for various deities worshipped in the temple at Elephantine (e.g Porten 1968, 160–64; *TADAE* C3.15; Porten and Yardeni 1993, 123–28). In the latter case, however, the purpose to which the silver was to be put is not stated, and while a logical deduction would be it was intended to fund temple operations, it has been suggested alternatively that it was to be used to create new deity statues (Cornell 2016, 298–309).

Once the temple in Jerusalem was rebuilt (23:18), the triannual pilgrimage calendar in Deut 16 would have become an important means of raising support for its operating costs. Significantly, no poll tax is

---

17 Many scholars noted that wives are nowhere listed among those who must attend the *ḥag* festivals. It is highly doubtful, however, that they were to remain to "hold down the fort" at home and protect the family property while everyone else was away. The most logical solution to this apparent anomaly is to remember that the smallest basic household unit was a husband and wife; a man did not set up his own house until he was married. Young couples might not have had any children yet but still constituted a household, with or without servants. Many women died in childbirth, so some households might have had no wife for a while, until the husband remarried. Even so, the definition of the basic household unit was a husband and wife.

mentioned in the book as a primary or supplementary means of funding the place Yhwh Elohim would place his name, as it is in Exod 30:13 and Neh 10:33–34. Were a pilgrimage site that would be used only three times a year envisioned, then no such tax would have been necessary. The vision presented in the book for these three festivals, which emphasizes their being occasions of rejoicing during which families were to eat their tithes, not use them to pay temple taxes or imperial taxes-in-kind, is consistent with a sacred site of pilgrimage without a full-time functioning temple and temple personnel.

Conclusion

Those responsible for Deuteronomy have reconceived the former royal cult of Yhwh Seba'ot and Asherah in many ways. They have moved to the idea of a single, invisible deity, Yhwh Elohim, that remains in heaven but places its name or reputation on earth. Yhwh Elohim is not to be presented in any sort of physical form. It is the god of Israel but also the deity that controls the fates of other groups. This deity is now the personal and family deity of every Israelite, replacing the former family god(s) and divinized ancestors.

This deity's will for its people has been revealed and written down in the scroll of teaching mediated by Moses. The three annual harvest festivals are now to be celebrated in honor of Yhwh Elohim alone, and all now commemorate Yhwh's saving act of the Exodus, enhancing the deity's reputation and making its presence felt among Israelites via stories about its saving deeds on behalf of its people. Observance of a weekly sabbath is to take place, also as a reminder of the foundational Exodus event. Meat may be procured without the use of an altar; the blood of the slaughtered animal is to be drained onto the ground. If part of the original conception and not a later addition, dietary laws, especially the avoidance of pork that was used in ancestral meals and probably also in the cult of Asherah, are to be followed. Visible reminders of Yhwh's personal protection will be provided through the inscription of words from the divine teaching on doorposts of houses, gates of housing complexes and possibly of walled settlements, and on amulets worn on the arm and around the head. Finally, acting in accordance with the divinely revealed and endorsed principles of justice within the community, toward fellow Israelites as well as resident non-natives, and respecting the decisions of higher authorities is envisioned as typifying the Israelite community. All of these ways of being a member of Israel can be observed inside or outside the promised land.

At the same time, the storyworld is set on the eve of the conquest and occupation of Cisjordan and conveys regulations for the community after it settles in this new home. The "final form" of the text envisions a single place Yhwh Elohim will choose to place his name, which will contain a temple staffed by priests. It will be the only legitimate venue for the practice of animal sacrifice to Yhwh Elohim. It also will house a court of appeals for legal disputes that cannot be decided locally. It will be the site where the three annual harvest celebrations in honor of Yhwh Elohim will take place communally. Three cities of refuge will operate in Cisjordan alongside the three allocated in Transjordan. These latter practices are specific to those Israelites who will inhabit the promised land.

Thus, Deuteronomy provides a blueprint for those who become members of the community of Israel wherever they live. It expects the majority to live within the promised land, where they can participate most fully in Israelite life; however, they also can be devoted Israelites in the Diaspora if they observe those practices and customs outlined in the teaching that do not specifically require performance at the central place or cities of refuge.

Works Cited

Ackerman, Susan. 1992. *Under Every Green Tree: Popular Religion in Sixth-Century Judah*. Harvard Semitic Monographs 46. Atlanta: Scholars.

Albertz, Rainer, Beth Alpert Nakhai, Saul M. Olyan, and Rüdiger Schmitt, eds. 2014. *Family and Household Religion: Toward a Synthesis of Old Testament Studies, Archaeology, Epigraphy, and Cultural Studies*. Winona Lake, IN: Eisenbrauns.

Albright, William F. 1958. "Palestinian Inscriptions." Pages 209–14 in *The Ancient Near East, Volume: An Anthology of Texts and Pictures*. Edited by James B. Pritchard. Princeton: Princeton University Press.

Altmann, Peter. 2011. *Festive Meals in Ancient Israel: Deuteronomy's Identity Politics in their Ancient Near Eastern Context*. Beihefte zur Zeitschrift für die alttestamentische Wissenschaft 424. Berlin: de Gruyter.

Amit, Yairah. 2000. *Hidden Polemics in Biblical Narratives*. Translated by Jonathan Chipman. Biblical Interpretation Series 35. Leiden: Brill.

Anderson, James S. 2016. *Monotheism and Yahweh's Appropriation of Baal*. Library of Hebrew Bible/Old Testament Studies 617. London: Bloomsbury.

Arnold, Bill T. 2016. "Israelite Worship as Envisioned and Prescribed in Deuteronomy 12." *Zeitschrift für altorientalische und biblische Rechtsgeschichte* 22: 161–75.

Binger, Tilde. 1997. *Asherah: Goddesses in Ugarit, Israel and the Old Testament.* Journal for the Study of the Old Testament Supplement Series 232; Copenhagen International Seminar 2. Sheffield: Sheffield Academic.

Blenkinsopp, Joseph. 1995. "Deuteronomy and the Politics of Post-Mortem Existence." *Vetus Testamentum* 45: 1-16.

Bloch-Smith, Elizabeth. 1992. *Judahite Burial Practices and Beliefs about the Dead.* American Schools of Oriental Research Monograph Series 7; Journal for the Study of the Old Testament Supplement Series 123. Sheffield: Sheffield Academic.

Braulik, Georg. 1994. "Deuteronomy and the Birth of Monotheism." Pages 99-130 in *The Theology of Deuteronomy: Collected Essays of Georg Braulik, O.S.B.* Translated by Ulrika Lindblad. Bibal Collected Essays 2. Richland Hill, TX: BIBAL.

Briant, Pierre. 2002. *From Cyrus to Alexander: A History of the Persian Empire.* Translated by Peter T. Daniels. Winona Lake, IN: Eisenbrauns.

Burnett, Joel S. 2001. *A Reassessment of Biblical Elohim.* Society of Biblical Literature Dissertation Series 183. Atlanta: Society of Biblical Literature.

Chavel, Simeon. 2015. "A Kingdom of Priests and its Earthen Altars in Exodus 19-24." *Vetus Testamentum* 65: 169-222.

Cohn, Yehudah B. 2008. *Tangled up in Text: Tefillin and the Ancient World.* Brown Judaic Studies 351. Providence, RI: Brown University.

Coleman, Simon and John Elsner. 1995. *Pilgrimage: Past and Present in the World Religions.* Cambridge, MA: Harvard University Press.

Cook, Stephen L. 2007. "Funerary Practices and Afterlife Expectations in Ancient Israel." *Religion Compass* 1: 660-83.

Cornell, Collin. 2016. "Cult Statuary in the Judean Temple at Yeb." *Journal for the Study of Judaism* 47: 291-309.

Darby, Erin. 2014. *Interpreting Judean Pillar Figurines: Gender and Empire in Judean Apotropaic Ritual.* Forschungen zum Alten Testament II 69. Tübingen: Mohr Siebeck.

Dever, William G. 2014. "The Judean 'Pillar-Base Figurines': Mothers or 'Mother-Goddesses'?" In *Family and Household Religion: Toward a Synthesis of Old Testament Studies, Archaeology, Epigraphy, and Cultural Studies,* edited by Rainer Albertz, Beth A. Nakhai, Saul M. Olyan, and Rudiger Schmitt. Winona Lake, IN: Eisenbrauns.

Edelman, Diana. 1995. "Tracking Observance of the Aniconic Tradition through Numismatics." Pages 185-225 in *The Triumph of 'Elohim: From Yahwisms to Judaisms.* Edited by D. V. Edelman. Contributions to Biblical Exegesis and Theology 3. Kampen, Netherlands: Kok Pharos.

------. 2009a. "God Rhetoric: Reconceptualizing Yahweh Sebaot as Yahweh Elohim in the Hebrew Bible." Pages 191-219 in *A Palimpsest: Rhetoric, Ideology, Stylistics and Language Relating to Persian Israel.* Edited by Ehud Ben Zvi, Diana Edelman, and Frank Polak. Piscataway, NJ: Gorgias.

———. 2009b. "From Prophets to Prophetic Books: Fixing the Divine Word." Pages 29–54 in *The Production of Prophecy: Constructing Prophecy and Prophets in Yehud*. Edited by Diana V. Edelman and Ehud Ben Zvi. BibleWorld. London: Equinox Publishing Ltd.

———. 2012. "Hidden Ancestor Polemics in the Book of Genesis?" Pages 35–56 in *Words, Ideas, World: Biblical Essays in Honour of Yairah Amit*. Edited by Athalya Brenner and Frank Polak. Sheffield: Sheffield Phoenix.

———. 2017a. "Adjusting Social Memory in the Hebrew Bible: The *Teraphim*." Pages 115–42 in *Congress Volume, Stellenbosch 2016*. Edited by Louis C. Jonker, Gideon R. Kotzé and Christl M. Maier. Supplements to Vetus Testamentum 177. Leiden: Brill.

———. 2017b "Living with Ancestral Spirits in Judah in the Iron Age and Persian Period." Pages 135–71 in *Entre dieux et hommes: anges, démons et autres … Actes du colloque organisé par le Collège de France, Paris, les 19-20 mai 2014*. Edited by Dominique Charpin, Thomas Römer, Bertrand Dufour, and Fabian Pfitzmann. Orbis Biblicus et Orientalis 286. Fribourg: Academic Press and Göttingen: Vandenhoeck & Ruprecht.

———. 2021. "Early Forms of Judaism as a Mixture of Strategies of Cultural Heterogeneity and the Re-embedding of Local Culture in Archaic Globalization." Pages 242–92 in *Levantine Entanglements: Local Dynamics of Globalization in a Contested Region*. Edited by Terje Stordalen and Øystein LaBianca. Sheffield: Equinox Publishing Ltd.

Flynn, Shawn. 2012. The Teraphim in Light of Mesopotamian and Egyptian Evidence." *Catholic Biblical Quarterly* 74: 694–711.

Frankfurter, David. 1998. "Introduction." Pages 3–48 in *Pilgrimage & Holy Space in Late Antique Egypt*. Edited by David Frankfurter. Religions in the Graeco-Roman World 134. Leiden: Brill.

Frevel, Christian. 1995. *Aschera und der Ausschließlichkeitsanspruch YHWHs. Beiträge zu Literarischen, religionsgeschichtlichen und ikonographischen Aspekten der Ascheradiskussion*. Weinheim: Beltz Athenäum.

Guillaume, Philippe. 2021. "Deuteronomy's *Māqōm* before Deuteronomy." Pages 195–217 in *Deuteronomy in the Making: Studies in the Production of Debarim*. Edited by Diana Edelman, Benedetta Rossi, Kåre Berge, and Philippe Guillaume. Beihefte zur Zeitschrift für die alttestamentische Wissenschaft 533. Berlin: de Gruyter.

Hadley, Judith M. 2000. *The Cult of Asherah in Ancient Israel and Judah: Evidence for a Hebrew Goddess*. University of Cambridge Oriental Publications 57. Cambridge and New York: Cambridge University Press.

Halpern, Baruch. 2009. "YHWH the Revolutionary: Reflections on the Rhetoric of Redistribution in the Social Context of Dawning Monotheism." Pages 179–212 in *From Gods to God: The Dynamics of Iron Age Cosmologies*. Edited by M. J. Adams. Forschungen zum Alten Testament 63. Tübingen: Mohr Siebeck.

------. 2021. "What Does Deuteronomy Centralize? Pages 97–162 in *Deuteronomy in the Making: Studies in the Production of Debarim*. Edited by Diana Edelman, Benedetta Rossi, Kåre Berge, and Philippe Guillaume. Beihefte zur Zeitschrift für die alttestamentische Wissenschaft 533. Berlin: De Gruyter.

Hays, Christopher B. 2011. *Death in the Iron Age II and in First Isaiah*. Forschungen zum Alten Testament 79. Tübingen: Mohr Siebeck.

Hillers, Delbert R. 1998. "Palmyrene Aramaic Inscriptions and the Bible." *Zeitschrift für Althebraistik* 11: 32–49.

Hulster, Izaak J. de. 2009. "A Yehud Coin with the Representation of a Sun Deity and Iconic Practice in Persian Period Palestine: An Elaboration on TC 242.5 / BMC Palestine XIX 29." 29 September, 2009. https://www.academia.edu/38727481/A_Yehud_coin_with_the_Representation_of_a_Sun_Deity_and_Iconic_Practice_in_Persian_Period_Palestine_An_Elaboration_on_TC_242.5_BMC_Palestine_XIX_29?auto

Hundley, Michael B. 2015. "Divine Presence in Ancient Near Eastern Temples." *Religion Compass* 9: 203–15.

Hutton, Jeremy. 2010. "Local Manifestations of YHWH and Worship in the Interstices: A Note on Kuntillet Ajrud." *Journal of Ancient Near Eastern Religions* 10: 177–210.

Keel, Othmar and Christophe Uehlinger. 1998. *God, Goddesses and Images of God: In Ancient Israel*. Translated by Thomas H. Trapp. Minneapolis: Fortress.

Kletter, Raz. 1996. *The Judean Pillar-Figurines and the Archaeology of Asherah*. British Archaeological Reports International Series 636. Oxford: Tempus Reparatum.

------. 2001. "Between Archaeology and Theology: The Pillar Figurines from Judah and the Asherah." Pages 179–216 in *Studies in the Archaeology of the Iron Age in Israel and Jordan*. Edited by Amihai Mazar with the assistance of Ginny Mathis. Journal for the Study of the Old Testament Supplement Series 331. Sheffield: Sheffield Academic.

Knoppers, Gary. 2013. *Jews and Samaritans: The Origins and History of their Early Relations*. Oxford: Oxford University Press.

Lemaire, André. 1995. "The Xanthos Trilingual Revisited." Pages 423–32 in *Solving Riddles and Untying Knots: Biblical, Epigraphic, and Semitic Studies in Honor of Jonas C. Greenfield*. Edited by Ziony Zevit, Seymour Gitin, and Michael Sokoloff. Winona Lake, IN: Eisenbrauns, 1995.

------. 2002. *Nouvelles inscriptions araméennes d'Idumée Tome II*. Paris: Gabalda.

------. 2015. *Levantine Epigraphy and History in the Achaemenid Period (539–332 BCE)*. Oxford: Oxford University Press.

Lewis, Theodore J. 1989. *Cults of the Dead in Ancient Israel and Ugarit*. Harvard Semitic Monographs 39: Atlanta: Scholars.

------. 2014. "Feasts for the Dead and Ancestor Veneration in Levantine Traditions." Pages 69–74 in *In Remembrance of Me: Feasting with the Dead in the Ancient Middle East*. Edited by Virginia Rimmer Herrmann and J. David Schloen. Chicago: Oriental Institute.

MacDonald, Nathan. 2003. *Deuteronomy and the Meaning of Monotheism*. 2nd ed. Forschungen zum Alten Testament 2.1. Tübingen: Mohr Siebeck.

Mayes, A. D. H. 1981. *Deuteronomy*. New Century Bible Commentary. Grand Rapids, MI: Eerdmans.

McCorriston, Joy. 2011. *Pilgrimage and Household in the Ancient Near East*. Cambridge: Cambridge University Press.

Mettinger, Tryggve N. D. 1995. *No Graven Image? Israelite Aniconism in Its Ancient Near Eastern Context*. Stockholm: Almqvist & Wicksell.

Meyers, Carol. 2010. "Household Religion." Pages 118–34 in *Religious Diversity in Ancient Israel and Judah*. Edited by Francesca Stavrakopoulou and John Barton. London: T & T Clark.

Minette de Tillesse, Georges. 1962. "Sections 'tu' et sections 'vous' dans le Deutéronome." *Vetus Testamentum* 12: 29–87.

Na'aman, Nadav. 2011. "The Inscriptions of Kuntillet 'Ajrud Through the Lens of Historical Research." *Ugarit Forschungen* 43: 299–324.

Nicholson, Ernest W. 1967. *Deuteronomy in History and Tradition*. Philadelphia: Fortress.

Niehr, Herbert. 1997. "In Search of YHWH's Cult Statue in the First Temple." Pages 73–95 in *The Image and the Book: Iconic Cults, Aniconism, and the Rise of Book Religion in Israel and the Ancient Near East*. Edited by Karel van der Toorn. Contributions to Biblical Exegesis and Theology 21. Leuven: Peeters.

———. 2003a. "The Changed Status of the Dead in Yehud." Pages 136–55 in *Yahwism After the Exile: Perspectives on Israelite Religion in the Persian Era: Papers Read at the First Meeting of the European Association for Biblical Studies, Utrecht, 6-9 August 2000*. Edited by Rainer Albertz and Bob Becking. Studies in Theology and Religion 5. Assen: Van Gorcum.

———. 2003b. "Götterbilder und Bilderverbot." Pages 227–47 in *Der eine Gott und die Götter. Polytheismus und Monotheismus im antiken Israël*. Edited by Manfred Oehming and Konrad Schmid. Abhandlungen zur Theologie des Alten und Neuen Testaments 82. Zurich: Theologischer Verlag.

Noth, Martin. 1967. *The Laws of the Pentateuch and Other Studies*. Translated by D. R. Ap-Thomas. Philadelphia: Fortress.

Nutkowicz, Hélène. 2006. *L'homme face à la mort au royaume de Juda: rites, pratiques et représentations*. Paris: Cerf.

Oestreicher, Theodor. 1923. *Das deuteronomische Grundgesetz*. Beiträge zur Förderung christlicher Theologie 27,4. Gütersloh: C. Bertelsmann.

Osborne, James F. 2011. "Secondary Mortuary Practice and the Bench Tomb: Structure and Practice in Iron Age Judah." *Journal of Near Eastern Studies* 70: 35–53.

Pessoa da Silva Pinto, Leonardo. 2019. "The Shema and the Devotion to Only One Deity." *Horizonte* 17: 20–42.

Phillips, Anthony. 1973. *Deuteronomy: Commentary*. Cambridge Bible Commentary 5. Cambridge: Cambridge University Press.
Porten, Bezalel. 1968. *Archives from Elephantine: The Life of an Ancient Jewish Military Colony*. Berkeley: University of California Press.
–––––– and Ada Yardeni. 1993. *Lists, Literary and Historical Texts*. Vol. 3 of *Textbook of Aramaic Documents from Ancient Egypt*. Jerusalem: Hebrew University. (=*TADAE*)
Rad, Gerhard von. 1953. *Studies in Deuteronomy*. Translated by David Stalker. Studies in Biblical Theology. Chicago: Henry Regnery.
Römer, Thomas. 2007. "Y avait-il une statue de YHWH dans le premier temple de Jérusalem? Enquêtes littéraires à travers la Bible hébraïque." *Asdiwal* 2: 41–58.
––––––. 2015. *The Invention of God*. Translated by R. Geuss. Cambridge, MA: Harvard University Press.
Rosenberg, Stephen. 2004. "The Jewish Temple at Elephantine." *Near Eastern Archaeology* 67: 4–13.
Rossi, Benedetta. 2021. "'Not by Bread Alone' (Deut 8:3): Elite Struggles over Cultic Prebends and Moses's Torah in Deuteronomy." Pages 329–63 in *Deuteronomy in the Making: Studies in the Production of Debarim*. Edited by Diana Edelman, Benedetta Rossi, Kåre Berge, and Philippe Guillaume. Beihefte zur Zeitschrift für die alttestamentische Wissenschaft 533. Berlin: de Gruyter.
Sanders, Seth. 2013. "The Appetites of the Dead: West Semitic Linguistic and Ritual Aspects of the Katumuwa Stele." *Bulletin of the American Schools of Oriental Research* 369: 85–105.
Sass, Benjamin. 1993. "The Pre-exilic Hebrew Seals: Iconism vs. Aniconism." Pages 194–256 in *Studies in the Iconography of Northwest Semitic Inscribed Seals: Proceedings of a Symposium Held in Fribourg on April 17–20, 1991*. Edited by Benjamin Sass and Christoph Uehlinger. Orbis Biblicus et Orientalis 125. Fribourg: University Press and Gottingen: Vandenhoeck & Ruprecht.
Sasson, Jack M. 2002. "On the Uses of Images in Israel and the Ancient Near East: A Response to Karel van der Toorn." Pages 63–70 in *Sacred Time Sacred Place: Archaeology and the Religion of Israel*. Edited by Barry M. Gittlen. Winona Lake, IN: Eisenbrauns.
Schmidt, Brian B. 1996. *Israel's Beneficent Dead: Ancestor Cult and Necromanacy in Israelite Religion and Tradition*. Winona Lake, IN: Eisenbrauns.
Schmitt, Rüdiger. 2012a. "Care for the Dead in the Context of the Household and Family." Pages 429–73 in *Family and Household Religion in Ancient Israel and the Levant*. Edited by Rainer Albertz and Rüdiger Schmitt. Winona Lake, IN: Eisenbrauns.
––––––. 2012b. "Rites of Family and Household Religion." Pages 387–428 in *Family and Household Religion in Ancient Israel and the Levant*. Edited by Rainer Albertz and Rüdiger Schmitt. Winona Lake, IN: Eisenbrauns.

Segal, Moses H. 1961. "The Composition of the Pentateuch-- A Fresh Examination." Pages 68–114 in *Studies in the Bible*. Edited by Chaim Rabin. *Scripta Hierosolymitana* 8. Jerusalem: Magnes Press.

Smith, George Adam. 1918. *The Book of Deuteronomy*. Cambridge: Cambridge University Press.

Stern, Ephraim. 1989. "What Happened to the Cult Figurines? Israelite Religion Purified after the Exile." *Biblical Archaeology Review* 15: 22–29, 53.

------. 1999. "Religion in Palestine in the Assyrian and Persian periods." Pages 245–55 in *Crisis of Israelite Religion: Transformation of Religious Tradition in Exilic and Post-exilic Times*. Edited by Bob Becking, and Marjo C. A. Korpel. Leiden: Brill.

------. 2006. "The Religious Revolution in Persian-period Judah." Pages 199–205 in *Judah and the Judeans in the Persian Period*. Edited by Oded Lipschits and Manfred Oeming. Winona Lake, IN: Eisenbrauns.

Teixidor, Javier. 1978. "The Aramaic Text in the Trilingual Stele from Xanthus." *Journal of Near Eastern Studies* 37: 180–85.

Thomas, Ryan. 2017. "The Meaning of *asherah* in Hebrew Inscriptions." *Semitica* 59: 157–218.

Tigay, Jeffrey H. 1982. "On the Meaning of T(W)TPT." *Vetus Testamentum* 101: 321–31.

Toorn, Karel van der. 1996. *Family Religion in Babylonia, Syria and Israel: Continuity and Change in the Forms of Religious Life*. Studies in the History and Culture of the Ancient Near East 7. Leiden: Brill.

------. 2002. "Israelite Figurines: A View from the Texts." Pages 45–62 in *Sacred Time Sacred Place: Archaeology and the Religion of Israel*. Edited by Barry M. Gittlen. Winona IN: Eisenbrauns.

------ and Theodore J. Lewis. 1995. "תרפים terapim." Pages 765–78 in *Theologisches Worterbuch zum Alten Testament*, vol. 8. Edited by H.-J. Fabry and Helmer Ringgren. Stuttgart: Kohlhammer.

Uehlinger, Christophe. 1997. "Anthropomorphic Cult Statuary in Iron Age Palestine and the Search for Yahweh's Cult Images." Pages 97–156 in *The Image and the Book: Iconic Cults, Aniconism, and the Rise of Book Religion in Israel and the Ancient Near East*. Edited by Karel Van der Toorn. Contributions to Biblical Exegesis and Theology 21. Leuven: Peeters.

Vorländer, Hermann. 1975. *Mein Gott: Die Vorstellungen vom persönlichen Gott im Alten Orient und im Alten Testament*. Alter Orient und Altes Testament 23. Kevelaer: Butzon & Bercker.

Welch, Adam C. 1924. *The Code of Deuteronomy: A New Theory of Its Origins*. London: James Clarke.

Wiggins, Steve A. 2007. *A Reassessment of Asherah: With Further Considerations of the Goddess*. Gorgias Ugaritic Studies 2. Piscataway, NJ: Gorgias.

Wolf, Eric. 1958. "The Virgin of Guadaloupe: Mexican National Symbol." *Journal of American Folklore* 71: 34–39.

Wyatt, N. 2012. "After Death Has Us Parted: Encounters between the Living and the Dead in the Ancient Semitic World." Pages 259–92 in *The Perfumes of Seven Tamarisks: Studies in Honour of Wilfred G. E. Watson*. Edited by Gregorio del Olmo Lete, Jordi Vidal, and Nicolas Wyatt. Alter Orient und Altes Testament 394. Münster: Ugarit.

Zevit, Ziony. 2001. *The Religions of Ancient Israel: A Synthesis of Parallactic Approaches*. New York: Continuum.

About the Author

Diana V. Edelman is professor emerita at the Faculty of Theology, University of Oslo. Her research interests focus on the history, archaeology, and literature of the ancient Southern Levant more generally, and on Judah and Samaria in the Iron Age, Neo-Babylonian, and Persian periods more specifically.

Chapter 8
Master-Scribe and Forefather of a Scribal Guild: Moses in Deuteronomy

Benedetta Rossi

Abstract

Among the various features of Moses' portrayal, the depiction of Moses as ancestor has received scant attention. In the following essay, I shall show that Deuteronomy portrays Moses as master-scribe and the founder of a scribal priestly class, the Levitical priests. The *sefer hattorah* is the legacy Moses bequeaths. It represents a fictionalized compendium of a complete scribal curriculum, reframed as Moses's farewell speech. As his personal bequest, the Torah scroll legitimized the authority of its keepers in relation to other priestly groups. In addition, Levitical priests use the *sefer hattorah* to put themselves forward as the authoritative and reliable guides of the community.

Keywords: Deuteronomy, Moses, Moses's Torah, scribal culture, Levitical priests

Starting from the legend of his birth, Moses assumes the traits of a heroic figure (Coats 1988, 9–36).[1] Throughout the desert, Moses exercises the functions of judge, intercessor for Israel (Aurelius 1988; Widmer 2004), lawgiver, covenant-mediator, as well as founder of the cult (Fischer 2000, 84–120; Otto 2006, 75–81; Otto 2010a, 568–71; Carr 2012; Kratz 2018, 61–63;

---

1   Outside the Pentateuch, Moses is mentioned in the Former Prophets, in Ezra, Nehemiah, and Chronicles. The references found in the prophets (Isa 63:11; Jer 15:1; Mic 6:4 and Mal 3:22) and in the Psalms (77:21; 90:1; 99:6–7; 105:25; 106:16, 23, 32–33) likely have been influenced by Dtr or post-exilic texts and thus would be late additions; cf. Römer 2004–2005, 100–1.

Edelman et al. 2012, 154–75; see Römer 2012 for marginal and extrabiblical traditions). What does Deuteronomy add to the portrait of Moses sketched previously in Exodus-Numbers? The depiction of Moses as a prophet is the first new feature (Deut 18:15; 34:10–12). Prophetic traits have also been identified in his oracles about the future of Israel (4:25–28; 29:21–28; 31:26–30), the Song in ch. 32, and his death beyond the Jordan outside the promised land (von Rad 1962, 292–95; Perlitt 1994; Sonnet 2016, 278–81; Otto 2021). Moses as a scribe, as archetype and model for scribes, is a second feature. It has also been extensively explored (Watts 1998; Otto 2005; Heckl 2013, 200–4; van der Toorn 2007, 167–69; Sonnet 2016, 278–81).

The depiction of Moses as an ancestor has received scant attention, however. Since genealogies play a marginal role in Moses's story, there has been a tendency to overlook his characterization as an "ancestor" (Edelman et al. 2012, 170), though Albert de Pury (1994; 2001) identified two competing ancestral legends, one relating to Jacob and the other to Moses. He suggests that they offer alternative models for belonging to Israel: through genealogy (Jacob) and through listening to Moses's teaching and accepting his mediation.

Moses's blessings in Deut 33 echo Jacob's blessings in Gen 49 to present Moses as a new Jacob (Schmid 2010, 84–86; Otto 2010b, 574; Otto 2017, 2,230–36), except that Moses does not function as an ancestor. Deuteronomy does not portray Israel as the successors of Moses (Sonnet 1997, 210–15), and in Exod 32 and Num 14 Moses explicitly refuses to be the ancestor of a people *via* genealogy. Joshua somewhat succeeds Moses, but less so than the Levitical priests upon whom Moses bestows the *sefer hattorah* (Deut 31:9), which ultimately is his true successor (Ska 2013). The Levitical priests are thereby foregrounded as priestly scribes (Deut 17:18) in charge of the reading and future interpretation of the Torah scroll (Deut 31:11–13). A group of scribal experts is a novelty within the Pentateuch. Besides Deuteronomy (Edelman 2023), only Exod 5 hints at a group with scribal-like features (שטרים), which it portrays negatively.

The *sefer hattorah* they receive from Moses confers on the Levitical priests much prestige and authority. In Deuteronomy, they appear as a new elite, as *homines novi* (Rossi 2021, 352–57). But where do they come from? Other priestly groups claim descent from Aaron. In Mesopotamia, Greece, and Egypt, scribal knowledge and expertise were transmitted from father to son, as colophons of scribal exercises testify (Hunger 1968, 16–20; Robson 2008, 231–36, 241–42, 245–51). It is plausible to think that Levitical priests also had an interest in building a pedigree. Levitical priests "claim the legacy of Moses" by referring to Moses as "their ancestor and their patron" (van der Toorn 2007, 167). Hence,

Karel van der Toorn (2007, 150–66) considers Deuteronomy a sample of scribal culture, i.e. the outcome of four successive editions: the Covenant Edition, the Torah Edition, the History Edition, and the Wisdom Edition. He defines Moses's legacy as scribal competence but does not go any further regarding the transmission of scribal skills and the contents of scribal training.

In the following, I shall show that Deuteronomy portrays Moses as a master-scribe and forefather of a scribal guild, the Levitical priests (§§1 and 2). In the absence of a common genealogy, they are ultimately responsible for depicting Moses as their ancestor, legitimizing their authority, and creating a background for their social ascent. The *sefer hattorah* represents precisely a compendium of the scribal expertise handed down by the forefather, Moses, to the scribes who were his heirs, i.e. the Levitical priests. Parallels from Mesopotamia and Egypt provide insightful evidence to support the claim (§3). An analysis of Moses's blessing over Levi (Deut 33:8–11) will reveal a challenge being made to the claim of superiority based on a priestly genealogical ancestry derived from Aaron and the claim that, ultimately, inherited expertise is the primary source of authority instead (§4). This can also shed light on the circumstances and reasons that impelled the Levitical priests to portray Moses as their ancestor and as a master-scribe (§5).

The picture that emerges in this contribution is slightly different from the one outlined by van der Toorn. In his view, the scribes behind Deuteronomy came from priestly families from the North. They were trained in priestly competence and later added scribal expertise to their skills and identified Moses as their ancestor (2007, 166–72). I argued elsewhere that Levitical priests arose from the administrative milieu of the Levites who served as tax collectors in the countryside and were involved in the administration of the temple (see the Levites "within your gates" in Deuteronomy and Neh 10:38–39; Rossi 2021, 357–58). Thanks to their scribal skills, they acquired prebendary privileges and performed some cultic duties, which spurred tensions with traditional priestly dynasties deputed in particular to sacrifices and blood-handling. Deuteronomy 18:1–8 transmits some traces of the quarrel over prebends (Rossi 2021, 341–50). Against this background, the Levitical priests claimed Moses, the master-scribe, as their ancestor and created a scribal pedigree to legitimize their position against the genealogical legitimation of priesthood.

1. The Farewell Address of a Scribe

Moses's scribal skills appear already in Exod 24, where he "writes all the words of Yhwh" (כתב, v. 4) and then reads aloud (קרא באזן, v. 7) the written *sefer habberit* to the people.[2] In Deuteronomy, however, Moses's portrait as a scribe takes a different direction from that in Exodus. A link between Exod 24:4, 7 and Deut 31:9, especially between the two scrolls written by Moses (i.e. the *sefer habberit* and the *sefer hattorah*), is often recognized. It is commonly held that the writing of the *sefer habberit* by Moses in Exod 24 is antecedent to the *sefer hattorah* in Deut 31:9, which is considered a response to the former (e.g. Markl 2020, 441). However, the question is not settled (see Rossi, forthcoming). In Deuteronomy Moses does not proclaim (קרא) the content of the written scroll to the people; only a tiny portion appended to the scroll (i.e. the Song of Deut 32) will be read after being inscribed (Deut 31:24). The public reading of the whole Torah scroll is the prerogative of the Levitical priests and delayed until entering the promised land (Deut 31:11–13).

Compared to the writing and reading skills at hand in Exod 24:4, 7, Deuteronomy provides further details about Moses's scribal expertise. Deuteronomy 1:5 summarizes Moses's words that follow with the expression: "Moses began to expound this Torah." The verb באר *piel* can be traced back to a scribal milieu, whether interpreted as "to explain," "to clarify" (< Akk. *bârum*; *CAD* B, 127), "to enforce" from a legal point of view (< Akk. *bârum* III), or to "interpret" (Otto 2005, 278–79; Ska 2007, 81–83). The etymological relation of the verb באר with בְּאֵר ("well") evokes teaching as a source of water and life, a likely link to wisdom and the scribal milieu (Edelman 2015, 318–25). Moses's activity in Deuteronomy is characterized as teaching (verb *lāmad*: 4:1, 5, 14; 5:31; 6:1; 31:22; but also *śym + tôrâ*: 4:44; *nātan + tôrâ*: 4:8; verb *ṣiwwah + tôrâ*: 33:4), a prerogative of scribal expertise and training.

Unlike Exod 24, Deuteronomy closely binds up Moses's scribal expertise with his succession. Interpretation and teaching (1:5) of the Torah are embedded in a sequence of four speeches (1:6–4:40; 4:44–28:68; 28:69–32:52; and 33:1–34:12) that Moses delivers before his death (Braulik and Lohfink 2021, 361–90). Already in the first speech (1:6–4:40), Moses evokes his death and succession (3:26–28). A quotation of Yhwh's words in 3:27 introduces the new reference to Moses's death in 31:2. The orders given by Yhwh for Joshua's succession, briefly mentioned in 3:28, are here carried out by Moses. The account of the writing of the *sefer* in 31:9 and the instructions given by Moses for its future transmission in 31:10–13

---

2   On Moses and writing in the Pentateuch, see Heckl 2013, 204–21.

interrupt the account of the investiture of Joshua in 31:7–8, 14. The Torah scroll thus comes to occupy a prominent place in the succession of Moses, eventually creating a parallel with Joshua himself. To a certain extent, the *sefer hattorah* is Moses's successor (so Ska 2013). The writing of the Song (31:24) appended to the book of Torah and its proclamation to the people (31:30) are also accompanied by hints about Moses's death and the events that will follow it (31:27, 29).

To sum up: two elements distinguish the depiction of Moses as scribe in Deuteronomy: a) references to his death and succession; and b) the use of lexemes and phrases that contribute to his characterization as a scribe, which are concentrated in the frames (chs. 1; 4; 5; 6; 31; 33). Whether the scribal characterization of Moses has been secondarily included together with the additional framing texts or was composed at the same time as the rest of the text, it is plausible that this characterization was meant as an interpretive key for the whole book. Deuteronomy is the farewell address of the scribe Moses who passes on his inheritance in the form of the Torah scroll and instructions for its transmission.

2. Scribal Skills as Moses's Legacy

According to Deut 31:9–13, the Torah scroll as well as instructions concerning its transmission are the heritage bestowed by Moses, the master-scribe, on Levitical priests. Some remarks are in order to clarify the elders' position, the stance of the whole of Israel toward the Torah, and its transmission.

2.1. The Elders and the Scroll

According to Deut 31:9, the Torah scroll is handed over to the Levitical priests and to "the elders of Israel." Yet, it is only the Levitical priests who are in charge of keeping the scroll and placing it beside the ark (31:25–26) they are required to transport. The Levitical priests are the custodians of the master-copy of the Torah, which will be transcribed by the king (17:18). Finally, Deut 31:10–12 shift from plural to singular addresses. Although the book is given to Levitical priests and elders, it is a singular "you" who shall "read this law before all Israel in their hearing" (Deut 31:11), which excludes the elders (Lundbom 2013, 835; Otto 2017, 2,116). The elders do not read the law, but their presence beside the Levitical priests in Deut 31:9 highlights the "lay" character of the Torah as opposed to the priestly Torah, which, according to Lev 10:10–11, is entrusted exclusively to Aaron (Otto 2017, 2,115).

2.2 A Legacy for the Entire Community?

The connection between the Torah and hereditary possession is made explicit in 33:4 by the noun מורשה "possession." The LXX translates this noun as κληρονομία "inheritance" (Wevers 1977). In particular, Deut 33:4 describes the Torah communicated orally by Moses (צוה) as a hereditary possession (מורשה) given to the whole "assembly of Jacob" (קהלת יעקב).[3] In Deut 33:4 the first-person plural who are speaking ("Moses commanded us a Torah," תורה צוה־לנו משה) can be understood as the intradiegetic recipients of Moses's speech in Moab, those who hear his oral teaching. According to Eckart Otto (2017, 2,221–2), in Deut 33:4 the interplay between verbal ("Moses commanded us a Torah," תורה צוה לנו משה) and nominal clauses ("a possession for the assembly of Jacob," מורשה קהלת יעקב) mirrors the shift between the Moab generation and the post-exilic addressees of Deuteronomy. If this is the case, the Torah is entrusted as an inherited possession to the entire, post-exilic Israel. However, the phrase קהלת יעקב ("assembly of Jacob") could also hint at the Moab congregation. In Deuteronomy, the nouns קהלה/קהל or the phrase קהל ישראל refer to the gathering at Horeb (Deut 9:10; 10:4; 18:16; see Lundbom 2013, 924), mirrored by the one in Moab, or to the same assembly in Moab before which Moses proclaims the Song (Deut 31:30). While Moses's oral communication of the Torah in Deut 33:4 is the hereditary possession of the Israelites gathered in Moab, i.e. the assembly of Jacob (מורשה קהלת יעקב), the written form of the same Torah is bequeathed to the Levitical priests (Deut 31:9).

2.3 Transmission of the Torah Scroll

Together with the scroll, Moses hands over to the Levites instructions for its future transmission. The Levitical priests are to read to the community the contents of the book Moses hands over to them once every seven years (31:11). This duty establishes a parallel with Moses's teaching at Horeb.

In Deut 4:10, Yhwh orders Moses to assemble the people ("assemble the people for me," הקהל־לי את־העם) and communicate the words so that

---

[3] The oral dimension of the Torah in 33:4 is further underlined in the Greek Deuteronomy by a textual variant in Codex Ambrosianus A147 (F): λογον, ον ενετειλατο ημιν Μωυσης ("a word, which Moses commanded us"); LXX: νομον, ον ενετειλατο ημιν Μωυσης; ("a law, which Moses commanded us") see Wevers 1977, 363. Nielsen 1995, 299: v. 4 is to be considered a gloss added to the text. However, the structure of the text and the parallel between 33:2 and 33:4 prevent the discarding of v. 4 as an addition; see Otto 2017, 2,242.

they can learn to fear Yhwh ("and I will let them listen to my words so that they may learn to fear me," ואשמעם את־דברי אשר ילמדון ליראה אתי). The roots שמע ("to listen/hear") and למד ("to learn") foreground the idea of instruction imparted orally. In 31:11–13, Moses invites the Levitical priests to gather the people every seven years (v. 12: "assemble the people," הקהל את־העם) to read and proclaim the scroll of "this Torah" (v. 11: "proclaim aloud this Torah," תקרא את־התורה הזאת) to all the people. As in 4:10, the objective of the reading is summarized by the verbs "listen, learn and fear" Yhwh (31:12: "so that they may hear and learn to fear Yhwh your God," למען ישמעו ולמען ילמדו ויראו את־יהוה אלהיכם). The following table summarizes the parallel:

At Horeb, Moses (4:10)	In Canaan, the Levitical priests (31:11–13)
assembled the people	assemble the people, men, women, children, immigrants
so that they listened to Yhwh's words	so that they listen
to learn	so that they learn
to fear Yhwh	and fear Yhwh and guard to do all the words of this Torah
and teach their children	and their sons will hear and learn to fear Yhwh

Before dying, Moses transfers his teaching role to Levitical priests. Along with the *sefer hattorah* (31:9), Moses conveys to them a teaching role, bound to the content of the *sefer* (Otto 2017, 2,117–18).

The transfer of Moses's scribal skills (including reading and teaching) to the Levitical priests is confirmed by the use of the root ירה in Deuteronomy: Deut 17:10–11 (instructions imparted by judges and Levitical priests), 24:8 (teaching of Levitical priests), and 33:10. Whereas the teaching of the Levites in 33:10 is supposedly based on the scroll Moses hands over to them and to the elders, the instructions Levitical priests give in 17:10–11 and 24:8 are seemingly received directly from Moses. The content of these instructions remains, however, inaccessible to the people (and the reader as well). Hence, besides the written Torah and the instructions for its teaching, Moses hands over to the Levitical priests other instructions (verb ירה) that are even less accessible to the rest of the community than those recorded in the Torah scroll stored beside the ark. Scribal teaching skills, expressed by the root ירה, linked to jurisprudence and medical lore, are not explicitly transmitted by the Torah. All in all, this is more akin to the secret knowledge typical of scribal circles in other cultures (Borger 1964; Hunger 1968, 13–14).

In summary, Moses bequeaths to the Levitical priests scribal crafts and skills, i.e. the *sefer hattorah*, its custody and control (31:26; 17:18), as well as the arrangements for its transmission (31:10–13). Additional instructions (ירה) not recorded in the Torah scroll reinforce the exclusive link between Moses and the guild of the Levitical priests, heirs of specific scribal functions. An examination of the content of the *sefer hattorah* provides further elements that support this link.

3. The *Sefer Hattorah:* A Fictional Scribal Curriculum

The extent of the book of the Torah written by Moses is debated. Jean Pierre Sonnet (1997, 248) and Dominik Markl (2012, 165) consider Deut 5–30 the plausible extent of the *sefer*. However, the references to "this Torah" in 1:5 and 4:44 make it clear that the written Torah in 31:9 is to be considered the writing of the Torah expounded (באר *piel*) by Moses in Moab, and thus also includes Deut 1–4. Therefore, the *sefer hattorah* can be identified with Deut 1:6–30:20 (Otto 2017, 2,111). However, following Deuteronomy, another chapter must be added to the *sefer hattorah*. According to Deut 31:22, 24, Moses wrote the song (Deut 32) as a supplement to the Torah (31:22: "Moses wrote this Song, that same day") and added it to the *sefer* (31:24: "when Moses finished writing <u>the words of this Torah</u> in a scroll, <u>to the end</u>," ויהי ככלות משה לכתב <u>את־דברי</u> <u>התורה־הזאת</u> על־ספר <u>עד תמם</u>). The interplay between Deut 31:22 and 31:24 shows that the *sefer hattorah* quite reasonably includes Deut 1:6–30:20 and Moses's Song (ch. 32), but probably not the entire book of Deuteronomy (against Blum 2007, 84–89).

Contentwise, the *sefer* presents a sequence of various literary genres held together in the frame of a farewell speech by Moses (van der Toorn 2007, 144; Edelman 2021). The first-person narrative of Deut 1:6–3:29, which offers a historical retrospective of the journey of Israel in the desert, occurs alongside parenetic exhortations (Deut 4–11; 29–30), laws and regulations (Deut 12–26), blessings and curses (Deut 27–28), a ritual text (Deut 27), and a song/hymn in poetic form (Deut 32). Although prevalent in the sections indicated, these literary genres appear mostly in a mixed format. For example, legal texts are intertwined with exhortations that urge the observance of prescriptions, illustrating their benefits. This peculiarity distinguishes the prescriptions in Deuteronomy from ancient Near Eastern legal codes (Edelman 2021, 40) and led Gerhard von Rad (1953, 15) to conclude that chs. 12–26 are not exactly a collection of laws but a sermon on the commandments. The Decalogue is also inserted into a typically parenetic section in a first-person narrative.

Following the hints provided in the framing texts (Deut 1:5; chs. 31 and 34), the mixture of literary genres has been interpreted as Torah-teaching in Moab, covenant treaty, or Moses's farewell speech. However, the apparent harmony of the text is misleading. As van der Toorn (2007, 144) observes, "the perspectives of a final teaching or Torah, on the one hand, and a treaty, on the other, are scarcely compatible." From a diachronic perspective, the "misleading" harmony of the materials is easily explained as the result of the accumulation of different textual layers over time. The question remains whether this is the best explanation or if the inclusion of a mixture of genres was a deliberate strategy for the composition of the *sefer hattorah*.

If we consider the material production of ancient texts, a tendency to insert additions in framing positions before or after the earlier text was the standard practice. The analysis of preserved manuscripts and tablets indicates that this was the most suitable and practical place to insert revisions and additions (Milstein 2016, 1-6; Carr 2020, 604-8). Bearing this is mind, it is plausible to investigate the nature and purpose of the *sefer hattorah* by starting with Deuteronomy's outer frames (Deut 1:1-5; ch. 31; chs. 33-34). These texts emphasize Moses's scribal skills, birth, and the vicissitudes of the Torah scroll; the same chapters envisage Moses's death and his succession.

As previously illustrated, the *sefer hattorah*, together with a series of scribal functions (teaching and the possession, reading, and transmission of the Torah scroll), is Moses's legacy to Levitical priests. On this basis, I argue that the *sefer hattorah* (Deut 1:6-30:20; 32) displays a collection of literary patterns typically taught in the curriculum of ancient scribes from Mesopotamia and Egypt. The sequence of patterns and genres scribes learned to master is then further framed as Moses's farewell speech. In this way, the curriculum is given a fictional story setting in which, on the eve of his death, Moses personally bequeaths its content to a scribal elite, the Levitical priests, thus legitimizing them as his professional "successors." Comparison with scribal education in Mesopotamia illustrates the overlap of genres in Deuteronomy and Mesopotamian scribal training texts. Late Egyptian Miscellanies provide a reference point for understanding the fictionalization of various genres by placing them in a literary setting.

3.1 Mesopotamian Scribal Training

Scribal education in Mesopotamia was made up of a series of steps and structured by the practice of various exercises, which progressed from the simplest exercises in writing to the reproduction of the most complex literary texts. Two levels of learning, elementary and advanced, typically can be distinguished for the Old, Neo and Late Babylonian periods (Veldhuis 2016; Gesche 2001, 58-198; Robson 2011, 562-64). In the Neo- and Late Babylonian periods, a fairly standard set of texts was employed for instruction, covering the various possible skills required of a scribe.[4] The identification of important and recurrent texts for the education of the scribes is based on the number of copies found and the frequency of references to the title of the work in scribal school tablets. Besides individual texts, it is equally important to recognize which text genres were part of the curriculum (see Gesche 2001, 173: "what is essential for an investigation of school teaching is above all to recognize which text genres, not which individual texts, were part of the curriculum [my translation]"). Thus, mastering different literary patterns, more than memorizing the content of individual texts, seems to have been the objective of scribal education. Vocabulary lists and proverbs belonged to the lowest level of instruction (Gesche 2001, 150). Exorcisms, prayers, administrative texts, fictional letters, law cases, and literary and historiographical texts were part of the second level.

In the course of scribal education, texts representing different genres were copied on the same tablet in a more or less fixed sequence (Gesche 2001, 44–57, 174–83). Tablets that witness to the lowest level of education with writing exercises, spelling primers, and vocabulary lists are easily distinguishable from tablets of a different format containing, in addition to the primers, extracts of incantations, exorcisms from various collections (Šurpu and Maqlû), prayers, and portions of literary texts such as the Enūma Eliš (Gesche 2001, 44–52; Robson 2011, 562–63). The writing of extracts from different texts on small school tablets is attested as late as the Hellenistic period. Cuneiform tablets with transliteration in Greek – the so-called Graeco-Babyloniaca – probably were written by Greek students who were being instructed in the Babylonian language and culture (Gesche 2001, 184–85). This practice attests to the stability of the scribal training system throughout the centuries. In Greco-Roman Egypt, scholastic and scribal training remained substantially similar to that in ancient Mesopotamia and earlier practice in Egypt (Cribiore 1996).

---

4   Concerning Old Babylonian schools, Herman L. J. Vanstiphout (1995, 7–8) identifies two main elements of the curriculum: lists and literary texts. Although specific examples could be used in different periods (Robson 2019, 10–48) these two categories remain the basis for the subsequent periods. Petra D. Gesche (2001, 172–73) asserts that in the Neo- and Late Babylonian periods, the pupils had as tools "a set canon of texts […] that they used in teaching (my translation)." Similarly, David M. Carr (2005, 22) also identifies a series of "model documents" that form part of the scribal curriculum in Babylonia, including "model letters, hymns, treaties, and certain classical documents". Although different language is used that might be confusing, all four scholars are agreeing that there was a standard set of genres taught in the curriculum, even if the specific examples of each changed over time.

Samples of different literary genres typical of the scribal curriculum are unified not only by writing them on a single tablet but also by titles and colophons (Hunger 1968; Gesche 2001, 153–66). These specify the name of the scribe and in some cases, his membership in a family of scribes. They also make explicit the purpose of the writing of the tablet, which often ends with invocations or prayers to deities or to the tablet itself. Examples include the Late Babylonian prayer to Nabû and the invocation to the tablet on the reverse of CTMMA 65 (Gesche 2005, 259–60) and BM 77665+ (Gesche 2005, 650–52).

Similar evidence of a collection of school exercises comes from Emar, an inland site in northern Syria (Cohen 2016, 124–25) and Ugarit, an ancient port in northern Syria (van Soldt 2016, 146–47). Both date to the late Bronze Age. Besides lexical lists, religious and literary texts also were copied and transmitted; as Yoram Cohen (2016, 124–25) points out, the contents of school texts – starting with lexical lists – were modified to fit local needs but the genres remained stable.

3.2 Fictionalizing a Scribal Curriculum: From Tablets to Scrolls

The Late Egyptian miscellanies offer an interesting additional comparison for observing the transition from tablet to scroll as well as more complex strategies of contextualization, including a kind of fictionalization of the scribal curriculum (Hagen 2006; Ragazzoli 2019, 84–99). The Late Egyptian miscellanies are "consecutive collections of short compositions of heterogeneous kinds" that went by the label, "instructions" (sbꜣyt) (Gardiner 1937, ix). According to Nili Shupak (1993, 31–34), the noun parallels biblical Hebrew מוסר. Similar to the Egyptian sbꜣyt, the Hebrew מוסר means both "instruction" (e.g. Prov 1:8) and "discipline" (Shupak 1993, 33). Among the genres collected in the miscellanies are letters (fictional or genuine), hymns, eulogies (about the king or the capital), instructions, exhortations, administrative texts, and lexical lists (Ragazzoli 2019, 267–326). A miscellaneous collection might sometimes appear in a scroll containing literary texts (didactic works, historical narratives), hymns, or magical texts.

The nature and purpose of the Late Egyptian miscellanies have been debated. The dominant view, proposed by Adolf Erman (1925) and also endorsed by Alan Gardiner (1937), is that the miscellanies papyri are collections of exercises produced by scribes-in-training (Hagen 2006, 86–93; Ragazzoli 2019, 96–98). Fredrik Hagen (2006, 86–93) critiques this view by pointing out that the handwriting and the literary quality of these texts make it unlikely the exercises were written by apprentice scribes. According to Stephen G. Quirke (1996, 383), "The potential of the passages for teaching is self-evident, but may be compared to the onomastica;

these might all be advanced learning, not teaching, devices." An analysis of the corrections in the margins of scrolls indicates they should not be considered corrections made by a teacher, as Erman (1925, 6–8) suggested, but rather, understood to be "self-corrections" made by scribes (Hagen 2006, 8). In Hagen's view, the attribution of the label "scribal exercises" to the Late Egyptian Miscellanies is misleading. What, then, are the characteristics and the possible uses of these miscellaneous manuscripts?

One of the most significant characteristics is that a sequence of different literary genres is re-contextualized by being copied onto a single scroll. Further literary strategies are then applied, like the use of titles, colophons, or epistolary formulas to frame sequences of prayers, eulogies, sapiential sayings, and even lists (Hagen 2006, 95–97). As Hagen (2006, 96) highlights, "The epistolary form, with the explicit mention of speaker and recipient, serves to contextualize the contents and make them relevant to the reader on a personal level."

In some cases, the collections are organized by thematic principles; Papyrus Lansing, for example, contains an array of texts about the scribal profession (Ragazzoli 2019, 292–93). Lexical lists are re-contextualized in fictional contexts, for example, that of temple taxes, tribute for foreign princes, or preparations for the arrival of Pharaoh (Ragazzoli 2019, 241–42). As Chloé Ragazzoli (2019, 246) explains, the reference to administrative use is thematic, not functional. In royal eulogies, in particular, the miscellanies appropriate texts from the monumental sphere, recontextualizing them literarily. She notes (2019, 326) that the miscellanies appear as "the archive and laboratory of the literate production of their time […] a kind of *vademecum* of the scribes' culture in the New Kingdom" (my translation). This process of recontextualization differentiates the Late Egyptian miscellanies from the purely educational sphere and makes them – according to Hagen's definition (2006, 96–97) – not primary but "secondary" educational texts. What, then, is the purpose of these collections?

Without excluding their use in education, Hagen argues that the Late Egyptian miscellanies, with their sampling of literary genres, serve as *reference works* for later compositions, like letter-writing (Hagen 2006, 95). Alongside this practical use, the miscellany collection also seems to provide a collection of "functional works" for consulting (Hagen 2006, 96). A development of the texts seems apparent; probably originating as scribal exercises, the Late Egyptian miscellanies would have become reference texts.[5]

---

5 Hagen 2006, 96–97 is cautious about using the term "exercises" to characterize the miscellanies. I interpret his phrase "cultural texts," he uses to characterize the final stage of development, to mean reference works.

These characteristics have led Ragazzoli (2019, 275) to define the Late Egyptian miscellanies papyri as scribal literature written by scribes and addressed to scribes. Through a combination of literary genres that reflect the elements of the scribal curriculum, the miscellaneous papyri extol the scribes' craft, set their standards, and construct their identity in opposition to other professions. The display of scribal art serves to emphasize their elite position. According to Ragazzoli's felicitous definition, scribal discourse takes the form of a sort of "rhetorical poaching" (my translation) used to construct one's elite identity. In Egyptian society, scribal art and the mastery of the scroll were instruments of social ascent and the legitimation of an elite class.

In short, the Late Egyptian miscellanies witness to a fictionalized scribal curriculum and become instruments of legitimation and progressive social ascent for the scribal class that produced them.

3.3 The Torah Scroll as Fictionalized Scribal Curriculum

Egyptian society was more complex than that of Israel-Samaria or Judah-Yehud. Moreover, the scarcity of data relating to the scribal curriculum in the latter two societies, when compared with the testimony available from Mesopotamia and Egypt, has been pointed out several times (Schniedewind 2017, 12–13). Comparison is fraught with difficulty, and short-cuts or generalizations are risky (e.g. Carr 2005, 112–16; Quick 2014, 11). Cuneiform artifacts that have been excavated in Middle and Late Bronze Age Canaan testify to the presence of the various genres characterizing the Mesopotamian scribal curriculum: lexical lists from Hazor, Aphek and Ashkelon, literary texts, omina, and excerpts from a series of laws (Cohen 2019, 248–49; Milstein 2021, 41–48; Horowitz et al. 2018). In contrast, however, once Hebrew replaced cuneiform in Canaan, we lack evidence of the genres and specific texts or examples that were used to train scribes in their craft.[6]

William Schniedewind (2017, 11) concludes that "no biblical texts are explicitly framed as scribal curriculum." I challenge his claim. On analogy with the Egyptian miscellanies, the *sefer hattorah* (Deut 1–30; 32)

---

6   It has been proposed that the jar inscriptions from the way station at Kuntillet 'Ajrud in northern Sinai from the end of the early eighth cent. BCE might have been scribal exercises; see Schniedewind 2014; 2017, 14–19; 2019, 23–48. In addition, the inscriptions made in black and red ink on plastered walls recovered in part from Deir 'Alla in Jordan, dated to ca. 840–760 BCE, have also been identified as school texts (Lemaire 1991, 54; Blum 2016, 35–40). This writing was displayed on a wall for viewing. The scribe who would have produced it would have been local- Ammonite perhaps.

can be considered a collection of various literary templates, re-arranged as a fictionalized compendium of a scribal curriculum. The following preliminary observations support this understanding. I start from the genres combined in the Torah scroll.

1. "Historiographical" narrative (Deut 1–3). The presence of "historiographical" texts within Mesopotamian scribal curriculum is attested by the "Weidner Chronicle," found on a school tablet initially dated to the Neo-Babylonian period, excavated in the temple at Sippar (Al-Rawi 1990). On the basis of the colophon, however, Hans Peter Schaudig (2009, 20–21) has lowered its dating to the end of the reign of Darius I (ca. 490–486 BCE). Gesche (2001, 148–49) refers to the Weidner Chronicle as the prototype of the historiographical texts copied in the scribal schools. David Carr (2005, 29) also has stressed the presence of historiographical texts in the scribal curriculum. The text incorporates a historiographical section within a letter of advice. Though there are differences, the idea of a theological rereading of history appears as a common feature in the historiography of the Weidner Chronicle and Deut 1–3 (Arnold 1994, 145–48).
2. Paraenesis, instructions (cf. 4–11; but also 12–26 *passim*; 29–30), and wisdom material. Didactic and wisdom material in the scribal curriculum of Mesopotamia is witnessed by the transmission of proverbs (Gesche 2001, 150–53), wisdom texts, and instructions (Edelman 2021, 55–66) among texts copied by scribes-in-training (Gesche 2001, 173). Wisdom texts were part of the scribal training at Ugarit as well (van Soldt 2016, 148).
3. Legal material (Deut 12–25). The use of legal texts in the scribal curriculum is well documented: extracts from law collections (esp. Hammurabi Laws) were copied (Wright 2009, 106–10; Gesche 2001, 217–18; Waetzoldt and Cavigneaux 2009, 302; Robson 2011, 569; Milstein 2021, 20–52). Legal phraseology and formulas were also used for model contracts and model court cases (Milstein, 2021, 20–52). As recently as 2021, Sara Milstein explored the link between scribal training exercises and biblical laws, showing that prescriptions concerning family, marriage, divorce, and inheritance are pedagogical fictional cases, typical of scribal training (2021, 53–89). That some prescriptions in Deut 12–25 interpret and rework material from the Covenant Code could also point to the importance given to the interpretation of texts in the scribal education in the ancient Near East (Carr 2005, 26, 137–38).
4. Curses and Blessings (Deut 28). The curses and blessings in Deut 28 have been typically interpreted against the background of the

covenant stipulation template. In particular, Esarhaddon's Succession Treaty or *adê* has been considered the point of reference for understanding a selection of curses in Deut 28 (Steymans 1995; Levinson and Stackert 2012, 128–39). In ch. 1 in this volume, Diana Edelman thoroughly challenges the proposal, and Laura Quick (2018a; 2018b) has placed Deut 28 and 13:9 within a broader north-west Semitic curse tradition. Cursing formulas are well documented in contracts and inscriptions. Both genres were learned and copied by student scribes. Curses are also found at the end of school tablets, together with wishes; this further confirms that this kind of phraseology was part of the scribal education (Hunger 1968, 12–14).

5. Ritual (Deut 27:11–26). Deuteronomy 27:11–26 contains instructions for a ritual ceremony to take place after crossing the Jordan. The Levites will pronounce curses and the people will answer in turn. Ritual texts have been found in school tablets from Ugarit (van Soldt 2016, 148) and Babylon (Gesche 2001, 172–73).
6. Song in poetic form (Deut 32): hymns and prayers are both literary genres that were included in scribal training (Gesche 2001, 177–78).
7. Lists: traces of lists are found in Deut 7:1; 20:17 (peoples); Deut 14:4–18 (pure and impure animals) (Schniedewind 2019, 87–94). Lexical lists are recognized as an element typical of scribal education both at the beginning and at more advanced levels (Gesche 2001, 66–146; Robson 2011, 563–64). "These early word-lists presumably influenced the arrangement of commodities in contemporaneous economic records, too" (Wagensonner 2010, 303). Ivan Hrůša (2010, 16–18) highlights the relationship between lexical lists (e.g. the list of synonyms *malku* = *šarru*) and literary texts: "Since an accumulation of synonyms often occurs in literary texts, a literary passage may recall a semantic word group of *mš* (my translation)." The parallels Hrůša highlights derive from Akkadian literature and stress bidirectional influence: from literary texts to *malku* = *šarru*, and vice versa, from *malku* = *šarru* to literary texts.

In short, the literary genres that make up the *sefer hattorah* (Deut 1–30; 32) were an integral part of the scribal curriculum in Mesopotamia and Egypt. Their combination is attested in both Mesopotamian school tablets (from the Old to the Late Babylonian periods) and in the Late Egyptian miscellanies, where they are reframed specifically under the title of "instruction," which also appears in the colophons (Ragazzoli 2019, 325, 399–401). In Deuteronomy, the literary genres that the Torah scroll are framed and rearranged as a farewell speech delivered by Moses, in the form of an instruction. Written in a scroll by Moses, the masterscribe, this fictionalized scribal curriculum is bequeathed to the Levitical priests.

Four additional elements confirm the proposed reading of the *sefer hattorah* as a compendium of a scribal curriculum.

1. According to Deut 31:26, the written *sefer hattorah* shall be put at the side of the ark (מצד ארון). Scholars have traditionally associated this provision with a stipulation found in many treaties that called for the deposit of a copy of the treaty in a temple (Weinfeld 1972, 63; Tigay 1996, 297). That practice tended to involve the placing of a treaty tablet in a chest that was set before the statue of the main city or national deity invoked to oversee the enforcement of the curses should the vassal break the terms of the treaty. Lundbom (2013, 846) has noted that ancient interpretations mistakenly believed the scroll was placed inside the ark, which would cohere well with the ancient practice of placing treaties inside chests. In the Babylonian Talmud, for example, it is concluded that the phrase "by the side of the ark" means that "the scroll is to be placed at the side of the tablets, and not between them; but even so, it was in the ark, only at the side" (*b. B. Bat* 14*b*). While many scholars have noted that the Masoretic Text places the scroll beside and not in the ark/chest, some have made the same mistake that Lundbom documents. Klaus Baltzer (1971, 88 n. 34), for example, considers the Torah scroll to have been "deposited in a sacred spot like a treaty."

   The phrase "to become a witness against you" is then seen to indicate that the scroll – supplemented by Moses's Song (Deut 32) – is to serve as witness to a formal contractual agreement. However, school tablets also were typically placed in temples as a votive gift to the divinity. The practice is attested by the colophons on many of the tablets (Gesche 2001, 153, 156–64; other examples in Hunger 1968, ##138:4; 139:8; 140:5; 140a:3). In some colophons of cuneiform tablets found in sanctuaries, the scribe addresses his tablet, asking it to intercede for him (Gesche 2001, 153–54). The tablet is apostrophized directly with the words: *qibi damiqti ša* PN "speak good words for PN" (Gesche 2001, 154, n. 568). Bearing this in mind, the phrase *hāyāh* + *bəkā* +*ləʿēd* might indicate that the Torah of Moses was being viewed as fulfilling the role of intercessor with Yhwh, which had been left vacant after the death of Moses (Rossi 2018, 220–23). Torah serves a reconciliatory function with Yhwh, especially in Deut 29 and 30. Ordinarily, an intercessor who intervenes on behalf of someone clearly shows the fault committed and seeks forgiveness for this fault. That the Torah scroll and the song in ch. 32 are to serve as witnesses against Israel is not inconsistent with their proposed intercessory role; the functions of accuser and intercessor are not mutually exclusive. The intercessory role assumed by the *sefer hattorah* could reinforce the closeness between the latter and the school tablets.

2. The scroll is not the only medium on which Moses' Torah will be written. In Deut 27:8, Moses commands that after crossing the Jordan, "all the words of this Torah" are to be inscribed on plastered stones erected like stelae (27:2-3). This command is typically interpreted in light of the stelae on which legal texts, including treaties, were inscribed (e.g. McCarthy 1978, 195-97; Sonnet 1997, 92-94; Otto 2017, 1,939). In this regard, Eckart Otto (2017, 1,937-39) mentions *kudurrū* stones, which were stelae inscribed with land grants that served as boundary markers. These proposed parallels focus on inscribed objects and their functions. However, since Deut 27:8 has a command to write, a shift in the interpretive focus towards the writing activity and those involved in it seems in order. Moreover, Deut 27:8 expects a complete replication of all the words written in the *sefer* by Moses (31:9) on the stelae (27:8): "all the words of this Torah/instruction."

In fact, only those who access the *sefer hattorah* can carry out the command and write a complete copy of all the words. The injunction in Deut 27:8 implies, therefore, the existence of a scribal group who can access the Torah scroll. This *scribal guild* can plausibly be identified with the Levitical priests who receive the *sefer hattorah* from Moses. The action this scribal guild (or one of their representatives) is supposed to perform (according to Deut 27:8) recalls Moses's writing (כתב) of the Torah scroll in 31:9. The verb באר (*piel*) in Deut 27:8 points back to the same function ascribed to Moses in 1:5.

Texts inscribed on stelae were part of scribal training. As Petra D. Gesche (2001, 149-50) highlights, these literary texts were typical of the first level of educational instruction, which included royal ideology and its relation to the cult as a standard topic. The fact that they were written on stelae is probably a sign of the interest in the texts and a perceived need to transmit them to future generations (Gesche 2001, 150). The transcription of *narû texts* was aimed at teaching scribes royal ideology, preparing them for working in the royal palace, and as Gesche (2001, 150) emphasizes, possibly also designing future royal inscriptions. Šulgi's hymns were copied as school texts but also registered as *narû* (Jonker

1995, 87–89). Designing stelae and composing inscriptions was, therefore, part of the scribal skill set.

3. According to Deut 17:18–20, the future king shall write a copy of "this Torah"; "it shall be with him and he shall read it" (והיתה עמו וקרא בו); the expression, והיתה עמו ("it shall be with him"), linked by a coordinative *waw* to קרא ("he shall read"), points to personal reading. Described in these terms, the king's actions closely mirror the practice of copying school texts, as is made clear by certain tablet *colophons* that testify to the existence of private tablet collections for personal use. Emblematic cases in this regard are the colophons attributed to Ashurbanipal but written in his name by royal scribes (Robson 2019, 124–127).

Personal reading is one purpose expressed in the *colophons* of Mesopotamian tablets: *ana tāmartīšu*, "for his personal reading/consultation." Specific examples provided by Hermann Hunger (1968, 11–12) include: ##110:3; 121:5; 297:5; 302: 4; 307: 4; 310:1, 379:3. The colophon of #379 explicitly states the scribe of the tablet is a student scribe: *Marduk-bān šamallû ṣeḫru* (379:2). In #302:4, private reading (probably silent) or consultation (*tāmartu*) is distinguished from recitation (*šitassû*). A similar formula about the scribe having written the text "for himself" appears in some papyri of the Late Egyptian miscellanies as well, making it a regionally diverse practice (Hagen 2006, 91). Other goals for copying texts are learning on the part of the scribe, *ana aḫazi* (e.g. Hunger # 91:4) and also fear/veneration of the divinity, *ana palāḫ bēlūtī-šu*, "for the fear/veneration of his lordship (of the divinity)" (Hunger 1968, 12).

Along with potential gains obtained from the text itself, colophons mention various aims of text-transcription. A prominent one is expected divine reward for carrying out the writing duty (Hunger 1968, 11). One form that can take is a long life, *arāk ūmī*, "length of days (of life)" (Hunger, # 91:4). In the colophons of the tablets from the so-called library of Ashurbanipal,[7] the king himself is depicted as a scribe and transcriber of texts. Here again, the purpose of the transcription is personal reading: #318:8: *ana tāmartīšu šarrūtiya* "to read for my majesty"; #319:8, *ana tāmartī*, "for reading" (Hunger 1968, 93–107). Gesche (2001, 153) highlights the difference between the colophons of school tablets and tablets belonging to

---

[7] Eleanor Robson (2019, 10–48) discusses at length the origin of the so-called "Assurbanipal's library." She shows convincingly that the idea of Assurbanipal's library as a collection of texts created by the royal figure is a modern ideological construct.

so-called libraries; the notation relating to reading is present in tablets of student scribes as well (e.g. Hunger 1968, #379:2).

The purposes stated in the colophons of copied Mesopotamian scribal texts overlap with those given for the royal copy of the Torah in Deut 17:18–19. A final conjunction (למען) introduces four purposes and aims: personal reading/consultation (קרא בו); learning (למען ילמד); fear/veneration of the divinity (ליראה את יהוה); and length of days (למען יאריך ימים). Collectively, they portray the king as a scribe. At the same time, the text to be copied ("a copy of this Torah", v. 18) appears to be a scribal text like those to be copied by scribes-in training as well as veteran scribes and made part of private collections for personal use.

4. According to Deut 31:9–13, the content of the *sefer hattorah* is supposed to be read and communicated to the people orally every seven years at the festival of Sukkot. Similarly, the Song in Deut 32, written by Moses as a supplement to the *sefer hattorah*, is intended for oral teaching and memorization (cf. 32:19). References to the memorization and oral teaching of words contained in the *sefer hattorah* can be also detected in 6:6–7. Texts typical of scribal curricula were also transmitted orally by the teacher and intended for mnemonic learning and recitation by student scribes (Gesche 2001, 168–69).

The above outlined observations provide new provisional insights concerning the *sefer hattorah* (i.e. Deut 1:6–30:20; 32), which can be considered a fictionalized compendium of a scribal curriculum transmitted by Moses to the scribal guild of Levitical priests as an inheritance. I am not claiming that Deuteronomy's objective is to provide didactic material for the whole community or for the nuclear family (Carr 2005, 134–42). Rather, the handing over of the *sefer hattorah* as the compendium of a scribal curriculum signifies the transmission of scribal knowledge and legitimizes a scribal class. Through the legacy of the *sefer hattorah* and the portrayal of Moses as master-scribe and forefather, an ancestry for the scribal group of the Levitical priests is constructed based on their expertise in composing texts.

4. From Genealogical Ancestry to Inherited Expertise (Deut 33:8–11)

The book Moses bequeaths to Levitical priests reinforces their authority and status. From this point of view, the transmission of scribal knowledge replaces genealogical ancestry as a legitimizing strategy. Deuteronomy 33 provides some clues in this regard.

Like Jacob (Gen 49), Moses (Deut 33) blesses the Israelites, tribe by tribe, before dying (Otto 2017, 2,230-36). The literary genre of patriarchal blessings (Isaac in Gen 27; Jacob in Gen 49) is grounded on genealogy. The genealogical bond between a patriarch and his descendants ensures the transmission of the blessings. Yet, Moses's blessings in Deut 33 not only take up the genealogical paradigm but also challenge it (Sonnet 1997, 210-15). In Deut 33:1, Moses is neither a father nor an ancestor blessing his children, as Jacob is in Gen 49:2. It is as *the* man of God (איש האלהים) that Moses bestowed his blessings on the children of Israel. Instead of beginning with his firstborn as Jacob does, Moses's blessing opens with a hymn to Yhwh (Sonnet 1997, 212). The next differences between Jacob and Moses' blessings are revealing.

Instead of Jacob's indictment of Levi and Simeon's violence (Gen 49:5-7), Moses's blessing of Levi (Deut 33:8-11) is a self-portrait as much as a celebration of Levi. Moses is present within Deut 33:8-11:[8] in all likelihood, your faithful or devout man (איש חסידך) in 33:8 alludes to Moses himself (Otto 2017, 2,246) rather than to the tribe of Levi (so Driver 1902, 399; Tigay 1996, 324; Lundbom 2013, 926-27). The reference to the trial at Massah and the waters of Meribah (33:8b) is irrelevant for Levi, because the Levites play no role at Massah and Meribah, neither in Exod 17:1-7 nor in Num 20:2-13. Is Moses referring to Aaron (Deut 33:8)? Aaron is not mentioned at all in Exod 17:1-7. He is mentioned as a onlooker in Num 20:1-13, whose goal is to clarify why both Moses and Aaron die before entering the land. On the contrary, Moses is present in both Exod 17:1-7 and Num 20:2-13, where he plays the central role. Since Moses is the one who utters the blessings (Deut 33:1), the faithful man tested at Massah and Meribah (33:8) is a self-reference . Relying on Moses himself, the blessing for Levi questions the principle of genealogy (Sonnet 1997, 213), a distinctive trait of the Aaronide priestly lineage. Priestly authority based on genealogy is replaced by an authority based on the transmission of competence. The onslaught against the Aaronite lineage is further illustrated with the denial of blood ties and the transmission of the Urim and Thummim.

Blood ties are invalidated in all three levels by "him who says to his father and to his mother: "I have not seen him" (33:9a). According to the

---

8   Otto 2017, 2,246-47. The shift from singular to plural (*Numeruswechsel*) has often been thought to signal an addition within the text. Applying this criterion, vv. 9d-10 (pl.) would have been added to a base layer (vv. 8-9ac, 11). However, the *Numeruswechsel* alone is not sufficient for assuming a diachronic division of vv. 8-11; see Nielsen 1995, 303; Otto 2017, 2,247-48. On closer inspection, the text consistently pursues a coherent goal in both the singular and plural verses: i.e. legitimizing Levitical priests at the expense of the Aaronide priesthood.

legend of his birth, Moses was indeed separated from his parents and brought up by Pharaoh's daughter (Exod 2:10). The second statement, "His brothers he did not recognize" (33:9b) can be read as the rejection of Aaron, Moses' elder brother, while "his son sons he did not know" (33:9c) targets Gershom, Moses's son (Exod 2:22), whom some priests claimed as ancestor (Judg 18:30), and possibly Eliezer, too (Exod 18:4). The Chroniclers seems aware of the identification of "your faithful man" with Moses, because Levi's genealogy mentions sons of Aaron but no sons of Moses (1 Chr 6). Despite the textual variants in Deut 33:9a-c (Otto 2017, 2,216), the challenge mounted against blood ties remains, in two directions: that of ancestry, toward the past (father and mother) and that of succession (children), toward the future.

According to Deut 33:8, Urim and Thummim are given to the איש חסי־דך ("your faithful man"), i.e. Moses himself.[9] The assignment of Urim and Thummim (v. 8) to Moses is peculiar; in Exod 28:30 and Lev 8:8, the Urim and Thummim are linked to the figure of Aaron and characterize his priestly status (Otto 2017, 2,246). In Num 27:21, the genealogical succession of the Aaronide priesthood is symbolically represented by the passage of the Urim and Thummim from Aaron to his son, Eleazar. The connection between the Urim and Thummim and priestly genealogy also is highlighted in Ezra 2:59–63. The sons of the priests Habaiah, Hakkoz, and Barzillai cannot prove their membership in priestly families through genealogy. Their names are not found written in the records and they are excluded as unclean. Their exclusion will persist until the arrival of a "priest with Urim and Thummim." The possession of Urim and Thummim is, thus, a distinctive sign of belonging to the priestly genealogy. The challenge that Deut 33:8–9 mounts to the principle of Aaronide priestly authority, based on genealogy, is twofold. On the one hand, the Urim and Thummim are entrusted to Moses, not to Aaron. On the other hand, the principle of genealogical transmission is denied.

Deuteronomy 33:9d confirms the challenge to the Aaronide genealogical priesthood and its authority. The change from singular to plural, from "*he* who says" to "*they* kept your words and upheld your covenant" (שמרו אמרתך ובריתך ינצרו), shifts the focus from the eponymous ancestor, Levi, to the group of Levites. Levitical fidelity to "your covenant"

---

9 Following 4QDeut[h] and 4QTest (as well as the Septuagint), the Thummim are to be given to Levi. The beginning of v. 8 runs: "bring (2 pl.) Levi [your Thummim]" (הבו ללו[י] תמד]). However, in 4QDeut[h] and 4QTest, the personal deixis ends up being inconsistent, as shown by the shift from 2 pl. (הבו) to 2 sing. (תמיד) addressees. The LXX harmonizes the inconsistency by changing the 2 sing. suffix (תמיד) into a 3 sing. pronoun (αὐτοῦ). Deut 33,8MT is, therefore, to be preferred. See Nielsen 1995, 297; Otto 2017, 2,216.

refers to the incident in Exod 32:26–29, where the Levites showed their loyalty to Yhwh by siding with Moses to punish those guilty of apostasy. This episode underlines the Levites' faithfulness as well as Aaron's sin and transgression. Aaron appears in Exod 32 in an entirely negative light (see esp. vv. 21–25, 35). In pointing back to Exod 32:26–29, Deut 33:9d conveys a negative view of Aaron and the Aaronide priesthood. No wonder the retelling of the episode in Deut 9 claims that Moses saved Aaron from Yhwh's wrath (9:20). The Levites are separated from Aaron and placed on Moses's side. Deuteronomy 33:10 then further specifies that the very relationship between Moses and the Levites is predicated on the transmission of competency related primarily to teaching and only later to worship. It is not genealogical, since it was already said of Moses that "he does not recognize his own son" (33:9). Nor does Deut 33:8–9 refer in any way to the transmission of Urim and Thummim from Moses to the Levites.

Deut 33:10 turns them into legal experts, teachers (ירה) of *mišpāṭîm* and *tôrâ* for Jacob and Israel. What is this all about? Typically, Torah is identified here with the transmission of cultic and priestly provisions. The parallel between *tôrâ* and *mišpāṭ*, as well as the pl. תורות in the Samaritan Pentateuch, seems to argue in favor of the identification. The use of the verb ירה in reference to Levites echoes Deut 24:8, where the same verb involves Levitical priests teaching cultic prescriptions linked to questions of purity. If the latter equation is accepted, Moses has issued commands (verb צוה) reserved exclusively for the Levites. Thus, the hand-over of knowledge – and more precisely the transmission of technical and scribal competence and other unspecified instructions shared only by this group – binds Moses to the Levites.

To recap, Levi's blessing in Deut 33:8–10 points to the figure of Moses as the authoritative ancestor of the Levites. The link between Moses and the Levites is not based on a genealogical principle, which is explicitly denied in 33:8, but on the transmission of scribal skills (33:10ab). Thus constituted, the link with Moses serves as the legitimating basis of the authority of the Levites. This is polemically opposed to the Aaronide priesthood, whose legitimacy is based on genealogy.

Deuteronomy 33:10cd confirms the proposed interpretation. The mention of the כליל offering "they place on your altar" hints at priestly prerogatives granted to the Levites. In Lev 6:15 [6:22 in English] the כליל offering is specifically reserved for the priest anointed to succeed Aaron from among his sons. The principle of priestly succession based on genealogy allows this particular type of offering to be presented. Similar to the Urim and Thummim in Deut 33:8, the כליל in v. 10 also is removed from the exclusive domain of the Aaronide priesthood – founded on genealogy – and handed over to the Levites. They are the custodians of

Moses's inheritance and are legitimized not by ancestry but by his bequeathed scribal competence (33:10). As in Deut 24:8, scribal competence and priestly prerogatives are combined in the group of Levitical priests. Through this scribal competence, the elite of the Levitical priests claim priestly privileges for themselves that otherwise had been reserved for Aaron's descendants (Rossi 2021, 355–60).

The involvement of scribes among cultic officials is well attested in Neo- and Late Babylonian documentation. Scribal expertise was transmitted within priestly families who enjoyed prebendary privileges. Analyzing a Late Babylonian tablet with a scribal exercise dedicated to Nabû (*CTMMA* 65, Gesche 2005, 258–61), Neik Veldhuis (2013, 177) concludes that "writing and education were part of the conceptual world that regulated the functioning of the temples and the prebendary families who used their prebends, as well as their literacy, to acquire and maintain their elite position in the city." The transmission of scribal expertise can be traced down multiple generations within a single family. As a case in point, a scribe reminds his son that Enlil has ordained for man that the son should follow his father's profession (Sjöberg 1973, 117; van der Toorn 2007, 59–63). Colophons of school tablets show sons copying a corpus of texts owned by their fathers as part of the transmission of the scribal expertise (Hunger 1968, ## 97:1; 98:2–3; 100:2–3).

Deuteronomy 33 reflects a similar situation. Moses is not only a prophet and man of God (v. 1) but also the ancestor of a specific group, the descendants of Levi (vv. 8–11). To them, Moses bequeaths his *torah*, the expertise to proclaim and teach it and supervise the production of its copy by the king. Ancestry based on the transmission of this scribal expertise replaces ancestry based on genealogy. It now remains to understand the reasons, the real issue, and the consequences of this replacement.

5. The Background and the Stakes

The previous observations suggest that it is the Levitical priests themselves who portrayed Moses as the first master-scribe and their non-genealogical forefather. Some provisional consideration of the reasons and circumstances that might have impelled the guild to elaborate such a portrait of Moses can be drawn.

- As an emerging scribal class within the Second Temple (Rossi 2021, 352–57), the Levitical priests felt the need to bolster their legitimacy. The gradual acquisition of power in juridical, political, and religious areas by this emerging scribal class, likely due to their entry into the administration of the rebuilt temple, impelled this

group to portray Moses as a master-scribe. The Torah scroll, a compendium typical of a scribal curriculum, is the legacy their received from Moses (Deut 31:9).
- The scribes are dependent on the power that employs them. Their expertise is indispensable to the ruling class for the administration and for the production of propaganda (e.g. royal inscriptions, court annals). At the service of the center of power, they end up conveying the culture of the regime in which they operate (Davies 1998, 17–19; Seibert 2006, 51–60. As Schniedewind (2004, 37) observes: "The scribes were not independent, but served at the discretion of the ruling groups who brought them into existence, provided for their sustenance, and controlled their access to the public." In the Persian period, scribes were employed in the highest ranks of the administration of the province of Yehud, but also, at a lower-middle level, as temple personnel (Schams 1998, 309–12). The legitimacy of scribes in the highest ranks of administration derived directly from their association with the Persian establishment. Involved in the local administration of the temple, the Levitical priests, an emerging scribal class, presumably sought an authoritative founder for themselves to legitimize their position.
- Struggles between priestly groups in the Second Temple priesthood probably urged Levitical priests to portray Moses as their "ancestral" master-scribe. Controversies over the distribution of prebends seem to point in this direction (Rossi 2021, 341–50). The challenge mounted to the transmission of symbols relating to priesthood (Urim and Tummim in Deut 33:8) further highlights controversies linked to the "business" of cult and sacrifice. Traces of such struggles are also found in Lev 10:16–20, where Moses scolds Aaron's sons Eleazar and Ithamar for not eating the victim of the sin-offering in the sanctuary according to his command (v. 18). Aaron's reply (v. 19) reduces Moses to silence (v. 20). Moses's silence before Aaron sounds like a yielding to the latter's interpretation; it is unique in the Pentateuch. In this instance, Aaron supplants Moses as "teacher" of the Torah (Nihan 2007, 602; Hiecke 2014, 394–98). The self-portrayal in Moses's benediction of Levi counters this claim and assigns Urim and Thummim to Moses.

In Deuteronomy, Moses is portrayed as the master-scribe *par excellence* and the founder of a scribal priestly class, the Levitical priests. They claim the legacy and sole possession of Moses's *sefer hattorah*, the fictional compendium of a complete scribal curriculum reframed as his farewell speech. Endowed with such a prestigious legacy, the Levitical priests put themselves forward as authoritative and reliable guides of the community. I will explore the function of the Torah within the community in ch. 9.

Works Cited

Al-Rawi, Farouk N. H. 1990. "Tablets from the Sippar Library. I. The 'Weidner Chronicle': A Supposititious Royal Letter Concerning a Vision." *Iraq* 52: 1–13.

Arnold, Bill. 1994. "The Weidner Chronicle and the Idea of History in Israel and Mesopotamia." Pages 129–48 in *Faith, Tradition and History: Old Testament Historiography in Its Near Eastern Context*. Edited by A. R. Millard, James K. Hoffmeier, and David W. Baker. Winona Lake, IN: Eisenbrauns.

Aurelius, Erik. 1988. *Der Fürbitter Israels. Eine Studie zum Mosebild im Alten Testament*. Coniectanea Biblica: Old Testament Series 27. Stockholm: Almqvist & Wiksell.

Baltzer, Klaus. 1971. *The Covenant Formulary in Old Testament, Jewish, and Early Christian Writings*. Translated by David E. Green. Philadelphia, PA: Fortress.

Blum, Erhard. 2007. "Pentateuch – Hexateuch – Enneateuch? Oder: Woran erkennt man ein literarisches Werk in der hebräischen Bibel." Pages 67–97 in *Les dernières rédactions du Pentateuque, de l'Hexeateuque et de l'Ennéateuque*. Edited by Thomas Römer and Konrad Schmid. Bibliotheca Ephemeridum Theologicarum Lovaniensium 203. Leuven: Peeters.

------. 2016. "Die altaramäischen Wandinschriften vom Tell Deir 'Alla und ihr institutioneller Kontext." Pages 21–52 in *Metatexte. Erzählungen von schrifttragenden Artefakten in der alttestamentlichen und mittelalterlichen Literatur*. Edited by Friedrich-Emanuel Focken and Michael R. Ott. Berlin: de Gruyter.

Borger, Riekele. 1964. "Geheimwissen." Pages 188–91 in vol. 3 of *Reallexikon der Assyriologie*. Edited by Erich Ebeling et. al. Berlin: de Gruyter.

Braulik, Georg and Norbert Lohfink. 2021. *Sprache und literarische Gestalt des Buches Deuteronomium. Beobachtungen und Studien*. Österreichische Biblische Studien 53. Berlin: Peter Lang.

Carr, David M. 2005. *Writing on the Tablet of the Heart: Origins of Scripture and Literature*. Oxford: Oxford University Press.

------. 2012. "The Moses Story. Literary-Historical Reflections." *Hebrew Bible and Ancient Israel* 1: 7–36.

------. 2020. "Rethinking the Materiality of Biblical Texts: From Source, Tradition and Redaction to a Scroll Approach." *Zeitschrift für die alttestamentliche Wissenschaft* 132: 594–621.

Coats, George W. 1988. *Moses: Heroic Man, Man of God*. Journal for the Study of the Old Testament Supplement Series 57. Sheffield: JSOT.

Cohen, Yoram. 2016. "The Scribal Traditions of Late Bronze Age Emar." Pages 119–31 in *Cultures and Societies in the Middle Euphrates and Habur Areas in the Second Millennium BC: Scribal Education and Scribal Tradition*. Edited by Shigeo Yamada and Daisuke Shibata. Studia Chaburensia 5. Wiesbaden: Harrassowitz.

———. 2019. "Cuneiform Writing in Bronze Age Canaan." Pages 245–64 in *The Social Archaeology of the Levant: From Prehistory to Present*. Edited by Assaf Yasur-Landau, Eric H. Cline, and Yorke Rowan. Cambridge: Cambridge University Press.

Cribiore, Raffaella. 1996. *Writing, Teachers, and Students in Graeco-Roman Egypt*. American Studies in Papyrology 36. Atlanta, GA: Scholars Press.

Davies, Philip R. 1998. *Scribes and Schools: The Canonization of the Hebrew Scriptures*. Louisville, KY: Westminster John Knox.

De Pury, Albert. 1994. "Erwägungen zu einem vorexilischen Stämmejahwismus. Hos 12 und die Auseinandersetzung um die Identität Israels und seines Gottes." Pages 413–39 in *Ein Gott allein? JHWH-Verherung und biblischer Monotheismus im Knotext der israelitischen und altorientalischen Religionsgeschichte*. Edited by Walter Dietrich and Martin A. Klopfenstein. Orbis Biblicus et Orientalis 139. Freiburg: Universitätsverlag and Göttingen: Vandenhoeck & Ruprecht.

———. 2001. "Le choix de l'ancêtre." *Theologische Zeitung* 57: 105–14.

Driver, Samuel Rolles. 1902. *A Critical and Exegetical Commentary on the Book of Deuteronomy*. International Critical Commentary 5. Edinburgh: T&T Clark.

Edelman, Diana. 2015. "The Metaphor of Torah as a Life-Giving Well in the Book of Deuteronomy." Pages 317–33 in *History, Memory, Hebrew Scriptures: A Festschrift for Ehud Ben Zvi*. Edited by Ian Douglas Wilson and Diana Edelman. Winona Lake, IN: Eisenbrauns.

———. 2021. "Deuteronomy as the Instructions of Moses and Yhwh vs. a Framed Legal Code." Pages 25–75 in *Deuteronomy in the Making: Studies in the Production of Debarim*. Edited by Diana Edelman, Benedetta Rossi, Kåre Berge, and Philippe Guillaume. Beihefte zur Zeitschrift für die Alttestamentische Wissenschaft 533. Berlin: de Gruyter.

———. 2023. "Scribes (šōṭᵉrîm) in Deuteronomy." *Scandinavian Journal of the Old Testament* 37/1: 34–57.

———, Philip R. Davies, Christophe Nihan, and Thomas Römer. 2012. *Opening the Books of Moses*. Sheffield: Equinox Publishing Ltd.

Erman, Adolf. 1925. *Die Ägyptischen Schülerhandschriften*. Berlin: Verlag der Akademie der Wissenschaften.

Fischer, Georg. 2000. "Das Mosebild der Hebräischen Bibel." Pages 84–120 in *Mose. Ägypten und das Alte Testament*. Stuttgarter Bibelstudien 189. Stuttgart: Verlag Katholisches Bibelwerk.

Gardiner, Alan. 1937. *Late-Egyptian Miscellanies*. Bibliotheca Aegyptiaca 7. Bruxelles: Édition de la fondation égyptologique Reine Élisabeth.
Gesche, Petra D. 2001. *Schulunterricht in Babylonien im ersten Jahrtausend v. Chr.* Alter Orient und Altes Testament 275. Münster: Ugarit.
------. 2005. "Nos. 65-66. Late Babylonian School Exercise Tablets." Pages 257-65 in *Literary and Scholastic Texts of the First Millennium B.C.* Edited by Ira Spar and Wilfred G. Lambert. Cuneiform Texts in the Metropolitan Museum of Art 2. New York: The Metropolitan Museum of Art.
Hagen, Fredrik. 2006. "Literature, Transmission, and the Late Egyptian Miscellanies." Pages 84-99 in *Proceedings of the Fifth Annual Symposium University of Durham 2004: Current Research in Egyptology 2004*. Edited by Rachel J. Dann. Oxford: Oxbow Books.
Heckl, Raik. 2013. "Mose als Schreiber. Am Ursprung der jüdischen Hermeneutik des Pentateuchs." *Zeitschrift für Altorientalische und Biblische Rechtsgeschichte* 19: 179-234.
Hiecke, Thomas. 2014. *Levitikus 1-15*. Herders Theologischer Kommentar zum Alten Testament. Freiburg i.B.: Herder.
Horowitz, Wayne, Takayoshi Oshima, and Seth Sanders. 2018. *Cuneiform in Canaan: The Next Generation*. Second Edition. University Park, PA: Eisenbrauns.
Hrůša, Ivan. 2010. *Die akkadische Synonymenliste* malku = šarru. *Eine Textedition mit Übersetzung und Kommentar*. Alter Orient und Altes Testament 50. Münster: Ugarit.
Hunger, Hermann. 1968. *Babylonische und assyrische Kolophone*. Alter Orient und Altes Testament 2. Neukirchen-Vluyn: Butzon & Bercker Kevelaer.
Jonker, Gerdien. 1995. *The Topography of Remembrance: The Dead, Tradition and Collective Memory in Mesopotamia*. Studies in the History of Religions 68. Leiden: Brill.
Kratz, Reinhard Gregor. 2018. "Moses: Creating a Founding Figure." *Archiv für Religionsgeschichte* 20/1: 61-75.
Lemaire, André. 1991. "Les inscriptions sur Plâtre de Deir ʿAlla et leur signification historique et Culturelle." Pages 33-57 in *The Balaam Text from Deir ʿAlla Re-evaluated: Proceedings of the International Symposium held at Leiden 21-24 August 1989*. Edited by Jacob Hoftijzer and Gerrit van der Kooij. Leiden: Brill.
Levinson, Bernard M. and Jeffrey Stackert. 2012. "Between the Covenant Code and Esarhaddon's Succession Treaty: Deuteronomy 13 and the Composition of Deuteronomy." *Journal of Ancient Judaism* 3: 123-40.
Lundbom, Jack R. 2013. *Deuteronomy: A Commentary*. Grand Rapids, MI: Eerdmans.
Markl, Dominik. 2012. *Gottes Volk im Deuteronomium*. Beihefte zur Zeitschrift für Altorientalische und Biblische Rechtsgeschichte 18. Wiesbaden: Harrassowitz.

------. 2020. "The Ambivalence of Authority in Deuteronomy: Reaction, Revision, Rewriting, Reception." *Cristianesimo nella Storia* 41: 427–61.

McCarthy, Dennis Joseph. 1978. *Treaty and Covenant: A Study in Form in the Ancient Oriental Documents and in the Old Testament.* Rome: Biblical Institute.

Milstein, Sara J. 2016. *Tracking the Master Scribe: Revision through Introduction in Biblical and Mesopotamian Literature.* Oxford: Oxford University Press.

------. 2021. *Making a Case: The Practical Roots of Biblical Law.* Oxford: Oxford University Press.

Nielsen, Eduard. 1995. *Deuteronomium.* Handbuch zum Alten Testament I/6. Tübingen: J.C.B. Mohr (Paul Siebeck).

Nihan, Christophe. 2007. *From Priestly Torah to Pentateuch: A Study in the Composition of the Book of Leviticus.* Forschungen zum Alten Testament II 25; Tübingen: Mohr Siebeck.

Otto, Eckart. 2005. "Mose, der erste Schriftgelehrte. Deuteronomium 1,5 in der Fabel des Pentateuch." Pages 273–84 in *L'Ecrit et L'Esprit. Etudes d'histoire du texte et de théologie biblique en hommage à Adrian Schenker.* Edited by Dieter Böhler, Innocent Himbaza, and Philippe Hugo. Orbis Biblicus et Orientalis 214. Fribourg: Academic Press and Göttingen: Vandenhoeck & Ruprecht.

------. 2006. *Mose. Geschichte und Legende.* Munich: C.H. Beck.

------. 2010a. "Moses. I. Old Testament." Pages 568–71 in vol. 8 of *Religion Past and Present: Encyclopedia of Theology and Religion.* Edited by Hans Dieter Betz et al. Leiden: Brill.

------. 2010b. "Moses, Blessing of/Song of." Page 574 in vol. 8 of *Religion Past and Present: Encyclopedia of Theology and Religion.* Edited by Hans Dieter Betz et al. Leiden: Brill.

------. 2017. *Deuteronomium 23,16–34,12.* Herders Theologischer Kommentar zum Alten Testament. Freiburg: Herder.

------. 2021. "The Suffering Moses in the Pentateuch and Psalms." *Old Testament Essays* 34: 240–53.

Perlitt, Lothar. 1994. "Mose als Prophet." Pages 1–19 in *Deuteronomium Studien.* Forschungen zum Alten Testament 8. Tübingen: Mohr Siebeck.

Quick, Laura. 2014. "Recent Research on Ancient Israelite Education: A Bibliographic Essay." *Currents in Biblical Research* 13: 9–33.

------. 2018a. *Deuteronomy 28 and the Aramaic Curse Tradition.* Oxford: Oxford University Press.

------. 2018b. "'But You Shall Surely Report Concerning Him': In Defense of the Priority of LXX Deuteronomy 13:9." *Zeitschrift für die alttestamentliche Wissenschaft* 130: 86–100.

Quirke, Stephen G. 1996. "Archive." Pages 379–401 in *Ancient Egyptian Literature: History and Forms.* Edited by Antonio Loprieno. Probleme der Ägyptologie 10. Leiden: Brill.

Rad, Gerhard von. 1953. *Studies in Deuteronomy*. Studies in Biblical Theology 9. London: SCM.

------. 1962. *Old Testament Theology. Volume I. The Theology of Israel's Historical Traditions*. Edinburgh: Oliver and Boyd.

Ragazzoli, Chloé. 2019. *Scribes. Les artisans du texte de l'Égypte ancienne (1550-1000)*. Paris: Les Belles Lettres.

Robson, Eleanor. 2008. *Mathematics in Ancient Iraq: A Social History*. Princeton: Princeton University Press.

------. 2011. "The Production and Dissemination of Scholarly Knowledge." Pages 556-76 in *The Oxford Handbook of Cuneiform Culture*. Edited by Karen Radner and Eleanor Robson. Oxford: Oxford University Press.

------. 2019. *Ancient Knowledge Networks: A Social Geography of Cuneiform Scholarship in First-Millennium Assyria and Babylonia*. London: UCL Press.

Römer, Thomas. 2004-2005. "The Construction of the Figure of Moses According to Biblical and Extrabiblical Sources." *Annual of the Japanese Biblical Institute* 30/31: 99-116.

------. 2012. "Tracking Some 'Censored' Moses Traditions Inside and Outside the Hebrew Bible." *Hebrew Bible and Ancient Israel* 1: 64-76.

Rossi, Benedetta. 2018. "Conflicting Patterns of Revelation: Jer 31,33-34 and Its Challenge to the Post-Mosaic Revelation Program." *Biblica* 98: 202-25.

------. 2021. "'Not by Bread Alone' (Deut 8:3): Elite Struggles over Cultic Prebends and Moses Torah in Deuteronomy." Pages 331-65 in *Deuteronomy in the Making: Studies in the Production of* Debarim. Edited by Diana V. Edelman, Benedetta Rossi, Kåre Berge, and Philippe Guillaume. Beihefte zur Zeitschrift für die alttestamentische Wissenschaft 533. Berlin: de Gruyter.

------. 2023. "Preaching the Law: Reconsidering the Relationship between the Covenant Code and Deuteronomy." *Scandinavian Journal of the Old Testament* 37: 148-165.

Schams, Christine. 1998. *Jewish Scribes in the Second-Temple Period*. Journal for the Study of the Old Testament Supplement Series 291. Sheffield: Sheffield Academic Press.

Schaudig, Hans Peter. 2009. "The Colophon of the Sippar Text of the 'Weidner Chronicle.'" *N.A.B.U.* 2009/1: 20-21.

Schmid, Konrad. 2010. *Genesis and the Moses Story: Israel's Dual Origins in the Hebrew Bible* Siphrut 3. Winona Lake, IN: Eisenbrauns.

Schniedewind, William M. 2004. *How the Bible Became a Book: The Textualization of Ancient Israel*. Cambridge: Cambridge University Press.

------. 2014. "Understanding Scribal Education in Ancient Israel: A View from Kuntillet ʿAjrud." *Maarav* 21/1-2: 271-93.

------. 2017. "Scribal Education in Ancient Israel and Judah into the Persian Period." Pages 11-28 in *Second Temple Jewish 'Paideia' in Context*. Edited by Jason Zurawski and Gabriele Boccaccini. Beihefte zur Zeitschrift für die neutestamentliche Wissenschaft 228. Berlin: de Gruyter.

———. 2019. *The Finger of the Scribe: How Scribes Learned to Write the Bible.* New York: Oxford University Press.

Seibert, Eric. 2006. *Subversive Scribes and the Solomonic Narrative: A Rereading of 1 Kings 1–11.* Library of Hebrew Bible/Old Testament Studies 436. New York: T&T Clark.

Shupak, Nili. 1993. *Where Can Wisdom Be Found? The Sage's Language in the Bible and in Ancient Egyptian Literature.* Orbis Biblicus et Orientalis 130. Fribourg: University Press and Göttingen: Vandenhoeck & Ruprecht.

Sjöberg, Åke W. 1973. "Der Vater und sein missratener Sohn." *Journal of Cuneiform Studies* 25: 105–69.

Ska, Jean-Louis. 2007. "Le début et la fin du Deutéronome (Dt 31:5 et 31:1)." *Textus* 23: 81–96.

———. 2013. "Qui est, dans le Deutéronome, le successeur de Moïse?" *La nouvelle revue théologique* 135: 353–70.

Soldt, Wilfried van. 2016. "School and Scribal Tradition in Ugarit." Pages 145–55 in *Cultures and Societies in the Middle Euphrates and Habur Areas in the Second Millennium BC I. Scribal Education and Scribal Traditions.* Edited by Shigeo Yamada and Daisuke Shibata. Studia Chaburensia 5. Wiesbaden: Harrassowitz.

Sonnet, Jean Pierre. 1997. *The Book Within the Book: Writing in Deuteronomy.* Biblical Interpretation Series 14. Leiden: Brill.

———. 2016. "Does the Pentateuch *Tell* of Its Redactional Genesis? The Characters of YHWH and Moses as Agents of *Fortschreibung* in the Pentateuch's Narrated World." Pages 269–82 in *The Formation of The Pentateuch: Bridging the Academic Cultures of Europe, Israel, and North America.* Edited by Jan C. Gertz, Bernard M. Levinson, and Dalit Rom-Shiloni. Forschungen zum Alten Testament 111. Tübingen: Mohr Siebeck.

Steymans, Hans Ulrich. 1995. *Deuteronomium 28 und die adê zur Thronfolgeregelung Asarhaddons. Segen und Fluch im Alten Orient und in Israel.* Orbis Biblicus et Orientalis 145. Freiburg: University Press.

Tigay, Jeffrey. 1996. *Deuteronomy [Devarim]: The Traditional Hebrew Text with the New JPS Translation.* Philadelphia, PA: The Jewish Publication Society.

Toorn, Karel van der. 2007. *Scribal Culture and the Making of the Hebrew Bible.* Cambridge, MA: Harvard University Press.

Vanstiphout, Herman L. J. 1995. "On the Old Babylonian Eduba Curriculum." Pages 3–16 in *Centres of Learning: Learning and Location in Pre-Modern Europe and the Near East.* Edited by Jan Willem Drijvers and Alasdair A. MacDonald. Brill's Studies in Intellectual History 61. Leiden: Brill.

Veldhuis, Neik. 2013. "Purity and Access: A Catalog of Lexical Texts Dedicated to Nabû." *Journal of Cuneiform Studies* 65: 169–80.

------. 2016. "Old Babylonian School Curricula." Pages 1–12 in *Cultures and Societies in the Middle Euphrates and Habur Areas in the Second Millennium BC I. Scribal Education and Scribal Traditions*. Edited by Shigeo Yamada and Daisuke Shibata. Studia Chaburensia 5. Wiesbaden: Harrassowitz.

Waetzoldt, Hartmut and Antoine Cavigneaux. 2009. "Schule." Pages 294–309 in vol. 12 of *Reallexikon der Assyriologie*. Edited by Erich Ebeling et al. Berlin: de Gruyter.

Wagensonner, Klaus. 2010. "Early Lexical Lists Revisited. Structures and Classification as a Mnemonic Device." Pages 285–310 in *Language in the Ancient Near East: Proceedings of the 53ᵉ Rencontre Assyriologique Internationale. Vol. 1, Part 1*. Edited by Leonid Kogan et al. Orientalia et Classica 30. Winona Lake, IN: Eisenbrauns.

Watts, James W. 1998. "The Legal Characterization of Moses in the Rhetoric of the Pentateuch." *Journal of Biblical Literature* 117: 415–26.

Weinfeld, Moshe. 1972. *Deuteronomy and the Deuteronomic School*. Oxford: Clarendon.

Wevers, John William (ed.). 1977. *Deuteronomium*. Septuaginta Vetus Testamentum Graecum Auctoritate Academiae Scientiarum Gottingensis editum III,2. Göttingen: Vandenhoeck & Ruprecht.

Widmer, Michael. 2004. *Moses, God, and the Dynamics of Intercessory Prayer: A Study of Exodus 32–34 and Numbers 13–14*. Forschungen zum Alten Testament II 8. Tübingen: Mohr Siebeck.

Wright, David P. 2009. *Inventing God's Law: How the Covenant Code of the Bible Used and Revised the Laws of Hammurabi*. Oxford: Oxford University Press.

About the Author

Benedetta Rossi is Associate Professor of Old Testament Exegesis at Pontifical Biblical Institute (Rome). Her research interests are Prophecy and the book of Jeremiah; Deuteronomy, its composition and production; the relation between Pentateuch and Prophetic Literature. She also focuses on Cultural Hegemony and the production of sacred texts in the Second Temple period. Her recent publications are articles and book chapters on Deuteronomy, Jeremiah, and prophetic books. She recently coedited with Diana Edelman, Kåre Berge and Philippe Guillaume the volume Deuteronomy in the Making. Studies in the Production of Debarim (De Gruyter: 2021).

CHAPTER 9
BETWEEN SELF-LEGITIMATION AND PROPAGANDA: TORAH IN DEUTERONOMY

Benedetta Rossi

Abstract

The following provides a fresh look at the Torah in Deuteronomy. Rather than an inclusive and democratizing instance within Israel, the Deuteronomic Torah separates one social class (the Levitical priests) from the others. Rather than serving as a mean to separate Israel from the nations, in the context of the Persian Empire, the Torah appears to have been influenced by *dāta*, a concept dear to the Persian imperial elite. Moving from the scribal realm to that of public, oral reception, the Torah emerges as an ideal tool for creating religious and political cohesion through propaganda. Not only does possession of the written Torah separate and legitimize an elite (i.e. the Levitical priests) ahead of potential competing groups, more importantly the oral transmission of the Torah proves an effective way to build the people's consensus.

Keywords: Deuteronomy; Torah; Levitical priests; hegemony; Achaemenid inscriptions; Old Persian dāta.

The meaning and function of the term Torah in Deuteronomy have been widely investigated, and certain interpretive trends have become mainstream. To provide a brief sketch, scholars stress that the semantic core conveyed by the noun Torah is basically that of "normativity" (Lindars 1968; Crüsemann 1992). In Deuteronomy, the meaning of Torah shifts from a single instruction to a *corpus* of instructions and, more precisely, from oral to written instructions (Lindars 1968; Braulik 1970; Crüsemann 1992). As Joseph Blenkinsopp (1977, 36) has stated, "The meaning of this shift is clear: there is now available an authoritative Torah which takes precedence over all other claims to provide guidance to the community." According to this standard view, the shift from the oral to the written Torah – basically retracing the storyline of Deuteronomy (from 1:5 to 31:9) – plays a decisive role in conferring authority on the Torah itself (see among others Sonnet 2012, 207–13; Vergari 2021, 128–36; on the authority of a written *medium*, see Markl 2021, 262–70).

The function of this authoritative Torah has been explored from two complementary points of view: the interaction between Israel and other peoples and its role within Israel.[1] First, Deuteronomy's Torah as a marker of Judean identity prevents the exiles from disappearing through assimilation among the nations (see Markl 2012; 2018; Collins, 2017, 41–42). According to this perspective, the "invention of Torah" in Deuteronomy (Collins 2017, 20–21) is the starting point for using "Torah" as a marker of Jewish exclusiveness and the "beginnings of Jewishness" (see Shaye Cohen's definition quoted by Schaper 2011, 36). Following this interpretation, the Torah plays a pivotal role in creating a claim of exclusivity for Israel. Second, within Israel, inclusivity instead of exclusivity is highlighted. In Deuteronomy, all institutions (king; priests; judges and prophets) and all Israelites are equally subjected to the Torah (Lohfink 1990, 321–322). The Torah is the sole sovereign power in Deuteronomy and takes on the authority of the king (see Levinson 2001, 511–521). Following Levinson, who speaks about a "Torah-monarchy" (2008, 85), no institution "is superior to the other, rather, each is equally subordinate to Deuteronomy's Torah." As a consequence, "Deuteronomy's laws of public offices emerge as the blueprint for a transformed society" (Levinson 2008, 81). As regards Israelites, the Torah is addressed to the whole of Israel, repeatedly depicted as a learning community (Deut 6:6–8; 11:18–21; 31:11–13) (see Finsterbusch 2005; Markl 2021, 266–268). Consequently, members of this learning community are ruled by the Torah and must transmit its instructions (Deut 6:6–8; 11:18–21). If the king as much as any other Israelite is equally subject to the Torah, the Torah is a kind of "democratizing" principle. Besides the so-called brotherhood ethics, this "democratizing" Torah would support the opinion that Israel was the "cradle of democracy" as much as Athens was (see Otto 1999, 378; Ska 2004, 148–54).

While these views have been widely accepted, there are reasons to question their legitimacy.

First, the presence and persistence of forms of Judaism not aligned with the Torah, like the Jewish community of Elephantine, cast doubts on the claim that the Torah was to serve as an exclusive identity marker

---

1   By the name "Israel" I refer here to the intra-diegetic addressees of Moses's Torah in Deuteronomy (see Deut 1:1).

within the community, much less one that distinguished Israelites from other peoples. The case of Elephantine may be explained as antecedent to the normative value of the Torah, but other forms of non-Mosaic Judaism remain without a logical explanation (Collins 2017, 62–79). Some wisdom traditions in the Hebrew Bible (e.g. Job; Qohelet) or narratives from the eastern diaspora (e.g. MT Esther and Daniel 1–6), as well as writings connected to Enochic (non-Mosaic) Judaism, indicate that the Torah could have been "one source of wisdom among many" (Collins 2017, 79) but was not the exclusive and essential identity-marker of Judaism.

A second weakness in the prevalent paradigm of a Jewish exclusivism is its underlying assumption that the Torah relies on the opposition between Judaism and other peoples and cultures. The administrative documents of the Āl-Yāḫūdu and Bīt Našar colonies (Pearce and Wunsch, 2014) provide evidence of the interaction and progressive integration of Jews with and into the social and economic fabric of the countries where they lived (Berlejung 2016; 2017). Some biblical texts, such as Second Isaiah (Isa 40–55) or Zech 1–8, also reflect a process of integration and a creative takeover from Persian ideology and elites rather than opposition to them (Silverman 2020).

Finally, it remains an open question whether the purported democratizing principle of Deuteronomy's Torah had any concrete expression in terms of social, political, or economic transformations (Levinson 2008, 83). For instance, the prescription of a seven-year teaching of the Torah addressed to the entire community during the feast of Sukkot (Deut 31:11–13), decisive for establishing the collective destination of the Torah, has little echo in the celebrations of the feast of Sukkot as prescribed in Lev 23:33–43, Num 29:12–38, or in later Jewish literature (see Lozinskyy 2022, 165–221, esp. 199).

In light of these contra-indications, I will argue that, far from being a democratizing instrument, the Torah establishes the outstanding position of a religious scribal elite, the Levitical priests. The interplay between the writing of the scroll and its envisioned transmission further enhances the role of this elite in controlling the content of the scroll and the dissemination of its knowledge. Employed by the elite group to stir up spontaneous consent, the Torah ends up being an instrument of hegemony. Moving from the scribal realm to that of public, oral reception, the Torah emerges as an ideal tool for creating religious and political cohesion through propaganda. Finally, I shall reconsider the role of the Torah in Israel's relationship with other peoples. Presented as a mark of Israel's identity among the nations (Deut 4:8), on closer inspection the Torah is, instead, a revival and adaptation of the Old Persian notion of *dāta*, a key instrument of Achaemenid political and religious discourse. This shows that the alleged exclusivism of Israel, based on the Torah, is rooted instead in the integration and cooperation of scribal and religious elites into and with the Persian Empire.

1. Transmitting the Torah and Setting an Elite Apart

In "Master-Scribe and Forefather of a Scribal Guild" (in this same volume), I argue that Moses's Torah begins as a scribal construct, the *sefer hattorah*. A compendium of a scribal curriculum bequeathed by Moses to Levitical priests and fictionalized as Moses's farewell speech, the *sefer hattorah* transmits a sample of the various literary genres typical of the scribal craft. Yet, the very first mention of the Torah is presented as an oral communication: "In the land of Moab, Moses began to explain this torah" (Deut 1:5). The oral communication of the Torah to "all Israel" (Deut 1:1) supports the idea that everyone could access the Torah, and each Israelite, including judges, priests, and the king, was equally subject to it. If Moses's Torah-teaching concerned all Israelites, three particular cases put the Levitical priests in a privileged position.

1.1 The Torah on Skin Disease (Deut 24:8)

The outbreak of a skin disease involves the Levitical priests as specialists whose instructions the Israelites are to be very careful to observe strictly and to do (השמר [...] לשמר מאד ולעשית). Moses justifies the skill of the Levitical priests by explaining that he has personally transmitted it to them: the people should act according to "whatever the Levitical priests instruct you (ככל אשר יורו אתכם) as I have commanded them (כאשר צויתם)." The Levitical priests thus teach (יורו) what Moses commanded them (צויתם). The actual contents of this command are revealed neither to the reader nor to Israel gathered in Moab. The Samaritan Pentateuch (SP) and the Septuagint (LXX) clarify the command received from Moses as Torah (or Law, Greek νόμος) itself:

> SP: "according to the Torah they will teach you." (ככל התורה אשר יורו אתכם)
>
> LXX: "you shall be careful to do according to all the law (κατὰ πάντα τὸν νόμον), whatever the priests, the Levites, may announce to you (ὃν ἐὰν ἀναγγείλωσιν ὑμῖν οἱ ἱερεῖς οἱ Λευῖται). As I commanded you (ὃν τρόπον ἐνετειλάμην ὑμῖν), be careful to do."

Whereas in the MT Moses invites the recipients of his speech to obey the orders (root צוה) he had given to the Levitical priests, in the Greek text Moses asks Israel gathered in Moab to obey the instructions he previously gave them (presumably Israel) rather than a knowledge to which only the Levitical priests were privy. The Septuagint probably smooths the text and resolves what appears to be an inconsistency (see McCarthy 2007, 70).

Eckart Otto (2017, 1836–37) sees in Deut 24:8 a possible reference to the priestly teaching outlined in Lev 10:10–11. However, in Lev 10:11 the contents of the Levitical teaching (ירה hi.) are the prescriptions (החקים) already given by Yhwh to the community through Moses ("all the prescriptions that Yhwh has spoken to them [אשר דבר יהוה אליהם] through Moses"). As Jacob Milgrom (1999, 617) has highlighted, in Lev 10:11 "the priests are not the recipients of the divine teachings. These teachings are imparted to Israel through the mediation of Moses." According to Milgrom, this indicates a break from the surrounding world, where, to the contrary, priests jealously guarded divine instructions. This is precisely the situation envisioned in Deut 24:8, where reference is made to an instruction not given directly to the community but reserved exclusively for Levitical priests.

The teaching of Levitical priests in Deut 24:8 can point back to the instructions (Torah) concerning leprosy in Lev 14. Deuteronomy 24:8 is the only instance where the noun צערה occurs in the Pentateuch outside Leviticus. Moreover, following Otto (2017, 1828–29), Deut 24:8–9 was a post-exilic rewriting (*Fortschreibung*), which in turn assumes P and its rewritings. The instructions concerning the leper and leprosy is communicated by Yhwh to Moses (Lev 14:1–32) and to Moses and Aaron (14:33–53). Unlike the Holiness Legislation (Lev 17–26) that is intended for public communication (from Moses to all Israelites) and established between Yhwh and all the people (26:46), the instructions concerning leprosy are reserved for Moses and later for Aaron. The possible link between Deut 24:8 and Lev 14 underlines once again the existence of an exclusive teaching reserved for a specific social class, represented in the case of Lev 14 by Moses and then Aaron, and by Levitical priests in Deut 24:8.

1.2 The Torah at the High Court

The Levitical priests are also granted the final power of adjudication for cases deemed too grave to be arbitrated at the local level on the evidence of (על פי) two to three witnesses (17:6). Difficult cases are thus referred to Levitical priests and a judge, who pronounce sentences that are to be carried out exactly "according to the Torah (על פי התורה) the Levitical priests (and the judge) will teach you" (17:11). Contrary to the common understanding of the Torah as a legal code of sorts, the Torah is the verdict pronounced by the Levitical priests, who function here as the supreme legal authority in addition to their supreme authority in medical matters (see Deut 24:8). The litigants have no option but to obey the verdicts that cannot be appealed and whose legality cannot be gauged against a written document. The Torah taught by Levitical priests and a judge (17:11) makes up for the lack of expertise in the local courts. At the *māqôm*, judgment based on the Torah replaces the judgment grounded on the word of two or three witnesses, which was sufficient to resolve cases in local courts (17:7) (Otto 2016, 1,474). The regulation concerning the high court (17:8-13) shows that the Torah needed for judgment is available neither to the whole community nor to the local courts.

In Deut 17:11 the sentence, "you shall not turn aside from the word they (i.e. Levitical priests and judge) will tell you either to the right or left (לא תסור מן־הדבר אשר־יגידו לך ימין ושמאל)" reinforces the authority of Levitical priests and judges. The commitment not to turn aside to the right or left (לא + סור + ימין ושמאל) in Deut 5:32 stresses the relevance of the Decalogue: "be careful to do as Yhwh your God has commanded you; you shall not turn to the right or to the left (לא תסרו ימין ושמאל)." Elsewhere, the same phrase emphasizes that Moses's instructions, whether orally transmitted (Deut 28:14 and also Josh 1:7) or written in the *sefer hattorah* (Deut 17:20; also Josh 23:6), are binding. The use of the same locution in Deut 5:32; 17:11, 20; and 28:14 parallels priestly judgments "according to the Torah" (על פי התורה) (in Deut 17:11) with the Decalogue (5:32) and the authority of Moses's instructions (Deut 17:20; 28:14). As a result, the peculiar expertise in the Torah shown by Levitical priests and judges at the high court elevates these two groups among the Israelites, while simultaneously enhancing the power of the high court over local ones. In addition, the phraseology employed in Deut 17:13-18 stresses the binding authority of the teaching of Levitical priests and judges, by paralleling it with Moses's teaching and Yhwh's Decalogue.

1.3 The Torah for the King

The regulations concerning the high court (Deut 17:8-13) (see Levinson 2008, 76) as well as the so-called "law of the king" (Deut 17:14-20) deprive the king of any involvement in the administration of justice. Following Deut 17:18, the king shall write for himself a copy of "this Torah, according to the one that is in the custody of Levitical Priests (מלפני הכהנים הלוים)." The king does not access the written Torah by himself; his access to the scroll is mediated by Levitical priests, who control the master-copy of the Torah. Verse 19 then describes the deference the king is to exercise toward the written Torah: he will constantly read (קרא) his copy of the

Torah scroll and learn (למד) from it. The king becomes a diligent and devout student and is *de facto* subject to the scribal elite of the Levitical priests.

The Temple Scroll (11Q19) goes a step further: "And when he sits upon the throne of his kingdom they shall write for him (וכתבו לו) this law according to this Torah which is before the priests" (56:20–21). Here, the Levitical priests do not even grant the king access to the master-copy of the Torah. They copy it for him (Paganini 2009, 145–148; Otto 2016, 1433). By writing a copy of the Torah, the Levitical priests mirror the actions of Moses, who writes the *sefer hattorah* in Moab (Deut 31:9).

To recap: the above observations show that while the Levitical priests are expected to obey the Torah, they do not seem subject to the Torah in the same way that all other Israelites and officials are. Expertise in the Torah and knowledge of its peculiar instructions, to the contrary, separate and legitimize them as an elite. At the same time, their social status is elevated in the eyes of the people. This poses a serious challenge to considering the Torah in Deuteronomy an intended form of democratization.

2. Storing the Scroll and Controlling Its Content

In Deut 31:9, Moses bestows the *sefer hattorah* he had written on two selected groups: the priests, the sons of Levi, who carry the ark, and the elders. In Deut 31:10 Moses gives instructions concerning the scroll exclusively to these two groups (ויצו משה אותם "and Moses commanded them"). For the first time in Deuteronomy, elders are grouped together with Levitical priests; the two are generally distinct.[2] Yet, the two remain separate entities rather than being merged. This situation is confirmed by the ensuing instruction for the future reading of the Torah in the land, addressed to a second person singular, in 31:11: "you shall read this Torah" (תקרא את־התורה הזאת). The latter verse highlights that once the people have entered the land, Levitical priests alone are to be in charge of transmitting the Torah to "all Israel" (see Otto 2017, 2,115–16). Then, in 31:25–26, only the Levites who carry the ark are the recipients of a second directive concerning the safe-keeping of the *sefer hattorah* (ויצו משה את־הלוים נשאי ארון ברית־יהוה "and Moses commanded the Levites

---

2   In most occurrences, the elders are related to the local jurisdiction of matters relating to family regulations (Deut 19:12; 21:2–3; 21:19–20; 22:15–18; 25:7–9). In two instances, they appear alongside the tribal chiefs (5:3) and other lay representatives as part of the community (29:9; 31:28) that enters the Moab covenant. Then, in 27:1, they stand with Moses in commanding prescriptions to the people.

who carried the ark of the covenant of Yhwh"). As representatives of the people, the elders witness the handing over of the *sefer hattorah* to the Levitical priests, who are in charge of both its safekeeping and its public readings later on (31:9). The presupposition is that the Levitical priests can read, while the elders are not necessarily able to read, nor do they need to. Therefore, the entrusting of the *sefer hattorah* and the addressing of instructions for its safekeeping and transmission only to Levitical priests emphasize the separation of one elite (i.e. the Levitical priests) from the rest of the people and from other groups such as the elders.

Deuteronomy 31:10–13 suggests an equivalence between Moses's oral teaching in Moab, his written Torah, and its future oral recitation by priests. The references to the Torah in the framing chapters show that the recipient of Moses's oral performance is "all Israel" gathered in Moab (1:5; 4:44). Similarly, the entire community ("men, women, little ones, and the sojourner within your gates," 31:12) will be the recipients of the public reading of the Torah scroll, which in the future will be performed by Levitical priests (31:9). At first glance, this seems to make the distinction between the entire community and a privileged scribal elite redundant. Everyone in Israel could access Moses's Torah, either via a written *medium* (i.e. Levitical priests) or an oral one (i.e. the entire people). Is the proposed separation of an elite through the Torah still sustainable? A comparison between the two *sefarim* written by Moses in the Pentateuch, the *sefer hattorah* (written in Deut 31:9) and the *sefer habbᵉrit* (written in Exod 24:3–9), provides clues to answer this question.

A relationship between Deut 31:9 and Exod 24:3–8 is commonly recognized (see Otto 2017, 2,111–12; Rossi 2023). Exod 24:3–8 displays movement "from *oral* performance to *writing* and from *writing* to *reading*" (Ska 2007, 165). In Exod 24:3–8, oral and written communication are intertwined.[3] As soon as Moses has narrated (ויספר) "all the words and ordinances of Yhwh" to the people, they commit themselves to do "all the words Yhwh has spoken we shall do" (כל־הדברים אשר־דבר יהוה נעשה). Only then does Moses *write* "all the words of Yhwh" (את כל־דברי יהוה) previously proclaimed (v. 4). After performing ritual actions (vv. 4b–6), Moses "took the book of the covenant (ספר הברית) and read it aloud (in the ears) to the people (ויקרא באזני העם)" (24:7), who, as a result, were in a position to verify that the contents of the book agreed with the previous oral proclamation (24:7). The text does not provide details of the content of the book written by Moses (vv. 3, 7): nonetheless, the reader can identify its content with the former legal prescriptions (the Decalogue +

---

3   As Ska (2007, 160–63) highlights, isolating different redactional layers in 24:3–8 seems unnecessary. The narrative displays an internal coherence.

the covenant code in Exod 20:22–23:19).⁴ Then the people commit themselves again to obedience: "All Yhwh has said (כל אשר־דבר יהוה) we will do and hear/obey (נעשה ונשמע)." The repeated answers in vv. 3 and 7 are not duplications. They fulfill different functions (Schenker 1996, 378–80; Ska 2007, 163–67). The first response in v. 3 is a preliminary agreement to the covenant. In the second approval in v. 7, the people implicitly recognize that the wording of the *sefer habberit* matches Moses's prior oral communication. As Jean-Louis Ska highlights, "For Israel, there is an identity between the words written in the book and the words spoken by Moses at the outset of the narrative, and these words are identified as Yhwh's words" (2007, 162). Hence, the document of the Sinai covenant, the *sefer habberit* (that contains the regulations previously communicated by Yhwh to Moses and by Moses to Israel) is duly double-checked by the people who enter the covenant.⁵

Deuteronomy 31:9–13 displays a crucial difference in depicting the relationship between oral performance, written record, and future oral recitation. First, Moses orally expounds the contents of "this Torah" (1:5) to all Israel gathered in Moab. The covenant is made in Moab (see 28:69): the collective response in 29:28 mirrors Israel's commitment to the covenant stipulations. In Deut 31:9, Moses's explanation of the Torah in Moab is finally put into writing, and the *sefer hattorah* finally is foregrounded. While in Exod 24:3–8 the written document is read and newly accepted by all Israel, in Deut 31:10–13 the reading of the *sefer hattorah* is displaced. The written document will be read later in the land, during a ritual septennial gathering.

In summary, in Exodus, the reading of the *sefer habberit* right after its production and the collective response to its reading clearly indicate that the book is "given" to the whole community. In Deuteronomy, to the contrary, the *sefer hattorah* is given to Levitical priests as the elders witness that act; it remains unread in Moab. The delayed and displaced reading of the *sefer hattorah* prevents all Israel from recognizing the identity between Moses's oral and written Torah. Instead, Israel can only accept the privileged position of those in charge of the future readings of the *sefer hattorah*. When the story of the events at Sinai are compared to those taking place in connection with the covenant in Moab, what becomes a displaced reading stresses the outstanding position of those in

---

4   According to Ska (2007, 167) the phrase "all the words of Yhwh" points back to the Decalogue (20:1–17), while the "ordinances" refer to the prescriptions of the Covenant Code.
5   As Ska (2007, 165–67) highlights, the narrative sequence clearly aims at showing the correspondence between the content of the written *sefer* and its oral transmission.

charge of the future readings of the *sefer hattorah* (i.e. Levitical priests). At the same time, this strategy of displacement legitimizes their authority in the eyes of the people.

Divesting the people of their ability to vouch for the contents of Deuteronomy's *sefer hattorah* by postponing its second reading by up to seven years (31:10) provides a motivation for the ensuing narrated events in Deut 31. According to v. 19, Yhwh commands that the "Song of Moses" should be written and learned by the Israelites as a future witness against them: "and now write this song for yourselves (ועתה כתבו לכם את־השירה הזאת) and teach [it] to the sons of Israel (ולמדה את־בני־ישראל) and put it in their mouth (שימה בפיהם)." While previously the deity had been addressing Moses only, here it seems to address Joshua as well (see Otto 2017, 2,092). Even so, it is Moses who complies immediately, writes down the song the same day, and proceeds to teach it personally to the children of Israel (v. 22). The song, then, becomes an interim memorized portion of the otherwise unread Torah (v. 24).

Deuteronomy 31:24 states clearly that the song became an integral part of the written *sefer hattorah*. Although he previously had written the Torah on a scroll he already had entrusted to the Levitical priests in front of the elders in 31:9, the opening clause of v. 24 states it was only when Moses wrote down the song that the written form of that Torah scroll became complete: "when Moses had finished writing the words of this Torah to the end" (ויהי ככלות משה לכתב את־דברי התורה־הזאת על־ספר עד תמם). In Deuteronomy, then, the contents of the song are part of the written Torah.

Expanding on the reported teaching of the song to Israel in 31:24, Moses proceeds to proclaim the song to the entire assembly of Israel. The narrator points out in 31:30, "Then Moses recited (וידבר) the words of this song in their entirety (עד תמם) for the whole assembly of Israel to hear." Moses's oral presentation of the song is highlighted by being recalled in Deut 32:44: "and Moses came and recited all the words of this song (את־כל־דברי השירה־הזאת) in the hearing of the people."

The sequence of writing followed by oral communication in Deut 31:22, 24, 30, while familiar from Exod 24:3–9, here serves to drive home a different point. Only a small portion of the written Torah – the song of Deut 32 – is immediately proclaimed to all Israel. In Deuteronomy, then, the majority of the *sefer hattorah* lies silent beside the ark. As a result, the Israelite recipients of Moses's instructions in Moab (see 1:5) cannot ascertain the correspondence between Moses's oral teaching ("this torah," 1:5) and the written *sefer* as they could at Sinai, according to Exod 24:3–8.

In his 1985 monograph, *Oral Tradition as History*, Jan Vansina discusses oral communication as a social product and investigates how social influences can alter the content and transmission of the message (Vansina 1985, 94). Focusing on the relationship between the message and its "social seat," Vansina identifies esoteric knowledge and copyright as tools to control information (1985, 96–98). Knowledge becomes esoteric when its access is reserved to a certain group, while copyright deals with the performance of the message: "traditions may thus be known but not repeated at will" (Vansina 1985, 98). In some cases, only certain groups can perform traditions. Though everyone may, indeed, hear the message, only some may tell it, and often only before an appropriate forum. The goal is to ensure accurate transmission and also "to keep control over the dissemination of information" (Vansina 1985, 98).

In Deuteronomy, the Levitical priests control Torah through the agency of esoteric knowledge and copyright. The use of the Torah to separate a scribal priestly elite from the rest of the community (see §1) points to the Torah, or at least some part of it, as a kind of esoteric knowledge. The issue of copyright as a means of controlling the performance of the Torah and its transmission is equally apparent in Deuteronomy. The content of the Torah is delivered orally to the whole community both in Moab (see 1:5 and Moses's oral teaching of "this Torah") and in the land (see 31:11–13 and the proclamation of the Torah during the septennial gathering). However, only a selected group (Levitical priests) can access the text, perform its content, and interpret it.

The control of the dissemination of tradition is further emphasized in Deuteronomy. In some cases, individuals will perform parts of the Torah in the land. On closer inspection, however, the performance is limited and regulated.

(1) In Deut 26:5–10, each Israelite will recite before the priest some ritual words that are embedded in the *sefer hattorah*. However, the words Israelites will pronounce during the offering of the first fruits are codified by Moses himself and cannot be subjected to variations.

(2) In Deut 6:7 and 11:19, the performance of Moses's words seems freely entrusted to the *pater familias*. He is supposed to recite "these words that I [Moses] am commanding you today (6:6)" (הדברים האלה אשר אנכי מצוך היום). However, two indications point to a limitation and control in the performance of the Torah within the family. First, both Deut 6:9 and 11:20 clarify that proclaimed words are to be written on the doorposts of "your house" and "your gates" (על־מזוזות ביתך ובשעריך), i.e. in private and public spaces. This means, first, that we are presumably dealing with an excerpt from the master-scroll of the Torah. Furthermore, the very act of writing, especially if it happens in a public space (בשעריך), is a way of limiting the performer's creativity. According to Deut 6:6–9 and 11:19–20, the words spoken will be the same as those fixed in writing; as a result, the individual performance of selected words from the master-scroll of

Torah that represented a compendium of scribal education reframed as Moses's farewell speech (Deut 1–30; 32) (see ch. 8 in this volume) will be subjected to a kind of public scrutiny.

(3) As discussed earlier in this section, Moses's Song in Deut 32 is the only part of the Torah delivered directly by Moses to all the Israelites for them to learn and recite (31:19: "put it in their mouths," שימה בפיהם). Again, the Israelites will be allowed to recite only a limited portion of the Torah, which is, moreover, clearly codified in the Torah itself (ch. 32).

To recapitulate, the writing of the *sefer hattorah* in Deut 31:9, the giving of the book exclusively to Levitical priests in the presence of witnessing elders (31:9), the apparent lack of a Torah-reading subsequent to its writing in Moab, and the displacement of the public reading until Israel has taken possession of Cisjordan (31:10–13) make Moses's Torah protected by copyright. Control over the dissemination of the Torah tradition in the land further highlights the issue at hand.

3. Torah and Hegemony

The Torah discourse in Deuteronomy outlined above is an instrument for generating and preserving the hegemony of a scribal elite. The concept of hegemony was developed by Antonio Gramsci to clarify the relationship between culture and power. It was then introduced into cultural studies by T. J. Jackson Lears (1985). Highlighting problems and possibilities for the application of this concept by historians, he points out how the concept of cultural hegemony "can aid intellectual historians trying to understand how ideas reinforce or undermine existing social structure" (1985, 568). Lears's analysis deals with modern historiography and cultural studies.

The 2021 volume, *Antonio Gramsci and the Ancient World*, stands as the first attempt to systematically apply some of Gramsci's insights to the ancient world, especially the Graeco-Roman world.[6] Hegemony occupies a prominent role. Three factors help define Gramsci's conception of hegemony[7]: (1) the presence of a *distinctive social group*, able to influence the rest of society, due to its prestige. Influence is wielded by (2) stirring

---

6   See Zucchetti and Cimino 2021. An investigation of Second Temple Judaism and the production and reception of biblical texts through the lens of cultural hegemony is still lacking. On this, see the volume *Cultural Hegemony, Ideological Conflicts, and Power in Second Temple Judaism* (eds. Danilo Verde and Benedetta Rossi, 2024. BETL 337. Leuven: Peeters).
7   As Zucchetti (2021, 2) highlights, Gramsci does not provide an explicit definition of hegemony/cultural hegemony. However, he outlines his ideas in this regard in the prison notebooks.

up *spontaneous consent*, (3) *through persuasion*, not through force. Hence, "achieving hegemony does not involve any top-down transmission of knowledge, but rather a 'spontaneous' consent, due to the penetration of some values and norms of the ruling group into common sense" (Zucchetti 2021, 2). These three elements are evident in the Torah discourse in Deuteronomy.

3.1 Elite and Prestige

I have shown that the exclusive knowledge of peculiar instructions as well as a monopoly over control of the written scroll of the Torah separate and legitimize the group of Levitical priests as an elite in Israel. More precisely, exclusive competence in the Torah displayed in the high court (§1.2) confers upon them prestige in the eyes of the rest of the community. Their outstanding position is further stressed by their relation to the king as well as by the control they exercise over the dissemination of the Torah in the land.

3.2 Spontaneous Consent Through Persuasion

Through ritualized public reading and interpreting (Deut 31:10–13), the elite group of Levitical priests is able to influence the habits and behavior of the rest of society. Deuteronomy displays various strategies for stirring up the spontaneous consent of the addressees, which becomes institutionalized as part of the Torah itself. The parenesis that runs through the book of Deuteronomy, which is intertwined with the instructions, exemplifies this situation. As a result, in Deuteronomy, the written Torah in particular (the *sefer hattorah*) secures not only its content but also the rhetorical and pragmatic devices that promote the speakers' reception (Moses in Moab; Levitical priests in the land) (see Rossi 2023). In addition, in Deut 29:28, the collective answer of the people, who commit themselves to the observance of "this Torah," reinforces its persuasive nature: "the hidden things belong to Yhwh our God, but the revealed things belong to us and to our children forever, to observe all the words of this Torah." According to Dominik Markl (2012, 106), the statement should be considered a commissive speech act by which the speakers commit themselves to practice the Torah. In Deuteronomy, this positive response to the requirements of the Torah becomes embedded in the written master-scroll. Moreover, Deuteronomy's persuasive strategy, aimed at stirring up the people's commitment to Moses's Torah, is effective: the people are ready to commit themselves to obey all the words of this Torah as well as all "the hidden things belonging to Yhwh our God"

(Deut 29:28). The separation between hidden and revealed things could hint at an intentional recognition of an elite within the community, or at any rate points to a different access to revelation mediated by the Torah of Moses within the community. Regardless, in Deuteronomy, the spontaneous consent of the community to the requirements of the Torah is an integral element of the written Torah.

3.3 Centralizing the Torah

Another element can be added to the above observations: the spatial setting of the Torah confirms its role in creating and fostering hegemony. In Deuteronomy, Moses's Torah is progressively subject to a process of centralization (Berge 2021), leading from the plains of Moab to the *māqôm*. The process of centralization guarantees the transmission of the Torah from the generation of Moab (Moses's interlocutors, i.e. intra-diegetic addressees) to the following generations (i.e. the extra-diegetic recipients). Outside Cisjordan, the Torah is expounded by Moses in Moab (1:5); the recipients of Torah-teaching are Moses's interlocutors (Israel in Moab). Following Deut 31:26, the written scroll of the Torah enters Cisjordan. Ensuing generations will access the Torah by going to the *māqôm*. There, the Levitical priests will instruct the people, gathered every seven years to take part in a public reading of Moses's Torah. In addition, at the *māqôm* the Levitical priests will administer a Torah that normally will not be accessible to the people in their hometowns (Deut 17:11; 24:8). In the place chosen by Yhwh, the Levitical priests will dispense the Torah and thus affirm their primacy over all other Israelites. The difference between Levitical priests and other Israelites is specifically marked by their possession of the Torah.

How does centralization link to hegemony? Following Julia Rhyder's insights (2019, 1-21; 66-90), centralization cannot be understood to limit certain actions to a central and single place of worship. Instead, centralization should be reconceptualized as "a dynamic and multifaceted network of processes" (Rhyder 2019, 4) that ultimately aims at creating a single authority. From this perspective, centralization strategies – e.g. creating standard ritual practices and restricting authority to one group (see Rhyder 2019, 4) – serve the purpose of fostering the hegemony of the dominant group over the rest of society perfectly.

According to Deut 30:1-10, Moses's Torah offers the way back to Yhwh for the people dispersed among the nations after having lost the land. However, the accessibility of the Torah to members of dispersed Israel is always mediated by the *sefer hattorah* (see 30:10), entrusted to Levitical priests and elders and transmitted once every seven years to the people gathered at the *māqôm* for a festival. The observance of the Deuteronomic Torah as a distinguishing feature of Israelites among the nations (e.g. Deut 4:8) should be seen to be an outcome of the hegemony built by the scribal priestly elite *via* the Torah.

4. Torah in Deuteronomy in Light of the Persian Concept, *Dāta*

So far, I have described Torah following the clues offered by the text of Deuteronomy. Torah as a tool used by a social elite to foster hegemony by stirring up consent shares some intriguing features with *dāta*, a key concept of Achaemenid political and religious propaganda.

The initial identification of *dāta* with a set of laws or a body of legislation in the form of a law-code (e.g. Dandamaev and Lukonin 1989, 117) is now considered outdated (see among others, Tuplin 2015, 88). So is the view that Torah represents a collection of laws. *Dāta* is currently understood as a set of regulations and prescriptions (e.g. in Babylonian and Elamite legal records and in the books of Daniel and Esther). At the same time, *dāta* is also considered a principle that governs social relations in the Empire according to order and justice (e.g. Achaemenid royal inscriptions) (see Pirngruber 2021, 1,087–90).

Starting from Ezra 7:11–26, Peter Frei (2001) has proposed that the relationship between Torah and *dāta* could point to Achaemenid influence on the Pentateuch in the form of alleged Persian imperial authorization of the Torah. While his concept of imperial authorization has been shown to be implausible (see Ska 2001, 164–70), his proposed relationship between Torah and *dāta* has not, as long as his equation of both with law-codes is updated.

Yishai Kiel (2017) tackles the question of the possible overlap between Torah and *dāta* by conducting a semantic analysis of the nouns תורה and דת/דתא. He concludes that in Ezra and Nehemiah, the concept of Yhwh's Torah is indebted to the concept of Ahura Mazda's *dāta*. He notes that in the ancient Near East, legal precepts were typically proclaimed and enforced by the king and commissioned by a national deity. A collection of prescriptions that emanates directly from God and exists beside the king's collection of prescriptions (see Ezra 7:26: "the law of your God [דתא די־אלהך] and the law of the king [ודתא די מלכא]") is, therefore, something new. Kiel (2017, 331–32) ascribes this innovation to the influence of the concept of divine revelation found in the Avesta and taken up in Xerxes's *daiva* inscription (XPh 46–56).[8]

---

8   For abbreviations, list and descriptions of Old Persian Achaemenid inscriptions, see Schmitt 2009, 7–32.

The issue of divine vs. royal prescriptions can be explored further by examining the function played by *dāta* within the communication system of Achaemenid ideology. As Gian Pietro Basello (2013, 40) states, royal Achaemenid inscriptions are "direct expressions of ideology. Therefore, they do not represent reality but are useful precisely to understand what image the empire wanted to give of reality and power" (my translation; see also Lincoln 2012, 105–86; Filippone 2012; Rollinger 2015).

Bruno Jacobs (2015; 2021) has questioned whether Achaemenid inscriptions and their accompanying iconography could have spread ideology within or throughout the Empire. His reservations stem from three observations. First, the inscriptions and iconography only rarely appear outside the center of the Empire. Second, they are foundation inscriptions (thus hidden) or are positioned too high to be read, making them "unsuitable for public oriented communication" (2021, 757–58). Third, the inscriptions are not addressed to a wide audience but to the heir to the throne. In his view, the top-down communication necessary for the maintenance of the Empire would have been conveyed by the imperial administration (Jacobs 2015).

Two counterarguments can be offered in rebuttal that involve the translation of Achaemenid inscriptions into languages employed by the administration in different segments of the Empire and the geographical and temporal diffusion of Achaemenid imperial propaganda. Paragraphs 60–61 and 70 of Darius's Bisitun Inscription (DB) (Rollinger 2015, 122; Huyse 1999, 45–51) illustrate both points. First, DB §§60–61 explicitly prescribe the dissemination of the contents of the inscription orally. Then, in DB §70 the transcription of the inscription on clay tablets and parchment is mentioned. According to DB §70, copies of the inscription are to be sent throughout the Empire. A copy of the text, translated into Aramaic, has been recovered from a reused papyrus found at the military colony on Elephantine Island in the Nile River in Egypt, dating prior to 400 BCE. The Aramaic translation of DB also includes a part of the inscription at Darius's tomb at Naqš-ī Rustam (DNb) (see Greenfield and Porten 1982; Porten and Yardeni 1993, 59–71). Then, a stela found in Babylon bears an adapted version of the Babylonian translation inscribed at Bisitun alongside the Old Persian and Elamite versions (von Voigtlander 1978, 63–66; Rollinger 2015, 121–23).

Jacobs thinks the Bisitun inscription could not have been read by a human audience at the crossroads intersection leading from Persia to Babylonia because of its placement high up a recessed cliff wall. However, this point, and more specifically the larger conclusions he draws from it, are outweighed by the evidence supplied by the abovementioned occurrences of the text. Its translation into Babylonian suggests a wider intended audience outside the Persian heartland was in view when the text was composed at the Persian court; DB §70 is missing from the Babylonian version carved in the Bisitun relief, which suggests it is precisely the text that was to be sent everywhere among the lands/peoples (Aspesi 2005, 19). The Aramaic version either was made from the Babylonian version, not the Old Persian or Elamite one, as a secondary development (Aspesi 2005, 20–21), or it was intended from the beginning to be sent to lands/peoples in the western part of the Empire, where Aramaic served as the official administrative language. Thus, Jacobs's reservations are unfounded.

The circulation of the text inscribed at Bisitun and other preserved and now lost Achaemenid texts within various areas of the Empire was probably done for didactic purposes (A. V. Rossi 2021, 75–76; 80 for lost texts). They would have been studied in scribal milieux and reproduced or adapted to "create something new" (Rollinger 2015, 126) locally. In the process, however, the borrowing of key terms and ideas, including *dāta* specifically (Tuplin 2015 who documents its appearance in several non-Persian languages), would have resulted in a certain accommodation to Achaemenid ideology. Considering the functions of *dāta* as an instrument of Achaemenid ideology therefore seems appropriate.

4.1 *Dāta* in the Rhetoric of the Empire

In most occurrences within Achaemenid inscriptions, *dāta* is an instrument of social cohesion. The *dāta* (subj. nominative), which belongs to the king (*dātam taya manā*, "my prescriptions"), holds (verb *adāraya* "held" < *dar*) the peoples (*dahyu-*) (DNa 21–22; DSe 20; XPh 18). Lists of peoples within the Empire usually follow. In DB I, 17–20 and 20–24; DNa 19; DSe 18, the function of *dāta* for the peoples is parallel to the tribute (*bāji-*) they are to deliver to the king. In the royal inscriptions, and especially in the reliefs that accompany them, tribute is the instrument through which the peoples actively and voluntarily participate in the building of the Empire (Lincoln 2012, 111–23). *Dāta* plays a similar role. Three characteristics of *dāta* emerge.

(1) A relationship to *dāta* distinguishes an elite, represented by the ruler (to whom *dāta* belongs)[9] but the Persian people more generally, as well. In Achaemenid royal inscriptions, the way peoples relate to the king's *dāta* displays a significant variation. In DB I, 14 Persia is mentioned in the first place among the peoples (*dāhyu-*) who follow (verb *pari-ay-*) Darius's *dāta* (I, 23). In DNa 21 (see also DSe 15–21 and XPh 15–19), on

---

9 See the formulas *dātam taya manā*, e.g. DNa 21; and *tayanā manā dāta*, e.g. DB I:23.

the other hand, Persia is absent from the list of peoples "held" (verb *dar-*) by the *dāta* itself[10] and subject to delivering tribute (*baji-*) to the king (see DNa 19; DSe 18; XPh 17). The wording in this second inscription might be intended to reflect the superior position of the Persian people with respect to the different *dahyāva*. Both inscriptions, in their own way, seem to underscore that a peculiar relation to *dāta* marks all Persians as an elite within the multi-ethnic Empire (see also Basello 2021, 863, who speaks of a dominant socio-ethnic class; see also Filippone 2012, 106–12).

(2) *Dāta* works as a principle of centralization, along with tribute. Held together by the king's *dāta*, the peoples participate actively in building the Empire.

(3) Lincoln (2012, 137–139) argues that the insistence on the cohesion of peoples produced by the king's *dāta* obscures the violent side of imperial domination. The exercise of force (attested in DB and DPe) is progressively replaced by *dāta* and its role in consolidating the Empire. In the rhetoric of Achaemenid inscriptions, the substitution of force with *dāta* indicates the latter was considered a tool for creating consensus through persuasion. A change in the representation of *dāta*, as well as the promises to those who follow the royal *dāta*, highlight this point.

In Xerxes's *daiva* inscription (XPh 46–56), *dāta* is not directly linked to the sovereign: rather, it is commanded (verb *ni-stā-*) by Ahura Mazda. XPh 46–56 equates the reverence to *dāta* with worship (of Ahura Mazda) performed using the correct ceremonial procedures. XPh 46–56 is the only instance in Achaemenid inscriptions where *dāta* does not belong to the king but only to the deity.

XPh 18–19, however, displays the most common formula that attributes *dāta* to the king and emphasizes its function in relation to peoples (*dātam taya manā avadiš adāraya*, "the set of prescriptions, which is mine, held them"). In XPh 46–56, the communicative context and the referent of *dāta* change. The communicative context is that of direct address by the king to a non-present individual (see the 2nd person singular in XPh 46–47: "you, who [will be] hereafter") seeking happiness in life and bliss after death. Xerxes advises his interlocutor to follow the *dāta* established by Ahura Mazda. To the individual who obeys the *dāta* of Ahura Mazda, the king promises happiness and bliss (XPh 52–56).

In short, within Achaemenid inscriptions, the only time *dāta* goes back to the deity and has an individual as a referent is within a predictive and persuasive speech addressed to a future interlocutor. *Dāta*'s belonging to Ahura Mazda reinforces the promise of happiness for those who follow

---

10   In the formula *dātam taya manā avadiš adāraya* ("the *dāta* which is mine held them"; e.g. DNa 21–22), the king's *dāta* is the subject of the verb, while peoples are the object.

its regulations. Moreover, in XPh the *dāta* of Ahura Mazda, elsewhere a specific possession of the king, seems accessible to anyone. Each person can individually seek happiness and bliss in life and after death by following the *dāta* of Ahura Mazda and venerating him with the right ceremonial acts.

4.2 *Dāta* and Deuteronomy's Torah

Against this background, four points of comparison between the function of *dāta* in Achaemenid inscriptions and *Torah* in Deuteronomy come to mind.

(1) In Achaemenid inscriptions, *dāta* ensures the cohesion of the Empire and establishes a criterion of belonging to it for the different population groups and also for the individual. In Deuteronomy, the idea of Torah does not provide a solution for how to build an imperial identity: rather, the issue is how to maintain cohesion among those scattered within the larger Empire, who share a religious identity. There is no need to keep a vast territory under control – the dilemma of the Achaemenid sovereigns – but rather, to "control" and influence the members of an ethnic group/religion scattered over a vast territory (Silverman 2020, 8).[11] The Deuteronomic Torah taught by Levitical priests provides a religious scribal elite with an instrument to create and maintain cohesion and control.[12] The rhetorical apparatus that supports its observance and authority seems to respond well to this need.

(2) As much as *dāta* works as a principle of centralization alongside tribute, Deuteronomy's Torah promotes cohesion through centralization. In the *fabula* of Deuteronomy, Torah moves from the plains of Moab to the promised land in Cisjordan. In addition, Torah advocates travel from

---

[11] The minority status of the Judeans in the Diaspora differed, depending on the areas within the Empire where they were located. Those in Babylon were a minority in a much larger context. Those in Yehud were a majority in a much smaller and more marginal part of the Empire. Jason Silverman (2020, 14) also underlines the different conditions of the Judean elites within the Persian Empire: in Yehud, we can speak of a post-collapse society; in Babylon and Assyria, descendants of those deported were integrated (e.g. the documents in Pearce and Wunsch 2014); in Elephantine, there was a military colony in the service of the Empire; while Samerina hosted long-term residents.

[12] This is possible within the political control exercised by Persian power. On the contrary, the idea of an identity with markedly political connotations would not be conceivable within a system of power that could be violent and was capable of promptly and cruelly repressing attempts of revolt and insubordination.

the peripheries to the *māqôm*, where Torah is taught by Levitical priests (during the septennial reading as well as at the high court).

(3) Though belonging to the sovereign and to Ahura Madza (cf. XPh), *dāta* is potentially accessible to the individual. The peacefulness of the Empire, produced by the subjection of peoples to the king's regulations and order, mirrors the happiness and bliss reserved for the individual who honors the *dāta* of Ahura Mazda. The same rhetorical dynamic can be seen in the Deuteronomic Torah: through the mediation of Levitical priests, Torah is accessible to the individual, even those scattered in the most distant lands (Deut 30). Torah allows a return to a symbolic and geographical center, the former expressed by obedience to Yhwh and his Torah and the latter in the return to the arable land after exile. At the same time, the observance of the Torah provides the way to a happy life (cf. the use of the root יטב).

(4) The Old Persian formula related to *dāta* and conveyed by the Achaemenid inscriptions may even appear in the blessing of Moses in Deut 33:2. The MT runs as follows: מימינו אשדת למו. Among other difficulties, the sequence of letters אשדת is difficult to comprehend. A marginal *qere* note suggests reading two words, אש דת, instead of one word, אשדת. Following this proposal, the phrase in v. 2 would read "from his right hand goes out a fire of law for them" (e.g. Otto 2017, 2,212), construing the word דת as a loanword from the old Persian noun *dāta* (Margulis 1969, 206; Otto 2017, 2,212). The Septuagint reads: ἐκ δεξιῶν αὐτοῦ ἄγγελοι μετ' αὐτοῦ ("from his right, angels with him"). The Septuagint rendering of אשדת with ἄγγελοι, "angels," is mistaken (Otto 2017, 2214).

In 2021, a new Italian translation of the Pentateuch appeared, in which Federico Giuntoli translates the *crux interpretum* in Deut 33:2 as follows: "dal sud un fuoco (מימינו אש), la Legge gli appartiene (דת למו)" (i.e. "a fire from the south, the Law belongs to him" [my translation]). Giuntoli considers the noun דת a loanword from Old Persian but goes a step further. He interprets the phrase דת למו in light of the old Persian formula, *dāta taya manā*, i.e. "the law which is mine" (see Giuntoli 2021, 567–8 n. G), which often appears in Achaemenid inscriptions. If Giuntoli's reading of Deut 33:2 is correct, the phrase דת למו would be an intentional link to Achaemenid ideology, conveyed by use of the Persian loan-word, *dāta*.

5. Concluding Remarks

The mainstream understanding of how the concepts of inclusivity and exclusivity describe the function of the Torah for Israel and the nations in Deuteronomy needs to be reversed. Rather than serving as an inclusive and democratizing instrument within Israel, the Deuteronomic Torah is characterized by a claim of exclusivity, since it separates one social class from the others. Rather than serving as a means to separate Israel from the nations, in the context of the Persian Empire, the Torah is characterized by a claim of inclusivity, since it appears to have been influenced by *dāta*, a concept dear to the Persian imperial elite.

If the connections highlighted above have any plausibility, the reformulation of the Torah in Deuteronomy against the background of the Old Persian *dāta*, a vehicle for Achaemenid propaganda, indicates the creative adoption and adaptation of an imperial cultural category by the scribes responsible for the composition. This would not be a case of intentional subversion of cultural categories of the Persian world, as proposed by some in the context of Assyrian imperialism (see Otto 2013). The sources do not, in fact, suggest any contrasting relationship between Judeans or Samarians and the Achaemenid imperial authorities that would supply a reason for resistance or ideological subversion (see Waerzeggers 2018; Silverman 2020, 19–20). Rather, we witness the assumption of some elements characteristic of Persian propaganda in order to build religious cohesion in a post-exilic, dispersed Israel. From this point of view, the phenomenon could be read with Jason Silverman (2020, 259) as one of the cases in which local elites reformulated their traditions in a way "useful" to the Empire.

This dynamism of creative interaction with one of the categories of imperial propaganda, as well as its adoption, finds further plausibility if we consider the connection of the Deuteronomic Torah with the Levitical priests and its function for the legitimation of this social and religious class. The role of the local priestly elites in the development and administration of the Persian Empire, beginning with the striking case of the clergy of Marduk in Babylon during the conquest of Cyrus as well as the use of religious propaganda as an instrument of empire cohesion,[13] could further confirm the hypothesis put forward.

Finally, the relationship between the written Torah and the oral transmission of the Torah in Deuteronomy is also worth reconsidering. If the observations made above are plausible, this is *not* a case of an oral tradition finally put down in writing. On the contrary, the Torah originates as a written product, a compendium of the scribal curriculum, fictionalized as Moses's farewell speech. The goal of this first phase of the Torah's "life" would have been the legitimization of the scribal elite. But this was not enough. The Torah is subsequently depicted as oral teaching imparted by Moses in Moab (1:5). The institutionalized septennial

---

13   E.g. the diffusion of worship of Mithra and Anahita during the reign of Artaxerxes II (Silverman 2020, 239–40).

reading in the land (31:11-13) follows. Not only does possession of the written Torah separate and legitimize an elite (i.e. the Levitical priests) ahead of potential competing groups, but, more importantly, the oral transmission of the Torah proves an effective way to build the people's consensus, direct their life, and ultimately forge their imagination.

Works Cited

Aspesi, Francesco. 2005. "La versione aramaica su papiro dell'iscrizione monumentale trilingue di Dario a Behistun." ACME. *Annali della Facoltà di lettere e filosofia dell'Università degli studi di Milano* 58: 15–27.

Basello, Giampiero. 2013. "Le unità amministrative dell'impero achemenide (satrapie): il potere percepito dai popoli sottomessi e le immagini di ritorno." Pages 37–97 in *Ciro chiamato per nome (Is 45,4): l'epoca persiana e la nascita dell'Israele biblico tra richiamo a Gerusalemme e diaspora perenne. Atti del XVII Convegno di studi veterotestamentari (Assisi, 5–7 Settembre 2011)*. Edited by Gian Luigi Prato. Bologna: EDB.

------. 2021. "Hierarchy and *ethno-classe dominante*." Pages 859–70 in *A Companion to The Achaemenid Persian Empire, Volume 2*. Edited by Bruno Jacobs and Robert Rollinger. Hoboken, NJ: Wiley Blackwell.

Berge, Kåre. 2021. "Dynamics of Power and the Re-Invention of "Israel." Pages 293–321 in *Persian Empire Judah. Levantine Entanglements - Cultural Productions, Long-Term Changes and Globalizations in the Eastern Mediterranean*. Edited by Terje Stordalen and Oystein S. LaBianca. Sheffield: Equinox Publishing Ltd eBooks. Doi: 10.1558/equinox.38448.

Berlejung, Angelika. 2016. "New Life, New Skills, New Friends: the Loss and Rise of Capitals of the Judeans in Babylonia." Pages 1–45 in *Alphabets, Texts and Artifacts in the Ancient Near East*. Edited by Israel Finkelstein, Christian Robin and Thomas Römer. Paris: Van Diren.

------. 2017. "Social Climbing the Babylonian Exile." Pages 101–24 in *Wandering Arameans: Arameans Outside Syria. Textual and Archaeological Perspectives*. Edited by Angelika Berlejung, Aren M. Maeir and Andreas Schüle. Wiesbaden: Harrassowitz.

Blenkinsopp, Joseph. 1977. *Prophecy and Canon. A Contribution to the Study of Jewish Origins*. Notre Dame, IN: University of Notre Dame Press.

Braulik, Georg. 1970. "Die Ausdrücke für „Gesetz" im Buch Deuteronomum." *Biblica* 51: 39–66.

Collins, John J. 2017. *The Invention of Judaism. Torah and Jewish Identity from Deuteronomy to Paul*. Oakland, CA: University of California Press.

Crüsemann, Frank. 1992. *Die Tora. Theologie und Sozialgeschichte des alttestamentlichen Gesetzes*. Munich: Kaiser.

Dandamaev, Muhammad A. and Vladimir G. Lukonin. 1989. *The Culture and Social Institutions of Ancient Iran*. Cambridge: Cambridge University Press.

Filippone, Ela. 2012. "DPd/DPe and the Political Discourse of King Darius." Pages 101–19 in *Dariosh Studies 2. Persepolis and Its Settlements: Territorial System and Ideology in the Achaemenid State*. Edited by Adriano Valerio Rossi and Gian Pietro Basello. Naples: Università degli Studi di Napoli "L'Orientale."

Finsterbusch, Karin. 2005. *Weisung für Israel: Studien zu religiösen Lehren und Lernen im Deuteronomium und in seinem Umfeld*. Forschungen zum Alten Testament 44. Tübingen: Mohr Siebeck.

Frei, Peter. 2001. "Persian Imperial Authorization. A Summary." Pages 5–40 in *Persia and Torah: The Theory of the Imperial Authorization of the Pentateuch*. Edited by James W. Watts. Atlanta, GA: SBL.

Giuntoli, Federico. 2021. "Deuteronomio." Pages 471–572 in *Bibbia, Volume 1*. Edited by Mario Cucca, Federico Giuntoli, and Ludwig Monti. Torino: Einaudi.

Greenfield, Jonas C. and Bezalel Porten. 1982. *The Bisitun Inscription of Darius the Great Aramaic Version: Text, Translation and Commentary*. Corpus Inscriptionum Iranicarum: Part 1 Inscriptions of Ancient Iran. Vol. 5 The Aramaic Versions of the Achaemenian Inscriptions. Texts 1. London: Lund Humphries, 1982.

Huyse, Philip. 1999. "Some Further Thoughts on the Bisitun Monument and the Genesis of Old Persian Cuneiform Script." *Bulletin of the Asian Institute* 13: 45–66.

Jackson Lears, Thomas J. 1985. "The Concept of Cultural Hegemony: Problems and Possibilities." *American Historical Review* 90: 567–93.

Jacobs, Bruno. 2015. "Achaemenid Royal Communication." *Encyclopaedia Iranica Online*, https://www.iranicaonline.org/articles/achaemenid-royal-communication (accessed on 13 April 2022).

------. 2021. "Achaemenid Art – Art in the Achaemenid Empire." Pages 749–67 in *A Companion to the Achaemenid Persian Empire, Volume 1*. Edited by Bruno Jacobs and Robert Rollinger. Hoboken, NJ: Wiley Blackwell.

Kiel, Yishai. 2017. "Reinventing Mosaic Torah in Ezra–Nehemiah the Light of the Law (*dāta*) of Ahura Mazda and Zarathustra." *Journal of Biblical Literature* 136: 323–45.

Levinson, Bernard M. 2001. "The Reconceptualization of Kingship in Deuteronomy and the Deuteronomistic History's Transformation of Torah." *Vetus Testamentum* 51: 511–34.

------. 2008. "Deuteronomy's Conception of Law as an 'Ideal Type': A Missing Chapter in the History of Constitutional Law." Pages 52–86 in *"The Right Chorale": Studies in Biblical Law and Interpretation*. Forschungen zum Alten Testament 54. Tübingen: Mohr Siebeck.

Lincoln, Bruce. 2012. *"Happiness for Mankind": Achaemenian Religion and the Imperial Project.* Acta Iranica 53. Leuven: Peeters.

Lindars, Barnabas. 1968. "Torah in Deuteronomy." Pages 117–36 in *Words and Meanings: Essays Presented to David Winton Thomas.* Edited by Peter R. Ackroyd and Barnabas Lindars. Cambridge: Cambridge University Press.

Lohfink, Norbert. 1990. "Die Sicherung der Wirksamkeit des Gotteswortes durch das Prinzip der schriftlichkeit der Tora und durch das Prinzip der Gewaltenteilung nach den Ämtergesetzen des Buches Deuteronomium (Dt 16,18–18,22)." Pages 305–23 in *Studien zum Deuteronomium und zur deuteronomistischen Literatur 1.* Stuttgarter biblische Aufsatzbände 8. Stuttgart: Katholisches Bibelwerk.

Lozinskyy, Hryhoriy. 2022. *The Feasts of the Calendar in the Book of Numbers. Num 28:16–30:1 in the Light of Related Biblical Texts and Some Ancient Sources of 200 BCE–100 CE.* Forschungen zum Alten Testament II 132. Tübingen: Mohr Siebeck.

Margulis, B. 1969. "Gen. XLIX 10/Deut XXXIII 2-3. A New Look at Old Problems." *Vetus Testamentum* 19: 202–10.

Markl, Dominik. 2012. *Gottes Volk im Deuteronomium.* Beihefte zur Zeitschrift für altorientalische und biblische Rechtsgeschichte 18. Wiesbaden: Harrassowitz.

———. 2018. "Deuteronomy's 'Anti-King': Historicized Etiology or Political Program?" Pages 165–86 in *Changing Faces of Kingship in Syria-Palestine 1500–500 BCE.* Edited by Augustinus Gianto and Peter Dubovsky. Alter Orient und Altes Testament 459. Münster: Ugarit.

———. 2021. "Media and Migration and the Emergence of Scriptural Authority." *Zeitschrift für Theologie und Philosophie* 143: 261–83.

McCarthy, Carmel. 2007. *Deuteronomy.* Biblia Hebraica Quinta 5. Stuttgart: Deutsche Bibelgesellschaft.

Milgrom, Jacob. 1999. *Leviticus 1–16: A New Translation with Introduction and Commentary.* Anchor Bible 3. New York: Doubleday.

Otto, Eckart. 1999. *Das Deuteronomium. Politische Theologie und Rechtsreform in Juda und Assyrien.* Beihefte zur Zeitschrift für die alttestamentliche Wissenschaft 284. Berlin: de Gruyter.

———. 2013. "The Book of Deuteronomy and Its Answer to the Persian State Ideology: the Legal Implications." Pages 112–22 in *Loi et Justice dans la Literature du Proch-Orient ancien.* Edited by Olivier Artus. Beihefte zur Zeitschrift für altorientalische und biblische Rechtsgeschichte 20. Wiesbaden: Harrassowitz.

———. 2016. *Deuteronomium 12,1–23,15.* Herders Theologischer Kommentar zum Alten Testament. Freiburg i.B.: Herder.

———. 2017. *Deuteronomium 23,16–34,12.* Herders Theologischer Kommentar zum Alten Testament. Freiburg: Herder.

Paganini, Simone. 2009. "Nicht darfst du zu diesen Wörtern etwas hinzufügen." *Die Rezeption des Deuteronomiums in der Tempelrolle: Sprache, Autoren, Hermeneutik*. Beihefte zur Zeitschrift für altorientalische und biblische Rechtsgeschichte 11. Wiesbaden: Harrassowitz.

Pearce, Laurie E. and Cornelia Wunsch. 2014. *Documents of Judean Exiles and West Semites in Babylon in the Collection of David Sofer*. Cornell University Studies in Assyriology and Sumerology 28. Bethesda: CDL.

Pirngruber, Reinhard. 2021. "Jurisdiction." Pages 1,087–96 in *A Companion to The Achaemenid Persian Empire, Volume 2*. Edited by Bruno Jacobs and Robert Rollinger. Hoboken, NJ: Wiley Blackwell.

Porten, Bezalel and Ada Yardeni. 1993. *Textbook of Aramaic Documents from Ancient Egypt: Volume 3 Literature, Accounts, Lists*. Winona Lake: Eisenbrauns.

Rhyder, Julia. 2019. *Centralizing the Cult: The Holiness Legislation in Leviticus 17–26*. Forschungen zum Alten Testament 134. Tübingen: Mohr Siebeck.

Rollinger, Robert. 2015. "Royal Strategies of Representation and the Language(s) of Power: Some Considerations on the Audience and the Dissemination of the Achaemenid Royal Inscriptions." Pages 117–30 in *Official Epistolography and the Language(s) of Power: Proceedings of the First International Conference of the Research Network Imperium & Officium. Comparative Studies in Ancient Bureaucracy and Officialdom. University of Vienna 10–12 November 2010*. Edited by Stephan Procházka, Lucian Reinfandt, and Sven Tost. Vienna: Österreichischen Akademie der Wissenschaften.

Rossi, Adriano Valerio. 2021. "The Inscriptions of the Achaemenids." Pages 75–85 in *A Companion to The Achaemenid Persian Empire. Volume 1*. Edited by Bruno Jacobs and Robert Rollinger. Hoboken, NJ: Wiley Blackwell.

Rossi, Benedetta. 2023. "Preaching the Law. Reconsidering the Relationship between the Covenant Code and Deuteronomy." *Scandinavian Journal of the Old Testament* 37/1: 148–165.

Schaper, Joachim. 2011. "Torah and Identity in the Persian Period." Pages 27–38 in *Judah and the Judeans in the Achaemenid Period: Negotiating Identity in an International Context*. Edited by Oded Lipschits, Gary N. Knoppers, and Manfred Oeming. Winona Lake, IN: Eisenbrauns.

Schenker, Adrian. 1996. "Drei Mosaiksteinchen. 'Königreich von Priestern', 'und Ihre Kinder gehen weg', 'wir tun und wir hören' (Exodus 19,6; 21,22; 24,7)." Pages 367–80 in *Studies in the Book of Exodus. Redaction – Reception – Interpretation*. Edited by Marc Vervenne. Bibliotheca Ephemeridum Theologicarum Lovaniensium 126). Leuven: Peeters.

Schmitt, Rüdiger. 2009. *Die altpersischen Inschriften der Achaimeniden. Editio minor mit deutscher Übersetzung*. Wiesbaden: Reichert.

Silverman, Jason. 2020. *Persian Royal-Judean Elite Engagements in the Achaemenid Empire. The King's Acolytes*. Library of Hebrew Bible/Old Testament Studies 690. London: T & T Clark.

Ska, Jean-Louis. 2001. "'Persian Imperial Authorization': Some Question Marks." Pages 161–82 in *Persia and Torah: The Theory of the Imperial Authorization of the Pentateuch*. Edited by James W. Watts. Atlanta, GA: SBL.

------. 2004. "Biblical Law and the Origins of Democracy." Pages 146–58 in *The Ten Commandments: The Reciprocity of Faithfulness*. Edited by William P. Brown. Louisville: Westminster John Knox Press.

------. 2007. "From History Writing to Library Building: the End of History and the Birth of the Book." Pages 145–69 in *The Pentateuch as Torah: New Models for Understanding Its Promulgation and Acceptance*. Edited by Gary N. Knoppers and Bernard M. Levinson. Winona Lake, IN: Eisenbrauns.

Tuplin, Christopher. 2015. "The Justice of Darius. Reflections on the Achaemenid Empire as a Rule-bound Environment." Pages 73–126 in *Assessing Biblical and Classical Sources or the Reconstruction of Persian Influence, History and Culture*. Edited by Anne Fitzpatrick-McKinley. Wiesbaden: Harrassowitz.

Vansina, Jan. 1985. *Oral Tradition as History*. Madison, WI: The University of Wisconsin Press.

Verde, Danilo and Rossi, Benedetta (eds.) 2024. *Cultural Hegemony, Ideological Conflicts, and Power in Second Temple Judaism*. BETL 337. Leuven: Peeters.

Vergari, Romina. 2021. *Toward a Contrastive Semantics of the Biblical Lexicon: the Nouns of Rules and Regulations in Biblical Hebrew Historical-Narrative Language and Their Greek Equivalents in the Septuagint*. Florence: Società Editrice Fiorentina.

Voigtlander, Elizabeth N. von. 1978. *The Bisitun Inscription of Darius the Great Babylonian Version*. Corpus Inscriptionum Iranicarum: Part 1 Inscriptions of Ancient Iran. Vol. 2. The Babylonian Versions of the Achaemenian Inscriptions. Texts 1. London: Lund Humphries.

Waerzeggers, Caroline. 2018. "The Network of Resistance: Archives and Political Action in Babylonia before 484 BCE." Pages 89–133 in *Xerxes and Babylonia: The Cuneiform Evidence*. Edited by Caroline Waerzeggers and Maarja Seire. Orientalia Lovaniensia Analecta 277. Leuven: Peeters.

Zucchetti, Emilio. 2021. "Introduction: The Reception of Gramsci's Thought in Historical and Classical Studies." Pages 1–43 in *Antonio Gramsci and the Ancient World*. Edited by Emilio Zucchetti and Anna Maria Cimino. Routledge Monographs in Classical Studies. London: Routledge.

Zucchetti, Emilio and Cimino, Anna Maria (eds.) 2021. *Antonio Gramsci and the Ancient World* (Routledge Monograph in Classical Studies). London: Routledge.

About the Author

Benedetta Rossi is Associate Professor of Old Testament Exegesis at the Pontifical Biblical Institute (Rome). Her research interests are prophecy and the book of Jeremiah; Deuteronomy, its composition and production; and the relation between the Pentateuch and prophetic literature. She also focuses on cultural hegemony and the production of sacred texts in the Second Temple period. Her recent publications are articles and book chapters on Deuteronomy, Jeremiah, and prophetic books. She recently coedited with Diana Edelman, Kåre Berge and Philippe Guillaume the volume, *Deuteronomy in the Making: Studies in the Production of Debarim* (De Gruyter, 2021).

Chapter 10
Deuteronomy's Fearsome "Pedagogy"

Kåre Berge

Abstract

Teaching and learning hold a central position in Deuteronomy. While most studies take a positive stance towards the "pedagogy" of Deuteronomy, this chapter is more critical, approaching it more from the perspective of social control. Before applying modern didactical terms like "pedagogy" to the biblical text, one should investigate all the terms used for teaching/learning, and its teachers. Given the tension between the different "classrooms" and the different "teachers" in Deuteronomy, fear may indeed be the best descriptor of Deuteronomic learning. Social control may thus encapsulate Deuteronomy's didactics as teaching, learning, and instruction that are considered more at the societal than the individual level. Little interest is given to the individual mind and heart, the internalization of practical and ethical skill and knowledge, what is termed *Bildung* in German.

Keywords: teaching teachers, learning, didactics, fear, Moses, Levitical priests

Throughout Deuteronomy Israel is urged to learn Yhwh's commands as it is a matter of life and death to observe them and behave accordingly instead of imitating the Canaanites once in their land. Therefore, the didactic interest of the book has been noted (Hogan 2017; Markl 2011). In general, didactics are understood as involving "learning by heart" followed by "existential appropriation" (Ego 2005, 1–2), but as we know very little about how education was conceived in Cisjordan in any period, modern theories are not necessarily relevant. Didactics have been applied to the biblical book of Proverbs (Jones 2003). Its "didactic sayings" inculcate lessons indirectly but leave no choice to the reader (Murphy 1996, 8; Perdue 2007, 49).

Given the importance it ascribes to teaching and learning, Deuteronomy is said to transmit a pedagogical theory (Otto 2017), or at least a "didactic temper" expressed by imperatives (4:9–10), *yiqtol* (6:2) and

Table 1: LMD in Deuteronomy

4:1	Israel, give heed to the statutes and ordinances that Yhwh is *teaching* you to observe, so that you may live to enter and occupy the land.
4:5	Moses now *teaches* you statutes and ordinances for you to observe in the land.
4:10	At Horeb they heard Yhwh's words so that they may *learn* to fear me as long as they live on the earth, and may teach their children so.
4:14	Yhwh charged Moses at that time to *teach* you statutes and ordinances for you to observe in the land.
5:1	Hear, O Israel, the statutes and ordinances that Moses is addressing to you today; you shall *learn* them and observe them diligently.
5:31	Yhwh will tell Moses all the commandments, the statutes and the ordinances, that he shall *teach* Israel.
6:1	This is the commandment – the statutes and the ordinances – that Yhwh your God charged Moses to *teach* you to observe in the land.
11:19	*Teach* these words to your children, talking about them when you are at home and when you are away, when you lie down…
14:23	You shall eat the tithes and the firstlings, so that you may *learn* to fear Yhwh your God always.
17:19	The copy of this law shall remain with the king and he shall read in it all the days of his life, so that he may *learn* to fear the Yhwh his God.
18:9	When you come into the land that Yhwh your God is giving you, you must not *learn* to imitate the abhorrent practices of those nations.
20:18	Annihilate the Hittites and the Amorites, the Canaanites and the Perizzites, the Hivites and the Jebusites, so that they may not *teach* you to do all the abhorrent things that they do for their gods.
31:12-13	Assemble the people – men, women, and children, as well as the aliens residing in your towns – so that they may hear and *learn* to fear Yhwh your God, so that their children may hear and *learn* to fear Yhwh your God.
31:19	Moses, write this song, and *teach* it to the Israelites; put it in their mouths, in order that this song may be a witness for me against them!
31:22	That very day Moses wrote this song and *taught* it to the Israelites.

weqatal (6:7, 21) forms (Weinfeld 1972, 298). While most studies take a positive stance towards the "pedagogy" of Deuteronomy, this chapter is more critical, approaching it more from the perspective of social control. This is not the place to discuss the pertinence of the technical terms "pedagogy" and "didactics," which, obviously, do not occur in the book. This chapter uses "didactics" without further theoretical qualifications, while reservations are raised against "pedagogy."

As a long discourse Moses pronounces on the plains of Moab, Deuteronomy presents the birth of Israel as a religious community of learning and teaching (Finsterbusch 2005a, 42; 2005b, 307). With Moses as teacher, *Debarim*'s educational program is expressed primarily with the verb *lmd* (למד) which occurs seventeen times (Finsterbusch, 2005b, 2) to express the acts of teaching and learning (Table 1).

Six teachings are designated as *ḥuqqîm ûmišpāṭîm*, two of them combined with a third term, *miṭwah* (5:31; 6:1). In 4:10 and 11:19, the teachings are the *debarim* of Yhwh or Moses. In chapters 18 and 20, Israel is taught not to learn the ways of the Canaanites. In 31:12-13, the fear of Yhwh is learnt by listening to the proclaimed "words of this torah." In 14:23, however, the fear of Yhwh is learnt by festive eating and drinking joyfully before him. Hence, the Deuteronomic Israel learns both by listening passively and by actively sharing communal meals. In the end, the two didactic strategies are somewhat combined in the act of learning the song Moses wrote, though Israel is never portrayed as actually singing it.

Other terms related to learning

The verb YRH (ירה "to instruct") refers to verdicts – literally "word" (*dabar*) and "this *torah*" – pronounced at the high court (17:10-11) or the "prescription" (*mišpaṭ*) of the Levitical priests about skin diseases (24:8). Moses's blessing of Levi in 33:10 summarizes the Levites' instructional mission: "They teach Jacob your *mišpaṭim*, and Israel your *torah*; they place incense before you, and whole burnt offerings on your altar."

The verb YSR (יסר "to discipline") refers to the divine education Israel received by hearing Yhwh's voice from the heavens (4:36), by the forty years of testing in the wilderness (8:5; 11:2 *musar*). Once in the land, discipline is shared between parents who are to discipline their own children, requesting the execution of a rebellious son if necessary (21:18), and elders who are to fine husbands who slander their wives (22:18).

The verb ṢVH (צוה "to command, instruct") is more common and is often used in the framing chapters of the book (1-11; 27-34) as a synonym of LMD in formulaic expressions, mostly in subordinate sentences with the structure: main sentence + (ka= / ke=kol) 'asher – (x) – ṣwh (38 cases).[1] Some superordinate sentences describe more specific commandments (4:23; 5:12, 15, 16; 12:14, 21; 13:6 TM; 20:17; 24:8), some of which address Israel as You (sg.). Despite the differences in the terms used to describe the content of the instruction, these subordinate sentences underline the authority of the commander, Yhwh or Moses.

The central part of Deuteronomy (chs. 12–25) uses ṢVH in the context of specific cases: sacrifices at the *maqom* (12:14, 21, 28), booty (13:18), credit (15:11, 15), cities of refuge (19:9), though it tends to refer to the entire corpus of Deuteronomic instructions.

Deuteronomy's "Classrooms"

All in all, learning and teaching occur in four specific locations.

The Scriptorium

The first task of Deuteronomy's Israelite king is to write for himself a copy of this Torah on a scroll under the supervision of the Levitical priests (17:18). Having completed the writing, the king is to read his scroll daily to learn to fear Yhwh, to observe all the matters of "this torah," and to practice these decrees without elevating his heart over his brothers, without turning to the right or to the left. He shall thus lengthen the days of his kingship and that of his sons in the midst of Israel (17:19–20).

This king is portrayed as a pupil undergoing scribal learning. He remains under the supervision of the Torah and of the teachers who supplied the master copy of the scroll and presumably checked his work for the common copying mistakes. The king is literate, but he never becomes a master scribe and never teaches the Torah except to himself. He is forbidden to multiply horses, women and gold, his only treasure is the book he reads every day, in order to overcome the temptation to behave as kings behave.

The Maqom

The so-called central place, the *maqom*, where all Israelite families gather, holds a central function as it is the location for three very different

---

1 Deut 4:5, 23, 40; 5:12, 15, 16; 6:2, 6, 17; 7:11; 8:1, 11; 9:12; 10:5, 13; 11:8; 12:14, 21, 28; 13:6 TM, 19 TM; 15:5; 18:18, 20; 19:9; 20:17; 26:13, 14; 27:10, 11; 28:1, 13, 15, 45; 20:2, 8, 11; 32:46.

kinds of learning. First, it is where "you" learn to fear Yhwh by eating and drinking the year's tithes before Yhwh joyfully (14:23-26). Second, the *maqom* is where difficult cases are referred to. No right of appeal is granted, and whoever refuses to accept the verdict pronounced there is to be executed (17:12), as are those who produce false witnesses there (19:20). Neither the means nor the location of the executions is stated. That no gates are mentioned (see below) may simply be the clue that the *maqom* is not conceived as a city, Jerusalem or else. If the executions at the *maqom* were carried out when all Israelite families gathered there to revel before Yhwh so that they witnessed them with their own eyes, the killings would have had a maximum teaching impact. Nothing better affirms the authority of the priest who, rightly or wrongly, passed the sentence for such an exemplary execution. "All the people will hear and fear and will not behave insolently (יזידון) again" (17:13). Priests are always right.

Finally, the *maqom* is where the priests, the sons of Levi, read aloud the Torah before the entire Israel – men, women, little ones, and immigrants as well. The exercise is to take place at the end of every seventh year during the festival of Sukkoth. The aim is again to learn to fear Yhwh (31:12-13), but the means differ radically. Hearing the words of the Torah once in every seven-year cycle is listening passively to a book (for wisdom teaching, see Shupak 2003, 417), while celebrating joyful yearly banquets is active learning by eating and drinking with family and friends.

The Home

Additional teaching means are prescribed at the local level: signs on hands, foreheads, and doorposts (6:8; 11:19-20). Nothing indicates that the inscribed signs (אתית) are actual words of the Torah. To illiterate Israelites, written commandments would be unreadable but they could recall the apotropaic sign on the doorposts in Exod 12:13. Even if unreadable, the materiality of these signs would convey power and efficacy (Stavrakopoulou 2013, 228-29).

In addition, the curriculum includes home education for Israelite sons by their fathers (Deut 6:6-9) as a continuation of the teaching of the adults (4:10b; 6:4-9, 20-25; 11:2, 18-21; 31:12-13). Rather than displaying a particular interest in the education of children, the father's role underscores the continuity of Israel as a people under Yhwh's commandments. Daughters might be included in the *ṭaf* (טף) since adult women are mentioned besides men in the audience of the Torah reading (31:12), but the common renderings of the word בנים as "children" rather than "sons" is a matter of political correctness. Deuteronomy only mentions the teaching of sons (4:9; 6:7.21; 11:19), to whom the *Shemaʿ Israel* should be repeated (שנה) and spoken (דבר) at home and while traveling, morning and evening (6:7).

The impression of mere rote and constant repetition is corrected in vv. 20–21, where the catechism is delivered in response to questions formulated by the sons. Later practice integrated these questions in the *seder* ritual, which does not exclude a possible awareness of the timeliness of lessons that are best learnt when pupils spontaneously formulate questions they are mature enough to integrate. Despite this possible hint about learning processes pinpointed by pedagogical science, the aim of home education is the same as for the king and for the other Israelites: learning to fear Yhwh.

The Gates

The last Deuteronomic schoolrooms are the gates of each settlement or the door of a particular house where public executions take place. The so-called *bi'artā* formula ("to purge the evil") is especially concentrated in the sex laws. Contrary to Leviticus, which considers any sexual activity impure, Deuteronomy equates proper relations between the sexes with exclusive fidelity to Yhwh (Edenburg 2009, 57). Sexual infringements of the exclusive rights of fathers, fiancés, and husbands (22:21–25; 24:7) are liable to capital punishment as much as worship of astral bodies (13:10), transgressions of the covenant (17:7), murder (19:13), and kidnap of persons belonging to one's brother (24:7).

Cynthia Edenburg's argument may be generalized to every aspect of daily life. The most striking case (pun intended) of purging the evil is that of the rebellious son, which is directly relevant to teaching:

ובערת הרע מקרבך וכל ישראל ישמעו ויראו

You shall purge the evil from your midst and all Israel shall hear and fear. (Deut 21:21)

Only the local men are involved in the stoning of the son who refused to listen to his father and mother, but this is a parade example of the use of fear for deterrence purposes. Though only men are directly involved in the stoning of the culprit, women, slaves, and children are sure to hear about it. The resulting fear is no mere philosophical notion. It is forcefully inculcated by the exemplary execution of all deviants: prophets, idolaters, those who do not abide by a judge's verdict, murderers, false witnesses, rebellious sons, women who were not virgins upon marriage, adulterers, and kidnappers. Such lessons are not easily forgotten, especially when it is at behest of the very parents of the culprit that the elders open the legal procedure. The Torah cuts through intra-familial solidarity.

Learning what?

In Deuteronomy, what is learnt is rendered by a versatile combination of general designations that are not easy to translate and differentiate from one another: decrees (חוקים), (common?) law (משפט), orders (מצות), testimonies (עדות), words (דברים), way (דרך), and the voice of Yhwh (קול יהוה) (Person 2021, 224–28). Instead of a clear exposition of the actual content of the curriculum, Yhwh and Moses seem to spend more time giving orders than explaining what their orders entail, as though their ultimate aim is blind submission and obedience to "everything I command you" (30:2, 16). To temper this impression, the Ten Commandments or the corpus of casuistic laws in chapters 12–26, or both, must be taken as the contents of what Israel must learn and practice.

As noted above, however, the mentions of actual acts of teaching and learning in chs. 12–26 mostly echo the authoritarian mood of the framing chapters. Moreover, the actual contents of "everything I command you" (12:14) are not easily identified. On the basis of 12:14, 21, 28, it could be the Israelite ways that are absorbed by meeting together with all Israelite families at the *maqom*. One can only suppose that the copy of this Torah that the king is to study is identical to "the words of this torah" mentioned in 29:28 and to the book Moses wrote down after he completed his speech (31:9–12). Yet, the abundance of designations suggests more a desire to be as inclusive as possible than any precise delimitation of the body of teaching.

As Deuteronomy stands as the last scroll of the Pentateuch, the contents of the previous scrolls may also be included in "everything I command you." Hence, the decrees, laws, orders, testimonies, words, and ways of Yhwh may be taken as instances of "nominalization," a technical term used to characterize the formal and impersonal prose in modern media news reports, political speeches, and bureaucratic discourses. Nominalization "elides grammatical voice, in such a way that the active or passive participants in a particular action are removed, leaving a reified, intransitive, and obscure given in their place" (Pickstock 1998, 92–93). If so, the audience of Deuteronomy is torn between the urgency to conform to the commands and the difficulty in identifying their contents. Some of the tension may be attributed to the plurality of teachers that adds to the plurality of "classrooms" discussed above.

Deuteronomy's Teachers

Apart from fathers who are to instruct their sons at home and the signs inscribed on doorposts and clothing, Deuteronomy has three main actors involved in teaching.

Moses as Writer

Mentioned by name about forty times, Moses is conceived as the mediator between Yhwh and Israel, the figure who heard the divine voice and eventually put the words down in writing. Yet, in the final chapters of Deuteronomy Moses discards his mediating role. He writes a book to indict Israel before it even had a chance to display its inability to observe the Torah, unless the testing in the wilderness (8:2) serves as an indicator for what would happen once in the land. Hence, Moses deepens the gulf between himself and Israel, setting himself above and apart from Israel which he had already blamed for his death before crossing the Jordan (4:21).

Moses turns wrathful in ch. 31 as he becomes aware that no one will replace him as mediator after his death, but wrongly so because 34:9 states that the people listened to Joshua, thus embodying the prophet as Moses announced in 18:15 (Sonnet 2013, 16). Does this mean that Israel is orphaned once in the land? Aren't the Levitical priests taking over his legacy?

The Levitical Priests as Readers

The Levitical priests who read the book of the Torah every seventh Succoth festival represent a second didactic agent besides Moses and after Moses. Yet, apart from this public reading, the Levitical priests are not involved in more substantial acts of Torah education. The reiteration of the Torah at such distant intervals can hardly rely on the efficacy of repetition (Ahmed 2004, 92; Butler 1993, 33) and Moses himself shows no confidence in it. Moses knows that Israel will not learn and obey the Torah, however often it is read to them.

Though the reading does set the Levitical priests as the legitimate successors of Moses, the aim is not to provide guidance in how to observe the Torah in Canaan because the Torah is not a body of laws destined to regulate society, as law codes are usually meant for. As heirs of the Mosaic legacy, the Levitical priests act as guardians of the original Torah penned by Moses. They prevent access to it and turn it into an invisible and mystified authority (Berge 2016). Only the king can copy it to read it all the days of his life (17:19), but never to teach it, though his daily interaction with it would make him the most apt teacher of the Mosaic heritage. Joshua would have needed it as much as the king to fulfill his mission, but he is not considered a potential student. The Levitical priests themselves would read the Torah at most a few times in their lives. They are pictured as having an almost innate knowledge of the Torah thanks to the book Moses gave them (31:9).

Instead of taking over Moses's mediating role, the Levitical priests step out once every eighty-four months and otherwise remain in the backstage, except as collectors of priestly dues (18:1–8) that are too generous to designate their beneficiaries as *personae miserae* as is often the case (e.g. Ebach 2018, 172).

As Torah specialists, the Levitical priests could be expected to be active in litigation. A priest is indeed involved at the high court to deliver final verdicts (17:12). A judge is mentioned besides the Levitical priests at the *maqom*'s supreme court (17:8–11), which could indicate the presence of a judiciary *collegium* there (Knoppers 1994, 78). King Jehoshaphat appoints such a *collegium* in Jerusalem (2 Chr 19:8), which includes heads of Israelite families besides Levites and priests.

The *maqom* court bears no comparison with Jehoshaphat's court and challenges the notion of a "democratic" system in Deuteronomy (against Oswald 2010). The nod to the token judge is swept aside in v. 12, where the verdict is ascribed to a single priest whose authority is underlined by making any contestation of his decisions liable to the death penalty. Deuteronomy has no interest in making the exercise of justice a collegial activity. The judge of 17:9 anticipates the elders of Israel who stand beside the Levitical priests when Moses hands over the book of the Torah (31:9, 28). This judge as much as these elders are window dressings that in no way challenge the primacy of the Levitical priests. The focus is on the priests, the sons of Levi, who take care of the Mosaic book as part of their mission to carry the ark of the covenant (31:9). If observing Yhwh's commands and decrees is a matter of life and death, one would expect these Torah specialists to teach it. Yet, it is parents who are to instruct their sons. Is the local Levite present in every settlement involved in Torah-teaching?

Apart from receiving the triennial tithes at the gate, his activities at the local level are never described. He is a consumer of tithes "in your gates" like the widow and the orphan. He is a consumer of tithes at the *maqom* too (18:1–8). The attribution of revenue is also a major concern in ch. 26 where a priest, rather than a Levite or a Levitical priest, acts as a kind of tax controller who makes sure that all dues have been set apart and disposed of in the proper way. Neither the priest nor the Levites are explicitly involved in teaching. Teaching is reserved for the Levitical priests, once every seventh year, if their reading of the Torah can be considered to be actual teaching.

Even if the distinctions between Levites, priests, and Levitical priests are ignored and it is assumed that they all refer to the same group, i.e., those who receive the book from Moses and read it at the *maqom*, Deuteronomy is silent over their activities besides the reading of the Torah once every seven years. In fact, these overwhelmingly idle figures need not do anything else. Their function is not in doing but in being embodiments of the authority of Moses in the land. Hence, Deuteronomy only uses the root *yrh* (ירה), from which the word "Torah" derives, with the Levitical priests or Levi as subjects (17:10–11; 24:8; 33:10).

One of Us

Moses is only the implicit speaker of the body of rules and regulations in Deut 5–26. Implicit, because Moses is never named in the core of the book that deals with very practical issues such as credit, family matters, agriculture, and justice. Hence, there is a third teacher at the heart of Deuteronomy, a teaching instance that cuts a different figure from the Moses who stands above and aloof from Israel.

As much as Hammurabi is named only in the prologue and epilogue of the legal collection inscribed on the stele that bears his image, Moses is named only in Deut 1:1–5:1 and 27:1–34:12. The Deuteronomic "laws" are pronounced by an anonymous figure perceived more as an equal to the "you" it addresses than as the towering figure that recapitulates the challenges it was to lead Israel through the wilderness (Deut 1–4), or the angry Moses of the final chapters. If the traditional title of Moses as "law-giver" mirrors that of Hammurabi's as the royal figure whose name is attached to the laws, Deuteronomy makes no attempt to portray Moses as the wise conceiver of rules and regulations who "made conflicts cease, improved the wellbeing of the nation, made the people lie down in well-watered pastures and let no one disturb their prosperity" as Hammurabi claims to have achieved in the Epilogue of the stele he set up in Babylon (Richardson 2000, 121).

Like Hammurabi (Richardson 2000, 125–35), Moses lists blessings and curses in the epilogue of Deuteronomy (chs. 27–28). Hammurabi writes his laws so that anyone who has a complaint may have the message on the stone read aloud so that its treasured words may resolve his complaint, and any future king who appears in his land may heed the righteous commands he inscribed on the stone and direct his land aright (Richardson 2000, 123–25). Unlike Hammurabi, Moses writes a book to indict his own people. Whatever the reason for this surprising phenomenon, it is coherent with the fact that the entire legal material at the heart of Deuteronomy is not explicitly stated as Mosaic. Instead of claiming authorship, the so-called lawgiver disowns the laws, suggesting that they are not his and that trying to teach them is a waste of time and energy. The lesson was not lost on subsequent readers. So loose is the relation between the book of the Torah and the prescriptions, prohibitions, and rules of Deut 12–26 that Rabbinic Judaism never considered itself "Mosaic" (Stemberger 2021, 119).

Making no effort to validate the legal material in Deut 5–26 and in the previous scrolls, Moses underlines its foreign origin. Instead of ascribing it to himself as Hammurabi does through bombastic self-praise (Richardson 2000, 118–23), Moses hints that the scribes who wrote and reinterpreted parallels from Exodus 21–23 in Deut 15–25 are not to be identified with the Levitical priests. To venture a step further in this hypothetical direction, one may even claim that Moses is aware of the kinship of the apodictic and casuistic material with the other ancient Near Eastern legal collections such as Hammurabi's, which ranks it close to the Canaanite ways that Israel must unlearn. No wonder, then, that Moses restricts its divulgation to public readings that defeat any pedagogical potential. Besides the stiff-neckedness of the Israelites (Exod 34:9), the pedagogical failure of the Torah should also be ascribed to Moses himself, who thus hardly deserves the title of "lawgiver." The law teachers are parents, elders, tribal heads, and any other authoritative figures other than Moses and the Levitical priests, i.e., Israelites. If so, what is left of didactics in Deuteronomy?

Fear and Obedience as the Outcomes of the Learning Process

Given the tension between the different "classrooms" and the different "teachers" in Deuteronomy, fear may indeed be the best descriptor of Deuteronomic learning (4:10; 5:29; 6:2, 13, 24; 8:6; 10:12, 20; 13:5; 14:23; 17:13 (see also 19:20; 21:21); 17:19; 28:58; 31:12, 13; about other people fearing Yhwh, 25:18 and 28:10). To fear him is what Yhwh demands (שׁאל) of Israel. It is defined as "to walk in all his ways, to love him, to serve Yhwh in all your heart and in all your breath (נפשׁך), keeping Yhwh's commandments (מצות) and his decrees (חקיו) that I commanded you today for your good" (10:12–13). The exhaustiveness of the list is of little help to figure out what fear entails practically. The instability of referents (Yhwh-him-I, Israel-you) and the string of six verbs simply stress the urgency and totality of the divine expectations. Is the pupil granted a chance to pass the test?

The answer depends on which part of Deuteronomy is considered. If Moses considers that Israel as a whole is doomed to fail the test, if the Levitical priests mostly restrict access to the Torah, the motivational clauses added to some of the casuistic laws do promise success as a result of obedience. For instance, much political clout is promised if debts are released in the seventh year (15:6). Divine blessings are tied to generous alms-giving, end-of-contract gifts, and interest-free loans (15:10, 18; 23:20). Land tenure is secured by impartiality in legal matters (16:20). Nothing in ch. 17 indicates that the king will disobey the Torah he studies daily. Territorial gains are promised in exchange for diligent observation of all this commandment (19:9). Abstaining from blood consumption, executing murderers, sparing the mother bird are necessary for well-being and long life (12:25; 19:13; 22:7). These common-sense economic and ethical measures have parallels in other ancient Near Eastern legal collections and the survival of an Israelite identity in the Levant is a sure sign that Israel did observe them.

Such didactics also involve forceful inculcation (Kugel 2017, 20–21), such as the public execution of deviants (13:9–10; 22:21, 23) or private and daily study for the king (17:19). Otherwise, fear is taught by eating and drinking the year's tithes joyfully, without Moses who by then will be dead.

The difference in the didactics of the joyful banquets and of exemplary executions of deviants should not necessarily be viewed as antithetic. They constitute the two prongs of a coherent strategy of social control. On the one hand, yearly tithes are generously granted to the tithes payers rather than to the priests. On the other hand, public hangings (21:22) and stonings are periodic reminders of the cost of disobedience. Rewards and punishments belong to the carrot-and-stick approach to maintain the hegemonic position of the priests, who pass final verdicts to settle disputes and outbreaks of skin diseases (24:8). To ensure "the internalization of the Torah" (Ego 2005, 1–2), this two-pronged didacticism is more efficient than the public reading of the Torah, which only serves to legitimate the right of the Levitical priests to collect priestly dues.

Social control may thus encapsulate Deuteronomy's didactics as teaching, learning, and instruction that are considered more at the societal than the individual level. The king is placed firmly under the control of a scroll of written instructions.[2] Little interest is given to the individual mind and heart, the internalization of practical and ethical skill and knowledge, what is termed *Bildung* in German. The men installed as leaders (1:13) are found wise and understanding without the agency of

---

2   On the concomitance of written law and the elimination of kings and nobles in Hesiod, see Naddaf 2002, 351.

the Torah. Joshua is equally full of the spirit of wisdom, not because he studied the Torah but because Moses laid hands on him (34:9). What the Torah inculcates is not wisdom but the fear of Yhwh into men, women, children, and the aliens alike.

This fear seems of a different nature from the fear of punishment that can be a powerful motivator for obedience or a disobedience deterrent. Hence, the curious consequence of a pupil who fears the teacher more than the punishment (exile) that he is constantly threatened with in Deuteronomy. But this is only a side-effect. The aim of Deuteronomic didactics is to coax a rebellious Israel into submission to ensure the smooth collection of dues to feed priests. Whether or not this is pedagogy is a matter of personal appreciation.

Works Cited

Ahmed, Sara. 2004. *The Cultural Politics of Emotion.* Edinburgh: Edinburgh University Press.

Berge, Kåre. 2016. "Mystified Authority: Legitimating Leadership through 'Lost Books.'" Pages 41–56 in *Leadership, Social Memory and Judean Discourse in the Fifth-Second Centuries BCE.* Edited by Diana Edelman and Ehud Ben Zvi. London: Equinox Publishing Ltd.

Butler, Judith. 1993. *Gender Trouble: Feminism and the Subversion of Identity.* New York: Routledge.

Ebach, Ruth. 2018. "'You Shall Walk Exactly on the Way which YHWH Your God has Commanded You': Characteristics of Deuteronomy's Concept of Leadership." Pages 159–77 in *Debating Authority. Concepts of Leadership in the Pentateuch and the Former Prophets.* Edited by Katharina Pyschny and Sarah Schulz. Beihefte Zeitschrift für die Alttestamentliche Wissenschaft 507. Berlin: de Gruyter.

Edenburg, Cynthia. 2009. "Ideology and Social Context of the Deuteronomic Women's Sex Laws (Deut 22:13–29)." *Journal of Biblical Literature* 128: 43–60.

Ego, Beate. 2005. "Zwischen Aufgabe und Gabe. Theologische Implikationen des Lernens in der alttestamentlichen und antik-jüdischen Überlieferung." Pages 1–26 in *Religiöses Lernen in der biblischen, frühjüdischen und frühchristlichen Überlieferung.* Edited by Beate Ego and Helmut Merkel. Tübingen: Mohr Siebeck.

Finsterbusch, Karin. 2005a. "'Du sollst sie lehren, auf dass sie tun ...' Mose als Lehrer der Tora im Buch Deuteronomium." Pages 27–43 in *Religiöses Lernen in der biblischen, frühjüdischen und frühchristlichen Überlieferung.* Edited by Beate Ego and Helmut Merkel. Tübingen: Mohr Siebeck.

———. 2005b. *Weisung für Israel. Studien zu religiösem Lehren und Lernen im Deuteronomium und in seinem Umfeld*. Forschungen zum Alten Testament 44. Tübingen: Mohr Siebeck.

Hogan, Karina M. 2017. "Introduction." Pages 1–12 in *Pedagogy in Ancient Judaism and Early Christianity*. Edited by Karina M. Hogan, Matthew Goff, and Emma Wassermann. Early Judaism and Its Literature 41. Atlanta: SBL Press.

Jones, Scott C. 2003. "Wisdom's Pedagogy: A Comparison of Proverbs vii and 4Q184." *Vetus Testament* 53: 65–80.

Knoppers, Gary N. 1994. "Jehoshaphat's Judiciary and 'The Scroll of Yhwh's Torah.'" *Journal of Biblical Literature* 113: 59–80.

Kugel, James L. 2017. "Ancient Israelite Pedagogy and Its Survival in Second Temple Interpretations of Scripture." Pages 15–58 in *Pedagogy in Ancient Judaism and Early Christianity*. Edited by Karina M. Hogan, Matthew Goff, and Emma Wasserman. Atlanta: SBL Press.

Markl, Dominik. 2011. "Deuteronomy's Frameworks in the Service of the Law (Deut 1–11; 26–34)." Pages 271–84 in *Deuteronomium - Tora für eine neue Generation*. Edited by Georg Fischer, Dominik Markl, and Simone Paganini. Wiesbaden: Harrassowitz.

Murphy, Roland E. 1996. *The Tree of Life: An Exploration of Biblical Wisdom Literature* (2nd ed.). New York: Doubleday.

Naddaf, Gerard. 2002. "Hesiod as Catalyst for Western Political *Padeia*." *The European Legacy: Toward New Paradigms* 7: 343–61. http://dx.doi.org/10.1080/10848770220132357.

Oswald, Wolfgang. 2010. "Early Democracy in Ancient Judah: Considerations on Ex 18–24 with an Outlook on Dtn 16–18." *Communio Viatorum* 52: 121–35.

Otto, Eckart. 2017. "Lehre und Lernen der Tora. Die Bildungstheorie der nachexilischen Deuteronomiums." *Zeitschrift für Altorientalische und Biblische Rechtsgeschichte* 23: 181–90.

Perdue, Leo. G. 2007. *Wisdom Literature: A Theological History*. Louisville and London: Westminster John Knox Press.

Person, Raymond F., Jr. 2021. "Self-Referential Phrases in Deuteronomy. A Reassessment Based on Recent Studies Concerning Scribal Performance and Memory." Pages 217–41 in *Collective Memory and Collective Identity. Deuteronomy and the Deuteronomistic History in their Context*. Edited by Johannes Unsok Ro and Diana Edelman. Beihefte Zeitschrift für die Alttestamentische Wissenschaft 534. Berlin: de Gruyter.

Pickstock, Catherine. 1998. *After Writing. On the Liturgical Consummation of Philosophy*. Oxford: Blackwell.

Richardson, Mervyn E. J. 2000. *Hammurabi's Laws. Text, Translation and Glossary*. Sheffield: Sheffield Academic Press.

Shupak, Nili. 2003. "Learning Methods in Ancient Israel." *Vetus Testament* 53: 416–26. doi: 10.1163/156853303768266380

Sonnet, Jean-Pierre. 2013. "If-Plots in Deuteronomy." *Vetus Testament* 63: 1–18. doi: 10.1163/15685330-12341117

Stavrakopoulou, Francesca. 2013. "Materialist Reading. Materialism, Materiality, and Biblical Cults of Writing." Pages 223–42 in *Biblical Interpretation and Method: Essays in Honour of John Barton*. Edited by Katharine J. Dell and Paul M. Joyce. Oxford: Oxford University Press.

Stemberger, Günter. 2021. "Is (Rabbinic) Judaism a Mosaic Religion? The Place of Moses in Israel's Foundation Story." Pages 109–21 in *"Written for our Discipline and Use". The Construction of Christian and Jewish Identities in Late Ancient Bible Interpretation*. Edited by Agnethe Siquans. Göttingen: Vandenhoeck & Ruprecht.

Weinfeld, Moshe. 1972. *Deuteronomy and the Deuteronomic School*. Oxford: Clarendon Press.

About the Author

Kåre Berge is Professor emeritus and guest researcher at the Faculty of Theology, University of Oslo. His studies cover the Pentateuch, especially Genesis, Exodus, and Deuteronomy, focusing on cultural memory, politics of identity, didacticism, and symbolization of power-relations. Among his more recent publications are "Law-didactic Torah Composition in the Exodus Narrative?," in R. Müller, U. Nõmmik and J. Pakkala (editors), *Fortgeschriebenes Gotteswort. Studien zu Geschichte, Theologie und Auslegung des Alten Testaments. FS Christoph Levin*, Tübingen: Mohr Siebeck, 2020, pp. 43–52; and "Deuteronomy and the Beginning of the Mosaic Torah," in A. Laato (editor), *The Challenge of the Mosaic Torah in Judaism, Christianity, and Islam*, Studies on the Children of Abraham 7, Leiden: Brill, 2020, pp. 3–18.

Chapter 11
Pragmatic, Utopian and Dystopian Deuteronomy

Philippe Guillaume

Abstract

The oft-repeated view of Deuteronomy's humanitarianism consequently gave rise to the notion that some of its laws are devoid of practical application and depict instead a utopia. Building upon the demonstration of the economic realism of Deuteronomy's laws in ch. 6 in this volume, this chapter nevertheless identifies some utopian as well as dystopian elements, ascribing them to different groups.

Does the priestly viewpoint of Leviticus and Numbers offer a more "realist or pragmatic approach" than Deuteronomy's "idealist, utopian vision" (Arnold 2016, 174)? To answer such a broad question, the most utopian components in Deuteronomy's vision need to be identified and distinguished from the book's more pragmatic parts. As with any body of laws, the Deuteronomic legal collection (DC) entails the presence of utopian elements as it seeks to prevent practices that the writer considered noxious for himself and his clan, and indeed for society at large, even though no legal system can effectively succeed in eliminating delinquency. The production of regulations and decrees strives for an unattainable aim, an ideal society in which laws and customs are observed every day by everyone. Nevertheless, many of Deuteronomy's laws promulgate rules of behavior that make sense in their ancient Israelite and Levantine context.

Keywords: utopia, dystopia, taxation, credit, Deuteronomy

1. Deuteronomy's Laws: From Unpractical Idealism to Utopia

In the late nineteenth and early twentieth centuries, the early critics of de Wette's hypothesis (1805) sought to demonstrate that Deuteronomy's laws could not reflect the cultic reform in 2 Kgs 22–23. They pointed to laws that could not be applied during the reign of Josiah. For instance, Hölscher (1922, 186–87) argued that it was inconceivable for the entire pre-exilic Judean population – slaves included – to gather in the courts of the Jerusalem temple to sacrifice their offerings while no one was left at home to care for the herds and flocks. The law that required the slaughter of an entire city to eradicate idolatry (Deut 13) could only be conceived in a time when national existence had been cancelled or suspended. Under such conditions the author could write theories without worrying about their practical application (Horst 1893, 141).

The consumption of a tenth of the yearly yield at the *maqom* (Deut 14:22–26) was judged excessive for wealthy families and outright unwise for the less affluent ones (Reuss 1879, 307; Hölscher 1922, 184). The *šmiṭṭah* debt release was equally deemed devoid of practical sense since a general and absolute release would dry out credit (Reuss 1879, 308; Hölscher 1922, 184). For this reason, the Rabbis later introduced the option of a legal recourse to avoid the *šmiṭṭah* through a declaration made before a court of justice at the time of lending that would exempt the loan in question from any future remission. As this measure, the *prosbol*, supposedly adapted the *šmiṭṭah* to the realities of the credit market, the conclusion was that Deut 15 did not take into account the practical impact of its ruling in real life but merely displayed an idealism that disregarded worldly realities (Hölscher 1922, 195). Despite these arguments, Deuteronomy's link to Josiah's purported reform remained popular and scholarship simply retained the general notion of the non-applicability of Deuteronomy's laws.

The notion of utopia was first applied in the sociology of knowledge (Mannheim 1991) and later in Marxist readings of literature (Jameson 2005). Various Deuteronomic themes were deemed utopian: the possession of the land (Davies 2014, 37), the destruction of the Canaanites (Berge 2017, 27), cult centralization (Otto 2007, 277), the idea of a *Groß Israel* (Otto 2012, 1065), the program of brotherly ethics, the freeing of slaves (Levin 2014, 50–59), as well as the law of the king (Arnold 2021, 183). In each case, a different understanding of utopia and utopian visions is presupposed (see Schweitzer 2006).

2. Utopia: Non-space or Dream of a Better Place

In its etymological sense, utopia corresponds to social processes unrelated to particular places (*u-topia* as non-space). Or it is a space for a better place (Portolano 2012, 118), or again, either a more or less realistic program, or a mere hope for a better life with few expectations for its realization. Utopia may also spring from an impulse and reflect a transcendent mentality that has the ability to break the bonds of the existing order and generate a new social one (Mannheim 1991, 205). Utopia may even be a book, i.e. Deuteronomy itself (Berge 2017, 30).

The public reading in Deut 31 supports the understanding of the aim of the laws as the formation of a common memory rather than the publication of laws regulating the life of the entire Israelite society (Berge 2012, 5). As a "*dream* for a better life" (Berge 2012, 7), the kind of utopia Deuteronomy displays could have had practical applications at least for "the small circle of literati themselves" (Berge 2012, 8), though what these practical applications could have been is not easy to fathom.

3. Economic Realism

The characterization of economic practices in Deuteronomy's laws as utopian is often the outcome of an insufficient grasp of ancient economic realities. In light of our current understanding of the ancient Near East (Jursa 2010), the laws in Deut 12–26 (the DC) are in their majority rooted in practices current in the world in which they were penned. In light of the Mesha stela published in the 1870s (Clermont-Ganneau 1875), the call to put to the sword the entire population of a given city (Deut 13) reflects a time of rising national existence rather than one of cancellation or suspension. The coherence of the economic measures advocated in the DC with the common economic practices delineated in ch. 6 of this volume sharply reduces the utopian nature of these laws.

For instance, the *šmiṭṭah*, as much as the debt releases attested to in Mesopotamia, was a set of practical measures to ease social tensions and bolster the popularity of the monarch who decreed them (Olivier 1997). A general and absolute release would indeed dry out credit (Reuss 1879, 308; Hölscher 1922, 184), but neither the *šmiṭṭah* nor the Mesopotamian edicts were general and absolute releases. Rather than dry out credit, they regulated the market by targeting specific types of debts. The *šmiṭṭah* only cancelled arrears on commercial loans between brothers. Subsistence loans merchants granted to farmers to tide them over until the next harvest were not concerned by the *šmiṭṭah* because neither the lender nor the borrower had any interest in "forgiving" arrears in the seventh year (Guillaume 2010; 2022).

A merchant had in practice little choice other than to lend more grain to farmers who already owed him grain but, through bad times, found themselves in arrears with their repayments. For the merchant to let them die of famine would have meant forfeiting any hope of ever recouping his loan. But by extending and even increasing the amount of credit to farmers in arrears, the merchant thereby awarded himself privileged access to future agricultural surpluses at prices below the going market rates.

As with the šmiṭṭah, interest-free loans (Deut 23:20) make sense within a closed circle of merchants where returns on investments are expected from a share of the profits rather than from interest charged on loan capital, as with modern banking practices. Who then are the beneficiaries of the two commands to "open your hand" (15:8 and 11)? The first one involves granting loans to a needy brother (15:7), even when the time of the release is drawing near (15:9–10). Such loans express the solidarity within the brotherhood. The second call to "open your hand" has nothing to do with lending. It concerns alms giving, generosity that by the same token increases the social capital of the alms giver, all the more so when the giving is made publicly. The problem is that both commands to "open your hand" are often taken as the "commandment concerning a loan to the poor" (Levin 2014, 57).

4. The Poor as a Key Feature of Faulty Understandings of Utopia

Lending to the poor makes no economic sense whatsoever, unless lenders judge the "poor" in question to be sufficiently creditworthy to be able to reimburse a loan. In such cases, the condition of being "poor" does not equate to being destitute but merely indicates a lack of own funds to carry out gainful economic activities. Conversely, to warrant a loan the "poor" persons that are destitute – i.e. who cannot offer a pledge or show a clean record of past repayments – have to rely for their survival on what others *give* them. No one proposes a loan to a beggar in the street. Deuteronomic scholarship also routinely uses the term "poor" to designate the beneficiaries of triennial tithes (14:28-29), of alms (15:10-11), of pledges returned at sunset (24:13), of salaries paid daily (24:14), of pledges other than a millstone (24:17), and of gleaning rights (24:19-22). This is misleading because, apart from alms, tithes, pledges, salaries, and gleanings all concern economic actors who are not destitute. Loans to the destitute appear neither in Deuteronomy nor in any actual economic system. As stated earlier, loans presuppose the lenders' belief in the creditworthiness of borrowers, thus their ability to reimburse the borrowed capital in one way or another, while no return is expected from alms apart from the social credit donors obtain through their reputation for generosity.

Hence, the image of the "poor" is a theological concept that is misleading when used in an economic and ethical context. Yet, that image has contributed much to the notion of Deuteronomy as a utopia, to the point that biblical laws supposedly regulate the "free and creative self-withdrawal of the strong for the benefit of the weak" (Welker 2013, 206). Such self-withdrawal supposedly aims at the restoration of a purported original equality. At most, this original equality could be identified with the Exodus era, the parenthesis between life in Egypt and life in Canaan, an ideal era, a parenthesis during which the miraculous provision of manna made the economy irrelevant.

In fact, biblical laws, in particular those of Deuteronomy, assume the coexistence of individuals of equal status (brothers) with persons of unequal status (ordinary Israelites, aliens, widows, Hebrews). If the lawgiver sought "the routine protection of the weak and the systematic safeguarding of their interest" (Welker 2013, 206), it is because the economically strong have every interest in safeguarding the interest of the weak. Setting aside tithes and gleanings, giving alms, returning pledges at sunset, paying salaries daily, and seizing pledges other than essential implements is no self-withdrawal of the strong for the benefit of the weak. On the contrary, it ensures the perpetuation of inequality as much as it ensures the survival of the weak.

The return of a pledged garment at sunset is simply the rational result of the reimbursement of a day loan. Giving borrowers the choice of the pledge they provide to secure a loan ensures optimal conditions for the debt to be honored because borrowers are best qualified to know what pledge would least impair their ability to honor their debt.

The prohibition to take a widow's garment as pledge (24:17) figures widows as potential borrowers and is thus a clue to their creditworthiness. They receive social support in the form of triennial tithes and gleaning rights, which indicates that their common designation as *personae miserae* is misleading (Lohfink 1991).

The decision to enslave oneself permanently to a master who can afford to feed another mouth year-round is a rational option for members of limited means, but hardly a utopian program. Most of Deuteronomy's laws promote modes of behavior essential to social life anywhere:

- Impartiality in trials by thorough inquiry (13:14), a high court for complex cases (17:8), the prohibition of bribes (16:19–20), the strict application of sentences (17:2–12), asylum to preserve the

presumption of innocence (19:1-13), more than a single witness (19:15-20), the punishment of false witnesses in proportion to their accusations (19:18), individual liability even within the family circle (24:16), and proportionality of punishments (25:1-3)
- Fairness in business: wages (24:14-15), weights and measures (25:13-16), protection of private property such as field boundaries (19:14), standing crops (23:24-25), and strays (22:1-4, 23:24-25)
- Protection of family honor: sexual laws (22) and rebellious sons (21:18)
- Basic hygiene (23:13-15; 24:8)

Nevertheless, there remain some elements in the DC that do bear the characteristics of a utopia.

5. Utopian Elements Despite Overall Economic Realism

However much the bulk of the Deuteronomic laws bear similarities to ancient economic practices (see ch. 5 in this volume), some elements do seem to make short-change of realities or to be somewhat over-optimistic in their ability to promote the envisioned world. Deuteronomy 12–26 displays a coherent vision of self-rule that renders the royal office dispensable and even extends Israel's hegemony over foreigners.

Did the writers really believe that the common-sense economic principle enumerated in Deut 12–26 could generate wealth to the point where the Israelite brothers could lend to foreigners against interest and never have to borrow from them (15:6)? What this verse imagines is no less than an Israel governed by an elite of international bankers with unlimited funds that are ever increasing thanks to interest earned on loans to the many nations over which they rule.

5.1 An Almost Kingless Israel

Though Israel is expected to rule over many nations, the king it may wish to establish would be a constitutional monarch not directly involved in ruling. He would spend his time studying the Torah (17:19). The war laws do not mention any king, and no taxes go to the palace. Yet, submission to another country seems out of the question. The expression "you cannot give over you a foreign man who (is) not your brother" (15:15) seems needlessly wordy. It is usually understood as insisting that the chosen king must be an Israelite brother and not a foreigner.[1] The writers assume that the observance of the rules and regulations they list can ensure the independence of their model society, ignoring political hierarchies and contingencies.

There were indeed times of a power vacuum when Near Eastern groups such as Aramean and Israelite tribes enjoyed self-rule with little interference from Mesopotamian, Hittite, or Egyptian Empires. Yet, the lawgiver's preference for a kingless Israel can hardly refer to such periods because he is aware of the existence of kings and empires commanding large armies (20:1), but he considers that Israel need not imitate the practices of the people around it. The elders, judges, and Levitical priests mentioned in the different laws are sufficient to guarantee Israel's independence. Hence, setting up a king over Israel is a divine concession to a human desire considered legitimate though superfluous (17:14). The main point of the law is to make the king subservient to Levitical priests in charge of the Torah (see ch. 8 in this volume).

5.2 An Almost Taxless Israel

At most, the Deuteronomic king is a brother among the brothers who represent the elite of international bankers *ruling* Israel and many nations. As merchants and financiers, such an elite would certainly favor an almost tax-free economy limited to triennial tithes set apart for social relief (14:28–29). Whether these tithes are collected every third year or on a yearly basis to average out yield variations, the overall yearly tax burden corresponds to a theoretical 3.33% of the agricultural yields because yearly tithes brought at the chosen place are for self-consumption, thus not in effect a tax. The priestly dues of 18:1–8 represent, however, a much heavier tax burden, but they may be secondary harmonizations with Exodus–Numbers (a possible but unprovable hypothesis).

Without denying the power of big men in international relations, could the writers realistically expect to conquer foreign cities, subduing or slaughtering their populations (20:10–14), without ever experiencing defeat and retaliation, in particular since the king was not to multiply horses (17:16)? And what if its fittest warriors remain behind because they built a new house, planted a vineyard, married a new wife, or simply when they are afraid (20:5–8)? Exemption of newly wed men is reflected in a range of ancient texts showing that ideally men should not risk their

---

1   The explicit mention of Edomite brothers who are permitted access to the assembly of the Lord (23:7) explains the insistence that the brother-king cannot be a foreigner such as Edomite brothers.

lives on the battlefield before having procreated (Wright 2011, 136-38). On its own, the exemption of newly weds thus reflects ordinary practice, but adding a new house, new vineyard, and even the fear in the face of death as grounds to shirk conscription belies serious consideration of military realities. Is this utopian view a mere exaggeration of the potential of the proposed model society to convince the audience to concur, or should those unrealistic elements be ascribed to a secondary process that introduced the figure of Moses, the Torah, priests, Levitical priests, and tribal heads in the legal core? Those figures and instances may indeed have been introduced within the older regulatory core because they introduce ideas consistent with views put forth in the framing chapters (Deut 1-11 and 27-34).

The first part of the war laws (20:1-9) feature elements that are either rare or unique in the core chapters:

- a reference to the Exodus in v. 1
- a priest instead of a Levite or levitical priests in v. 2
- officials (שטרים) in vv. 5,8,9 found also in 1:15; 16:8; 29:10; 31:28.

The towering figure of Moses introduces new elements that directly challenge the elite of international bankers of the Deuteronomic utopia. But instead of adding elements that would seem to make the utopia easier to attain, the Torah turns the utopia into a dystopia. The Torah-studying king is deprived of military means to protect Israel from invasions. The šōṭ^{e}rîm send back home the fittest elements of his army.

5.3 Blaming Israel for the Failure to Achieve Utopia

The framing chapters recall the Baal of Peor (4:3), Israel's inherent stubbornness (9:6), and Aaron's idolatrous golden calf (9:20) for a dystopian figuration of the wilderness era (Davies 2006). But instead of using such a bleak past to work out a vision for the future (Ben Zvi 2006, 73), Moses foretells the repetition of the dystopian past in the future. Why?

One likely target for the rejection of any utopian future is the utopia of the international elite (including Edomite brothers, see 23:8) discussed above. Though the blessings and curses listed in Deuteronomy's final chapters can be read as urgent calls to avoid the recurrence of the dystopian past (Sasson 2006, 31), Moses's knowledge that once in the land Israel will be complacent, idolatrous and will inevitably be exiled (4:25-28) serves the interest of the Levitical priests who guard the Torah.[2] Moses's prediction is confirmed by Yhwh himself who announces that soon after Moses's death the people will begin to prostitute themselves (31:16-18). The present is sandwiched between both a past and a future dystopia.[3] The present is thus an irrelevant parenthesis. With a future as dystopian as the past was, the notion of rule through a financial brotherhood is rejected.

This scenario is not challenged by pointing out the expected change of heart in exile that is coupled with the promise that Yhwh will neither abandon nor destroy Israel and that he shall not forget the covenant with the ancestors (4:31). This is a vague promise, devoid of any precise political realization that could provide a basis for a utopian society such as the rule of the international brotherhood in the core chapters. Lending to other nations (28:12) is now conditioned to the strict observation of the terms of the covenant. These terms are repeated every seven years (31:10-13), but Israel's ability to obey and at least partly realize the utopia is voided in advance by the foretelling of future disobedience and exile (4:25-28). The promised change of heart and restoration (4:31) is not echoed in the gruesome descriptions of the consequences of disobedience in ch. 28. At best, the audience is locked into the fatality of cyclical political defeats and restorations similar to the cycle of disobedience, distress, calls for help, and deliverance in Judg 2-16: hardly a utopian program.

Contrary to the idolatrous brother or city that should be put to the sword (Deut 13:6-12) it is over the entire Israel that the Damocles sword of idolatry hangs and will surely fall. Israel shall not live long in Canaan (4:26). The final chapters turn any utopian elements into dystopia caused by Yhwh himself:

- the *ger* becomes the head and Israel the tail (28:43-44), though the *ger* laws do not present the alien as the tail and it is many people

---

[2] Modern translations of 4:25 introduce a conditionality that is not necessarily rendered by the Hebrew particle כי "when", which opens the verse. It is the LXX's Ἐὰν δὲ that clearly leaves the possibility of obedience to the Torah open. Translations that begin v. 25 as "when you have had children" often continue with "should you become corrupt" (see Tigay 1996, 51; McConville 2002, 98). Goeman (2020) argues, however, that כי in 4:29 does not express a condition "if you seek him with all your heart and all your soul" but the reason for Israel's latter return to Yhwh: Israel will find Yhwh *because* they will seek him wholeheartedly. Therefore, 4:25-26 can be rendered as "when you have fathered sons and grandsons... and made idols... I will call heaven and earth to witness against you and you will soon perish from the land..."

[3] The outcome of Moses's dialogues with Yhwh in chs 3 and 9 also exculpates Moses and adds blame on Israel. See Paganini 2018, 35.

(גוים ראבים) rather than the alien in your gates (compared 15:6 with 28:43) who would borrow from Israelites when Israel is blessed.
- Israel suffers defeat, dispossession, slavery, and exile (28:28–49). Instead of entire families feasting joyfully before Yhwh, Yhwh will cause Israel to eat its own children (28:53–57).
- the social distinction between brothers, neighbors, aliens, foreigners, widows, and orphans gives place to an Israel cursed as a whole, and addressed as "you" (28:15–68).

6. Rooting Utopia and Dystopia in Different Groups

Ou-topia as the absence of a geographical *topos* must nevertheless be rooted in sociology and represents the interest of the particular group that generates it. Yet, one's utopian vision may be perceived by another contemporary segment of the same society as a nightmare. The realistic, utopian and dystopian elements in Deuteronomy should thus be related to particular groups. As the description of a "good society that is better than that of the author's present" (Schweitzer 2006, 16), utopia identifies the group to which the author belongs and the interests of that group at a particular point. Hence, the realism of the laws dealing with the regulation of economic interactions reflects the interest of the financial brotherhood mentioned above. Realistic as they are, these laws represent a utopia in the sense that their application would, from the point of view of this elite, be a great improvement on their previous situation. Or their present application is already a great improvement on the previous situation, which can be teased out as the rule of a foreign king who multiplied horses and chariots, ignored field boundaries, press-ganged laborers, corrupted witnesses, rendered summary judgments and dispensed with careful enquiry, left empaled corpses rotting in the sun and flogged men to death, raped women before selling them as slaves, appropriated oxen, sheep, and donkeys by claiming them as strays, appropriated the inheritance of orphans, ravaged standing crops, and used different weights and measures.

Depending on whether or not the authors of the first legal collection had achieved a hegemonic position, their laws were either an honor code for their own ranks to preserve that hegemony or they were a utopia, i.e. a blueprint for a reality that could be achieved precisely because it is based on practical common sense to ensure fairness rather than relying on military force and extortion.

In case the authors had not yet achieved a strong position but were still suffering from a context they experienced as nightmarish, the common-sensical aspect of the economic practices in Deut 14–25 (in contrast to

Deut 12–13 and 26) indicates that their revolutionary element was indeed a challenge to the status quo. They could not be blueprints of an ideal society dreamt by a powerless group that could only hope for a complete reversal of their present condition. Rather, much of Deut 14–25 reflects the interests of an affluent group that strove after political influence at the measure of the wealth it had acquired and wished to develop further. This wealthy group sought to replace the old nobility or was already replacing it. As much as the farmers, these merchants and lenders longed for the peace and stability needed for their trade to flourish. Hence, rule through credit rather than by military might indicates that the DC with the brotherhood at its core was an innovative work indicating a reality that could come about if the laws were applied. In this sense, the legal collection would become a work of legitimation of the present reality (see Schweitzer 2006, 19) if the international elite ever replaced the foreign domination the brothers viewed as tyrannical.

In this case, the war laws of ch. 20 reflect the hands of two rival groups, though not necessarily multiple redactional layers (Schweitzer 2006, 23). Like the brother king uninvolved in war, the war laws display war as a chivalrous sport for the few warriors left after the majority is excused for having more urgent tasks to perform. On the one hand, any town attacked by such a small band is unlikely to be impressed enough to accept the terms of peace (15:10–11). On the other hand, acceptance of the offered terms of peace is irrelevant if the financial elite is already ruling it through the interest-bearing loans it grants to foreigners (15:5–6; 23:20). The long siege of towns that reject the terms of peace is equally irrelevant. There is no need to cut down the orchards around them (20:19–20) because they already belong indirectly to the besieging troop![4] Only the total annihilation of the Canaanite nations in 20:15–18 can be suspected to belong to a later hand as it pushes the rule-through-credit utopia to the extreme and turns it into pies-in-the-sky. Such a transformation of the accomplishable utopia into wild dreams of conquered distant cities (20:15) is the mirror image of Moses's rejection of the brotherhood's utopia by foretelling future exiles.

Conclusion

Do Deuteronomy's brotherly ethics imply that all fellow Judahites are to be treated as brothers (Van Seters 1999, 111; Otto 2007, 135), including women (Reuter 1993, 150–151; Otto 1998, 183) and slaves (Weinfeld 1993,

---

4 On Egyptian and Assyrian parallels to the practice of destroying orchards in war see Beukenhorst 2021, 281–2.

34), to the point that even the rich may wish to become poor in order to be close to God as is the case in the Psalms (Levin 2014, 59)?

Indeed not. Instead of any attempt to restore a purported original equality, Moses's warning that Israel will disobey the Torah sets the guardians of that Torah apart from a supposedly rebellious Israelite populace. The Levitical priests who supervise the king's Torah are thus set above the brother king in order to dethrone the brotherhood elite to whom the Deuteronomic king belongs.

Whereas the rule of the financial brotherhood rendered war unnecessary, Moses envisages Yhwh's punishment of Israel for its incapacity to observe the Torah as the result of conquest and deportation (4:26–27). The change indicates the presence of rivals who reject the brothers' utopia and are unable or unwilling to present a viable alternative. One way to explain the difference is to postulate that the core's views were altered substantially when the core was set within the frames, a scenario that can never be definitively established (Edelman 2021, 67–71). What is certain is that the frames succeeded in rendering the vision of a banker-led society invisible to modern scholarship.

Is Deuteronomy's vision more idealistic and utopian that Leviticus and Numbers? The answer varies depending upon which part of Deuteronomy is used for the comparison. The bulk of Deuteronomy's laws is far more practical than the sacrificial economy of Leviticus and Numbers that ignores the producers of the animals required to pacify Yhwh and feed Aaron's priestly dynasty. Therefore, the sacrificial economy of Leviticus and Numbers has little affinity with Deuteronomy, not even as the fifth volume of the Torah and Moses's last words that cast a bleak outlook upon Israel's future in the land he is prevented from entering and present both Israel's past and future as dystopian. The dystopia relies on the fear of the consequences of disobedience to motivate obedience to the Torah and its guardians, the Levitical priests. There lies the closest similarity of Deuteronomy with the hegemony of the priestly caste in Leviticus and Numbers. Fear replaces any thoughtful consideration of the reasonable possibility of achieving a level of security, thanks to the hold on trade and credit of a rival brotherhood. In sharp contrast to current readings of the DC as the description of an egalitarian society frozen in timeless and unreachable perfection, the brotherhood at the core of Deuteronomy claimed the ability to implement a better though not ideal society. The trouble with this somewhat utopian vision is that it kept priests and Levitical priests at the margin. Such a square peg had to be rounded to fit it at the end of the Torah, a process that equally overdid the fear of the consequences of disobedience. Laws that were originally presented as mildly utopian ended up as a dystopian vision of an Israelite brotherhood doomed to disobedience. Yet, it is the notion of a kingless Israel that ensured the survival of Israel as a resilient sociological movement – Judaism – throughout centuries of kingless and stateless existence.

Works Cited

Arnold, Bill T. 2016. "Israelite Worship as Envisioned and Prescribed in Deuteronomy 12." *Zeitschrift für Altorientalische und Biblische Rechtsgeschichte* 22: 161–75.

------. 2021. "Innovations of the Deuteronomic Law and the History of its Composition." Pages 163–94 in *Deuteronomy in the Making*. Edited by Diana Edelman, Benedetta Rossi, Kåre Berge and Philippe Guillaume. Beihefte Zeitschrift für die Wissenschaft 533. Berlin: de Gruyter.

Ben Zvi, Ehud. 2006. "Utopias, Multiple Utopias, and Why Utopias at All? The Social Roles of Utopian Visions in Prophetic Books within Their Historical Context." Pages 5–85 in *Utopia and Dystopia in Prophetic Literature*. Edited by Ehud Ben Zvi. Helsinki/Göttingen: Finnish Exegetical Society/Vandenhoeck & Ruprecht.

Berge, Kåre. 2012. "Literacy, Utopia and Memory: Is there a Public Teaching in Deuteronomy?" *Journal of Hebrew Scriptures* 12: 1–19.

------. 2017. "Ṣedaqa and the Community of the Scribes in Postexilic Deuteronomy." Pages 19–36 in *Ṣedaqa and Torah in Postexilic Discourse*. Edited by Susanne Gillmayr-Bucher and Maria Häusl. London: Bloomsbury.

Beukenhorst, Martijn. 2021. "The War Laws in Deuteronomy." Pages 271–288 in *Deuteronomy in the Making*. Edited by Diana Edelman, Benedetta Rossi, Kåre Berge and Philippe Guillaume. Beihefte Zeitschrift für die Wissenschaft 533. Berlin: de Gruyter.

Clermont-Ganneau, Charles. 1875. "Stèle de mésa," *Revue critique* 2: 166–74.

Davies, Philip R. 2006. "The Wilderness Years: Utopia and Dystopia in the Book of Hosea." Pages 160–174 in *Utopia and Dystopia in Prophetic Literature*. Edited by Ehud Ben Zvi. Göttingen: Vandenhoeck & Ruprecht.

------. 2014. "The Authority of Deuteronomy." Pages 27–47 in *Deuteronomy-Kings as Emerging Authoritative Books. A Conversation*. Edited by Diana V. Edelman. Ancient Near Eastern Monographs 6. Atlanta: SBL.

De Wette, Wilhelm. M. L. 1805. *Dissertatio critico-exegetica qua Deuteronomium a prioribus libris Pentateuchi diversum, alius cuiusdam recentioris auctoris opus esse monstratur*. PhD diss., University of Jena: Etzdorf.

Edelman, Diana V. 2021. "Deuteronomy as the Instructions of Moses and Yhwh vs. a Framed Legal Core." Pages 25–75 in *Deuteronomy in the Making*. Edited by Diana Edelman, Benedetta Rossi, Kåre Berge and Philippe Guillaume. Beihefte Zeitschrift für die Wissenschaft 533. Berlin: de Gruyter.

Goeman, Peter. 2020. "Towards a New Proposal for Translating the Conjunction khy in Deuteronomy 4:29." *Bible Translator* 71: 158–178.
Guillaume, Philippe. 2010. "The Hidden Benefits of Patronage: Debt." Pages 107–125 in *Anthropology and the Bible*. Edited by Emanuel Pfoh. Piscataway: Gorgias Press. Reprint, pages 223–240 in *Patronage in Ancient Palestine and in the Hebrew Bible: A Reader*. Edited by Emanuel Pfoh. Sheffield Phoenix Press, 2022.
------. 2022. *The Economy of Deuteronomy's Core*. Sheffield: Equinox Publishing Ltd.
Hölscher, Gustav. 1922. "Komposition und Ursprung des Deuteronomiums," *Zeitschrift für die alttestamentliche Wissenschaft* 40: 161–255.
Horst, Louis. 1893. "Etudes sur le Deutéronome: II – Les sources et la date du Deutéronome (suite et fin)." *Revue de l'histoire des religions* 27: 119–76.
Jameson, Fredric. 2005. *Archaeologies of the Future*. London: Verso.
Jursa, Michael. 2010. *Aspects of the Economic History of Babylonia in the First Millennium BC: Economic Geography, Economic Mentalities, Agriculture, the Use of Money and the Problem of Economic Growth*. Münster: Ugarit Verlag.
Levin, Christoph. 2014. "Rereading Deuteronomy in the Persian and Hellenistic periods: The Ethics of Brotherhood and the Care of the Poor." Pages 48–71 in *Deuteronomy-Kings as Emerging Authoritative Books: A Conversation*. Edited by Diana V. Edelman. Ancient Near Eastern Monographs 6, Society of Biblical Literature, Atlanta.
Lohfink, Norbert. 1991. "Poverty in the Laws of the Ancient Near East and of the Bible." *Theological Studies* 52: 34–50.
Mannheim, Karl. 1991. *Ideology and Utopia. Introduction to the Sociology of Knowledge*. London: Routledge. German edition: *Ideologie und Utopie*. Bonn: F. Cohen, 1929.
McConville, J. Gordon. 2002. *Deuteronomy*. Leicester, Apollos.
Olivier, Johannes P. J. 1997. "Restitution as Economic Redress: The Fine Print of the Old Babylonian *mēšarum*-Edict of Ammiṣsduqa." *Zeitschrift für Altorientalische und Biblische Rechtsgeschichte* 3: 12–25.
Otto, Eckart. 1998. "False Weights in the Scales of Biblical Justice? Different Views of Women from Patriarchal Hierarchy to Religious Equality in the Book of Deuteronomy." Pages 128–46 in *Gender and Law in the Hebrew Bible and the Ancient Near East*. Edited by Victor H. Matthews, Bernard M. Levinson and Tikva Frymer-Kensky. Sheffield: Sheffield Academic Press.
------. 2007. *Das Gesetz des Moses*. Darmstadt: Wissenschaftliche Buchgesellschaft.
------. 2012. *Deuteronomium*. HthKAT. Freiburg: Herder.
Paganini, Simone. 2018. "Chronology, Dischronology and the Search for Meaning in the Plot of Deuteronomy." Pages 22–36 in *Perception du*

temps dans la Bible. Edited by Marc Leroy and Martin Staszak. Leuven: Peters.

Portolano, Mariana. 2012. "The Rhetorical Function of Utopia: An Exploration of the Concept of Utopia in Rhetorical Theory." *Utopia Studies* 23: 113–141.

Reuss, Eduard. 1879. *L'histoire sainte et la Loi : (Pentateuque et Josué)*. Paris : Librairie Sandoz et Fischbacher.

Reuter, Eleonore. 1993. *Kultzentralisation. Entstehung und Theologie von Dtn 12*. BBB 87. Frankfort: Hain.

Sasson, Jack M. 2006. "Utopian and Dystopian Images in Mari Prophetic Texts." Pages 27–40 in *Utopia and Dystopia in Prophetic Literature*. Edited by Ehud Ben Zvi. Publications of the Finnish Exegetical Society 92. Göttingen: Vandenhoeck & Ruprecht.

Schweitzer, Steven James. 2006. "Utopia and Utopian Literary Theory: Some Preliminary Observations." Pages 13–26 in *Utopia and Dystopia in Prophetic Literature*. Edited by Ehud Ben Zvi. Göttingen: Vandenhoeck & Ruprecht.

Tigay, Jeffrey. 1996. *The JPS Torah Commentary: Deuteronomy*. Philadelphia: Jewish Publication Society.

Van Seters, John. 1999. *The Pentateuch*. Sheffield: Sheffield Academic Press.

Weinfeld, Moshe. 1993. "Deuteronomy: The Present State of the Field." Pages 21–35 in *A Song of Power and the Power of Song*. Edited by Duane L. Christensen. Winona Lake: Eisenbrauns.

Welker, Michael. 2013. "Justice – Mercy – Worship. The 'Weighty Matters' of the Biblical Law." Pages 205–24 in *Concepts of Law in the Sciences, Legal Studies, and Theology*. Edited by Michael Welker and Gregor Etzelmüller. Tübingen: Mohr Siebeck.

Wright, Jacob L. 2011. "Making a Name for Oneself: Martial Valor, Heroic Death, and Procreation in the Hebrew Bible." *Journal for the Study of the Old Testament* 36: 131–62.

About the Author

Philippe Guillaume is a trained agriculturist and a lecturer at the Biblical Institute of the University of Berne (Switzerland). His current research focuses on the ancient Near East economy and agrarian matters related to biblical texts and laws, in particular in Deuteronomy with a volume dedicated to *The Economy of Deuteronomy's Core* (Sheffield: Equinox Publishing Ltd, 2022).

Chapter 12
Deuteronomic Parenting

Philippe Guillaume

Abstract

Current studies of biblical laws dealing with family matters display much interest in sexual issues and rightly denounce their patriarchal bias. Focusing on parenting provides a more balanced appreciation of the role of mothers and the place of women within a male-dominated society. An analysis of the levirate law, the rebuttal of a slanderous husband, and primogeniture show that the aim of the lawgivers was to maximize the chances to produce offspring and fulfill the Genesis mandate to multiply. Procreation, however, is but the first stage of the life-long process of parenting that involves both parents, even after the death of the father, if necessary. Thus, women and mothers are shielded from abusive repudiation by the production of a bloodied sheet, while any disrespect toward parents or disobedience to their commands is liable to the death penalty, except in certain cases for daughters, who are given a chance to overturn parental opposition.

Keywords: Deuteronomy, marriage, discipline, mother, fertility

In Arabic cultures, parenting is a major status-changer signified by the acquisition of an additional title, *abu* "father of" and *umm* "mother of" besides *ibn* "son of" and *banat* "daughter of." The Bible displays no such change; men and women are designated as sons or daughters, whether they are parents or not. Nevertheless, from its very first chapter, the Hebrew Bible places a heavy emphasis on procreation. Jacob Wright (2011) has identified a biblical predilection for procreation over heroic death as the means to make a name for oneself.

Procreation is but the initial stage of the long process of parenting, a process that does not necessarily end when children marry and become parents in turn. Yet, biblical Hebrew has no term for parents. Parent(s) in modern biblical translations *always* render the term "father" (אב), most of the time in reference to the biblical patriarchs (Abraham, Isaac, and Jacob) or to anonymous ancestors of the Israelites. Mothers occur rarely. Does this mean that their role as parents is depreciated?

It is tempting to think so, because the Bible is the product of a patriarchal society and was written by men and for men. For this reason, parenting in Middle Eastern societies has been analyzed through the prism of the notions of *paterfamilias* and *patria potestas*. Husbands supposedly "had exclusive financial, sexual, and legal jurisdiction over their wives and fathers over their daughters" (Bidmead 2014, 404). Yet, the actual powers Roman law granted to the *paterfamilias* over his wives and children were more limited than generally presumed (Thompson 2006). Nevertheless, the *paterfamilias* is a favorite target among feminist and womanist biblical exegetes (Pressler 1991; Case 2020), though Simone Paganini (2010, 21) warns that the biblical *paterfamilias* is used as an overly convenient straw man.

The Bible was, indeed, produced within a patriarchal society, though the biblical patriarch is no more dictatorial than those with the same status in other comparable ancient legal collections. Ancient Near Eastern societies as a whole were not phallocracies (Cardascia 1980, 7). In fact, biblical laws grant mothers powers equal to those of fathers in certain cases. Whereas the debate has focused on the powers of men as fathers and husbands, parenting, i.e. fathering and mothering, offers a fresh perspective for reconsidering gender roles in the Hebrew Bible.

The second volume of the *Handbook of Parenting* has four pages on ancient Israel, drawing clues from the entire biblical corpus—narratives, laws, prophetic material, novella (Ruth, Esther), Psalms, and proverbs (French 2002, 254–58). Cynthia Chapman's monograph (2016) focuses on maternal kin in biblical narrative and poetry but ignores several laws pertaining to mothering. Therefore, the focus here is on legal material that deals specifically with mothering and fathering.

Legal texts are no more faithful witnesses to ancient Israelite reality than stories and poetry. Laws convey a utopian element but are not pie-in-the-sky. Utopia has no appeal if the vision of the future it promotes is perceived by its intended audience as an unlikely solution to a problematic present (Ben Zvi 2006, 73; Berge 2012). However ideal the behaviors biblical laws recommend, they deal with issues that the lawgivers considered problematic in the world in which they lived, Iron Age Palestine.

Table 1: Mothers and fathers in biblical legal collections

Context	Exodus	Leviticus	Deuteronomy
idolatry			13:7 father + mother
striking	21:15 father + mother		
disrespect	21:17 father + mother	20:9 father + mother	
revering		19:3 father + mother	
rebellious son			21:18–19 father + mother
jealousy			22:15–21 father + mother
fine for rape	22:17 father		22:29 father
"incest"		18:1–18; 20:11–23	23:1 father's wife
liability	20:5 father	26:39 father	personal 24:16, father

Fathers and Mothers in Biblical Laws

As direct biological genitors, fathers and mothers occur in the passages listed in Table 1 above.

The term "mother" is far less common than the term "father." Mothers are *never* mentioned alone, except in reference to animals (Table 2).

Ewes and Birds as Paradigmatic Mothers

Table 2 shows that over a quarter of the occurrences of the word "mother" (אם) in biblical laws refer to animals (6/22, 27%): a kid who should not be boiled in its mother's milk (Exod 23:19; 34:26; Deut 14:21), firstborns left with their mothers for seven days before being given over to god (Exod 22:30; Lev 22:27), and a brooding mother who should be allowed to escape when collecting its eggs or fledglings (Deut 22:6).

Why grant such a large space to non-human mothers? Eckart Otto (2016, 1686) attributes the law of the mother bird to Deuteronomy's *Tierethik* because it is found in a passage that also requires the return

Table 2: Animal mothers in biblical laws

	Exodus	Leviticus	Deuteronomy
Firstborn males with their mother for a week	22:29	22:27	
Do not boil a kid in its mother's milk	23:19; 34:26		14:21
Let the mother bird on its nest go free			22:6
Total	3/5	1/11	2/6

of strays to their owner and relieving fallen beasts of burden (Deut 22:1-10). In fact, such laws simply reflect practical wisdom. In the long run, overloading beasts of burden is as self-defeating as eating the mother bird with its eggs or fledglings in the nest. Ethical concerns for the animals are subservient to human interest. Nothing indicates that a mother bird is less attached to its fledglings than a cow or ewe to its unweaned offspring. Letting the mother bird live ensures a future supply of eggs and fledglings for humans. Letting newborns suckle their mothers for a week before sacrificing them activates the production of milk that is more palatable for humans than colostrum.

The motivation of the ban on boiling a kid in its mother's milk is debated, but the proposals based on the supposed inhumanity of the practice are the least likely (Cooper 2012).[1] This particular law, as much as the previous ones, makes animal wellbeing subservient to the economic interests of humans. Though the animal metaphors for human mothering might seem to be yet another example of patriarchal demeaning of women, they also acknowledge that a man labors in vain if the fruits of his labor are not destined to raise the fruits of his wife's labor. The expulsion from the mythical garden of Eden underlines the intimate relation between Eve's labor pains and Adam's sweaty brow (Gen 3:16-19). Fathers and mothers contribute differently to parenting, but both are necessary.

Procreation and Parenting: Seed of the Father *and* of the Mother

The Bible generally uses the term seed (זרע) to designate the father's role in procreation and his descent. Yet, it is also used for Eve, Hagar, and Rebekah's offspring (Gen 3:15; 16:10; 24:60, Chapman 2016, 269 n. 6). Hence women are not viewed as mere gardens into which males plant a seed, as Carol Delaney's notion of "monogenetic procreation" (2001, 454) would have it. The ancients were well aware that mothers contribute far more than fathers to the production of the next generation.

Table 3 lists the laws explicitly or implicitly relevant to parenting in Deuteronomy, the most detailed biblical collection of such materials, especially in relation to the life of non-priestly elites. Though these cases do not mention the term "mother," their number somewhat corrects the dearth of the term mother in biblical laws and shows the importance

---

[1] The view of Gloria London (2016, 138-41) that boiling meat in a pot previously used for dairy foods whose residue would sour and spoil the meat is somewhat countered by the attested Palestinian diet of *leben ummo*, which consists of cooking meat in yogurt (Bauer 1903, 203-4).

Table 3: Laws relevant to parenting in Deuteronomy

Deut	Context	Implications for Parenting
12:7,18; 14:26	Yearly banquets	Building a common identity by feasting together
13:7	Idolatry	Danger of close kin influences
14:28–29	Triennial tithes	Provisions for fatherless households
15:16–17	Self-indenture	Life-long position in a wealthy family
17:17	Royal harem	Limits the number of pretenders to the throne
20:7; 24:5	Military exemption	Ensures procreation before enrollment
20:14	Women as booty	Increases procreation potential
21:10–14	War captive	Increases procreation potential
21:15–16	Hated wife	Secures firstborn rights
21:18–21	Rebellious son	Prevents squandering
22:13–19	Post-marital slander	Limits grounds for repudiation
22:20–21	Pre-marital pregnancy	Warning to unmarried women
22:22–27	Adultery and rape	Controls paternity
22:28–29	Abduction	Overrides parental refusal
24:1–4	Remarriage of repudiated wife	Repudiation reversible in certain cases
24:17	Not pledging widow's garment	Secures minimal conditions to raise orphans
24:19–21	Widow's gleaning rights	Secures minimal conditions to raise orphans
25:5–9	Wife of deceased brother	Protects partnership from immediate dissolution
25:11	Grabbing wife	Protects male potency

granted to parenting. The majority of the listed laws displays a strong interest in fertility, i.e. the production of children, and the necessary conditions for raising them. Yearly banquets with entire families ensure the transmission of family values (chs. 12 and 14) and reduce the risk of idolatry (ch. 13). Becoming a mother made a woman less dispensable than before she bore a child, all the more so a son. Fathering was equally important, to the point that many ancient legal collections envisage post-mortem fathering. Tithes, gleaning rights, and special regulations for pledging (chs. 14 and 24) are meant to help widows raise their children.

The following paragraphs focus on a selection of these passages.

Post-Mortem Procreation: Law of Levirate

In the Bible, only Deuteronomy considers the case of the untimely death of a married man who dies before having sired a son. When faced with such a case, a brother is expected to impregnate the widow to ensure a descendant for the deceased. In light of a Roman law, this custom is commonly designated as the law of the levirate, from the Latin term *levir*, though the Latin translation of the Bible does not use it. Additional confusion results when Deuteronomy's so-called law of the levirate is read in light of the stories of Tamar (Gen 38) and of Ruth (Mathias 2020a, 193–96).

Of the six verses dedicated to this law (Deut 25:5–10), four explain how the widow can compel the so-called *levir* to "perpetuate his brother's name in Israel" so that it "may not be blotted out of Israel" (vv. 6–7). The entire passage expects the widow to appeal to her local elders, pressuring an unwilling brother-in-law to the extent of spitting publicly in his face to shame him. Nevertheless, the man retains the right to decline, but at the cost of being remembered in future generations as having failed in his duty.

Modern translations commonly render the woman as "widow," the brother as her "brother-in-law," and their union as "marriage," three problematic designations. The text avoids the term "widow" and systematically refers to the woman as the "wife of the dead" (אשת המת), because her status is not legally akin to that of a widow (אלמנה), to whom Deut 14:28–29 grants tithes and gleaning rights.

Verse 5 narrows the scope of this law to brothers who "resided together" (ישבו יחדו). As the term "brother" in Deuteronomy and in the ancient Near East in general designated a male sibling as much as a business partner (Milstein 2019, 56), economic considerations are at least as important as kinship. Whether the brothers were siblings working their paternal estate in common or were partners who had pooled funds to finance a common enterprise, the post-mortem birth of an heir secures the continuation of the partnership until his coming of age as the legal heir.

Marriage is equally confusing, as neither Roman law nor Deuteronomy necessarily envisages a permanent union (Mace 1953, 95). The Hebrew does use the standard formulation for marriage, i.e. "to take her for himself as wife" (לקחה לו לאשה in v. 5), but the Greek translation rendered the "taking" of the wife of the dead by the surviving brother as συνοικέω "cohabitation," implying that the wife of the deceased merely cohabits with the surviving partner. The expected son (or child in the Greek text) is designated as firstborn (בכיר), implying that his birth releases his mother from her duties (Coats 1972). After the birth of an heir, the mother may be free to contract a proper marriage with a man outside (חוצה) the partnership because, at that point, the matter of the transmission of the estate of the deceased has been resolved (Weisberg 2009, 27; Davies 2020, 116). In the interim, the partnership survives while the guardianship of the heir's share in the partnership and of any of the rest of the estate not entirely invested in the partnership is assumed by the surviving brother or by the heir's mother, as with the wives of Assyrian traders who acted as independent businesswomen after the deaths of their husbands (Schlüter 2021). In either case, the matter is not the inheritance of the widow (see Mathias 2020a, 52–56) to ensure her subsistence (so Verburg 2019) but rather the securing of the inheritance of the deceased brother's estate. The lawgiver has the entire process of parenting in view, including the transmission of assets from one generation to the next. Sexuality, the framework within which the Levirate is considered in current scholarship (Mathias 2020b, 231), is a side issue.

The reluctance of the surviving brother to sire an heir for his deceased partner makes sense if he otherwise stands to inherit the assets of his late partner. In this case, fathering a son through the wife of the dead effectively disinherits him "through his own actions" (Davies 2020, 116, quoting Weisberg 2009, 27). Conversely, the wife of the dead man has an immediate vested interest in the survival of the partnership if her late husband had, as was often the case, invested part or all of her dowry in it. Hence, death did not necessarily terminate the outstanding duty to ensure generational continuity. Though the so-called levir is the biological father of the child borne by the wife of the dead, the child is legally both the heir of his genitor and the posthumous heir of his mother's husband. The business partner retained the option of desisting from impregnating his partner's wife, in which case he had to liberate funds to reimburse the dowry and any sums owed to the legal heirs of his deceased partner, blood brothers, cousins, and any creditor who, having granted loans to the deceased man or to the partnership, now required settlement. The liquidation of the partnership to liberate funds at an unpropitious time could land the surviving brother in dire financial difficulties.

Consummation and Fatherhood: Law of the Slanderous Husband

The importance of making sure that one's wife bears one's own children and not someone else's are at the root of the prohibitions of extramarital relations and the limitation of rape to extra-conjugal relations that sought to remedy the impossibility of guaranteeing the identity of male genitors. Deuteronomy's adultery laws are introduced with a theoretical case to illustrate the basic principle of negative prescription, i.e. the inadmissibility of accusations made when the passing of time has made it impossible to confirm or deny their validity. The production of a stained sheet by the parents of a wife accused of premarital unchastity by her husband is enough to rebuff the accusation (Deut 22:13–21).

Due to the overdetermination regarding virginity in Christianity, the sheet produced by the parents has long been understood as evidence of defloration, hence the perpetuation of semi-public defloration rituals on the wedding night and the lucrative trade of hymen restoration. Yet, the *betulim* on the sheet produced by the mother and father were more likely to have been taken as menstrual blood and evidence that their daughter was not pregnant when the accusing husband took her (Chapman 2016, 93; Wenham 1972).[2]

Parents did not necessarily store the physical proof of their daughter's honor, though signs of pregnancy within the months following the wedding or a birth about nine months later could indeed be taken by a suspicious husband as evidence that his wife was not in the expected state of chastity when he married her. Any sheet stained with any blood is deemed sufficient to fine the accusing husband one hundred shekels as compensation to the woman's father in addition to the loss of the right of repudiation (Frymer-Kensky 1998, 95). Hence, the act of marriage automatically ascribes fatherhood and secures the marital status of mothers against "dry" repudiation, that is repudiation without the return of the dowry.

All the duties pertaining to fatherhood are automatically ascribed to the mother's husband when the child is born. The identity of actual male genitors is irrelevant because unprovable, which shields mothers from malevolent accusations.

Post-Marital Parenting: Married Women and their Paternal House

It is a common presupposition that a wedded woman "legally belonged to the house of her husband" (Wright 2011, 134). The designation of a husband as *baʻal*, "master, owner," indeed suggests that marriage transferred a nubile girl from the authority of her father to that of her husband, thus severing her filial bond to graft her onto another lineage. The tenth commandment is also evoked as proof that the wives were regarded as property (Pietersen 2021, 4):

2 On the Akkadian cognate *batultu* as a nubile girl and menstrual blood, see Cassin 1987.

> You shall not covet your neighbor's house, you shall not covet your neighbor's wife and his slave and his servant and his ox and his donkey and everything that (is) to/for your neighbor. (Exod 20:17)

Here, the neighbor's wife is listed between the neighbor's house and his other assets, suggesting that she is one item of property among others. The Deuteronomic version of the Decalogue, however, underlines the difference between the wife and the neighbor's properties by mentioning the wife in a first prohibition, and the house and other properties in a second prohibition:

> You shall not covet your neighbor's wife.
>
> You shall not covet your neighbor's house: his field and his slave and his servant, his ox and his donkey and everything that (is) to/for your neighbor. (Deut 5:21)

Deuteronomy's placement of the wife in a separate commandment is a clue that she does not belong to the master of the house in the same way as his land, slaves, and animals. According to Deuteronomy at least, marriage does not make the wife's personhood "an object of her husband's property" as Sandra Jacobs (2018, 346) claims. In fact, Tracy Lemos (2017, 77) warns that referring to women as property is inaccurate and confusing. At most, the common notion that a daughter and a wife conventionally belong "to her father, or husband, who remained at liberty to gift, sell, or even prostitute, her" (Jacobs 2018, 348) is only accurate when "belonging" is used in a very broad and loose way. Strictly speaking, giving or selling one's wife implies the right to alienate one's property by transferring it to another owner for free or at a price. This is the highest level of ownership in the complex gradation of use-rights (Thompson 1978, 328).

Lower levels of ownership imply possession without the right to transfer to another user. In Roman law, *abusus* designates the right not only to use (*usus*) but also to alienate the possession. *Abusus* belongs to full ownership or freehold, while *usus* rights (without *abusus*) correspond to leasehold. Applied to the marital sphere, marriage grants a husband the right and duty to possess his wife, but not to abuse her, neither in the sense of giving or selling her to another man nor in the sense of mistreating her.

The conclusion is that, despite the Hebrew designation of a husband as *ba'al*, marriage confers a lesser level of ownership over a wife than over slaves. A slave master owns the personhood of his slaves to the point where he can beat them to death without being accused of manslaughter (Exod 21:26–27). A husband does not own his wife's person. In biblical Hebrew, marriage does not alter the spouses' personhood. There are no specific terms for "wives" and "husbands." A woman remains a woman when her man takes her for himself (לקח לו) as *his* woman.

Therefore, the term "patron" accurately expresses the duty of fathers and husbands to provide the sustenance of their daughters and wives (Edenburg 2009, 57–58). As duties imply rights, what rights does marriage confer on the husband over his wife?

Marriage as the Acquisition of a Woman's Fertility

Using property terminology to illustrate a point, marriage is closer to leasehold than to freehold. Marriage transfers the duty of providing for a woman's maintenance from father to husband. Marriage also grants the husband the usufruct of his wife's fertility, a right not necessarily granted to the father.[3] Even in the doubtful hypothesis that a husband was allowed to prostitute his wife, i.e. granting his usufruct over her body to another man, prostituting one's wife does not entail the right to give or sell her. Were a husband at liberty to sell his wife, he would receive a price in exchange for the loss of his purported property. This is not the case because the right of repudiation entails the duty to return the dowry received from the wife's father at the time of marriage as advancement— the technical term for the daughter's use of her share of her father's estate during his lifetime without having to wait for his death or the partition of his estate. Instead, repudiation meant for the husband a loss of available capital in the form of the dowry as well as the exclusive use (usufruct) of the wife's fertility.

The conclusion is that biblical legal material does not conceive of marriage as severing the parental bond established through birth (Barmash 2020, 59). The difference over the status of the wife in the two versions of the Decalogue (see above) reflects the difference between Roman *sine manu* marriage in which the wife remained under the legal control of her father and earlier concepts of marriage such as the Roman *cum manu* marriage that transferred wives to the legal control of their husbands (Hylen 2019, 508). In Deuteronomy at least, husbands merely hire the reproductive potential of their wives from the parental line of the women.

Unfortunately, the assets exchanged during marriage negotiations (Ugaritic *mhr*, Hebrew *mohar*, Arabic *mahr*) are often designated as "brideprice," which suggests a sale that makes the husband owner of the woman. "Bride wealth" is the accurate term. It focuses on the wife's total

---

3 On the omission of father-daughter incest in Lev 18, see Cardascia (1980) and Ziskind (1996).

capital rather than establishing dubious distinctions between the dowry she received from her father, the gifts she received from her husband, and the gifts presented by the prospective husband to the girl's kin (Stol 2016, 126–27). The point of marriage was to create "a network of relationships, rights, and duties between the parties and their natal families" (Barmash 2020, 63).

Parenting and Polygamy: Primogeniture

As was customary in the ancient Near East (Davies 1993), a double share of the paternal estate was granted to the firstborn son. Deuteronomy 21:15–17 insists that the principle applies even to sons born from a wife the father hates. One may ask why this man does not repudiate the wife he hates, or at least demote her to secondary status to promote the second wife he loves. The simple answer is that the hated wife has given birth to a son, which strengthens her position in the household.

This is not a case of a man taking on a second wife because the first one has not yet produced him a son. Here, both women gave birth to sons and the father has not divorced the first wife he hates. Why not? The less simple answer is that he has no ground to do so, which means that divorcing her would entail forfeiting his right to retain her dowry (Wells 2013, 304).

The Deuteronomic principle of primogeniture underlines the prevalence of the biological life cycle over any personal preferences, probably to overturn the "traditional practice of allowing fathers to assign the status of firstborn to sons other than the biologically oldest one" (Wells 2013, 301). The episode of Adonijah's request to be granted Abishag the Shunammite as wife in compensation for the loss of the throne is indirect evidence of such a practice since Solomon admits that Adonijah is his older brother, though not necessarily the firstborn (1 Kgs 2:22).

As was the case in Mesopotamia, the double share granted to the firstborn compensated for his duty to perform funerary rituals for parents and ancestors, a duty that involved the provision of offerings (Wright 2011, 135 n. 8; Jonker 1995, 187–88; Tsukimoto 1985, 34–38; Brichto 1973, 21). Instead of unfairness towards the younger siblings, the double share attributed solely on the basis of the birth order condemns favoritism, an issue as common as it is cruel for the children and the mothers who suffer from it.

A second law reveals the Deuteronomic lawgiver's concern with the consequences of abusive parenting and offers a loophole to avoid them.

Parenting against Parental Choice: The Law of the "Raped Virgin"

Deuteronomy's sexual laws (22:22–30) distinguish four categories of women with whom sexual relations are prohibited: married women other than one's wife, promised (engaged, betrothed) women, women not yet promised, and the wife of one's father, probably including any other wives besides one's mother, whether repudiated during the father's lifetime or widowed.

In the matter of parenting, the most interesting is the law of the raped but not yet promised girl (Deut 22:28–29). Contrary to the case of the promised girl (Deut 22:23–27), the place where the intercourse took place (there is no word for "rape" in the Bible)—in town or out in the open country—is irrelevant. The decisive factor is the presence of witnesses testifying that they caught the pair *in flagranti* and that the girl was indeed forcefully taken and thus a non-consenting victim. While the man who slept with another's wife or with a promised girl is executed, the rapist's "penalties" for the rape of a not yet promised girl is marriage to his victim, a "fine" of fifty shekels of silver for the girl's father, and the loss of any right of repudiation.

Contrary to Exod 22:17, Deuteronomy denies the father's right to cash the silver and keep his daughter. Therefore, Paganini (2010, 26) is certainly correct in reading Deut 22 as the protection of the daughter from the arbitrariness of her father and of her rapist. Feminist readings legitimately denounce the harshness of forcing a woman into a life-long marriage with her rapist (Ochshorn 1981, 207). Yet, for a young woman whose rape is publicly known, marrying her rapist remains the only option she has left to find a husband (Weinfeld 1972, 285).

In fact, this law protects a young woman against parental arbitrariness more than it deters rape. As long as the negotiations regarding her marriage have not been finalized, the prospective bride can easily find accomplices to confirm the use of violence and thus preserve her honor and that of her family, while the same violence enhances the virtue of the "rapist" (Fleishman 2004, 13). This is exactly what happens in the well-attested practice of marriage by elopement (Evans-Grubbs 1989). As is the case in ancient Near Eastern laws in general, the guilt of the victim is determined in inverse proportion to the violence she suffered, while the violence has little impact on the guilt of the rapist (Wells 2020, 5).

Deuteronomy implies that the marriage is recognized on the spot and forever, instead of the several years of cohabitation required by Mesopotamian law (Stol 2016, 92). Therefore, the lawgiver places a high premium on the ability of an enterprising girl to overcome parental preferences and choose the "husband of her heart," as Mesopotamian laws designate a freely chosen mate (Stol 2016, 86 and 232). Cynthia

Edenburg (2009, 56) even detects in Deuteronomy "an interest in limiting parental discretion in resolving matters of sexual violation." But there is more.

Deuteronomy's interest exceeds matters of sexual violation. The law is consistent with a deeper view concerning parenting: giving a say to a young woman in the choice of the man whose children she will bear and raise, and also giving an enterprising man a way to eliminate rival suitors (Frymer-Kensky 1998, 85), in particular if the bride's family is wealthy. The fifty shekels, if they represent a fine, present a safeguard and a deterrent against the rape of a woman of superior status (Otto 2017, 1724). Elopement is thus a viable option only for grooms of superior social standing whose parents oppose the arrival of a lower status bride in the family. A husband whose family can afford the fine secures a more favorable economic context for a bride of lower status to raise children. Nevertheless, a lower status groom may view the need to pay the fine as an investment, the price to be paid to overrule parental opposition on both sides and force his way into a wealthy family. Having raped the daughter, he is in a position to negotiate the payment of the fine in installments or force his parents to find the necessary funds.

Parenting and Discipline

Discipline is a crucial element of parenting. The refrain about the jealous god who punishes a number of subsequent generations for the sins of a forefather is the transposition onto the divine sphere of a keen awareness of the challenge of transmitting parental values and valuables down the generations. Like gardens, children spontaneously produce weeds. Uncultivated, they become thorns and brambles. While education is a matter dealt with at great length in the biblical book of Proverbs, the case of the rebellious and drunken son (Deut 21:18–21) is paradigmatic for the entire educational aspect of parenting. The "fearful" aspect of Deuteronomy's pedagogy underlines the importance of raising children in preparation for their role in the preservation and perpetuation of the group's assets.

Both parents are to agree to seize (תפש) the problematic son and accuse him before the local elders of not listening to his parents. There is no need for the elders to investigate the truth of the charge (Dion 1993, 77). They merely rubber-stamp the parents' charge and order stoning to death by the adult males of the local community (Deut 21:18–19).

Deuteronomy also mentions both parents jointly when dealing with a slanderous husband (see above) and with particularly grave cases of idolatry, whether committed by the father's son or the mother's son (Deut

13:7). Exodus and Leviticus mention father and mother together in cases of parental disrespect (see Table 1). Does this mean that in Deuteronomy, fathers and mothers are "quietly treated as equals" (Hagedorn 2000, 105)?

Equality may be a slight exaggeration, but the involvement of the mother as well as the father in bringing the charge, the referral of the case to the elders, and the participation of all the local males in the execution is certainly an additional reason to discount the common designation of the biblical father as *pater familias*. The testimony of the mother besides that of the father fulfills the minimal requirement that a death sentence requires the testimony of two witnesses (Deut 17:7). It also dispenses the local elders from having to ascertain the validity of the parental accusations. That father and mother must speak with a single voice shows that the biblical father has no more sole right of life and death over his family than fathers had under Roman law (Thompson 2006) or in Hammurabi's code (§§168–168; see Otto 2016, 658; Marcus 1981, 43). Nonetheless, one should not infer that father and mother are equals.

The involvement of the father in the execution of his son is debated. The Greek text differs from the received Hebrew text in failing to render the word "all" (כל) to avoid the possible implication in the Hebrew text that the father is involved in the stoning by *all* the men (כל אנשי). The Septuagint renders this expression as "the men of the city" (οἱ ἄνδρες τῆς πόλεως), which can be read as sparing the father as much as the mother from the duty of throwing the first stone, as is required of the witnesses upon whose testimonies a death sentence is secured (Deut 17:7). If so, the uniqueness of parent-child relations is taken into account. The execution of the rebellious son is a special case that excuses parents from performing the execution of their problematic son, even though they were the ones to request it.

The execution of a son old enough to have developed traits of ingrained rebellion is a major loss for his kin. Nevertheless, this blood is the price to pay to cleanse the family honor (Hagedorn 2000). The text lists no shameful deeds specifically, because shame results from a fuzzy constellation of attitudes and traits of behavior rather than from precise actions. Nevertheless, the result is tangible economic losses: the squandering of the family's capital in the form of savings, revenues, and reputation. Requesting the loss of one's son prevents further damage for the parents who are held legally responsible for the behavior of their children, whatever the age of their offspring and regardless of whether or not the parents are still married. As the specifics of what confers honor and shame vary from one region to another, even within the Mediterranean ambit (Pina-Cabral 1989), it is up to the parents themselves to decide if the loss of a child is a more profitable option than the loss of honor. Just as the mother bird is to be left to escape, the parents are to agree to the loss of a problematic son. Rather than a mark of psychopathy (so Rotenberg and Diamond 1971), the sacrifice is the price to be paid to remove shame and protect the family's hard-won resources to ensure that other sons have the ability to care for their parents in their old age.

The aim of parenting is to turn the next generation into productive members and prevent a child from turning into a "non-contributing parasite" (Bellefontaine 1979, 21). The harshness of the Mediterranean climate and its irregular rainfall did not allow squandering behavior when endemic food scarcity as well as neonatal child and mother mortality were prevalent.

Conclusion: Deuteronomy's Shift from Procreation to Parenting

Biblical legal passages, Deuteronomy's in particular, consider the challenges and practical aspects of the Genesis mandate to "fructify, multiply, and fill the land" (Gen 1:28; 8:17). The Hebrew Bible is, indeed, the product of a patriarchal society in which mothers feature less often than fathers and often as ewes and mother birds, rather than women. This could seem to confirm the lawgivers' strong bias against women. Yet, in cases of adultery and fornication, both culprits, the male as much as the female, are liable to receive the death penalty. The aim of the sexual laws is to maximize the chances to produce offspring. Thus, women and mothers are shielded from abusive repudiation by the production of a bloodied sheet. The Deuteronomic lawgiver grants a rebellious daughter the means of overturning parental opposition with a guarantee against future repudiation, while a rebellious son is to be executed at the request of both of his parents.

Procreation without parenting defeats the point of procreation. The aim is to produce viable and thriving future generations. Procreation is but the first stage of the life-long process of parenting that involves both parents.

Works Cited

Barmash, Pamela. 2020. *The Laws of Hammurabi. At the Confluence of Royal and Scribal Traditions*. Oxford: Oxford University Press.
Bauer, Leonard. 1903. *Volksleben in Land der Bibel*. Leipzig, Wallmann.
Bellefontaine, Elizabeth. 1979. "Deuteronomy 21.18-21: Reviewing the Case of the Rebellious Son." *Journal for the Study of the Old Testament* 13:13–31.

Ben Zvi, Ehud. 2006. "Utopias, Multiple Utopias, and Why Utopias at All? The Social Roles of Utopian Visions in Prophetic Books within Their Historical Context." Pages 5–85 in *Utopia and Dystopia in Prophetic Literature*. Edited by Ehud Ben Zvi. Publications of the. Finnish Exegetical Society 92. Helsinki and Göttingen: Finnish Exegetical Society and Vandenhoeck & Ruprecht.

Berge, Kåre. 2012. "Literacy, Utopia and Memory: Is there a Public Teaching in Deuteronomy?" *Journal of Hebrew Scriptures* 12:1–19.

Bidmead, Julye. 2014. "Legal Status: Ancient Near East." Pages 403–408 in *The Oxford Encyclopedia of the Bible and Gender Studies 1*. Edited by J. M. O'Brien. Oxford and New York: Oxford University Press.

Brichto, Herbert Chanan. 1973. "Kin, Cult, Land and Afterlife: A Biblical Complex." *Hebrew Union College Annual* 44:1–54.

Cardascia, Guillaume. 1980. "Egalité et Inégalité des sexes en matière d'atteinte aux mœurs dans le Proche-Orient Ancient." *Die Welt des Orients* 11:7–16.

Case, M. L. 2020. "The Inheritance Injunction of Numbers 36: Zelophehad's Daughters and the Intersection of Ancestral Land and Sex Regulations." Pages 194–216 in *Sexuality and Law in the Torah*. Edited by Hilary Lipka and BruceWells. LHB/OTS 675. London: T.&T. Clark.

Cassin, Elena. 1987. "Virginité et stratégie du sexe." Pages 338–57 in *Le semblable et le différent: Symbolismes du pouvoir dans le Proche-Orient ancien*. Edited by Elena Cassin. Paris: La découverte.

Chapman, Cynthia R. 2016. *The House of the Mother. The Social Roles of Maternal Kin in Biblical Hebrew Narrative and Poetry*. Anchor Yale Reference Library. New Haven, CT: Yale University.

Coats, Georges W. 1972. "Widow's Rights: A Crux in the Structure of Genesis 38." *Catholic Biblical Quarterly* 34:461–66.

Cooper, Alan. 2012. "On Again Seething a Kid in its Mother's Milk." *Jewish Studies Internet Journal* 10: 109–43.

Davies, Eryl W. 1993. "The Inheritance of the Firstborn in Israel and the Ancient Near East." *Journal of Semitic Studies* 38: 175–91.

------. 2020. "Judah, Tamar, and the Law of Levirate Marriage." Pages 111–22 in Sexuality and Law in the Torah. Edited by Hilary Lipka and Bruce Wells. LHB/OTS 675. London: T.&T. Clark.

Delaney, Carol. 2001 "Cutting the Ties that Bind: The Sacrifice of Abraham and Patriarchal Kinship." Pages 445–67 in *Relative Values: Reconfiguring Kinship Studies*. Edited by Sarah Franklin and Susan McKinnon. Durham, N.C.: Duke University.

Dion, Paul E. 1993. "La procédure d'élimination du fils rebelle (Deut 21,18-21): Sens littéral et signes de développement juridique." Pages 73–82 in *Biblische Theologie und gesellschaftlicher Wandel*. Edited by Georg Braulik. Freiburg: Herder.

Edenburg, Cynthia 2009. "Ideology and Social Context of the Deuteronomic Women's Sex Laws (Deuteronomy 22:13–29)." *Journal of Biblical Literature* 128:43–60.

Evans-Grubbs, Judith. 1989. "Abduction Marriage in Antiquity: A Law of Constantine and its Social Context." *Journal of Roman Studies* 79:63–64.

Fleishman, Joseph. 2004. "Exodus 22:15–16 and Deuteronomy 22:28–29—Seduction and Rape or Elopement and Abduction Marriage?" Pages 59–73 in *The Jerusalem 2002 Conference Volume*. Edited by Hillel Gamoran. Binghamton NY: Global Academic Publishing.

French, Valerie. 2002. "History of Parenting: The Ancient Mediterranean World." Pages 345–76 in *Handbook of Parenting. Volume 2 Biology and Ecology of Parenting*. Edited by Marc H. Bornstein. Mahwah, NJ & London: Lawrence Erlbaum.

Frymer-Kensky, Tikva. 1998. "Virginity in the Bible." Pages 79–96 in *Gender and Law in the Bible and the Ancient Near East*. Edited by Victor H. Matthews, Tikva Frymer-Kensky and Bernard M. Levinson. JSOTSup 262. Sheffield: Sheffield Academic Press.

Hagedorn, Anselm C. 2000. "Guarding the Parents' Honour—Deuteronomy 21.18-21." *Journal for the Study of the Old Testament* 88:101–21.

Hylen, Susan E. 2019. "Women, Children, Slaves, and the Law of the New Testament Period." Pages 505–18 in *The Oxford Handbook of Biblical Law*. Edited by Pamela Barmash. Oxford: Oxford University Press.

Jacobs, Sandra 2018. "The Disposable Wife as Property in the Hebrew Bible." Pages 337–55 in *Gender and Methodology in the Ancient Near East*. Edited by Stephanie L. Budin, Megan Cifarelli, Agnès Garcia-Ventura and Adelina Millet Albà. Barcelona: Edicions de la Universitat de Barcelona.

Jonker, Gerdien. 1995. *The Topography of Remembrance: The Dead, Tradition and Collective Memory in Mesopotamia*. NUMEN 68. Leiden: Brill.

Lemos, Tracy M. 2017. *Violence and Personhood in Ancient Israel and Comparative Contexts*. Oxford: Oxford University Press.

London, Gloria. 2016. *Ancient Cookware from the Levant: An Ethnoarchaeological Perspective*. WANEM; Sheffield, Equinox Publishing Ltd.

Mace, David R. 1953. *Hebrew Marriage. A Sociological Study*. London: Epworth.

Marcus, David. 1981. "Juvenile Delinquency in the Bible and the Ancient Near East." *Journal of the American Near Eastern Society* 13:31–52.

Mathias, Steffan. 2020a. *Paternity, Progeny, and Perpetuation*. LHB/OTS 596. London: T.&T. Clark.

------. (2020b). "Reproducing Torah: Human and Divine Sexuality in the Book of Deuteronomy." Pages 217–38 in *Sexuality and Law in the Torah*. Edited by Hilary Lipka and Bruce Wells. LHB/OTS 675. London: T.&T. Clark.

Milstein, Sara J. 2019. "Will and (Old) Testament: Reconsidering the Roots of Deuteronomy 25,5-10." Pages 49–64 in *Writing, Rewriting, and*

Overwriting in the Books of Deuteronomy and the Former Prophets. Essays in Honour of Cynthia Edenburg. Edited by Ido Koch, Thomas Römer and Omer Sergi. BETL 304. Leuven: Peeters.

Ochshorn, Judith. 1981. *The Female Experience and the Nature of the Divine.* Bloomington: Indiana University Press.

Otto, Eckart. 2016. *Deuteronomium 12,1–23,15.* HThKAT. Freiburg: Herder.

––––––. (2017). *Deuteronomium 23,16–34,12.* HthKAT. Freiburg: Herder.

Paganini, Simone. 2010. "Gesetze für, gegen bzw. über Frauen im Buch Deuteronomium." *Protokol zur Bibel* 19:21–34.

Pietersen, Christo. 2021. "Women Treated as Property: The Influence of the Ancient Near East on the Covenant Code." *Journal for Semitics* 30:1–13. https://doi.org/10.25159/2663-6573/8476.

Pina-Cabral, Joao de. 1989. "The Mediterranean as a Category of Regional Comparison: A Critical View." *Current Anthropology* 30:399–406.

Pressler, Carolyn. 1991. *The View of Women Found in the Deuteronomic Family Laws.* BZAW 216. Berlin: de Gruyter.

Rotenberg, Mordechai and Bernard L. Diamond. 1971. "The Biblical Conception of Psychopathy: The Law of the Rebellious Son." *Journal for the History of the Behavioral Sciences* 7:29–38.

Schlüter, Sarah P. 2021. "Madawada. Portrait of a Businesswoman?" Pages 145–53 in *Distant Worlds Journal Special Issue 3.* Edited by Beatrice Baragli, Patrizia Heindl, Polly Lohmann and Sarah P. Schlüter. Heidelberg: Propylaeum. https://doi.org/10.11588/propylaeum.886.c11956.

Stol, Marten. 2016. *Women in the Ancient Near East.* Berlin: de Gruyter.

Thompson, E. P. 1978. "The Grid of Inheritance." Pages 328–60 in *Family and Inheritance.* Edited by Jack Goody, Joan Thirsk and E. P. Thompson. Cambridge: Cambridge University Press.

Thompson, Steven. 2006. "Was Ancient Rome a Dead Wives Society? What did the Roman Paterfamilias Get Away With?" *Journal of Family History* 31:3–27.

Tsukimoto, Akio. 1985. *Untersuchungen zur Totenpflege (kispum) im alten Mesopotamien.* Neukirchen-Vluyn: Neukirchener Verlag.

Verburg, Jelle. 2019. "Women's Property Rights in Egypt and the Law of Levirate Marriage in the LXX." *Zeitschrift für die alttestamentliche Wissenschaft* 131: 595–97.

Weinfeld, Moshe. 1972. *Deuteronomy and the Deuteronomic School.* Oxford: Clarendon Press.

Weisberg, Dvora E. 2009. *Levirate Marriage and the Family in Ancient Judaism.* Waltham: Brandeis University Press.

Wells, Bruce. 2020. "Review of Law and Gender in the Ancient Near East and the Hebrew Bible, by Ilan Peled," New York: Routledge, 2020. *Review of Biblical Literature* 12.

––––––. 2013 "Is it Law or Religion? Legal Motivations in Deuteronomic and Neo-Babylonian Texts." Pages 287–309 in *Law and Religion in the Eastern*

Mediterranean: From Antiquity to Early Islam. Edited by Anselm C. Hagedorn and Reinhard G. Kratz. Oxford: Oxford University Press.

Wenham, Gordon J. 1972. "B^etûlāh: a Girl of Marriageable Age." *Vetus Testamentum* 22: 326–48.

Wright, Jacob L. 2011. "Making a Name for Oneself: Martial Valor, Heroic Death, and Procreation in the Hebrew Bible." *Journal for the Study of the Old Testament* 36:131–62.

Ziskind, Jonathan R. (1996). "The Missing Daughter in Leviticus XVIII." *Vetus Testamentum* 46:125–30.

About the Author

Philippe Guillaume is a trained agriculturist and a lecturer at the Biblical Institute of the University of Berne (Switzerland). His current research focuses on the ancient Near East economy and agrarian matters related to biblical texts and laws, in particular in Deuteronomy, with a volume on *The Economy of Deuteronomy's Core* (Sheffield: Equinox Publishing Ltd, 2022).

Chapter 13
Deuteronomy as Utopia: New Possibilities for Reading an Old Friend/Foe

Madhavi Nevader

Abstract

Scholars have long held Deuteronomy up as a classic example of utopian literature in the Hebrew Bible but have not always rigorously engaged with the implications of doing so for the interpretation of the book. This chapter sets out to redress the imbalance by asking two fundamental questions: can we in fact read Deuteronomy as a utopia and what happens if we do? In response to the first, the chapter demonstrates that Deuteronomy exhibits many of the structural features typical of a literary utopia and can consequently be read as such. In response to the second, it goes on to explore some of the hermeneutical dividends for reading, utilizing work done by Utopian Studies on the social and political function of utopias. While the interpretive outcomes are manifold, reading the book as utopia brings into particular focus how Deuteronomy works as critical literature, and how its alternative, imagined world contributes to wider discussions of ancient political discourse and theory.

Keywords: utopia, Deuteronomy, political discourse, utopian literature, political theory, Utopian Studies

1. Introduction

To read Deuteronomy as utopia – a term coined in the early decades of the sixteenth century by the Englishman, Sir Thomas More (1989) – is to embark on one epic, anachronistic exercise in academic play. But it is also to play a game well known in Biblical Studies in so far as Deuteronomy, or aspects thereof, is often held up as one of the clearest examples of utopian thinking in the Hebrew Bible (e.g. Hölscher 1922; Lohfink 1993; Collins 2000; Hagedorn 2004; Levinson 2006; Berge 2012). The rules, however, are very fuzzy indeed – on the one hand because scholars use the term utopia with little precision and on the other because rarely is the labelling of Deuteronomy as "utopia" or "utopian" the result of critical engagement with the concept. My aim in this chapter is, therefore, quite straightforward. First and foremost, I will demonstrate that we *can* read Deuteronomy as a utopia in a strict(ish) literary sense.

Above and beyond the text having utopian aspects or some of its legislation striving for a social ideal, I will suggest that the book of Deuteronomy exhibits many, if not all, of the structural and conceptual categories that come to define "utopia" as a literary genre. But to what end? I will use the second part of this chapter to explore what any of it might mean for interpreters and for this particular book. For interpreters, reading Deuteronomy as utopia can raise new(ish) questions about impulse, audience, and function. For the book, reading Deuteronomy as utopia provides a new vantage point from which to examine and to understand this most complicated piece of writing.

2. Utopia: A Problem of Definitions

First to definitions. Here we run immediately into a problematic truism: there are as many definitions of utopia as there are manuscripts of Deuteronomy, ranging from a particular type of text (Kumar 2003) to a Weberian ideal type (Uhlenbruch 2015), from wish for a better life (e.g. Giesecke 2003) to a feeling of estrangement (e.g. Suvin 1979). To sort through the definitional quagmire, Stephen Schweitzer (2007, 14) has helpfully offered an analogy based on how we now differentiate between "apocalypse" (genre), "apocalyptic" (ideology), "apocalypticism" (sociological movement), such that by "utopia" we mean the genre, by "utopian" we mean the ideology, and finally, by "utopianism" we mean a (sociological) movement. With respect to a definition of utopia as a literary genre, I have found the one proposed by Gerrie Snyman (2016) most helpful. For him, a utopia is a *literary* text that constructs an *imaginary* world as a disjunctive *alternative* to the contemporaneous *social reality* of the targeted audience who experiences their reality as *deficient* – a fictional reality in which an imagined community is thought to be at a better place – although not *perfect* – than the one the readers currently inhabit. (Snyman 2016, 43)

The definition is careful and reflects the many voices from, and concerns raised within, the now multidisciplinary field of Utopian Studies (Levitas 2013; Marks, Wagner-Lawlor, and Vieira 2022; Sargent 2022). At its most basic, for something to be a utopia, it must be a *literary* text that creates an alternative or imaginary world ("social reality") deemed better than that inhabited by the reader. Importantly, utopia is *not* perfection-seeking, and in not being so, we can and must distinguish the constructed ideal society of a utopia from that of the nostalgic idealism of Golden Age thinking. Both are concerned with ideal or model iterations of a good society (eutopia, "good place"), but they differ on a temporal, perhaps even orientational horizon. Golden Age thinking is a return (or longing to return) *to* something that was once purportedly experienced in the past (e.g. Eden or David *redivivus* traditions in the Hebrew Bible). Utopia, by contrast, is never a return. It is always a turn to an alternative–regardless of whether set in the past, present, or future.

One of the strengths of Snyman's definition is that it accounts for the close relationship that has developed since the mid-twentieth century between Utopian Studies and science fiction (Jameson 2005; Moylan 2018; Suvin 1979), as well as its phoenix-like re-emergence as a viable political and philosophical discourse within our secular/post-secular, liberal/post-liberal, colonial/postcolonial world (e.g. Moylan and Baccolini 2007; Levitas 2013; Ashcroft 2017). To the contours of this debate and the possibilities deriving from it for reading Deuteronomy, I return in due course. But beyond a basic function shared with utopia *qua* genre, I think it is possible to demonstrate that Deuteronomy shares many of the *structural features* on display in traditional literary iterations of utopia.

3. Deuteronomy as a Literary Utopia

Because utopia as term, literary genre, and concept has undergone manifold transformations since More's work (Hölscher 1996), it is less common to define utopia by its literary attributes, as to do so might leave certain texts outside the umbrella of consideration (Vieira 2010). Nevertheless, there are a number of features that tend to recur in classic, literary iterations of utopia, which will aid us in our initial foray into

Deuteronomy's utopian nature (Pinheiro 2006; Schweitzer 2007, 14–27; Vieira 2010). These include: 1) a basic narrative structure of journey – tour – explanation of ideal society – presumed return; 2) spatial, and in some instances temporal, displacement; 3) human, as opposed to divine, orientation and agency; 4) the careful and heavily organized nature of the ideal society with special attention paid in societal systems and hierarchies; 5) a particular interest in the political organization of society.

3.1 Literary Structure

The first structural feature is a relatively fixed literary structure: a utopia normally pictures a journey (by sea, land, or air) of an individual to an unknown place (an island, a country, or a continent); once there, the utopian traveler is usually offered a guided tour of the society, and provided with an explanation of its social, political, economic, and religious organization. Looking at Deuteronomy from this perspective, we are not off to a great start – it (unlike, say 1 Enoch or Ezekiel's temple vision in Ezek 40–48) is not a journey or a tour. And yet, the events that transpire in Deuteronomy take place while Israel and Moses are on the journey of all journeys. More pointedly, while Moses is not transported to a specific place, the entire narrative fiction of Deuteronomy is that he is recalling/teaching material that he obtained having journeyed *up* a mountain, a mountain which incidentally is said to be beyond the wilderness (Exod 3:1). No one greets Moses atop the mountain, but the Torah that he receives is recounted to him directly by Yhwh and endeavors to cover the full breadth of Israelite society – a tour of society, albeit with a legal guide (for Torah, see chs. 3 and 9 in this volume). Finally, the very premise of Deuteronomy – a retelling of the law to Israel in a formal speech – functions to provide an explanation of the social, political, economic, and religious organization of society to Israel as audience.

3.2 Spatial and Temporal Displacement

One of the grammatical building blocks of More's coined neologism "utopia" is *ouk topos* – no place – which points to the second aspect of classical, literary utopias: radical spatial displacement. Here we are on safer ground with Deuteronomy. As already noted, Horeb is "beyond the wilderness," the closest the Bible gets to "no man's land." More importantly, while the mountain is named, it is outside the land and geographically other – neither in Egypt nor the promised land; neither Sinai nor Zion. Explicit temporal displacement will not become a defining aspect of utopian literature until the Enlightenment, but Deuteronomy's own *temporal* ambiguities are suggestive as well: it is a text set in the distant past, but ultimately presented as a speech delivered in the present about a society that will come to be only in the future.

3.3 Human Orientation

The spatial and temporal dislocation of Deuteronomy does not by any reckoning render it irrational, like Aristophanes' *Nephelokokkugia*, "Cloud-cuckoo-land." To be sure, Deuteronomy displays elements of the "idealistic": it assumes, for example, that there will never be anyone in need amongst the community (Deut 15:4; for a practical, non-utopian option of reading of the book, see ch. 11 in this volume). But the ideal is nonetheless soundly anchored in a believable space-time continuum. With Deuteronomy, it is worth remembering that the point of the Torah given by Yhwh is to order large swathes of Israelite society, ranging from slavery and women to judicial procedure and licit religious practice. The breadth of the instruction, while not fully comprehensive, nonetheless firmly grounds it in the lives of the Israel to whom it is addressed and who are envisioned as that group who will enact the world envisioned in the text.

3.4 Social Organization

A fourth characteristic of the classical literary utopia, speculative discourse on the organization of society, strikes me as the very *raison d'être* of Deut 12–26. Deuteronomy is not simply a compendium of legal material (see e.g. Wells 2008 and ch. 3 in this volume), nor a scientific text manipulated by the wider historical story into which it has now been set. Rather, it endeavors to structure and to organize Israel, defining hierarchies and systematizing the interactions of different players within the larger chess board of society. Deuteronomy organizes its society around the demands made by and obedience to divinely revealed Torah, which in turn comes to dominate a complex network of peoples and institutions. In this way the insistence on "One God – One Cult – One Nation" (Kratz and Spieckermann 2010) works to reconfigure the various institutions that define Israel according to a (radically) different paradigm of social organization: different both in terms of what comes before it in narrative sequence (Levinson 1997) and what archaeology tells us was the lived reality of Iron Age II–III Judah (e.g. Stern 2010). For our present purposes, the importance of this project is not its content, but that it is achieved through careful and purposeful systematization and legislation, effectively organizing the nation to a tee.

3.5 Political Structuring

Finally, utopias show a particular concern for and interest in describing the political organization of the society deemed ideal (Destrée, Opsomer, and Roskam 2021, viii), which brings us directly to Deut 16:18–18:22, the so-called "Law of Offices." Though scholars cannot seem to agree on the date of the unit or how precisely it works, most appear to read it as a political "constitution" of one sort or another (e.g. McBride 1987; Lohfink 1993; Miller 2005; Wilson 2005; Levinson 2006; Strawn 2018; for an exception, see Edelman 2021). While the scholarly terminology may be anachronistic, Deut 16:18–18:22 remains the only text in the Hebrew Bible to lay out comprehensively the manner in which Israel ought to be politically ordered. The players (judge, king, priest, prophet) are traditional and what one would expect of a small, Levantine city-state, but only in this biblical text are their duties, privileges, limits, and connections to one another set out as fixed and unchanging.

So, if I am correct that Deuteronomy displays many, if not all of the core features of a literary utopia, then I think our conclusion is pretty straightforward: Deuteronomy can be read – in addition to many other things – as a utopia in the strict, "classical" sense. It is not that Deuteronomy has utopian aspects or adopts a utopian outlook or even that it is painting a picture of an "ideal Israel." Deuteronomy can be read as a literary utopia. But... so what? Or better yet, what are the hermeneutical dividends of reading it as such?

4. Hermeneutical Dividends

In the first instance, identifying Deuteronomy as a utopia opens up a number of new possibilities regarding what precisely Deuteronomy is doing (*qua* text, *qua* utopia). Indeed, by asking, as many do outside Biblical Studies, "What are utopias and what do they accomplish?" we can ask those same questions of our reading of Deuteronomy. And so, if most would agree that utopias are exploratory thought experiments and as such are radical polemic, then we ought to think about what that means for our understanding of Deuteronomy. Whether we read Deuteronomy's utopia as cultural imagination (Ricœur 1986), social dreaming (Sargent 1994; Sargisson 2007), or desire for a better world (Levitas 1990), approaching the text from a utopian framework opens up a whole myriad of possible readings of and for Deuteronomy.

4.1 The Implications of Alternative Worlds: Deuteronomy between History, Literature, and "Reality"

Whether as imagination, dream, or desire, most would agree that a utopia depicts an ideal form of social life which, by definition, does not currently exist for/in the world of the author(s) (Goodwin and Taylor 1982). In my mind, this has a whole array of consequences and possibilities for Deuteronomy, but let's begin with the most obvious: If Deuteronomy is a utopia, then its world does not exist. And if its world does not exist, then its ideal society is not one that we should expect to see necessarily "in place" at any point in Israelite or Judahite history. For Deuteronomy in particular, one of the most important implications of this rupture between text and history is that we are forced to separate the book's envisioned society from the putative cult reform of King Josiah as narrated in 2 Kgs 22–23, which scholars, since the work of Wilhelm de Wette in the early nineteenth century, have taken as mirror images of one another: either Josiah is putting in place the world of Deuteronomy or the world of Deuteronomy is a retrojection of Josiah's reform. To be sure, the overall structure of the so-called "Deuteronomistic History" (Deut–2 Kgs) pivots on the connection between Deuteronomy and Josiah as the book that legitimates the royal reform (Römer 2005; see Berge 2016), but we ought to appreciate it as an intentional literary and theological connection, not a "historical" one. More crucially still, the utopian-ness (let's pretend that's a word) of Deuteronomy makes the historical reflection, let alone historical reconstruction, impossible, since it is purposefully describing a world that is *not*.

Unmooring Deuteronomy's alternative society from history does not require that the book be late or early – scholars have quite different positions on this thorny issue (see Pakkala 2009, 2011; MacDonald 2010) – but it suggests that Deuteronomy is not intended to be a record of society as lived at any one point and, as such, should not be treated as a sort of archaeological, if textual, artifact by which we can reconstruct Israelite/Judahite history. One opportunity this affords is the ability to appreciate that Deuteronomy is *literature* and as literature, Deuteronomy is *fiction* (see Boer 1997; Berge 2012). Doing so does not excuse us from asking historical or critical questions of the text. Nevertheless, allowing Deuteronomy to be fiction may, in fact, emancipate it from some of the constraints we have imposed upon it by making it or some earlier form of it (its *Urtext*) *only* a "law code" (e.g. Noth 1981), treaty text (e.g. Kline 1963), constitution (e.g. McBride 1987; Miller 2005), or even more generously, instruction (Edelman 2021).

One particular vantage point that opens up to us is reading Deuteronomy as polemic literature, since as Bill Ashcroft notes, "all utopias are critical" (Ashcroft 2007, 149). In positing an alternative better world (*eu-topos*), utopia takes a critical stance against the world known to and experienced by its authors, thus engaging "in a significant polemic with the dominant culture" (Bauman 1976, 47). But surely here is where history finally bares its fangs. How, after all, can we know what the utopia of Deuteronomy is critiquing if we do not know when it was written – the historical given known to and experienced by its authors? Let's map the problem out using the "Law of the King" (Deut 17:14–20), Deuteronomy's unique vision for the future Israelite monarch. The "law" pivots around three injunctions: that the appointed king may not be a foreigner but chosen from amongst the community (Deut 17:15); that he not accumulate excess horses, women, or wealth (Deut 17:16–17); and that his days be filled with the study of Torah so that he remain pious and not exalt himself over his brethren (Deut 17:19–20). Deuteronomy's royal vision is by all accounts idiosyncratic, leading most to read it as a critique of the larger theological underpinnings of the royal institution (e.g. the king as warrior, guardian of the realm, and cult sponsor; Levinson 2001) alive in Israel and Judah as it was elsewhere in the wider Ancient Near East. But how are we supposed to date the critique? Are the text's idiosyncrasies a protest against the supposed foreign dalliances of Solomon (e.g. Sweeney 1995) or the kowtowing and political aspirations of the "wicked" Manasseh in the seventh century BCE (e.g. Levinson 2001)? Are they a late monarchic response to Assyrian imperial hegemony (e.g. Wazana 2016) or a post-exilic pushback against Persian imperial hegemony (e.g. Nicholson 2006; Wilson 2017)? Or, are they an exilic attempt to recalibrate power away from kingship toward the more charismatic institution of prophecy (e.g. Lohfink 1993)? History baring its fangs indeed!

Raising this thorny issue is not intended to bog us down in the vicissitudes of scholarly reconstructions, nor do I wish to imply that reading Deuteronomy as utopia is a cure-all for resolving or ignoring complicated issues of textual dating. But I do believe that thinking about Deuteronomy as a utopia can help us understand better the/a target of the book's criticism. So, while many tend to read Deuteronomy oriented outwardly as reacting against the threat of foreign, colonial domination (e.g. Otto 1999) or worse, advancing beyond "oriental kingship" (McConville 1998), the utopian vantage point may bring something much closer to home into critical view. Interestingly, the emancipatory discourse that governs colonized and postcolonial utopia writing (Ashcroft 2017; Sargent 2010) is *not* at work in Deuteronomy. The ways in which kingship is reconfigured in Deuteronomy is, instead, more emblematic of authors writing against the dominant culture of their own society. I am less convinced than others that this allows us to locate the origin of the book in the (pre-exilic) North (e.g. Davies 2021; contrast Edenburg and Müller 2015) or to read it as an intra-Israelite ethnicity debate in response to the influx of post-722, Northern refugees (e.g. Crouch 2014).

The nature of utopia writing allows us to appreciate that Deuteronomy is writing against dominant Judahite culture, making its world with a Torah-gagged king a radical upheaval of native Judahite royal theology (e.g. Isa 11:1–4; Ps 2; 18; 45; 72; 89), not simply a disavowal of foreign political domination. Is Deuteronomy's alternative world one with an Assyrian or Babylonian king, the very image of God (Machinist 2006; Winter 2008), on the throne? No. But neither is it one with a traditional Judahite king, Yhwh's anointed son, on the throne either! The point I'm driving at here has less to do with the when or even necessarily the who of Deuteronomy's polemic, than it does with the impulse driving it along. Where readings oriented towards the rejection of the "foreign"/"imperial" in Deuteronomy make the text fundamentally reactive, reading Deuteronomy as utopia allows us to consider the radical ways in which its authors are also overturning long held, foundational tenets of Judahite theology in the process of their utopia writing.

Kings and dates (even dating Kings!) to one side, I think there remain two interpretive hurdles in our discussion of Deuteronomy as utopia that need addressing: the temporal setting of the book and the question of intended achievability. First to consider is time. If Deuteronomy is a utopia, in using the past as its canvas for creating an alternative world, it is temporally oriented against the grain of non-biblical utopias that dream predominantly in the present or future. But as Steven J. Schweitzer's work (2007) on Chronicles or Molly Zahn's work (2023) on the Temple Scroll has shown, the past is precisely where our scribes go to construct their alternative worlds and histories.

In turning to the past, the authors of Chronicles or the Temple Scroll are not interested in rewriting history or explaining why the present is as it is, but rather are in the business of articulating how the past ought to have been by constructing an ideal that never was (Schweitzer 2007, 30; Zahn 2023, 396). We ought to understand Deuteronomy as engaging in a very similar exercise, which in turn allows us to explain the text's temporal orientation in two mutually informative ways. On the one hand, set in the distant past and anchored (likely legitimized) by the figure of Moses, Deuteronomy is a very fine example of the antiquarian tendency that comes to dominate Near Eastern literature starting in the second half of the first millennium BCE (Beaulieu 1994; compare the literature that develops around the figure of Enoch). On the other, Deuteronomy is playing with time in a profound way. It opens up the distant past *not* as an ideal now lost (compare, e.g., Jer 7 or Ezek 16), but as a space it manipulates in order to construct a counterfactual Israel.

This brings us to the question of achievability, where we run into *the* question that plagues scholars of Deuteronomy and utopia alike. Many insist that utopias fulfil their radical, social function only because they are unrealized, "a dream unrealized, but not unrealizable" (Déjacque 1971, 131). Indeed, some have suggested that there is fine line between utopianism and totalitarianism, which disappears precisely at the point that efforts are made to actualize or realize utopia (see further Rothstein 2003; Villoro 2006). As such issues relate to Deuteronomy, we know that the counterfactual world of Deuteronomy never became Israel or Judah's lived experience, and attempts in history to actualize it have, at best, fallen short, at worst, led to unspeakable atrocity (Deist 1994; Mohawk 2000).

To address the lesser of these two problems, I wonder whether returning again to Deuteronomy as literature may provide a means by which to realize Deuteronomy's utopia without realizing Deuteronomy's utopia. Here I turn to the work of Hannah Liss (2006) on Ezekiel's temple vision (Ezek 40–48). She suggests that the fictive nature of Ezek 40–48 is the key to unlocking the temple restoration envisioned therein. By reading the vision of the rebuilt temple, the temple is rebuilt in the mind of the text's reader as she progresses through the text verse by verse. The question of whether the temple is *meant* to be rebuilt then becomes moot since it textually *is*. This strikes me as a very helpful way of addressing the question of achievability in Deuteronomy. Did its authors hope for the utopia to be realized? This question we *cannot* and will never be able to answer despite scholarly suggestions otherwise (e.g. Markl 2018; Miller 2005; Stordalen 2023). More fundamentally, the question itself is the wrong one to ask. The point is that Deuteronomy's utopia *is* realized in the process of reading the text and is kept ever alive by virtue of the command to study and teach the Torah – that is, the utopia – constantly and in perpetuity (Deut 6:6–9).

4.2 Deuteronomy as Political Theory

The final topic to consider is what consequence reading Deuteronomy as utopia has for our understanding of the book's political discourse. Barbara Goodwin and Keith Taylor note that "Any utopia fulfilling the condition of social criticism through the depiction of an alternative society must be regarded as the stuff of political theory" (Goodwin and Taylor 1982, 29). If they are correct, then I think we need to think afresh about Deuteronomy as some form of political theory. Here Classics is well ahead of us. In his examination of ancient utopian writing, Doyne Dawson (1992, 7–8) divides the corpus into a two-part typology. The first consists of utopian works of myth, fantasy, or messianism, which Dawson dismisses as deriving from "some misty Indo-European past ...[with] analogies the world over" (Dawson 1992, 7). Problems of distant origin and ubiquity notwithstanding, Dawson's first type does not map well onto the world of Deuteronomy (though interestingly, it does onto other texts in the Hebrew Bible, e.g. Ezek 37). His second type, texts as political utopianism, is, however, more instructive. Here Dawson identifies texts whose purpose is to set out a program for an ideal city-state, which in doing so critique the existing institutions or leaders of the day, but also act as a more oblique model for political speculation. Plato's *Republic* is the pinnacle of the type, though Dawson sees it also at work in the Cynic and Stoic utopias of the third century CE.

It strikes me that even the most cursory reading of Deuteronomy allows us to bring the book into Dawson's discussion not simply of ancient utopias, but of political utopianism in particular. To be sure, Deuteronomy does not set out to organize a city-state in the Hellenic mold, but, as discussed earlier, it remains a program for the ideal political configuration of Israel, be it as "polity" or "people." I have only touched on the critique underlying Deuteronomy's model king, but the many other institutions addressed – judiciary, priesthood, prophecy, sacrificial practice, cult objects, divination – all pivot on a critical reconfiguration of what we know was normative practice in Judah (Stavrakopoulou and Barton 2010). Because that reconfiguration has for so long been associated with the "religious" reforms of King Josiah, it is less common to read it as political speculation beyond its possible contribution to the history of political thought (e.g. Levinson 2006; Miller 2011) or western constitutionalism (e.g. McBride 1987; Lohfink 1993). But the stuff that Deuteronomy is made of – its comprehensive program for a polity – makes it, in the first place, political utopianism (as argued by Dawson), and in the second, *complex* political theory (as argued by Goodwin and Taylor).

4.3 Deuteronomy and the Wider Utopian Tradition

Let us turn the table of hermeneutical gain and look briefly at the possible contribution of Deuteronomy to wider discussions of utopia. It is common to speak of Homer's epic poems as "pre-texts" of the utopian genre in literature (Pradeau 2000, 83), acting as literary and conceptual building blocks for the genre as it will come to develop. Without necessarily pivoting Deuteronomy to Greece (e.g. Hagedorn 2004) or claiming its temporal or epistemological priority (e.g. Berman 2011), it seems possible that we can cautiously suggest that Deuteronomy also acts as a pre-text of utopian literature. Utopian literature may begin "properly" with Plato, but the circumstances of the scribes, authors, and theologians responsible for Deuteronomy were such that they, too, turned to counterfactual world building to reflect not only on the ideal way in which a society might be governed but also as a means of moving beyond the very fact that their own differed so profoundly. In this respect, Deuteronomy provides us with the beginnings of a semitic utopian tradition that will have as long an afterlife as the Greek and one which Utopian Studies itself may find instructive to explore.

5. Conclusion

I began this chapter with the admission that to read Deuteronomy as a utopia is an anachronistic exercise. Indeed, to speak of anything as a utopia before the sixteenth century would fall foul of the anachronism police! Nevertheless, many within Utopian Studies acknowledge that there is a rich, antecedent utopian tradition that comes from the Greco-Roman world. I have suggested that this antecedent tradition should also include the book of Deuteronomy. Quite apart from using the tools of Utopian Studies to unpick the problems of Deuteronomy or arguing that the text displays utopian impulses (e.g. hope, social dreaming, world construction), I've proposed that the book can, in fact, be read as a literary utopia. This needn't be to the exclusion of the other functions that the book may serve (e.g. instructional speech). But Deuteronomy displays all of the formal features of literary utopias, which brings with it a number of hermeneutical dividends. Chief amongst these is an appreciation of Deuteronomy as critical literature, which allows us as readers to appreciate its alternate, counterfactual vision of Israel and the fundamentally political nature of the book's world construction. Deuteronomy does not display the same theoretical discourse as Plato, but it remains as complex a form of political utopianism as we have from the Greek world.

Robert R. Wilson once wrote: "Deuteronomy is intended to be a polity, a constitution for an actual state, and scholars are not free to ignore the implications of that observation" (Wilson 2005, 123). I hope that I've shown exactly the *opposite* – that Deuteronomy is intended to be a utopia, a dream of an alternative state. Scholars can, of course, ignore the implications, but our understanding of Deuteronomy is all the richer if we, as students and scholars alike, do not.

Works Cited

Ashcroft, Bill. 2007. "Critical Utopias." *Textual Practice* 21:411–31.

———. 2017. *Utopianism in Postcolonial Literatures*. London: Routledge.
Bauman, Zygmunt. 1976. *Socialism: The Active Utopia*. London: Allen and Unwin.
Beaulieu, Paul-Alain. 1994. "Antiquarianism and the Concern for the Past in the Neo-Babylonian Period." *Bulletin of the Canadian Society for Mesopotamian Studies* 28:37–42.
Berge, Kåre. 2012. "Literacy, Utopia and Memory: Is there a Public Teaching in Deuteronomy?" *Journal of Hebrew Scriptures* 12:1–19.
———. 2016. "Mystified Authority: Legitimating Leadership Through 'Lost Books.'" Pages 41–56 in *Leadership, Social Memory and Judean Discourse in the Fifth-Second Centuries BCE*. Edited by Diana V. Edelman and Ehud Ben Zvi. Sheffield: Equinox Publishing Ltd.
Berman, Joshua. 2011. *Created Equal: How the Bible Broke with Ancient Political Thought*. New York: Oxford University Press.
Boer, Roland. 1997. *Novel Histories: The Fiction of Biblical Criticism*. Sheffield: Sheffield Academic Press.
Collins, John J. 2000. "Models of Utopia in the Biblical Tradition." Pages 51–67 in *A Wise and Discerning Mind: Essays in Honor of Burke O. Long*. Edited by Saul M. Olyan and Robert C. Culley. Brown Judaic Studies 325. Providence, RI: Brown Judaic Studies.
Crouch, Carly L. 2014. *The Making of Israel: Cultural Diversity in the Southern Levant and the Formation of Ethnic Identity in Deuteronomy*. Vetus Testamentum Supplements 162. Leiden: Brill.
Davies, Philip R. 2021. "From Where Did Deuteronomy Originate?" Pages 13–24 in *Deuteronomy in the Making*. Edited by Diana Edelman, Benedetta Rossi, Kåre Berge, and Philippe Guillaume. Beihefte zur Zeitschrift für die alttestamentische Wissenschaft 533. Berlin: De Gruyter.
Dawson, Doyne. 1992. *Cities of the Gods: Communist Utopias in Greek Thought*. Oxford: Oxford University Press.
Deist, Ferdinand E. 1994. "The Dangers of Deuteronomy: A Page from the Reception History of the Book." Pages 13–29 in *Studies in Deuteronomy: In Honour of C. J. Labuschagne on the Occasion of his 65th Birthday*. Edited by F. García-Martínez, A. Hilhorst, J. T. A. G. M. van Ruiten, and A. S. van der Woude. Supplements to Vetus Testamentum 53. Leiden: Brill.
Déjacque, Joseph. 1971. *A bas les chefs: écrits libertaires* (1847–1863). Edited by Valentine Pelosse. Paris: Champ Libre.
Destrée, Pierre, Jan Opsomer, and Geert Roskam, eds. 2021. *Utopias in Ancient Thought*. Berlin: De Gruyter.
Edelman, Diana V. 2021. "Deuteronomy as the Instructions of Moses and Yhwh vs. a Framed Legal Core." Pages 25–75 in *Deuteronomy in the Making*. Edited by Diana Edelman, Benedetta Rossi, Kåre Berge, and Philippe Guillaume. Beihefte zur Zeitschrift für die alttestamentische Wissenschaft 533. Berlin: De Gruyter.

Edenburg, Cynthia, and Reinhard Müller. 2015. "A Northern Provenance for Deuteronomy? A Critical Review." *Hebrew Bible and Ancient Israel* 2:148–61.

Giesecke, Annette Lucia. 2003. "Homer's Eutopolis: Epic Journeys and the Search for an Ideal Society." *Utopian Studies* 14:23–40.

Goodwin, Barbara, and Keith Taylor. 1982. *The Politics of Utopia: A Study in Theory and Practice*. Reprinted 2009 edition. Bern: Peter Lang.

Hagedorn, Anselm C. 2004. *Between Moses and Plato: Individual and Society in Deuteronomy and Ancient Greek Law*. Forschungen zur Religion und Literatur des Alten und Neuen Testaments 204. Göttingen: Vandenhoeck & Ruprecht.

Hölscher, Gustav. 1922. "Komposition und Ursprung des Deuteronomiums." *Zeitschrift für die alttestamentliche Wissenschaft* 40:161–255.

Hölscher, Lucian. 1996. "Utopie." *Utopian Studies* 65–7:1.

Jameson, Fredric. 2005. *Archaeologies of the Future: The Desire Called Utopia and Other Science Fictions*. London: Verso.

Kline, Meredith G. 1963. *Treat of the Great King: The Covenant Structure of Deuteronomy – Studies and Commentary*. Grand Rapids, MI: Eerdmans.

Kratz, Reinhard G., and Hermann Spieckermann, eds. 2010. *One God – One Cult – One Nation: Archaeological and Biblical Perspectives*. Beihefte fur Zeitschrift für die alttestamentische Wissenschaft 405. Berlin: De Gruyter.

Kumar, Krisham. 2003. "Aspects of the Western Utopian Tradition." *History of the Human Sciences* 16:63–77.

Levinson, Bernard M. 1997. *Deuteronomy and the Hermeneutics of Legal Innovation*. New York: Oxford University Press.

------. 2001. "The Reconceptualization of Kingship in Deuteronomy and the Deuteronomistic History's Transformation of Torah." *Vetus Testamentum* 51:511–34.

------. 2006. "The First Constitution: Rethinking the Origins of Rule of Law and Separation of Powers in Light of Deuteronomy." *Cardozo Law Review* 27:1,853–88.

Levitas, Ruth. 1990. *The Concept of Utopia*. New York: Philip Allan.

------. 2013. *Utopia as Method: The Imaginary Reconstitution of Society*. London: Palgrave Macmillan.

Liss, Hannah. 2006. "'Describe the Temple to the House of Israel': Preliminary Remarks on the Temple Vision in the Book of Ezekiel and the Question of the Fictionality in Priestly Literatures." Pages 122–43 in *Utopia and Dystopia in Prophetic Literature*. Edited by Ehud Ben Zvi. Publications of the Finnish Exegetical Society 92. Göttingen: Vandenhoeck & Ruprecht.

Lohfink, Norbert. 1993. "Distribution of the Functions of Power: The Laws Concerning Public Office in Deut 16:18–18:22." Pages 336–52 in *A Song of Power and the Power of Song: Essays on the Book of Deuteronomy*. Edited by D. L. Christensen. Winona Lake, IN: Eisenbrauns.

MacDonald, Nathan. 2010. "Issues and Questions in the Dating of Deuteronomy: A Response to Juha Pakkala." *Zeitschrift für die alttestamentliche Wissenschaft* 122:431–35.

Machinist, Peter. 2006. "Kingship and Divinity in Imperial Assyria." Pages 152–88 in *Text, Artifact, and Image: Revealing Ancient Israelite Religion*. Edited by Gary Beckman and Theodore J. Lewis. Providence RI: Brown Judaic Studies.

Markl, Dominik. 2018. "Deuteronomy's 'Anti-King': Historicized Etiology or Political Program?" Pages 165–87 in *Changing Faces of Kingship in Syria-Palestine 1500-500 BCE*. Edited by Agustinus Gianto and Peter Dubovsky. AOAT 459. Münster: Ugarit-Verlag.

Marks, Peter, Jennifer A. Wagner-Lawlor, and Fátima Vieira, eds. 2022. *The Palgrave Handbook of Utopian and Dystopian Literatures*. London: Palgrave Macmillan.

McBride, S. Dean, Jr. 1987. "Polity of the Covenant People: The Book of Deuteronomy." *Interpretation* 41:229–44.

McConville, J. Gordon. 1998. "King and Messiah in Deuteronomy and the Deuteronomistic History." Pages 271–95 in *King and Messiah in Israel and the Ancient Near East*. Edited by John Day. Journal for the Study of the Old Testament Supplement Series 270. Sheffield: Sheffield Academic Press.

Miller, Geoffrey P. 2011. *The Ways of a King: Legal and Political Ideas in the Bible*. Journal of Ancient Judaism Supplements 7. Göttingen: Vandenhoeck & Ruprecht.

Miller, Patrick D. 2005. "Constitution or Instruction? The Purpose of Deuteronomy." Pages 125–41 in *Constituting the Community: Studies on the Polity of Ancient Israel in Honor of S. Dean McBride*. Edited by John T. Strong and Steven S. Tuell. Winona Lake, MI: Eisenbrauns.

Mohawk, John C. 2000. *Utopian Legacies: A History of Conquest and Oppression in the Western World*. Santa Fe, NM: Clear Light Publishers.

More, Thomas. 1989. *Utopia*. Edited by George M. Logan and Robert M. Adams. Cambridge Texts in the History of Political Thought. Cambridge: Cambridge University Press.

Moylan, Tom, and Raffaella Baccolini, eds. 2007. *Utopia Method Vision: The Use Value of Social Dreaming*. Ralahine Utopian Studies 1. Oxford: Peter Lang.

Moylan, Tom. 2018. *Scraps of the Untainted Sky: Science Fiction, Utopia, Dystopia*. New York: Routledge.

Nicholson, Ernest. 2006. "'Do Not Dare to Set a Foreigner Over You': The King in Deuteronomy and 'The Great King.'" *Zeitschrift für die alttestamentliche Wissenschaft* 118:46–61.

Noth, Martin. 1981. *The Deuteronomistic History.* Journal for the Study of the Old Testament Supplement Series 15. Sheffield: JSOT Press.

Otto, Eckart. 1999. *Das Deuteronomium: Politische Theologie und Rechtsreformen in Juda und Assyrien.* Beihefte fur Zeitschrift für die alttestamentische Wissenschaft 284. Berlin: De Gruyter.

Pakkala, Juha. 2009. "The Date of the Oldest Edition of Deuteronomy." *Zeitschrift für die alttestamentliche Wissenschaft* 121: 388–401.

———. 2011. "The Dating of Deuteronomy: A Response to Nathan MacDonald." *Zeitschrift für die alttestamentliche Wissenschaft* 123:431–36.

Pinheiro, Marília F. 2006. "Utopia and Utopias: A Study on a Literary Genre in Antiquity." Pages 147–71 in *Authors, Authority, and Interpreters in the Ancient Novel: Essays in Honor of Gareth L. Schmeling.* Edited by Shannon N. Byrne and Jean Alvares. Groningen: Barkhuis Publishing.

Pradeau, Jean-François. 2000. "Plato's Atlantis: The True Utopia." Pages 83–91 in *Utopia: The Search for the Ideal Society in the Western World.* Edited by Roland Schaer, Gregory Claeys, and Lyman Tower Sargent. New York: Oxford University Press.

Ricœur, Paul. 1986. *Lectures on Ideology and Utopia.* New York: Columbia University Press.

Römer, Thomas. 2005. *The So-Called Deuteronomistic History: A Sociological, Historical and Literary Introduction.* London New York: T. & T. Clark International.

Rothstein, Edward. 2003. "Utopia and Its Discontents." Pages 1–28 in *Visions of Utopia.* Edited by Edward Rothstein, Herbert Muschamp, and Martin E. Marty. New York: Oxford University Press.

Sargent, Lyman Tower. 1994. "The Three Faces of Utopianism Revisited." *Utopian Studies* 5:1–37.

———. 2010. "Colonial and Postcolonial Utopias." Pages 200–22 in *The Cambridge Companion to Utopian Literature.* Edited by Gregory Claeys. Cambridge: Cambridge University Press.

———. 2022. *Rethinking Utopia and Utopianism: The Three Faces of Utopianism Revisited and Other Essays.* Ralahine Utopian Studies 26. Oxford: Peter Lang.

Sargisson, Lucy. 2007. "The Curious Relationship Between Politics and Utopia." Pages 25–46 in *Utopia Method Vision: The Use Value of Social Dreaming.* Edited by Tom Moylan and Raffaella Baccolini. Bern: Peter Lang.

Schweitzer, Steven J. 2007. *Reading Utopia in Chronicles.* Library of Hebrew Bible/Old Testament Studies 442. London: T. & T. Clark International.

Snyman, Gerrie. 2016. "Utopia Where It Is to Be Hoped that the Coffee Is A Little Less Sour? Dr Who's 'Utopia' and 'Chronicles.'" Pages 38–58 in *Worlds that Could Not Be: Utopia in Chronicles, Ezra and Nehemiah.* Edited by Frauke Uhlenbruch and Stephen J. Schweitzer. Library of Hebrew Bible/Old Testament Studies 620. New York: Bloomsbury T. & T. Clark Publishing.

Stavrakopoulou, Francesca, and John Barton, eds. 2010. *Religious Diversity in Ancient Israel and Judah*. London: T. & T. Clark International.

Stern, Ephraim. 2010. "From Many Gods to the One God: The Archaeological Evidence." Pages 395–403 in *One God - One Cult - One Nation: Archaeological and Biblical Perspectives*. Edited by Reinhard G. Kratz and Hermann Spieckermann. Beihefte fur Zeitschrift für die alttestamentische Wissenschaft 405. Berlin: De Gruyter.

Stordalen, Terje. 2023. "Book Religion? The Role of the Scroll in Deuteronomy." *Scandinavian Journal of the Old Testament* 37:166–83.

Strawn, Brent A. 2018. "Moses at Moab, Lincoln at Gettysburg? On the Genre of Deuteronomy, Again." *Zeitschrift für altorientalische und biblische Rechtsgeschichte* 24:153–210.

Suvin, Darko. 1979. *Metamorphoses of Science Fiction: On the Poetics and History of a Literary Genre*. New Haven, CT: Yale University Press.

Sweeney, Marvin A. 1995. "The Critique of Solomon in the Josianic Edition of the Deuteronomistic History." *Journal of Biblical Literature* 22–114:607.

Uhlenbruch, Frauke. 2015. *The Nowhere Bible: Utopia, Dystopia, Science Fiction*. Studies of the Bible and Its Reception 4. Berlin: De Gruyter.

Vieira, Fátima. 2010. "The Concept of Utopia." Pages 3–27 in *The Cambridge Companion to Utopian Literature*. Edited by Gregory Claeys. Cambridge: Cambridge University Press.

Villoro, Luis. 2006. "The Triple Confusion of Utopia." *Diogenes* 53:5–10.

Wazana, Nili. 2016. "The Law of the King (Deuteronomy 17:14–20) in the Light of Empire and Destruction." Pages 169–94 in *The Fall of Jerusalem and the Rise of the Torah*. Edited by Peter Dubovsky, Dominik Markl, and Jean-Pierre Sonnet. Forschungen zum Alten Testament 107. Tübingen: Mohr Siebeck.

Wells, Bruce. 2008. "What is Biblical Law? A Look at Pentateuchal Rules and Near Eastern Practice." *Catholic Biblical Quarterly* 70:223–43.

Wilson, Ian D. 2017. *Kingship and Memory in Ancient Judah*. New York: Oxford University Press.

Wilson, Robert R. 2005. "Deuteronomy, Ethnicity, and Reform: Reflections on the Social Setting of the Book of Deuteronomy." Pages 107–24 in *Constituting the Community: Studies on the Polity of Ancient Israel in Honor of S. Dean McBride*. Edited by John T. Strong and Steven S. Tuell. Winona Lake, MI: Eisenbrauns.

Winter, Irene J. 2008. "Touched by the Gods: Visual Evidence for the Divine Status of Rulers in the Ancient Near East." Pages 75–101 in *Religion and Power: Divine Kingship in the Ancient World and Beyond*. Edited by Nicole Brisch. Oriental Institute Seminars 14. Chicago: The University of Chicago Press.

Zahn, Molly M. 2023. "The Utopian Vision of the Temple Scroll." *Journal of Ancient Judaism* 23:1–25.

About the Author

Dr Madhavi Nevader is Lecturer in Hebrew Bible/Old Testament at the University of St Andrews. Her main areas of research include the political institutions and theologies of the Hebrew Bible and other ancient Near Eastern texts, Biblical and Near Eastern Prophecy, and Israelite/Judahite religion. She is currently working on a larger project looking at political utopianism in the Hebrew Bible.

Chapter 14
The Role of Deuteronomy in the Pentateuch

Richard D. Nelson

Abstract

Readers of the Tetrateuch encounter Deuteronomy as a disruptive experience that "bends" what is being read into a distinctive direction. The preceding journey-oriented narrative is replaced by quoted speech of Moses. Striking differences in language, tone, viewpoint, and presentation pile up. Expected plot progression is delayed. Linguistic changes, emergence of the testament genre, theological divergences, and the abrupt appearance of a book, disorient readers and grab their attention. When post-monarchical readers arrived at its last chapter, as viewed through the lens of the Song of Moses, the Pentateuch as a whole afforded them an effective metanarrative. It provided an explanatory, organizing archetype to a society existing precariously under the shadow of imperial domination and alien gods. It offered Israel a pattern for belief and the construction of meaning that made possible their survival as a people.

Keywords: covenant, Deuteronomy, metanarrative, Moses, Tetrateuch, Pentateuch

1. Metanarrative

The notion of metanarrative in literary theory is rooted in the work of Jean-François Lyotard (1924–1998). He introduced the term as part of a study of post-modernism, in order to designate an overarching, explanatory background story. Such a metanarrative is understood within a culture as providing an explanation or interpretation of "the way things are" and "how the world works." A society collectively deems certain past events (not necessarily historical) and present circumstances as offering a pattern or model for the way meaning is constructed and beliefs are shaped. Through its metanarratives, a culture comes to shared understandings of fundamental questions such as morality, the meaning of existence, and the proper way to structure society. Metanarratives are not individual stories but comprehensive narrative frameworks that tie stories together. They are canonical in the sense of exercising accepted authority over people's perceptions, values, and actions. For its ancient readers, the Pentateuch provided a metanarrative, encompassing creation and fall, election and liberation, law-giving and the promise of land. It disseminated a meaningful, archetypical profile about who Israel was and was to be as the people of Yahweh.

The grand narrative of the Pentateuch flows from the books of Genesis through Numbers (the Tetrateuch) before the reader encounters Deuteronomy as a disruptive experience. It interrupts, modifies, and "bends" the narrative of the Tetrateuch in a distinctive direction. As a result, when readers arrive at the last chapter of the Pentateuch, as viewed through the lens of Deuteronomy, the whole five-book unity could serve as an effective metanarrative for its post-monarchical audience. The Tetrateuch plus Deuteronomy provided an explanatory, organizing archetype for a theocentric urban society with a written scripture, existing precariously under the shadow of culturally ascendant imperial domination and the lure of alien gods.

What follows investigates the role of Deuteronomy in the Pentateuch from a synchronic perspective, reflecting the experience of a reader who encounters first the Tetrateuch and then Deuteronomy. (For a review of diachronic issues, that is, how the relationship between the Pentateuch and an evolving Deuteronomy developed over time, see Stackert 2022, 52–85, 110–25, 134–58).

2. The Story Line of the Tetrateuch

Each book of the Tetrateuch has its own literary integrity and begins and ends with discernible literary markers. At the same time, the four books are linked together by rhetorical bridges. Exodus 1:1–6 recapitulates Gen 46:8–27 and repeats the death of Joseph. Leviticus 1:1 picks up the tent of meeting from Exod 40:34. Numbers utilizes the formula that Leviticus repeats thirty-two times, "Yahweh spoke to Moses, [saying]," just as consistently (forty-two times).

Together, the four books of the Tetrateuch tell a coherent story. After recounting how Israel's ancestors were initiated into a special relationship with Yahweh and how they migrated to Egypt, the narrative starts in earnest with the book of Exodus. The pivotal events of the exodus are followed by various proclamations of divine law and Israel's fraught journey toward the land of promise. Beginning with Exod 15:22, verbs of journeying ("set out," "came to") recur relentlessly in Exodus and Numbers until the people reach the edge of the promised land "in the plains of Moab" (Num 33:48–49). As this journey unfolds, narrative movement is stopped periodically for the proclamation of law, first by God directly at Sinai (Exod 20), and then as mediated by Moses (Exod 20:22–23:33; 25:1–31:18; 34:11–26). After Israel leaves Sinai, law is promulgated all the way through Leviticus and then in shorter sections in Numbers. Nevertheless, the *reported speech* (direct discourse) of law-giving is always unambiguously incorporated into and subordinated to the ongoing plot action described in *narrative discourse* (storytelling), often by means of the formula "Yahweh spoke to Moses."

3. Deuteronomy: Discontinuity and Disorientation

Upon reaching Deuteronomy, however, the reader encounters a sharp discontinuity. Immediately, one detects an abrupt change from the *narrative discourse* that dominates the Tetrateuch to chapters and chapters of *reported speech* (direct discourse): "These are the words that Moses spoke" (Deut 1:1; compare 4:44–46; 5:1; 29:1 [28:69 in Hebrew]; 33:1). Almost everything that follows, until the reader reaches chs. 31 and 34, consists of the quoted speech of Moses: laws (Torah), exhortations, reconsidered events, blessings, curses, and poetry (for more on Torah, see ch. 9. In this volume).

Switching away from the direct narration format of the Tetrateuch, Deuteronomy describes events by subordinating them into the speech of Moses. He retrospectively reviews incidents (1:6–3:29; 9:8–10:11), characterizing them by a repeated formula, "at that time" (fourteen times between 1:9 and 10:8). In so doing, he reviews the past in order to throw light on the present moment of hearing on the plains of Moab ("today," 1:10; 5:1, 3; 29:10, 12–15 [29:9, 11–14 in Hebrew]; 32:46 and elsewhere). To reiterate: Deuteronomy's format of the direct discourse of reported speech sharply contrasts with the Tetrateuch, where narrative discourse dominates. The reader is thus alerted that something new is at hand and perhaps becomes disoriented.

Eventually, near the end of Deuteronomy, the balance between direct discourse and narrated events evens out, particularly in chs. 31 and 34.

Nevertheless, quoted speech continues to dominate, notably in chs. 28–30 and 32–33. The narrator interjects parenthetical background data at 2:10–12, 20–23; 4:41–43, 46–49; 10:6–9.

A sudden change in point of view creates a second experience of dislocation for readers. According to the narrator, Moses gives his address "beyond the Jordan" (1:1, 5). This usually means "on the opposite side," east or west of the river depending on the viewpoint of the narrator or speaker. Here, the expression clearly refers to Moab on the east bank as the "other side." This point of view is not that of Moses and Israel in the world of the narrative, but of the narrator and readers who are located west of the river (contrast Num 32:19). This startling change of viewpoint creates a sharp break in the narrative flow.

Third, the reader experiences a sudden postponement in plot advancement when encountering Deuteronomy. The sequence of events in Numbers leads the reader to expect a plot development that does not occur but is unexpectedly delayed. At the end of Numbers, the nation is poised on the brink of the Jordan, at the plains of Moab by Jericho (Num 22:1; 36:13), ready to begin the conquest and settlement of the land. Yahweh has given instructions for the conquest and described the boundaries of the land (Num 33:50–34:15). But instead of conquest, the disconcerting formula, "these are the words" (Deut 1:1), breaks into the expected plot line. Without warning, Moses starts to review recent events, gives exhortations to obedience, and proclaims new or revised laws. What the reader expects does not take place. It is only near the end of Deuteronomy that events leading to the conquest begin to unfold, with the appointment of Joshua and the death of Moses (31:1–8, 23; 34:5–9).

Related to this interruption in expected developments, the reader experiences yet a fourth discontinuity in that the flow of narrative time is stalled at the static "today" (1:10; 5:1) of Moses's extended address. The Tetrateuch is structured as a narrative shaped largely by journeys: Abraham to Canaan, Jacob away from there and back, Joseph and his brothers to Egypt, the exodus escape, and the wilderness wandering. As stated above, Deuteronomy exhibits a static, speech-oriented format instead. The narrator presents the words of Moses by means of four deictic headings ("these are/this is," 1:1–5; 4:44–49; 29:1–2 [HB 28:69–29:1]; 33:1–2a). There are few narrated actions (Moses set aside cities, 4:41–43; Moses wrote, 31:9; Moses and Aaron appear at the tent, 31:15). Important happenings are communicated to the reader indirectly, within speeches: "You stand assembled...I am making this covenant" (29:10, 14 [HB 29:9, 13]). All the words are spoken and all events take place on a single day at a single place (Beth-peor, 4:46; 34:6).

A fifth dislocation occurs in that Moses unexpectedly circles back to review recent history (1:6–3:29; 9:8–10:11). This review signals a new start in the sense that the audience in Moab (and the book's readers) are stopped short and invited to rethink the meaning or significance of past events: the appointment of judges to ensure impartial justice, Israel's disobedience and resulting punishments, the roundabout journey from Kadesh-barnea, and two victorious conquests. These themes are, of course, important to Deuteronomy (for instance, 7:17; 8:2–5; 9:3; 16:18). What Moses leaves out as he condenses so much text of the Tetrateuch into a few chapters also calls for some rethinking on the part of readers. The tabernacle, Aaron, and controversies over priestly credentials are apparently unimportant.

3.1 Structures and Genre

Numerous other divergences from the Tetrateuch alert the reader that Deuteronomy is offering a conceptual perspective different from that of the Tetrateuch. For example, compared to the Tetrateuch, the structural style of Deuteronomy is rich in framing patterns that use *inclusio* (repetitions to bracket blocks of text) and chiasms (concentric structures forming an x-pattern when outlined). An example of an *inclusio* is 11:26–32, which begins and ends with "I am setting before you today." The Hebrew word order of 2:14–15 presents a chiasm:

>had perished ...
>>from the camp ...
>>>Yahweh had sworn ...
>>>Yahweh's hand ...
>>from the camp ...
>had perished.

These rhetorical structures call the audience's attention more emphatically to the words they are hearing or reading. The density and sophistication of these linguistic patterns sets Deuteronomy off from the Tetrateuch, where they are sometimes present but much less prevalent (Lundbom 1996).

As Deuteronomy nears its conclusion, readers are reminded of its dramatic setting as an address by ever more frequent examples of introductions to speech acts (for example, 27:1a, 9, 11; 31:1–2; 7). In the end, the topic of Moses's death is highlighted (31:2, 14, 29; 32:50; 33:1). This emphasis would cause an ancient reader to recognize the overall literary form or genre of Deuteronomy as an extended *testament*. The testament genre consists of advice given as death draws near by a king to his subjects or by a father to his children (for example, Gen 49; 1 Kgs

2:1-9). As a testament, the words of Moses are thus addressed directly to readers in an effective way.

3.2 Deuteronomistic Language and Persuasive Rhetoric

Another dislocation experienced by the reader is a sharp change in linguistic style. The language of Deuteronomy is distinctively different from that which dominates in the Tetrateuch. Sentences are long and complex. Balanced phrases roll out in rhythmic parallelism. Synonymous nouns are repeated by twos and threes ("statutes and ordinances," "the alien, the orphan, and the widow," "a mighty hand and an outstretched arm," "your heart and soul"). Frequently repeated expressions become clichés: "remember that you were a slave," "you shall purge the evil from your midst," "the entire commandment that I command you today," and so forth. Another idiosyncratic stylistic feature is a puzzling interchange between second person singular and plural address.

Deuteronomy's rhetoric is designed to evoke emotion: fear, joy, kinship solidarity, abhorrence. Emotions are harnessed to motivate the reader to be loyal to God and obey the law. Moses relentlessly encourages obedience by appealing to Israel's election and liberation, Yahweh's benevolence, and a sense of social obligation, along with the promise of blessing and the threat of curse. The emotional temperature is intense: "Israel will hear and be afraid" (13:11 [13:12 in Hebrew]); "rejoice before Yahweh" (16:11). It reaches a boiling point with horrible curses in 28:32–24, 53–57, 65–67.

3.3 Suddenly, There is a Book

Events take a stunning turn when the law that Moses has been proclaiming orally unexpectedly becomes a book (Sonnet 2012, 207–13). By being written down in book form, transmitted by Levitical priests and elders, and read out periodically (29:21 [29:20 in Hebrew], 31:9-11, 24–26), his previously oral presentation is concretized and directed toward the future generations who would read Deuteronomy. Moses creates a book to survive his death (31:27–29). To be sure, the Sinai/Horeb covenant agreement focused on a book of the covenant (Exod 24:4, 7; presumably 20:22–23:33). But the radical difference in Deuteronomy is that the book Moses writes is self-referential. That is to say, Deuteronomy does not just portray the book of the law; it *is itself* the book it describes. A scroll was needed to hold all that Moses had said and to be accessible for constant reading, in order to inculcate obedience (as in the case of the king, Deut 17:18–19). The whole text of this law was also to be displayed on a public monument in the new land (27:2-4, 8) and periodically read aloud to groups who could not be expected to be literate (31:12-13).

The book is to be distributed as widely as possible, from children even to the king. In this way, Deuteronomy moves the whole of the Pentateuch well on the way to becoming canonical scripture made up of individual books. The Pentateuch becomes what Deuteronomy is: authoritative in its written form, read aloud in public, and intended to be consulted. Moreover, as we shall see below (section 5.3), there are perceptible variations between Deuteronomy and some of the laws in the Tetrateuch. This means that readers of the Pentateuch would have to learn to engage in comparative interpretation, another step on the way to the notion of scripture. Strictly speaking, the Tetrateuch is anonymous. Rounding it off with a fifth book spoken and written by Moses converted the resulting whole into the Book of Moses (Ezra 6:18; Neh 13:1).

In summary, as the reader passes from the Tetrateuch to Deuteronomy, striking differences in language, tone, viewpoint, and presentation pile up. As a result, the reader experiences a sharp discontinuity, a sense of disjointedness, a fracture point. The expected course of the narrative has been delayed and twisted. Rhetorical changes, a plot delay, the testament genre, and the unexpected manifestation of a book disorient readers and grab their attention. The metanarrative of the Tetrateuch is being altered and redirected by Deuteronomy.

4. Connections to the Tetrateuch

Nevertheless, Deuteronomy remains a connected part of the Pentateuch. For all its differences from the Tetrateuch (and its similarities to Joshua), Israel came to treat Deuteronomy as the fifth of five books and canonized it as such. This development took place even though it seems likely that Deuteronomy was at one time the first part of the Deuteronomistic History, a single complex that incorporated the books of Joshua through 2 Kings. Grand themes hold the whole of the Pentateuch together, for example Yahweh's pledge to the patriarchs, Israel's election and its concomitant responsibilities, and the promise of a land. A common narrative arc (summarized in Deut 26:1-9) extends from promise to bondage to exodus to anticipated occupation of the land. Most obviously, Deuteronomy plugs tightly into the journey sequence of the Tetrateuch by situating itself in the plains of Moab where Numbers leaves off and retelling events from Exodus and Numbers. Deuteronomy 1:3 carries on the timeline established in Numbers (Num 33:38). Later on, Deuteronomy repeats the appointment of Joshua (Num 27:12-23; Deut 31:14-15, 23) and assumes that its readers will know the stories of Balaam (23:4-5), Miriam

(24:9), and Sodom (29:23 [29:22 in Hebrew]). Deuteronomy 32:48-52 looks back to Aaron's death in a way that parallels Num 20:24-29.

Another linkage to the Tetrateuch is that elements of Deuteronomy's characteristic phraseology occur infrequently in the Tetrateuch, making them already somewhat familiar to the reader when they are encountered in the fifth book. For example, Deuteronomy's standard list of adversary nations appears several times in Genesis and Exodus, and Exodus and Numbers speak of the land of milk and honey (compare Deut 6:3). Remarkably, the Ten Commandments appear in Exodus in distinctively Deuteronomistic garb (notably in Exod 20:2-3, 5, 10).

Deuteronomy' last chapter wraps up the career of Moses with language similar to that describing the deaths of Joseph and Aaron (Gen 50:26; Num 20:29; 33:39). An inclusive framework is formed by parallel deathbed poems spoken by Jacob in Gen 49 and Moses in Deut 33. The Moses praised in Deut 34:10-12 is the very same Moses portrayed in the Tetrateuch: the wonder-working prophet who listens and speaks directly with God (Exod 33:11; Num 12:8; compare Deut 5:4).

5. Theological Differences

Theologically, Deuteronomy is markedly different from the Tetrateuch. These differences would have had an impact on an ancient reader whose views had been shaped by experience with the previous four books. Deuteronomy's rhetorical intensity, explored above (section 3.2), suggests that such an impact would have been profound. Deuteronomy sets its readers into a time of decision and crisis. They are placed on the edge of a new land, a new world. There are battles to win, dangers to face, decisions to be made. This is a watershed moment that demands decision. In Deut 30:11-20, as the book draws to a close, Moses presents the alternatives starkly: obedience leading to life and prosperity as opposed to apostasy leading to death. Verse 19 is climactic: "Choose life." Blessings and curses motivate his demand and appeal (11: 26-28; ch. 28), along with threats of defeat (32:19-25) and many promises of flourishing (for example, 5:33, 7:13 and often).

Deuteronomy's dissimilarities in theology and worldview from the Tetrateuch are not so much matters of outright contradiction but of different emphasis and perspective. More stress and space is given to particular traditions and topics, or a new theological idea is introduced into the ideological mix. Deuteronomy's divergences in ideology and practice resulted from at least three factors. First, the bulk of the Tetrateuch was written at a different time than Deuteronomy, some parts certainly earlier and others apparently later. Second, the social location of those responsible for Deuteronomy, usually thought to be scribes, savants, and Levitical priests, differed from those groups from which the earlier and later components of the Tetrateuch emerged (for Moses as a master scribe, see ch. 8 in this volume). Third, core ideas in Deuteronomy are often seen to stem from the northern tribes and the Northern Kingdom rather than from Judah and Jerusalem.

The most important issues of theological divergence from the Tetrateuch involve 1) Yahweh's nature and manifestation, 2) the unitary nature of the place of Israel's worship and the purpose and character of sacrifice, 3) a rethinking of parts of the law, 4) matters of polity and social relationship, and 5) the contours of the convent that bound Israel and Yahweh together.

5.1 Yahweh is Transcendent and Radically One

The nature of the deity Deuteronomy describes is unitary in the sense of allowing no room for multiple names and local manifestations. This contrasts with the wider access to Yahweh at different holy sites under various traditional names described in the Tetrateuch (Gen 35:1; Exod 6:3; 17:15). Yahweh is one Yahweh and is to be the only God with whom Israel is to have a relationship (Deut 6:4). As a corollary to this, Yahweh is completely intolerant of rival gods, demanding that all their religious installations and any Israelite worship of them be eradicated. Moreover, Yahweh is a deity who is heard only and not seen. This contrasts to what Genesis describes about the patriarchs (Gen 17:1; 18:1) and what Exodus reports about events at Sinai (Exod 24:9–11). According to Deuteronomy, at Horeb the people heard a voice only; they saw no form (Deut 4:12, 15, 36; 5:22–26 (for more on Yhwh Elohim, see chs. 7 and 16 in this volume).

5.2 Joyous Worship at a Single Sanctuary

Deuteronomy's Yahweh dwells transcendently in the heavens (4:36; 26:15), not in or at any earthly holy place. It is only through the placement of Yahweh's name at the single place of sacrificial worship so that it may be said to dwell there (12:5, 11) that Yahweh associates with an altar and sanctuary (Richter 2007, 343–49). This concept deemphasizes notions of divine localization and presence that appear in the Tetrateuch, particularly the concept of Yahweh's immanent glory that plays such a large role in descriptions of the tabernacle (Exod 40:34, compare 24:16–17). In a similar way, the ark of the covenant in Deuteronomy functions as a container for stone tablets and the location next to which the book of the law was to be placed (Deut 10:1-5; 31:26) in contrast to the Tetrateuch, where it is a locus of Yahweh's presence (Exod 25:22; Num 10:33-36).

Large swaths of the Tetrateuch are taken up with the sacrificial system and its proper operation. Deuteronomy concerns itself with hardly any of this detail and focuses instead on the effects sacrifice is to have on the populace. Concepts of purification and atonement for sin are absent, although purity, as it impacted one's diet and participation in communal feasts, is important (Deut 12:15, 22; ch. 14). Sacrifice is celebrated as a matter of memory and community joy, with an emphasis on the inclusive banquet (12:15, 12, 18; 16:11, 14; 26:12). There are priests in Deuteronomy, but their family qualifications and duties differ from what is promoted in Leviticus and Numbers. When Deuteronomy reformulates the festival calendar already encountered by the reader in Exod 23:14-17; 34:18-23, the celebrations become pilgrimages to the central holy place marked by rejoicing (Deut 16:11, 14, 15). Similarly, the reader is induced to rethink previous guidelines about the offering of firstlings and the Feast of Weeks (Deut 15:19-23; 26:1-11).

5.3 Another Perspective on the Law

The law given at the mountain by Yahweh and proclaimed there and then later by Moses in the Tetrateuch is brought forward to the readership of Deuteronomy by an authorial technique. In both the Tetrateuch and Deuteronomy, Yahweh speaks the Ten Commandments at the mountain, and then Moses assumes the task of receiving and revealing the rest of the law. In the Tetrateuch, Moses is commanded to reveal the rest of the law, some right away at Sinai/Horeb and other decrees on the way to the land. However, Deuteronomy appears to be ambiguous about exactly when Moses first proclaims the law apart from the Ten Commandments. According to Deut 1:5, forty years after the exodus Moses "undertook to expound" (better, "state clearly") "this law" on a day called "today." "This law" refers to what Moses proclaims in chs. 12-26 (see 17:18-19; 27:3; 31:9), often referred to as "statutes and ordinances" (for example, 4:14; 5:1; 12:1; 26:16). But is Moses repeating and explicating law that he had *already* spoken or has he waited until arriving at Moab before promulgating this law for the very first time? The latter scenario is as at least suggested by Deut 4:5 (translating "I now teach you" with NRSV), 8, 14, 44-45 (translating "after they had left" with NJPS); 5:31.

Whatever the case, when one reads Deuteronomy after the Tetrateuch, confusion occurs, because the law that Moses now sets forth is not the same as what was transmitted in Exodus, Leviticus, and Numbers (Levinson 1997, 23-52, 98-143; Mattison 2018, 29-173). The problem is not so much that there is additional legal material beyond what has already been read. Moses has been supplementing the first tranche of post-Ten Commandments laws in Exodus with additional directives throughout Leviticus and Numbers. What seems problematic is that when Deuteronomy's law covers the same topics as preceding laws, there are often apparent (or actual) differences that need to be considered and negotiated. To the extent that the precepts contained in Exod 20:22–23:33 (the Book of the Covenant) must be rethought after reading Deuteronomy's version of these laws, the reader must learn to become a comparative interpreter. Among such restatements are Exod 21:12–14 by Deut 19:1–13 and Exod 21:2–11 by Deut 15:12–18. The same situation obtains with the festival calendars and food laws. It is not enough just to hear and obey; now one must also think about what one reads (for more on law in Deuteronomy, see ch. 3). The addition of Deuteronomy to the Tetrateuch means that all of the Pentateuch has become a book that requires interpretation.

5.4 Life Together in the Land

Readers of the whole Pentateuch would find elements of Deuteronomy's social and political backdrop more familiar than some of the more distant and archaic elements of the Tetrateuch. Israel has no king in the Tetrateuch, only hints about a future one (Gen 49:10; Num 24:17). In contrast, Deuteronomy envisions a king and wants him to be close to the people and loyal to the law (Deut 17:14–20). The possibilities of a king's exile and of a non-native ruler are on the horizon (17:15; 28:36). Deuteronomy envisions an active social support system (14:28–29; 15:1–11; 21:10–17; 24:19–20) and some amelioration of the plight of women, debt slaves, and other unfortunates, although such concerns are not totally alien to laws set forth in the Tetrateuch and should not be over-idealized.

Deuteronomy shows evidence of cultural anxieties. For example, prophets, who feature in the Tetrateuch only in an impromptu sense, come to the fore in Deuteronomy as a source of both revelation and danger (13:1–5 [13:2–6 in Hebrew]; 18:15–22), suggesting uncertainty over the trustworthiness of claimed revelation.

In Deuteronomy, the regulation of war emerges as an important topic (ch.20; 21:10–14; 23:9–14 [23:10–15 in Hebrew]; 24:5), much more so than in the Tetrateuch. The war laws of Deuteronomy may communicate a reaction against royal military campaigns with their costs to the citizenry (17:16) and seem to suggest that older, pre-monarchic military patterns would be preferable. Especially serious among these war laws are those involving ḥērem, which refers to the status of things or people deemed to be irrevocably owned by Yahweh. In the Tetrateuch, this proscribed category applies to fields, animals, and persons vowed to Yahweh. Deuteronomy applies *ḥērem* to the annihilation of captives and booty acquired in war and also uses it to mandate the elimination of alien religious elements (7:2, 26; 13:15 [13:16 in Hebrew]). Whether or not the demand that all or part of an enemy population be exterminated was seriously intended or ever carried out in Israel is entirely uncertain, although at least one neighboring people did so ("The Inscription of King Mesha," ANET 320–21; COS 2.23:137–38). The existence of *ḥērem* laws demonstrates a sense of existential danger. In addition, excluding particular "others" from communal worship (23:3–8 [4–9 in Hebrew]) reveals the panic of a society that sees itself under threat. Thus, Deuteronomy highlights the legal tradition of *ḥērem* as a xenophobic way of prosecuting war and, at the same time, shapes it into a guarantee of religious loyalty (similar to Exod 22:20 [22:19 in Hebrew]).

5.5 Intersecting Covenants

In the Pentateuch, the concept of covenant serves as the dominant metaphor describing the relationship between Yahweh and Israel. it is commonplace to speak of two categories of covenant. Genesis 15 and 17 provide the classic accounts of Yahweh's grant of land and promise of progeny made to Abraham. This Abrahamic covenant emphasizes Yahweh's choice and promise and there is no notion of potential termination implicit in it (Gen 13:15). In Deuteronomy also, Yahweh's covenant promise to the patriarchs lies behind Israel's election (Deut 7:7–8) and the gift of land (6:10; 9:5). But in Deuteronomy the Abrahamic covenant is not absolutely unconditional. Rather, it is shadowed by the thought that the land is potentially dangerous and is likely to produce a level of disobedience that would result in its loss (6:11–15; 8:19–20; 11:17; 31:16–20). Thus, in Deuteronomy's view, no promises made to the patriarchs can actually be unconditional but must ultimately depend on obedience. Abrahamic covenant promises do not obviate impending defeat and exile (4:25–28; 8:19–20; 28:36–37, 29:22–27 [HB 29:21–26]; 30:17–18) but must be understood only as prospects for the survival of a diminished remnant (4:29–31; 30:1–10; 32:26–27).

A second covenant was established at Sinai/Horeb, one associated with the Ten Commandments and the rest of the law. This articulation of covenant relationship puts emphasis on what Israel must do in order to maintain its relationship with Yahweh. Its classic formulation is "I will take you as my people, and I will be your God" (Exod 6:7), echoed in Deut 26:17–18; 29:13 [29:12 in Hebrew]. In Deuteronomy Moses extensively reminds Israel of this Sinai/Horeb covenant in chs. 4–5, 9–10 as he prepares his audience to receive the laws he will proclaim in chs. 12–26. "Yahweh our God made a covenant with us at Horeb" (5:2; for more on covenant, see ch. 2 in this volume).

However, Deuteronomy also goes on to confront its readers with a striking modification of how they have learned to understand the Sinai/Horeb covenant. In a remarkable and surprising rhetorical move, Deuteronomy adds another element to the theology of covenant and thereby pulls readers themselves into the covenant-making process. In Deuteronomy, the Sinai/Horeb covenant is supplemented by and coordinated with a matching covenant, when Yahweh commands Moses to make a covenant "in the land of Moab" with the people assembled there (29:1–29 [28:69–29:28 in Hebrew]). This Moab covenant is both something old and something new. It is parallel to the past covenant already cited by Moses as having been made at Horeb with this "today" generation (5:2–3, compare 4:13, 23). It is also "in addition to" that Horeb covenant and established on the "today" when the action of Deuteronomy occurs (29:1, 12 [28:69; 29:11 in Hebrew]), so that readers themselves become the "you" who "stand assembled today . . . to enter into the covenant" (29:10–12 [29:9–11 in Hebrew]). Readers are also incorporated in that the Moab covenant is being made explicitly with future generations. It adds "those not here with us today" to those "here with us today" (29:14–15 [29:13–14 in Hebrew]). The Horeb and Moab covenants are tightly intertwined together, two sides of the same coin, made with Israelites of the past, the present, and the future. (For more on Israel as an ethnos, see ch. 5 in this volume.)

Deuteronomy introduces yet another convolution to the reader's Tetrateuch-based conception of covenant. It modifies the older metaphor of covenant by adding to it elements from the contemporary world of imperial treaties. Specifically, it imitates the loyalty treaties that Assyrian monarchs imposed on dependent kings who were their vassals. The harsh demands for uncompromising loyalty set forth in Deut 13 and the curses threatening the faithless in 28:27–35, 53–57 have been seen to show direct knowledge of these Assyrian treaties (principally "Esarhaddon's Succession Treaty," *COS* 4.36:155–66; *ANET* 534–41; Crouch 2014, 47–92, 167–78; Levinson and Stackert 2012, 127–32; for a rebuttal, see ch. 1 in this volume).

Analogous to the loyalty demanded by an Assyrian overlord, Israel's absolute fidelity to Yahweh is the center of the covenant relationship, and disloyal service to other gods would be the supreme violation of it (11:16–17 and often). The probable influence of Assyrian treaty practices is also reflected in Deuteronomy's strong emphasis on blessings and (especially) curses as a way of promoting obedience to the covenant (11:27–28; 27:13–26; ch. 28). The standard language of international relations demanded that vassals "love" their overlords, in the sense of showing fidelity and obedience, and Deuteronomy picks this up by calling on Israel to love Yahweh (6:5; 10:12; 11:1, 13; 30:6).

6. Relating to the World of the Pentateuchal Reader

In ways that seem less true of the Tetrateuch, Deuteronomy is strongly oriented toward its future, to the time of those reading the book. Law and national story are to be taught to the children (6:20–25) (for pedagogy in Deut, see ch. 10). The book of the law is to be read out on a regular basis (31:10–13), and the Song of Moses will continue to caution future generations (31:21; 32:46). Curses and blessings presage future scenarios.

Those who read the five books of the Pentateuch would know of problematic native kings and foreign domination. For them, the land of promise was a place of uncertain ownership or even of longing by those who had been forced to leave it behind and could only hope to return. Social change and economic distress were rampant. In response, Deuteronomy seeks to ameliorate social conditions and promote justice. There were powerful temptations to syncretism or apostasy with respect to the apparently more successful gods of dominant empires, to the venerable traditions of non-Yahwistic local religion, or to quasi-orthodox forms of Yahwism. In response, Deuteronomy is more radically theocentric than the Tetrateuch, promoting an aniconic, unitary god with a unique and exclusive name (6:13; 10:20) and a centralized sanctuary. A perceived threat from alien ideas and peoples provided fruitful soil for xenophobia.

6.1 The Song of Moses as Metanarrative

Near the end of Deuteronomy, the Song of Moses (ch. 32) offers readers an overarching perspective on Israel's origin, history, and future (Nelson 2004, 362–80). In effect, it presents a compact metanarrative for readers of the whole Pentateuch. The Song is intended for future readers in that Moses is not just to recite it but to write and teach it (31:19, 22), so that it will remain "in their mouths" (that is, internalized, 30:14). Moses speaks it in the ears of all (31:30, 32:44), and they are to communicate it to their offspring (32:46). The Song is so vital that it is comparable to the law itself. Both are witnesses (31:19, 21, 26) and both are communicated "to the very end" (31:24, 30).

The Song tracks Israel's story back to primeval, mythic time ("of old" v. 7), when Yahweh chose Jacob as "his people" (v. 9). This pushes the time horizon back earlier than the Pentateuch's other election stories.

Citing the alternate election tradition of wilderness-finding (v. 10 MT; Hos 9:10) reinforces this difference. What is more, Israel's relationship to Yahweh has a mythic flavor, that of father-like creation (vv. 6, 18). Yahweh transports Israel to the rich and nurturing land (vv. 11-14). But the story then turns sour as over-fed Israel forgets its Rock and sacrifices to strange gods (vv. 16-17).

At this point, the poem takes up God's viewpoint and recounts Yahweh's plans to destroy Israel and the reasons for this (vv. 19-24). Israel has "provoked" and "made jealous" (vv. 16, 21a) with their "no faithfulness" involving what is "no god" (vv. 20, 21a). Yahweh proposes to turn things around and employ a "no people" (foreign aggressors) against them, in order to provoke Israel and make them jealous in turn (v. 21b). The Divine Warrior tradition (Yahweh conceptualized as wielding weapons of destruction) provides a rhetoric of terror and complete destruction (vv. 22-25).

Yet Yahweh relents (vv. 26-27)! For the reader of Deuteronomy, it is astonishing that God's change of heart has nothing to do with repentance or renewed obedience on the part of Israel (contrast 30:1-10). This narrative turnaround is driven solely by internal, theocentric motives. Yahweh cares about personal reputation and integrity (v. 27, 39), is distressed by Israel's desperate situation (v. 36), and thirsts for personal vindication (vv. 41, 43).

This poem presents readers with a metanarrative, a way to conceptualize their election and life in the land, both in times of prosperity and of peril and disaster. The gods that tempt them are subordinate and impotent (vv. 8, 17, 31, 37-38). In contrast, it is Yahweh the Divine Warrior (vv. 39-42) who controls events. Hope is possible. Indeed, it is the proper response to Yahweh's praiseworthy greatness (vv. 3-4, 43). From start to finish, Israel remains "his people" (vv. 9, 36, 43).

6.2 Deuteronomy, Pentateuch, and Metanarrative

Deuteronomy's "today" is a moment of new challenges, a new start. Readers are once more on the verge of promised land, living as they do in an era of incomplete and threatened possession of their territory. Their land is held tentatively, shadowed by imperial aggression, exile, and long-term colonial domination. "Today" is a time for making decisions (30:15, 19) and re-initiating the covenant relationship (26:17-18, 29:10, 12-13 [29:9, 11-12 in Hebrew]).

In a sense, Deuteronomy's "today" is also the "today" of the entire Pentateuch. The death of Moses rounds off the Pentateuch and makes it a completed whole. Readers of the Pentateuch are in a different place by the time they have reached the last words of Deuteronomy. They are motivated to remember, love, and obey. They have been offered resources to live through the crises that are looming on their horizon or are happening contemporaneously.

To oversimplify a complex and poorly understood process, the Pentateuch was formed by adding Deuteronomy to the Tetrateuch, a development usually dated to the fifth century BCE during the Persian period. This amalgamation brought the reality of a profoundly broken covenant into view and consequently the issue of the people's destruction, exile, and continued domination by imperial powers. For readers in the Persian period, this situation would be both a traumatic memory and a catastrophic reality. Consequently, Israel needed to hear the hopeful message that repentance and renewed obedience could lead to the restoration of their relationship with Yahweh. It was Yahweh alone who could circumcise their hearts (30:6) and thus resolve the problem of their fickle infidelity (9:6; 10:16; 31:27). They can trust, or at least hope, that their covenant relationship with Yahweh has a future. It is fitting, then, that the Pentateuch should end in the incomplete, open-ended circumstances of Deuteronomy. The Jordan has not yet been crossed, and Joshua's leadership mission has hardly begun (34:9). "Today" is the time to "choose life" (30:19).

Light is refracted as it travels from one medium to another and bent as it passes through the gravitational field of a star. Similarly, their encounter with Deuteronomy bends what readers of the complete Pentateuch have inherited from the Tetrateuch into new and somewhat unexpected directions. The resulting whole offered Israel a viable metanarrative, providing a shared pattern or structure for belief, the construction of meaning, accepted morality, and survival as a people.

Works Cited

Crouch, Carly. 2014. *Israel and the Assyrians: Deuteronomy, the Succession Treaty of Esarhaddon, and the Nature of Subversion.* Ancient Near Eastern Monographs 8. Atlanta: SBL Press.

Levinson, Bernard M. 1997. *Deuteronomy and the Hermeneutics of Legal Innovation.* Oxford: Oxford University Press.

Levinson, Bernard M., and Jeffrey Stackert. 2012. "Between the Covenant Code and Esarhaddon's Succession Treaty: Deuteronomy 13 and the Composition of Deuteronomy." *Journal of Ancient Judaism* 3:123–40.

Lundbom, Jack O. 1996. "The Inclusion and Other Framing Devices in Deuteronomy i–xxviii." *VT* 46:296–315.

Lyotard, Jean-François. 1984. *The Postmodern Condition: A Report on Knowledge.* Theory and History of Literature 10. Minneapolis: University of Minnesota.

Mattison, Kevin. 2018. *Rewriting and Revision as Amendment in the Laws of Deuteronomy.* FAT 2, 100. Tübingen: Mohr Siebeck.

Nelson, Richard D. 2002. *Deuteronomy.* Old Testament Library. Louisville: Westminster John Knox.

Richter, Sandra L. 2007. "The Place of the Name in Deuteronomy." *VT* 57:342–66.

Sonnet, Jean-Pierre. 2012. "The Fifth Book of the Pentateuch." *Journal of Ancient Judaism* 3:197–234.

Stackert, Jeffrey. 2022. *Deuteronomy and the Pentateuch.* New Haven: Yale University Press.

About the Author

Richard D. Nelson is a professor emeritus of Biblical Hebrew and Old Testament Interpretation at Perkins School of Theology, Southern Methodist University. He is the author of ten books on the interpretation, history, and theology of the Hebrew Bible.

CHAPTER 15
DEUTERONOMY: THE SAMARITAN VERSION

Sidnie White Crawford

Abstract

The version of Deuteronomy that is the canonical text of the Samaritans differs in important ways from the Masoretic version of Deuteronomy. Examining those differences yields important information regarding the textual history of Deuteronomy as well as the history of the relations between Samaritans and Jews.

Keywords: Deuteronomy, Samaritan Pentateuch, Samaritans, Masoretic Text, textual criticism, canon

1. The Origins and History of the Samaritans

While most readers will be familiar with the Samaritans from the New Testament narratives (e.g. Lk 10:29–37, Jn 4:4–42), the Samaritan community had been in existence much longer than the New Testament period. Their name is taken from the northern kingdom of Israel's capital city, Samaria. According to their own origin story, the Samaritans consider themselves the true Israelite community, being members of the tribes of Levi (their priesthood) and Ephraim and Manasseh. They trace the origin of their community back to the period of the Judges. They claim that Eli, the priest of Shiloh (1 Sam 1–4), split from the legitimate Israelite sanctuary on Mount Gerizim and its high priest Uzzi and set up a schismatic sanctuary in Shiloh. The Samaritans maintain that their religious practice and belief are based on the authentic worship practices of the first sanctuary on Mount Gerizim. Even more importantly, they claim that their line of high priests, which still exists today, descends from the Gerizim high priest Uzzi, who in turn was a descendant of Aaron, the first high priest in Israel (Pummer 2016, 9–13, 297–98).

The traditional Jewish view of the origins of the Samaritans is based on the narrative of the destruction of the northern kingdom of Israel found in 2 Kgs 17, augmented by the narratives of Josephus, the first-century Jewish historian. This view holds that the Samaritans are a mixed people descended from the intermarriage of native Israelites and foreigners imported into Israel by the Assyrians after 722 BCE, who continued idolatrous practices mixed with the worship of Yhwh, the god of Israel (2 Kgs 17: 24–41). Thus, in Judaism, the Samaritans are a heretical sect and cannot be considered true worshippers of God (Pummer 2016, 13–14).

Modern scholars consider that both accounts contain legendary elements that cannot be verified historically. Rather, scholars posit that the Samarian community (later known as the Samaritans) are descendants of those Israelites who remained in the northern kingdom after 722 BCE. These Samarians continued to worship Yhwh, the god of Israel, eventually establishing a sanctuary on Mount Gerizim, an important cult site in the northern territory, where they continued the worship of Yhwh (Knoppers 2013, 65–70). The sanctuary on Mount Gerizim was established in the middle to late fifth century BCE and continued in existence until its destruction by the Hasmonean king John Hyrcanus in 110 BCE (Magen 2008, 1). Mount Gerizim is still a sacred place for the Samaritans today, and most of the surviving community continues to live in its vicinity, for example in Palestinian cities such as Nablus.

2. The Samaritan Pentateuch

The Samaritans consider only the Pentateuch, the first five books of Moses (Genesis, Exodus, Leviticus, Numbers, and Deuteronomy), to be their canonical scripture. The Samaritan Pentateuch, like the MT, is written in the Hebrew language but differs from the MT in several important respects.

First, the Samaritan Pentateuch is preserved in a version written in a script derived from the ancient Israelite script. This ancient Israelite script is found in Iron Age inscriptions and ostraca in the territories of Israel and Judah. In the Persian period (539–332 BCE) this script fell out of everyday use among both Samarians and Judeans; the Aramaic language became the ordinary language of commerce and government, and documents began to be written in Aramaic square script. For example, the Wadi ed-Daliyeh papyri, discovered in the cave of Abu Shinjeh halfway between Samaria and

Jericho, which are the personal documents of leading Samarian families fleeing the Macedonian army after their rebellion against Alexander the Great in 331 BCE, are all written in Aramaic, although some of their seals are in the ancient Israelite script.

The Judean or Jewish community eventually adopted the Aramaic square script for copying their sacred scripture, as remains the case today (Table 1). Most of the Dead Sea Scrolls biblical manuscripts, which date from the third century BCE until the first century CE, are written in the Aramaic square script. However, the Samaritans continued to copy their sacred scripture in a later version of the ancient Israelite script, which in Second Temple period texts and inscriptions is known as paleo-Hebrew. Scholars date the paleo-Hebrew script in which the Samaritan Pentateuch is copied to the first century BCE (Purvis 1968, 18–21).

Second, the Samaritan Pentateuch, which is copied in consonants only, without the vowel points found in the MT, is written using a "fuller" (*plene*) orthography than is found in most of the MT. This orthography is characterized by the more frequent use of certain consonants (*waw, yod, heh,* and sometimes *'aleph*) to signal vowels in the text. These consonants are known as vowel letters or *matres lectionis* ("mothers of reading"). The Samaritan Pentateuch prefers to use a vowel letter to represent long vowels, especially long *o* and long *u*, even in unaccented syllables. It also prefers to use *heh* to represent final long *a* (Purvis 1968, 54–57). This fuller spelling practice also occurs in many of the manuscripts from the Qumran caves, indicating that a fuller orthography is a Second Temple period scribal phenomenon in both Samaria and Judea; it was not unique to the Samaritan community (Table 2).

Third, the Samaritan reading tradition, which refers to the way the text was pronounced out loud when read in worship or study settings, differs from the Masoretic reading tradition in many respects. This is

Table 1: Paleo-Hebrew script and Aramaic square script

Letter name	'alep (a)	bet (b)	gimel (g)	dalet (d)
Paleo-Hebrew script	✔	𝟡	ๅ	◁
Aramaic square script	א	ב	ג	ד

Table 2: The word תחתם ("under them") written in the SP, the MT and Paleo-Hebrew

SP in Aramaic Square Script (plene spelling)	MT	Samaritan (paleo-) Hebrew
תחתיהם	תחתם	𐤌𐤄𐤉𐤕𐤇𐤕
takhtêhem	takhtăm	takhtêhem

illustrated by a transcription of Deut 1:1 in contemporary Samaritan pronunciation:

These are the words which Mooshe spoke to all Yishraael across the Yaardaan, in the desert, in the prairie, opposite Sof, between Faaraan and Atfaal, and Libban, and Aahseerote, and Dee Zaahb (Tsedaka and Sullivan 2013, 405).

Scholars agree that this reading tradition is ancient, reflecting Hebrew pronunciation in the first centuries BCE and CE (Tsedaka and Sullivan 2013, xxx–xxxi).

Finally, the text of the Samaritan Pentateuch differs from the text of MT Pentateuch in major ways. Like the Septuagint version of the Pentateuch, SP is an expansive text, longer than the version found in MT. These expansions include small harmonizing changes, clarifying small additions, and large-scale additions and harmonizations comprising several verses. In addition, the ancient scribes of the SP added a layer of specifically Samaritan editorial changes (mainly references to their holy place, Mount Gerizim), to conform their Pentateuch to Samaritan theology. Further, the SP exhibits editorial changes that "update" the text, removing orthographic peculiarities and grammatical infelicities, or correcting perceived problems in the text (Crawford 2016, 167–68). These textual differences will be demonstrated below with examples from Deuteronomy.

3. The History of the Samaritan Text

The oldest copies of the Samaritan Pentateuch date from the twelfth and thirteenth centuries CE. An important witness to the text is the 'Abisha Scroll, revered by the Samaritans as supposedly coming from the hand of 'Abisha, the great-grandson of Aaron. Portions of this manuscript date to the twelfth century, and it contains the entire book of Deuteronomy (Pummer 2016, 198). Its text is often used as the base text in a critical edition of the Samaritan Deuteronomy.

The Samaritan Pentateuch first came to the attention of western scholarship in 1616, when Pietro della Valle brought a complete manuscript of the text to Europe (Crawford 2016, 169). Because of the expansive character of the text, it was judged to be inferior to the MT and dismissed as "popular" or "vulgar," a product of Samaritan scribes after their rupture with Judaism. This view was the majority opinion of textual critics until the discovery of the Dead Sea Scrolls in the mid-twentieth century (Crawford 2016, 169–71).

The scrolls found in the Qumran caves revealed biblical manuscripts with a consonantal text very close to the text of the Samaritan Pentateuch, without the specifically Samaritan content. These biblical manuscripts came to be characterized as "pre-Samaritan." The manuscripts in question are 4QpaleoExod^m, 4QExod-Lev^f, 4QLev^d, 4QNum^b, 4Q158, 4Q364, and 4Q175.* These manuscripts all date paleographically (by handwriting) to no later than the first century BCE; 4QExod-Lev^f dates to the third century BCE.

Since the Qumran settlement was inhabited by Jews in the first centuries BCE–CE, it was obvious that the "pre-Samaritan" text found in these manuscripts was in circulation among both Jews and Samaritans in the late Second Temple period and was claimed as an authentic version of the Pentateuch by both communities. Thus, the base text of the Samaritan Pentateuch was revealed as a text of great antiquity, and its history had to be re-evaluated.

Current scholarship agrees that the pre-Samaritan text of the Pentateuch is an ancient version of the text of the Pentateuch that circulated in Palestine (Judea and Samaria) at least as early as the third century BCE. This date is supported by the fact that the pre-Samaritan version shares many small expansions (two, three, or more words) with the Greek Septuagint (LXX) version of the Pentateuch. Since the LXX Pentateuch was translated into Greek from a Hebrew base text(s) in the mid-third century BCE, that Hebrew base text must have been in circulation by the early third century BCE. Thus, the pre-Samaritan version and the LXX version of the Pentateuch share a common Hebrew ancestor that differed from the Masoretic Text (Crawford 2021, 55).

Sometime in the third century BCE, that ancestor underwent the more large-scale alterations that are characteristic of the pre-Samaritan manuscripts. These large-scale alterations include 1) a revised chronology in the genealogies in Genesis 5 and 11, solving the problem, preserved in MT, that three of the patriarchs, Jared, Methusaleh, and Lamech, seem to have survived the Flood. 2) The plague narratives in Exodus 6–11 have ten plusses, all of which record the fulfillment of the divine command to Moses and Aaron to warn Pharaoh before each plague. 3) Sections of Deuteronomy 1–3, Moses's exhortation on the plains of Moab, are retrojected back into the corresponding narrative in Exodus and Numbers if there is disagreement between the two (Crawford 2016, 167–68). Specific editorial changes to pre-Samaritan Deuteronomy will be examined below. All of

---

* The sigla indicate the salient information about each manuscript. For example, 4QpaleoExod^m indicates that the manuscript was found in Cave 4, Qumran; that it is written in paleo-Hebrew; that it is a manuscript of Exodus; and that it is the thirteenth (m) manuscript of Exodus found in Cave 4. If it has only a number (4Q158); it indicates that it was found in Cave 4, Qumran, and its number is 158 according to the system in Tov 2010.

these scribal changes may have been the product of cooperation among Samaritan and Judean scribes, working in their respective communities and sharing their work with each other.

The Samaritan and Judean communities experienced a final rupture, never to be repaired, when the Hasmonean ruler John Hyrcanus destroyed the Samaritan sanctuary on Mount Gerizim in 110 BCE. At that point the Samaritans separated from the Judeans, choosing as their canonical text the pre-Samaritan text already in circulation in Palestine. Their scribes then added to this base text a thin veneer of purely Samaritan editing, primarily the "Samaritan Tenth Commandment" to build a sanctuary on Mount Gerizim (see below). This historical reconstruction is supported by the paleographic dating of the Samaritan paleo-Hebrew script to the late second century BCE, the orthography of the SP, reflecting late Second Temple orthographic practice, and the reading tradition of the Samaritans, which developed in the late second to early first centuries BCE (Crawford 2016, 169; Schorch 1997, 1999). Later, in the late first century CE, the Jewish community would solidify their choice of the MT textual version as their canonical Pentateuch.

4. Deuteronomy in its Samaritan Version

Deuteronomy in its pre-Samaritan and Samaritan versions must always be considered in relation to the other books of the Pentateuch, since, by the third century BCE, the five books of Moses were considered one complete unit. This is demonstrated by the fact that scribal editorial changes, especially the harmonizations between Deut 1–3 and the narratives of Exodus and Numbers, take place across individual books.

Bearing that in mind, Deuteronomy in the SP exhibits unique textual characteristics. Some of these characteristics were most likely already in its pre-Samaritan version. Unfortunately, we do not possess an entire pre-Samaritan manuscript of Deuteronomy, but 4Q364, a pre-Samaritan manuscript, contains fragments of Deuteronomy. Other textual characteristics in SP Deuteronomy are clearly the product of Samaritan editing. I will describe the editorial characteristics of SP Deuteronomy in roughly chronological order, beginning with the small expansions and other changes found only in the SP or shared with LXX Deuteronomy and ending with the specifically Samaritan changes. The variants described below are all *intentional* or *deliberate* variants; that is, they were made deliberately by a scribe(s) and were not the result of unintentional changes such as orthographic differences, confusion of consonants, oral/aural misunderstandings, and the like. There are approximately 568 intentional variants in SP Deuteronomy (McCarthy 2004, 122).

4.1 Minor Additions and Word Changes

Deuteronomy has a distinctive rhetorical style, replete with formulaic phrases that repeat throughout the book. Examples include "[the commandments] that the Lord your/our God is commanding you/has commanded you [today];" "with a mighty hand and an outstretched arm"; "which the Lord your God is giving to you"; "the land that the Lord your God is giving you to possess"; and "statutes, (commandments), and ordinances." Because of this repetition, the Deuteronomy text in SP (and LXX) often expands to include more of the formula than was in the earlier text form. For example, at Deut 4:2, MT has the phrase "that I am commanding you." After "you," both SP and LXX add "today." At 24:1, MT reads "If a man takes a woman and becomes her husband ..." SP has a longer reading: "If a man takes a woman and he goes into her and becomes her husband ..." The longer reading of SP, with the addition of "and he goes into her," echoes the wording of 22:13.

The text of the Samaritan Pentateuch sometimes is "updated" to use a more common or "modern" word than that found in MT (it is often difficult to determine what word LXX is translating). For example, at Deut 16:8 SP Deut has חג, "festival," rather than עצרת, "assembly." These sorts of small changes most likely were part of pre-Samaritan Deuteronomy.

4.2 Large-Scale Editorial and Harmonistic Changes

The pre-Samaritan group of texts, of which the Samaritan Pentateuch is a descendant, as a whole is characterized by large-scale editorial (or scribal) changes and harmonizations, in which textual material from one part of the Pentateuch is inserted into another part of the Pentateuch (harmonization) or textual material is added to the base text (editorial change). There are, according to Magnar Kartveit, forty of these large-scale expansions in the pre-Samaritan Pentateuch text (Kartveit 2009, 265). These pre-Samaritan readings are preserved in Qumran manuscripts 4QExod-Lev[f], 4QpaleoExod[m], 4QNum[b], 4Q364, and 4Q158, as well as a quotation in 4QTestimonia (4Q175). The purpose of these scribal insertions is to create a more "perfect" version of the text of the Pentateuch by filling in perceived gaps in the Pentateuchal narrative (this type of editorial activity does not take place in the legal sections of the Pentateuch). With regards to Deuteronomy, this scribal activity is especially evident in the story of the desert wanderings, first narrated in Exodus and Numbers and then re-told by Moses on the Plains of Moab in Deut 1–3. Relevant material from Deut 1–3 is retrojected back into the narratives of Exodus and Numbers at the appropriate points in the narrative. Two examples of harmonization from Deut 1–3 into Exodus and Numbers follow, the first from 4QpaleoExod^m and the second from 4QNum^b.

4.2.1 The Appointment of Judges
4QpaleoExod^m: Exod 18:24 + Deut 1:9–18 + Exod 18:26 (the Deuteronomy text is in italics):

$^{\text{Exod 18:24}}$ And Moses listened to the voice of his father-in-law and did all that he had said. $^{\text{Deut 1:9-18}}$ *And Moses said to the people, I alone am not able to bear you. The Lord your God has multiplied you, and here you are today as the stars of heaven in multitude. May the Lord, the God of your forefathers make you a thousand times more numerous than you are and bless you as He has promised you. How can I alone bear your problems, and your burdens, and your complaints? You choose wise, understanding, and knowledgeable men from among your tribes and I will assign them as heads over you. And they answered and said, the thing which you have said to do is good. And he took the heads of their tribes, wise and understanding men, and made them heads over them, commanders of thousands, and commanders of hundreds, commanders of fifties, and commanders of tens, and officials in their tribes. And he commanded their judges, saying, hear the cases between your brethren, and judge righteously between a man and his brother, or his proselyte. You shall not show partiality in judgment, you shall hear the small as well as the great. You shall not be afraid in any man's presence, for the judgment is God's. The case that is too hard for you, bring to me, and I will hear it. And he commanded them all the things which they should do.* $^{\text{Exod 18:26}}$ And they judged the people at all times. The hard cases they would bring to Moses, but every minor dispute they themselves would judge. (Translation from Tsedaka and Sullivan 2013, 169–70, with alterations).

Note that the scribe has altered his source text, Deut 1:9—18, from the direct, first-person speech of Moses to the third person, to fit the third-person narrative voice of Exodus. Otherwise, the Deuteronomy text is simply inserted into the Exodus narrative, bringing the two versions of the story together. As separate narratives they could be viewed as disagreeing with each other, since in Exodus it is Jethro, Moses' father-in-law, who proposes the idea of judges, while in Deuteronomy Moses acts on his own. The scribe solves that perceived problem with his harmonization.

4.2.2 Avoidance of Ammon
4QNum^b: Num 21:12 + Deut 2:17–19 + Num 21:13 (the Deuteronomy text is in italics):

$^{\text{Num 21:12}}$ From there they traveled and camped in the brook of Zered. $^{\text{Deut 2:17-19}}$ *And the Lord spoke to Moses, saying, This day you are to cross over at Ar on the border of Moab. And you will come near the sons of Ammon. Don't harass them or meddle with them, for I will not give you any of the land of the sons of Ammon as an inheritance, because I have given it to the sons of Lot as an inheritance.* ^(Exod 21:13) And they traveled from the brook of Zered and they camped on the side of the Arnon, on the desert that goes out of the border of the Amorites (Translation from Tsedaka and Sullivan 2013, 361, with alterations).

In this passage it is not necessary to change the grammatical person of the Deuteronomy passage, since it is a quotation of Yhwh speaking to Moses. The scribe only had to insert it into the Numbers narrative.

4.2.3 Harmonization in the Text of Deuteronomy

There are only two instances in the pre-Samaritan text of Deuteronomy where material is inserted into Deuteronomy from the earlier narratives of Exodus and Numbers. They are found at Deut 2:7 and 10:6. Both instances are found in 4Q364 as well as SP Deuteronomy, indicating they are part of pre-Samaritan Deuteronomy.

Deut 2:7 + Num 20:14, 17–18 + Deut 2:8 (the Numbers text is in italics):
^(Deut 2:7) For the Lord your God has blessed you in all the work of your hands. He has known your going through this great desert. These forty years the Lord your God has been with you, you have not lacked a thing. ^(Exod 20:14, 17–18) *And I have sent messengers to the king of Edom, saying, I will pass through your land, I will not turn aside through field or through vineyard, and we will not drink water from a well. We will go along the King's Way. We will not turn right or left until we will pass your border. And he said, You shall not pass through me or I will come out with the sword against you.* ^(Deut 2:8) And we passed beyond our brothers the sons of Esau, who dwell in Seir, away from the desert road, away from Elath and from Ezion-Geber (Translation from Tsedaka and Sullivan 2013, 409, with alterations).

Since this insertion is placed into Deuteronomy from Numbers, the grammatical person changes from third person narration to the first-person speech of Moses and then the first- person speech of the king of Edom. It is otherwise unchanged.

Deut 10:6a + Num 33:31–37a + Deut 10:6b (the Numbers text is in italics):
^(Deut 10:6a) And the sons of Israel set out ^(Num 33:31–37a) *from Moserah and they camped in Bene-jaakan. From there they journeyed and camped in Hor-haggidgad. From there they journeyed and camped in Jorbathah, a land of streams of water. From there they journeyed and camped in Abronah. From there they journeyed and camped in Ezion-Geber. From there they journeyed and camped in the desert of Zin, it is Kadesh. From there they journeyed and camped in Mount Hor. And Aaron died there,* ^(Deut 10:6b) and he was buried. And Eleazar his son ministered as priest in his place (Translation from Tsedaka and Sullivan 2013, 431, with alterations).

This text has a more complicated insertion. The scribe has altered the text of Deut 10:6 in order to make the insertion from Numbers fit into the text smoothly. In MT Deut 10:6 the death of Aaron is placed in Moserah, where he is buried and Eleazar succeeds him; the Israelites then journey to Gudgodah and then on to Jotbathah. SP Deuteronomy does not record the death of Aaron at Moserah but instead begins the insertion from Numbers. In Numbers, Jorbathah/Jotbathah is not otherwise described, but in Deuteronomy it is described as "a land of streams of water," which the scribe retained in the text. The text then picks up Numbers again, moving the Israelites all the way to Mount Hor. In Numbers, Aaron dies at Mount Hor, not at the more obscure Moserah, which this scribe retains here in Deuteronomy. After the death of Aaron, the text resumes with Deut 10:6b. This insertion displays the skill of the scribe, who does not simply insert one text into another but interweaves the two texts, resulting in one smooth, non-contradictory narrative.

4.3 Ancient Variants between Pre-Samaritan Deuteronomy and MT Deuteronomy

The Samaritan text of Deuteronomy contains two important variants from MT Deuteronomy that are ancient, stemming from the pre-Samaritan version of Deuteronomy. Because the variants are ancient and well-established in their respective traditions, it is difficult to determine which reading was earlier and which reading was a deliberate (later) change.

4.3.1 Deut 12:5, the רחבי/רחב ("chose/will choose") variant

This variant appears in the Deuteronomic formula המקום אשר יבחר/בחר יהוה אלהיכם לשים את שמו שם, "the place where Yhwh your God will choose/has chosen to set his name," which first appears at Deut 12:5 and then recurs twenty-one times throughout the book.** The formula refers to the location where Israel is to meet to make sacrifices and offerings (Deut 12:6-7), a place that was eventually understood as where Yhwh's temple was to be built, which in the Samaritan tradition is Mount Gerizim and in the Judean tradition is Jerusalem. SP consistently reads בחר, "has chosen," referring to Mount Gerizim (Deut 11:29), while MT has יבחר, "will choose," referring to the future choice of Jerusalem, fulfilled under David and Solomon (1 Kgs 8:16//2 Chr 6:5-6). Unfortunately, no Qumran manuscripts of Deuteronomy preserve this phrase. Until very recently, most scholars argued that the Samaritan reading was ideological, a change made once the Samaritans adopted the pre-Samaritan version of the Pentateuch as their canonical text and altered it to fit with their

---

**   Deut 12:5, 11, 14, 18, 21, 26; 14:23, 24, 25; 15:20; 16:2, 6, 7, 11, 15, 16; 17:8, 10, 15; 18:6; 26:2; and 31:11.

election theology of Mount Gerizim (see, e.g. Tov 2022, 190–91). However, Adrian Schenker has collected twelve instances in the Greek tradition where the independent reading "has chosen" (Gk. aorist tense) occurs (Deut 12:5 [2x], 12:11, 12:14, 12:26, 14:23, 14:24 [2x], 14:25 [2x], 16:2, and 17:8) (Schenker 2008; 2010). These readings indicate that the reading "has chosen" is ancient, existing before the Greek and the pre-Samaritan textual traditions of Deuteronomy separated. Since that is the case, any argument about which reading is earlier must be made on other grounds than the traditional argument that the Samaritans simply adopted the Judean Pentateuch and altered it. In fact, the notion that God has already chosen Mount Gerizim for his sanctuary fits better within the narrative of Deuteronomy, since it is already hinted at in Deut 11:29: "When the Lord your God has brought you into the land that you are entering to occupy, you shall set the blessing on *Mount Gerizim* and the curse on Mount Ebal" (emphasis mine). Thus, Mount Gerizim is the mountain of blessing and as such an obvious choice for Yhwh's sanctuary in the holy land. On the other hand, the MT formula "will choose" only makes sense within the broader contours of the Former Prophets (Joshua through 2 Kings, with Deuteronomy as a prologue), in which Jerusalem does not even become part of the Israelite territory until David's conquest in 2 Sam 5:6–9. Therefore, it can be argued that the MT reading "will choose" is just as ideological as the Samaritan reading "has chosen," and that both must be accepted as equally ancient and valid readings (Crawford 2017, 102–03).

4.3.2 Deut 27:4: Gerizim vs. Ebal

This important variant is related to the chose/will choose variant. In Deut 27, Moses is commanding the people concerning what they should do when they cross the Jordan into the promised land. Deuteronomy 27:4 reads: "So when you have crossed over the Jordan, you shall set up these stones, about which I am commanding you today, on Mount Gerizim/Ebal, and you shall cover them with plaster." Perhaps not surprisingly, the Samaritan Pentateuch reads "on Mount Gerizim (בהרגריזים)," reflecting their understanding that Mount Gerizim has been chosen by God as the mount of blessing (Deut 11:29). Much more surprising is the MT reading "on Mount Ebal (בהר עיבל)." Mount Ebal is the mount of cursing in Deut 11:29, so why should an altar be built there? Simply on literary grounds, the SP Gerizim reading would seem to be earlier, and the MT Ebal reading a later, polemical change (Schorch 2011, 28–30). Further, recently two independent witnesses to the Samaritan reading have been discovered: the first is a Latin manuscript (Codex Lugdunensis) and the second a Greek papyrus (Papyrus Giessen 19). Thus, once again it is clear that the Samaritan reading is as ancient as the MT reading; in this case a persuasive argument can be made that the Samaritan reading of Mount

Gerizim is the earlier of the two, and MT's reading "Mount Ebal" is a later polemical change.

4.4 The Samaritan Tenth Commandment

After relations between the Samaritan and Judean communities were irreparably ruptured by the Hasmonean destruction of the Samaritan sanctuary on Mount Gerizim in 110 BCE, the Samaritans chose the pre-Samaritan version of the Pentateuch, already in circulation in Palestine and shared by both communities, as their canonical text of the Pentateuch. That text was then edited by Samaritan scribes to conform more closely to Samaritan theology. The most prominent change was the addition of the so-called Samaritan Tenth Commandment at the end of the Decalogue in Exod 20 and Deut 5, placing in the Decalogue a command to build an altar on Mount Gerizim. To accomplish this while keeping the traditional number of ten commandments, the Samaritans reorganized the Decalogue, taking Deut 5:6-7, "I am the Lord your God, who brought you out of the land of Egypt, out of the house of slavery. You shall have no other gods before me," not as the first commandment but as part of the preamble. They then added a tenth commandment after 5:18:

And when the Lord your God brings you to the land of the Canaanites that you are entering to possess, you shall set up large stones for yourself and cover them with plaster. And you shall write on the stones all the words of this law. And when you have crossed the Jordan, set up these stones on Mount Gerizim as I command you today. Build there an altar to the Lord your God, an altar of stones. Do not use any iron tool on them. Build the altar of the Lord your God with unhewn stones and offer burnt offerings on it to the Lord your God. That mountain is across the Jordan, westwards toward the setting sun, in the territory of the Canaanites who dwell in the Arabah facing Gilgal, near the oak of Moreh, facing Shechem.

In keeping with the scribal technique found in pre-Samaritan Deuteronomy, where passages are harmonized by using passages from elsewhere in the Pentateuch, this commandment is woven from Deut 11:29, 27:2-7, and 11:30, with some alterations. These passages, as we have seen above, identify Mount Gerizim, according to the pre-Samaritan text, as the mount of blessing and direct the erection of an altar there. This additional commandment in the Decalogue simply reinforces that instruction, making the location of the altar completely clear by specifying the location of the mountain. This command may also be seen as polemical, given that the actual altar on Gerizim had been recently destroyed by the Judeans (Kartveit 2009, 293). It is the only major change that the

Samaritan community made to the pre-Samaritan version of Deuteronomy after the split with the Judeans.

Around the same time that the Samaritans chose the pre-Samaritan version of the Pentateuch as their canonical text, the Judean community, led by the Temple priesthood in Jerusalem, favored the textual ancestor of the Masoretic Text, to the extent that by the second century CE, all our manuscript evidence from the Judean Desert caves preserves the pre-Masoretic consonantal text (Crawford 2021, 54). It may be during that time that the MT consonantal text of Deuteronomy was altered to read "Mount Ebal" at Deut 27:4.

In conclusion, the Samaritan Pentateuch contains a text of Deuteronomy that is ancient, authoritative, and accepted by both the Judean community and the Samaritan community. It was not until after the rupture between the Samaritans and the Judeans in the late second century BCE that the pre-Samaritan text slowly fell out of use in the Jewish community.

Works Cited

Crawford, Sidnie White. 2016. "1.2.3 Samaritan Pentateuch." Pages 166–75 in *Textual History of the Bible: The Hebrew Bible*, Vol. 1A. Edited by Armin Lange and Emanuel Tov. Leiden/Boston: Brill.

––––––. 2017. "2.2.4.5 Deuteronomy." Pages 101–5 in *Textual History of the Bible: The Hebrew Bible*, Vol. 1B. Edited by Armin Lange and Emanuel Tov. Leiden/Boston: Brill.

––––––. 2021. "The Text of the Pentateuch." Pages 41–60 in *The Oxford Handbook of the Pentateuch*. Edited by Joel S. Baden and Jeffrey Stackert. New York: Oxford University Press.

Kartveit, Magnar. 2009. *The Origins of the Samaritans*. Supplements to Vetus Testamentum 128. Leiden/Boston: Brill.

Knoppers, Gary N. 2013. *Jews and Samaritans. The Origins and History of their Early Relations*. New York: Oxford University Press.

Magen, Yitzhak. 2008. *A Temple City*. Vol. 2 of *Mount Gerizim Excavations*. Judea and Samaria Publications 8. Jerusalem: Israel Antiquities Authority.

McCarthy, Carmel. 2004. "Samaritan Pentateuch Readings in Deuteronomy." Pages 118–30 in *Biblical and Near Eastern Essays: Studies in Honour of Kevin J. Cathcart*. Edited by Carmel McCarthy and John F. Healey. Journal for the Study of the Old Testament Supplement Series 375. New York/London: T. & T/ Clark.

Pummer, Reinhard. 2016. *The Samaritans: A Profile*. Grand Rapids: W. B. Eerdmans.

Purvis, James D. 1968. *The Samaritan Pentateuch and the Origin of the Samaritan Sect*. Harvard Semitic Monographs 2. Cambridge, MA: Harvard University Press.

Schenker, Adrian. 2008. "Le Seigneur choisir-t-il le lieu de son nom ou l' a-t-il choisi? L'apport de la Bible grecque ancienne à l'histoire du texte samaritain et massorétique." Pages 339–52 in *Scripture in Transition: Essays on Septuagint, Hebrew Bible, and Dead Sea Scrolls in Honour of Raija Sollamo*. Edited by Annsi Voitila and Jutta Jokiranta. Supplements to the Journal for the Study of Judaism 126. Leiden: Brill.

------. 2010. "Textgeschichtliches zum Samaritanischen Pentateuch und Samareitikon." Pages 105–21 in *Samaritans: Past and Present: Current Studies*. Edited by Menachem Mor and Friedrich V. Reiterer. Studia Samaritana 53. Berlin: de Gruyter.

Schorch, Stefan. 1997. "Die Bedeutung der samaritanischen mündlichen Tradition für die Textgeschichte des Pentateuch (II)." *Mitteilungen und Beiträge der Forschungsstelle Judentum, Theologische Fakultät Leipzig* 12–13: 53–64.

------. 1999. "Die Bedeutung der samaritanischen mündlichen Tradition für die Exegese des Pentateuch." *Wort und Dienst* 25: 77–91.

------. 2011. "The Samaritan Version of Deuteronomy and the Origin of Deuteronomy." Pages 23–38 in *Samaria, Samarians, Samaritans: Studies on Bible, History and Linguistics*. Edited by József Zsengellér. Studia Judaica 66/Studia Samaritana 6. Berlin: de Gruyter.

Tov, Emanuel. 2010. *Revised Lists of the Texts from the Judaean Desert*. Leiden/Boston: Brill.

------. 2022. *Textual Criticism of the Hebrew Bible*. 4th ed. Minneapolis: Fortress.

Tsedaka, Benyamim and Sharon Sullivan. 2013. *The Israelite Samaritan Version of the Torah*. Grand Rapids: W. B. Eerdmans.

About the Author

Sidnie White Crawford is Professor emerita of Hebrew Bible and Second Temple Judaism at the University of Nebraska-Lincoln. She edited nine Qumran Deuteronomy manuscripts for the series Discoveries in the Judaean Desert and is an internationally recognized expert in the textual criticism of the Pentateuch.

Chapter 16
Where and When Might Deuteronomy Have Been Written?

Diana V. Edelman

Abstract

The proposal that Deuteronomy exhibits northern/Israelite ideology is evaluated and found to be inconclusive. Three suggested dating indicators thought to point to the initial composition of the scroll either soon after 722 BCE or during the reign of King Josiah are then assessed: the expansion of Jerusalem in the late eighth century BCE, the hypothetical dependence of small portions of Deuteronomy on Esarhaddon's Succession Oath Documents, and the equation of the scroll of Torah purportedly found in the temple during repairs under Josiah with Deuteronomy (2 Kgs 22:8–10). The first and third are found to be inconclusive and the second erroneous. The religious worldview associated with Yhwh Elohim found in the book is argued to be a more reliable indicator of the book's initial creation in either the Neo-Babylonian or early Persian period. Finally, options for the place of composition in Yehud or Babylonia during the Neo-Babylonian period and in Yehud, Babylonia, or on Mt Gerizim in the early Achaemenid period are evaluated.

Keywords: Deuteronomy, northern ideology, Yhwh Elohim, Torah, scribes, Mt. Gerizim, Jerusalem, Josiah, Esarhaddon

1. Introduction

The books comprising the Hebrew Bible are all anonymous, as are their places of composition. In the case of the first five books in particular, Genesis Exodus, Leviticus, Numbers, and Deuteronomy, where and when they were written become especially important to consider, because only these five books came to be accepted as authoritative by both the Judean community in Jerusalem and the Samarian community on Mt. Gerizim. Beginning within the Hellenistic period (ca. 332–63 BCE), some scholars prefer to refer to the latter religious community as Samaritans, to distinguish them from the wider population of the province of Samaria. The remaining books are generally thought to have been written in Jerusalem. In theory, any or all of the first five books could have been written in the kingdom of Israel or its successor, the province of Samerina/Samaria, or in the kingdom of Judah or its successor, the province of Yehud. The main clues we have concerning who composed each book, and where, however, are internal indicators in the books themselves, and scholars do not always agree on what constitutes a reliable indicator.

The most popular view has been that all five of these books were written by scribes in Jerusalem, either during the later monarchy (ca. 700–586 BCE), during the Neo-Babylonian period, represented in biblical chronology as "the Exile" (586–532 BCE), or in the first half of the Achaemenid period (ca. 538–438 BCE), conceived of as "the post-exilic" period in the biblical corpus. Different rationales underlie each period, and these can differ among the five books.

The typical scholarly understanding considers chs 12:1–26:15 to be a self-contained unit of "laws," often dubbed the Deuteronomic Code (DC), that was framed initially by 4:44–11:32 and 27–30. According to the common view, Deut 4:44–30:20 should have formed the earliest version of the book (e.g. Noth 1981 [1943], 16). Eventually, a second outer frame is thought to have been added: 1:1–4:43 and 31–34. There are variations, however. Thomas Römer, for example, defines the earliest form to begin with Deut 6:4–5 (6–7a), go on to include much of chs 12–26, and end with ch. 28, although he thinks 30:19a could have followed ch. 28 directly as the closing verse (2005, 78–81).

There has been a longstanding view that the scroll of Deuteronomy reflects "Northern/Israelite ideology." But even with that, the place of composition has been identified differently. The more common view places it in Jerusalem, with the ideas carried by refugees who fled to Judah after the fall of Samaria in 722 BCE, while a less common view places it in Samaria soon after 722 BCE, as the end-product of a program to teach the new population groups like the Assyrians who moved into the province about the ways of the native deity of the land.

The issue of the place of composition, however, needs revisiting in the light of more recent developments. A new possibility has surfaced with an interesting twist: the book might have been composed on Mt. Gerizim, the site of the Samarian temple dedicated to Yhwh Elohim, by Judean scribes who had moved there to help staff the new temple.

2. What is "Northern" about Deuteronomy?

Deuteronomy feels "different" from the other books in the Pentateuch when read. It acknowledges various roles of priests; they will dispense justice (17:9, 12; 19:17; 21:5) and make medical diagnoses of contagious skin disease (24:8). As cultic functionaries, they will be entitled to temple prebends and portions of any sacrifices made by private citizens that they officiate over (18:1-3). The officiating priest is to receive the basket of first fruits (Deut 26:3-4) at Sukkôt, and as bearers of the Ark, the priests are entrusted with the Torah, alongside the elders (31:9). A priest will speak to the troops before battle (Deut 20:2), and priests will supervise the writing of a copy of the Torah for the king to study (17:18). Yet, the book has relatively little to say about the sacrificial cult associated with the altar (e.g. 12:17-18; 18:3-4), especially in contrast to Leviticus, or about the temple, which occurs explicitly in a single passage in the book (Deut 23:18). There is no mention of Jerusalem. A case could be made that most if not all such references to sacrifices at the temple are secondary additions.

Instead, Deuteronomy focuses on Israel as a community; how it is to be administered and which social and legal norms are to prevail after the conquest of Canaan. The book is commonly ascribed to the worldview of Levites (e.g. von Rad 1953, 60-68), i.e. scribal bureaucrats who are separate from priests, even though both are assigned to membership in the tribe of Levi; while all priests are "Levites," not all Levites are priests (contra von Rad). Priests are thought to be responsible for Leviticus and Numbers, as well as parts of Genesis and Exodus. This distinction alone could account for the different outlook, rather than assuming a geographical distinction associated with differing understandings of the cult of Yhwh in Israel/Samaria vs. Judah/Yehud.

"Northern" is the typical way to refer to ideas or material that originated either in the kingdom of Israel (ca. 1000-722 BCE) or in its successor province, named after the capital city, Samaria. It is called Samerina in the Assyrian and Babylonian texts and on coins minted in the province during the Persian period, which reflects the Hebrew spelling of the name of the city: Shomron. "Southern," then, refers to ideas or content that originated either in the kingdom of Judah (ca. 975–587 BCE) or in its successor province, Yehud. The latter name is Aramaic instead of Hebrew.

In the mid-twentieth century, a segment of biblical scholars accepted the theory that Deuteronomy derived directly or indirectly from premonarchic-era traditions associated with Israel's existence as a twelve-tribe amphictyonic league associated with a sequence of central sanctuary locations, especially Shechem, Shiloh, Bethel, and Gilgal. It was believed a ceremony of covenant renewal commemorating the covenant, the formal agreement sealed by oath made between Yhwh and Israel at Mt. Sinai, took place at the central sanctuary periodically, perhaps even annually. These "early" traditions were thought to have been transmitted within the Northern Kingdom at sites like Shechem, Bethel, and Gilgal (see e.g. Nicholson 1967, 58–65).

It needs to be recognized, however, that according to the logic of this theory, any such traditions would have been shared by northern and southern tribes, so none would have been "northern" specifically. Being preserved at northern sanctuaries does not mean that a tradition might not also have been preserved within "southern" tradition and eventually recorded and archived. To claim Deuteronomy is "northern" on an amphictyonic basis means only that any older traditions the book builds on were accessed from Israelite archives, not that the ideas they reflect were only believed or followed by Israelites or Samarians but not Judahites or Judeans.

Assuming this amphictyonic background, it was argued that Yhwh's kingship over Israel explains why the powers of the human king are so restricted in Deut 17:14–20, why the regulations concerning "holy war" (ḥerem) are present (Deut 20:16–17), and why there is an emphasis on rejecting "the gods" worshiped by the Canaanites and other nations throughout the book. Deuteronomic "name theology" (see e.g. Mettinger 1982, 38–79) asserts that the otherwise invisible deity is present on earth via its šem, "name" or "reputation," which the deity will set in its chosen place, to dwell or reside (e.g. Deut 12:5, 11, 21; 14:23–24; 16:2, 6, 11; 26:2).[1]

According to Ernest Nicholson (1967, 66–82), "name theology" went hand in hand with a reconceptualization in northern understanding of the Ark, from the throne (or footstool of the throne) of Yhwh to a container for the two stone tablets upon which were written the ten commandments, symbolizing Yhwh Elohim's Torah "teaching." Both were to

---

1 Here I follow the West Semitic meanings of the Hebrew terms in this wording (lešakkēn šemô šām), not the East Semitic (Akkadian) idioms used on royal monuments that fell out of use before Judah or Israel had contact with Assyria, as Sandra Richter prefers (2002).

have taken place during the period of the kingdom of Israel, after David moved the Ark to Jerusalem.

The theory of early Israel constituting a religiously based amphictyonic league is now passé. As a result, any argument about a northern origin of Deuteronomy that rests on it will need to be reframed in order to be valid. Nevertheless, the possibility that the book might have drawn upon traditions that originated in the kingdom of Israel or the province of Samerina or was composed there remain viable options to be explored.

It is noteworthy that in the Pentateuch, including Deuteronomy, the deity is never referred to as Yhwh Ṣebā'ôt, "Yhwh of Hosts," the title of the god associated with the temple in Jerusalem during the Judahite monarchy. Neither is it designated Yhwh Shomron, the apparent name of the territorial deity of the kingdom of Israel or the city deity of Samaria, found in a ninth-century inscription at Kuntillet ʿAjrud in the northern Sinai. Instead, the form of Yhwh in Deuteronomy is consistently identified as Elohim, "God" or "divinity," always with a pronominal suffix – my, our, your, his, their. So, this idea is not specifically "northern."

On the other hand, however, the book names very few sites in Cisjordan, and of those, the Shechem Valley stands out in importance as the place where a cultic ceremony is to take place. In 27:4–8, 12–13 Moses commands the people to erect large, plastered stones containing "all the words of this teaching" on Mt. Gerizim after the completion of the conquest of Canaan, as well as an altar. A growing number of scholars accepts that the reading, Mt. Ebal, found in the Jewish Masoretic text (MT), has been altered over time from the original reading, Mt. Gerizim, found in the Samaritan Pentateuch (SP) and in Old Greek (OG) manuscripts. A few verses later, there is to be to a ceremony involving the blessing and cursing of the tribes, half of whom will stand opposite Mt. Gerizim and half opposite Mt. Ebal. These two mountains are located on either side of the Shechem Valley, squarely within the territory of the kingdom of Israel and its successor, the province of Samerina/Samaria.

The patriarch Jacob, whose name Elohim changes to Israel (Gen 32:24–32), is thought to have roots within northern tradition and is specifically said to have bought land near Shechem (Gen 33:18) or taken Shechem ("a shoulder") from the hand of the Amorites with his sword and bow (Gen 48:22) and have dwelt in the Shechem Valley (Gen 33:18–35:5). He was to have established an altar to Yhwh there (33:20) and to have buried the foreign gods, likely ancestral figurines (Edelman 2017) his family had traveled to Canaan with from their home in Haran (35:2–4) (Edelman 2012). In contrast, Abraham and possibly Isaac seem to have had roots in southern tradition, based on the places each dwell in Genesis (e.g. Römer 2012).

Scholars debate the antiquity of Jacob's connection to Shechem. While it used to be considered an early, pre-monarchic and/or amphictyonic tradition, some now suspect it is monarchic or later (for various views, see e.g. Nielsen 1955; de Pury 2006; Blum 2012; Na'aman 2014b; Finkelstein and Römer 2014; Hensel 2021). In addition, there almost certainly has been some tampering with the text of Deut 27 concerning the location in Cisjordan where the large inscribed, plastered stones that Moses commands to be established are to be erected and the timing of the action.

In Deut 27:2–3, on the one hand, the stones are to be set up near the Jordan River on the very day Israel crosses the Jordan into the promised land. The fulfillment of this command appears to be narrated initially in Josh 4, except that instead of two, twelve stones, one for each tribe, are taken from the midst of the Jordan River and erected at Gilgal near Jericho, where the Israelites encamp after entering Cisjordan. Also, the twelve are not plastered, and "all the words of this teaching" (27:2) are not inscribed on them. Ultimately, this story provides an etiology for the cult site of Gilgal instead, which apparently contained a circle of *maṣṣēbôt* (standing stones).

On the other hand, immediately after the first order issued in Deut 27:2–3, Moses commands the Israelites a second time to set up the large stones, but this time on Mt. Gerizim (Mt. Ebal in the MT), along with an altar of unhewn stones, and to inscribe on the large stones "all the words of this teaching," after they cross the Jordan. They are to offer whole burnt offerings on the altar and sacrifices of well-being, after which they are to eat there and rejoice (27:4–8). Mt. Gerizim lies about 26 miles from Jericho using current Israeli road systems. On foot, this would have been a minimum journey of two to three days northwest from Gilgal for the envisioned hundreds of thousands of multi-generational families carrying their tents and possessions.

The second command has no indicator as to when the stones and accompanying celebration are to take place other than "after the crossing of the Jordan." The fulfillment of this second command is narrated in Josh 8:30–35 and takes place after the destruction of Ai. Then, a subsequent ceremony led by Joshua takes place in the vicinity of Shechem in final chapter of the book, Josh 24. He writes the words of a formal agreement the people enter into there on "the scroll of the Torah of God" and sets up a large stone under the oak in the sanctuary of Yhwh, which seems to be a reference to the oak of Moreh ("Teaching") in Gen 35:4. The oaks (pl.) of Moreh also appear in Deut 11:31, but in a context that either places them beside Gilgal or beside Mt. Ebal and Mt. Gerizim, if the final prepositional phrase is a dangling modifier.

It seems unlikely that both commands in Deut 27 were original to the book. The present wording can be construed to propose two separate ceremonies to take place at two sites that are remembered as having had sacred associations; a Gilgal near Jericho during the monarchic era (e.g.

1 Sam 15:21, 33; 2 Kgs 2:1; 4:38; Hos 4:15; 9:15; 12:11; Amos 4:4–5) and Mt. Gerizim, possibly also a sacred site in the Iron IIC period according to the results of excavations (Arie 2021), but definitely one in the Persian period (Magen 2008; Edelman forth. c). One was to take place immediately upon entering the land and the other later on, at an unspecified point during or after the conquest. Had both been original, one would have expected more clarity about the two separate ceremonies, the timing of the second one, and no reference to the plastering and inscribing of stones in the first. The command to conduct a blessing and cursing ceremony at Mt. Gerizim and Mt. Ebal is anticipated in Deut 11:29–30, where the wording signals more clearly that the event will take place after Yhwh has caused the people to enter the land they are entering to inherit, as opposed to after having crossed over [the Jordan]. Which of the two in Deut 27:2–8 is original and which has been added is a point of debate, as is the reason for the alteration (e.g. Nielsen 1955, 39–85).

It also has been argued that both commands in Deut 27:2–3 and 4–8 are secondary additions, evidenced by how ch. 27 in its entirety breaks the otherwise logical continuity between Deut 26:16–19 and 28:1 (Nicholson 1967, 34). Those who accept his argument consider the references to Mt. Gerizim and Mt. Ebal in Deut 11 and 27 to be irrelevant, therefore, to the date and setting of the origin of Deuteronomy (e.g. Nihan 2007, 200–14; Edenburg and Müller 2015, 152, 157). Given the contradictions present, one still would have to postulate two layers within this purported "addition."

There are five references in Deut 4:44–30:20 (6:10; 9:5, 27; 29:13; 30:20) to the trio of patriarchs, Abraham, Isaac, and Jacob, with another found in 1:8. Some consider these to be later additions to the text, inserted to tie the book more closely to Genesis. Thomas Römer (1990, 319), for example, has argued that the wording in the book initially was "fathers" generically, in all instances, which designated all disobedient generations after the conquest. Others consider them original, building either on the existing text of Genesis or drawing on older traditions that eventually were recounted in Genesis (e.g. Arnold 2017). The inclusion of all three patriarchs in a standard formula presumes the perspective of Israel as twelve tribes encompassing both north and south, so this is not specifically northern either.

Some argue that the emphasis on the theme of the Exodus in this book reflects a tradition of northern origin. It is noteworthy that uniquely, all three pilgrimage festivals are made to commemorate the escape from Egypt in Deuteronomy (Deut 16; 26:1–11). In contrast, in Exod 23; 34 and Num 28–29, it is associated only with Passover; in Lev 23 it commemorates both Passover and Sukkôt. Many scholars believe that the references to the Exodus in Hosea 8:13, 9:3, 6; 11:1, 5; 12:9, 13; 13:4 and Amos 2:10–11;

3:1; 4:10 provide evidence that this tradition originated in the North, not the South (e.g. Burney 1918, xlv–vi). Both are considered the earliest prophetic books, dating somewhere from 762–700 BCE, during the reign of King Jeroboam II (ruled ca. 793–752 BCE) or shortly thereafter. Both focus on indicting the kingdom of Israel and predict its destruction. Hosea is portrayed as a native Israelite and Amos as a Judahite who goes to the Israelite royal temple in Bethel to prophesy.

Caution is needed, however, in concluding the Exodus is a northern tradition. All the prophetic books were created by scribes in Judah or Yehud; none form part of the official repertoire of northern Samaritan scripture. Within the Book of the Twelve (also called the Minor Prophets), these two compositions focus primarily on the destruction of the kingdom of Israel for apostasy. Israel's conversion to the province of Samerina serves as an object lesson for the kingdom of Judah, which eventually falls, allegedly for the same reason, as outlined in nine of the remaining ten books (excluding Jonah) named after prophets who are associated with the southern kingdom and the province of Yehud. Whatever actual words from historical prophets might be preserved in the two books, both reflect, ultimately, a southern perspective (e.g. Ben Zvi 2015; 2019). That being the case, it is hard to be certain whether the references to the Exodus were from historical prophets named Hosea or Amos or whether they derive from the Judahite or Judean scribes who created books, as part of their theological interpretations and understandings.

A review of possible "northern" content in Deuteronomy has not yielded anything definitive. By the same token, there is nothing explicitly "southern" in the content either.

3. How Reliable are Proposed Dating Indicators?

Those who propose a date for the composition of Deuteronomy during the monarchy tend to rely on three factors.

3.1 Archaeological Evidence for the Growth of Jerusalem in the Late Eighth century BCE

The first factor is external to the book itself. It concerns the substantial growth of the city of Jerusalem, with the building of a second wall to enclose a new western quarter, sometime near the end of the eighth century BCE. A number of scholars attribute this event to the arrival of a flood of refugees from Israel at the time of, or in the wake of, the Assyrian conquest of the kingdom in 722 BCE and its conversion to the province of Samerina (e.g. Broshi 1974; Finkelstein and Silberman 2001, 243; 2006; Schniedewind 2003, 380, 385–86; Finkelstein 2008; Burke 2012).

According to this theory, among those seeking asylum were scribes, who took with them their precious scrolls (e.g. Grabbe 2007, 169–70). This scenario requires that after they arrived, they found employment at the royal court in Jerusalem and became so influential that King Hezekiah (reigned ca. 716/15–687/86) adopted their traditions and ideas. Or, like the Assyrian king Ashurbanipal (reigned 669–631 BCE) who was a bibliophile and built a library from materials gathered from near and far, Hezekiah had their scrolls copied and added to the archives or library located in Jerusalem, possibly in the temple complex. In the latter case, they either could have been used to compose Deuteronomy and perhaps the other four Pentateuchal books; or, an early form of the book, already composed, could have become part of the scribal reading repertoire. So, this historical reconstruction would allow a composition of the scroll of Deuteronomy somewhere in Israel prior to 722 BCE by an Israelite scribe or sometime after 722 BCE in Jerusalem in Judah, either by a Judahite court scribe or by an immigrant Israelite scribe who found work at the royal court.

The problem with this entire reconstruction is that there is no proof that the occupants of the new "second quarter" in Jerusalem were primarily displaced Israelites. In fact, since Judah already was an Assyrian vassal at this time, the terms of its treaty would have required it to return any such refugees to the imperially appointed overseers of the new Assyrian province or suffer the consequences of treaty violation (Na'aman 2007, 31–35).

Those who cite the alleged presence of Israelites at Hezekiah's Passover festival reported in 2 Chr 30:25 as a historically reliable, corroborating text need to explain how this information was preserved for some 400 years and in the wake of the burning and destruction of Jerusalem in 587 BCE. It is part of the Chronicler's own agenda concerning the re-uniting of Israel and Judah; it does not appear in the account of Hezekiah's reign in 2 Kgs 18–20 but may have been inspired by the report of King Josiah's subsequent celebration of the Passover as prescribed in the "book of the oath-bound agreement" or more commonly, "the book of the covenant," for the first time since before the days of the judges (2 Kgs 23:21–23). There is no reference to the participation of northern Israelites living in various Assyrian provinces in the latter account, however; this was the Chronicler's own contribution.

An alternate historical reconstruction proposes that the occupants of the expanded city resulted from the natural growth of the city's population together with the arrival of Judahites from the countryside who voluntarily or involuntarily had moved there, some for economic opportunities and others for protection from an anticipated Assyrian invasion and siege after King Hezekiah rebelled and withheld his annual vassal tribute prior to 701 BCE (e.g. Na'aman 2007, 2009; 2014a; Guillaume 2008). If one considers this latter proposal more likely, then the expansion of the city of Jerusalem in the late eighth century has no relevance for when or where Deuteronomy was written. One has to find a different corroborating factor to explain the perceived though hard-to-find "northern ideology" in the book if (s)he wants to argue for its ultimate composition in Jerusalem during the monarchy.

A more historically plausible scenario for explaining the perceived "northern ideology" of the book rejects the flood of Israelite refugees heading to Jerusalem in favor of its composition soon after 722 BCE in the city of Samaria, the administrative seat of the new Assyrian province of Samerina, or in Bethel, which housed a royally established cult for Yhwh of Samaria. The Assyrians sent into exile a significant percentage of the Israelite population and replaced them with new groups forcefully resettled in Samerina in their stead. According to 2 Kgs 17:24, the incoming groups originated from Babylon, Cuthah, Avva, Hamath, and Sepharvaim and established the worship of their home deities alongside taking up the worship of the native deity, Yhwh Shomron of Samaria (vv. 29–41). Albrecht Alt (1953, 250–51), who wrote before the excavations in Jerusalem had uncovered the "second quarter," argued that Deuteronomy had been composed in Samerina shortly after 722 BCE by "northern circles" for a "northern" audience as a restoration program. This theory was never widely embraced, however, as formulated.

Building on Alt's proposed historical setting, however, Philip R. Davies (2021) more recently proposed that Deuteronomy was the end-product of a project whose aim was to enculturate the recent immigrants into Samaria into existing and ongoing Israelite customs, practices, and the worship of the native Yhwh Shomron as part of a large enterprise of reasserting and redefining the identity of Israel within Samaria after 722 BCE. According to this theory, then, Deuteronomy was composed in the post-monarchic province of Samerina/Samaria and reflects northern content throughout its earliest version as a coherent composition. We know that subsequent changes were made editorially, but the bulk of what is in the book today would also have been included by the scribe who created the scroll. In the case of both Alt and Davies, however, no accompanying explanation is offered for how or why the book was adopted and applied in Judah or Yehud as well.

3.2 Deuteronomy as the Scroll of the Torah Rediscovered in the Reign of Josiah

The second factor ties the call for a single place that Yhwh Elohim will choose to place "his" name to dwell in multiple passages within Deuteronomy to the claim that "the scroll, the scroll of the Torah ['teaching']" that was found during the reign of King Josiah during temple repairs (2 Kgs 22:8–10), was Deuteronomy. After it was read to the king, "the scroll of the oath-bound agreement (*seper habbᵉrît*)" found in the temple of Yhwh (2 Kgs 23:2) prompted the closing of all temples and shrines in Judah other than the main temple in Jerusalem (2 Kgs 23:4–13). As a logical corollary, the scroll, whether it is Deuteronomy alone or included some other books within the Pentateuch as well, would have been composed in Jerusalem at some point prior to its discovery, by a Judahite scribe.

The identity of Deuteronomy with the scroll of the Torah/scroll of the oath-bound agreement allegedly found in the temple during Josiah's reign (ca. 640–609 BCE) is often associated with the doctoral thesis of Wilhem M. L. de Wette approved in 1805. But, as demonstrated by Paul B. Harvey and Baruch Halpern (2008), the idea predates this individual, who did not, in fact, offer a compelling argument for identifying Deuteronomy with the Josianic "Book of the Torah." Notwithstanding, a form of this theory remains popular today, even if there has been a stream of challenges to it, most of which doubt the historical reliability of the reported scroll-finding event (e.g. Nicholson 1967, 1–17 for an early overview; Davies 2005; Ben Zvi 2008; Nicholson 2014, 16–40). Those who take the latter stance generally assume Deuteronomy was written during the Neo-Babylonian or early Persian period and has been retrojected to the late monarchic period under one of the most pious kings according to the evaluation of the scribe who created the scroll containing 1–2 Kgs, in order to create a memory of continuity between the cult of Yhwh Ṣebā'ôt under the monarchy and that practiced in the rebuilt temple in Jerusalem in the early Persian period, dedicated to Yhwh Elohim.

One way some traditional cultures deal with innovation is to deny anything is new and breaks with past tradition by claiming that the practice or idea in question has always existed or been part of tradition for a long time. No change is acknowledged (e.g. Peel 1984). From this viewpoint, the scroll of the Torah (teaching), also identified as the scroll of the *berît* (oath-bound agreement), would have been something that had been created and gained prominence after the monarchy had ended.

A minority position, however, advocates a variation on this principle that allows the historicity of the finding of the scroll during temple repairs to be upheld. Thomas Römer has pointed to the multicultural practice of planting a new composition somewhere to be discovered that would then allow the claim to be made that it was very old (e.g. 1997, 5–10; 2005, 51–53). An example from Babylonian history is the cruciform monument of Manistushu (reigned ca. 2270–2255 BCE), the third king of the Akkadian Empire and son of Sargon the Great. It likely was created by a priest or scribe associated with the temple of the sun deity Shamash in Sippar during the reign of Nabonidus (reigned ca. 556–539 BCE), to assert that Manistushu had bestowed a number of endowments on the temple that needed to be honored by future kings, including Nabonidus. Nabonidus strongly favored the cult of the moon god Sin (e.g. Gelb 1949; Finkel and Fletcher 2016, 239–45). Following this line of thinking in combination with the assumption a scroll was actually "discovered" during temple repairs, Deuteronomy would have been composed during the reign of Josiah by a Judahite scribe who probably had been associated with the temple in Jerusalem. He would have deposited it in the temple so it could be "found" and claimed to be very old and authoritative; somehow, it had been "misplaced" for hundreds of years inside the temple.

Arguing against the latter approach, many point out that it is historically implausible that the regulations incumbent upon the king in Deut 17:14–20 could have been written during the existence of the monarchy. They make him a pious studier of the Torah so that he can follow its expected behaviors and worldview. There is no endorsement of his normal royal functions of leading the army in war or administering justice. Instead, he is to defer to the priestly court to render decisions on the most difficult cases that could not be resolved in local courts. These verses effectively undercut the authority of the king; would a reigning monarch endorse such limitations to his power and authority? Those who maintain a date of origin for Deuteronomy during Josiah's reign solve this challenge by suggesting that this particular passage is a later, post-monarchic editorial insertion.

3.3 Deuteronomy's Inclusion of Segments of Esarhaddon's Succession Oath Document

The final proposed dating indicator asserts that the scribe who composed Deuteronomy had access to a copy of the succession oath documents (abbreviated ESOD, VTE, or EST) produced by King Esarhaddon (reigned 681–669 BCE) to secure the succession of his son Ashurbanipal to the throne of Assyria after his death. The king imposed it on all the citizens of the Assyrian Empire in 672 BCE. It has been argued that the scribe responsible for Deuteronomy incorporated a few segments of this specific document into the earliest textual form of the book in Deut 6:5; 13:1 [12:32 in English], 2–6 [1–5 in English] and 7–12 [6–11 in English]; and 28:15–45.

It is further suggested that this appropriation of Assyrian ideology that is then applied to bolster the Judahite vassal's self-understanding, as a way to undermine the original message, was a deliberate strategy of subaltern resistance, a concept derived from post-colonial studies (e.g. Otto 2000, 62–65; 2016, 1, 238–41; Levinson 2009, 32; Morrow 2009, 228–29, 231–33; for resistance, see e.g. Jefferess 2008). As a result, the book would have been written sometime after 672 BCE, when the ESOD was officially promulgated. In theory, it could have been within a year or within the ensuing century, as long as a copy of ESOD was accessible in an archive or temple. But those who espouse this reconstruction tend to tie this idea to the second factor, to reinforce a date of composition under Josiah.

In ch. 1 in this volume, I present a detailed rebuttal of this proposal (Edelman 2022a). Judah was a vassal kingdom of Assyria at the time ESOD was enacted, not an Assyrian province. There is no evidence that any vassals participated in the Empire-wide oath-bound ceremonies that took place within the confines of Assyrian territory. As a result, a copy of the document would not have ended up in Judah. In addition, a review of the alleged borrowings of wording indicates that the overlapping language cannot be attributed specifically to the ESOD but instead, reflects standard phraseology found in international treaties and their curses. This third date indicator must be rejected altogether; it is invalid. Even so, it illustrates how one's assumptions influence how one reads texts and creates an interpretative framework.

None of the three proposed date indicators provides undisputed, airtight information or evidence that points to a specific time of composition for the first version of the scroll of Deuteronomy, no matter how a scholar might choose to define that composition.

4. A New Dating Indicator and Its Implication for the Time and Place of Composition

4.1 A New Dating Indicator

A fourth dating indicator that is not yet widely acknowledged but holds more chronological promise than the first three is the conception of Yhwh as Elohim and the accompanying traits of that deity in Deuteronomy (Edelman forth. a). The conception is not limited to this book alone; it is found throughout the Pentateuch, in other books, and in Psalms 42–83, a collection within the larger book that emphasizes (Yhwh as) Elohim (see e.g. Gosse 2023; see ch. 18 in this volume). The concept of Yhwh Elohim carries with it a number of correlates that break with what is known about the cults of Yhwh in the monarchic period. A full discussion is provided in ch. 7 in this volume (Edelman 2022b).

Summarizing the main traits: there is a single, universal deity (Deut 6:4) that is imageless (Deut 4:12, 15–19) but which will choose either a single place or "a type of place that might be instantiated in multiple locations over time" to set its šem, "name" or "reputation" on earth (Ben Zvi 2023, 21–23, quote from p. 22). Practically speaking, the deity is accessible via its instruction contained in Moses's Torah, "teaching" (Edelman 2009, 87–91). The divine teaching is symbolically represented by the tablets inside the Ark inscribed with the ten commandments by the finger of Elohim (Deut 9:10), which also are recorded in the scroll of Deuteronomy that is to be placed beside the Ark (Deut 31:24–26). The worship of Asherah, his former divine wife, represented by a living tree, is no longer to be tolerated (Deut 16:21). Ancestors are no longer to be divinized nor consulted by their living relatives (Deut 18:11). The explicit prohibition of the worship of other gods mentioned frequently in the book (e.g. Deut 5:7–9; 6:14–15; 7:2–6; 8:19–20; 10:20; 11:16, 28; 12:2–7; 13; 17:2–5 et passim) means the former household gods no longer are to be consulted either. Yhwh Elohim is now to be the sole divinity honored and prayed to directly by all Israelite households in household cult.

This new henotheistic conception of Yhwh Elohim almost certainly emerged among a group of Judean exiles somewhere in Babylonia (Edelman 2021, 264–78; Lebel 2022, 95–102). Their forced exile and immersion in a pluralistic cultural setting where they constituted a small, powerless ethnic minority prompted adaptation to new circumstances to maintain or create group cohesion and identity. The former territorial god of Judah became conceived of as a non-territorial "divinity" that oversaw all realms formerly associated with other divinities in the Judahite pantheon. Its worship no longer required a temple and regular animal sacrifices; instead, it became embedded in the household cult of members of the new movement.

In contrast, there was no crisis among the non-exiled Judeans after 587 BCE or among non-exiled Samarians after 722 BCE that would have required or stimulated the adaptation of the cult of the main territorial divine couple, Yhwh Ṣebā'ôt and his Asherah, or Yhwh of Samaria and his Asherah. Both would have continued uninterrupted, even if they now lacked the royal patronage both had enjoyed during the monarchies of Israel and Judah. Established temples for the worship of the first outside Jerusalem and the second in Samaria and elsewhere in the province likely would have had sufficient pre-existing endowments and non-royal revenue streams to be able to continue to function, offering prebendary portions that passed down from generation to generation within the priestly and bureaucratic families based at each.

The likely origination of the concept of Yhwh as Elohim by a priest or a scribe among the exiled Judeans in Babylonia leads to a number of options for where and when the scroll of Deuteronomy would have been created. One would have been in Babylonia, as a manifesto of sorts for the core members of the new Yhwh Elohim movement. However, it is equally possible that the book would not have been created immediately but only after adherents of this new religious outlook were repatriated to Yehud under the Achaemenids. In the latter circumstance, the book could have been written either in Jerusalem, right before or soon after the rebuilding of the temple, or among the temple community of Mt. Gerizim.

Adherents of this new concept of Yhwh as Elohim would have been among the Judeans repatriated to Yehud by the Achaemenid imperial administration, probably in order to build up the local agricultural workforce in preparation for a planned conquest of Egypt (Hoglund 1992, 242–44; Edelman 2005, 334–51). It would supply needed food and possibly wine for the troops *en route* to Egypt. In addition to farmers, literate bureaucrats (trained scribes) would have been needed to manage and keep accounts of the movement of grain to storage facilities on the border of Egypt and disbursements to authorized personnel and troops.

4.2 The Possible Composition of Deuteronomy in Yehud during the Neo-Babylonian Period

Deuteronomy's composition in Yehud under the Neo-Babylonian imperial administration is implausible in light of the likely origin of the concept of Yhwh as Elohim and its concurrent changes in worldview in Babylonia. The cult of Yhwh Ṣebā'ôt and Asherah should have been able to continue in place at ongoing sanctuaries in Yehud. The new god concept is unlikely to have impacted Judean society until some of its adherents repatriated to Yehud and actively sought to persuade those still espousing the monarchic-era worldview of the divine realm to adopt their alternate views and practices.

One is hard-pressed to find a scholar who has posited that Deuteronomy was first assembled in Yehud under the Neo-Babylonians. However, in the nineteenth century, Carl Peter Wilhelm Gramberg (1829, 153–54, 305) advanced this possibility alongside a post-exilic one. And in 1906, Robert Hatch Kennett argued the book was "the outcome of the labours of the reforming party in Palestine during the generation after the destruction of Jerusalem" (1906, 490). In his view, it must have been substantially completed and accepted in Samaria as well as in Yehud by the time Zerubbabel arrived on the scene. "The composition belongs to the generation which closed around 520 BCE" (Kennett 1906, 500). Kennett found the twelve-tribe orientation that pervades the book and the call for a single sanctuary to reflect an exilic development in which a religious reunification of north and south took place that included a compromise that led to the closure of Bethel and the migration of its Aaronide priests to Jerusalem (1905, 170–75; 1906, 498).

A third advocate of this setting was Gustav Hölscher (1922). His analysis of Deut 1–30 led him to conclude that Deuteronomy arose in Jerusalem among one circle of the Levitical priesthood as their ideological lawbook containing their ideas for a program of reform that included ways to ensure their own financial support. The program was a reaction against the "more or less vulgar folk religion" of the time (1922, 228–29, 251, 253, 255; quote from p. 251). His arguments are applicable to either the Neo-Babylonian or the early Achaemenid period; they always are against a Josianic date, with the exile as the earliest possible starting point for dating the book. Although it contained some laws from the monarchic period, in his view, Deuteronomy probably would not have functioned as the public law in Jerusalem or among the wider Jewish community. This was due, on the one hand, to the impracticality of some of its laws, like those about debt relief, and on the other hand, because it does not legislate for all areas of life (1922, 252–53).

More recently, citing Hölscher with approval, Juha Pakkala (2009; 2011) has argued for a date for the composition of chs 12–26, the so-called Deuteronomic Law Code (DC), post 587 BCE and prior to the rebuilding of the temple in Jerusalem, be that in 518 BCE or ca. 450 BCE. Thus, his arguments could be situated equally under the early Achaemenid administration. He fails to say specifically, however, where he envisions the scribe to have been living.

He notes that the monarchy plays no role in the original work; he considers 17:14–20 to be a later addition. There also is a lack of state infrastructure and organization, and no references to Judah, which one might have expected had these chapters been intended to regulate the cultic activity of the kingdom of that name. Instead, Israel is conceived of as a religious community, not as inhabitants of a state. The failure to mention the temple (23:19 is a later addition) or Jerusalem in the earliest version presumes the author wrote when there was no longer a functioning temple, and the twelve-tribe scheme and name theology are thought to be post-monarchic as well. Finally, the Judean military colony resident on Elephantine Island in the Nile is unacquainted with rules in the book or any alleged cult centralization that had taken place under Josiah when they write to gain assistance to rebuild their destroyed temple ca. 410 BCE and have to be instructed concerning how to celebrate the festival of Massot, with or without Passover, ca. 419 BCE. Of these points, only the one concerning name-theology engages with the revolutionary religious agenda that permeates the book, and his discussion seems unaware of the wider aspects of this agenda.

Even if an exilic setting in Yehud has never been a popular option for the initial assembling of Deuteronomy, it has been and continues to be common to assert that the purported first version of the late monarchic Judahite scroll of Deuteronomy underwent further editing in Yehud during the exile. According to Martin Noth, a non-exiled Judahite scribe attached to the regional seat located at Mizpah or the temple in Bethel (1981 [1943], 85, 141, n. 9, 142, n. 10) revised the existing text of Deuteronomy (4:44–30:20) ca. 560 BCE (1981 [1943], 12, 16–17) as part of a larger project to provide a rationale to explain Judah's loss of independence. He was thought to have created the sequence of books comprising Joshua, Judges, Samuel, and Kings, in which he applied teachings from Deuteronomy to different stretches of the past conceived of as the Mosaic age, the conquest or occupation west of the Jordan River, the period of settled life under the judges, the united monarchy under Saul, David, and Solomon, and the period of the kingdoms of Israel and Judah. He did so by claiming that the king and people had worshiped other gods over and over, failing to follow Torah. Thus, Yhwh chose to punish them by invoking the sanctions spelled out in the formal agreements (covenants) struck between Yhwh and Israel at Mt. Sinai/Horeb and in the plains of Moab; their deity had not been defeated by the Babylonian gods.

Although Noth's single authorship of a grand "history" was not adopted wholesale by the scholarly guild, the label "Deuteronomistic History" has become commonplace for the books consisting of Joshua-Kings, although the alternate designation, DHC, "Deuteronomistic historical collection," has been proposed by Ehud Ben Zvi (2013, 75), to emphasize that this group of books have disparate origins, even if they share similar ideological outlooks in many ways. In either case, there has been agreement among European and English-speaking scholars that both Deuteronomy and the remaining books underwent one or more redactions during the exile (see conveniently Römer 2005, 27–31; for one example, see Otto 2023).

4.3 The Possible Composition of Deuteronomy in Babylonia during the Neo-Babylonian Period

Ernest W. Nicholson (2014, 41–73) is one scholar in the twenty-first century who has posited that Deuteronomy was created in Babylonia. In his view, exiled Judean "authors and redactors" "gave thought and taught and wrote, not for an interim situation requiring 'survival strategies', but for a new age in the history of their people, who were now no longer identified simply as the resident population of the ancestral homeland, but embraced also what we have come to describe as the Diaspora, in this instance specifically the Babylonian Diaspora" (Nicholson 2014, 50–51). Citing Louis Stulman (1990) and Nathaniel B. Levtow (2008), he notes the repeated stress in the book on not making any anthropomorphic or theriomorphic deity image and the strong contrast drawn between the "Israelite way" and the "Canaanite" way, which he believes is leveled at other Judean exiles who are acculturating, reflected in Moses's warning about forgetting past traditions (e.g. Deut 4:9; 6:10–15) as well as his vision of future exile and idolatry (Deut 28:63–64) (Nicholson 2014, 55–59). He also considers as a probable exilic development the emphasis on the family, where parents are to teach and thereby transmit Torah and the events at Mt. Sinai/Horeb to their children (Deut 4:9; 6:7–10, 20–25; 11:18–21; 31:12–13; 32:46), and children are to honor their parents (Deut 5:16; 21:18–21), alongside the sanctification of the weekly sabbath day, to be done within the family, possibly involving local neighborhood gatherings for worship (Nicholson 2014, 60–62). In his view, Deuteronomy emerged in reaction to the religious, moral, and spiritual needs of the permanent Judean Diaspora community in Babylonia (Nicholson 2014, 71). Thus, he, too, considers the book to be grounded in religious changes some Judeans were making in their new environment, but ones the person who created the book disapproved of.

Nicholson did not take on board, however, the novelty of the views expressed in Deuteronomy when set beside the monarchic-era cult of Yhwh Ṣebā'ôt and his Asherah and household cult in Judah during that period (e.g. Edelman 2021). Instead, he seems to think that the authors and redactors of the book were upholding older, existing views of Yhwh for the most part.

Had the cult of Yhwh Ṣebā'ôt already been henotheistic during the monarchy, there would have been little reason to emphasize the need not to worship gods other than Yhwh. Even if the Neo-Babylonians claimed their gods had defeated Yhwh, that would not have eliminated this particular deity from the divine realm or prevented his worshipers from continuing to honor and petition him for help.

One might suggest that some Judeans decided there was no point in continuing to appeal to Yhwh Ṣebā'ôt since they no longer lived inside his territory; it would have been more efficacious to petition the native Babylonian gods whose territory they now inhabited, where Yhwh would have become a middle or lower-tier god instead of a top-tier god, as he had been in Judah. Even so, Yhwh would have become a divine intermediary, like the ancestors and family gods had been, so there would have been no need for the displaced Judahites to eliminate his worship altogether; it would have been a matter of continuing to honor him alongside joining in the cult of the gods that controlled their new placed of residence.

Nicholson is presuming the henotheistic outlook expressed in Deuteronomy existed during the monarchy. Yet it seems the monarchic cult in Judah had been headed by a divine couple and had embraced a worldview in which there were divine entities with varying levels of influence, as in other polytheistic cultures. As such, embracing the worship of influential Babylonian gods would have been a logical option for exiled Judahites to pursue.

It is rather the concept that Yhwh is Elohim, abstract "divinity" that encompasses all the normal divine entities that formed imperial and national pantheons, which is new and radical. The emphasis on not worshiping other gods is necessitated by the older, "normative" Judahite worldview that acknowledged the existence of multiple deities with various levels of influence, which would have informed the decisions made by fellow exiles about which deities would have been of most help in their new environment. Turning Yhwh into a non-territorial, imageless divine abstraction that could be petitioned directly at home, without the need of a temple or sacrifices, was the brainchild of a radical thinker, who set about to convince others to share this bold new understanding and its vision for the future. The first form of Deuteronomy could have been penned by this individual or by an early convert to his message, to target fellow literate exiles and create a new religious movement in Babylonia, with some changes made by other members in the group as it grew and solidified its core principles.

4.4 The Possible Composition of Deuteronomy in Jerusalem under the Achaemenids

Deuteronomy's origin in the early Achaemenid period was argued for in the first half of the twentieth century in the English-speaking world by, for example, George Ricker Berry (1940). He argued that the book's combination of "a prophetic spirit mingled constantly with priestly interest" (1940, 136) matches the situation and attitude of the prophets Haggai and Zechariah, whose immediate concern was the rebuilding of the temple in Jerusalem. In his view, the book would have been written in Jerusalem a few years after 520 BCE, when the two prophets had begun to preach, "to meet all the requirements of the new national life" (1940, 135). His rationale did not build specifically on the religious innovations found in the book that have been presented here as dating indicators.

When Jerusalem was rebuilt as the regional seat of Yehud under the Achaemenid King Artaxerxes, the former temple of Yhwh Ṣebā'ôt and his Asherah probably also was rebuilt, although not in ca. 518 BCE as the dates in the books of Haggai and Zechariah imply. The dates in the early years of the reign of Darius I probably reflect an attempt to show the fulfillment of the prediction of 70 years of ruination for Judah found in Jer 25:11–12 with 27:6–7 and 29:10 (Edelman 2005, 90–139). When rebuilt, the temple housed a cult dedicated to Yhwh Elohim, who initially was equated with the former deity, Yhwh Ṣebā'ôt (Haggai and Zech 1–7). The invisible god was now present, however, in the form of his *šem*, "name" or "reputation," which came to be represented and made manifest by its Torah ("teaching").The temple appears to have become the administrative center of the province, whose personnel handled the collection of imperial taxes and were supported by receiving prebendary portions of its daily animal sacrifices as well as designated parts of private sacrifices they conducted for worshipers.

The book of Deuteronomy sets forth a vision of how the community of Israel will live by the revealed teachings (Torah) associated with the deity, Yhwh Elohim, in the promised land, where the deity will choose a place (*māqôm*) to set its name/reputation to dwell/remain, to which the community will make three annual pilgrimages. The concept of the single chosen place represents a modification of what likely was the original core belief and practice system of the Yhwh Elohim movement, as part of a strategy to gain a large number of new members in Yehud, that would allow the small, core group to become mainstream (Lebel 2022, 67–73). The modified vision now embraced a single temple and sacrificial system that probably had not been deemed necessary in Babylonia.

If this sketchy reconstruction is more or less accurate, then we could posit that Deuteronomy would have been written in the fifth century BCE, right before or soon after the rebuilding of the temple in Jerusalem. It espoused an understanding of deity that only emerged during the Babylonian exile. Its target audience would have included other literate scribes and priests among both returnees and the non-exiled, who had not yet embraced this new concept of Yhwh as Elohim and its concomitant implications, as well as the larger illiterate populations in Yehud and Babylonia who, it was hoped, would slowly embrace its henotheism and new understanding of household cult. Efi Lebel has labeled those Judeans who continued to embrace the monarchic-era mindset and worldview, no matter where they lived, "Templians" (Lebel 2022, 89, 143–94). How the books of the Pentateuch would have been mediated to the temple on Mt. Gerizim will be discussed in the ensuing section. Briefly, familial ties between its staff and the personnel at the temple in Jerusalem and the sharing of the concept of Yhwh as Elohim in common would have facilitated such exchange.

4.5 The Possible Composition of Deuteronomy by a Member of the Immigratory Judean Temple Staff on Mt. Gerizim

Excavations of the Samaritan sacred complex on Mt. Gerizim tend to indicate that it was operating by the second half of the fifth century BCE, if not already sometime closer to 475 BCE, with adjoining housing occupied by its full-time staff (Magen 2007; 2008; Lemaire 2014, 411; Regev and Greenfeld 2023; Edelman forth. b). It may have been completed before the temple in Jerusalem, which could account for why the books of Haggai and Zechariah have set the rebuilding of the Jerusalemite temple under King Darius I (522–486 BCE) instead of its likely rebuilding under King Artaxerxes (465–425 BCE). In Zech 7:5, the dating is explicitly justified as the fulfillment of a 70-year prophecy of destruction found in Jer 25:11–12; 29:10 (Edelman 2005, 90–95, 103–7). While many scholars would date these two prophetic books close to the events they describe in the fifth century BCE, they may well be closer in time to the books of Ezra and Nehemiah, which are either late Persian or more likely, Hellenistic (332–37 BCE) in date. By the early Hellenistic period, the rivalry between the two temples was already heating up and the Judean priesthood was keen to assert the chronological primacy of its temple, even if the claim were not historically accurate.

The book of Ezra is eager to give Torah, the teaching of Moses, a pedigree that traces to the monarchic-era temple in Jerusalem. It is said that Ezra the scribe dedicated himself to studying Mosaic Torah, observing it personally and teaching it to other exiles (Ezra 7:6, 10). By implication, the Torah had gone with Judahite exiles to Babylonia and returned again with Ezra the scribe, who is given a seventeen-generation Aaronide pedigree (Ezra 7:1–5). Later, under the native Judean Hasmonean rulers of priestly descent (ca. 140–37 BCE), the explicit claim was made in 2 Macc 2:2–3 that the late monarchic prophet Jeremiah had given the Torah to the deportees to observe in Babylonia (Edelman forth. c.). By implication, they may have been countering a claim to primacy by the staff of the temple on Mt Gerizim.

A second point that will prove to be of interest is that, by the time the Hasmoneans gained power, Nehemiah, governor of Yehud, had become a counter-hero to Sanballat, governor of Samerina. This had already occurred earlier in the Hellenistic period, as evidenced by the portrayal of Sanballat as a "bad guy" who opposed Nehemiah's plan to rebuild Jerusalem in the book of Nehemiah. His name and epithet was revocalized to Sanballat the Horonite from its apparent original form, Sinuballiṭ the Haranite, probably in order to sever any positive associations with the city of Haran, which features prominently in the book of Genesis as the temporary home of both Abraham and Jacob. In fact, it is possible that those references were meant to honor Sanballat/Sinuballiṭ originally (Edelman forth. b).

Again in 2 Macc, written under the Hasmoneans, Nehemiah becomes the rebuilder of the temple in Jerusalem, not Sheshbazzar or Zerubbabel as in Hag 2:23; Zech 4; Ezra 1:1–10; 3:8; 5:14–17), and dedicates the altar (1:18–36), paralleling his fellow governor to the north, who builds the "illegitimate" temple on Gerizim. He also establishes a library in Jerusalem (2 Macc 2:13); by implication, this would parallel a similar library Sinuballiṭ had sponsored on Gerizim.

The deity to whom the sacred complex on Mt. Gerizim was dedicated was, apparently, Yhwh Elohim, and its priesthood was of Aaronide descent (Magen, Misgav, and Tsafania 2004, 260), as was the priesthood of the temple rebuilt in Jerusalem (Edelman forth. b and c). At the time it was built, there almost certainly was an ongoing, longstanding cult dedicated to Yhwh of Samaria and his Asherah in the regional seat, the city of Samaria.

The choice of Mt. Gerizim to house the Samarian temple of Yhwh Elohim will have been influenced by various factors. It cannot be coincidental, however, that this is the very site where, in Deut 11:26–28 and 27:4–8, 12–13, a commemorative ceremony celebrating the giving of the Torah on the plains of Moab was to take place, associated with divine blessing. This is the case whether these verses are original to the book or secondary additions. In the eyes of the founders of this temple, they were honoring the site in Samaria where Yhwh Elohim had chosen to place its name/reputation to dwell/remain, as stated or would be stated in the scroll of Deuteronomy.

Centuries later, the Jewish historian Josephus (ca. 37/38–100 CE) reported that the temple on Gerizim had been built by the governor of Samerina, Sanballat the Horonite, for his son-in-law Manasseh, the son of Johanan the high priest and brother of Jaddua; the latter succeeded their father in office in Jerusalem. Josephus also claims that a number of priests and Levites who also had married Samarian wives defected to Manasseh in Samaria and were given money, land, and houses by Sanballat, in order to gratify his son-in law (*Ant.* 11.302-12, 321-25). Sanballat purportedly "deemed it a great reward that his daughter's children should have th[e] dignity" (11.324) of a father who served as high priest in the newly built temple on Mt. Gerizim, one of whose male heirs would succeed him in office down through the generations, while other sons could serve also as priests.

It is widely recognized that Josephus's story is an elaboration of the statement in Neh 13:28 that a grandson of the high priest of Jerusalem, Eliashib, had married the daughter of Sanballat and that Nehemiah, governor of Yehud, had driven him out, literally, "caused him to cross over" from his presence, presumably, from Jerusalem and the province of Yehud. Whether Josephus drew on any other sources or not is debated (e.g. Kartveit 2002, 71–108; Pummer 2016, 54–66; Edelman 2024). The passage in Nehemiah mentions nothing of a temple being built for the son-in-law.

It is probable, however, that Josephus deliberately misdated Sinuballiṭ's governorship to the end of the fourth century BCE and the building of the temple under Alexander, well after the temple in Jerusalem had been functioning for over 100 years. This allowed him to give the impression that the temple in Jerusalem had been the first of the two to be built and, therefore, was the only legitimate "place Yhwh will choose to set his name/reputation to dwell/remain." On the basis of extrabiblical evidence, Sinuballiṭ's term in office can be firmly dated in the fifth century BCE (e.g. Edelman 2005, 38–53; Dušek 2012).

Establishing a sacred complex on Mt. Gerizim would have allowed Sinuballiṭ to appoint a new hereditary priesthood to be supported by a prebendary system established at the time the temple was dedicated, to sustain its new, full-time staff. He could not have inserted his son-in-law into the long-established hereditary priesthood and its prebendary system at the temple for Yhwh Shomron in the regional seat in the city of Samaria, which was still in full operation during his governorship and until 332 BCE. Appointing him to a newly established temple, however, would have guaranteed the bloodline descendants through this couple a secured, prestigious future.

Thus, even if Josephus may have linked the building of the temple on Gerizim to Sanballat/Sinuballiṭ, guessed at his motivation for doing so, and assumed that other priests and scribes would have moved there with the son-in-law from Jerusalem to become its new staff, his hunches are, in fact, consistent with the few facts we can verify. The construction of the sacred complex atop Gerizim was completed by the mid-fifth century BCE. It probably included a temple from its foundation, and definitely had adjoining housing outside its perimeter, occupied by temple personnel. Sinuballiṭ would have been governor in this period. Josephus's deduction explains how an Aaronide priesthood became established at Gerizim, whose presence is confirmed in the inscriptions recovered from the sanctuary debris. And, it is consistent with the governor's inability to add his son-in-law to the longstanding, hereditary temple staff at the temple to Yhwh in the regional seat at Samaria, even though Josephus seems to have been unaware of this situation.

The sourcing of the Gerizim temple staff from Jerusalem would open up the possibility that Deuteronomy and perhaps other books of the Pentateuch, particularly Genesis with its Jacob traditions and the references to Haran, were written by scribes of Judean origin who became attached to the Samarian sacred complex in the fifth century BCE, during the governorship and under the patronage of Sanballat/Sinuballiṭ. The concept of Yhwh Elohim arguably has its roots in Babylonia among exiled Judean priestly and bureaucratic personnel. But members of the movement who had returned to Yehud might have seen an opportunity to advance their understanding and its implications when the situation arose offering employment on Mt. Gerizim. It could afford the possibility for the core group to experience exponential growth and become mainstream by implementing their new form of Yhwh in a temple where their livelihoods would be guaranteed for generations to come. Once rebuilding began in Jerusalem as well, the opportunity to envision a twelve-tribe Israel that embraced the customs and practices associated with Yhwh Elohim, realized at two sites, may have prompted the composition of Genesis, Exodus, and Deuteronomy on Mt. Gerizim and their eager adoption by members of the movement in Jerusalem, who would become part of the temple staff there. Leviticus and Numbers might also have been written on Mt. Gerizim, or perhaps in Jerusalem, once the cult became operational.

5. Conclusion

A review of possible "northern" content in Deuteronomy has tended to indicate that the ideas it espouses are neither "northern" nor "southern," except for the altar to be built on Mt Gerizim and the ceremony to take place there. Its religious worldview is new and likely arose in the mind of an exiled Judahite scribe or priest when faced with being a new minority in an imperial setting, where the typical philosophy of the victors would have argued that Yhwh had been defeated by the gods of Babylonia and so was a powerless deity not worth worshiping. He began a core movement, some of whose members appear to have been repatriated to Yehud under the Achaemenid imperial administration. A consideration of a possible northern provenance for its composition has proven to be inconclusive.

Five options for the book's initial composition have been considered: in Judah under King Josiah, in Yehud during the exile, in Babylonia during the exile, in Jerusalem under the Achaemenids, and on Mt. Gerizim under the Achaemenids. The first two have been rejected, but a case could be made for any of the latter three. It appears, however, that elements in the core group's initial thinking have been modified, particularly the endorsement of "the place Yhwh will choose to set his name/reputation" in the ancestral homeland and acceptance of animal sacrifice; neither makes sense if one believes in an invisible, universal deity that should not need to be fed. On this basis, it would make better sense to eliminate the third option as well and to focus on its composition in the Persian period, either in Jerusalem or on Mt. Gerizim.

Either remaining option then has a plausible explanation for how it and the other Pentateuchal books came to be shared as an authoritative collection associated with the two temples in these locations: the marriage of an Aaronide priest from Jerusalem to the daughter of Sanballat. This resulted in the construction of the temple on Mt. Gerizim dedicated to Yhwh as Elohim, and the likely move of other priests and scribes to become its new priests and administrators. This circumstance would have allowed ongoing interaction and exchange between the two sets of Aaronide temple staff who served in both temples dedicated to Yhwh Elohim.

Works Cited

Alt, Albrecht. 1953. "Die Heimat des Deuteronomiums." Pages 250–75 in *Kleine Schriften zur Geschichte des Volkes Israel*, Vol. 2. Munich: C. H. Beck.

Arie, Eran. 2021. "Revisiting Mt. Gerizim: The Foundation of the Sacred Precinct and the Proto-Ionic Capitals." Pages 39*–63* in *New Studies in the Archaeology of Jerusalem and Its Region*. Edited by Yehiel Zelinger, Orit Peleg-Barkat, Joseph Uziel, and Yuval Gadot. Collected Papers 14. Jerusalem: The Israel Antiquities Authority.

Arnold, Bill. 2017. "Reexamining the 'Fathers' in Deuteronomy's Framework." Pages 10–41 in *Torah and Tradition: Papers Read at the Sixteenth Joint Meeting of the Society for Old Testament Study and the Oudtestamentische Werkgezelchap, Edinburgh, 2015*. Edited by Klaas Spronk and Hans Barstad. Oudtestamentische Studiën 70. Leiden: Brill.

Ben Zvi, Ehud. 2008. "Imagining Josiah's Book and the Implications of Imagining It in Early Persian Yehud." Pages 193–212 in *Berührungspunkte. Studien zur Sozial - und Religionsgeschichte Israels und seiner Umwelt: Festschrift für Rainer Albertz zu seinem 65. Geburtstag*. Edited by Ingo Gottsieper, Rüdiger Schmitt, and Jakob Wöhrle. Münster: Ugarit Verlag, 2008.

------. 2013. "Prophetic Memories in the Deuteronomistic Historical and the Prophetic Collections of Books." Pages 75–102 in *Israelite Prophecy and the Deuteronomistic History: Portrait, Reality and the Formation of a History*. Edited by Mignon R. Jacobs and Raymond E. Person, Jr. Society of Biblical Literature Ancient Israel and Its Literature 314. Atlanta: Society of Biblical Literature.

------. 2015. "Remembering Hosea: The Prophet Hosea as a Site of Memory in Persian Period Yehud." Pages 37–57 in *Poets, Prophets, and Texts in Play: Studies in Biblical Poetry and Prophecy in Honour of Francis Landy*. Edited by Ehud Ben Zvi, Claudia V. Camp, David M. Gunn, and A. W.

Hughes. Library of Hebrew Bible/Old Testament Studies 597. London: Bloomsbury T & T Clark. Reprinted as pages 274–93 in *Social Memory among the Literati of Yehud*. Beihefte zur Zeitschrift für die alttestamentliche Wissenschaft 509. Berlin: De Gruyter.

———. 2019. "Reading the Book of Hosea, Remembering Hosea and Thinking of Exile in Yehud." Pages 294–303 in *Social Memory among the Literati of Yehud*. Beihefte zur Zeitschrift für die alttestamentliche Wissenschaft 509. Berlin: De Gruyter.

———. 2023. "'Your Gates' – Evoking a Landscape of Fortified Cities in Deuteronomy: Meanings, Implications, and Comparative Considerations with Other Constructions of the Israelite Past." *Scandinavian Journal of the Old Testament* 37.1: 17–33.

Berry, George Ricker. 1940. "The Date of Deuteronomy." *Journal of Biblical Literature* 59: 133–39.

Blum, Erhard. 2012. "Jacob Tradition." Pages 181–211 in *The Book of Genesis: Composition, Reception, and Interpretation*. Edited by Carl A. Evans. Supplements to Vetus Testamentum 152. Leiden: Brill.

Broshi, Magen. 1974. "The Expansion of Jerusalem in the Reigns of Hezekiah and Manasseh." *Israel Exploration Journal* 24: 21–26.

Burke, Aaron. 2012. "Coping with the Effects of War." Pages 263–87 in *Disaster and Relief Management = Katastrophen und ihre Bewaltigung*. Edited by Angelika Berlejung. Forschungen zum Alten Testament 81. Tübingen: Mohr Siebeck.

Burney, Charles Fox. 1918. *The Book of Judges with Introduction and Notes*. London: Rivingtons.

Davies, Philip R. 2005. "Josiah and the Law Book." Pages 65–77 in *Good Kings and Bad Kings: The Kingdom of Judah in the Seventh Century BCE*. Edited by Lester L. Grabbe. Library of Hebrew Bible/Old Testament Studies 393 and European Seminar in Historical Methodology 5. London: T & T Clark.

———. 2021. "From Where Did Deuteronomy Originate?" Pages 13–24 in *Deuteronomy in the Making: Studies in the Production of* Debarim. Edited by Diana V. Edelman, Benedetta Rossi, Kåre Berge, and Philippe Guillaume. Beihefte zur Zeitschrift für die alttestamentliche Wissenschaft 533. Berlin: De Gruyter.

Dušek, Jan. 2012. "Archaeology and Texts in the Persian Period: Focus on Sanballat." Pages 117–32 in *Congress Volume Helsinki 2010*. Edited by Martti Nissinen. Supplements to Vetus Testamentum 148. Leiden: Brill.

Edelman, Diana V. 2005. *The Origins of the "Second" Temple: Persian Imperial Policy and the Rebuilding of Jerusalem*. BibleWorld. Sheffield: Equinox Publishing Ltd.

———. 2009. "God Rhetoric: Reconceptualizing Yahweh Sebaot as Yahweh Elohim in the Hebrew Bible." Pages 81–107 in *A Palimpsest: Rhetoric,*

Ideology, Stylistics and Language Relating to Persian Israel. Edited by Ehud Ben Zvi, Diana Edelman, and Frank Polak. Piscataway NJ: Gorgias.

——. 2012. "Hidden Ancestor Polemics in the Book of Genesis?" Pages 35–56 in *Words, Ideas, World: Biblical Essays in Honour of Yairah Amit*. Edited by Athalya Brenner and Frank Polak. Sheffield: Sheffield Phoenix.

——. 2017 "Adjusting Social Memory in the Hebrew Bible: The *Teraphim*." Pages 115–42 in *Congress Volume, Stellenbosch 2016*. Edited by Louis Jonker, Gideon R. Kotzé, and Christl M. Supplements to Vetus Testamentum 177. Leiden: Brill.

——. 2021. "Early Forms of Judaism as a Mixture of Strategies of Cultural Heterogeneity and the Re-embedding of Local Culture in Archaic Globalization." Pages 242–92 in *Levantine Entanglements: Local Dynamics of Globalization in a Contested Region*. Edited by Terje Stordalen and Øystein LaBianca. Sheffield: Equinox Publishing Ltd.

——. 2022a. "Saying Goodbye to the Theory of the Influence of Esarhaddon's Succession *Adê* on Deuteronomy 13 and 28." https://www.equinoxpub.com/home/view-chapter/?id=44273.

——. 2022b. "Yhwh (ha)Elohim and a Reconceived Yahwism in the Book of Deuteronomy." https://www.equinoxpub.com/home/view-chapter/?id=44585.

——. 2024. "Yhwh Shomron and Yhwh Elohim in the Achaemenid Province of Samaria." Pages 35–80 in *Yahwism under the Achaemenid Empire: Prof. Shaul Shaked in Memoriam*. Edited by Gad Barnea and Reinhard Kratz. Beihefte zur Zeitschrift die alttestamentliche Wissenschaft. Berlin: De Gruyter.

——. Forthcoming a. "The Case for Post-Exilic Deuteronomy." In *The Book of Deuteronomy: Composition, Contexts, Interpretation, and Reception*. Edited by Kyung S. Baek and Dominik Markl. Formation and Interpretation of Old Testament Literature; Supplements to Vetus Testamentum. Leiden: Brill.

——. Forthcoming b. "Sanballat, Abraham, and Jacob." In a *Festschrift for Thomas Römer*. Edited by Christoph Nihan and Jean-Daniel Macchi. Beihefte zur Zeitschrift die alttestamentliche Wissenschaft. Berlin: De Gruyter.

Edenburg, Cynthia and Reinhard Müller. 2015. "A Northern Provenance for Deuteronomy? A Critical Review." *Hebrew Bible and Ancient Israel* 4: 148–61.

Finkel, Irving and Alexandra Fletcher. 2016. "Thinking Outside the Box: The Case of the Sun-God Tablet and the Cruciform Monument." *Bulletin of the American Schools of Oriental Research* 375.1: 215–48.

Finkelstein, Israel. 2008. "The Settlement History of Jerusalem in the Eighth and Seventh Centuries BC." *Revue biblique* 115: 499–515.

Finkelstein, Israel and Neil Silberman. 2001. *The Bible Unearthed: Archaeology's New Vision of Ancient Israel and the Origin of Its Sacred Texts*. New York: Free.

——. 2006. "Temple and Dynasty: Hezekiah, the Remaking of Judah and the Rise of the Pan-Israelite Ideology." *Journal for the Study of the Old Testament* 30.3: 259–85.

Finkelstein, Israel and Thomas Römer. 2014. "Comments on the Historical Background of the Jacob Narrative in Genesis." *Zeitschrift für die alttestamentliche Wissenschaft* 126.3: 317–38.

Gelb, Ignace J. 1949. "The Date of the Cruciform Monument of Maništušu." *Journal of Near Eastern Studies* 8.4: 346–48.

Gosse, Bernard. 2023. Deuteronomy's Influence on the Formation of the Psalter." https://www.equinoxpub.com/home/view-chapter/?id=45364.

Grabbe, Lester. L. 2007. *Ancient Israel: What Do We Know and How Do We Know It?* London: T & T Clark.

Gramberg, Carl Peter Wilhelm. 1829. *Kritische Geschichte der Religionsideen des altenTestaments*, Vol. 1. Berlin: Duncker und Humblot.

Guillaume, Philippe. 2008. "Jerusalem 720–705 BCE. No Flood of Israelite Refugees." *Scandinavian Journal of the Old Testament* 22.2: 195–211.

Harvey, Paul B., Jr. and Baruch Halpern. 2008. "W. M. L. de Wette's '*Dissertatio Critica* …': Context and Translation." *Zeitschrift für altorientalische und biblische Rechtsgeschichte* 14: 47–85.

Hensel, Benedikt. 2021. "Edom in the Jacob Cycle (Gen *25–35): New Insights on Its Positive Relations with Israel, the Literary-Historical Development of Its Role, and Its Historical Background(s)." Pages 57–133 in *The History of the Jacob Cycle (Genesis 25–35): Recent Research on the Compilation, the Redaction, and the Reception of the Biblical Narrative and Its Historical and Cultural Contexts*. Edited by Benedikt Hensel. Archaeology and the Bible 4. Tübingen: Mohr Siebeck.

Hoglund, Kenneth. 1992. *Achaemenid Imperial Administration in Syria-Palestine and the Mission of Ezra and Nehemiah*. Society of Biblical Literature Dissertation Series 125. Atlanta: Scholars.

Hölscher, Gustav. 1922. "Komposition und Ursprung des Deuteronomiums." *Zeitschrift für die alttestamentliche Wissenschaft* 40: 161–255.

Jefferess, David. 2008. *Postcolonial Resistance: Culture, Liberation, and Transformation*. Toronto: University of Toronto Press.

Josephus, Flavius. 1994. *The Works of Josephus Complete and Unabridged*. Translated by William Whiston. New updated version. Peabody MA: Hendrickson.

Kartveit, Magnar. 2002. *The Origins of the Samaritans*. Supplements to Vetus Testamentum 128. Leiden: Brill.

Kennett, R. H. 1905. "The Origin of the Aaronic Priesthood." *Journal of Theological Studies* 6: 161–86.

———. 1906. "The Date of Deuteronomy." *Journal of Theological Studies* 7: 481–600.

Lebel, Efi. 2022. "The Survival of Identity Groups: A Case Study of the Jewish People's Survival during the Second Temple Period." PhD dissertation, University of Haifa.

Lemaire, André. 2014. "Fifth- and Fourth-Century Issues." Pages 406–25 in *Ancient Israel's History: An Introduction to Issues and Sources*. Edited by Bill T. Arnold and Richard S. Hess. Grand Rapids: Baker Academic.

Levinson, Bernard M. 2009. "The Neo-Assyrian Origins of the Canon Formula in Deuteronomy 13:1." Pages 26–43 in *Scriptural Exegesis: The Shapes of Culture and the Religious Imagination. Essays in Honor of Michael Fishbane*. Edited by Deborah A. Green and Laura S. Lieber. Oxford: Oxford University Press.

Levtow, Nathaniel B. 2008. *Images of Others: Iconic Politics in Ancient Israel*. Biblical and Judaic Studies 11. Winona Lake IN: Eisenbrauns.

Magen, Yitzhak. 2007. "The Dating of the First Phase of the Samaritan Temple on Mt Gerizim in Light of Archaeological Evidence." Pages 157–212 in *Judah and the Judeans in the Fourth Century B.C.E.* Edited by Oded Lipschits, Gary N. Knoppers, and Rainer Albertz. Winona Lake IN: Eisenbrauns.

———. 2008. *Mount Gerizim Excavations*. Vol. 2, *A Temple City*. Judea and Samaria Publications 8. Jerusalem: Israel Antiquities Authority.

Magen, Yitzhak, Haggai Misgav, and Levana Tsafania. *Mount Gerizim Excavations*. Vol. 1, *The Aramaic, Hebrew and Greek Inscriptions*. Judea and Samaria Publications 2. Jerusalem: Israel Antiquities Authority, 2004.

Mettinger, Tryggve N. D. 1982. *The Dethronement of Sabaoth: Studies in the Shem and Kabod Theologies*. Translated by Fred Cryer. Coniectana Biblica Old Testament Series 18. Lund: CWK Gleerup.

Morrow, William B. 2009. "The Paradox of Deuteronomy 13: A Post-Colonial Reading." Pages 227–39 in *"Gerechtigkeit und Recht zu üben" (Gen 18, 19). Studien zur altorientalischen unde biblischen Rechtsgeschichte, zur Religionsgeschichte Israels, und zur Religionssoziologie: Festschrift für Eckart Otto zum 65. Geburtstag*. Edited by Reinhard Achenbach and Martin Arneth. Wiesbaden: Harrassowitz.

Na'aman, Nadav. 2007. "When and How Did Jerusalem Become a Great City? The Rise of Jerusalem as Judah's Premier City in the Eighth-Seventh Centuries B.C.E." *Bulletin of the American Schools of Oriental Research* 347: 21–56.

———. 2009. "The Growth and Development of Judah and Jerusalem in the Eighth Century BCE: A Rejoinder." *Revue biblique* 116.3: 321–35.

———. 2014a. "Dismissing the Myth of a Flood of Israelite Refugees in the Late Eighth Century BCE." *Zeitschrift für die alttestamentliche Wissenschaft* 126.1: 1–14.

------. 2014b. "The Jacob Story and the Formation of Biblical Israel." *Tel Aviv* 41: 95–125.
Nicholson, Ernest W. 1967. *Deuteronomy and Tradition*. Philadelphia: Fortress.
------. 2014. *Deuteronomy and the Judaean Diaspora*. Oxford: Oxford University Press.
Nielsen, Eduard. 1955. *Shechem: A Traditio-Historical Investigation*. Copenhagen: G. E. C. Gad.
Nihan, Christophe. 2007. "The Torah between Samaria and Judah: Shechem and Gerizim in Deuteronomy and Joshua." Pages 187–223 in *The Pentateuch as Torah: New Models for Understanding Its Promulgation and Acceptance*. Edited by Gary N. Knoppers and Bernard M. Levinson. Winona Lake IN: Eisenbrauns.
Noth, Martin. 1981 [1943 original]. *The Deuteronomistic History*. Translated by Michael D. Rutter. Supplements to the Journal for the Study of the Old Testament 15. Sheffield: Department of Biblical Studies.
Otto, Eckart. 2000. "Political Theology in Judah and Assyria: The Beginning of the Hebrew Bible as Literature." *Svensk exegetisk årsbok* 65: 59–76.
------. 2016. *Deuteronomium 12:1-23,15*. Herders Theologischer Kommentar zum Alten Testament. Freiburg: Herder.
------. 2023. "Deuteronomy: Rewritten to Reflect on the Exile and Future Redemption." Pages 1–10. *TheTorah.com*. https://thetorah.com/article/deuteronomy-rewritten-to-reflect-on-the-exile-and-future-redemption.
Pakkala, Juha. 2009. "The Date of the Oldest Edition of Deuteronomy." *Zeitschrift für die alttestamentliche Wissenschaft* 121(3): 388–401.
------. 2011. "The Dating of Deuteronomy: A Response to Nathan MacDonald." *Zeitschrift für die alttestamentliche Wissenschaft* 123: 431–36.
Peel, J. D. Y. 1984. "Making History: The Past in the Ijesho Present." *Man* New Series 19.1: 111–32.
Pummer, Reinhard. 2016. *The Samaritans: A Profile*. Grand Rapids, MI: Eerdmans.
Pury, Albert de. 2006. "The Jacob Story and the Beginning of the Formation of the Pentateuch." Pages 51–72 in *A Farewell to the Yahwist? The Composition of the Pentateuch in Recent European Interpretation*. Edited by Thomas B. Dozeman and Konrad Schmid. Society of Biblical Literature Symposium Series 34. Atlanta: Society of Biblical Literature.
Rad, Gerhard von. 1953. *Studies in Deuteronomy*. Translated by David Stalker. Studies in Biblical Theology 9. Chicago: Henry Regnery.
Regev, Dalit and Uzi Greenfeld. 2023. "The Persian Pottery from the Salvage Excavations at Har Gerizim (2019–2021): Preliminary Findings." Pages 65–88 in *Identity Perspectives from Israel, Judah, Egypt, and Transjordan in Biblical Traditions: Yahwistic Diversity and the Hebrew Bible II*. Edited by Benedikt Hensel, Dany Nocquet, and Bartosz Adamczewski. Forschungen zum Alten Testament. Tübingen: Mohr Siebeck.

Richter, Sandra L. 2002. *The Deuteronomistic History and Name Theology:* lᵉšakkēn šemô šām *in the Bible and the Ancient Near East.* Beihefte zur Zeitschrift für die alttestamentliche Wissenschaft 318. Berlin: De Gruyter.

Römer, Thomas C. 1990. *Israels Väter. Untersuchungen zur Väterthematik im Deuteronomium und in der deuteronomistischen Tradition.* Orbis Biblicus et Orientalis 319. Freiburg: Universitätsverlag and Göttingen: Vandenhoeck & Ruprecht.

------. 1997. "Transformations in Deuteronomistic and Biblical Historiography: On 'Book-Finding' and other Literary Strategies." *Zeitschrift für die alttestamentliche Wissenschaft* 109.1: 1–11.

------. 2005. *The So-Called Deuteronomistic History.* London: T&T Clark.

------. 2012. "Abraham Traditions in the Hebrew Bible." Pages 159–80 in *The Book of Genesis: Composition, Reception and Interpretation.* Edited by Craig A. Evans, Joel N. Lohr, and David L. Petersen. Supplements to Vetus Testamentum 152. Leiden: Brill.

Schniedewind, William M. 2003. "Jerusalem, the Late Judaean Monarchy, and the Composition of Biblical Texts." Pages 375–93 in *Jerusalem in Bible and Archaeology: The First Temple Period.* Edited by Andrew G. Vaughn and Anne E. Killebrew. SBL Symposium Series 18. Atlanta: Society of Biblical Literature.

Stulman, Louis. 1990. "Encroachment in Deuteronomy: An Analysis of the Social World of the D Code." *Journal of Biblical Literature* 109: 613–32.

Wette, Wilhelm Martin Leberecht de. 1805. *Dissertatio critica, qua Deuteronomium a prioribus Pentateuchi libris diversum, alius cuiusdam recentioris auctoris opus esse monstratur.* Jena: Literis Etzdorfii.

About the Author

Diana V. Edelman is professor emerita at the Faculty of Theology, University of Oslo. Her research interests focus on the history, archaeology, and literature of the ancient Southern Levant more generally, and on Judah and Samaria in the Iron Age, Neo-Babylonian, and Persian periods more specifically.

Chapter 17
Deuteronomy's Ethics[*]

Georg Braulik

Abstract

After an initial outline of the methodology I use to generate an ethics of the Old Testament and a presentation of three other recent approaches, this chapter delineates Deuteronomy's theonomous ethics of "choosing life" and the rich blessing of God in the realization of the covenant of Israel with Yhwh. The short ethical formulations of the Decalogue are specified in the individual provisions of the Deuteronomic legal code. In the Moab covenant, Moses commits the general assembly of Israel to this ethics of the Torah for upcoming life in the promised land. Thanks to the circumcision of hearts, it can be realized even after episodes of disobedience. Israel's basic requirement is love for Yhwh or fear of God, which is expressed in obedience to the individual commandments of the Deuteronomic collection. The justice of the ethics of the Torah is praised even by the other peoples.

Keywords: Deuteronomy, ethics, covenant, paraenesis, Decalogue, brotherly ethics, social legislation

This chapter introduces the ethical conceptions of the book of Deuteronomy. Because my contribution rests on a reading of the final form of the text, it consciously excludes questions relating to the history of origin and redaction of the text. Likewise, it will not be possible to address

---

[*] This article is dedicated to Gerhard Lohfink as an expression of gratitude and friendship. I thank Norbert Lohfink and Ingeborg Gabriel for their comments on the manuscript, and Hanneke Friedl for her assistance in proof-reading the translation.

comparisons with the other two legal codes of the Pentateuch in the books of Exodus and Leviticus. After outlining my methodological approach and sketching the most recent views of the ethics of the Old Testament, I will present my own contribution to understanding Deuteronomy's ethical outlook, which can be summarized as "Choose life!" in a society ruled by the moral and judicial laws of the Old Testament. It should be noted, however, that my approach is not identical with that of J. Gary Millar (1998) in his monograph, *Now Choose Life: Theology and Ethics in Deuteronomy*, whose viewpoints fail to account for certain aspects of modern exegesis. Whereas he had chosen the categories of covenant, journey, law, the nations, and human nature as leading ideas, I distinguish between the Horeb and Moab covenantal charters; furthermore, I focus on divine grace and forgiveness as well as two pillars of Deuteronomic ethics: a personal relationship with God, characterized by love, and the concept of paraenesis. I close with considerations relating to cultic law, social law, the law of public offices, and the law of warfare in Deuteronomy.

1. Methodological Approach

I work, then, primarily with the MT (Masoretic Text) version, which has deliberately been standardized by the rabbis. I acknowledge that there is no single "final form" of the text of Deuteronomy; there are dozens of variant readings within the extant preserved manuscripts of this book in its various ancient translations (e.g. Greek, Latin, Syriac, Ethiopic).

Although the ethical norms of Deuteronomy were written to deal with concrete ancient social and economic conditions, the specific socio-historical context of the scribe who produced the earliest form of Deuteronomy is disputed. As a result, I am limiting myself here to the insights of the "Fifth Book of Moses" and not exploring their application in ancient or modern societies.

Though the Torah may serve as the basis of a biblically oriented Christian ethics, it addresses Israel specifically rather than humanity more generally (Crüsemann 1996, 424–25). In Deuteronomy, Moses conveys ethical principles as interpretations of the Decalogue, the document of the Sinai/Horeb covenant. As such, it is valid *for* Israel and should not be misunderstood as a general humanitarian moral document. Apart from its future biblical development at the hands of a "prophet like Moses" (Deut 18:18), it can neither be abstracted historically nor theologically into a timeless, universally binding, moral catalogue . This understanding differs significantly from the widespread view that the biblical ethos, the characteristic spirit of Israelite culture as manifested in its beliefs and aspirations, only serves purposes of illustration. For Israel, that is, within the community of the people of God, it indeed has normative, morally binding power. This power is based on the fact that Israel was liberated from Egypt by God, which we will discuss again when considering the value and purpose of the Decalogue more closely.

2. Recent Views about Old Testament Ethics

In his "Ethics in Ancient Israel" (2014), John Barton focuses on topics of ethical thinking encountered in Israelite social history, which he selects on the basis of modern anthropological questions. Barton does not mention the Hebrew Bible at all because he argues that "the documents we have from ancient Israel do not portray ethical obligation exclusively in terms of obedience to the declared will of God." Although he is not concerned, then, with the relevance of biblical ethics, Barton is convinced "that there was critical reflection on moral issues in ancient Israel [...] [such] that Israelite thinkers did put forward general claims about how a well-lived life was to be understood, and how moral norms were grounded" (Barton 2014, 12–13; see Soete 1987, 257–81).

My essay does not focus on the relevance of key ethical issues of Deuteronomy for modern discourses or current problems. Instead, it is concerned with the ethical implications of matters that belong to the systematic program offered by the book of Deuteronomy. Although in the past there has been a tendency to base biblical ethics on relevant passages drawn from throughout the Old and New Testaments, a focus on the ethical stance of a single book is not unusual today. Two notable book-length studies in German of the ethics of the Old Testament each contain a chapter devoted to the ethics of Deuteronomy (Otto 1994; Kessler 2017). Thus, there has been a growing recognition that there is not a monolithic Israelite ethos but rather, even though there is significant overlap, different ethical views are endorsed in various books.

Eckart Otto's *Theologische Ethik des Alten Testaments* focuses on the reception of the system of norms within the Old Testament; it is primarily descriptive in terms of cultural history. He describes the Deuteronomic social order from the late pre-exilic legal code to the project of the post-exilic New Israel, based on his own reconstruction of redactors and their ethical profiles. His main thesis is that the Deuteronomic ethos evolved from secular law but obtained its theological legitimacy by refraining from imposing sanctions, contrary to Mesopotamian legal concepts (Otto 1994, 81–116).

Otto considers the biblical ethos to have resulted from the theologizing of law, which was subsequently integrated into the tradition of ethics, i.e. as the subordination of law to the will of God (Otto 1993, 907,

n. 6). According to Annette Soete (1987, 119-120), the biblical ethos is expressed in the form of traditional law that seeks the preservation of ethos. The ethos, in turn, is the founding context of the meaning of the law and thus precedes it. Both are grounded in the salvation-historical experience of being "with Yhwh" and are subject to a process of learning and change.

Rainer Kessler (2017, 192) emphasizes, however, that sentences without sanctions and apodictic formulations that are legally binding were and are characteristic of both ancient and modern law. Hence, the plausibility of Otto's analysis is debatable; from a legal-historical point of view, much of it remains hypothetical. Above all, the ethics of the Old Testament cannot be limited to the regulations of social action in legal and wisdom texts.

In Deuteronomy, the collection of individual laws has narrative flashbacks and paraenesis relating to the first commandment interspersed within it. The term "paraenesis" is understood here as a separate speech act that serves as an admonition to behave correctly rather than as a command to do something (Braulik 2017f, 272). There is, however, a difference between an exegetical and an ethical approach to paraenesis. Ethics is concerned with the question of what needs to be done, while paraenesis aims at implementing these ethically standardized provisions. Where there is no agreement on what is morally or legally required, argumentation rather than paraenesis is appropriate (Schüller 1980, 17). Werner Wolbert (1981, 18–19) defines paraenesis as the manner of ethical discourse that inculcates a moral commandment or prohibition, where it is always presupposed that the subject and addressee of the paraenesis agree in their assessment of the action in question. It is opposed to "normative ethics," where this agreement does not exist. Normative ethics aim at recognizing what is morally right; paraenesis aims at doing what is morally good. Paraenesis aims at moral value, while normative ethics determine which moral values to strive for (Wolbert 1981, 39).

The Deuteronomic interweaving of narrative and law is described by Dominik Markl (2015, 325–26) as "narrative law-interpretation": the narratives mostly deal with ethical issues, while many legal texts explicitly develop ethical norms. Law and ethos perform reciprocal functions; they are interconnected, and both are embedded in theology, especially that of God's people. Hence, the different language forms related to ethics and theological justification must always be considered (see Schwienhorst-Schönberger 2015, 63–67).

Because the Old Testament conveys a multiplicity of ethics, Kessler's *Ethik des Alten Testaments* (2017; see 2021a; 2021b) treats them from a canonical perspective, closer to the scope and reading order of the Hebrew Bible. It preserves both the polyphony and unity of Old Testament ethics.

Kessler structures the main narrative of the Pentateuch according to a "two-pillared model." Blessing and deliverance are the two pillars on which the theme of justice rests and which is predominantly discussed in the legal provisions of the Torah. Deuteronomic ethics contain an "option for the poor" (cf. likewise Markl 2015, 324). Kessler (2017, 243–67) sees Deuteronomy's most important contribution to modern ethical problems in the notions of blessing as the basis and goal and of justice as the condition of ecologically and socially-oriented economic and social ethics. In addition, Kessler takes into account the stories of Genesis, the revelation and proclamation of the legal documents, and the complex structure of meaning of the covenants into which they are built.

3. Choose Life! Deuteronomic Ethics

Deuteronomy is the first book to provide us with a systematization of various traditions of Israel's obligation to the exclusive service of its God, Yhwh, in the form of a contractual relationship, a "covenant" (*berît*). In the envisaged society, all areas of life are drawn into this relationship with God. According to the literary fiction of the book, Moses constitutes an assembly of Israel "today," on the day of his death, at Beth Peor on the east bank of the Jordan River (Deut 5:1; 29:1; see Braulik and Lohfink 2021, 433–39).

Handing over Moses's leadership to Joshua requires a reconfirmation of the Horeb covenant. It occurs at the conclusion of the covenant in Moab (Deut 28:69) immediately before the entry into the promised land and involves the various figures lined up before Moses: tribal leaders, elders, officials, all men, children, women, and strangers, from woodworkers to water carriers (29:9–10). Although there is no express reference to the future, the Moab covenant also applies to all generations to come. Moses makes the covenant with "those who stand here today before Yhwh and with those who today are not with us" (29:14). The whole society of Israel, as a partner to the covenant of God, is fundamentally subject to the law in its differentiation, including women, children, dependants, and future descendants. The last of the ritual texts of Deut 29–30 urgently summons Israel to decide to enter the Moab covenant (30:15–20). After that, there is no indication of how the people will react; everything remains open. The readers of later times should draw the right conclusions for their own situation. This legally relevant final section explains in a condensed form that which implicitly characterizes the ethics of Deuteronomy. Although Moses's speech to the general assembly of Israel ends in 30:20, it occurs before the actual act of commitment to the covenant ceremony:

See, I set before you today life and prosperity, death and adversity. If you obey the commandments of Yhwh your God that I am commanding you today, by loving Yhwh your God, walking in his ways, and observing his commandments, decrees, and ordinances, you shall live and become numerous, and Yhwh your God will bless you in the land that you are entering to possess. But if your heart turns away and you do not hear but are led astray to bow down to other gods and serve them, I declare to you today that you shall perish; you shall not live long in the land that you are crossing the Jordan to enter and possess. I call heaven and earth to witness against you today that I set before you life and death, blessings and curses. Choose life so that you and your descendants may live, loving Yhwh your God, obeying him, and holding fast to him; because he is your life and length of days, so that you may reside in the land that Yhwh swore to your ancestors, to Abraham, to Isaac, and to Jacob, to give to them. (Deut 30:15–20, my translation)

The choice is not between autonomy or submission. It is a response to Yhwh's continuous loyalty in the past (29:1–8, see Braulik 2021a, 19–29). The privilege of being able to choose makes the people responsible for their future (Würthwein 1982, 35–36; Reuter 2011). The emphasis is on the choice between "life and happiness" (*haṭṭôb*, "the good") and "death and misfortune" (*hārāʿ*, "the evil") (v. 15), as expressed in "blessing and curse" (v. 19). This presents the ethics for the Israel assembled in the Moab plain as a question about the good life, about happiness, and as a binding answer to it (Kessler 2017, 21–23; Brumlik 2004, 28–29; Markl 2014). Furthermore, v. 16 links the question, "What shall we do to live happily?" to the commandment to love God, which goes beyond regular loyalty since it applies exclusively to Yhwh. The alternative would be to allow oneself to be seduced into worshiping other gods, with the result that the settlement in the land would fail (vv. 17–18). The concluding paraenesis specifies that the love of God and obedience to the deity results in "remaining alive" (v. 19b), "loving, listening to the voice and clinging to him who is your life" (v. 20). The space in which this is realized is the land that God has already sworn to give to the patriarchs (v. 20). The promised blessing is ultimately due to the pure grace of the divine oath sworn to the fathers, the covenant with the patriarchs.

Deuteronomy 30:15–20 places the question Moses put forward with his Torah instruction about "what we should do" before the existential decision between life and death. The traditional legal scheme of these verses, in particular the invocation of heaven and earth as cosmic witnesses when taking the oath and the sanctions of blessing and curse (30:19), refers to the ethics of the covenant tradition (L'Hour 1967; Van Oyen 1967; Testa 1981).

Despite the principle of theonomy represented by the Torah (5:31; 6:1; 26:16), ethics is not externally determined but characterized by free, mutual behavior: whatever good things the deity offers of its own accord should be chosen independently and accepted with conscious consent (30:15–16). "Theonomy," the Christian ethical view that society should be ruled by the moral and judicial laws of the Old Testament, does not mean blind submission to a holy right or a divine will but rather, an awareness of the gratitude of freedom. When I turn to God as the source of my freedom, my claim to freedom remains undiminished. However, it has changed insofar as the free individual is no longer fixated on his or her own autonomy, and the free collective is protected from the hubris of comprehensive planning and design in all areas of life (Joas 2020, 287). The liberty of Israel is closely related to its obligation, and these two opposites lend Israel's obedience its typical character and value. The covenant is always about fulfilling the will of another in free decision (L'Hour 1967, 48). The dialogic character of the morality of the covenant is shown in the concluding exhortation of the Moab covenant:

> Today you have accepted the agreement of Yhwh. He declares that He will be your God; and you will walk in his ways, keep his statutes, commandments, and ordinances, and obey his voice. And today Yhwh has accepted your agreement: You declare that you will be his own people, as he had promised you. You will keep his commandments, and He will set you high above all nations that He has made, as praise and as fame and as honor; and that you will be a people holy to Yhwh your God, as he had promised. (Deut 26:17–19; my translation)

Moses summarizes the content of the contract that God and Israel conclude. He thereby documents what the declarations of consent (see 27:1, 9–10) mean theologically and legally (Braulik and Lohfink 2021, 89–90). According to the complicated but clear legal structure of 26:17–19, each contracting party explains to the other what it is willing to undertake as an obligation and what it demands of the other in return. The other swears to assume the required contractual performance (Lohfink 1990b, 235–36).

As can be seen from ancient Near Eastern parallels, Israel's relationship with God is understood by analogy with state treaties. But the duties of the partners are completely different, despite the formal parallels. The established relationship is by no means one between equals. Nevertheless, the covenant formula "your God – my people" to which God commits and the obedience to the commandments the people swear an oath to uphold necessarily belong together, according to the model of the contract. Deuteronomy justifies the pragmatism of its ethics of happiness neither anthropologically nor sociologically, although these two factors are, indeed, co-determiners of its ethical pragmatism; rather, it does so in terms of salvation history, with the unique relationship between Yhwh and Israel, which is described as a covenant (*berît*) (5:2–3; 29:11–13). The personal form of address again underlines the conversational character of ethics.

Many texts of Deuteronomy are shaped by ideas and language forms of this covenantal theology. They have their blueprints in ancient Near Eastern political treaty law traditions, in particular, the Hittite vassal treaties and the Neo-Assyrian Succession Treaty of Esarhaddon (Lohfink 1963; McCarthy 1978, 157–205; Koch 2008; Steymans 2003; 2013; 2016; 2019).

After a brief characterization of the documents of Horeb and Moab, the further structure of my essay loosely follows the legal structure of the contract form, which traditionally regulated the relationship of the great king to a vassal and was transferred to the religious relationship of Israel to its God. The crucial elements of this formal structure are: 1) the history of past benevolence as the legal basis of God's claims on the society of Israel; 2) the paraenesis of the declaration of principles, with the principal commandment defining the fundamental and individually comprehensive attitude of Israel before its God and its practical application in particular cases; and finally 3) the associated conditional promises of blessing of a good, successful life in exchange for faithfulness to the contract or curses for breach of contract.

4. The Horeb and Moab Charters

The covenant ceremony in Moab renews the founding act of the Horeb covenant (5:2–3), but it also surpasses it (Braulik 2021a; Versluis 2022). Its contractual document is the written Deuteronomic Torah (Deut 5–28) that God had communicated only to Moses at Horeb (5:23–31). It connects the Decalogue (5:6–21), the document of the Horeb covenant, with its interpretation in "the words of this Torah" or in the whole commandment (6:1–26:16). It consists of the paraenesis of the first Decalogue commandment (6:1–11:32), followed by a collection of individual commandments (12:1–26:16). I shall here confine myself to the content of the Decalogue and its commentary in the Deuteronomic code.

4.1 The Decalogue

The Decalogue, the "ten words" (Deut 4:13; 10:4), is considered a summary of God's will (Otto 1994, 215–19; cf., however, Crüsemann 1996, 8,

80). It should not, however, be misunderstood as a comprehensive and universally valid human ethos (Dohmen 1993). It is not a timeless catalog of morality that can be isolated from its reinterpretations in other parts of the Bible, including that in the Book of the Covenant (Exod 21–23). In Deut 5, the Decalogue forms a compendium of the subsequent Deuteronomic law. The Decalogue and the other laws differ from each other. On the one hand, the Decalogue is the unsurpassable will of God; on the other, it is a changeable and time-dependent literary expression (Lohfink 1993, 236; Irsigler 2021, 749).

As a short ethical formula that does not claim to be complete, the Decalogue formulates basic rules for the preservation and practice of freedom, which Israel owes to Yhwh's delivery from the "house of slaves" in Egypt. This cipher represents the possibility of living in the land in close communion with God and enjoying its riches without enslaving labor. Above all, the Decalogue marks the boundaries that protect the relationship to God and the freedom granted to the individual. It does not address the socio-legal consequences for the classic *personae miserae* of ancient Near Eastern societies. They are only taken into account in the case of Sabbath rest but are given full consideration in the individual laws that comment on the Sabbath commandment. Most of the differences between the Exodus and Deuteronomy versions of the Decalogue are, indeed, related to the Sabbath commandment.

While Exod 20:11 argues in terms of the theology of creation, where God rests on the seventh day, Deut 5:15 justifies the cessation of work on the Sabbath for all family members as well as for strangers and slaves as being analogous to the existence of Israel as guest citizens and slaves in Egypt (Markl 2015, 326–33). The sanctification of the day of rest, which is referred to here as the Sabbath, is not determined by the cult. It serves Israel's identity in relation to its environment as a repetitive symbol of liberation from Egyptian slavery, and it structures the life and work of the entire domestic and economic community, including their animals. The Sabbath commandment occupies the largest space in the Deuteronomic Decalogue. It forms a new whole through the correspondence of keywords and sentences (Lohfink 1990a). In Deuteronomy, the Sabbath commandment (5:12–15) becomes the first commandment or, in the covenantal context, the primary commandment. It is proclaimed by God to the people immediately at Horeb (5:4–5 and 22) and is valid always and everywhere.

Both the Sabbath commandment and that concerning the honoring of parents use the formula "as Yhwh your God has commanded you" (5:12 and 16; see Braulik 2017b). Moses or the narrator interrupts the presentation of the Decalogue twice with this remark. On the level of the final text of Deuteronomy, it refers to God's commandments, which were issued after the revelation of the Decalogue. The formula thus serves as an inner-Deuteronomic reference to individual laws, especially the provisions of the festival calendar (16:1–17) and the law of the offices (16:18–18:22), which are loosely associated with the Sabbath commandment and the commandment regarding the honoring of parents. This peculiarity already demonstrates that in the composition of its individual laws, the Deuteronomic legal code is an interpretation of the Horeb Decalogue under the conditions of life in Canaan (4:5; 12:1).

4.2 Primary Commandment and Individual Laws

In Deut 5, Moses summarizes the legally relevant words of God in quotations in accordance with the ancient Near Eastern legal technique. After the Decalogue, he reports God's affirmative answer to the request of the people's representatives to appoint him as mediator of the law (5:28–31). Hence, it is to Moses that God communicates the whole commandment, the laws, and the judgments. What is meant is the paraenesis of the primary commandment (Deut 6–11) and the collection of individual laws (Deut 12–26). However, Moses does not present it to the general assembly of Israel until they are in Moab (6:1).

The Decalogue forms the basis of the textual framework of Deuteronomy (Braulik 2019b). Its prologue and the first commandment, with Yhwh's exclusive claim to Israel, are contained in the paraenetic material in chapters 6–11. They are both taken up several times and interpreted in paraphrasing terms for different situations (Lohfink 1963, 139–236). For example, the prohibition against other gods (5:7) is included in 6:14 "You shall not follow other gods." The paraenesis in 4:16–18 develops the phrase, "You shall not make for yourself a cult image, or likeness, of anything in heaven above, or on the earth beneath, or in the water under the earth" (5:8). The expression "do not bow down to them [other gods] and do not serve them" (5:9) is applied in 4:19 to cultic rites before the sun, moon, and stars. Oaths (6:13) must follow the recurrent theme (*Leitmotiv*) of the Horeb theophany (5:5, 29), with the reminder that "Yhwh, your God, alone you shall fear." The commentary on the main commandment, "Take heed not to forget Yhwh, who brought you out of Egypt, the house of slaves" (6:12; see 5:6) is even commented on again for a time of prosperity: "Be careful that your heart does not become proud and you do not forget Yhwh your God" (8:14). Beyond the beginning of the Decalogue, individual words and phrases also link the Decalogue with individual provisions of the Deuteronomic collection (Markl 2007, 212–17). Terms like "command" are only used by Yhwh. Israel is to "fear" and "serve." "Love," however, is used alternately by both covenant partners.

The collection of individual laws supplements and clarifies the fields of action that are generally regulated by the Decalogue but are otherwise still open. To a certain extent, it contains the implementing regulations for the Decalogue. In addition, in the disposition of its legal propositions, it follows the arrangement of the Decalogue commandments as a kind of grid (Braulik 1991). The composition of the law follows the systematization techniques of ancient Near Eastern legal codifications. This means, for example, that legal clauses are often strung together associatively. The fact that the correspondences between the Decalogue commandments and the provisions that specify them appear to differ in clarity is primarily due to the history of development of three blocks of individual commandments (12:2–17; 16:18–18:22; 19:1–25:16). The actual Decalogical editing of the legal code may only have taken place in connection with the last great expansion of the legislative material (Braulik 2017b, 66 n. 20; Kilchör 2015, 63–70). It also shows that the Deuteronomic body of laws in its final form claims to apply to the overall book. The following table mentions the themes of the groups of laws according to the relevant sections of the Decalogue (Braulik 2017a, 27):

Commandment against	Deuteronomy
1 Idols and images	12:2–13:19 One God – one cultic place
2 Misuse of the Name	14:1–21 Living as Yhwh's holy people in ritual distinction from the peoples that serve other gods
3 Work on the Sabbath	14:22–16:17 Calendar of cultic and "brotherly" activities
4 Dishonoring parents	16:18–18:22 Respect for Israel's officials and authorities
5 Murder	19–21 Protecting life. 22:1–12 Transitions between the fifth and sixth commandments
6 Adultery	22:13–23:15 Preserving human dignity
7 Stealing	23:16–24:7 Placing human needs above property rights
8 False witness	24:8–25:4 Preserving the rights of the poor, those socially disadvantaged, and of legal offenders
9 Coveting a neighbor's wife	25:5–12 Ensuring offspring
10 Coveting a neighbor's belongings	25:13–16 Using a single set of weights

5. Divine Grace and Forgiveness

What Israel is and what Israel should do results directly from what God is for Israel and what the deity does for Israel. Since the morality of the covenant is primarily a morality of response in a historical dialogue, one must ask about the normative roots of Deuteronomic ethics (L'Hour 1967, 15 and 63).

5.1 From Pharaoh's Rule to Justice before Yhwh (Deut 6:20–25)

Israel owes its social order to the saving deeds of its God. They establish a history of freedom that enables Israel to act ethically, shaped by decision and responsibility, so that it can live in a just society. According to 6:20–25, the ethos of salvation and justice is to be retained in the cultural memory of the people by an easily memorized short formula of faith for subsequent generations (Barbiero 2002; Perlitt 1994b). As the adults regularly recite the paraenesis of the primary commandment and the collection of the individual laws (Deut 6–26), the children learn them by heart (6:6–7, see Braulik 2017c, 99–106). One day they ask: "Why (these) legal declarations, rules, and legal specifications that Yhwh our God has obliged you to follow?" (Deut 6:20). The wording can be clarified on the basis of the subsequent family catechesis (vv. 21–25): "Are we acting correctly if we observe this whole law closely before Yhwh, our God?" It is an enquiry after the inner meaning of the laws, which for an Israelite immediately becomes a question of the origin of the law and its binding force. The answer must necessarily be historical. It is recounted how the covenant obligation came about (Lohfink 1963, 161). Despite the temporal distance from the founding event, the parents not only pass on the religious knowledge of Israel, they also identify themselves in the collective "we" and "us" with the slaves who came out of Egypt:

> ... then you shall say to your children, "We were Pharaoh's slaves in Egypt, but the LORD brought us out of Egypt with a mighty hand. The LORD displayed before our eyes great and awesome signs and wonders against Egypt, against Pharaoh and all his household. He brought us out from there in order to bring us in, to give us the land that he promised on oath to our ancestors" (Deut 6:21–23 NRSV).

This confession uses manumission as a legal-theological argument for following the whole law. It affects an entire people and is effected by God. It assumes that a slave could be ransomed or freed by using force. Because Pharaoh had unjustly enslaved Israel, using "a strong hand" was legitimate (Schulmeister 2010, 160–61). Yhwh demonstrated his right and abilities by mighty, ominous signs and wonders, not only to Egypt and its king but also before Israel, who confirmed the events as eyewitnesses. Leading out and leading in are, therefore, legal processes. Whoever "brings out" (yṣ' hiphil) a slave from someone else's property becomes his new master. According to the legal meaning of the verb *bwʾ* (hiphil), he can "lead him in" to make him his slave. Israel was led from the realm of slavery, the land of Egypt, into a new realm, the land sworn to the fathers. Although the "leading in" is only formulated in the final sentence, it is part of the reasoning. The goal toward which the whole history of liberation is directed is formulated in the next main proposition: the imposition of the Deuteronomic laws and the fear of God. The logical implication of the manumission model is not stated explicitly: Yhwh now made Israel his own slave in his home. The emancipation of Israel from Egyptian slavery was a legal act in which Israel was led out of the dominion of Pharaoh to the dominion of Yhwh; thus, it constituted the abolition of human dominion. The legal act does not subjugate; it gives life through a new social order. Through emancipated Israel, God institutes a society ruled in justice; a society that stands in contrast to the system from which Israel emerged (Braulik 2001a, 47):

> Then the LORD commanded us to observe all these statutes, to fear the LORD our God, for our lasting good, so as to keep us alive, as is now the case. If we diligently observe this entire commandment before the LORD our God, as he has commanded us, we will be in the right. (Deut 6:24–25 NRSV)

Mutual obligations follow from the gift of freedom. The personal relationship of the Israelites to Yhwh, namely, to fear the deity in the sense of exclusive and faithful worship (Becker 1965, 93), is realized in the fact that they live according to the law. As their new master, Yhwh not only tells them what he wants from them but also provides for their sustenance. Therefore, the positive consequences of obedience can also be understood to be: "God will provide our livelihood without time limit" (*leḥayyōtēnû* 6:24) (Lohfink 1995b, 269). If it is also "in the right" (*ûṣedāqâ tihyeh lānû*), Israel shall remain in the state of salvation of a fulfilled life in the land "as we have it today" (6:24) i.e., if it keeps the entire commandment Yhwh has commanded (Braulik 2017d, 16–17; see 24:13 and Barbiero 2002, 162–63).

In fact, the Exodus from Egypt and the settlement in Canaan are a return to the unconditional divine love and election of the patriarchs (Braulik 2022). The return to the patriarchs' Canaan establishes the gracious intervention of God (4:37; 7:7–8) and his unique relationship with Israel. It enables the people to love in return, as well as to obey (7:9) and thus enjoy a happy life by maintaining the Deuteronomic social order (4:40; 7:11–16).

5.2 Moses's Intercession (9:26-29) and God's Faithfulness (29:1-7)

In addition to the myths of the patriarchs and Egypt (6:21-23), Deuteronomy recalls a third myth of origin, i.e. the primordial event of the revelation at Horeb, with the Decalogue as the covenant document that founds the Deuteronomic law (Lohfink 2005a, 114; Geiger 2010, 308). The Horeb covenant had to be upheld against Israel's apostasy from the very hour it was made (9:12,16). But in Deuteronomy, there is neither a breach nor a renewal of the covenant. It only knows the intercession of Moses for Israel at Horeb (9:26-29). In the story of sin at Horeb, Moses develops a narrative that unites everything that happened to Israel in terms of sin and divine forbearance over the past forty years (Lohfink 2005b, 154). In view of the continuous history of sin among his people, God remains free to grant pardon. Moses's entreaty not to ruin "your people and your inheritance" (v. 26aα) can prevent the destruction of Israel (Braulik 2023). "Your people and your inheritance" underline Yhwh's commitment toward Israel. The people owe their privileged existence exclusively to their redemption from Egyptian slavery: God bought them free with power and brought them out of Egypt with a strong hand (v. 26aβb; see v. 29). This does not constitute a right to be spared. In view of the failure of Israel and its sin, Moses justifies his intercession beyond the original story told in the catechesis (6:21-25) with the memory of "your servants Abraham, Isaac, and Jacob" (9:27). God listened to Moses and did not abandon the people to perdition (10:10).

Although Israel rebels against Yhwh throughout the desert journey (9:7,24), a covenant is again possible in Moab. Despite all the rebelliousness, God does not shirk his freely accepted responsibility. Israel's relationship with God at the time of the covenant at Horeb and in Moab remains one and the same; the time interval between the two is virtually eliminated (5:2-3). The Moab covenant takes up and confirms the Horeb covenant. However, the two covenants differ in their swearing-in rituals and contractual documents (28:69). When Moses reminds Israel of its history in 29:1b-6a, he neglects the difference between the Exodus-Horeb and Moab generations and thereby places those addressed in their true identity (Lohfink 1991a, 20-25). Because of this merging of generations, the people gathered before him were eyewitnesses to the great deeds of God in Egypt (29:1b-2), although until now they have lacked the necessary ability to see and understand (29:3). The events at Horeb are not mentioned, and above all, the infringement of the ban on images is passed over in silence. God recalls the forty wilderness years when under his guidance, the Israelites did not end up in rags and received food and drink in a miraculous way (29:4-5a). What God intended there he reveals only now, at the end of the journey to Moab: "You should recognize: I am Yhwh your God" (v. 5b). Sin and punishments fade away; only the wonderful guidance of Yhwh to this point stands before one's eyes. Everything that filled the time in the wilderness was God-directed and God-supported prehistory, without an actual encounter with God, leading up to this moment when Israel will recognize their God, Yhwh (Gomes de Araújo 1999, 328).

The formula, "I am Yhwh your God" (29:5b), also opens the Decalogue, the contract document of Horeb (5:6). Above all, however, it points ahead to the covenant made in Moab, which aims "to make you his people today and to become your God" (29:12). In the Moab covenant, then, there is seeing, hearing, and discerning what Israel had not previously perceived. The sojourn in Egypt and in the desert can only be understood by reading "in this day" (v. 3a) and "in this place" (v. 6a) against the background of chs. 1–3. For 29:1b takes up the wording of 1:30b: "All that he [Yhwh your God] did with you in Egypt before your eyes." The concluding remark in 29:6a, however, has a parallel in 1:31: "...until you came to this place." The short report that follows in 29:6b–7 only summarizes 2:32–3:13, so it is limited to the last two years of the wilderness and the conquests in Transjordan. The unbelief of the people at Kadesh-Barnea (1:32) and the subsequent thirty-eight years of punitive extinction of the Egypt-Horeb generation in the desert are left out (2:14). The memory of Israel's blessed past concludes the covenant in Moab. Only Yhwh's unilaterally sustained loyalty makes it possible to include the covenant made at Horeb in the oath ritual of Moab. Everything Israel learned from Yhwh in the past was intended to prepare for his unchanged promise: "I am Yhwh, your God" (29:5) who "appoints you today as his people" (29:12; see 26:17–19; Braulik 2021a, 28–29).

5.3 The Circumcision of the Heart (30:6)

Israel will break the Moab covenant and go into exile. Nevertheless, Moses foresees that despite the punishment, God will not expose the exiles to destruction, because he knows that he is bound by an oath to the fathers (4:31). Israel will take to heart its covenantal duty of returning to Yhwh and hearing the divine voice (30:1–2). For God will have mercy on his people, gather them, bring them back to the land of their fathers, and make them even happier than their ancestors (30:3–5). Above all, he will bring about a radical inner renewal through a cardiological intervention (Braulik 2020b, 86–91). This is the prerequisite for the gracious conversion and change in the circumstances of life: "Yhwh, your God, will circumcise (LXX: purify) your heart and the heart of your seed so that you love Yhwh your God with all your heart and with all your soul, that you may have life" (30:6).

Whereas 10:16 required the Israelites to circumcise the foreskins of their hearts and give up their stubbornness, God now effects the transformation. The change not only affects the barrier of the foreskin but eliminates the unfitness and inability of the organ. In addition, it is not limited to the generation of returnees but also applies to their descendants. Through a circumcision of the heart, God enables Israel to love him again with all their spirit and vitality, i.e. to keep the main commandment of love of God (6:5) and to enjoy life in abundance (30:6). This circumcision will prove effective in the Deuteronomic social order as recorded in the Torah of the Moab covenant (30:10). God will bestow on this society a rich agricultural harvest, an increase in offspring, and fertility in cattle and agriculture. He will rejoice in Israel again (30:9).

What is decisive is what ensues as a result of the divine circumcision of the heart in 30:11–14 regarding the obligation and possibility of following the main and individual commandments. Israel can change its ways while in exile because it is never overwhelmed by the commitment to obedience and need not search after God's will:

> Surely, this commandment that I am commanding you today is not too hard for you, nor is it too far away. It is not in heaven [...] Neither is it beyond the sea [...] No, the word is very near to you; it is in your mouth and in your heart for you to observe. (Deut 30:11–14 NRSV)

The verses form a coda to vv. 1–10 and are tied back to the causal series in vv. 9b–10 by the introductory "because." They refer to the love commandment in 30:6 and integrate the learning process of 6:6–7, which in turn follows the love commandment in 6:5. By constantly reciting it, one carries the commandment, that is, the whole of the covenantal ethic concretized in the paraenesis and individual laws of the Torah to which Moses now binds the people in Moab (30:11). The commandment is internalized in the heart to ensure the ability of the people to act upon it, both individually and communally (30:14). The very near word is the place of encounter with God through the circumcised heart (30:6). It is a word of grace and of accepting faith. The call to choose life and happiness, not death and misfortune (30:15–20), shows, however, that this ability to love God and a just society is entrusted to a risky freedom.

5.4 Ethics from a Guilty History: Israel's Original Sins

Moses's first speech recapitulates the journey from Horeb to Kadesh-Barnea on the edge of the promised land. At this point, the first complete narrative of the book begins; it is the only one dealing with Israel's guilt without paraenesis and commandments. A second, even more extensive story will tell of the collective defection to the molten calf and of the delay in concluding the covenant on the mountain of God Horeb (Braulik 2021b, 177). Both stories are paradigmatic as they create a fundamental framework of collective unbelief and rebellion, to which God's reaction to sin adds ungraciousness (Braulik 2021b; 2023; forthcoming). Both narratives reflect the decisive foundations of Deuteronomic ethics in a model-like manner, albeit based on experiences of guilt and in contrast to the behavior God expected from Israel.

At the oasis of Kadesh-Barnea, the people demanded that spies be sent out to explore the hill country of the Amorite, despite the divine assurance that it was ready for the taking (Deut 1:20–21). Moses agrees to go ahead with this suggestion (vv. 22–23), thus becoming co-responsible for the looming guilt. Like the other members of the Exodus generation, he is not allowed to enter the promised land (Braulik and Lohfink 2021, 440–55). Upon the spies' return, the people balk, despite their report about the magnificent land (vv. 24–25):

> But you were unwilling to go up. You rebelled against the mouth of Yhwh your God; you grumbled in your tents and said, "It is because Yhwh hates us that he has brought us out of the land of Egypt, to hand us over to the Amorites to destroy us." (Deut 1:26–27; my translation)

Not only does Israel decide willfully not to obey God's command, but it is also the first time in the Pentateuch that Israel's collective disobedience is characterized as "rebellion against the mouth of Yhwh" (*mrh* [*hiphil*] *'et pî Yhwh*). The monstrosity lies in the "slander" (*rgn* [*niphal*]) of God.

Yhwh's alleged hatred and his intention to use the Amorites to exterminate the people voids the entire process of liberation from Egypt and, thus, the center of the creed. Moses's evocation of previous episodes of deliverance fails to counter the horror of the giant offspring of the Anakim (v. 28). The people's inner resistance translates as the inability to trust that God will fulfill his promise to bring them into the promised land (v. 32). Because of this unbelief, Israel proves itself unwilling at the beginning of its history to let God lead it into the promised good life. Therefore, the act of bestowal of the land, which should have been accepted through its occupation, is transferred from the Exodus generation to the next, the Moab generation. Guilt and punishment remain limited to "this corrupt generation" that must die in the desert (v. 35).

The rebellion continues when, despite an express divine prohibition, they go up to fight the Amorites, who defeat them (vv. 43–44). The pattern of rebellion against God and of lack of trust in him is the archetypal sin in which all later transgressions are rooted (2 Kgs 17:14; Pss 78 and

106). Ultimately, Moses's reminder about the rebellion of the Exodus generation at Kadesh-Barnea (Deut 1:19–46) explains why "today," at the end of his life, he must appoint Joshua to be his successor. According to verse 38, "he is the one who is to give Israel its possession." Considering Israel's collective guilt, they are still in need of a mediator to lead them and plead with God on their behalf.

The second story of collective guilt is the Golden Calf episode. This sin (9:21) crowns the entire wilderness period as a time of constant rebellion against Yhwh (vv. 7, 24) and forms the *Leitmotiv* of the Deuteronomistic history. Following the detailed description of the misconduct at Horeb (9:8–21), other places are listed where the people provoked the displeasure of Yhwh (*qṣp* hifil vv. 7, 8, 22; see *qṣp* qal 1:34; 9:19). After recalling the sin at Kadesh-Barnea, Moses concludes that Israel has been rebellious against Yhwh "ever since I have known you" (9:24, compare v. 7). Unlike at Kadesh-Barnea, it is not directed against "Yhwh's mouth," i.e. against a specific command, but against God in general.

6. The Pillars of Deuteronomic Ethics

6.1 Basic Requirement: Personal Relationship with God

Ancient Near Eastern vassal contracts defined the relationship between the contracting parties in terms of the vassal's loyalty delineated in the observation of the individual regulations. The loyalty principle is neither the first commandment nor the most important; it is the very soul of all commandments, which it sums up and surpasses. The ethical value of each law derives primarily from the basic requirement of loyalty and only secondarily from its own content (L'Hour 1967, 64).

In Deuteronomy, loyalty is mentioned above all in the paraenesis in chapters 4–11. The verbs that formulate the relationship to Yhwh or to other gods are decisive (Lohfink 1963, 73–80). They can occur individually or in a series. In the following sections, I limit myself to the two most frequent expressions related to Yhwh, "to love" (*ʾhb*) and "to fear" (*yrʾ*). They are used exclusively for Israel's relationship with Yhwh, as are the more marginal "to cling to" (*dbq*) and "not to forget" (*škḥ*).

6.1.1 The Mutual Love between Yhwh and Israel
Deuteronomy uses the verb "to love" (*ʾhb*) relatively frequently compared to other biblical books (Braulik 2017b; 2022): Yhwh loves his people or their fathers five times (4:37; 7:8 as noun; 7:13; 10:15; 23:6), and once he loves the stranger in Israel (10:19). But twelve times it is Israel who loves or should love its God (5:10; 6:5; 7:9; 10:12; 11:1,13, 22; 13:4; 19:9;

30:6,16,20) and once strangers, too (10:19). Apart from Josh 22:5; 23:11, only Deuteronomy calls the audience in the story world on the plains of Moab, as well as the reader/hearer, to love God. These appellatives belong to the peculiarities of its theology.

Historical summaries primarily point to God's love, past or present; it grounds His action, expressly or implicitly, toward or on behalf of Israel. Although the Deuteronomic use of the word "to love" originates in the legal rhetoric of ancient Near Eastern vassal treaties, including Esarhaddon's Succession Treaty, it is emotionally charged. Two verbs used in this context make this clear: when God loves, he "sets his heart to cling to someone" (*'šq* in 7:7; 10:15); when Israel loves, they "cleave to God, cling to him" (*dbq* in 11:22; 13:5; 30:20).

The commandment to love Yhwh (6:5) is preceded by a summary of former ages, the first such summary of God's dealings on behalf of Israel in the Pentateuch:

> And because he loved your fathers and chose their descendants after them, he brought you out of Egypt with his own presence, by his great power, to exterminate before you nations greater and mightier than yourselves, to bring you in, giving you their land for your heritage, as it is today. (Deut 4:37–38; my translation)

The unique rescue event stems from God's creative love for the patriarchs and reaches into the Mosaic present. Yhwh's past salvation of Israel makes it possible for the deity to be recognized as the only God who is powerful in heaven and on earth: "So acknowledge today and take to heart that Yhwh is God in heaven above and on the earth beneath; there is no other" (v. 39). This insight is to become a matter of heart and conviction for Israel and finally leads to the request: "Therefore, you should keep his laws and his commandments, which I enjoin on you today, so that you and your children after you will be fine and you shall live long on the land which Yhwh your God gives you for all time" (v. 40). Thus, the first discourse of Moses places the knowledge of God programmatically at the service of social ethics. Israel's obedience to the commandment results from a free decision and a genuine responsibility for a happy future. Ultimately, however, it is made possible by the love of God, which is revealed in historical experience and monotheistic conviction (Braulik 2006).

The first commandment of the Decalogue is the ban on foreign gods, which characterizes Israel as those who love Yhwh and keep his commandments (5:9–10). Here, too, the principle of grace applies to love and obedience to the commandments. They are preceded by the emancipation from slavery in Egypt, i.e. by God-given freedom. To preserve it, Israel must refrain from having any other gods because there is a dialectic between the image of God and the order of society. Ultimately, enslaving, inhumane social systems are connected with other deities. Moses comments on Yhwh's claim to exclusivity subsequently in chs 6–11, introduced by Israel's confession to Yhwh as its "only one" to whom it is to be linked in love as its God and to him alone: "Listen, Israel! Yhwh our God, Yhwh is one! Then love Yhwh your God with all your heart and with all your soul and with all your strength! (6:4–5). The entire paraenesis of the commandment is rooted in this *amor ex auditu* (love based on hearing).

What is meant is a legally imposed relationship of loyalty, a complete devotion in obedience. It encompasses gratitude and trust and is realized in an emotionally experienced relationship. "Hear, O Israel!" calls the collective Israelite "you" to love, and only then does the individual Israelite do so. Israel expresses its love for Yhwh in fulfilling his social and societal order, which becomes a reality when the people as a whole carry it out because it is a "civilization of love" and corresponds to Yhwh's ideal for the people he loves (Braulik 2017e, 246). Should Israel break the covenant and be banished from its land, Moses prophetically promises that God will circumcise Israel's heart and thereby remove the inability to love him (30:6). The last admonition of the final paraenesis of the Moab covenant repeats the commandment: "Love Yhwh your God, listen to his voice and hold fast to him; for he is your life" (30:20). The principle of love thus embraces the Torah and the Covenant (Deut 5–30).

The extent to which the reciprocal love between God and Israel is mutually determined by each other is illustrated in 7:7–13 and 10:12–19. In 10:12–13 and 19, Israel is asked to love Yhwh or the stranger, but in 10:14–15 and 17–18 it is God who sets his heart to love the patriarchs and the stranger. However, one can only fulfill the demand to love God if one also keeps his commandments according to the cultic and the social order of the Deuteronomic Torah. These commandments assure the realization of Israel's loyalty to God in all dimensions of its communal life, and accordingly, they assure that Israel prospers. In the question in vv. 12–13, Moses formulates what God expects of Israel and clarifies that "loving" is what the fear of God means:

> So now, O Israel, what does Yhwh your God require of you? Only to fear Yhwh your God, by walking in all his ways and loving him and serving Yhwh your God with all your heart and with all your soul, and by keeping the commandments of Yhwh your God and his laws, which I enjoin on you today, for your own well-being. (Deut 10:12–13; my translation)

In this divine paraenesis, "fear" and "love" are not opposed to each other. They complement each other as two aspects of an intense, positive, emotionally oriented, and respectful relationship (Markl 2012, 58). This relationship, combined with the observance of his laws, is what God asks of his people (see 10:12).

6.1.2 Fear of Yhwh and Obedience

The fear of God describes Israel's reaction to the theophany at Horeb, the experience of Yhwh as a counterpart that calls fascination and shuddering to the fore (Braulik and Lohfink 2021, 122–26). The fear experienced on God's mountain (5:5) ascribes a specific meaning to the ancient Near Eastern concepts of religion and belief. Only in 25:18 does "fearing God" designate a universally valid human ethos. In Deuteronomy, the verb "to fear" (yrʾ), combined with the name of God, evokes the experience of Horeb and Israel's relationship with God resulting from it (Lohfink 2005a, 128). The fear of Yhwh is said to continue in Israel through the generations (4:10; 5:29). It is actualized every year when the annual tithes are consumed in a lavish feast (14:23). At the Feast of Tabernacles in every seventh year, when the provisions of the Torah are read and taught to the assembly of all Israel, they are to be combined with the social experience of the egalitarian joy of the debt-free people (31:9–13). The future king will daily experience this divine awe because he is obliged to read the Torah every day, which is supposed to awaken the fear of Yhwh in him (17:19). These are all occasions when "to fear Yhwh" can and should become internalized as the immediate reaction to hearing the Decalogue or the Laws, but also in a joint celebration (4:10; 6:2; 14:23; 17:19; 31:12, 13). The latter is something that is unique to Deuteronomy.

The "fear of Yhwh" occurs fourteen times (4:10; 5:29; 6:2,13,24; 8:6; 10:12,20; 13:5; 14:23; 17:19; 28:58; 31:12.13) and outnumbers all other phrases having Yhwh as the direct object of a verb. The subject is always Israel; only once is it the king, as a model Israelite.

"Fear" can be combined with other verbs of relationship with God (10:12; 13:5). Above all, however, the expression is used alongside verbs of general injunction. Within the framework of the covenant, the fear of Yhwh expresses allegiance to the divine partner. The individual provisions are subordinate to this bond and only offer proof of fundamental fidelity. Consequently, one must not identify "fearing Yhwh" with a sense of being afraid of the consequences of disobedience but rather, as an act of worship (Becker 1965, 87–91).

6.1.3 Relationship with God and Observance of the Law

The two complementary verbs denoting the relationship with God, "love" and "fear," denote a lasting attitude within Israel. The other verbs of relationship with the divine, "to cling to" (dbq), "to serve" (ʿbd), and "to follow" (hlk ʾaḥărê), are used synonymously with them, even though they do not describe a state of being. Instead, they are all active verbs that involve some manner of commandment observance. Or, conversely, these activities are summarized by verbs that denote a relationship with God. The two groups of verbs are linked together in mixed sets of infinitive clauses in different ways. Their syntax is relevant to the theological relationship between observing the law and relating to God (Braulik and Lohfink 2021, 248–55). The conjunction "and" (*syndesis*) between them leaves the relationship open; on the other hand, the ideas found in the infinitive clauses are not linked by conjunctions (*asyndesis*) but rather, they are linked to one another by adding "[where]by" to clarify meaning. Deuteronomy 10:12–13, quoted above, can serve as an example: The verses set explicit syntactical connections such as "by walking in all his ways" and "by keeping the commandments of Yhwh and his laws" against implicit connections such as "and love him and serve Yhwh your God with all your heart and with all your soul" to illustrate the alternation between infinitive clauses denoting relationship with God and the observance of the commandments.

The infinitive clauses imply that the relationship with God does not simply consist in obedience to the commandment and must not be equated with it. Belonging to Yhwh is neither the consequence ("so that") nor the purpose ("in order to") of observing the commandments, because it has always been given to Israel prior to all obligations. But love and fear of Yhwh as well as the other designations of the relationship to God find their authentic expression willed by God in the observance of the law: "by" in the sense of "by means of" or "as a demonstration that." Loving God or fearing him is realized in obedience to the commandments. Because the infinitive clauses also only form examples of attitudes and actions, relationship with God and obedience to the commandments are not identical (Braulik and Lohfink 2021, 254–55).

6.2 The General Paraenesis of Laws and the "Paraenetic Scheme"

Deuteronomic paraenesis is not, as in other ancient literature, about interpersonal instruction, admonition, or warning in different situations (Braulik 2017f). Rather, it concerns Israel's relationship with God and "the whole commandment" (*kol hammiṣwâ* 5:31, i.e. Deut 6–26) and within it, the collection of individual laws, "the laws and judgements" (*haḥuqqîm wehammišpāṭîm*, Deut 12–26). Like other ancient Near Eastern legal collections, "the biblical law collections were (each in their own way) similarly meant to inculcate community beliefs and values, rather than dictate what to do and what not to do or to serve as the basis of adjudication. This type of authority is epistemic [intellectual, cognitive] rather than practical" (Vroom 2018, 211).

Paraenesis can be general or can refer to specific laws or groups of laws. Because Deuteronomy is largely the speech of Moses quoted by the narrator, the paraenesis occurs in the form of address. The explicit execution of the direct general legal paraenesis corresponds to chs. 4–11 (without chs. 5 and 9–10). It therefore does not appear in the legal code (Deut 12–26) and in the ritual texts of the Moab covenant (Deut 29–30; see Braulik 2017f, 276–79). Verbs expressing a desire to perform their action as part of observing the law constitute the basic framework. These verbs are followed by one or more expressions for "law." In addition, Moses uses the commitment formula – "which I enjoin on you today." It focuses on the Moab covenant and shows that paraenesis not only appeals and motivates but also argues in a legally binding manner. Finally, general paraenesis can also be part of a larger context of form, the so-called "paraenetic scheme" that 1) calls for obedience to the law and 2) promises God's blessing in return. It serves as a framing and structuring element in the presentation. This two-part structure and its typical features can be found, for example, in 8:1:

> The whole commandment that I enjoin on you today, 1) you shall observe to do,
>
> 2) that you may live and multiply and may enter and possess the land which Yhwh swore to your fathers.

According to ancient Near Eastern learning and educational practices, "observe" (*šmr*) refers to the memorization of the laws learned by heart, while "to do" (*'śh*) means their realization. These core verbs of paraenesis prove that knowing and keeping the whole commandment cannot be separated. In addition, the paraenesis of laws and the paraenetic scheme fulfill a deeper function: they serve the inner unity. They repeatedly steer the speech toward the entirety and that which is essential. Furthermore, they sharpen the one, basic attitude that transcends and interweaves every individual action, which is ultimately what matters. In addition, the paraenetic scheme places the people as listeners in the tension between the currently required action and the resulting future blessings. This phenomenon is another unique feature of the book of Deuteronomy (Braulik 2017f, 296–97; Lohfink 1963, 96–97).

7. Examples of Deuteronomic Ethics from the Collection of the Individual Commandments

7.1 Keeping the Sacrificial Meal and Rejoicing: The Cultic Laws

The legal collection of Deuteronomy turns sacrifices and pilgrimage festivals into the primary settings of Israel's interpretation of their world and of their socialization. The meal also had a ritual character before and after the conquest (Braulik 2019c). Deuteronomy concentrates all sacrifices and festivals in the single "resting" place (Deut 12:9), commonly understood as the temple of Jerusalem on the basis of 1 Kgs 8:56 (Braulik 1988, 220–24), even though the so-called "place" (*māqôm*) is never located (against Pyschny 2019, 304–10). It envisions its own pilgrimage scheme and ritual framework around the activities at the "place" Yhwh will choose. The aim of the cultic regulations is to ensure that Israel experiences pure joy before its God through a festive sacrificial meal (Lohfink 1995a, 239). In so doing, it gains its identity as the people of Yhwh.

The Deuteronomic festival theory prescribes the chosen site as the location of all animal and vegetable sacrifices, combined with the special treatment of blood, as well as the time of the three pilgrimage festivals to be celebrated "for Yhwh": Pesach, the Feast of Weeks, and the Feast of Tabernacles. Because the worship of Yhwh should take place as a community, it is characterized by social responsibility. "Eating" (*'kl*) and "rejoicing" (*śmḥ*) before (*lipnê*) Yhwh are at the heart of all Deuteronomic cultic regulations. The two actions are not interchangeable. "Eating" connotes sacrificial meals, which is not the focus of the joyful harvest festivals. Deuteronomy knows no other joy than that at sacrifice and feast. It is the basic Deuteronomic liturgical attitude. "Rejoicing" is profound gratitude "for all that your hands have created, because Yhwh your God has blessed you" (12:8) or "for all the good things that Yhwh your God has given you" (26:11). The joint feast is the response to these blessings. Of the seven cultic laws, six connect rejoicing with a shorter or longer list of participants (12:7,12; 14:26; 16:11,14; 26:11); only 12:18 sets rejoicing in the wake of a sacrificial meal.

The family is at the center of the joyful communal meal (12:7; 14:26; 15:20). The list of household members is highly significant: the sons, daughters, and the male and female slaves of the addressee designated as "you" (12:12,18; 16:11,14). Despite claims to the contrary (Pyschny 2019, 309–12; Jacobs 2020, 9), the wife is implicitly granted the right to direct the sacrificial ritual (Braulik 2001b, 85–87; Ebach 2014, 133–35).

The family unit is followed by outsiders who have no land and therefore no crops. At the sacrifices, attention is given to the "Levites in your towns" (12:12,18; 14:27) and at the harvest to the "strangers, orphans, and widows in your towns" (14:29, 16:11, 14). Here, cultic regulations and social legislation regarding the supply of victuals intertwine. At the Feast of Weeks and Tabernacles (16:11,14) the symbolic number of seven groups of participants expresses the all-inclusiveness of the participation. The requirement to travel to the central sanctuary focuses on the theological intention of the celebration, not on its practical details concerning the celebration. All members of the "family of Yhwh" ('*am Yhwh*) should celebrate the highlights of the farming year on an equal footing, despite their differences in social status. The joyful eating together in the central sanctuary becomes a real symbol of the united people of God (Braulik 2019c, 134). The fact that everything happens "before Yhwh" not only underlines the presence of God in the temple but also points to mystical depths more accessible through the joy of feasting together than during sacrificial rites at the altar.

Within the framework of the sacrificial laws, Deut 12 deals with the destruction of foreign places of worship together with their cultic symbols (vv. 2-3) and the prohibition of their cultic practices (vv. 29-31). This is done to illustrate the distinctively Israelite aspect of the cult of Yhwh.

In four paragraphs, Deut 12 regulates the where, when, what, and how of everyone's share of the common sacrifice. With juridical logic, each section unfolds one aspect of the meal: the offerings that may only be brought to the chosen place of worship (vv. 4-7), the time when the cult regulations come into force (vv. 8-12), the difference between sacrifice and slaughter, or slaughter at the sanctuary and slaughter in the localities, together with their prohibitions concerning eating, which result from cult centralization (vv. 13-19), and the treatment of blood (vv. 20-28).

Notably, the word "unclean" occurs in 12:15 and 22 and is the key word of 14:3-21. These regulations apply to Israel as a whole, while Deuteronomy lists no particular purity regulations for priests. Purity is a reflection of holiness, which, in Deuteronomy, separates Israel from other peoples rather than drawing a line between priests and non-priests within Israel (Lohfink 1995a, 245). The focus is not on who is allowed to slaughter or to sacrifice but on how the blood is treated: poured on the ground in the case of home slaughter or poured out on the altar at the sanctuary in the case of sacrifice.

Burnt offerings and communal sacrifices correspond to the two forms of hospitality offered to God. The burnt offering corresponds to a meal to honor the guest, namely God, because the animal is reserved for him alone. In contrast, communal sacrifices practice a more general type of hospitality, in which God is the guest of the hosting family and both guest and hosts share the meal. In the sacrifices made from agricultural products, God accepts this meal from the food of Israel and thus testifies to his special bond with the people and their land (Marx 2000, 136).

The pilgrimage calendar in 16:1–17 fixes not only the place but also the times when all of Israel is to gather for the celebration and festival "for Yhwh," thus to a degree determining day and night, spring and autumn, and work and harvest. It builds on experiences that result from folk history or from the rhythm of nature. Pesach (vv. 1–8) is the only sacrifice that bears a name and is specifically scheduled to be performed. Because it brings together all families and social classes to build a common identity for the entire people, there is no list of participants. It is observed in spring, in the month or new moon of Abib.

The older seven-day festival of unleavened bread may also have begun on this date (see v. 16), which is merged with Pesach in Deuteronomy without any calendar change. The celebration symbolizes the time and food of the nocturnal Exodus from Egypt, the primeval date of Israel's own history, and the commemorative figure of Israel's identity: "For in the month of Abib, Yhwh your God brought you out of Egypt at night" (v. 1). The Passover must be slaughtered at the chosen place (v. 2) and on the evening of the first day (v. 4), "at the hour when you came out of Egypt" (v. 6). "You shall not eat anything leavened. Seven days you shall eat unleavened bread, the food of distress, for you came out of Egypt in haste" (v. 3). Matzah is bread for the journey, made from unleavened dough before it had time to rise. It is the "food of distress" as a symbol of the hasty departure. Eating unleavened bread as a commemoration of suffering has an almost sacramental symbolic value here.

Such a broad outlook on the celebration of Pesach seeks to change Israel's social awareness "every day" (v. 3; see Deut 5:15; 15:15; 16:12; 24:18, 22; Veijola 2008, 60). Ethically it is not a matter of gratitude for one's own liberation but of one's own liberating action made possible by the gift of freedom (Noichl 2002, 98). Biblical ethics is, therefore, not a slave morality but a morality of the liberated (Markl 2015, 338).

In contrast, the Feast of Weeks celebrated seven weeks after the beginning of the grain harvest is a joyous harvest festival (vv. 9–12). The freely offered gift illustrates the blessing received from God. Finally, in autumn, at the end of the farming year after the grain harvest and grape harvest, the Feast of Tabernacles is celebrated for seven days (vv. 13–15). It is "your feast" (v. 14) to celebrate the hard-won agricultural produce "when Yhwh your God has blessed you in all things, in your harvest and in the work of your hands, then you shall really rejoice" (v .15). With this "joy before Yhwh" it becomes possible to experience what Israel is in terms of its social organization. The liturgical reform produces the nucleus and the climax of a comprehensive social reform.

7.2 A Society without Poor: The Poor and Welfare Law

Ancient Near Eastern cultures know a high ethos of care of the poor, which particularly the ruling elite was expected to practice. Israel shares these ethical convictions (Lohfink 1989; Braulik 2019a). Unlike the gods of Israel's neighbors, however, Yhwh was not content with an "option for the poor" that seeks to alleviate misery. Yhwh intervened in the system that produced economic exploitation and social declassification and wrested the Hebrews, i.e. the entire lower class, from the slave state of Egypt, giving them a new legal order as his people on Sinai/Horeb to ensure that Israel could succeed in their own country. Only the Deuteronomic Torah constructs a just and therefore blessed society in which there need not be any poor.

Deuteronomy uses the terms *'ebyôn* "poor" and *'anî* "destitute" only to describe a process of increasing indebtedness. Because these are misfortunes that could threaten the small farmers of Palestine at any time, the credit regulations endeavor to reduce the burden of excessive indebtedness. If, for example, one needed a loan due to crop failures, the addressee is admonished to lend at his own risk (15:7-11). When a creditor takes a pledge, he must not do so in a manner that humiliates the debtor (24:12-13). Whoever hires day laborers must pay their wages daily (24:14-15).

Deuteronomy groups the "strangers, orphans and widows" in a fixed triad (Glanville 2020). While they are often understood as representative of the poor and designated as *personae miserae*, they are, in fact, preserved from poverty (Lohfink 1991b, 43). Deuteronomy describes an elaborate economic system that includes social relief for the groups who, like the Levites, are deprived of land lots. It changes the structure of society and allows them, as full members of God's people, to participate in the entire life of Israel, especially in the joy of its festivals. The strangers, orphans, and widows find themselves at the fringes of the problematic area of justice and jurisprudence. This is the case for the strangers due to their legal accountability despite their ethnic and religious foreignness (1:16-17), and for the widows and orphans (24:17-18; 27:19), because they cannot appear in court themselves and therefore must be protected. However, this does not imply that they are considered poor.

Ultimately, all ethical behavior toward the social outsiders in Israel must imitate God's work in their favor as "he [Yhwh, your God,] establishes justice for orphans and widows and he loves strangers so that he gives them food and clothing" (10:18). This action of God results in an associative obligation on the part of the Israelites, which is not tied to any specific circumstances and is motivated by their own positive historical experience: "You, too, should love the stranger, for you (yourself) were strangers in the land of Egypt" (10:19; see Glanville 2018; Braulik 2020a, 43–44; Friedl 2021, 246–61).

Deuteronomy envisions a society without any marginal groups in 15:4–6. This idea is wedged between the requirement to waive debts every seventh year (15:1–3) and the paraenesis about credit assistance to impoverished Israelites (15:7–11):

> There should, however, be no one in need among you, because Yhwh is sure to bless you in the land that Yhwh your God is giving you for your inheritance, if only you pay careful attention to the voice of Yhwh your God by keeping and observing this entire commandment that I enjoin on you today. When Yhwh your God has blessed you, as he promised you, you will lend to many nations, but you will not borrow; you will rule over many nations, but they will not rule over you. (Deut 15:4–6; my translation)

Yhwh's blessing is the basis of the absence of a poor class in the land that he has given to his people as an inheritance; a land "where you have built magnificent houses and live in them, where your cattle, sheep and goats will multiply, and your silver and gold will multiply, and all your possessions will multiply" (8:12–13). However, this material wealth and economic activity arising from the fullness of blessing depend on the obedience of the whole people. Only when everyone puts the Deuteronomic social order into action can the world of social justice become reality.

Divine blessing will even enable prosperity by allowing Israelites to make interest-bearing loans to non-Israelites; Israelites should avoid borrowing from them to avoid becoming economically dependent on them. In the present context, however, this promise is in tension with the realistic statement: "The poor will never disappear completely from your country. Therefore, I make it your duty: You shall open your hand to your needy and poor brother who lives in your country" (15:11). That means that in the face of rising poverty, fellow Israelites have to react to any pressing need with a loan that would help the poor survive. But there is no legal enforcement for this generosity. The "brother ethos" demanded here cannot really be put into legal terms. As is a matter of course in a family, fellow Israelites must be helped to get out of their misery as soon as a threat of poverty arises, even if it involves significant financial sacrifices (Braulik 2019a, 26; Kessler 2021c). This prevents any single group within Israel from becoming entrenched in poverty.

7.3 A Brotherly People: Social Laws and the Laws of Public Offices

In Deuteronomy, the word "brother" (*'aḥ*) serves above all as a leitmotif of a particular Israelite ethic and is embedded in the theology of the people (Friedl 2021). Beyond family ties, it primarily refers to fellow citizens, in contrast to "foreigners" (*nokrî*), and can be used gender-inclusively (see 15:12). The documents can be found in the social laws and the laws of the offices but are used differently in terms of grammar and semantics. They form a bridge between the agrarian and the cultural-urban background of the two groups of texts. In contrast, cultic regulations never refer to a "brother" – it is not a liturgical title. Apparently, people without a financial or power-political basis are nurtured at the sacrifices and feasts. Here the fraternal society is already symbolically realized.

Deuteronomy's social legislation is found in 15:1–18 and 22:1–4; 23:20–21; 24:7, 10–15; 25:5–10. The key texts of ch. 15 deal with the remittance of debts in the fallow year, the granting of loans shortly before the seventh year, and the release of Hebrew slaves in the seventh year. These texts concretize fraternity as liberation from the hard-hearted thinking associated with mere profitability by explicating the apodictic commandment of Deut 15:1: "At the end of every seven years you shall grant a remission of debts." Exodus 23:10–11 had already ordered that fields, vineyards, and olive trees should lie fallow (*šmṭ*), so that the "poor of your people" (*'ebyon 'ammekā*) could benefit from it.

The legal interpretation of this text in Deut 15:2 alters the agrarian outlook to a financial "decree" (*šemiṭṭâ*). A creditor who had granted a consumer loan under personal liability is called upon to release what he has loaned to his neighbor (*bᵉrē'ēhû*); he shall not exact it of his neighbor, insofar as he is his brother, because he has proclaimed a remission (*šemiṭṭâ*) for Yhwh. The place of the "poor man" in Exod 23:11 is taken by "your brother," which constitutes a religious and quite emotional particularization of the traditional expression "your neighbor." Interpersonal relationships are thus opened toward the egalitarian community of those who live the liberating love of God. As a brother, the Israelite demands greater, even the highest attention from fellow Israelites (Perlitt 1994a, 64; Friedl 2021, 79–90).

Because this solidarity forms a "decree before Yhwh" (v. 2), the "foreigner" is excluded from it (v. 3; see 23:21), so that the international rules of loan granting remain valid in the case of transactions with foreigners. The cancellation of debt ultimately aims at freeing the people of God from poverty "for Yhwh will bless you richly… if you observe this commandment and keep it" (15:4–5). The "you" mentioned no longer refers merely to the creditor but to the whole of Israel as a society (Ebach 2014, 135). The "brother" as a person in need is contrasted to the person who enjoys prosperity. The former appeals to the social responsibility of the latter. He pleads for a turn in attitude, for a return to the original ideal of equality: "Actually, there should be no poor among you" (15:4). In other economic regulations, all of them related to debts and aiming at human dignity and solidarity, the "brother" is expressly associated with the poor (*'ebyôn*) and destitute (*'ānî*) (15:7,9,11; 24:12,14,15) but never with the "strangers, orphans and widows," who certainly also deserve protection and support but who are no longer considered among the classical poor at the fringes of society because Deuteronomy legally shifts them to the center of economic provision.

While the social laws deal with a brother who has fallen into poverty, the brother appears as a full citizen with equal rights in the laws concerning public officials (16:18–18:22, the so-called "laws of the offices"). Whereas the brother stands in contrast to the addressee of the social laws, the laws of the offices integrate him into the collective "you" that is addressed in these laws (Friedl 2021, 233–36; Kessler 2021d, 282–83). Both groups of laws mention the "brother" seven times each (15:2,3,7,7,9,11,12 and 17:15,20; 18:2,7,15,18; 20:8), but the word primarily occurs in the plural in the laws of the offices. The brotherly relationship eliminates the social distance between those above and those below and removes the scandal of class formation. Even the God-chosen king must be a brother who must not "exalt his heart above his brothers" (17:20). God will raise a prophet in the midst of his brothers (18:15,18). The tribe of Levi is to "dwell amidst its brethren," (18:2) and each Levite may serve as his Levitical brethren do at the central sanctuary (18:7), where he receives the same allocation (18:8). Even the war laws (20:1–9) embody brotherly ethics in a special way (Friedl 2021, 137). It is the people who make decisions regarding war. Apart from the priest, only the administrative officers (16,18), who are installed by the people and who are operative in mustering the army and appointing its leaders, are mentioned. The king is never mentioned in the context of war. The faint-hearted are sent back home to avoid discouraging their brothers (20:8). Yet, the discouraged and the brave are given equal status as brothers (Friedl 2021, 138).

The "draft constitution" (16:18–18:22) displays a utopian theory critical of monarchy with a separation of powers regulated by the Torah (Lohfink 1985, 69–73; Schäfer-Lichtenberger 1995). The previous concentration of power in the hands of kings and priests is thus dismantled in favor of the judge and prophet. The balance of power between judiciary, royal government, temple priesthood, and free charisma guarantees that these powers together are at the service of the efficacy of the divine word, or more precisely: the rule of Yhwh through the written Torah and the word of his prophet. While the Torah given to Moses at Horeb is entrusted to the priests for safekeeping and teaching (31:9), it is to be adapted to future situations by the prophet, while the judges must administer justice according to it and the king must learn from it each day, as should every other Israelite (Braulik 1992, 121; Lohfink 1985, 73-75).

7.4 The Metaphorization of War and the Nations

The notion of a complete conquest of the promised land and of the extermination of its population, outlined in Deuteronomy and narrated in the Book of Joshua, is an ideal construct (Braulik 2001c, 115-18; 2022, 113-22). The sacred war of annihilation against the inhabitants of the land never occurred. This idea dates back to the time of King Josiah in the seventh century at the earliest (against Versluis 2017, 320). At that time, the peoples who were supposed to be wiped out no longer existed, and Israel itself had already lost most of its land. The concept of land grab systematizes and consciously generalizes older elements of tradition: reports of victories with the renunciation of booty and the dedication of humans, cattle, and goods to the deity (ḥerem); lists of extinct or legendary peoples who have already perished; promises of territorial conquest with the expulsion of local populations. Individual motifs such as the depiction of the terrors of war may have been inspired by the language and imagery of Neo-Assyrian blood-soaked war propaganda, which the ḥerem seeks to counteract with a boost of self-confidence for an Israel whose strengths are dwindling (Lohfink 1982, 211). The commandment to utterly destroy (haḥarēm taḥarîm) the seven mightier nations was meant to be a spiritual parable from the start. It refers exclusively to the upcoming war of conquest and to future returns from exile. It differs from later wars envisaged in the war laws of 20:10-15 that list the previous inhabitants of Israel by name (20:17; see 7:1) but expressly rejects a later strategy of annihilation by granting peace to those who surrender (20:10-12). Had the elimination of the Canaanites been realistic, the law would have made an unfounded requirement. In fact, it commits its original addressees to something other than a war of annihilation.

Apart from the historical impossibility, there are factual contradictions in the conquest program that make ḥerem appear as a theological construct. The total annihilation of all human beings goes hand in hand with prohibitions that presuppose the coexistence of the Canaanite peoples with the Israelites. The social distance necessary to prevent religious coexistence requires the theoretical annihilation of the previous inhabitants and the destruction of their places of worship and of everything that could lead to cultic seduction and apostasy from Yhwh. This model can only be described as a fictional expression of the demand for undivided and exclusive worship of the only God (Irsigler 2021, 810). The ḥerem texts, then, concern above all the identity of Israel as the people of Yhwh and exclude all who threaten the covenant, whether inside or outside Israel (Reeder 2011; Glanville 2021). Therefore, the annihilation of an entire city is restricted to one that has fallen away from Yhwh (13:13–19). Rahab's group and the Gibeonites are not submitted to the ḥerem because they have confessed Yhwh (Josh 2:8–11; 9:9–10, 24). The latter even take part in the covenant in Moab as "the strangers in your camp, from the woodworkers to the water carrier" (Deut 29:10; Josh 9:27). In general, the intolerant provisions of Deut 7 apply exclusively to those who hinder Israel's possession of the promised land and to potential seducers (Schäfer-Lichtenberger 1996, 195).

Yet, Deut 9:1–7, like 7:1, presents the conquest of Canaan as a war of God. Yhwh crosses the Jordan like a consuming fire and destroys the mighty Canaanites before Israel so that it can wipe them out. But this account serves only as a strictly theological argument about grace and merit. It places the injustice of the other peoples on the same level as Israel's stubbornness, so that neither of them has any legal claim to the land. That Israel, despite its continued failure to be faithful, is granted Canaan is entirely due to Yhwh's faithfulness to his oath to the patriarchs; thus, the land is a gift of pure grace.

The foreigners mentioned in relation to the foretold exile (29:21–27) witness the catastrophe and confess with Israel the justice of Yhwh's punishment. If other people take possession of the land again during Israel's exile, no war and destruction are mentioned when Israel returns (30:1–10). Israel's return is no longer associated with violence (Braulik 2001c, 144–49).

The radicalism with which the land is to be conquered under Joshua serves as a narrative symbol for the radicalism of the trust expected of Israel to let God do his work. The war imagery from the early period, with its direct belief in God, forms a striking contrast to the history that failed after centuries of state existence (MacDonald 2003, 113–22; but see Lohr 2009, 167–72). When Israel again trusts in God, Yhwh will give back the lost land, for he is victorious over all who oppose him and in favor of all who believe in and obey him (Stipp 2017).

The future high point in the relationship between Israel and the peoples is already formulated in ch. 4:

> You must observe them [his laws and judgements] diligently, for this will show your wisdom and discernment to the peoples, who, when they hear all these laws, will say, "Surely this great nation is a wise and discerning people!" For what other great nation has a god so near to it as Yhwh our God is whenever/wherever we call to him? And what

other great nation has laws and judgements as just as this entire Torah that I am setting before you today? (Deut 4:5–8; my translation)

Wisdom and discernment motivate the preservation and observance of the laws admired even by foreign peoples (Braulik 2019d, 192–201).

The special position of Israel among the peoples results from its religious-ethical greatness gained from the unique closeness of its God and the incomparable justice of its Torah. The Deuteronomic usage of the expression "calling to Yhwh" (qrʾ ʾel Yhwh) shows that brotherly ethics is the foundation of Yhwh's closeness, which allows Israel to call on him anywhere and at any time. The phrase is found in two regulations that concern the brother. In 15:9, a poor man cries out to Yhwh when a fellow Israelites refuses to grant him a loan shortly before the year of remission. Conversely, when the wages of a day laborer are paid before sunset, he will not need to call on God (24:15), and the employer will not incur guilt before God. Hence, the economically and socially weak have a constitutive role in the determination of sin (15:9; 24:15) and righteousness (24:13). It is the theological dignity of the poor that Deuteronomy puts at the service of its legal paraenesis, which is addressed to the Israelite who lives as a free person without financial obligations. That this is not a marginal matter is underlined by the fact that in the entire Deuteronomic law, righteousness (ṣedāqāh) is mentioned only in 24:13 (Kessler 2009, 265).

The phrase "just laws and judgements" (ḥuqqîm ûmišpāṭîm ṣaddîqim) in 4:8 may allude to the "just judgements" (dînat mišārim) in the epilogue of King Hammurabi's collection of laws. However, despite all its legal erudition, Hammurabi's stele hardly claims to protect the weak, orphans, and widows. Moral appeals are missing in the purely rational secular law of the stele of this self-proclaimed "king of justice" (Richardson 2000, 121–23; see Russell 2020; Milstein 2022, 249). On the contrary, Israel was very aware of the uniqueness of its revealed legal collection, in which all peoples were expected to see the proof of God's special nearness and immediacy (von Rad 1982, 108).

At the end of his prayer for the dedication of the temple, Solomon asks God to hear the supplications of his people Israel "whenever they call to you" (1 Kgs 8:52; see Deut 4:7). In the blessing that follows, Solomon asks that the words with which he pleaded before Yhwh remain near Yhwh day and night (1 Kgs 8:59; see Deut 4:7) so that all the people of the earth may know that Yhwh is Lord. This should motivate Israelites to devote themselves entirely to Yhwh and obey his laws and statutes (1 Kgs 8:61). Moses and Solomon therefore unite with the people in their confession of "Yhwh our God" (Deut 4:7; 1 Kgs 8:59) to combine obedience to the commandments with closeness to Israel. This ethics has the peoples of the entire world in mind for a worldwide recognition that no one is God but Yhwh alone (1 Kgs 8:60; see Deut 4:35; Braulik 2019d, 196).

To summarize: the ethical concept of the book of Deuteronomy is founded upon the summons to "choose life." As a partner in God's covenant, Israel becomes the legal subject of its ethics, which concerns not only the free male citizens, but also the women, children, dependents, and Israel's future generations. It is this covenantal structure that has guided our exploration of the ethics represented by the book of Deuteronomy. The legal code of Deuteronomy commences with the Decalogue, which serves as the structure for the further development of its legal paraenesis and the explication of its individual laws. After having been slaves in Egypt and having been liberated from there by the strong hand of Yhwh, Israel was brought into the promised land. This obliges Israel to act in accordance with the requirements of its God, who in turn will always provide for its needs. As a people who may live from the joy of abundance in the context of its cultic provisions, Israel is therefore called upon to generously supply for the needs of the poor and destitute among them.

Works Cited

Barbiero, Gianni. 2002. "Höre Israel (Dtn 6,4-25)." Pages 93–167 in *Studien zu alttestamentlichen Texten*. Edited by Gianni Barbiero. Stuttgarter Biblische Aufsatzbände 34. Stuttgart: Katholisches Bibelwerk.

Barton, John. 2014. *Ethics in Ancient Israel*. Oxford: Oxford University Press.

Becker, Joachim. 1965. *Gottesfurcht im Alten Testament*. Analecta Biblica 25. Rome: Pontifical Biblical Institute.

Braulik, Georg. 1988. "Zur deuteronomistischen Konzeption von Freiheit und Frieden." Pages 219–30 in *Studien zur Theologie des Deuteronomiums*. Edited by Georg Braulik. Stuttgarter Biblische Aufsatzbände 2. Stuttgart: Katholisches Bibelwerk.

------. 1991. *Die deuteronomischen Gesetze und der Dekalog. Studien zum Aufbau von Deuteronomium 12-26*. Stuttgarter Bibelstudien 145. Stuttgart: Katholisches Bibelwerk.

------. 1992. *Deuteronomium II, 16,18–34,12*. Neue Echter Bibel 28. Würzburg: Echter. Second Edition 2003.

------. 2001a. "Konservative Reform. Das Deuteronomium in wissenssoziologischer Sicht." Pages 39–55 in *Studien zum Deuteronomium und seiner Nachgeschichte*. Edited by Georg Braulik. Stuttgarter Biblische Aufsatzbände 33. Stuttgart: Katholisches Bibelwerk.

------. 2001b. "Durften auch Frauen in Israel opfern? Beobachtungen zur Sinn und Feiergestalt des Opfers im Deuteronomium." Pages 59–89 in

Studien zum Deuteronomium und seiner Nachgeschichte. Edited by Georg Braulik. Stuttgarter Biblische Aufsatzbände 33. Stuttgart: Katholisches Bibelwerk.

------. 2001c. "Die Völkervernichtung und die Rückkehr Israels ins Verheißungsland. Hermeneutische Bemerkungen zum Buch Deuteronomium." Pages 113–50 in *Studien zum Deuteronomium und seiner Nachgeschichte*. Edited by Georg Braulik. Stuttgarter Biblische Aufsatzbände 33. Stuttgart: Katholisches Bibelwerk.

------. 2006. "Geschichtserinnerung und Gotteserkenntnis. Zu zwei Kleinformen im Buch Deuteronomium." Pages 165–83 in *Studien zu den Methoden der Deuteronomiumsexegese*. Edited by Georg Braulik. Stuttgarter Biblische Aufsatzbände 42. Stuttgart: Katholisches Bibelwerk.

------. 2017a. "Das Buch Deuteronomium." Pages 11–50 in *Studien zu Buch und Sprache des Deuteronomiums*. Edited by Georg Braulik. Stuttgarter Biblische Aufsatzbände 63. Stuttgart: Katholisches Bibelwerk.

------. 2017b. "Der unterbrochene Dekalog. Zu Deuteronomium 5,12 und 16 und ihrer Bedeutung für den deuteronomischen Gesetzeskodex." Pages 61–74 in *Studien zu Buch und Sprache des Deuteronomiums*. Edited by Georg Braulik. Stuttgarter Biblische Aufsatzbände 63. Stuttgart: Katholisches Bibelwerk.

------. 2017c. "Die 'Worte' (*haddebārîm*) in Deuteronomium 1–11." Pages 89–107 in *Studien zu Buch und Sprache des Deuteronomiums*. Edited by Georg Braulik. Stuttgarter Biblische Aufsatzbände 63. Stuttgart: Katholisches Bibelwerk.

------. 2017d. "Die Glaubensgerechtigkeit im Buch Deuteronomium. Ein Beitrag zu den alttestamentlichen Wurzeln der paulinischen Rechtfertigungslehre." Pages 213–39 in *Studien zu Buch und Sprache des Deuteronomiums*. Edited by Georg Braulik. Stuttgarter Biblische Aufsatzbände 63. Stuttgart: Katholisches Bibelwerk.

------. 2017e. "Die Liebe zwischen Gott und Israel. Zur theologischen Mitte des Buches Deuteronomium." Pages 241–59 in *Studien zu Buch und Sprache des Deuteronomiums*. Edited by Georg Braulik. Stuttgarter Biblische Aufsatzbände 63. Stuttgart: Katholisches Bibelwerk.

------. 2017f. "Die allgemeine Gesetzesparänese und das 'paränetische Schema' im Buch Deuteronomium." Pages 271–99 in *Studien zu Buch und Sprache des Deuteronomiums*. Edited by Georg Braulik. Stuttgarter Biblische Aufsatzbände 63. Stuttgart: Katholisches Bibelwerk.

------. 2019a. "Eine Gesellschaft ohne Arme. Das altorientalische Armenethos und die biblische Vision." Pages 13–30 in *Tora und Fest. Aufsätze zum Deuteronomium und zur Liturgie*. Edited by Georg Braulik. Stuttgarter Biblische Aufsatzbände 69. Stuttgart: Katholisches Bibelwerk.

------. 2019b. "Das Ende einer Karriere. Zum Dekalog in Deuteronomium 5 nach der revidierten Einheitsübersetzung." Pages 82–99 in *Tora und Fest. Aufsätze zum Deuteronomium und zur Liturgie*. Edited by Georg

Braulik. Stuttgarter Biblische Aufsatzbände 69. Stuttgart: Katholisches Bibelwerk.
──────. 2019c. "Alltägliche Ernährung und festliches Mahl im Buch Deuteronomium. Vom Essen Israels in der Wüste, im Verheißungsland und im Tempel." Pages 100–41 in *Tora und Fest. Aufsätze zum Deuteronomium und zur Liturgie*. Edited by Georg Braulik. Stuttgarter Biblische Aufsatzbände 69. Stuttgart: Katholisches Bibelwerk.
──────. 2019d. "Hat Gott die Religionen der Völker gestiftet? Deuteronomium 4,19 im Kontext von Kultbilderverbot und Monotheismus." Pages 142–251 in *Tora und Fest. Aufsätze zum Deuteronomium und zur Liturgie*. Edited by Georg Braulik. Stuttgarter Biblische Aufsatzbände 69. Stuttgart: Katholisches Bibelwerk.
──────. 2020a. "Der blinde Fleck – das Gebot, den Fremden zu lieben. Zur sozialethischen Forderung von Deuteronomium 10,19." Pages 41–63 in *Menschenrechte und Gerechtigkeit als bleibende Aufgaben. Beiträge aus Religion, Theologie, Ethik, Recht und Wirtschaft. Festschrift für Ingeborg G. Gabriel*. Edited by Irene Klissenbauer et al. Göttingen: V&R Unipress.
──────. 2020b. "Die Beschneidung an Vorhaut und Herz. Zu Gebot und Gnade des Bundeszeichens im Alten Testament." Pages 63–95 in *Die Beschneidung Jesu. Was sie Juden und Christen heute bedeutet*. Edited by Jan-Heiner Tück. Freiburg im Breisgau: Herder.
──────. 2021a. "Horebbund und Moabbund. Ihre Einheit und Verschiedenheit nach Dtn 5,1–5 und 29,1–8." *Biblica* 102: 1–29.
──────. 2021b. "Kollektive Schuld und gerechte Vergeltung. Zur 'Ursünde' des Gottesvolks im Buch Deuteronomium." *Münchener Theologische Zeitschrift* 72: 171–95.
──────. 2022. "Die Erwählung Israels im Buch Deuteronomium." Pages 99–141 in *Dein Wort ist meinem Fuß eine Leuchte. Festschrift für Ludger Schwienhorst-Schönberger*. Edited by Georg Braulik, Agnethe Siquans, and Jan-Heiner Tück. Freiburg im Breisgau: Herder.
──────. 2023. "Gottesbund und Gnade im Deuteronomium." *Biblische Zeitschrift* 67: 1–42.
──────. forthcoming. "Sich auflehnen" (*mrh* Qal / Hifil) gegen Gott und ihn 'auf die Probe stellen' (*nsh* Piel). Zu einer Geschichtstheologie kollektiven Unglaubens."
Braulik, Georg and Norbert Lohfink. 2021. *Sprache und literarische Gestalt des Buches Deuteronomium. Beobachtungen und Studien*. Österreichische Biblische Studien 53. Berlin: Peter Lang.
Brumlik, Micha. 2004. *Advokatorische Ethik. Zur Legitimation pädagogischer Eingriffe*. Berlin-Vienna: Philo.
Crüsemann, Frank. 1996. *The Torah: Theology and Social History of Old Testament Law*. Minneapolis: Fortress.
Dohmen, Christoph. 1993. "Freiheit für Israel oder Gesetz für alle Völker? Die Geltungsfrage des Dekalogs im Horizont des jüdisch-christlichen

Verhältnisses." Pages 187–201 in *Zion - Ort der Begegnung. Festschrift für Laurentius Klein zur Vollendung des 65. Lebensjahres*. Edited by Ferdinand Hahn *et al*. Bonner Biblische Beiträge 90. Bodenheim: Athenäum.

Ebach, Ruth. 2014. *Das Fremde und das Eigene. Die Fremddarstellungen des Deuteronomiums im Kontext israelitischer Identitätskonstruktionen*. Beihefte zur Zeitschrift für die alttestamentliche Wissenschaft 471. Berlin: de Gruyter.

Friedl, Johanna. 2021. *Ein brüderliches Volk. Das 'Bruder' -Konzept im Heiligkeitsgesetz und deuteronomischen Gesetz*. Österreichische Biblische Studien 52. Berlin: Peter Lang.

Geiger, Michaela. 2010. *Gottesräume. Die literarische und theologische Konzeption von Raum im Deuteronomium*. Beiträge zur Wissenschaft vom Alten und Neuen Testament 183. Stuttgart: Kohlhammer.

Glanville, Mark R. 2018. "The *Gēr* (Stranger) in Deuteronomy: Family for the Displaced." *Journal of Biblical Literature* 137: 599–623.

———. 2020. "The Stranger, Fatherless and Widow in Deuteronomy." In *The Oxford Handbook of Deuteronomy*. Edited by Don C. Benjamin. Oxford: Oxford University Press.

———. 2021. "ḥrm (ḥērœm) as Israelite Identity Formation: Canaanite Destruction and the Stranger (gr, gēr)." *Catholic Biblical Quarterly* 83: 547–70.

Gomes de Araújo, Reginaldo. 1999. *Theologie der Wüste im Deuteronomium*. Österreichische Biblische Studien 17. Frankfurt am Main: Peter Lang.

Irsigler, Hubert. 2021. *Gottesbilder des Alten Testaments. Von Israels Anfängen bis zum Ende der exilischen Epoche*. Teilband II. Freiburg im Breisgau: Herder.

Jacobs, Sandra. 2020. "Women in Deuteronomy." in *The Oxford Handbook of Deuteronomy*. Edited by Don C. Benjamin. Oxford: Oxford University Press.

Joas, Hans. 2020. *Im Bannkreis der Freiheit. Religionstheorie nach Hegel und Nietzsche*. Berlin: Suhrkamp.

Kessler, Rainer. 2009. "Die Rolle des Armen für Gerechtigkeit und Sünde des Reichen." Pages 256–66 in *Studien zur Sozialgeschichte Israels*. Edited by Rainer Kessler. Stuttgarter Biblische Aufsatzbände 46. Stuttgart: Katholisches Bibelwerk.

———. 2017. *Der Weg zum Leben. Ethik des Alten Testaments*. Gütersloh: Gütersloher.

———. 2021a. "Was ist und wozu brauchen wir eine Ethik des Alten Testaments?" Pages 203–26 in *Leben und Handeln in der Gesellschaft. Studien zur Sozialgeschichte Israels und Ethik des Alten Testaments*. Edited by Rainer Kessler. Stuttgarter Biblische Aufsatzbände 73. Stuttgart: Katholisches Bibelwerk.

———. 2021b. "A Strange Land: alttestamentliche Ethik beiderseits von Ärmelkanal und Atlantik." Pages 227–53 in *Leben und Handeln in der*

Gesellschaft. Studien zur Sozialgeschichte Israels und Ethik des Alten Testaments. Edited by Rainer Kessler. Stuttgarter Biblische Aufsatzbände 73. Stuttgart: Katholisches Bibelwerk.

———. 2021c. "Altes Testament und gegenwärtige ethische Herausforderungen. Das Beispiel der Wirtschaftsethik." Pages 254–73 in *Leben und Handeln in der Gesellschaft. Studien zur Sozialgeschichte Israels und Ethik des Alten Testaments.* Edited by Rainer Kessler. Stuttgarter Biblische Aufsatzbände 73. Stuttgart: Katholisches Bibelwerk.

———. 2021d. "Tora und Menschenrechte." Pages 274–86 in *Leben und Handeln in der Gesellschaft. Studien zur Sozialgeschichte Israels und Ethik des Alten Testaments.* Edited by Rainer Kessler. Stuttgarter Biblische Aufsatzbände 73. Stuttgart: Katholisches Bibelwerk.

Kilchör, Benjamin. 2015. *Mosetora und Jahwetora. Das Verhältnis von Deuteronomium 12–26 zu Exodus, Levitikus und Numeri.* Beihefte zur Zeitschrift für Altorientalische und Biblische Rechtsgeschichte 21. Wiesbaden: Harrassowitz.

Koch, Christoph. 2008. *Vertrag, Treueid und Bund. Studien zur Rezeption des altorientalischen Vertragsrechts im Deuteronomium und zur Ausbildung der Bundestheologie im Alten Testament.* Beihefte zur Zeitschrift für die alttestamentliche Wissenschaft 383. Berlin: de Gruyter.

L'Hour, Jean. 1967. *Die Ethik der Bundestradition im Alten Testament.* Stuttgarter Bibelstudien 14. Stuttgart: Katholisches Bibelwerk.

Lohfink, Norbert. 1963. *Das Hauptgebot. Eine Untersuchung literarischer Einleitungsfragen zu Dtn 5–11.* Analecta Biblica 20. Rome: Pontifical Biblical Institute.

———. 1982. "ḥāram ḥēræm." Pages 192–213 in *Theologisches Wörterbuch zum Alten Testament III.* Edited by G. Johannes Botterweck. Stuttgart: Kohlhammer.

———. 1985. "Gewaltenteilung." Pages 57–75 in *Unsere großen Wörter. Das Alte Testament zu Themen dieser Jahre.* Freiburg im Breisgau: Herder. First Edition 1977.

———. 1989. "Gott auf der Seite der Armen. Zur 'Option für die Armen' im Alten Orient und in der Bibel." Pages 122–43 in *Das Jüdische am Christentum. Die verlorene Dimension.* Edited by Norbert Lohfink. Freiburg im Breisgau: Herder.

———. 1990a. "Zur Dekalogfassung von Dt 5." Pages 193–209 in *Studien zum Deuteronomium und zur deuteronomistischen Literatur I.* Edited by Norbert Lohfink. Stuttgarter Biblische Aufsatzbände 8. Stuttgart: Katholisches Bibelwerk.

———. 1990b. "Dt 26,17–19 und die Bundesformel." Pages 211–61 in *Studien zum Deuteronomium und zur deuteronomistischen Literatur I.* Edited by Norbert Lohfink. Stuttgarter Biblische Aufsatzbände 8. Stuttgart: Katholisches Bibelwerk.

------. 1991a. *Die Väter Israels im Deuteronomium. Mit einer Stellungnahme von Thomas Römer.* Orbis biblicus et Orientalis 111. Fribourg – Göttingen: Universitätsverlag – Vandenhoeck & Ruprecht.

------. 1991b. "Poverty in the Laws of the Ancient Near East and of the Bible." *Theological Studies* 52: 34–50.

------. 1993. "Kennt das Alte Testament einen Unterschied von 'Gebot' und 'Gesetz'? Zur bibeltheologischen Einstufung des Dekalogs." Pages 206–38 in *Studien zur biblischen Theologie.* Edited by Norbert Lohfink. Stuttgarter Biblische Aufsatzbände 16. Stuttgart: Katholisches Bibelwerk.

------. 1995a "Opferzentralisation, Säkularisierungsthese und mimetische Theorie." Pages 219–60 in *Studien zum Deuteronomium und zur deuteronomistischen Literatur III.* Edited by Norbert Lohfink. Stuttgarter Biblische Aufsatzbände 20. Stuttgart: Katholisches Bibelwerk.

------. 1995b. "Deuteronomium 6,24: *leḥayyotenû* 'für unseren Unterhalt aufkommen'" Pages 269–78 in *Studien zum Deuteronomium und zur deuteronomistischen Literatur III.* Edited by Norbert Lohfink. Stuttgarter Biblische Aufsatzbände 20. Stuttgart: Katholisches Bibelwerk.

------. 2005a. "Deuteronomium 5 als Erzählung." Pages 111–30 in *Studien zum Deuteronomium und zur deuteronomistischen Literatur V.* Edited by Norbert Lohfink. Stuttgarter Biblische Aufsatzbände 38. Stuttgart: Katholisches Bibelwerk.

------. 2005b. "Deuteronomium 9,1–10,11 und Exodus 32–34. Zu Endtextstruktur, Intertextualität, Schichtung und Abhängigkeiten." Pages 131–80 in *Studien zum Deuteronomium und zur deuteronomistischen Literatur V.* Edited by Norbert Lohfink. Stuttgarter Biblische Aufsatzbände 38. Stuttgart: Katholisches Bibelwerk.

Lohr, Joel N. 2009. *Chosen and Unchosen: Conceptions of Election in the Pentateuch and Jewish-Christian Interpretation.* Siphrut 2. Winona Lake IN: Eisenbrauns.

MacDonald, Nathan. 2003. *Deuteronomy and the Making of Monotheism.* Forschungen zum Alten Testament 2,1). Tübingen: Mohr Siebeck.

Markl, Dominik. 2007. *Der Dekalog als Verfassung des Gottesvolkes. Die Brennpunkte einer Rechtshermeneutik des Pentateuch in Ex 19–24 und Dtn 5.* Herders biblische Studien 49. Freiburg im Breisgau: Herder.

------. 2012. *Gottes Volk im Deuteronomium.* Beihefte zur Zeitschrift für Altorientalische und Biblische Rechtsgeschichte 18. Wiesbaden: Harrassowitz.

------. 2014. "This Word is Your Life. The Theology of Life in Deuteronomy." Pages 71–96 in *Gottes Wort im Menschenwort. Festschrift für Georg Fischer SJ zum 60. Geburtstag.* Edited by Dominik Markl, Claudia Paganini, and Simone Paganini. Österreichische biblische Studien 43. Frankfurt am Main: Peter Lang.

------. 2015. "Israels Moral der Befreiten. Zur Begründung der 'Option für die Armen' in der geschichtlichen Identität Israels." Pages 324–44 in *Mehr als Zehn Worte? Zur Bedeutung des Alten Testaments in ethischen Fragen*. Edited by Christian Frevel. Quaestiones Disputatae 272. Freiburg im Breisgau: Herder.
Marx, Alfred. 2000. "Opferlogik im alten Israel." Pages 129–49 in *Opfer. Theologische und kulturelle Kontexte*. Edited by Bernd Janowski and Michael Welker. Suhrkamp Taschenbuch Wissenschaft 1454. Frankfurt am Main: Suhrkamp.
McCarthy, Dennis J. 1978. *Treaty and Covenant. A Study in Form in the Ancient Oriental Document and in the Old Testament*. New Edition completely rewritten. Analecta Biblica 21. Rome: Pontifical Biblical Institute.
Millar, J. Gary. 1998. *Now Choose Life. Theology and Ethics in Deuteronomy* (NSBT), Leicester: Apollos.
Milstein, Sara. 2022. "The Origins of Deuteronomic 'Law.'" Pages 237–50 in *Congress Volume Aberdeen 2019*. Edited by Grant Macaskill, Christl M. Maier, and Joachim Schaper. Supplements to Vetus Testamentum 192. Leiden: Brill.
Noichl, Franz. 2002. *Ethische Schriftauslegung. Biblische Weisung und moraltheologische Argumentation*. Freiburger theologische Studien 165. Freiburg im Breisgau: Herder.
Otto, Eckart. 1993. "Die Tora in Israels Rechtsgeschichte." *Theologische Literaturzeitung* 118: 903–10.
------. 1994. *Theologische Ethik des Alten Testaments*. Theologische Wissenschaft 3,2. Stuttgart: Kohlhammer.
Oyen, Hendrik van. 1967. *Ethik des Alten Testaments*. Gütersloh: Gütersloher.
Perlitt, Lothar. 1994a. "'Ein einzig *Volk* von Brüdern.' Zur deuteronomischen Herkunft der biblischen Bezeichnung Bruder." Pages 50–73 in *Deuteronomium-Studien*. Edited by Lothar Perlitt. Forschungen zum Alten Testament 8. Tübingen: Mohr Siebeck.
------. 1994b "Deuteronomium 6, 20–25: eine Ermutigung zu Bekenntnis und Lehre." Pages 144–56 in *Deuteronomium-Studien*. Edited by Lothar Perlitt. Forschungen zum Alten Testament 8. Tübingen: Mohr Siebeck.
Pyschny, Katharina. 2019. "From Core to Centre: Issues of Centralization in Numbers and Deuteronomy." *Hebrew Bible and Ancient Israel* 8: 287–312.
Rad, Gerhard von. 1982. *Theologie des Alten Testaments. Band 1: Die Theologie der geschichtlichen Überlieferungen Israels*. Munich: Kaiser.
Reeder, Caryn A. 2011. "Community Violence in Deuteronomy." Pages 36–50 in *The Cambridge Companion to the Hebrew Bible and Ethics*. Edited by Carly L. Crouch. Cambridge: Cambridge University Press.
Reuter, Hans-Richard. 2011. "Das ethische Stichwort Verantwortung." *Zeitschrift für Evangelische Ethik* 55: 301–04.
Richardson, Mervyn E. J. 2000. *Hammurabi's Laws. Text, Translation and Glossary*. The Biblical Seminar 72. Sheffield: Sheffield Academic.

Russell, Stephen C. 2020. "Near Eastern Practice of Law in Deuteronomy." in *The Oxford Handbook of Deuteronomy*. Edited by Don C. Benjamin. Oxford: Oxford University Press.

Schäfer-Lichtenberger, Christa. 1995. "Der deuteronomische Verfassungsentwurf. Theologische Vorgaben als Gestaltungsprinzipien sozialer Realität." Pages 105–18 in *Bundesdokument und Gesetz. Studien zum Deuteronomium*. Edited by Georg Braulik. Herders biblische Studien 4. Freiburg: Herder.

------. 1996. "JHWH, Israel und die Völker aus der Perspektive von Dtn 7." *Biblische Zeitschrift* 40: 194–218.

Schüller, Bruno. 1980. *Die Begründung sittlicher Urteile. Typen ethischer Argumentation in der Moraltheologie*. Düsseldorf: Patmos.

Schulmeister, Irene. 2010. *Israels Befreiung aus Ägypten. Eine Formeluntersuchung zur Theologie des Deuteronomiums*. Österreichische Biblische Studien 36. Frankfurt am Main: Peter Lang.

Schwienhorst-Schönberger, Ludger. 2015. "Recht und Ethik im Alten Testament." Pages 60–91 in *Mehr als Zehn Worte? Zur Bedeutung des Alten Testaments in ethischen Fragen*. Edited by Christian Frevel. Quaestiones Disputatae 272. Freiburg im Breisgau: Herder.

Soete, Annette. 1987. *Ethos der Rettung – Ethos der Gerechtigkeit. Studien zur Struktur von Normbegründung und Urteilsfindung im Alten Testament und ihrer Relevanz für die ethische Diskussion der Gegenwart*. Würzburg: Echter.

Steymans, Hans Ulrich. 2003. "Die neuassyrische *Vertragsrhetorik* der 'Vassal Treaties of Esarhaddon' und das Deuteronomium." Pages 89–152 in *Das Deuteronomium*. Edited by Georg Braulik. Österreichische Biblische Studien 23. Frankfurt am Main: Peter Lang.

------. 2013. "Deuteronomy 28 and Tell Tayinat." *Verbum et Ecclesia* 34/2: 1–13.

------. 2016. "Recension of Carly Crouch, *Israel and the Assyrians*." *Review of Biblical Literature* 02/2016<https://www.academia.edu/30541314/Review_Crouch_Israel_and_the_Assyrians_in_RBL_02_2016>.

------. 2019. "Deuteronomy 13 in Comparison with Hittite, Aramaic and Assyrian Treaties." *Hebrew Bible and Ancient Israel* 8/2: 101–32.

Stipp, Hermann-Josef. 2017. "Monotheismus, Monolatrie, Gewalt und Identität. Alttestamentliche Gesichtspunkte zu den Monotheismus-Thesen von Jan Assmann." *Münchener Theologische Zeitschrift* 68: 99–130.

Testa, Emmanuele. 1981. *La morale dell'Antico Testamento*. Brescia: Morcelliana.

Veijola, Timo. 2008. "'Du sollst daran denken, dass du Sklave gewesen bist im Lande Ägypten'. Zur literarischen Stellung und theologischen Bedeutung einer Kernaussage des Deuteronomiums." Pages 48–68 in *Leben nach der Weisung. Exegetisch-historische Studien zum Alten Testament*. Edited by Timo Veijola, Walter Dietrich, and Marko Martilla.

Forschungen zur Religion und Literatur des Alten und Neuen Testaments 224. Göttingen: Vandenhoeck & Ruprecht.
Versluis, Arie. 2017. *The Command to Exterminate the Canaanites: Deuteronomy 7*. Oudtestamentische Studien 71. Leiden: Brill.
------. 2022. "Covenant in Deuteronomy: The Relationship between the Moab, Horeb, and Patriarchal Covenant." Pages 79–100 in *Covenant: A Vital Element of Reformed Theology. Biblical, Historical, and Systematic-Theological Perspectives*. Edited by Hans Burger, Gert Kwakkel, and Michael Mulder. Studies in Reformed Theology 42. Leiden: Brill.
Vroom, Jonathan. 2018. *The Authority of Law in the Hebrew Bible and Early Judaism. Tracing the Origins of Legal Obligation from Ezra to Qumran*. Supplements to the Journal for the Study of Judaism 187. Leiden: Brill.
Wolbert, Werner. 1981. *Ethische Argumentation und Paränese in 1 Kor 7*. Düsseldorf: Patmos.
Würthwein, Ernst. 1982. "Verantwortung im Alten Testament." Pages 9–116 in *Verantwortung*. Edited by Ernst Würthwein and Otto Merk. Kohlhammer-Taschenbücher 1009. Stuttgart: Kohlhammer.

About the Author

Father Georg Braulik OSB is an emeritus member of the Faculty of Roman Catholic Theology of the University of Vienna. He is the author and editor of about twenty-five monographs and has written more than 220 scientific articles, many of them translated into various languages. He is also the founder and editor of the series, Österreichische Biblische Studien.

Chapter 18
Deuteronomy's Influence on the Formation of the Psalter

Bernard Gosse

Abstract

After a review of the distinctive traits of each of the five books that turn the Psalter into a second Pentateuch, eight semantic or conceptual cases are identified as likely references to Deuteronomy, shoring up Jamie Grant's view of the influence of the law of the king, but broadened to other parts of Deuteronomy.

Keywords: Psalms, King David, Deuteronomy 17, Deuteronomy 28, Aaron, Psalm 132, Zion

1. Introduction

The interactions between the Psalter and parts of 2 Isaiah (chs 40–55) have come under scrutiny for several decades (see Berges 2022), but what common ground might the Psalter share with Deuteronomy? There is no equivalent to the legal material at the heart of Deuteronomy in wisdom literature. Nevertheless, the Psalter begins with a psalm celebrating *torah*, "teaching," but which frequently is translated "law," (Ps 1) and continues in Pss 19 and 119 (Torah and seven synonyms) to make *torah* tower over other themes in the first and last books of the Psalter (Grant 2004, 255). In addition, the Psalter imitates the Pentateuch's structure with five "books" that contain references to Abraham, Isaac, Jacob, Moses, Aaron, and Pharaoh. Among these Pentateuchal echoes, is it possible to detect any particular influence of Deuteronomy?

2. The Structure of the Book of Psalms

The Psalter opens with a general introduction comprising Pss 1 and 2. Psalm 1 praises those who delight in Yhwh's *torah* and compares them to a tree planted beside a stream that produces its fruit in season and whose leaves do not wither. Psalm 2 then emphasizes the theme of kingship: Yhwh scoffs at earthly rulers and enthrones his own king in Zion. Zion evokes David, who is named 88 times in the book (75 times in the titles of psalms and 13 times in the text) and the books of Samuel and Kings, where his life story covers 42 chapters (1 Sam 16–1 Kgs 2). Since, however, Ps 1 has, right from the beginning, established the primacy of *torah*, the architecture of the Psalter looks beyond King David. The first letters of each line of Ps 2 also form an acrostic that reads, "For Yannay and his wife" (ליעני ואשתו), celebrating the wedding of Yannai (Alexander Jannaeus) and Salome Alexandra (ca. 100 BCE; Atkinson 2008; Knauf 2009). He was the second king of the Hasmonean dynasty, of priestly, not Davidic origin.

Although there are many more mentions of David than Moses overall in the Psalter and David is the focus of Books 1, 2, 3, and 5, as will be seen, Moses replaces him as the focus of Book 4. Table 1 lists the number of occurrences of David and Moses in each of the five books of the Psalter to illustrate the articulation of the two figures.

Table 1: David and Moses in the Psalter (Hebrew numbering)

	David			Moses		
Book	Titles	Text	Total	Titles	Text	Total
1	37×	18:51	1			0
2	20×	72:20	1			0
3	1×	78:70; 89:4, 21, 36, 50	5		77:21	1
4	2×			1	99:6; 103:7; 105:26; 106:16, 23, 32	6
5a (107–119)			7			7
5b (120–150)	15×*	122:5; 132:1, 10, 11, 17; 144:10				0
Total	75	13	88	1	7	8

*In the title of Pss 108; 109; 110; 122; 124; 131; 133; 138; 139; 140; 141; 142; 143; 144; 145.

A first glance is enough to note that Moses occurs almost exclusively in Book 4 of the Psalter, precisely where David is the least present. As Ps 119 echoes Ps 1 and makes a fitting conclusion to a Torah Psalter, the text of a Psalter limited to Pss 1–119 without any titles struck a perfect balance between the two main biblical figures: seven occurrences for David between Ps 18:51 and 89:49, and seven for Moses between Ps 77:21 and 106:32.[1] The six additional mentions of David in the post-119 psalms (122–144) break the balance; none of these psalms mention Moses. Yet, the conceivers of the titles generated a tenfold advantage in favor of David with a grand total of 88 references against 8 occurrences for Moses.

2.1 Book 1 (Pss 3–41)[2]

The *Leitmotiv* of the body of the psalms of Book 1 is Yhwh's care of the poor (Pss 9:13, 19; 10:2,9, 12; 12:6; 14:6; 18:28; 22:25; 25:16; 34:7; 40:18). Every titled psalm in Book 1 mentions David, who is thus identified with the figure of the poor (עָנִי) and who appears as the victim of the wicked who persecute the poor (10:2) and lurk in secret like a lion to "seize the poor and drag them off in their net" (10:9 NRSV).[3]

2.2 Book 2 (Pss 42–72)

Book 2 comprises two groupings: Pss 42–49, attributed to the Korahites, are followed by a first Psalm of Asaph (Ps 50) that marks the transition to a second group attributed to David (Pss 51–72). The Korahite psalms are attributed to the sons of Korah (see below §2.3), who appear in titles that fall into two clusters (42–49 and 84–85; 87–88) with a symbolic total of 12 (Mitchell 2006, 366). The Korah collection opens both Book 2 as well as the Elohistic Psalter (Pss 42–83) and closes Book 3 (though Ps 89 is not attributed to the sons of Korah but to Ethan the Ezrahite).

---

1 A parallel discussed in Midrash Tehilim on Ps 1:1 (see Choi 2009, 453).
2 All references in the Psalms cite the Hebrew numbering followed by the corresponding numbers for chapters and verses in English Bibles in square brackets when they differ from the Hebrew.
3 In the Hebrew, Pss 9 and 10 constitute a complete alphabetic acrostic (aleph to kaph in Ps 9; lamed to tav in Ps 10, with a few irregularities). Though the acrostic is lost in translation, the Greek and Latin versions take into account the alphabetic structure by counting the two as a single psalm; this is the source of the difference in numbering between Pss 11–113 (Hebrew numbering) or 10–112 (Greek and Latin numbering). Further differences occur further on: Hebrew Pss 114 and 115 = Ps 113 in Greek and Latin; Hebrew Ps 116 = Greek and Latin Pss 114 and 115; Hebrew 117–46 = Greek and Latin 116–45; Hebrew 147 = Greek and Latin 146–47.

Whereas the titles of Pss 51–72 recall David's wars from the books of Samuel, the Korahite psalms shift the focus away from David toward Jerusalem and Zion, which are saved miraculously by the Lord of hosts (יהוה צבאות):

> As we have heard, so have we seen in the city of the Lord of hosts, in the city of our God, which God establishes forever. (Ps 48:9 NRSV)

This shift away from the figure of David prepares the reader for the doubts expressed in Ps 89 concerning the continuation of his dynasty.

2.3 Book 3 (Pss 73–89)

Book 3 begins with psalms of Asaph (73–83) that focus on the fall of Jerusalem (74; 79). Ps 77:21 [20] contains the sole mention of Moses outside Book 4; it anticipates his function as a counterpart to David (78:70–72). The second part of Book 3 (particularly Pss 84–85 and 87–89) underlines the failure of the promises made to David following the fall of Jerusalem and the destruction of the temple.

The title of Ps 86, "David's Prayer," signals a shift of focus away from David by connecting David with the self-description of the psalmist in the initial verse as "poor and needy" (עני ואביון, Ps 86:1). While in the Psalms this formulation is not negative in itself, its association with David prepares the way for the note about the demise of the Davidic dynasty in Ps 89:50 at the end of Book 3. At the same time, it reaffirms Yahwism, which has been downplayed in the Elohistic Psalter (42–83):[4]

> Remember, O Adonai, how your servant is taunted; how I bear in my bosom the insults of the peoples, with which your enemies taunt, O Yhwh, with which they taunted the footsteps of your anointed. (89:50–51)

The fact that the Elohistic Psalter spans Books 2–3 is a crucial element of Deuteronomy's influence on the Psalter. Deuteronomy expressly advocates the concept of Yahweh as Elohim (Edelman 2022), so the chunk of psalms that use Elohim as title for Yhwh can be argued to reflect Deuteronomic theology and be programmatic for use in the temples in Jerusalem and Samaria in the Persian period.

---

4   The so-called "Elohist Psalter" consists of 42 psalms, each with at least one mention of Elohim but only 39 mentions of Yhwh throughout the collection. On the symbolism of the number 42 in the Bible, in Egypt, and in Mesopotamia, see Gosse 2018; Mitchell 2006, n. 4.

2.4 Book 4 (Pss 90–106)

Books 4 and 5 may not be later than the previous books, but the evidence from the 41 manuscripts recovered from the Qumran caves show that the sequence and contents of the last two books were still in flux at the turn of the era and that other pieces of poetry and non-biblical psalms were intermixed with the canonical psalms (Flint 1997).

Moses is the central figure of Book 4; Ps. 90:1 is entitled, "A Prayer of Moses, the Man of God." He is named subsequently in 99:6; 103:7; 105:26; 106:16, 23, 32, all passages that are discussed in detail below. The Yahwistic faith is reaffirmed in this book as well, as a way to shift attention "from the kingship of David and his progeny back to Yahweh as king" (Vassar 2003, 165).

2.5 Book 5 (Pss 107–50)

Books 1 and 5 form a frame around Books 2 to 4. The first psalm of Book 5 (107) underlines Yhwh's steadfast love that endures forever, to indicate that the eclipse of David in Book 4 is not final. David reappears 21 times in Book 5 (Table 1). His first mention in the text of Book 5 (rather than in titles) is in reference to Jerusalem, which attracts all the tribes to worship Yhwh (122:3–7). There were set the thrones of David's dynasty. This is a memory of the days of old when David's house sat there to pronounce judgment. The audience is invited to intercede for the peace of Jerusalem, its walls and its towers, but not for its palace. Book 5 does not encourage hope in the re-enthronement of a descendant of David.

Then, Ps 132 evokes David's efforts to bring the ark to rest in Zion, the place that Yhwh chose for himself (v. 13). The sure oath that Yhwh had sworn to David is recalled: "From the fruit of your entrails I will set a throne for you" (132:11). This promise was fulfilled by the reign of his first successor, Solomon. After him, however, dynastic continuity became conditional:

> If your sons observe my *berit* and my decrees (עדות) that I will teach them, their sons also shall sit on your throne forever more. (132:12)

The fulfillment of the divine oath depends on the ability of David's sons to hold fast to the *berit* and the *edut*. Yet, a wedge is driven between David's throne and Zion. Whatever happens to David's line, Zion is forever Yhwh's choice (בחר) for his residence (מושב), his resting place (מנוח). Yhwh will indeed cause a horn to sprout up there for David and prepare a lamp for his anointed one (132:17). The oil this horn may contain is at best for anointing the priests mentioned in the previous verse (and already in v. 9), but not to anoint a king. The royal office is discredited, and Ps 132 closes with the evocation of his *nazir* (נזרו), rendered in the NRSV as "but on him (i.e. David), his crown will gleam" (132:18).

This "crown" is a sign of consecration that refers primarily to the priestly office (Exod 28; 29:6; 39:30; Lev 8:9). It endows David with a priestly rather than royal role.[5] This is already suggested by Ps 110, where the anonymous figure sitting at Yhwh's right hand is a priest of the order of Melchizedek (Ps 110:4, see Gen 14:18 that refers to Abram).

With its Davidic title (לדוד), Ps 110 has David himself state that a priestly figure has supplanted the soldier and king, revealing the crucial role titles play in shaping the five books of the Psalter. Overall, the focus is on David's transfer of the ark (132:3-5), re-enacted in the liturgical pilgrimage of the Songs of Ascent (Pss 120-134 [119-133]), a transfer that leads up to the house of Yhwh and into the courts of his house (135:2). Yhwh – not David – killed mighty kings (135:10), and the houses that are to be blessed are priestly ones, those of Aaron and Levi (135:19-20), not David's.

Then, Psalm 144 evokes David's musical skills as the psalmist strikes up a new song upon a ten-stringed harp to "the one who gives victory to kings, who rescues his servant, David" (144:10). The implication of this new song is that Yhwh saves David but not his royal dynasty. The Davidic monarchy is dispensable (McCann 1993, 156). David becomes the tutelary figure of harp players, who accompany the final doxology (Pss 146-150) with the instruments listed in the final verses of the Psalter (150:3-6).

3. Deuteronomy's Influence on the Architecture of the Psalter

The above review of the interplay of the figures of Moses and David suggests that it is at the meta-level of the Psalter that the influence of Deuteronomy is likely to be found. The five books of the Psalter recall the architecture of the Pentateuch and articulate the figures of Moses, Aaron, David and kingship in general in such a way as to make the first five books the key to interpret these human figures and principles.

3.1 Zion as the Location of Deuteronomy's *māqôm* in Psalm 132

One of the most significant features of Deuteronomy is the centralization of worship at a place designated as the *māqôm*, "the place that Yhwh will choose (יבחר) as a dwelling (משכן) for his name." Though Deuteronomy

---

5   Instead of a crown, the Septuagint refer to τὸ ἁγίασμμά μου (Ps 131:18) rendered as "my sanctuary" or "my sanctity" (NETS), none of which refers to David.

itself never indicates the location of the *māqôm*, a majority of scholars still read it as a reference to Jerusalem, though this silence may be intentional. It can reflect the need to change the site of Israel's feasting before Yhwh from year to year to prevent groups that would otherwise find themselves forever at the periphery from being tempted to meet on their own closer to home, as illustrated by the incident in Josh 22 (see Von Rad 1966, 94; Halpern 2021, 103; Guillaume 2021a, 205–206).

Psalm 132 fills in Deuteronomy's silence over the location of the *māqôm* by depicting David's tireless efforts to settle the Ark in Zion (Ps 132:3–8). The doubts over the continuation of David's line are compensated by Zion, Yhwh's choice (בחר) for his residence (מושב) and resting place (מנוח) forever. The choice (בחר) echoes the 17 occurrences of the expression המקום אשר יבחר, "the place he will choose," in the Deuteronomic centralization formula (12:5, 11, 14, 21, 26; 14:23, 24; 15:20; 16:2, 6, 7, 11, 15, 16; 17:8; 18:6; 26:2). Yet, arguably, it is precisely because of Deuteronomy's silence over the location of the *māqôm* that Ps 132:7 and 13 describe Zion as Yhwh's "habitation" (מושב) and v. 14 as his desired "resting place" (מנוח). Both terms seem to replace the more temporary Deuteronomic expressions, "to settle" (שכן) or "put" (שום) his name at the *māqôm*. In Deut 14:28, the triennial tithes find a resting place (הנחת) at the gate of each settlement to feed the local Levite, alien, orphan, and widow (Deut 14:28), a decentralization the psalmist has no interest in whatsoever. Thus, instead of mimicking the Deuteronomic formula, Ps 132 underlines the stability of Zion as Yhwh's choice forever. This contrast presumes the demise of the Davidic dynasty at the time of the creation of the book of Psalms and a transition to the temple and its leadership as the center of power in a "post-exilic" setting.

3.2 David's Seven Enemies in Book 2 and Those Fleeing You in Seven Ways (Deut 28:7)

After locating Deuteronomy's chosen place of worship, a direct reference to Deuteronomy's catalogue of blessings and curse is found in Book 2. The title of Ps 18 presents it as a song of victory following Yhwh's support of David against his enemies, in particular King Saul, whose name appears again only in some titles in Book 2 (Pss 52:1; 54:1; 57:1; 59:1). Psalm 18 has a close parallel in 2 Sam 22, placed after a chapter that notes David's declining physical abilities (2 Sam 21:15). It ascribes the killing of Goliath to Elhanan (2 Sam 21:19; see Edelman 2021). Verses 21–25 of this psalm depict David as a blameless observer of Yhwh's judgments (משפטים) and decrees (חוקים), thus ascribing to David the blessings Deut 28:1–14 promises to Israel if it obeys Yhwh and diligently observes all his commandments. The closing verse of the psalm applies the blessing of the fruit of the womb of the obedient (Deut 28:4a) to David's dynasty:

> (Yhwh is) a tower of salvation for his king, he shows loyalty to his anointed, to David and to his seed forever. (2 Sam 22:51 // Ps 18:51)

Shifting the focus away from the ageing king toward his everlasting dynasty anticipates the troubles David encounters during his reign that are evoked in the titles of Book 2 (see Gosse 2022) and read as illustrations of the victories Yhwh grants to the faithful over those who oppose them:

> Yhwh will cause your enemies who rise against you to be defeated before you. They will come out against you in one way but will flee before you in seven ways. (Deut 28:7)

Those seven ways are given concrete expression in specific crises in King David's career recalled in the titles of seven psalms in Book 2:

> When Nathan Accused Him in Relation to the Bathsheba affair (Ps 51:2; 2 Sam 12:1)
>
> When Doeg the Edomite Reported His Hideout to Saul (Ps 52:1; 1 Sam 22:9–10)
>
> When the Zifites Reported His Hideout to Saul (Ps 54:1; 1 Sam 23:19)
>
> When the Philistines Caught Him in Gath (Ps 56:1; 1 Sam 21:11–13)
>
> When He Hid in a Cave (Ps 57:1 // 142:1; 1 Sam 22:1–2; 24:1–9)
>
> When Saul Sought to Pin Him to the Wall (Ps 59:1; 1 Sam 19:10)
>
> When He Sent Joab to Fight the Arameans (Ps 60:2; 2 Sam 10)

None of the other mentions of the number seven or the adjective seventh in the psalms (12:6 purified silver; 119:164 daily praise) refers to enemies defeated by Yhwh. These titles thus apply the Deuteronomic promise of victory in 28:7 specifically to King David.

3.3 Moses versus David in Book 4

As noted above, Moses is first introduced beside Aaron in Book 3 to recall his leading of God's people – rather than Yhwh's people – since this psalm belongs to the Elohistic Psalter:

> Like a flock (צאן), you led (נחית) your people by the hand of Moses and Aaron. (77:21[20])

David is the target of this portrayal of Moses as a shepherd; the next psalm ascribes a similar role to David:

He chose David his servant; he took him from the folds of the sheep (צאן); from tending the nursing ewes he brought him to shepherd Jacob, his people and Israel, his inheritance. With upright heart he tended them and guided them with skillful palms (כפיו). (Ps 78:70–72)

Introduced as possessing leadership skills that equal David's, Moses is ready to become the towering figure of Book 4 who will eclipse David and his dynasty in the previous books. Hence, Ps 89:4 (the last psalm of Book 3) recalls the promise of an everlasting dynasty to David but ends on a despairing note:

How long, O Lord? Will you hide yourself forever? How long will your wrath burn like fire?... Remember, O Lord, how your servant is taunted; how I bear in my bosom the insults of the peoples. (89:47 and 50)

The next psalm – the first of Book 4 – names Moses in its title; this is the sole mention of Moses in a psalm title (90:1). From the outset, the identity of David's challenger is clear. Moses's name appears another six times in the body of Book 4 (see Table 1 above).

Moses is mentioned as belonging to the priests as much as Aaron and Samuel (99:6–7):

They called to the Lord, and he answered them. He spoke to them in the pillar of cloud; they kept his testimony (עדיו) and the decree (חק) he gave him (למו).

Since the pillar of cloud is a reference to the Exodus, Samuel is the odd man out. And although Aaron and Moses both experience Yhwh in the pillar of cloud, Moses is the sole recipient of the decree. After repeating that Yhwh answered them, v. 8 states that he was a forgiving God to them, but an avenger of their wrongdoings (נקם על עלילותם). It is unclear whether the wrongdoings are Israel's in general or specifically those committed by Moses, Aaron, and Samuel. Whether or not these charges target Moses in relation to the Meribah episode (Num 20), what is significant here is that the term *'alîlâh/'alîlôt* occurs only twice in the Pentateuch, in Deut 22:14, 17, in reference to charges brought up by a husband accusing his wife of premarital infidelity. As this prescription is unique to Deuteronomy, it constitutes another clue of the influence of Deuteronomy on the Psalter.

The fact that even Moses's record is not entirely clean underlines the theological point of this entire psalm: Yhwh is king, the only true lover of justice. Moses, Aaron, and Samuel remain priests, but David's kingship is discounted.

Then, Moses is presented as the sole recipient of the revelation of Yhwh's ways for Israel (103:7). Yhwh's mercy toward Moses, repeated throughout this psalm, may be a response to the allusion to the wrongdoings of Samuel, Aaron, and Moses. Merciful and gracious, Yhwh "will not accuse always" (103:8-9). Samuel, Aaron, and Moses are vindicated, whatever wrongdoings they had committed. The reference to youth renewed like the eagle's (103:3 and 5) is most fitting for Moses among the three, however, since his sight was unimpaired when he died in full vigor at age 120 (Deut 34:7).

Psalm 105 in his second part (see Ps 105:1-15 and 1 Ch 16:8-22 with the identification of the messiahs (plural) to the descendants of Abraham) recalls Yhwh's wondrous works for Israel. Before evoking the plagues that struck Egypt (vv. 28-36), v. 26 refers to Moses and Aaron by name:

שלח משה עבדו אהרן אשר בחר בו

He sent Moses his servant, Aaron whom he had chosen. (Ps 105:26)

The secondary position of Aaron reflects his late arrival on the Exodus scene to overcome Moses's hesitations (Exod 4:14), but the two brothers are not placed on an equal footing. Moses's status as divine servant evokes the crises he encountered in the last psalm of Book 4: Dathan and Abiram (Num 16; Deut 11:6; Ps 106:16), the Golden Calf incident (Exod 32; Deut 9:15-21; Ps 106:23) and the Meribah incident (Exod 17:1-7; Num 20:24; Deut 33:8; Pss 81:8[7]; 95:8; 106:32).

Contrary to Num 16 and 26:9-11 that mention Korah beside Dathan and Abiram, neither Deuteronomy nor the Psalms mention Korah. This could be a clue that the writer of Ps 106 was intending to recall the Deuteronomic version of the rebellion rather than the more detailed version in Numbers.

Psalm 106 recalls the Golden Calf episode in vv. 19-23 to underline Moses's role as the sole intercessor who overturned the divine desire to destroy Israel (v. 23). The designation of the calf as "an image (תבנית) of an ox that eats grass" (Ps 106:20) echoes the prohibition against divine images in Deut 4:15-18, where the word *tabnit* occurs five times. In Exodus, *tabnit* occurs twice (25:9, 40), but both occurrences refer to the model for the tabernacle. Hence, a reference to Deuteronomy here is clear, confirming the prior impression that the version of the Dathan and Abiram story being drawn upon also is the one in this particular book. The evidence is not overwhelming, but it is possible to argue that the wording of the Deuteronomic version of the different crises Moses faced had a greater impact on the person who composed Ps 106 than versions of those same events found in other Pentateuchal books.

3.4 The Center of the Psalter and Deuteronomy's Law of the Firstborn

As noted above, Book 4 uses the figure of Moses to downplay the central position of David in the previous books. The antagonism is introduced already in Book 3 with the mention of Moses in Ps 77:21 [20] and the references to the fall of Jerusalem and the destruction of the temple in Pss 74 and 79. Yet, Book 4 also closes upon a discordant note that sets Aaron apart as Yhwh's chosen one (Ps 105:26). Hence, a second polemical layer arises, one that targets Moses.

The middle verse of the 2,516 verses of the present form of the Psalter when the titles are included in the count refers to the last plague that struck Egypt:

(Ps 78:51 Book 3) ויך כל בכור במצרים ראשית אונים באהלי חם

He struck every firstborn in Egypt, the first fruit of the virilities in the tents of Ham.

This verse is repeated almost exactly in Book 4:

(Ps 105:36) ויך כל בכור במצרים ראשית לכל אונם

He struck every firstborn in Egypt, the first fruit of all their virility.

Such a collocation of the words "firstborn" (בכור) or "first fruit, prime" (ראשית) with the term "virility, generative strength" (און) is found in the law of the firstborn:

את הבכר בן השנואה יכיר לתת לו פי שנים בכל אשר ימצא לו ראשית אנו לו (Deut 21:17)

The firstborn of the hated (wife) he shall acknowledge as firstborn, giving to him twice in all that will be found his, because he is the first [issue] of his virility.

Pure coincidence? Besides the reference to Reuben as Jacob's firstborn in Gen 49:3 (ראשית אוני), Deut 21:17 and Pss 78:51; 105:36 are the sole verses to use the term און in the sense of a man's virility.[6] There is thus a strong probability that a version of the Psalter very similar to the one transmitted by the Masoretic text constructs a deliberate echo of the law of the firstborn with a double reference in Pss 78 and 105 to evoke the double

---

6 און in the sense of physical power rather than the more common meanings of "disaster, deception" and for the less common sense of "wealth", otherwise refers to the Creator's might (Isa 40:26), Jacob's fight at the Jabbok (Hos 12:4), the shortened strong steps of the wicked (Job 18:7) and the physical strength of the hippopotamus (Job 40:16).

share to be granted to the firstborn of the demoted wife.[7] As this law is not found in the other legal collections of the Pentateuch, the reference to Deuteronomy is undeniable. Placing a reference to the firstborn that uses terminology similar to the law of the firstborn right at the center of the Psalter underlines the pivotal role the scribes who organized the final shape of the Psalter attributed to Deuteronomy.

In the Exodus story, Aaron is Moses's older brother and the firstborn son of their parents. "Amram took Jochebed his father's sister as wife and she bore him Aaron and Moses" (Exod 6:20a). Exodus 7:7 indicates a three-year difference between the brothers; "Moses was eighty years old and Aaron eighty-three when they spoke to Pharaoh." Therefore, the scribal game consists of combining the double reference to the plague of the firstborn in Book 3 and 4 with Deuteronomy's mandate to provide a double share of the paternal estate to the firstborn son in order to evoke Aaron and Moses. Was the aim to set Aaron against Moses in the same way as Book 4 sets Moses against David? Or is the reference to the firstborn allude to Israel among the nations, as Yhwh's firstborn?

In any case, the importance of the titles and their distribution across the Psalter supports the suggestion of Kent Sparks (2008, 306) that the final shape of the Psalter reflects "influences from the whole post-exilic Torah tradition, which included not only Deuteronomy but also P [the Priestly Source or Writer]." Nevertheless, the influence of Deuteronomy remains particularly significant, as the so-called law of the king shows.

3.5 Kingship in the Psalms in Light of Deut 17?

The challenge to the validity of David's dynastic promises in Book 4 begins already in the last psalm of Book 3 with a list of violations that would void the promise and prevent the royal line from enduring as long as the heavens (89:29–30 [Eng. 28–29]). Were the king's sons to abandon my *torah* (יעזבו בניו תורתי), not walk according to my customs (משפטי), violate my decrees (חקתי), or not keep my commandments (מציתי), their transgressions will be punished with the rod (89:33 [32]).

Each of these terms – torah, customs, decrees, and commandments – are common designations occurring throughout the Pentateuch, which leads John Vassar (2003, 145–201) to note no particular link between the law of the king and the Psalter.

---

7   On the understanding of the expression "hated" (שנואה) as expressing the demotion of the wife without legitimate legal grounds, despite the fact that she gave birth to a son, see Wells (2013, 304).

Table 2: "Torah" and its synonyms in the law of the king and in the Psalter

	Deuteronomy	Psalms								
Chapter	17	1	19	37	40	78	89	94	105	119
תוראה	18, 19	2	8	31	9	1,5,10	31	12	45	25x
חקה/חוק	19		8			7	32			22x
מצוה	20		8			7	32			22x
שמר	19						32			
משפט	8.9.11	5	10				15, 31			23x
Total		2	4	1	1	5	6	1	1	96

In fact, the collocation of the Hebrew terms used as synonyms for "Torah" in the so-called "law of the king" (Deut 17) and in the Psalter is significant enough to demonstrate that the architecture of the Psalter does echo Deuteronomy's subordination of the king to the Torah (Table 2).

Sparks challenges Grant's view of the importance of the messianic expectations of the editors of the Psalter. He suggests instead that "royal psalms such as Psalm 89 anticipated the historical restoration of David's house, so that one could as easily suppose that the editors of the Psalter had this rather than eschatology in mind" (Sparks 2008, 306). Grant may have exaggerated the importance of messianism because he had Jesus Christ in view as Israel's coming messiah (Grant 2004, 295; Sparks 2008, 305).

The acrostic of Ps 2 makes no mention of the royal title king, even though coins minted for Alexander Janneaus (reigned 103–76 BCE) feature the words *basileus* and *mlk* (see Knauf and Guillaume 2016, 212). Clearly, then, he followed the precedent set by his brother Aristobulus I (reigned 104–103 BCE), who was the first Hasmonean to take for himself the title of king. It is therefore significant that the acrostic of Ps 2 ("For Yannay and his wife") denies Alexander the royal title he used on his coins, all the more so since kingship is the main theme of that psalm. One likely explanation is that the author anticipated the restoration of a king of Davidic descent, which then made him anti-Hasmonean, because that family did not descend from the expected bloodline. The re-conceptualization of kingship in Deut 17 (Levinson 2001) provided the biblical justification for the critique of the Hasmonean rulers.

Mentioned after 13 verses on judicial procedures that grant no function to the king, Deut 17 does not make the election of a monarch a prerequisite for life in Canaan. The addressees may discuss (אמרת) the matter, but the motivation "to set up a king over me like all the people around me" (Deut 17:14) signals the narrator's lack of enthusiasm for the project. The expression "people (גוים or עמים) around" is encountered earlier to refer to idolatry (Deut 6:14; 13:8). Deuteronomy 17:15 strongly emphasizes that the royal candidate must be a brother (מקרב אחיך) whose candidacy must be rubber-stamped by Yhwh. Even so, this king is divested of all duties and privileges pertaining to the royal office to the point that the law of the king may well be considered "anti-king" (so Markl 2018). Prevented from accumulating horses, wives, silver, and gold, the Deuteronomic optional ruler is deprived of military, diplomatic, and economic functions. Instead, he is to copy the Torah scroll supplied by the Levitical priests and study it day and night, without having a chance to practice its prescriptions beyond his private life (see Rossi 2021).

Such an unroyal portrayal of kingship in Deut 17 contributes to the hypostatization of the Torah as a powerful identity marker devoid of any judicial function beyond circumcision, pork taboo, and Sabbath observance, the (sole?) practices that were recognized as distinctive of Judaism from the Hellenistic era on (Collins 2022; Stern 1974). Apart from these, a transition from descriptive to prescriptive law can hardly be identified in Judaism or Samaritanism. The Torah remains on the level of formative ideal with very little normative function in both the Diaspora and in Palestine.

3.6 David as Messiah or as Torah Reader?

Table 3 lists uses of the term "anointed, messiah" in the Psalter, to detect how it re-conceptualizes kingship.

Table 3: משיח in the Psalter and its referents

Book	Psalm	Referent
1	2:2	king
	18:51[50]	king
	20:6	king? see v. 9
	28:8	people?
2	45:7	king
3	84:10[9]	Israel?
	89:20 (verb), 39[38]; 52[51]	David
4	105:15	Prophets
5	132:10, 17	David

Out of these 12 occurrences of the anointed one,[8] only five are clear references to David. Books 1 and 2 refer to an anonymous king. Book 3 clarifies the identity of the messiah as David in Ps 89, while the reference to prophets in 105:15 is coherent with the anti-Davidic trend of Book 4. Despite their clear attribution of the term "messiah" to David, the two usages in Book 5 provide a rather narrow base for the identification of a solid trend regarding a non-royal Davidic messiah.

Though Ps 132:10–17 confirms the identification of the messiah with David in Ps 89, it affirms the conditionality of the Davidic dynasty. The ability of David's descendants to rule depends on their obedience to Yhwh's *berit* and *'edut* that he will teach them (see above §1.5). In contrast, it is Zion, Yhwh's everlasting residence and resting place (v. 13–14), which replaces the Davidic dynasty as unconditional.

Yhwh himself assumes royal functions such as supplying bread for the needy (v. 15) and clothing for the priests (v. 16). Though David was eager to find a place for Yhwh (vv. 1–5), the ability of his sons to succeed him on the throne is not guaranteed; but Yhwh's presence in Zion is. What the horn, the lamp, and the crown that Yhwh prepares for David (132:17–18) mean practically is left in limbo. At most, the Psalter models David's dynasty on the lines of the idle Deuteronomic king who copies and studies the Torah all the days of his life (Deut 17:19).

3.7 The Sons of Korah and Deuteronomy 23:8[7]

Who are the sons of Korah (קרח) to whom 12 psalms are attributed (by splitting Ps 42 into Pss 42 and 43, see Mitchell 2006, n. 2)? They are usually related to the second son of Levi, Kohath, who had four sons: Amram, the father of Aaron and Moses; Izhar, the father of Korah, Nepheg, and Zichri; Hebron, and Uzziel (Exod 6:16–21; Num 16:1; 1 Chr 6:7 [22]). Hence, the Korah who led the rebellion recalled in Num 16 would be a "first cousin" to Aaron and Moses. Whether this genealogy should be taken at face value to reflect true blood lines or seen to be a means to create artificial kinship within a profession does not affect the larger point.

The first biblical mention of a person named Korah refers, however, to an Edomite, a son of Esau by his Hivite wife (Gen 36:5, 16). The Chronicler, on the other hand, associates the Korahites with Judahite (1 Chr 2:43) and Benjaminite (2 Chr 12:6) clans, underlining their close family ties. It is unclear if the Chronicler has suppressed any "Edomite" character of the sons of Korah he might have been aware of, perhaps due to their presence

---

8 89:20 is the thirteenth and can be ignored as it is a verbal form "I anointed him" (משחתיו).

in the titles of some psalms. He might have assumed they must have been of "native" Levitical ancestry.

We cannot be certain which Korahite ancestry is being assumed by the psalmist. If, however, the son of Esau in Gen 36:5,16 was meant to be called to mind, then there might be an intentional allusion to Deut 23:8[7] in this text, which forbids abhorring an Edomite "because he is your brother." Moses, Aaron, and the Korahites would be related, though more distantly, as third cousins, with Korah a first cousin to Levi. This brotherly status is a thorn in the flesh of the common understanding of Israel as a brotherhood that includes women and slaves but excludes foreigners. Scholars strive to downplay its significance to salvage the ethnic purity of the *qehal-Yhwh*, the assembly of Yhwh. Deuteronomy 23:9[8] clearly states, however, that third generation Edomites and Egyptians are granted full membership in this assembly, which does not necessarily refer to Israel (see Guillaume 2021b, 311–16).

This is not the place to discuss the identity of this particular *qahal*, the dating of the titles of the Korahite psalms, of Deut 23, or of the Edomite genealogies. Put simply, Deut 23 cannot be ignored as an insignificant marginal note. It fits the overall Edomite portrayal in the Hebrew Bible and constitutes another possible clue concerning Deuteronomy's influence on the Psalter.

Another hint pointing to this potential Deuteronomic influence is found in the Korahite Ps 44:6[5]. The verb נגח refers to a violent action against foes. According to David Mitchell (2006, 371 and n. 21), it "derives from Ephraimite military ideology which made much of the Josephite ox of Deut 33:17 goring the nations."

As a final observation, Nissim Amzallag (2014) has noted that the most cosmopolitan chapters of the Psalter have been attributed to Korah, in particular Ps 87. This is in spite of the downgrading of the Korahites to mere guards in 1 Chr 9:17–32, probably because of their challenges to the continuity of the Davidic royal dynasty. If so, the Edomite connection is hardly surprising, and it can only be explained in reference to Deut 23.

Conclusion

This chapter has mapped the Psalter's gradual remodeling of the figure of David. Book 1 ends with him being a poor victim of evildoers. In Book 2 he is displaced by Zion, and Book 3 closes by recalling the fall of his city. In Book 4, Moses takes center stage, challenging the legitimacy of the Davidic dynasty. Finally Book 5 features the return of David as a Torah student along the lines of Deuteronomy's Law of the King.

Though the Psalter's structure is meant to mirror the entire Pentateuch, several cases indicate a specifically Deuteronomic influence. The seven ways the enemies shall flee (Deut 28:7) are given concrete illustration in the titles of Book 2; they evoke seven foes and crises King David faced.

The mention of wrongdoings forgiven by Yhwh in Ps 99 is likely to allude to the law of post-marital accusations (Deut 22:13–21). The term עלילותם in vv. 6–7 occurs only twice in the Pentateuch, both times in Deut 22:14, 17 in reference to charges brought up by a husband accusing his wife of premarital infidelity. One may well find here an ironic echo to the Bathsheba affair.

Another semantic influence from Deuteronomy appears in the Korahite Ps 44:6[5] that uses the verb נגח to express the "pushing down of our foes" (NRSV) but refers more precisely to their goring, as is the case with Joseph in Deut 33:17, who gores the nations.

The prohibition against abhorring an Edomite brother in Deut 23:8 is one element that could have contributed to the attribution of two groups of psalms to Korah, despite his possible Edomite antecedents.

The reference to youth renewed like the eagle's in Psalm 103:3 and 5 is a likely echo of Moses who, according to Deut 34:7, died with unimpaired sight and in full vigor.

The introduction of the Coraites in Number 16 is posterior to Psalm 106 (see Achenbach 2003, 53, 129). He notes the opposition of the Asaphites and Ezrahites to the Korachites.

The term *"tabnit"* applied to the Golden Calf in Ps 106:20 echoes the five uses of that term in Deut 4:16–18 in relation to idolatry rather than its two occurrences in Exodus (25:9, 40) for the tabernacle.

The Egyptian firstborn mentioned in the middle verse of the entire Psalter (Ps 78:51) when titles are included in the count reveals an elaborate scribal game that establishes a link with Aaron, Moses's older brother, who was granted the priesthood as a distant echo of the Law of the firstborn to whom fathers must grant a double share of their estate (Deut 21:17).

Yet, the strongest clue to Deuteronomy's influence is the effort Ps 132 deploys to anchor the Deuteronomic *māqôm* at Zion, efforts necessary because Deuteronomy resists such an identification.

The entire scroll of Deuteronomy is thus mined (from chs. 4–34). No difference is evinced between legal and parenetic passages, which is coherent with the hypostatization of the Torah as an entity in which law and narrative are indistinct.

This chapter corroborates Grant's view (2004) of the influence of Deut 17 in the psalms but not his understanding of messianism. Though the Psalter became the most quoted Hebrew Bible book in the New Testament (over 60 quotes), the Psalter itself remains as discreet about a messianic David as it is regarding the Hasmonean assumption of the royal title. In the Psalms, David is a zealous believer and a tormented poet. While his enemies are active, "David wanders the realm of poetry and bares his broken heart before God" (Kara-Ivanov Kaniel 2019, 69). The Korah psalms promise a resurrection of the messiah, a promise that is fulfilled in Ps 92 and confirmed in Ps 110, where the messiah appears from heaven (Mitchell 1997, 253–67 and 281–84).

Finally, Deuteronomy's influence on the organization of the Psalter as a second Pentateuch is reflected in the Dead Sea scrolls, where Deuteronomy is only second to the Psalter in the number of attested biblical books (Washburn 2002). It also is reflected in the New Testament, where it is the third most quoted Hebrew book after Isaiah (55 times) and psalms (129 of the 150 are quoted) thus reflecting the notion that Jesus came not to abolish the law but to fulfill it (Matt 5:17). With a mere three quotes, the books of Samuel are almost ignored, which underlines the popularity of the Psalter's re-conceptualization of the figure of David into a non-political figure (Brooke and Najman 2016).

Works Cited

Achenbach, Reinhard. 2003. *Die Vollendung der Tora: Studien zur Redaktiongeschichte des Numberbucher im Kontext von Hexateuch und Pentateuch"* 53, 129. Beheifte zur Zeitschrift für altorientalische und biblische Rechtsgeschichte 3. Wiesbaden: Harrasowitz Verlag.

Amzallag, Nissim. 2014. "The Cosmopolitan Character of the Korahite Musical Congregation: Evidence from Psalm 87." *Vetus Testamentum* 64: 361–81.

Atkinson, Kenneth. 2008. "The Salome No One Knows." *Biblical Archaeology Review* 34(4): 60–65, 72.

Berges, Ulrich. 2022. "Isaiah 55–66 and the Psalms: Shared Viewpoints, Literary Similarities and Neighboring Authors." *Journal of Biblical Literature* 141: 277–99.

Brooke, George J. and Hindy Najman. 2016. "Dethroning David and Enthroning Messiah: Jewish and Christian Perspectives." Pages 111–27 in *On Prophets, Warriors and Kings*. Edited by Georges J. Brooke and Ariel Feldman. Berlin: de Gruyter.

Choi, John H. 2009. *Traditions at Odds. A Study of the Reception History of the Pentateuch in Biblical and Second Temple Literature*. Dissertation Hebrew Union College-Jewish Institute of Religion.

Collins, John J. 2022. "The Torah in its Symbolic and Prescriptive Functions." *Hebrew Bible and Ancient Israel* 11: 3–18.

Edelman, Diana V. 2021. "How Starting Assumptions Affect Results: The Story of David's Slaying of Goliath (1 Samuel 17; 2 Samuel 21:19) Interpreted in Terms of Orality, Scribalism, and Cultural Memory." Pages 259–92 in *De l'oral à l'écrit, Actes du colloque organisé par le Collège de France, Paris, 19–20 mai, 2016*. Edited by Thomas Römer, Hervé Gonzalez, Lionel Marti and Jan Rückl. Leuven: Peeters.

———. 2022. "Yhwh (ha)Elohim and a Reconceived Yahwism in the Book of Deuteronomy." Pages 1–38 in *Deuteronomy: Outside the Box*. Edited by Diana Edelman and Philippe Guillaume. Sheffield: Equinox Publishing Ltd eBooks. https://www.equinoxpub.com/home/view-chapter/?id=44585. http://dx.doi.org/10.1515/9783110713312

Flint, Peter W. 1997. *The Dead Sea Psalms Scrolls and the Book of Psalms*. Leiden: Brill.

Gosse, Bernard. 2018. "The 42 Generations of the Genealogy of Jesus in Matthew 1:1–17 and the Symbolism of Number 42 : Curse or Blessing in the Bible and in Egypt." *Studia Biblica Slovaca* 10: 142–51.

———. 2022. "Le Psautier comme prière du David des livres de Samuel selon le Psaume 18 et 2 Samuel 22 / The Psalter as a Prayer of the David of the Books of Samuel according to Psalm 18 and 2 Samuel 22." *Revue d'histoire et de philosophie religieuses* 102/2: 145–74.

Grant, Jamie A. 2004. *The King as Exemplar. The Function of Deuteronomy's Kingship Law in the Shaping of the Book of Psalms*. Boston: Brill.

Guillaume, Philippe. 2021a. "Deuteronomy's *Māqôm* before Deuteronomy." Pages 195–217 in *Deuteronomy in the Making. Studies in the Production of Debarim*. Edited by Diana Edelman, Benedetta Rossi, Kåre Berge, and Philippe Guillaume. BZAW 533; Berlin: de Gruyter.

———. 2021b. "Brothers in Deuteronomy: Zoom in on Lothar Perlitt's *Volk von Brüdern*." Pages 289–327 in *Deuteronomy in the Making. Studies in the Production of Debarim*. Edited by Diana Edelman, Benedetta Rossi, Kåre Berge, and Philippe Guillaume. BZAW 533; Berlin: de Gruyter.

Halpern, Baruch. 2021. "What does Deuteronomy Centralize?" Pages 97–162 in *Deuteronomy in the Making. Studies in the Production of Debarim*. Edited by Diana Edelman, Benedetta Rossi, Kåre Berge and Philippe Guillaume. BZAW 533; Berlin: de Gruyter.

Kara-Ivanov Kaniel, Ruth. 2019. "David and Jerusalem: From Psalms to the Zohar." Pages 67–108 in *Psalms in/on Jerusalem*. Edited by Ilana Pardes and Ophir Münz-Manor. Berlin: de Gruyter.

Knauf, Ernst Axel. 2009. "Salome Alexandra and the Final Redaction of Psalms." *Lectio Difficilior* 2. Online: http://www.lectio.unibe.ch/09_2/knauf_salome_alexandra.html

———. and Philippe Guillaume. 2016. *A History of Biblical Israel. The Fate of the Tribes of Israel from Merenptah to Bar Kochba*. Sheffield: Equinox Publishing Ltd.

Levinson, Bernard M. 2001. "The Reconceptualization of Kingship in Deuteronomy and the Deuteronomistic History's Transformation of Torah." *Vetus Testamentum* 51: 511–34.
McCann, J. Clinton. 1993. *A Theological Introduction to the Book of Psalms.* Nashville: Abingdon.
Mitchell, David C. 1997. *The Message of the Psalter: An Eschatological Programme in the Book of Psalms.* JSOTSup, 252; Sheffield: Sheffield Academic Press.
------. 2006. "'God Will Redeem My Soul from Sheol: The Psalms of the Sons of Korah." *Journal for the Study of the Old Testament* 30: 365–84.
Rossi, Benedetta. 2021. "'Not by Bread Alone' (Deut 8,3): Elite Struggles over Cultic Prebends and Moses's Torah in Deuteronomy." Pages 329–63 in *Deuteronomy in the Making, Studies in the Production of* Debarim. Edited by Diana Edelman, Benedetta Rossi, Kåre Berge and Philippe Guillaume. BZAW 533; Berlin: de Gruyter.
Sparks, Kent. 2008. "Review of *The King as Exemplar: The Function of Deuteronomy's Kingship Law in the Shaping of the Book of Psalms* by Jamie A. Grant." *Journal of Near Eastern Studies* 67: 305–307.
Stern, Menahem. 1974. *Greek and Latin Authors on Jews and Judaism.* Jerusalem: The Israel Academy of Sciences and Humanities.
Vassar, John S. 2007. *Recalling a Story Once Told. An Intertextual Reading of the Psalter and the Pentateuch.* Macon, GA: Mercer University Press.
Von Rad, Gerhard. 1966. *Deuteronomy: A Commentary.* Translated by Dorothea Barton. Philadelphia: Westminster.
Washburn, David L. 2002. *A Catalog of Biblical Passages in the Dead Sea Scrolls.* Atlanta: SBL.
Wells, Bruce. 2013. "Is it Law or Religion? Legal Motivations in Deuteronomic and Neo-Babylonian Texts." Pages 287–309 in *Law and Religion in the Eastern Mediterranean: From Antiquity to Early Islam.* Edited by Anselm C. Hagedorn and Reinhard G. Kratz. Oxford: Oxford University Press.

About the Author

Bernard Gosse earned a doctorate from the Sorbonne in Paris. His latest publications include *David and Abraham: Persian Period Traditions* (Paris: Gabalda, 2010); *L'Espérance messianique davidique et la structuration du Psautier* (Paris: Gabalda, 2015); "Moïse dans le Psautier," *Revue Biblique* 126 (2019): 52–63; "Remarques sur le Psautier Coréite et Asaphite Ps 42–49; 84–85.87–89," *Biblishe Zeitschrift* 66 (2022): 93–107; "La rédaction du Psautier par inclusion en cinq livres, les fonctions des titres des psaumes, le rôle du psautier Elohiste (Ps 42–83) et les théologies des chantres lévites Asaphites, Coréites et Ezrahites dans le cadre du Psautier en confrontation avec les livres des chroniques," *Biblische Notizen* 191 (2021): 31–48; "David and Moses in Post-Exilic Time," in Jill Middlemas, *Innovation in Persian Judah* 43–58 (Tübingen: Mohr Siebeck, 2023).

19
LANDSCAPE IN DEUTERONOMY: WHAT WERE THE LITERATI IMAGINING AND WHY?[1]

Ehud Ben Zvi

Abstract

This chapter is about constructions of internal territorial space and its ideological implications. It discusses the lay of the land of the Israelite society that the literati "saw" when reading Deuteronomy. A non-hierarchical arrangement of cities and "the place" strongly characterize the book. Neither the imaginary landscape of the Israelite polity nor the polity itself evoked by Deuteronomy were consistent with those evoked by any of the "historiographical" works in Yehud (Gen–Kgs and Chr, Ezr, Neh). As a result, its literati had to assume either that such a landscape had never actually been fulfilled in any period of the past or try to conform to Deuteronomy's landscape to other past-shaping, ideological texts and related memories that existed in their core repertoire, or both, in a complementary, balancing way.

Keywords: Deuteronomy, Deuteronomy's landscapes, ancient Israelite political thought, constructions of territorial space, intellectual history of Yehud, social memory

---

1 This chapter is a revised version of an article entitled "'Your Gates' – Evoking a Landscape of Fortified Cities in Deuteronomy: Meanings, Implications, and Comparative Considerations with Other Constructions of the Israelite Past," published in *Scandinavian Journal of the Old Testament* 37.1 (2023): 17–33. We thank Taylor and Francis for granting copyright permission to reuse about 85% of the text of the original version.

1. Introduction

Reading the book of Deuteronomy, not any partial forerunner, conjured among the historical target readership (i.e., the few literati able to read the book in the Persian period) an image of the land of the Israelite settlement/polity. Since they "saw" that land while reading through the eyes of Yhwh and Moses, the lay of the land that they observed and which characterized the Israelite settlement was set mainly in the (normative) future of the narrative.[2] From the perspective of the literati among whom the book of Deuteronomy emerged, Moses and his period were in the foundational past. But was the lay of the land that they "saw" also in their past? Or was it an atemporal foundational image? Or perhaps an image to be fulfilled in the future? Or some combination of the above? Whatever the case might be, since Deuteronomy was a culturally and ideologically central, authoritative book for the literati, which voiced Yhwh and Moses to them, the lay of the land communicated by Deuteronomy conjured in the very least a model for the lay of the settled land. Whether fulfilled or not in the past, that model still represented a kind of ideological standard, a paradigmatic map against which all others (e.g., those emerging from Kings or Chronicles) may be compared.

By "lay of the land," I am not referring to physical geography. Within the world portrayed in Deuteronomy and the imaginary that it evokes, and unlike the case of the mental maps shaped in e.g., Ezek 47:1–48; 49 and Zech 14:3–11, rivers, hills, lowlands, coastal areas, and even the land's economic potential do not change when it becomes Israel's (for economic dimensions of Deut, see ch.6 in this volume). Certainly, within Deuteronomy, Yhwh's choice of the land and Yhwh's promise to give it to Israel transform the land. But the lay of the physical land, alongside its economic potential, remains the same before and after Israel's settlement, as does, seemingly, Yhwh's care for that land.

It is "a land that Yhwh your God looks after. The eyes of Yhwh your God are always on it, from the beginning of the year to the end of the year" (Deut 11:12). The idea that Yhwh cares particularly for the land likely connoted for the readership how the land is always under divine "observation," and if those who reside in it are wrongdoers, calamity may befall them.

---

2 Deuteronomy is multivocal in relation to the boundaries of the promised land and the beginning of the conquest. Some of its literary units clearly communicate that the Jordan is its eastern border and that Moses did not conquer any portion of it (e.g., Deut 1:6–8; 7:16–23; 8:7–9; 11:22–25; 12:8–28; 27:1–8; 30:17–18; 32:49), but others include the territory north of the Arnon River (Deut 2:24–3:22) and portray Moses as beginning the process of conquest; see also Deut 34:1–4.

What the Israelite settlement brings about is a transformation of the cultural, social, and political lay of the land. This approach in Deuteronomy is consistent with its main concern: the establishment of a particular Israelite polity that is structured by and around Yhwh's will – as construed and communicated by the book. Deuteronomy is a book about change and discontinuity in the social-cultural, human sphere against the backdrop of a stable, constant physical world.

From a general, comparative perspective, Deuteronomy's construction of the Israelite-settled land represents a case of a transcultural common pattern: using the core conceptual metaphor of a "place" as a container to transform physical space into a "place" due to its particular contents.

This basic core metaphor applies not only to "the land" as a whole but also to any space that is socially or culturally understood as a "place." Place has been widely used to conceptualize, inter alia, homes, in contradistinction to physical houses or apartments and cities (Vermeulen 2020; for the ancient Near East, see e.g., Van Leeuwen 2010). The generative container-metaphor and its related images underlie much of the widely attested, ancient Near Eastern motif of house-building and house.

Pragmatically, a generative grammar that utilizes this basic metaphor also emphasizes contrasts. Two differences in particular between what is "seen" in the imagined social geography of the land portrayed in Deuteronomy, a book that bears much authority among the historical, target readership, and other circumstances of the audience are noteworthy. First, how does what they see in Deuteronomy differ from what they "see" when they look into the monarchic period – as they construed it to be through readings of other books in their core repertoire? Second, how does it differ from what they "see" when they look at the social lay of the land in their own time?

To "see" here refers explicitly to a historically contingent social act of imagination and meaning construction. To a significant extent, what is seemingly only physically "seen" is also dependent on cultural norms, expectations, and socially shared habits of thought (Nisbett and Masuda 2003). Humans can physically see streets, houses, walls, gates, fields, hills, and valleys but not the socially organized land. Precisely because the latter is a socially shared landscape, acts of "seeing" in this sense serve to socialize those sharing them into accepting and performing ideological norms. They "see" what should be "seen."

It is worth stressing that what is stated above holds true whether the "seen" landscape faithfully reflects aspects of a perceived or directly experienced external reality or has no reference whatsoever to physical landscapes. The same applies to anything between these two opposite poles.³

Whether the "seen" landscapes of the socially organized territory are utopian or dystopian, hopeful or disturbing, "factual" or "fictive," such landscapes by necessity shape and communicate, inter alia, an image of the polity that exists in the particular territory. In what follows I will focus on the lay of the land of the Israelite, Deuteronomy-organized society that the literati "saw." What were its most prominent, systemic features? What did these features imply in terms of the polity in the remembered or imagined territory? What did the mentioned features of the lay of the land and the implications of their polity-characterization suggest about the place of the latter within the world of the literati, among whom Deuteronomy emerged? Finally, and following up some of the issues that surface alongside the last question, some features of the landscape of Deuteronomy's socially organized territory will be compared with that conjured by Chronicles, a book that in *some ways* is more "deuteronomistic" than the Deuteronomistic Historical Collection (Josh–2 Kgs; hereafter, DHC; so e.g., Knoppers 2012) but which recalls and, as we shall see, cannot but recall a different social territory. The implications of this difference will be explored.

2. The Land of the Israelite Polity is One of Cities and "The Place"

Deuteronomy portrays a land of cities (e.g., Frese 2015). The land certainly has valleys, mountains, rivers, wheat and barley fields, fruit trees, vineyards, iron stones, copper mines and the like (see, e.g., Deut 8:7-9; Marlow 2018), but none of these reflects the way in which the Israelite settlement as a new polity is organized within Deuteronomy. The literati reading Deuteronomy saw the territory (to be) settled by Israel as socially and ritually organized around the crucial differentiation between (a) cities, which go basically unmarked and thus represent the "ordinary" and "default" social place for the Israelites (e.g., Zerubavel 2018, passim) and (b) a "place" shared by the population settled in the cities that is identified by the phrasing, "the place that Yhwh will/may choose/chooses" in various formats (hereafter *hammāqôm*) (Deut 12:5|–7, 14, 18; 14:23; 15:20; 16:2, 7, 11, 15–17; 23:17; 31:11). *Hammāqôm* is clearly a marked place.

3   This and related observations touch on matters usually discussed in contemporary Critical-Spatial Theory. For an updated summary and discussion of its relevance for studies of ancient Israel, among which, and for which many of the books that ended up in the HB emerged as such, see Vermeulen (2020, 16–36). My thanks to Dr. Karolien Vermeulen, my conversation partner, on some of the issues discussed in this piece.

There are crucial activities in the world of Deuteronomy that are forbidden in the cities or anywhere but *hammāqôm*. Offering various types of sacrifices (Deut 12:13–14, 26–27; 15:19–20), eating "the tithe of your grain, your wine, and your oil, the firstlings of your herds and your flocks, any of your votive gifts that you vow, your freewill offerings, or your donations" (Deut 12:17; NRSV) and the mandated reading of the torah/instruction written by Moses to all Israel (Deut 31:10–13) are restricted to *hammāqôm*. Justice cases that cannot be addressed by the leadership of the city, either because of their technical character or because they involve more than one city (see Deut 17:8–13), are also to be decided at *hammāqôm*. Finally, the three annual pan-Israelite festivals are to be celebrated at "the place" (Deut 16).

Pan-Israelite activities that further and are necessary for the social cohesiveness of the Israel that dwells in "the cities" are associated with *hammāqôm*.[4] This is not surprising; *hammāqôm* is the only substantial trans-city place in the landscape conjured by Deuteronomy. Also unsurprisingly, most of the activities associated solely with *hammāqôm* involve worship of some kind or other. Given that the Israelites in the cities were supposed to worship at shared, set times together, it seems natural for Deuteronomy's non-hierarchical system of cities (see below) to select a separate, marked place, i.e., *hammāqôm*, for worship activity.

The selection of *hammāqôm* and the way the latter is marked are rooted in and reaffirm the widespread notion that the people cannot freely decide among themselves when, where, or how to worship their deity but must worship Yhwh in the way that Yhwh instructs them to do, i.e., in a place chosen by Yhwh, at prescribed times and in specified ways, and by the personnel Yhwh has selected for that role (see Tigay 1996, 122 for the history of interpretation of Deut 12).

In Deuteronomy, and anywhere in the ancient Near East, the proper relation with the deity involves more than narrowly understood cultic matters. Living in accordance with Yhwh's will is made accessible to the Israelites through the act of reading Deuteronomy. This reading was tantamount to learning from Yhwh and from Moses, the paradigmatic

---

4   This includes the mandated reading of the torah/instruction written by Moses to all Israel (Deut 31:10–13). According to Deut, unmarked, "regular" godly instruction is to take place within the family, which means, within the cities. Fathers are responsible for it (e.g., Deut 6:7; 11:19). But family instruction, even when set within clear ideological parameters, needs to be complemented within the world of Deut by a pan-Israelite, symbolically powerful event at *hammāqôm*. Both through the actual text being read and, as importantly, the power of the ceremony, the public reading of the torah every seven years instills among its participants (i.e., "all Israel") that the torah does not "belong" to a family or a city, but to all Israel.

prophet (Deut 31:9-13). Deuteronomy contains the divine torah ("teaching") that Moses wrote and gave to the priests, sons of Levi, as part and parcel of the pan-Israelite, trans-city role of *hammāqôm* (for more on Torah, see ch.9 in this volume).

The key question is what is the impact of *hammāqôm* in the lay of the land conjured by Deuteronomy. On the one hand, it is undeniable that the literati who read Deuteronomy within a Jerusalemite world of knowledge and ideology identified *hammāqôm* with the Jerusalemite temple from the moment the latter was established, and likely with Shiloh before that (e.g., Jer 7:12-15). Likewise, it is undeniable that their Samarian counterparts would strongly disagree with that Jerusalem-centered reading and argue instead that "the place" was Mt. Gerizim (for the Samaritan version of Deut, see ch.15 in this volume). But on the other hand, whether Samarian or Yehudite, these literati could not but notice that their shared text of Deuteronomy was extremely vague, not only in relation to the physical location and layout of *hammāqôm* but also in relation to the question of whether it refers to a single place or a type of place that might be instantiated in multiple locations over time (see e.g., Greenspahn 2014; Halpern 2021, 98-110; Guillaume 2021).

In Deuteronomy, *hammāqôm* is construed without any explicit reference to a particular city chosen to serve as a "container"; there is no "place" within a specifically named city that marks the city and makes it unique. This contrasts with the explicit and emphatic language of 1 Kgs 8:16, 44, 48; 11:13, 32, 36; 14:21; 2 Kgs 21:7; 23:27; 2 Chr 6:5-6, 34, 38; 7:12, 16; 12:13; 33:7, which directly associates Jerusalem with Yhwh's temple. In addition, although *hammāqôm* is obviously a cultic place, its architectural features are undefined. *Hammāqôm* may be imagined and was later understood in terms of a temple, but nothing in Deuteronomy requires it to be one; an open space sanctuary may also be imagined.

Moreover, it is also worth noting that there is only a single reference to the "house" or temple of Yhwh in the book (23:19), and it is unconnected to the supposedly "centralizing" texts or those referring to the festivals. In contrast, this expression appears often in the books of Kings, the prophetic collection, the psalms, and the books of Chronicles. The occurrence of the term "the house of Yhwh" in Exod 23:19; 34:26; Josh 6:24; Judg 19:18; 1 Sam 1:7, 24; 3:15; 2 Sam 12:20 means that its single use in Deuteronomy cannot be explained away by appealing to the setting of the world portrayed in the book in a time that preceded the building of the temple in Jerusalem. The verses mentioned above all use this term in the context of textual worlds that preceded Solomon's temple. Those who wrote, redacted, and edited the book of Deuteronomy could have used that term, especially in the context of centralization, but they chose not to. Those reading it within the same literati circles in which the book as such emerged would have been aware of this textually inscribed preference.

Within all the textually inscribed blurring that creates a potentially fluid image of *hammāqôm* in Deuteronomy, one thing is clear: conceptually, *hammāqôm*, whether a single place or a type of place that may be instantiated at multiple localities, is projected as a place outside the system of cities in which Israel dwells, as a necessary complement to it. This *hammāqôm* is defined by what happens there that cannot take place in any of the cities populated by Israel. At the same time, it evokes no clear geographical or architectural anchor in terms of the imagined landscape of the Israelite territory conjured by Deuteronomy. The lack of any reference to how *hammāqôm* looks or should look is consistent with the tendency to allow Samarians and Yehudites to read in their own ways. Mt. Gerizim and Jerusalem were very different sites. The projected "place" is not clearly anchored in space and in time, and activities that could be conducted only at *hammāqôm* are only loosely anchored in time (see, e.g., Deut 16:1–17).

Although in the landscape of the Israelite settlement evoked by Deuteronomy *hammāqôm* is certainly portrayed as physically existing in a geographical, spatial sense, its physical mark in the same landscape is fuzzy, unclear, and certainly not emphasized. The physicality of "the place" is additionally conveyed by explicit references to Israelites who live far away from it (see Deut 12:21; 14:24). However, if ancient readers of Deuteronomy had to draw among themselves a mental map of the land without recourse to their additional knowledge, they would have been unable to place *hammāqôm* anywhere on the map and would have been unable to draw any architectural feature associated with it that might serve as a signifier.

In their mental landscape, the majority non-*hammāqôm* space is structured in terms of cities. The latter are the regular places in which not only the imagined male "citizen" of Deuteronomy dwells but also all his dependants – sons, daughters, and [male and female] slaves),[5] as well as widows, levites, *gerim*, and fatherless individuals, i.e., the entire

---

5 It is well-known that wives are regularly unstated and implicitly subsumed under their husbands in these and similar lists in Deut (see, e.g., Deut 5:14 [cf. Exod 20:10]; 6:2; 12:12,18; 16:11, 14). The phrase "your wife" does not appear in Deut; "your women/wives" occurs twice in the book, once in a context of exclusion (Deut 3:19), where wives/women are to remain in the safe/protected space of cities, and once for inclusion (Deut 29:10), in a list of participants at the assembly to confirm the covenant being entered into. In both instances, the referent is more likely to be "your women" than "your wives." Linguistic choices about what goes stated or unstated shed important light in the ideological world of those writing and reading these texts on what was "invisible" to them, particularly in cases in which daughters and female slaves are not included by implication but

community (for parenting in Deut, see ch.12 in this volume). In fact, the expression "who is in your gates" is explicitly, textually marked as equivalent to "who is among you" (see Deut 16:11, 14), excluding the possibility of a significant "you" outside the cities (see also Deut 24:14). The same city-based landscape holds true in the world of Deuteronomy even before the Israelite conquest (Deut 1:28; 3:5; 6:10–11; 9:1; 28:52).

While the Israelite settlement does not affect the dominance of cities in the socio-political landscape, it does create a sense of a pan-Israelite polity that has no counterpart in the preceding period. The new polity requires the establishment of hammāqôm – discussed above – but also, and directly relevant to the life of the people in almost all places and times, an Israelitization of the cities. Such a process is not construed in physical terms. After all, the physical geography of the land remains unchanged after Israelite settlement. Nor is it marked by the presence of new types of buildings or by changes in the names of cities after the conquest, to mark them now as Israelite (for this process, see also ch.4 in this volume). The latter practice was common among kings claiming sovereignty over new territory. In Deuteronomy, very few cities are mentioned specifically by name; the focus, then, is on an array of occupied cities more generally.

Further, the text communicates that the physical location of a city and its environs make no difference worth mentioning or remembering because whether the city is large or small, in a valley or on a hill, it makes no difference in terms of how its entire population should behave. Within the book of Deuteronomy, the Israelite character of the cities is to be manifested in the behavior of the population and the rules governing such behavior, which are encoded in the book.

All the preceding observations are consistent with, reflect, and contribute to the shaping and communication of the conceptualization of Israel and its polity in the land within the world within Deuteronomy. Its Israel is certainly not construed as unified around a royal city, nor around a royal dynasty or even a temple. Instead, the city-organized polity and people are construed around a set of divine teachings associated with Moses, which include memories about past divine deliverances, Israel's failures, admonitions, prophetic announcements of justified punishment and exile, and announcements of return to the land by means of divine agency (for Moses in Deut, see ch.8 in this volume). Above all, rules about how to behave in the territory, which cover what we would understand as social, political, ritual, and economic areas, are included in the Mosaic teaching. The people and the polity are thus unified primarily around

are explicitly mentioned, while wives are not. For a general survey of women in Deut and bibliography, see Jacobs (2020).

Yhwh, the deity's teachings as communicated by Deuteronomy, and the figure of the remembered prophet, i.e., around Deuteronomy.

Imagining Israel unified around Yhwh and the god's divine teachings may go hand in hand with imagining a hierarchical landscape dominated by one central place (see e.g., Isa 2:2–4; Mic 4:1–5 and *passim* in prophetic literature, Kgs, Chr, Sir), whether controlled or not by a monarchic dynasty. Nevertheless, the fact that Deuteronomy creates a drastically different world is even more remarkable and raises substantial questions. Most of these questions require exploration in separate contributions, but one narrow group of issues can be further discussed here.

3. The Cities, the Israelite Polity, and Mental Landscapes

Whatever is contained in a house and the manner in which it is spatially displayed sheds light on the people who call it home. The same can be said of the contents and organization of a bookshelf and the like. Likewise, what is contained in the territory of a polity sheds light on its social and political structure. Thus, for instance, informed by the context of ancient Greece, Aristotle wrote:

> As to fortified positions, what is expedient is not the same for all forms of constitution; for example, a citadel-hill is suitable for oligarchy and monarchy and a level site for democracy; neither is favorable to an aristocracy but rather several strong positions. (Aristotle, *Politics* 7, 1330b)

Within an ancient Near Eastern context, to evoke a landscape of a relatively small polity dominated by a single city and its remarkable fortifications is likely to recall the image of a centralized or centralizing local kingdom. This is the case whether the power of the king and court is fully and effectively asserted over the land or not. Moreover, once the basic nature of the landscape is construed as marked by the presence of this royal city, the presence of secondary, fortified cities in the land would be seen as an attestation of the agency and control of the center.[6]

---

6 Cf. the reference to the forty-six fortified walled cities of Hezekiah conquered by Sennacherib according to various versions of that king's annals (e.g., Rassam Cylinder; Cylinder C=BM 022508; Taylor/Oriental Institute Prism [see Sennacherib 004, Sennacherib 15, and Sennacherib 022 at http://oracc.museum.upenn.edu/rinap/ corpus/]). They construe the image of a powerful Hezekiah, in order to enhance the achievements and military prowess Sennacherib, the king who defeated him. These and similar remarks in these royal texts served to rhetorically compensate for the lack of an account about the conquest of Jerusalem. The reliefs depicting the siege and capture of Lachish play a similar role.

What is true of country-landscapes holds true as well for city-landscapes. If the latter is dominated by the royal palace and the temple/s of the deity/ies that provide ideological support to the king and proclaim his rightful place as king of the land, then the landscape evokes the image of a polity with a king at its center. Such an imagined king is associated both directly or indirectly, via previous kings in the same dynasty, with the production of that city-landscape by (re)building and maintaining activities within the capital city particularly associated with its temple/s, fortifying and embellishing the city, bringing goods and honor to it, and the like. In these cases, a positive feedback loop is activated: the king's activities produce the landscape, and the latter communicates the grandeur of the king at the center of the polity. If the ruler is a High Priest, as in Sir 50, then the latter becomes a kingly figure, and such activities point to his grandeur and piety. But if so, what does the horizontal, non-hierarchical arrangement of an array of cities suggest in terms of the polity that Deuteronomy shapes, one without a real counterpart in any of the "historical" narratives of ancient Israel or the social memories that the latter evoked?

Due to my focus on memory and intellectual history, "ancient Israel" here refers to the Israel that first construed, remembered, and identified itself with an Israel that existed only in the world of knowledge and memory of the literati and which was centered around what they considered to be a divine torah encoded in a specific textual repertoire. This Israel, due to their cultural production, literary repertoire, social memory, and imagination, shaped the first Israel that shared some basic, conceptual resemblance with the variety of Israels that later appeared throughout history within Jewish, Christian, and Muslim circles. This ancient Israel could not have appeared in history before the Achaemenid period, due, inter alia, to the date of the Pentateuch. It also emerged in the form of two inter-related versions, one Samarian and one Jerusalem-centered (Ben Zvi 2012; 2019, passim. For the possible origin of Deut, see ch.16 in this volume).

Clearly, Deuteronomy shows a consistent tendency against constructing a clear-cut political center when it refers to cities and elsewhere. As Jeffrey Tigay (1996, 159) states, "By dispersing authority and prestige among various officials and limiting their powers, Deuteronomy seeks to prevent the development of a single, strong focus of prestige and power." Thus, although Deuteronomy refers to a human royal figure (Deut 17:14–20), even as it constructs it to a large extent as a reverse image of an ancient Near Eastern king, it does not construe a royal "place" within the human/social geography it projects. There is no capital city, royal palace, or royally supported temple. None of the usual buildings that characterize the center of power within a polity, be it a monarchy or not, are present.

The "king" conjured by Deuteronomy exists, but no special space is allocated to him, and he has no impact on the imagined lay of the land or in the landscape of the polity. He is not the usual hero king who expands territory; he is absent from the rules for conducting war in Deut 20, which is consistent with the trend to avoid constructions of solidified, centralized power. The same holds true, for instance, for the priest in charge of pan-Israelite judgment in Deut 17:12, where the text never states he occupies a permanent position, or the priests/judges in Deut 17:8–13. Their judgment, their torah is at the center. No physical building, clear-cut location, or anything that might impact on the mental map of the Israelite polity is mentioned, as though any of these might detract from the centrality of what these figures may teach Israel, according to Deuteronomy.

From a conceptual viewpoint, this approach is fully consistent with a position according to which physical buildings, including temples and palaces, and political structures are essentially impermanent. They can easily be overturned by an enemy, unlike torah, provided its teachers and texts continue from generation to generation. Only polities that exist in texts written on fragile material (like Deuteronomy) and in the minds of those reading them are impervious to the vicissitudes of history. Although this would have been obvious to the literati living among the ruins in Jerusalem, Samarian literati also would have understood the point very well. In the ideal world of Deuteronomy, the main transgenerational teachers of torah, i.e., the permanent successors of Moses, are not a particular group in most circumstances but the Israelite male addressed directly in the book as "you" (masculine singular), who resides each in his own city.

The tendency to place a book (Deut) at the center shapes and reflects a mindscape in which land and territory are important and in in which physical "spaces" become special "places," but one in which no political center is allowed to be prominent.[7] The result is a horizontal, decentralized landscape, but matters go both ways. A horizontal decentralized landscape communicates a polity that lacks any substantial political

---

7 It is worth stressing that this strong tendency is present even in seemingly unexpected contexts. For instance, the book evokes among its readers scenarios in which drastic actions have to be taken against a city. Such actions would require effective leadership that goes beyond the level of the single city. One might have expected a reference to some form of prominent pan-Israelite authority; instead, the agents who bear the responsibility to take action are simply referred to by the generic (2ms) "you," i.e., the male Israelite who is the addressee in the book. See Deut 13:13–18. No explicit leadership or leadership structures are mentioned.

center and its usual physical manifestations, which is partially consistent with a historical context of living in provinces (Samaria and Yehud) within an empire, with little self-determination. Further, the leadership roles of town elders and local judges (Rofé 2001; Willis 2001; Tigay 2011; Berge 2021, 89–91) in every city, with no specification of any central institution making the appointments, suggests that each of the local centers is organized in terms consistent with a local aristocratic oligarchy, as opposed to monarchy, democracy, or a centralized theocracy. The seemingly oligarchic organization evokes particular features that characterize these cities, and vice versa; cities that contain these features project an implied polity in which a local aristocratic oligarchy holds positions of leadership.

The divine instruction communicated by Deuteronomy is presented as normative, but neither as a practical constitution for Israel nor as a reflection of how the monarchic polities of Israel and Judah worked in reality or even how they were remembered to work. Reading Deuteronomy meant imagining and constructing a utopian world, but one easily accessible to those immersed in the discursive world shared by the literati (Ben Zvi forth.; cf. Berge 2016, 190–95; chs.11 and 13 in this volume).

In sum, in ordinary times and spaces, the entire Israelite settlement is imagined in Deuteronomy to function as a horizontal array of autonomous cities; the social-political landscape evoked by the book provides the readers with the most suitable mental landscape. There are particular marked times and places that bring the various cities together, creating social cohesion among inter-city/all Israel that also constitutes the latter as a people around Deuteronomy and the practices and ideology that it communicates. From a systemic, socio-anthropological perspective, the existence of such marked times and places is a basic requirement to unite an array of autonomous cities into a single, social entity. However, the existence of such a unified entity does not require the mentioned horizontally arrayed autonomous cities; plenty of polities were imagined as a centralized unit held together by a king.

4. Imagining the Cities in Deuteronomy

Since the entire Israelite settlement is envisioned to function as a horizontal array of autonomous cities, and since cities are partially construed in terms of containers, it is not surprising that these cities would be imagined containing some unmarked and unremarkable physical structures or places associated with local leadership. Given the emphasis on living in a community governed by and set around the divine instruction (commandment) encoded in Deuteronomy, the most obvious candidate for such a place is the city gate (e.g., Walsh 2014). There is nothing unusual in conceiving the city gate as, e.g., a place for public legal resolution (e.g., Deut 21:19; 22:15). But what is surely out of the ordinary is the repeated, non-standard, rhetorical use of the term "your gates" while clearly referring to "your cities." This is a metaphor or a case of a metonymical reference. But metaphors are not "just" metaphors, and linguistic, metonymical choices are never meaningless; they shape concepts efficiently. What is the pragmatic role of this rare and repeatedly attested linguistic choice in Deuteronomy?

First, gates are integral parts of walls. A city characterized by and referred to by its gates evokes the image of a walled city. The depicted landscape is not just one of a non-hierarchical array of cities but of walled, fortified cities (Deut 1:18; 3:5; 9:1; 28:52). References to walls and gates communicate that the city is protected. Walls and gates "naturally" evoke protection against besieging armies. But, in the world of Deuteronomy, the threat of foreign troops is, at best, a secondary motif. So why are gates (and implicitly walled cities) so ubiquitous in the world of the book? What purpose do they serve?

Gates and walls also demarcate boundaries. As such, they play an important role in the conceptualization of the city as a container, which, by definition, must call forth an image of enclosure (Vermeulen 2020, 167–69). For obvious reasons, gates rather than walls are usually associated with openings. Gates are liminal places for flowing into or out of the inner place and permeable spaces for bringing goods and the like in or sending them out. But gates may also be imagined as marking and enclosing spaces in which internal disputes among members of the in-group are publicly discussed and resolved. Gates may evoke permeability, but also impermeability.

Given the general trends in Deuteronomy and its focus on governing the life of the Israelites in their cities, in ordinary times and places, it is not surprising that gates in the world portrayed in this book are associated primarily with an image of maintaining inner social containment. Images of the inner social group crossing the gates tend to be associated with going to normative places at normative times, including *hammāqôm*. Not only does the group explicitly exit the city for socially contained places; it remains closely associated with its "gates" and the inner world of the latter. Within an ideological, conceptual world in which being in "your land" goes explicitly and markedly with "being in your cities" (Deut 24:14), and being in "your cities" is explicitly, textually marked as equivalent to "being among you" (Deut 16:11, 14), being outside "your gates" is (metaphorically) impossible for any proper member of the in-group.

In addition, gates are the places explicitly associated with forced, social elimination of members of the in-group who defy established norms

(Deut 17:2-5; 21:18-21; 22:23-24). In Deuteronomy, the term "gates" does not evoke images of permeability. It is not a place to meet foreigners or residents of other cities, conduct trade, or the like. Within the implied conceptual map of Deuteronomy, gates primarily communicate enclosure and social containment. They and the implied walls in which they are set are associated with boundaries, both physical and ideological, which are construed as rooted in the divine instructions of Deuteronomy, the main centralizing text that stands at the center of the life of each city and of the territory encompassed by them, i.e., "the land."

In the world of Deuteronomy, the main danger for the Israelites in the land is never a foreign army invading the country or laying siege to the cities; instead, it is the possibility that Israel will abandon Yhwh's ways as encoded in the book. In fact, the book, Moses, Yhwh, and the readers of the book are all aware that this possibility will be actualized with tragic consequences for the people (Deut 28:15-68; 29:13-27; 30:1-5, 17-19; 31:19-22; 32:19-25; Ben Zvi 2019, 221-23). Since gates are presented time and again as providing protection by shaping local enclosures, it seems there is little reason for an abundance of explicit rhetorical references to walls in the text.

That said, walls are explicitly mentioned in Deut 28:52. That text recalls Deut 9:1, which refers to the pre-Israelite settlement cities (see also Deut 1:28; 3:5). In all four passages, the point is that high and fortified walls, even if they reach up to the heavens, do not provide protection against Yhwh, who can seize any city. The Israelite cities are fortified, and even in that sense, they and the landscape they shape resembles the situation prior to the anticipated settlement. Within this discourse, both are and cannot but be imagined as great cities, and great cities cannot but be imagined as heavily fortified. In this respect, the discourse invokes well known ancient Near Eastern literary and ideological motifs. In royal Assyrian texts, for example, enemies boast of protection from fortifications, difficult-to-cross rivers, and impassable mountains, but to no avail. Assur and the Assyrian king, his deputy, defeat them, contributing to the heroic characterization of both the king and the deity.

Deuteronomy communicates that walls do not provide Canaanites hoped-for protection against Yhwh; nor will they protect their successors, the Israelites who will inhabit these fortified cities, either. Protection follows from observing Yhwh's instructions. For such a message, gates working as social enclosures are far more worthy of mention and remembrance, as is an entire country whose population is horizontally organized around them (and thus, fortified cities) and around Deuteronomy, as opposed to any central authority.

5. The Landscape and Polity of Deuteronomy in Other Past-Shaping Texts and Implications about the World of Deuteronomy

Neither the imaginary landscape of the Israelite polity nor the polity itself evoked by Deuteronomy are consistent with those conjured by any of the historiographic works in Yehud. To resolve this dilemma, readers of Deuteronomy would have had two basic options. Either they would have to assume that neither of the conflicting portrayals reflected past reality as far as they were aware, or they would have to try to conform Deuteronomy to other past-shaping, ideological texts in their core repertoire and social memory in some complementary and balancing way.

The latter approach is well attested. *Hammāqôm* undoubtedly was understood and reconfigured to refer to Jerusalem and its temple in the minds of Judean literati who read Deuteronomy in a way strongly informed by the books of Kings or Chronicles. Such an approach led to the construction of a hierarchical, centralized, and centralizing system of cities with Jerusalem at its center, overwriting the one in Deuteronomy per se. Was this reading so dominant among these literati that the voice of Deuteronomy by itself was never heard, or did there exist a creative, generative tension between these two readings, facilitated by a world of social memory in which Jerusalem becomes *hammāqôm* for Israel only from David's days? |If the latter, the situation would have shaped a playground for safely exploring multiple readings and their potential ideological implications and relevance when thinking about the future polity of Israel, as expressed both in the historical and prophetic book collections (Ben Zvi 2019, passim).

In any event, the image of an array of fortified cities populating the country does not necessarily stand in tension with that evoked in the historical books, even if gates are nowhere near as emphasized as in Deuteronomy. But the books of Kings and even more Chronicles construe not only a past territory of fortified cities, but one in which kings fortified cities, and thus one in which their presence points to royal achievements. Moreover, Chronicles, in particular, tends to associate this type of building activity with divine blessing. Although the book strongly conveys the idea that city fortifications and army-building per se have no actual protective role, like Deuteronomy, the very act of establishing them serves as an indication of the piety of the king and of Yhwh's blessing at the time in which the king is undertaking the relevant endeavors. Thus, engaging with fortified cities brings to mind the matter of the king.

In the books of Kings and Chronicles, the king, both the office and the persona, plays a central role. Both books portray a centralized and centralizing, hierarchical polity at whose center stood the king and his officers. However, the extent to which the monarchic center in the kingdom of Judah exerted power over local groups is an open question (see e.g., Maier and Shai 2016; for the same issue in early Mesopotamia, see e.g., Richardson 2017) that stands in direct tension with the authoritative Israelite world evoked by Deuteronomy. Both the landscape conjured by Deuteronomy and the related polity shape an image and a memory of a world in which a "normal" king has no place. Yet, the book also blocks the option of assigning all of the above to a pre-monarchic past, because Deuteronomy's world explicitly contains a king, even if he lacks all the usual attributes and powers.

Deuteronomy, thus, shapes a polity and a related landscape of memory that cannot fit well in any possible period of the remembered past. Instead, it serves as a mental blueprint for what the Israelite settlement should be and should have been. But Deuteronomy was never an island; it existed as part and parcel of a textual eco-system that included the past-shaping historiographical books mentioned above. Memories from a Yehudite perspective of what should have been and partially was here and there informed those about what the past "was" and *vice versa*. They raised questions about what the future might be in a community organized around divine instruction. Moreover, all this takes place within an ideological discourse in which the people are also, even if partially, conceptualized in royal terms, which by necessity meant some reconfiguration of the concept of kingship. Of equal import, it occurs within a context in which the torah-student "king" of Deuteronomy becomes a type of the literati's ideal people whom they instruct as they continue the teaching role of Moses in their own generation (e.g., Ben Zvi 2016; Markl 2018; Ben Zvi 2019, passim) in a territory in which Israelite fortified cities do not (yet?) populate the land.

Works Cited

Ben Zvi, Ehud. 2012. "How 'Historical" is Ancient Israel?" Pages 25–34 in *The Wiley-Blackwell History of Jews and Judaism*. Edited by Alan T. Levenson. Malden, MA: Wiley-Blackwell.

——. 2016. "Memory and Political Thought in the Late Persian/Early Hellenistic Yehud/Judah: Some Observations." Pages 9–26 in *Leadership, Social Memory and Judean Discourse in the 5th–2nd Centuries BCE*. Edited by Diana V. Edelman and Ehud Ben Zvi. London: Equinox Publishing Ltd.

——. 2019. *Social Memory among the Literati of Yehud*. Beihefte zur Zeitschrift für die alttestamentaliche Wissenschaft 509, Forschungen zum Alten Testament 128. Berlin: De Gruyter.

———. forth. "Deuteronomy and Utopia: Reading, Imagination, and Memory among Yehudite Literati."

Berge, Kåre. 2016. "Are There Centres and Peripheries in Deuteronomy?" Pages 181–95 in *Centres and Peripheries in the Early Second Temple Period*. Edited by Ehud Ben Zvi and Christoph Levin. Forschungen zum Alten Testament 108.Tübingen: Mohr-Siebeck.

———. 2021. "Cities in Deuteronomy: Imperial Ideology, Resilience, and the Imagination of Yahwistic Religion." Pages 77–96 in *Deuteronomy in the Making: Studies in the Production of* Debarim. Edited by Diana Edelman, Benedetta Rossi, Kåre Berge, and Philippe Guillaume. Beihefte zur Zeitschrift für die alttestamentaliche Wissenschaft 533. Berlin: De Gruyter.

Frese, Daniel A. 2015. "A Land of Gates: Covenant Communities in the Book of Deuteronomy." *Vetus Testamentum* 65: 33–52.

Greenspahn, Fred E. 2014. "Deuteronomy and Centralization." *Vetus Testamentum* 64: 227–35.

Guillaume, Philippe. 2021. "Deuteronomy's *Māqôm* before Deuteronomy." Pages 195–217 in *Deuteronomy in the Making: Studies in the Production of* Debarim. Edited by Diana Edelman, Benedetta Rossi, Kåre Berge, and Philippe Guillaume. BZAW 533. Berlin: De Gruyter.

Halpern, Baruch. 2021. "What does Deuteronomy Centralize?" Pages 97–162 in *Deuteronomy in the Making: Studies in the Production of* Debarim. Edited by Diana Edelman, Benedetta Rossi, Kåre Berge, and Philippe Guillaume. Beihefte zur Zeitschrift für die alttestamentaliche Wissenschaft 533. Berlin: De Gruyter.

Jacobs, Sandra. 2020. "Women in Deuteronomy." 24 pages in The Oxford Handbook of Deuteronomy. Edited by Don C. Benjamin. https://doi.org/10.1093/oxfordhb/9780190273552.013.13.

Knoppers, Gary N. 2012. "The Relationship of the Deuteronomistic History to Chronicles: Was the Chronicler a Deuteronomist?" Pages 307–41 in *Congress Volume Helsinki 2010*. Edited by Martti Nissenen. Supplements to Vetus Testamentum 148. Leiden: Brill.

Maeir, Aren M. and Itzhaq Shai. 2016. "Reassessing the Character of the Judahite Kingdom: Archaeological Evidence for Non-Centralized, Kinship-Based Components." Pages 323–40 in *From Sha'ar Hagolan to Shaaraim: Essays in Honor of Prof. Yosef Garfinkel*. Edited by Saar Ganor, Igor Kreimerman, Katharina Streit, and Madeleine Mumcuogluet. Jerusalem: Israel Exploration Society.

Markl, Dominik. 2018. "Deuteronomy's 'Anti King': Historicized Etiology or Political Project?" Pages 165–86 in A (eds.) *Changing Faces of Kingship in Syria-Palestine 1500-500 BCE*. Edited by Agustinus Gianto and Peter Dubovský. Alter Orient und Altes Testament 459. Münster: Ugarit Verlag.

Marlow, Hilary F. 2018. "'A Land with Fine Large Cities': Mapping the Landscapes of Deuteronomy." Pages 73–88 in *The City in the Hebrew Bible: Critical, Literary and Exegetical Approaches*. Edited by James K. Aitken and Hilary F. Marlow. The Library of Hebrew Bible/Old Testament Studies 672. London: T&T Clark.

Nisbett, Richard E. and Takahito Masuda. 2003. "Culture and Point of View." *Proceedings of the National Academy of Sciences* 100.9: 11,163–70; https://doi.org/10.1073/pnas.1934527100.

Richardson, Seth. 2017. "Before Things Worked: A 'Low- Power' Model of Early Mesopotamia." Pages in 17–62 in *Ancient States and Infrastructural Power: Europe, Asia, and America*. Edited by Clifford Ando and Seth Richardson. Philadelphia: University of Pennsylvania Press.

Rofé, Alexander. 2001. "The Organization of the Judiciary in Deuteronomy (Deut. 16,18-20; 17,8-13; 19,15; 21,22-23; 24,16)." Pages 92–112 in *The World of the Aramaeans: Biblical Studies in Honour of Paul-Eugène Dion*, Vol. 1. Edited by P. M. Michèle Daviau, John W. Wevers, and Michael Weigl. Journal for the Study of the Old Testament Supplement Series 324. Sheffield: Sheffield Academic Press.

Tigay, Jeffrey H. 1996. *Deuteronomy*. Philadelphia: Jewish Publication Society.

------. 2011. "The Role of the Elders in the Laws of Deuteronomy." Pages 89–96 in *A Common Cultural Heritage: Studies on Mesopotamia and the Biblical World in Honor of Barry L. Eichler*. Edited by Grant Frame, Erle Leichty, Karen Sonik, Jeffrey H. Tigay, and Steve Tinney. Bethesda, MD: CDL.

Van Leeuwen, Raymond C. 2010. "Cosmos, Temple, House: Building and Wisdom in Ancient Mesopotamia and Israel." Pages 399–421 in *From the Foundations to the Crenellations: Essays on Temple Building in the Ancient Near East and Hebrew Bible*. Edited by Mark J. Boda and Jamie Novotny. Alter Orient und Altes Testament 366. Münster: Ugarit-Verlag.

Vermeulen, Karolien. 2020. *Conceptualizing Biblical Cities: A Stylistic Study*. Cham, Switzerland: Palgrave Macmillan.

Walsh, Carey. 2014. "Testing Entry: The Social Functions of City Gates in Biblical Memory." Pages 43–59 in *Memory and the City in Ancient Israel*. Edited by Diana V. Edelman and Ehud Ben Zvi. Winona Lake, IN: Eisenbrauns.

Willis, Timothy M. 2001. *The Elders of the City: A Study of the Elders-Laws in Deuteronomy*. Society of Biblical Literature Monograph Series 55. Atlanta: SBL.

Zerubavel, Eviatar. 2018. *Taken for Granted: The Remarkable Power of the Unremarkable*. Princeton: Princeton University Press.

About the Author

Ehud Ben Zvi is a professor (emeritus) in the Department of History, Classics, and Religion at the University of Alberta in Edmonton, Alberta, Canada. He has published extensively on ancient Israel, its intellectual history, social memory, historiography, and prophetic books. He explores how ancient Israelites construed their past and future and the significance of these images of the past and future for them. His recent work has focused, though not exclusively, on matters of Social Memory in late Persian/early Hellenistic Israel.

Author Index

Achenbach, Reinhard 124, 492
Ackerman, Susan 24, 217, 226
Aspesi, Francesco 294
Ahlström, G. W. 106, 126
Ahmed, Sara 312
Al-Rawi, Farouk N. H. 260
Albertz, Rainer 219
Allen, Spencer L. 14
Albright, William F. 232
Alt, Albrecht 47, 76, 412
Altman, Amnon 40, 41, 43
Altmann, Peter 236
Amit, Yairah 118, 219
Amzallag, Nissim 491
Anbar, Moshe 119, 120
Anderson, Benedict 139–140
Anderson, Gary A. 168
Anderson, James S. 217
Arie, Eran 409
Arnold, Bill T. 24, 37, 116, 193, 225, 260, 320, 321, 409
Arubas, Benjamin 11
Ashcroft, Bill 356, 360, 361
Assmann, Jan 158
Athanassiou, Homer 7
Atkinson, Kenneth 477
Aurelius, Erik 124, 148, 247

Baccolini, Raffaella 356
Baltzer, Klaus 262
Barbiero, Gianni 445, 446
Barcina, Cristina 4
Barmash, Pamela 102, 103, 344, 345
Barth, Fredrik 136, 137
Barton, John 364, 436
Bartor, Assnat 49, 75, 76
Basello, Giampiero 293, 295
Batto, Bernard F. 106
Bauer, Leonard 338
Bauman, Zygmunt 361
Beaulieu, Paul-Alain 362

Becker, Gary S. 169
Becker, Joachim 446, 454
Becker, Uwe 124
Beckman, Gary 43
Bellefontaine, Elizabeth 349
Ben Zvi, Ehud 37, 99, 327, 336, 410, 416, 419, 509, 510, 511
Bennett, Harold V. 175
Berge, Kåre 56, 99, 157, 158, 161, 291, 312, 321, 322, 336, 355, 360, 507
Berges, Ulrich 476
Berlejung, Angelika 11, 280
Berlinerblau, Jacques 136
Berman, Joshua A. 18, 19, 82, 364
Berquist, Jon L. 155
Berry, George Ricker 421
Beukenhorst, Martijn 330
Bidmead, Julye 336
Binger, Tilde 217
Blenkinsopp, Joseph 148, 221, 222, 278
Bloch-Smith, Elizabeth 134, 136, 137, 153, 220
Blum, Erhard 119, 122, 123, 254, 259, 408
Boer, Roland 170, 186, 188, 360
Borger, Riekele 12, 253
Borowski, Oded 97
Boston, James R. 50
Bottéro, Jean 79, 80–82
Bourdieu, Pierre 152, 162, 192, 197
Braulik, Georg 250, 278, 437, 438, 439, 440–458, 460, 461, 464–467
Brekelmans, Christianus 38
Brettler, Marc 119, 123
Briant, Pierre 55, 237
Brichto, Herbert Chanan 345
Brooke, George J. 493
Broshi, Magen 411
Brubaker, Rogers 161
Brumlik, Micha 439
Burke, Aaron 411

Burnett, Joel S.   212, 220, 223
Burney, Charles Fox   410
Butler, Judith   312

Cardascia, Guillaume   336, 344
Carmichael, Calum M.   47, 48, 50
Carr, David M.   247, 255, 256, 259, 260, 265
Case, M. L.   336
Casey, Edward S.   99, 101, 102
Cassin, Elena   342
Cavigneaux, Antoine   260
Chapman, Cynthia R.   338, 342
Charpin, Dominique   81, 82, 173, 189
Chavel, Simeon   224
Choi, John H.   478,
Cimino, Anna Maria   289
Clements, Ronald E.   102,
Clermont-Ganneau, Charles   322
Coats, George W.   247, 340
Cogan, Morton   6
Cohen, Abner   56, 155, 157, 158
Cohen, Yoram   50, 257, 259
Cohn, Yehudah B.   224
Coin-Longeray, Sandrine   174
Coleman, Simon   236
Collins, John J.   279, 280, 355, 489
Connor, Walker   135
Cook, Stephen L.   220
Cooper, Alan   338
Cornell, Collin   237
Crane, Eva   97
Crawford, Sidnie White   392–394, 399, 401
Crenshaw, James L.   50
Cresswell, Tim   101
Cribiore, Raffaella   256
Cross, Frank Moore, Jr   53
Crouch, Carly L.   15, 18, 83, 362, 384
Crüsemann, Frank   154, 155, 278, 435, 441
Csabai, Zoltán   178

Dandamaev, Muhammad A.   292
Darby, Erin   217
Davies, Eryl W.   341, 345
Davies, Philip R.   57, 63, 84, 97, 137–139, 151, 270, 327, 361, 412, 413
Dawson, Doyne   363, 364
De Pury, Albert   248, 408
de Vaux, Roland   47, 49, 50, 52
De Wette, Wilhelm. M. L.   360, 413
Deist, Ferdinand E.   363

Déjacque, Joseph   363
Delaney, Carol   338
Démare-Lafont, Sophie   80
Destrée, Pierre   359
Dever, William G.   217
Diamond, Bernard L.   349
Dion, Paul E.   16, 19, 347
Dohmen, Christoph   442
Donner, Herbert   53
Doron, Pinchas   49
Dorsey, David A.   114
Dozeman, Thomas
Driver, Samuel Rolles   22, 126, 266
Durand, Jean-Marie   3, 36, 42
Dušek, Jan   425

Ebach, Ruth   313, 457, 462
Edelman, Diana V.   39, 40, 42, 43, 48, 55, 62, 75, 76, 83, 107, 112, 134, 137, 151, 153, 216, 218, 219, 220, 222, 223, 230, 248, 250, 254, 260, 261, 331, 359, 360, 407, 409, 415–417, 420, 422–425, 479, 482
Edenburg, Cynthia   44, 77, 84–88, 120, 122, 126, 310, 344, 347, 361, 409
Ego, Beate   305, 316
Eichler, Barry L.   81
Eilers, Wilhelm   79
Elsner, John   236
Eph'al-Jaruzelska, Izabela   3, 7
Eriksen, Thomas Hylland   136,
Erman, Adolf   257, 258
Evans-Grubbs, Judith   346

Filippone, Ela   293, 295
Finkel, Irving   414
Finkelstein, Israel   58–60, 153, 408, 411
Finkelstein, J. J.   81
Finsterbusch, Karin
Fischer, Georg   247
Fishbane, Michael   116
Fitzmyer, Joseph A.   3, 42,
Fitzpatrick-McKinley, Anne   80–83
Fleishman, Joseph   346
Fleming, Daniel   60, 80, 153
Fletcher, Alexandra   414
Flint, Peter W.   480
Flynn, Shawn   220
Foxhall, Lin   197
François, Mark S.   14, 15
Frankena, Rintja   10, 13, 14, 25
Frankfurter, David   236
Fleming, Daniel   60, 80, 153

Author Index

French, Valerie 336
Frese, Daniel A. 499
Frei, Peter 292
Frevel, Christian 62, 217
Fried, Lisbeth 81, 82
Friedl, Johanna 434, 461, 462, 463
Frymer-Kensky, Tikva 76, 342, 347

Gadot, Yuval 11
Gall, A. Freiherr von 110
Gamoran, Hillel 181
Gardiner, Alan 257
Garmann, Sebastian 137, 139
Geiger, Michaela 447
Gelb, Ignace J. 414
Geller, Stephen A. 50
Gemser, Berend 49, 76
George, Andrew R. 172
Gesche, Petra D. 255–257, 260–265, 269
Giblin, Charles H. 120
Giesecke, Annette Lucia 355
Giuntoli, Federico 297
Glanville, Mark R. 460, 461, 465
Goeman, Peter 328
Gomes de Araújo, Reginaldo 448
Goodwin, Barbara 360, 363, 364
Gosse, Bernard 415, 479, 483
Grabbe, Lester. L. 411
Gramberg, Carl Peter Wilhelm 417
Grant, Jamie A. 476, 488
Greenfeld, Uzi
Greenfield, Jonas C. 293
Greengus, Samuel 78, 79
Greenspahn, Fred E. 501
Grosby, Steven E. 137, 148, 154
Guibernau, Montserrat 136
Guillaume, Philippe 99, 102, 139, 186, 229, 323, 482, 488, 412, 491, 501
Guillory, John 158

Hadley, Judith M. 217
Hagedorn, Anselm C. 21, 22, 348, 355, 364
Hagen, Fredrik 257, 258, 264
Hall, Jonathan M. 139, 142, 153
Hallo, William W. 40, 41
Hallock, Richard T. 141
Halpern, Baruch 74, 212, 228, 413, 482, 501
Hansen, Mogens H. 142
Haque, Ziaul 187
Hardmeier, Christof 24,
Harvey, Paul B., Jr 74, 413

Hays, Christopher B. 220
Heckl, Raik 248, 250
Henkelman, Wouter F. M. 140, 141
Hensel, Benedikt 408
Herrenschmidt, Clarisse 55
Hiecke, Thomas 270
Hillers, Delbert R. 12, 24, 212
Hogan, Karina M. 305
Hoglund, Kenneth 417
Hölscher, Gustav 321, 322, 355, 418
Hölscher, Lucian 356
Horowitz, Wayne 85, 259,
Horst, Louis 321
Hrůša, Ivan 261
Huddlestun, John R. 106
Hulster, Izaak J. de 216
Hundley, Michael B. 230
Hunger, Hermann 248, 253, 257, 261, 262, 264, 265, 269
Hutchinson, John 136
Hutton, Jeremy 15, 211
Huyse, Philip 293
Hyatt, J. P. 110
Hylen, Susan E. 344

Irsigler, Hubert 442, 464

Jackson, Bernard S. 83
Jackson Lears, Thomas J. 289
Jacobs, Bruno 293
Jacobs, Sandra 343, 457
James, Paul W. 139
Jameson, Fredric 321, 356
Jefferess, David 415
Joas, Hans 440
Jones, Henry Stuart 174
Jones, Scott C. 305
Jonker, Gerdien 263, 345
Jursa, Michael 170, 322

Kara-Ivanov Kaniel, Ruth 493
Kartveit, Magnar 395, 400, 425
Kawashima, Robert. S. 85
Keel, Othmar 216
Kennett, R. H. 417
Kessler, John 56
Kessler, Rainer 436–439, 461, 463, 466
Kiel, Yishai 292
Kilchör, Benjamin 444
Killebrew, Ann E. 153, 155
Kinnier Wilson, J. V. 8
Kitchen, Kenneth A. 21
Kletter, Raz 153, 217

Kline, Meredith G.   360
Knauf, Ernest Axel   125, 126, 477, 488
Knoppers, Gary N.   229, 313, 390, 499
Knox, Paul L.   100, 101
Koch, Christoph   13, 16, 18, 19, 441
Koopmans, William T.   120
Korošec, Viktor   43
Kratz, Reinhard G.   124, 145, 247, 358
Kraus, F. R.   79–81
Krause, Joachim J.   122–124
Kugel, James L.   316
Kumar, Krisham   355
Kutsch, Ernst   47, 50

L'Hour, Jean   439, 440, 445, 451
Lafont, Sophie, see Démare-Lafont
Lambert, Thomas E.   171, 179
Lambert, Wilfred G.   160
Lanfranchi, Giovanni B.   4–6
Landsberger, Benno   79
Lang, Bernhard   25
Lauinger, Jacob   2–7, 23, 36, 41, 42, 46
Launderville, Dale   158
Lawrence, Paul J. N.   21
Lebel, Efi   63, 416, 422
LeFebvre, Michael   83, 84
Leichty, Erle   3
Lemaire, André   229, 237, 259, 423
Lemos, Tracy M.   343
Leoussi, Athena S.   137
Levin, Christoph   47, 172, 177, 321, 323, 331
Levinson, Bernard M.   10, 13, 16, 18, 21–23, 25, 74, 77, 261, 279, 280, 283, 355, 358, 359, 361, 364, 381, 384, 415, 488
Levitas, Ruth   356, 359
Levtow, Nathaniel B.   420
Lewis, Theodore J.   52, 53, 220
Liddell, Henry Georges   174
Lincoln, Bruce   55, 293–295
Lindars, Barnabas   50, 278
Lipiński, Eduard   7
Lipschits, Oded   11
Liss, Hannah   363
Liverani, Mario   6
Lohfink, Norbert   174, 250, 279, 324, 355, 359, 361, 364, 438, 440–443, 445–447, 450, 451, 454–458, 460, 463, 464
Lohr, Joel N.   465
London, Gloria   338
Lozinskyy, Hryhoriy   280
Lukonin, Vladimir G.   292

Lundbom, Jack   251, 252, 262, 266, 376
Lyotard, Jean-François   372

Mace, David R.   340
Machinist, Peter   142, 362
Mackil, Emily   142
MacDonald, Nathan   215, 360, 465
Magen, Yitzhak   390, 409, 423, 424
Mäkipelto, Ville   119, 120, 122, 124, 126
Maier, Aren   511
Malfroy, Jean   50
Malul, Meir   81
Mannheim, Karl   321, 322
Marcus, David   348
Margulis, B.   297
Markl, Dominik   63, 139, 145, 155, 250, 254, 279, 290, 305, 363, 437–439, 442, 443, 453, 459, 489, 511
Marks, Peter   356
Marlow, Hilary F.   499
Marston, Sallie A.   100, 101
Marx, Alfred   459
Masuda, Takahito   498
Mathias, Steffan   340, 341
Mattison, Kevin   381
Mayes, Andrew D. H.   22, 126, 221, 228
McBride, S. Dean, Jr.   154, 359, 360, 364
McCann, J. Clinton   481
McCarthy, Carmel   282, 394
McCarthy, Dennis J.   24, 39, 263, 441
McConville, J. Gordon   328, 361
McCorriston, Joy   236, 237
McKay, J. W.   24
McKeating, Henry   88
Mettinger, Tryggve N. D.   219, 406
Meyers, Carol   219
Milgrom, Jacob   96, 282
Millar, J. Gary   435
Miller, Geoffrey P.   364
Miller, James C.   135
Miller, Jared   44, 45
Miller, Patrick D.   126, 359, 360, 363
Misgav, Haggai   424
Milstein, Sara J.   48, 80, 84, 85, 87, 88, 198, 255, 259, 260, 340, 466
Minette de Tillesse, Georges   228
Mitchell, David C.   478, 479, 490, 491, 493
Mohawk, John C.   363
Moran, William L.   24
More, Thomas   355
Moreno García, Juan Carlos   175
Morrow, William B.   11, 20, 25, 36, 38, 48, 55, 76, 83, 415

Mousourakis, George 79
Moylan, Tom 356
Murphy, Roland E. 50, 306

Na'aman, Nadav 9, 57–59, 114, 117, 122, 211, 408, 411, 412
Nadan, Amos 187
Naddaf, Gerard 316
Najman, Hindi 493
Nash, Alan E. 100, 101
Nasuti, Harry P. 76
Nelson, Richard D. 123, 385
Nestor, Dermot Anthony 136
Nicholson, Ernest W. 125, 154–156, 160, 228, 361, 406, 409, 413, 419–421
Niehr, Herbert 216, 220
Nielsen, Eduard 114, 115, 119, 122, 252, 266, 267, 408, 409
Niemann, Hermann Michael 61, 62
Nihan, Christophe 117, 119, 122, 124, 270, 409
Nilsen, Tina D. 159
Nisbett, Richard E. 498
Nissinen, Martti 52
Noichl, Franz 459
Noth, Martin 122, 226, 360, 404, 419
Novotny, Jamie 3
Nutkowicz, Hélène 220

O'Dowd, Ryan 50
Ochshorn, Judith 201, 346
Oeming, Manfred 11, 20, 23
Oestreicher, Theodor 228
Olivier, Johannes P. J. 172, 322
Opsomer, Jan 359
Osborne, James F. 220
Oshima, Takayoshi 85
Oswald, Wolfgang 51, 313
Otto, Eckart 16, 22, 24–26, 36, 52, 74, 81–84, 86–88, 124, 159, 160, 198, 247, 248, 250–254, 263, 266, 267, 279, 282–287, 297, 298, 306, 321, 330, 337, 347, 348, 361, 415, 419, 436, 441
Oyen, Hendrik van 439

Paganini, Simone 284, 328, 336, 346
Pakkala, Juha 18, 74, 83, 360, 418
Parpola, Simo 3, 5, 8, 13–17, 22, 36, 41, 45, 46, 52
Patrick, Dale 83
Paul, Shalom M. 48, 49, 76
Pearce, Laurie 11, 142, 179, 183, 186, 280, 296

Peel, J. D. Y. 413
Perdue, Leo. G. 306
Perlitt, Lothar 110, 122, 248, 445, 462
Person, Raymond F. Jr 311
Pessoa da Silva Pinto, Leonardo 214
Philips, Anthony 126
Pickstock, Catherine 311
Pietersen, Christo 342
Pina-Cabral, Joao de 348
Pinheiro, Marília P. Futre 357
Pirie, Fernanda 82
Pirngruber, Reinhard 175, 292
Polanyi, Karl 175
Pongratz-Leisten, Beate 4
Popović, Mladen 122
Porten, Bezalel 229, 237, 293
Portolano, Mariana 322
Pradeau, Jean-François 364
Pressler, Carolyn 84, 88, 336
Pummer, Reinhard 390, 392, 425
Purvis, James D. 391
Pyschny, Katharina 457

Quick, Laura 16, 259, 261
Quirke, Stephen G. 257

Rad, Gerhard von 126, 223, 248, 254, 405, 466, 482
Radner, Karen 2–11, 16, 42, 46, 171, 172
Ragazzoli, Chloé 257–261
Ramos, Melissa 16
Reeder, Caryn A. 465
Regev, Dalit 423
Reuss, Eduard 321, 322
Reuter, Eleonore 21, 22, 330
Reuter, Hans-Richard 439
Rhyder, Julia 291
Richardson, Mervyn Edwin John 190, 314, 315, 466
Richardson, Seth 511
Richter, Sandra L. 380, 406
Ricœur, Paul 359
Ro, Johannes. U. 170
Robson, Eleanor 248, 255, 256, 260, 261, 264
Rofé, Alexander 84–88, 102, 507
Röllig, Wolfgang 53
Römer, Thomas 37, 112, 116, 119, 122–124, 161, 215, 216, 247, 248, 360, 404, 407–409, 413, 419
Rosenberg, Stephen 229
Roskam, Geert 359
Rossi, Adriano Valerio 294

Rossi, Benedetta 56, 158, 186, 230, 248–250, 262, 269, 270, 285, 290, 489
Rotenberg, Mordechai 349
Roth, Martha T. 20, 51, 75, 79–82
Rothstein, Edward 363
Royce, Anya P. 135–137, 151, 155, 156
Russell, Stephen C. 466
Rüterswörden, Udo 16, 22, 23, 25

Saley, Richard J. 53
Sanders, Seth 85, 219, 231
Sargent, Lyman Tower 356, 359, 361
Sargisson, Lucy 359
Sass, Benjamin 216
Sasson, Jack M. 216, 327
Schäfer-Lichtenberger, Christa 463, 465
Schams, Christine 270
Schaper, Joachim 279
Schaudig, Hans Peter 260
Scheffler, E. H. 174
Schenker, Adrian
Schlüter, Sarah P. 341
Schmid, Konrad 77, 83, 119, 122, 124, 248
Schmidt, Brian B. 220
Schmitt, Rüdiger 219, 220, 292
Schniedewind, William M. 85, 154, 259, 261, 270, 411
Schorch, Stefan 394, 399
Schüller, Bruno 437
Schulmeister, Irene 445
Schütte, Wolfgang 60, 61
Schwartz, Seth 143, 154, 157
Schweitzer, Steven James 321, 329, 330, 355, 357, 362
Schwemer, Daniel 8
Schwienhorst-Schönberger, Ludger 437
Scott, Robert 174
Segal, Moses H. 110, 228
Seibert, Eric 270
Seitz, G. 77
Sergi, Omer 61
Shai, Itzhaq 511
Shupak, Nili 257, 309
Sider, Ronald. J. 178
Silberman, Neil A. 58–60, 411
Silverman, Jason M. 55, 158, 280, 296, 298
Simkins, Ronald A. 170
Singer, Itamar 21
Singletary, Jennifer 3
Sjöberg, Åke W. 269

Ska, Jean-Louis 279, 285, 286, 292, 248, 250, 251
Small, David 137, 153
Smith, Anthony D. 136, 137, 139, 144, 150
Smith, Sir George Adam 126, 221
Snaith, N. H. 106
Sneed, Mark 50
Snyman, Gerrie 355, 356
Soete, Annette 436
Sonnet, Jean Pierre 248, 254, 263, 266, 279, 312, 377
Sonsino, Rifat 48, 76
Sparks, Kenton L. 136–138, 142, 143, 159, 487, 488
Sperling, S. David 119, 120, 122
Stackert, Jeffrey 10, 13, 23, 25, 74, 102, 261, 373, 384
Starr, Ivan 7
Stern, Ephraim 217, 358
Stern, Menahem 126, 489
Steymans, Hans Ulrich 4–16, 261, 441
Stipp, Hermann-Josef 465
Stol, Marten 180, 201, 345, 346
Stolper, Matthew W. 140, 141
Stordalen, Terje 363
Stavrakopoulou, Francesca 309, 364
Stemberger, Günter 315
Strawn, Brent A. 359
Streck, Maximillian 6
Stulman, Louis 420
Sullivan, Sharon 392, 396, 397
Suvin, Darko 355, 356
Sweeney, Marvin A. 361

Tadmor, Hayim 3, 5, 6, 10, 42
Taggar-Cohen, Ada 21, 36, 44, 54
Taylor, Keith 360, 363, 364
Testa, Emmanuele 439
Teixidor, Javier 237
Thomas, Ryan 211
Thompson, E. P. 343, 348
Thompson, Steven 336
Tigay, Jeffrey H. 13, 24, 75, 199, 224, 262, 266, 334, 500, 507
Tsafania, Levana 424
Tsai, Daisy Y. 193
Tsedaka, Benyamim 392, 396, 397
Tsukimoto, Akio 345
Tuplin, Christopher 292, 294

Uhlenbruch, Frauke 355
Uelinger, Christophe 216

Van de Mieroop, Marc   170
Van der Toorn, Karel   216, 219, 220, 223, 248, 249, 254, 255, 269
Van Leeuwen, Raymond C.   498
Van Seters, John   37, 77, 117, 120, 122, 126
Van Soldt, Wilfried   257, 260, 261
Vansina, Jan   287, 288
Vanstiphout, Herman L. J.   256
Vassar, John S.   480, 487
Veijola, Timo   18, 19, 22, 459
Veldhuis, Neik   255, 269
Vermeulen, Karolien   498, 508
Versluis, Arie   441, 464
Verburg, Jelle   198, 341
Verde, Danilo   289
Vergari, Romina   279
Vieira, Fátima   356, 357
Villoro, Luis   363
Vogt, Peter   172
Voigtlander, Elizabeth N. von   293
Vorländer, Hermann
Vriezen, Theodor C.   43
Vroom, Jonathan   84, 455

Waetzoldt, Harmut   180, 260
Waerzeggers, Caroline   158, 298
Wagensonner, Klaus   261
Wagner-Lawlor, Jennifer A.   356
Wagner-Tsukamoto, Sigmund A.   202
Walsh, Carey   508
Washburn, David L.   493
Watanabe, Kazuko   2–17, 22–24, 36, 41, 42, 45, 46
Watts, James W.   76, 248
Wazana, Nili   361
Weber, Max   156, 158
Welborn, Larry L.   170
Welch, Adam C.   228
Wells, Bruce   74, 77, 78–84, 88, 345, 346, 358, 487
Weinfeld, Moshe   12–13, 18–19, 21, 24–26, 36, 39, 47, 50, 193, 201, 262, 307, 330, 346,
Weingart, Kristin   60, 61
Welker, Michael   324
Wenham, Gordon J.   115, 342
Westbrook, Raymond   74, 79–84
Wevers, John William   252
Whybray, Roger N.   50
Wildenboer, Johan   122, 124
Widmer, Michael   247
Wiggins, Steve A.   217
Williamson, Hugh G. M.   60
Willis, Timothy M.   507
Wilson, Ian D.   144, 361
Wilson, Robert R.   144, 154, 359, 365
Winter, Irene J.   362
Wiseman, Donald J.   4, 7, 12
Wolbert, Werner   437
Wolf, Eric   236
Wood, Diana   178
Wormald, Patrick   82
Wright, David P.   78, 260
Wright, Jacob L.   327, 335, 342, 345
Wunsch, Cornelia   142, 179, 183, 186, 280, 296
Würthwein, Ernst   439
Wyatt, N.   220

Yardeni, Ada   237, 293
Yeivin, Shmuel   47, 50

Zaccagnini, Carlo   186
Zadok, Ran   142
Zahn, Molly M.   362
Zehnder, Markus   6, 7, 15, 19, 20, 24
Zerubavel, Eviatar   499
Zevit, Ziony   53, 211, 226
Ziskind, Jonathan R.   344
Zohary, Michael   97, 98
Zucchetti, Emilio   289, 290

Biblical Index

Genesis
1:28 349
3:15–19 338
5 393
8:17 349
11 393
12 120
12:1–5 107, 115
12:6–7 113, 114, 118, 124
12:10–20 109, 115
13:5–13 97, 107
13:14–17 144
13:15 383
14:6 105, 109
15 383
15:5 115
15:13 109
15:18 96
16:10 338
17:1 380
17:5–20 115
18:1 380
18:18 115
19:30–38 107
21:13–18 115
22:17 115
23 144
24:60 338
25:19–27:45 109
28:10–22 112
31 220
32:24–32 408
32:4 105, 109
33:14–20 105, 109, 114, 144, 408
35:1 380
35:2–4 118, 120, 220, 408
35:4 408
35:11 115
36:1–30 105, 107, 109
36:5–16 490
38 198, 340

38:8 199
38:14 114
41:37–46 109
46:3 115
46:8–27 373
46:31–47:12 109
49 115, 376, 379
49:3 486
49:10 382
50:26 379

Exodus
1:1–6 373
3:1 110, 111, 357
4:14
6–11 393
6:3–4 380
6:7 383, 487
6:16–21 490
7:7 487
12:13 309
13:9 123
14:21–31 117
15:22 374
15:25 122
16:1 110
16:4–28 123
17:6 110
17:15 380
18–24 51
18:16–20 123
18:21 83
19–24 127, 225
19:1–2 110
19:6 224, 226
19:21 213
20:1 442
20:2–10 379
20:5 337
20:10 502
20:17 343

Biblical Index

20:22–34:26 374
20:22–23:19 55, 74, 286, 377
20:24–26 117, 122, 224
20:24 74, 117
21–23 442
21:2–22:17 77–78
21:2–14 103–105, 382
21:26–27 343
22:15–16 87, 337
22:17 337, 346
22:20 383
22:29 337
23 231, 409
23:1–8 83
23:10–11 462
23:14–17 381
23:15 232
23:19 337, 501
23:31 96
24:3–8 285
24:4–7 250
24:5 225
24:9–11 213, 215, 380
24:12 123
25:9–40 492
28:3 125
30:13 238
31:19–35 220
32 248
33:6 110
33:11 379
34 231, 238, 409
34:9 315
34:18–25 232, 381
34:26 337, 501
40:34 373, 380

Leviticus
1:1 373
8:9 481
10:10–11 251, 282
14 282
17:26 74
18:1–18 337
19:3 337
19:19 108
19:27–28 221
20:9–23 337
22:27 337
23 231–238
23:5–8 232
23:33–43 280
25:22 381
25:36 181
26:39 337

Numbers
10:33–36 381
12:8 379
14 248
14:6 122
16–18 108
16 485
16:1 490
16:3 224
16:34 146
20:24–29 379
21:33 114
22–24 108
22:1 375
24:17 382
25:2 220
26:9–11 485
27:1–11 199, 378
28–29 231–238, 409
28:16–29:39 232
29:12–38 280
32:19 375
33:38 278
33:39 379
33:48–49 374
33:50–34:15 375
36:13 375

Deuteronomy
1–30 260–265, 279
1–4 254
1–3 138, 378, 393
1:1–5:1 314
1:1–5 36, 39, 41, 42, 105, 107, 111, 114, 115, 144–146
1:1 392
1:3 147
1:5 298, 375
1:6–30:20 254
1:6–11:32 39, 111
1:6–4:43 75
1:6–3:29 254, 255, 374, 375
1:6–8 96, 497
1:8 39, 409
1:10–11 115, 375
1:11–21 222
1:16–17 83, 122, 139
1:18 508
1:19–46 451
1:20–27 450

1:21 39
1:26–28 39
1:28 503, 509
1:38 125, 145
1:46–2:29 105
2:4–9 106, 107, 109, 114, 144, 149
2:10–23 275
2:12 145
2:14–15 376
2:19–23 144
2:24–3:22 497
2:28–36 97, 98, 108
3:1 114
3:3–7 98
3:5 503, 508, 509
3:8–20 97, 98
3:18–20 139
3:19 502
3:21–28 125
3:12 148
3:17 97
3:18 147
3:28 149
4–34 492
4:1 145, 222, 250, 306
4:1–45 122
4:2 16, 20, 21, 395
4:3–5 39
4:5–8 465–66
4:6–8 115, 149–151, 381
4:7 467
4:8 47, 50, 75, 123, 280
4:9–10 111, 252, 306, 307, 315, 420
4:9 420
4:10 454
4:12–33 215
4:14 382
4:15–19 215, 219, 416, 443, 485
4:16–18 492
4:19 212
4:20 102, 149
4:21 312
4:25–30 96, 248, 328, 383
4:26 40–42
4:29–31 383
4:31 328
4:34 150, 328
4:35–39 214
4:36 307, 380
4:37–38 39, 446, 452
4:41–26:19 37
4:41–43 102, 375
4:44–30:20 419

4:44–28:69 39, 75
4:44–11:32 404
4:44–46 123, 147, 254, 374, 375
4:45 47, 50, 75
4:47–49 97
5–26 138
5–30 254
5:1 122, 145, 146, 157, 306, 375, 381, 438
5:2–3 441
5:2 111
5:4 379
5:5 454
5:6–21 442
5:7 100, 215, 416, 443
5:10 451
5:12–15 442
5:14 502
5:15 459
5:16 420
5:18 400
5:21 343
5:23–31 441
5:28–31 443
5:28 149
5:29 454
5:22 215
5:29 315
5:30 440
5:31–32 47, 50, 122, 157, 250, 283, 307
6:1–26:16 441
6:1–3 42, 75, 122, 145, 157, 222
6:1 250, 307, 440
6:2 502
6:2–24 315
6:3 379
6:4–11:25 113, 416
6:4–5 2, 24–25, 74, 83, 214, 385, 414
6:5 451, 452
6:6–8 279, 309, 363
6:7–25 420
6:7–9 76, 100, 224, 500
6:8 224
6:10 138, 139, 383, 409, 503
6:11–15 383, 385, 416, 420, 443
6:14 443, 489
6:19 97
6:20–25 445, 446
6:20 47, 50, 75, 122, 385
6:23–34 222
7:1 98, 100
7:2–26 383
7:2–6 416
7:4 215

Biblical Index

7:6 102, 224
7:7-13 453
7:7-9 446
7:7 452
7:8 39, 54, 138, 222, 383, 451
7:9 451
7:11 47, 50, 75, 122
7:12 115, 222
7:13 217, 222, 451
7:16-23 497
7:17 376
7:22 98
7:66 149
8:1-18 222
8:1 456
8:2-5 376
8:6 315
8:7-14 97-99, 443
8:7-9 497
8:12-13 461
8:19-20 383, 416
8:35 122
9:1-7 465
9:1 98, 145, 503, 508, 509
9:3 376
9:5 39, 383, 409
9:6-29 102, 149
9:6 327, 387
9:8-10:11 374, 375
9:8-21 451
9:10-11 215, 252, 416
9:15-21 485
9:20 327
9:26-29 447-448
9:27 409
10:1-8 213, 230
10:1-5 39, 215, 381
10:2 145
10:3-9 56, 101-103, 139
10:4 252
10:6-7 147, 148, 375
10:8 217, 225
10:11 149, 222
10:12-20 315, 385, 453
10:12 451, 454
10:15 222, 451, 452
10:16 387
10:18 460
10:19 452
10:20 215, 385, 416
10:22 116
11:1-22 451
11:1 47, 50, 385

11:6 146, 485
11:9-21 222, 309
11:11-15 97, 99
11:12 497
11:13-12:8 40, 4211:15 98
11:14 217
11:16-28 41, 42, 100, 416
11:17 383, 384
11:18-21 224, 279, 420
11:19 306, 309, 500
11:22-25 497
11:22 452
11:24 96
11:26-28 424
11:29-31 101, 113, 113, 116-119, 127, 409
11:32 47, 75, 122
11:35 408
12-25 154, 322, 404, 441
12-18 76
12-13 330
12:1-26:15 39, 41, 42, 43, 47-51, 55, 64, 74, 76, 99, 102
12 458
12:1-16:15 50, 100
12:1 122, 222, 381
12:2-13:19 444
12:2-7 416
12:5-26 482, 499
12:5 112, 148, 380, 398-99, 406
12:6-27 101, 103, 193, 339
12:6-11 225
12:7 457
12:8-28 497
12:8-9 457
12:12-18 457, 502
12:13-19 228
12:13-14 500
12:14 148
12:15-24 225, 311, 381, 405
12:17 500
12:18 457
12:21 502
12:25 316
12:26-27 225, 500
13 416
13:1-12[12:32-13:11] 2, 16-25, 74, 83, 87, 88, 100, 414
13:2-17 139, 382
13:4 451
13:5 87, 452, 454
13:6-12 328
13:7-16 221

13:7   197, 337, 339
13:8   489
13:9–10   316
13:10   149
13:12   146, 377
13:13–19   465, 506
13:14   324
13:15–16   383
14–25   329
14:1–21   444
14:1   221
14:2–21   98, 100, 102, 139, 149, 224, 226–227, 337
14:19   458
14:20–29   175, 198, 230
14:22–26   102, 175, 193, 194, 196, 309, 315, 321, 406
14:22–16:17   444
14:23   307, 454, 499
14:24   502
14:26   339, 457
14:27   457
14:28–29   323, 326, 339
15:1–18   462
15:1–6   189, 193, 194, 316, 330, 358
15:1   462
15:4–6   461
15:7–12   139, 189, 323, 330, 460
15:9   466
15:10–18   316
15:11   174, 192, 324, 461
15:12   63, 186, 200, 382
15:14   202
15:15   76, 325, 459
15:16–17   193, 200, 339
15:19–23   101, 103, 381, 500
15:20   457, 499
16   500
16:1–16   102, 140, 230, 231, 406, 459
16:1–5   228, 232
16:2–17   499
16:8   395
16:11–14   100, 193, 215, 377, 381, 458, 502, 503, 508
16:16–17   231
16:18–18:22   359, 443, 444, 463
16:18–20   83, 88, 99, 140, 148, 149, 151, 221, 316, 324, 376
16:21–22   215, 218, 219, 416
17   492
17:2–25   88, 145
17:2–7   212, 228, 324, 416, 509
17:4–10   140
17:5–7   87, 88
17:7–16   149
17:8–14   101, 139, 151, 152, 221, 230, 282, 283, 313, 500, 506
17:8   324
17:9   313, 405
17:10–11   253, 291, 307
17:12   101, 506
17:13–20   139, 154, 283, 284, 315, 361, 382, 406, 418, 488–89, 506
17:14   326
17:17   339, 348
17:18–20   39, 40, 51, 56, 83, 145, 230, 308, 377, 381, 405
17:19   192, 313, 316, 325, 454, 490
18:1–8   56, 101, 103, 111, 145, 148, 225, 230, 249, 326
18:1–3   405
18:2–18   139, 149, 151
18:5   216, 225
18:6   146, 228
18:9–16   100, 105, 111, 126, 219, 221
18:11   223, 416
18:15   248, 312, 382
18:16   252
19–25   77–78
19:1–22:12   444
19:1–13   221
19:1   98
19:1–13   102, 104, 325, 382
19:4–6   84, 104, 151, 228
19:8   196
19:9   451
19:11   48
19:13   145, 316
19:14   98, 325
19:15–21   193, 221, 230, 325
19:17   56, 405
19:18   325
19:19   316
20   506
20:1–8   193, 326, 339, 382
20:2–9   149, 230
20:2   56, 405
20:3   145
20:10–20   98, 195, 197, 326, 327, 339, 406
20:10–15   464
20:19   97, 193, 196, 330
21–25   84
21:1–9   221, 230
21:1   146
21:4   97
21:5   48, 56, 101, 216, 405

21:7   193
21:8   145, 149
21:10–21   339
21:10–14   193, 195, 382
21:15–25:10   77–78, 84
21:15–17   75, 139, 151, 193, 197, 221, 345
21:17   486, 493
21:18–21   347, 420, 509
21:18   48, 308, 325, 337
21:19–26   47, 508
21:19   145
21:20   197
21:21   310
21:22   151, 193, 196, 316
22:1–10   338
22:1–4   462
22:1–2   47, 122, 325
22:4   172
22:6–7   193, 196, 316, 337
22:8   193
22:10–11   108, 196
22:13–29   48, 75, 84–88, 145, 337, 339, 342
22:13–23:15   444
22:13–21   492
22:13   395
22:14–17   484
22:15   197, 508
22:17   201
22:21–23   316
22:23–24   509
22:22–27   197, 201, 310, 346
22:29   201, 346
23:1–8   26, 107, 109
23:1[22:30]   200, 337
23:3–9   383
23:6   451
23:8–9   106, 172, 327, 491, 492
23:9–15   382
23:16–24:7   444
23:15-16   193, 197, 221
23:17   499
23:17–18   147, 228, 230
23:19   101, 103, 194, 214, 419, 501
23:20–21   181, 188, 316, 323, 330, 462
23:24–26   97, 193, 194, 325
24:1–8   48, 56, 75, 84, 339, 395
24:4   193, 197
24:5   339, 382
24:6–13   185, 194, 195
24:7   139, 147, 310, 462
24:8–25:4   444

24:8   230, 253, 281–282, 291, 307, 316, 405
24:10–11   194
24:12–18   460
24:14   193, 202, 323, 325, 503, 508
24:15   466
24:16   325, 337, 380
24:17   100, 139, 151, 323, 324
24:19–21   97, 173, 175, 193, 197, 339
24:26   120
25:1–7   48, 139, 151, 152, 193, 325
25:3   196
25:4   193, 196
25:5–12   76, 84, 145, 198, 339, 444
25:5   199, 200
25:5–10   340, 462
25:13–16   202, 325, 444
25:18   454
26:1–9   378, 381, 406, 409
26:3–4   56, 230, 405
26:5   150
26:6   47
26:11   100, 236
26:12–15   219, 222, 380, 381
26:15–19   97, 101, 112, 145, 149, 224, 383
26:16–19   41, 42, 54, 75, 102, 117, 122, 386, 409
26:16   381, 440
26:17–19   440
27:1–34:12   314
27–30   404
27–28   314
27   114
27:1–8   101, 113, 116–120, 127, 149, 376, 378, 381, 440, 497
27:2–8   408, 409
27:4–13   424
27:4   399, 401
27:9–14   42, 145, 146, 149, 407
27:14–28:45   40–42
27:17–19   98, 100, 460
28   377
28:1   409
28:2–14   40, 42, 102, 149
28:4–18   217
28:4–7   482–83
28:7   483
28:9   224
28:12–24   97, 328
28:15–68   509
28:15–45   12–16, 23–25, 41, 42, 55, 74, 97, 98, 414
28:36   382
28:38–52   217, 328, 329

28:52 98, 503, 508, 509
28:58–69 96, 105, 111, 115, 147, 315, 375, 384
28:63–64 420
29:1–30:20 75, 438
29:1–8 439, 447–448
29:2 146
29:7–20 148
29:9–10 438
29:10 145, 465, 502
29:11–27 42, 54,115, 149, 222, 283, 386
29:11–13 441
29:13–27 509
29:13 409
29:21–28 248, 291, 377, 465
29:28 311
30:1–8 96, 383, 385, 387, 465, 509
30:6–20 448–449, 452
30:10 123
30:11–20 379
30:15–19 40, 42, 63, 386, 387, 438, 439, 439, 509
30:15–16 440
30:17–18 497
30:20 222, 409, 452, 453
31:1–11 146, 149, 292, 375, 376
31:3–23 125
31:7–20 222
31:9–30 39–42, 56, 83, 96, 102, 112, 116, 145, 230, 313, 377
31:9–13 248, 250, 253, 279, 280, 284–290, 311, 454
31:9 313, 381, 405
31:10–13 299, 307, 309, 315, 328, 378, 385, 420, 500
31:11 499
31:14–23 379, 385
31:16–18 328, 383
31:19–23 147, 250, 385, 509
31:22 250
31:24–26 416
31:26–30 214, 248, 253, 381
31:27 387
31:28 148
31:30 252
32 385–386
32:1–46 40, 149
32:2 97
32:4 151
32:8–52 147
32:8–9 212
32:13–14 97, 98
32:19–25 509
32:21–28 151, 370, 383
32:39 214
32:41 151
32:44 125
32:45 146
32:46 40, 385, 420
32:48–52 379
32:49 497
33 379
33:1 147
33:2–29 145, 149
33:2 105, 111, 297
33:4 250, 252
33:5 148
33:8–11 56, 151, 249, 265–269
33:8 485
33:10 253, 307
33:16–24 139, 151
33:17 491, 492
34 115
34:1–4 96, 497
34:4 222
34:7 485, 492
34:8–9 147, 375, 387
34:9 125, 312
34:10–12 145, 146, 248, 379
39:4 125

Joshua
1:2–6 125
1:7 123
2:8–11 465
3:1–4:24 117
4:19–34 117
5:11 178
6:24 501
8:30–35 116–119, 122, 123, 127, 408
8:38 83, 112
9:9–10 465
9:27 465
18:21–24 58
22:5 122, 452
23:6 123
23:11 452
24 126
24:1–28 116–124
31:7–28 251

Judges
9 124
11:24 212
17–18 220
18:5–14 220

19:18 501

Ruth 340
2 193
4 198

1 Samuel
1–4 389
1:7–24 501
2:11 215
3:15 501
4:4 210, 212, 213
10 83
10:17–19 120
10:25 121
12 121
14:18–19 213, 215
15:21–33 409
15:23 220
16:12 114
19:10 483
19:13–16 220
21:11–13 483
22:1–2 483
22:9–10 483
23:9 215
23:19 483
28:13 220
30:7 215
30:25 122

2 Samuel
6:2 210
7:8–16 52
9–20 60
10 483
12:1 483
12:20 501
22:51 483
23:1–7 52

1 Kings
1–2 60
2:1–9 376–77
2:3 123
2:22 345
8:9–21 213, 501
8:44–48 501
8:52–61 466, 467
11:13–36 501
12 124
12:20 124
14:21 501

15:13 218
18:28 220
19:8 110

2 Kings
2:1 409
4:38 409
10:31 123
11:4–20 47, 52
14:21 47
17:14 450
17:24–41 390
17:24 412
17:34–37 123
18–20 411
18:4 218
19:15 210
21:1–3 47, 218
21:7–8 123, 218, 501
21:19
22–23 74, 321, 360
22:8–10 413
23 58
23:1–5 83, 121, 123
23:2 413
23:6–15 218, 413
23:21–23 411
23:24 220
23:27 501
24:20 10

1 Chronicles
2:43 490
6:7 490
9:17–32 491
16:8–22 485
16:40 123

2 Chronicles
6:5–6 501
6:34–38 501
7:12–16 501
12:6 490
12:13 501
15:16 218
17:9 123
19:8 313
30:25 411
23:11 52
23:18 123
25:4 123
30:16 123
31:3 123

33:8 123
33:7 501
35:26 123

Ezra 56
1:1–10 424
3:2 123
3:8 424
5:14–17 424
6:18 378
7:1–10 423
7:10 122, 123
7:11–26 292
9:1–10:3 121

Nehemiah 56
2:3 123
8:3–9:3 123, 124
8:14 123
8:18 123
9:13–14 123
10:28–29 123
10:33–34 238
10:38–39 249
13:1 378
13:28 424

Esther

Job 280

Psalms
1–119 478
1 476
2 362
2:2 489
3–41 478
12:6 483
18:51 478, 489
19 476
20:6 489
28:6 489
42–83 415
42–72 478–79
44:5–6 491
45 362
45:7 489
51:2 483
52:1 483
54:1 483
56:1 483
57:1 483
59:1 483

60:2 483
72 362
73–89 479
77:20–21 483, 486
78 450
78:10 123
78:41 60
78:51 486, 492
78:70–72 484
80:2 210
81:5 122
81:8[7] 485
84:10 489
87 491
89 362
89:20–38 52
89:20–51 489
89:28–33 488
89:47 484
89:49 478
90–106 480
92 493
95:8 485
99 492
99:1 210
99:6–7 484
103:3–9 485
105:1–15 485
10515 489
105:26 485, 486
105:36 486
106 450–51
106:16 485
106:20 492
106:23 485
106:28 220
106:32 485
107–150 480–81
110 493
119 476
119:164 183
132 492
132:3–8 482
132:8 213
132:10–17 489, 290
132:11–12 52
142:1 483

Proverbs 306
1:8 257
3:16 192
6:20 76
28:27 173

30:5-6   20

Qohelet/Ecclesiastes   280
1   193
3:14   20

Song of Songs   203

Isaiah
1-11   60
1:10   123
2:2-4   504
6:1-7   215
8:19-20   220
11:1-4   362
11:2   125
37:16   210
40-55   280, 476
65:4   226
66:17   226

Jeremiah
2   60
7   363
16:6   221
24   218
25:11   422, 423
26:2   20
27:6   422
29:10   422, 423
31:21   216

Ezekiel
1:4-28   215
7:18   221
10:1-22   215
16   362
20:23   216
21:26   220
27   171
37   364
40-48   357, 363
44:12   216
47-1-48   497
49   497

Daniel
1-6   280
9:11-13   123

Hosea
2:10-15[8-13]   217
3:4   220

4:15   409
5:9   60
8:13   409
9:3   409
9:10   386
9:15   409
12:7   171
12:9-13   409
12:11   409
13:4   409

Amos
2:10-11   409
3:1   410
4:4-5   409
4:10   410
8:4-8   171

Micah
1-3   60
1:5   60
1:16   221
3:1-10   60
4:1-5   504
4:6   123
5:13[14]   218
6:10-13   171

Haggai   422
2:23   424

Zechariah
1-8   280, 422
4   424
7:5   423
9:6   108
10:2   220
14:3-11   497

Malachi
3:22[4:4]   123

Deuterocanonical Books
Sirach 50   504
2 Maccabees
1:18-36   424
2:2-3   423, 424
2:13   424

Pseudepigrapha
Enoch   280, 357

Dead Sea Scrolls

4QpaleoExod^m 393
4QExod-Lev^f 393
4QLev^d 393
4QNum^b 393
4Q158 393
4Q364 393
4Q175 393
11Q19 284, 362

Ancient Jewish Writers
Josephus, Ant. 11.302–12, 321–25 424

New Testament
Matthew
5:17 493
6:3 192
22:24 198

Luke
10:29–37 389

John
4:4–42 389

Classical Authors

Aristotle, Politics 174, 179, 504
Homer 364
Plato, Republic 364

Rabbinic Works
m. Ter. 11:2–3 97
m. Bik. 1:3, 3:9 97
m. Ned. 6:8–9 97

Early Christian Writings

Ancient Near Eastern Writings
Bisitun 293–296
CTH 133 20
CTH 378 21
Dna
DSe
HL
LH
MAL
Naqš-ī Rustam 293
Papyrus Lansing 258
Saa 10 3
TADAE 237
XPh

SUBJECT INDEX

Adad (god) 7, 8
adê, adû 3, 6, 9, 16, 21, 36, 41, 64, 261
'ālâ 36, 43
Aleppo 21, 23
altruism 193
al-yahudu 280
altar 4, 22, 74, 101, 103–105, 113–120, 128, 147, 215, 218, 223–232, 238, 268, 307, 380, 389, 400, 405, 407, 408, 424, 426, 458
amulet/s 100, 224, 238
Anat 7, 8, 53
antichresis 185, 186, 190, 191, 200, 203
Anu 12, 14, 51
Arad 61
Arameans 7–10, 26, 38, 43, 54, 101, 234, 326, 483
Arnon 97, 397, 497
Ashdod 9, 10, 108
Asherah 59, 64, 211, 215218, 226, 227, 238, 416, 417, 420, 422, 424
Ashur (city) 2, 4, 8, 171
Aššur (god) 3, 4, 12–14, 23, 46, 52, 53

Baal (god) 8, 53, 217, 220, 221, 327
Benjamin 57–61, 64, 490
berit 36, 37, 41, 43, 44, 46, 47, 52–55, 64, 213, 250, 285, 286, 413, 438, 441, 480, 490
Bethel
 (god) 7, 8
 (place) 57–59, 112, 117, 218, 406, 410, 412, 418, 419
Bethlehem 61, 62
blood 14, 101, 102–105, 220, 225, 226, 229, 238, 249, 316, 335, 342, 348, 348, 457, 458, 464
blood ties 147, 149, 221, 266, 267, 341, 425, 488, 490

capital
 cultural 158

financial 172, 176, 179–184, 189, 192, 203, 324, 344, 345, 348
 social 192, 194, 197, 323, 348
Carchemish 8
central/izing/ation 59, 63, 74, 77, 96, 101, 127, 146, 152, 175, 213, 219, 223–224, 227–231, 233–236, 239, 291, 295, 308, 321, 385, 406, 418, 458, 463, 481, 482, , 501, 504, 506, 507, 509, 510
cities 503
collateral 185, 187, 203
credit/or, creditworthiness 171, 173, 175, 176, 178, 179–182, 185–189, 191–197, 202, 203, 308, 314, 322–324, 330, 331, 341, 462
cult
 astral 414, 443
 ancestor 220–222, 227, 238, 420
 of divine couple 8, 416, 417, 420, 421, 424, 460
 fertility 226
 household, domestic 63, 219–224, 227, 416, 420, 422
 iconic 218, 364, 443, 458
 Jerusalem 59, 101, 118, 218, 268, 413, 418, 422, 426
 joyful 457
 monolatrous 62, 420, 444
 mortuary 221
 northern 59, 60, 117, 390, 407, 412
 reform 26, 47, 58, 59, 74, 77, 218, 223, 230, 238, 321, 360, 416, 418
 sacrificial 229, 249, 270, 405, 458
curse 2, 6, 10, 12–16, 21, 35, 47, 261, 377, 399, 439
 of Balaam 108
 at Ebal 113, 116–117, 120
 of Joshua 120
 in Psalms 482

Dan 57, 61, 64, 96, 101

David (king) 52, 57–62, 125, 356, 398, 399, 407, 419, 477, 478–484, 486–493, 510
debt/or 168, 169, 172, 176, 177, 180, 184, 186–193, 202–205, 235, 292, 216, 321–324, 382, 418, 454, 460–463
debt release 172, 173, 186, 188–192, 202–204, 302, 303, 311–323, 462
decentralized, see central
discontinuity 498–499
divination 219, 220, 266–270, 364

Ebal 42, 95, 105, 113, 114, 116, 118–120, 128, 160, 399–401, 407–409
ēdō/ut 36, 43, 47, 50, 75, 214, 480, 490
Edom/ite 101, 105–110, 115, 128, 141, 143, 172, 212, 229, 326–327, 397, 483, 490–492
Egypt/ian 3, 7, 9, 21, 52, 57, 62, 101, 106, 109, 120, 141, 150, 151, 153, 168, 175, 218, 229, 237, 293, 324, 357, 374, 417, 486, 491, 492
  Brook of 96, 101
  culture 248, 249, 255–264, 330
  slavery 55, 76, 95, 108, 109, 110, 126, 138, 147, 213, 222, 232–236, 400, 409, 436, 442–459, 467
Ekron 7, 9, 11, 25
Elam/ite 7, 141, 292–294
Elephantine 237, 279, 280, 293, 296, 418
Emar 85, 257
Enneateuch 37, 124, 127
Ephraim 61, 63, 104, 389, 491
Esarhaddon Succession Treaty 2–27, 45–46, 52, 74, 261, 384, 414, 452

fathers 500
future 497

gates 99, 146, 195, 224, 228, 249, 285, 288, 309–313, 329, 503, 508
Gath 9, 483
ger/im (stranger) 108, 109, 152, 236, 328, 502
Gerizim 101, 105, 113, 114120, 127, 128, 160, 229, 389, 390, 392, 394, 398–400, 404–409, 417, 422–427, 501, 502
Gilgal 99, 114, 117, 121, 126, 400, 406, 408

Hammurabi 20, 23, 51, 75, 79, 189, 190, 260, 314, 315, 348, 466

Heshbon 96, 99, 108, 144
Hezekiah 59, 61, 62, 159, 160, 218, 411, 412, 504
Hittite/s 7, 19–21, 26, 35, 36, 38–45, 48, 54, 64, 75, 98, 306, 326, 441
holy
  convocation 231–234
  of holies 213
  ones 53
  people 37, 100, 102, 150, 209, 221, 224–266, 440, 444
  qedeshah 145
  right 440
  sites 380, 381, 392, 399
  war 149, 406,
Horeb 23, 37, 41, 54, 102, 105, 106, 109–113, 120, 128, 139, 213–215, 252, 253, 306, 357, 377, 380, 381, 383, 384, 419, 420, 435, 438, 441–443, 447–451, 454, 460, 463
house/s 498
  of Yhwh 501
ḥuqqîm 35, 43, 47–51, 75, 117, 122, 125, 233, 307, 466

interest/s 88, 152, 169, 172, 176–192, 202, 203, 204, 222, 248, 263, 305, 309, 313, 316, 323–325, 328–330, 338–314, 347, 357, 359, 412, 423, 461,
išḫiul 36, 39, 44

Jericho 99, 375, 391, 408
Jerusalem 501–502, 506, 510
Jordan 36, 64, 97, 101, 107, 114, 117, 126, 159, 248, 261, 263, 312, 375, 387, 399, 400, 408, 409, 419, 438, 439, 465, 497
Josiah 25, 27, 47, 58, 74, 121, 136, 138, 154, 159, 160, 218, 321, 360, 364, 411, 413–415, 418, 426, 464
Judah
  document 25, 55, 83, 419
  kingdom 51, 57, 152–155, 160, 210, 404, 406, 407, 410, 415, 426
  land 7, 8, 10, 11, 12, 20, 57–64, 84, 104, 138, 143, 217, 218, 232, 358, 390, 418
  oath 25–26
  people 37
  scribes 2, 11, 24, 38, 59, 78, 84, 85, 410, 411, 413, 414, 419
  tradition 20, 39, 43, 54, 362, 421

Subject Index 535

Kadesh Barnea 96, 106, 122, 376, 448–451
Kalḫu 2, 4, 5, 8, 46
Khirbet Beit Lei 211
Kinalua (see Tayinat)
king 10–22, 25–26, 37–47, 51–59, 64, 77, 81–83, 88, 98–99, 108, 121, 145, 150, 172, 190–192, 222, 230, 251, 257, 264–269, 279, 280–284, 290–296, 306–316, 325–331, 359, 361–364 ,382, 405–406, 414, 419, 441, 454, 463–464, 477, 480–491, 504–506, 509, 511
koinon 142, 143

landscape 498–511
law/s
 case 47, 49, 76, 87, 256, 311, 316
 centralization 74
 code 47, 48, 79, 80, 82, 156, 292, 312, 329, 360
 collections 23, 49, 74–86, 260, 455
 common 82, 311
 court 101
 cultic 47, 88, 117, 224, 281, 331, 383, 435, 457–459
 customary 80, 147, 152
 economic 170, 173, 178, 181, 182, 189, 190, 194–198, 200, 322, 324–325, 329, 338, 460–466
 Exodus 54, 74, 77, 86, 382
 Deuteronomic 20, 74–78, 83–88, 169, 172, 193, 201, 254, 314, 357, 381, 404, 436, 442
 dietary 226–227, 382
 humanitarian 193, 196, 197, 199–201, 221, 346–347
 Joshua 120, 125
 Josiah 321
 king 283–284, 292, 297, 306, 316, 321, 325, 326, 330, 361, 382
 levirate 198–199, 340–341
 Levitical 74, 310, 382
 Moab 23, 381, 435, 438, 443, 456
 Moses 247, 252, 314, 315, 327, 375, 377, 378, 381, 396, 456
 narrative 49, 50, 75, 373, 437
 philosophy 50, 83, 87, 158, 279, 281, 338, 445, 455
 reading 116, 140, 251, 306, 322, 385
 regulation 36
 Roman 343, 348
 Seidel's 22, 116

Sinai/Horeb 23, 120, 374, 381, 383, 384, 435, 443, 447
utopian 88, 203, 321, 328, 329, 331, 336, 359, 418
Yhwh's 73, 76, 83, 88, 374, 446, 449, 451
Lebanon 96
Levi 56, 148, 157, 230, 249, 266, 268–270, 284, 307, 309–314, 389, 405, 463, 481, 490–491, 501, 502
Levites 101, 103, 146, 152, 158, 175, 194, 213–217, 230, 249, 252, 261, 266–268, 284, 307, 313, 405, 424, 457, 460
literati 55–56, 61, 135, 157, 160, 162, 322, 501
loan 173–191, 194, 195, 200, 203–205, 316, 321–325, 330, 341, 460–462, 466,
love 13, 24–25, 77, 152, 200, 203, 315, 345, 385, 387, 435, 439, 443, 446, 449, 451–455, 460, 462, 480, 484
loyalty 2–11, 17, 19, 24, 44, 73, 74, 88, 119, 126, 227, 268, 453, 483
 oath 25–26, 45, 76, 222, 384
 Yhwh's 384, 439, 448
 unconditional 83, 384, 451, 453

Manasseh (king) 2, 6, 11, 25, 26, 97, 160, 361
map/s (mental) 497, 502, 506, 509
maqom see place
Maṣṣôt 231, 232, 235, 237, 418, 459
memory 505, 510–511
milk 98, 217, 227, 337, 338, 379
mišpāṭîm 43, 47–51, 74–77, 117, 122, 125, 217, 268, 307, 455, 466
Moab
 covenant 51, 64, 95, 102, 113, 115, 121, 147, 156, 254, 384, 419, 434, 438, 440–451, 456, 465
 generation 116, 252, 291
 land 143
 plains of 23, 36, 37, 42, 51, 64, 74, 75, 97, 107, 110, 112, 139, 252, 281, 291, 307, 374, 381 378, 395, 396, 439
 torah 281–291, 296, 298, 424
 wilderness 107, 114
Moabites 101, 107–109, 141, 144, 212,
mourning 195, 221, 226
Moses
 blessings 248, 249, 266, 307, 314, 379
 biography 116, 247, 267

death 376
despairing 312, 316, 327, 331, 385, 420, 448
diviner 267, 270
eyes of 497
fighter 106
intercessor 447
interpreter 381, 382
and Joshua 126, 287, 317, 375, 438
judge 247, 396
law-giver 49, 76, 77, 96, 116, 314, 315, 357, 381
Levite 268, 269
master scribe 23, 102, 248-263, 269, 279, 375
mediator 112, 119, 238, 282, 312, 442
miracle 110
memory 36, 139
narrator 75
new Jacob 248, 266, 268
past leader 120-124, 127
prophet 125, 248, 269, 328, 330, 435, 453, 500
in Psalms 477-481, 483-487, 490-492
servant 116
sinner 147, 266, 450
Song of 40-42, 254, 262, 265, 287, 485, 486
speaker 39, 43, 75, 97, 113, 145-146, 285, 289, 314, 374, 375, 377
tablets of 213
teacher 49, 50, 99, 113, 114, 151, 157, 160, 250, 306-307, 311, 314
torah 116, 123, 151, 248, 252-254, 281, 285, 286, 290, 291, 327, 378, 416
writer 500

Nabu (god) 2, 4, 229, 257, 269

orphans see, widows
ostraca/on 229, 232, 390

palace 506
patriarchalism 288, 336-337, 348, 349
Passover 100, 231, 232, 234, 23213, 4837, 409, 411, 418, 457, 459, 495
Philistines 7, 9, 101, 108, 141,
pilgrimage 59, 102, 112, 128, 129, 148, 155, 209, 219, 229, 230-238, 281, 409, 422, 457, 459, 481
place 498-50.....
pledge, see collateral

prophet/ic 16-19, 23, 77, 83, 119, 120, 125-126, 139, 171, 172, 211, 216, 248, 269, 279, 310, 312, 336, 359, 379, 382, 410, 421, 423, 435, 463, 489, 490

Quntillet ʿAjrud 61, 211

Ramat Raḥel 11, 25, 26
responsa 82

Šala (god) 7, 8
sacrifice 52, 77, 105, 118, 138, 193, 194, 221, 380, 405, 457, 458, 462, 500
animal 114, 100, 128, 225, 229, 239, 249, 416, 422, 426
business of 270
effect 381
financial 461
for the dead 220
holocaust 116, 225, 228, 232, 233
maqom 398, 457
peace 225
portions 422
of son 349
slaughter 458
temple 405, 421
to strange gods 386
voluntary 101, 230
well-being 408
Samaria/n 52, 59, 62-63, 98, 118, 159, 211, 232, 390, 404-417, 424-425, 501, 506, 507
Samaritan 113-119, 227, 268, 281, 389-401, 407, 410, 423, , 501
Saul 57-61, 121, 213, 220, 419, 482, 483
Sennakerib 504
Sefire 19, 42, 43, 53
Seir 105-111, 114, 115, 128, 397
Shamash 9, 13
Shariʿa 82, 181, 182
Shavuʿôt 231, 232
Shiloh 119, 215, 389, 406, 501
Sidon 7-9, 141
Sîn (god) 12, 13, 14, 109, 110, 414
Sinai 23, 37, 54, 95, 105, 107, 109-118, 120, 128, 147, 211, 215, 259, 286, 287, 357, 374, 377, 380, 381-384, 406, 407, 419, 420, 435, 460
šmiṭṭah, see debt release
standing stones 126, 215, 219, 408
stele
  Babylon 293

Dan 61, 62
Hammurabi 79, 314, 466
Katumuwa 219
Mesha 383
Sukkôt 100, 117, 121, 219, 231, 233, 234, 235, 237, 265, 280, 309, 321, 405, 409, 454, 457–459

tablet
  in ark 416
  clay 293
  school 264, 265, 269
  stone 406
Tabernacles (see Sukkot)
Tayinat, Tell 2, 4–7, 17, 45
temple/s
  at Bethel 410, 419
  in Deuteronomy 230, 398, 501, 505
  Ezekiel's 357, 363
  at Elephantine 229, 237,
  on Gerizim 118, 127, 405, 417, 423–427
  Hittite 39–45
  at Jerusalem 20, 25, 27, 47, 55–60, 103, 111, 121, 125, 155, 160, 215, 218, 222, 269, 231, 237, 269–270, 321, 401, 407, 411, 413, 418, 421, 422, 457, 479, 482, 486, 506
  maqom 101–103, 105, 114, 214, 501, 510
  Mesopotamian 2–6, 175, 180, 260, 414
  Solomon's 213, 466, 501
  taxes 258
  in Transjordan 229
  Scroll 284, 362,
teraphim 221
tithes 500

Ugarit 85, 217, 257, 260, 261, 344
unleaven bread, see Maṣṣôt
urim and thummim, see divination
usufruct 185, 203, 204, 344

usury 178–182, 204
utopia 88, 135, 140, 143, 146, 154, 172, 197, 203, 321–331, 336, 355–365, 499

weeks (feast) 100, 233, 235, 381, 457–459
widow/s 173–175, 196–200, 203, 233–236, 313, 340, 341, 377, 482, 502
wife/ves 12, 237, 502
  abducted 346
  Abishag 345
  adulterous 85, 86
  Asherah 59, 217, 218, 416
  Aššur's 13, 14
  demoted 487
  Esau's 490
  father's 200, 337
  fertility 344
  grabbing 339
  hated 339, 345, 486, 492
  Jochebed 487
  in levirate 198, 199, 340, 341
  Melqart's 8
  missing in Deut 502
  new 326
  neighbor's 343, 444
  Rebekah 109
  Rapā's 180, 181
  repudiated 339
  sacrificing 457
  slandered 342, 484
  Yannay's 477, 488
wool 98, 171, 188, 217, 225

Yhwh Elohim 18, 37, 39, 51–53, 56, 62, 64, 96, 100, 101, 103, 111, 112, 119, 120, 123, 125, 209, 211, 214, 216, 219, 220, 222–239, 380, 403, 405, 406, 413, 415–417, 422–426
Yhwh Ṣebaot 51, 59, 64

Zagros 2–6, 46
Zoar 96. 97

www.ingramcontent.com/pod-product-compliance
Lightning Source LLC
LaVergne TN
LVHW050426250825
819359LV00040B/696